The Origins of Yahwism

Beihefte zur Zeitschrift für die alttestamentliche Wissenschaft

Edited by
John Barton, Ronald Hendel, Reinhard G. Kratz,
and Markus Witte

Band 484

The Origins
of Yahwism

Edited by Jürgen van Oorschot
and Markus Witte

DE GRUYTER

ISBN 978-3-11-042538-3
e-ISBN (PDF) 978-3-11-044822-1
e-ISBN (EPUB) 978-3-11-044711-8
ISSN 0934-2575

Library of Congress Cataloging-in-Publication Data
A CIP catalog record for this book has been applied for at the Library of Congress.

Bibliografic information published by the Deutsche Nationalbibliothek
The Deutsche Nationalbibliothek lists this publication in the Deutschen Nationalbibliografie;
detailed bibliografic data are available on the Internet at http://dnb.dnb.de.

© 2017 Walter de Gruyter GmbH, Berlin/Boston
Printing and binding: CPI books GmbH, Leck
♾ Printed on acid-free paper
Printed in Germany

www.degruyter.com

MIX
Papier aus verantwor-
tungsvollen Quellen
FSC
www.fsc.org   FSC® C083411

Table of Contents

Introduction —— VII

Josef Tropper
The Divine Name *Yahwa —— 1

Mark S. Smith
YHWH's Original Character: Questions about an Unknown God —— 23

Manfred Krebernik
The Beginnings of Yahwism from an Assyriological Perspective —— 45

Angelika Berlejung
The Origins and Beginnings of the Worship of YHWH: The Iconographic
Evidence —— 67

Faried Adrom and Matthias Müller
The Tetragrammaton in Egyptian Sources – Facts and Fiction —— 93

Henrik Pfeiffer
The Origin of YHWH and its Attestation —— 115

Jörg Jeremias
Three Theses on the Early History of Israel —— 145

Martin Leuenberger
YHWH's Provenance from the South
A New Evaluation of the Arguments pro and contra —— 157

Christoph Berner
"I am YHWH your God, who brought you out of the land of Egypt" (Exod 20:2)
Reflections on the Status of the Exodus Creed in the History of Israel and
the Literary History of the Hebrew Bible —— 181

Reinhard Müller
The Origins of YHWH in Light of the Earliest Psalms —— 207

Ronald Hendel
God and the Gods in the Tetrateuch —— 239

Juha Pakkala
The Origins of Yahwism from the Perspective of Deuteronomism —— 267

Friedhelm Hartenstein
The Beginnings of YHWH and "Longing for the Origin"
A historico-hermeneutical query —— **283**

Bibliography —— 309

Authors —— 341

Index of Modern Authors —— 343

Index of Subjects and Names —— 349

Index of Ancient Sources —— 355

Introduction

The question of the beginning and origin of the worship of the god YHWH goes to the heart of Israelite-Jewish self-understanding and touches upon essential aspects of biblical theology. On the one hand, according to the Old Testament tradition the early historical revelation of YHWH grants Israel its *status* as the people of God (cf. Exod 19; Deut 7). The establishment of the historical and literary role of the figure of Moses and the Exodus narrative are closely related, but so too are those of kings Hezekiah and Josiah. On the other hand, the question of the beginning and origin of YHWH worship directly converges with the determination of YHWH's essence, as is reflected in the various different theologies of the Hebrew Bible.

Furthermore, the beginnings of Yahwism relate to the unresolved problems of the Israelite-Jewish history of religion. One solution, if a solution is to be found, is to achieve an interplay between philology and literary history, epigraphy and religious history, archaeology and cultural studies. Accordingly, the present volume offers a multifaceted analysis of relevant epigraphic, iconographic and biblical sources. In the process, it discusses various exegetical methods and research trajectories. The foundation of the volume is built on seven articles first published in German in 2012 in the *Berliner Theologischen Zeitschrift*.[1] For this publication those articles were updated, translated into English, and juxtaposed with five articles commissioned for this volume.[2] An updated English version of the philological analysis of the Tetragrammaton by Josef Tropper published in *Vetus Testamentum* in 2001 has also been newly added; in the estimation of the editors of this volume, Tropper's analysis has thus far received too little attention in the scholarly literature. The thirteen contributions brought together here illustrate the plurality of positions in the fierce debate to clarify whether YHWH originated in the South or the North, and provide a further evaluation of the arguments put forward in this discussion. Insofar as this volume includes European and North American scholars from different generations and confessions, as well as various disciplinary perspectives on the ancient world and religious history, it represents the present state of scholarship and fulfils the function of a current reference work.

---

1 The essays by Faried Adrom and Matthias Müller, Angelika Berlejung, Christoph Berner, Friedhelm Hartenstein, Manfred Krebernik, Reinhard Müller and Henrik Pfeiffer.
2 The essays by Ronald Hendel, Jörg Jeremias, Martin Leuenberger, Juha Pakkala and Mark S. Smith.

The volume's opening contribution from *Josef Tropper* (Berlin), which proceeds from the Akkadian transcription of North-West Semitic names and the grammatical structure of the Tetragrammaton, subjects the philological derivations of the YHWH-name proposed in previous studies to a critical appraisal. Tropper himself develops the thesis that the godlike name YHWH is a genuine nominal foundation, which fits seamlessly into the grammatical system of North-West Semitic onomastics. Tropper thereby deals extensively with the phenomenon of the long form *yhwh* and the short form *yhw/yh*; he discusses the relevant inscriptions from Kuntillet 'Ajrud and Khirbet el-Kom, which are also taken into account by all of the subsequent contributions to this volume, and touches upon the central questions of Northern Syrian-Palestinian religious symbolism.

The clarification of the beginnings and origins of YHWH worship is inseparably bound up with the determination of the profile of YHWH, and closely related to questions about to which type of deity YHWH ought to be assigned, both originally and in his religious-historical transformations, and how YHWH fits into the broader world of Ancient Near Eastern deities. The spectrum here ranges from a storm and thunder god to a weather god, all the way to a sun god; and in all these cases substantial affinities with a war god are present. Hence *Mark S. Smith* (Princeton) provides an overview of identifications of the oldest manifestations of YHWH with Baal, El, Athtar suggested in the literature, and correlates these with corresponding Egyptian, Ugaritic and biblical traditions and texts. It is clear that there are interferences between theological and regional classifications, and the worship of YHWH as a universal creator and the lord of history is a product of the theological reflection of the Persian-Hellenistic period.

Insofar as ancient Israel and Judah were always a part of the Ancient Near Eastern world and participated in the cultural and religious developments of Mesopotamia, Asia Minor, Northern Syria and Egypt, taking them up and altering them over time, the question arises as to how YHWH and early YHWH worship are represented from the perspective of the religious history of the Ancient Near East. This question is pursued by the assyriologist *Manfred Krebernik* (Jena) in his presentation: like Smith, he also considers the northern Syrian region, with its late Bronze Age Ugaritic texts which are immensely important for the elucidation of the Syrian-Palestinian religious and linguistic history, and reads central biblical sources such as Ps 29 from the perspective of Ancient Oriental Studies.

The introductory philological and religious-historical essays already cite important inscriptions such as the Moabite Mesha-Stele, in which, according to our current understanding, an East Jordanian king mentions YHWH as the state god of Israel for the first time in the middle of the 9th century BCE, and the inscriptions from Kuntillet 'Ajrud (8th century BCE), in which not only the inscription

"Yhwh and (his) Ashera" appears, but also pictures of gods/demons and animals next to the name Yhwh. The Egyptologists *Faried Adrom* and *Matthias Müller* (both from Basel) therefore subject all of the Egyptian texts which have been cited as supporting documents for the name of Yhwh to a critical review. Late Bronze Age Egyptian place name lists (from Amarah-West and Soleb), which are repeatedly suggested as a local terminal point for the oldest Yhwh worship in the North Arabian (Edomite and Midianite) region, are subject to especially meticulous philological and tradition-historical evaluation.

The archaeological findings in Judah point to worship of Yhwh without images from at least the Persian period, and in pagan world of the Hellenistic period the imageless cult is considered a Jewish speciality. Nevertheless, the precise age of the Old Testament prohibition against images is open to question; so too is whether, contrary to the Mosaic fiction, images still existed during the older Yhwh cult of the Late Bronze Age and Iron Age, and what they looked like. *Angelika Berlejung* (Leipzig/Stellenbosch) supplies the relevant overview, and describes the fundamental problem of assigning artefacts bearing images of gods to concrete gods and goddesses. In the process she achieves a foundational iconographic and theological contribution to the identification of a god and the relationship between god and image.

The contribution of *Henrik Pfeiffer* (Erlangen) again illustrates the theory which has for some time been known as the Berlin hypothesis,[3] namely that Yhwh, as a type of Syrian Baal-Hadad, was not imported from the South to Israel-Palestine, but rather originates in the North, hence from within the Syrian-Palestinian area itself. Here the texts already briefly exegeted by Smith, Judg 5, Ps 68, Deut 33 and Hab 3, may be expected to play a special role. The remarks of Pfeiffer are contrasted with two contributions which attempt to substantiate the classical derivation of Yhwh worship from the area of Edom: on the one hand, a thesis of *Jörg Jeremias*, professor emeritus of Old Testament at Marburg, who offers an exemplary historical sketch of the Jacob narratives; on the other hand, an overview oriented towards a detailed history of scholarship and methodology from *Martin Leuenberger* (Tübingen). The polarity between Pfeiffer's essay on the one hand, and Jeremias's and Leuenberger's on the

---

3 More precisely, it is a Giessen-Munich-Berlin hypothesis, since a crucial impetus for the formation of this theory dates back to an inaugural lecture by Christoph Levin at the University of Giessen in 1996. However, the lecture was only published after Levin moved to the Ludwig-Maximilians-Universität (Munich) ("Das vorstaatliche Israel." ZTK 97 [2000]: 385–403, here: 390). This was extended to a model of the history of religions in Berlin through the work of Henrik Pfeiffer und Matthias Köckert, accompanied by further observations made by Christoph Levin and his student Reinhard Müller (formerly of Munich, now in Münster).

other, illustrates the open questions surrounding both theories and signal directions for future research. In particular, future research should clarify whether the mediation of YHWH worship, if it is not completely indigenous, originates from the (Northern-)Syrian area or from the Edomite, Northern-Arabian region.

Christoph Berner (Göttingen) and *Reinhard Müller* (Münster) critically evaluate Exodus and selected Psalms, supposedly the oldest literary witnesses of YHWH worship, in this volume. The focus on the book of Exodus is explained by the claims made by the text itself: for in the context of modern research, Moses, if not the "founder of religion", is still viewed as an essential figure in the historical (or remembered) beginnings of the YHWH cult. The attention paid to selected Psalms is due to the insight from literary studies and history of religions that oldest elements (motifs, mythologies, traditions) of a religion have been preserved in cultic lyrics. Thus Reinhard Müller's analysis deepens the key poetic texts already addressed in the contributions from Mark S. Smith, Manfred Krebernik, Henrik Pfeiffer, Jörg Jeremias and Martin Leuenberger, namely Deut 33, Judg 5, Hab 3, Ps 29 and Ps 68, and juxtapose them with exegesis of Psalms 18, 24, 36, 48, 65, 93, 97 and 98.

The question of the beginnings of YHWH worship is not first posed from outside the biblical text, but is already being negotiated within the texts themselves,[4] such that one can speak of a multifaceted interdependence between a 'native history' and a 'scholarly history'. If the preceding essays represent above all a 'scholarly history', the contributions from *Ronald Hendel* (Berkeley) and *Juha Pakkala* (Helsinki) instead emphasise a literary-historical 'native history'. Hendel sketches – in the paradigm of a simplified documentary hypothesis and using the rubric of cultural memory – the origin narratives of the revelation of YHWH from the 'Elohist', 'Jahwist', and from the 'priestly writer' in the context of Genesis through to Exodus; the relation of YHWH to the gods of other peoples; and the beginnings of YHWH monotheism. Pakkala investigates the development of Yahwism in the deuteronomistic literature and determines, as Hendel elucidated for the theology of P, the destruction of Jerusalem in 587 BCE as an essential factor in the transition from YHWH-monolatrism during the monarchy to YHWH-monotheism and shows the shift of the centre YHWH-religion, at least that shaped by the Deuteronomist, from the temple to the text of the nascent Torah.

The considerations of *Friedhelm Hartenstein* (Munich) at the end of the volume are conceived as a more religion-theoretically and systematically applied

---

4 Cf. Gen 4:26; 12:8; 17:1; Exod 3:13–18; 6:2–8; Jos 18:1 (cf. Jer 7:12); 24:2–6; 1Sam 14:35; 2Sam 7:1 –16; 1Kgs 8.

summation of the religious-historical and exegetical essays. They pursue, on the one hand, the historical and philosophical premises and intentions of the search for the beginnings and origins in research which has taken place since the 19th century. On the other hand, they again expressly reflect the fact that the question of the beginnings of Yhwh worship is bound up with the relationship between monotheism and polytheism, as well as the iridescence of the concept of revelation.

The present volume cannot deliver a clear and indisputable answer to the question of the historical beginning and origin of the worship of Yhwh. The findings of the history of religion are too fragmentary, and the capacity of literary and reception historical analyses of biblical and extra-biblical sources are too limited, to designate historically the time and place where Yhwh worship begins. At the same time, detailed insights into the world of ancient eastern gods towards the second and early first millennia before Christ are possible. It is with this milieu that the Israelite and Judean dynastic and state god Yhwh arose and in the course of the sixth through to the forth centuries, through a complex tapestry of literary and theological-historical processes, ascended from the exclusively worshiped among the world of the gods, to one and only absolutely sovereign God. That the Hebrew Bible, in contrast to the myths of its surroundings, does not decree any theogony and that this Yhwh, who in contrast to his numerous typologically corresponding relatives in the panthea of Mesopotamia, Syria, Egypt or Greece has no genealogy, is only theologically appropriate if a grandeur is seen in him as the one who stands over against the world as its creator, history as its guide and life as the founder of its meaning. As such, Yhwh can have no beginning, and only he himself can be the source of his worship. From a theological perspective, what the letter to the Hebrews ascribes to the mysterious Melchizedek of Salem (Gen 14:18–22) as a model for Christ Jesus (Heb 7:3a) also applies to him: 'He is without a father, without a mother, without a genealogy, having neither beginning of days nor end of life.'

The historical search for the beginnings of the worship of this God can, then, only arrive at a relative goal, and merely marks points according to the present knowledge of the sources, showing for the first time a recognition of Yhwh as the sense of a greatness in the corresponding personal names, in individual rites and in religious texts. The determination of the historical origin of this worship, whether it be an historical (and as such reconstructable) experience of rescue from slaves fleeing Egypt, or in a manifestation in nature as thunder, downpour or storm, is likewise always only a relative possibility and must be newly revised for individual phases of literary history and history of religion.

We warmly thank the authors of this volume for making their contributions available to us, for readily fulfilling the wishes of the editors, and for having waited patiently for the publication. We would like to thank the *Evangelische Verlagsanstalt* (Leipzig) which published the previously mentioned volume of the *Berliner Theologische Zeitschrift*, and the *Brill publishing house* (Leiden) which published a German version of the article by Josef Tropper, for granting permission to print updated and translated versions of the original publications. We are also grateful to the editors of the BZAW series, John Barton, Reinhard G. Kratz, Nathan McDonald and Carol Newsom, for the inclusion of this anthology in the series, and to the staff of *de Gruyter publishing house* (Berlin), in particular Dr. Sophie Wagenhofer and Sabina Dabrowski, for their collaboration which has proven excellent throughout. During the corrections, the creation of typeset proofs and the preparation of the index we were ably supported by Heye Jensen, Gesine Meier and Brinthanan Puvaneswaran (all from Berlin) and also by Bianca Breunig and PD Dr. Lars Allolio-Näcke (both from Erlangen) and are thankful for all their efforts.

For preparing and reviewing the English translations of the articles written originally in German we would like to thank Stephen Germany (San Francisco, CA), Stephen Hamilton (Erlangen) and Tobias Tan (Oxford, UK).

Berlin and Erlangen, October 2016
Markus Witte

Jürgen van Oorschot

Josef Tropper
The Divine Name *Yahwa

1. It has long been known that the divine name "Yahweh," which is attested in Jewish personal names in Akkadian cuneiform texts of the neo-Babylonian and Achaemenid periods, appears in syllabic script[1] either as *ia-a-ḫu-ú* (and similar)[2] or as *ia-a-ma* (and similar).[3] The use of the two variants is dependent on the position in the name: the *ia-a-ḫu-ú*-variant is used when the divine name forms the first component of the name as a theophoric element (type: *ia-a-ḫu-ú*-X), while the *ia-a-ma* form appears only in second (last) position (X-*ia-a-ma*).[4] Both variants can be preceded by the determinative "dingir" (for deity); it occurs quite frequently before *ia-a-ḫu-ú* but only very rarely in front of *ia-a-ma*.

It is certain that syllabic *ia-a-ḫu-ú* stands for /yahû/ and thus corresponds to the alphabetical writing *yhw*. The interpretation of *ia-a-ma* is not quite as unanimous. That this, too, is a rendition of the "Yahwe"-name is undisputed. Following Cross (1962, 253, n. 122)[5], Coogan (1976, 53) and others, it is usually postulated that *ia-a-ma* stands for /yaw/ and consequently corresponds to the alphabetical writing *yw*. This presupposes, firstly, that the sign MA can have the phonetic value wa_6 in Late Babylonian (an unproblematic assumption),[6] and, secondly, that the final vowel was not articulated and is irrelevant for the interpretation.

In the following, the syllabic writing *ia-a-ma*, or better *ia-a-wa₆*, will be examined more closely. Despite the fact that is attested well over 100 times and

---

1 Concerning spelling variants and attestations in detail see especially M.D. Coogan, *West Semitic Personal Names in the Murašû Documents* (HSM 7; Missoula, Montana 1976), 49–50.52–53 and R. Zadok, *The Jews in Babylonia During the Chaldean and Achaemenid Periods Accordung to the Babylonian Sources* (Haifa 1979), 7–8; see also F. Joannès and A. Lemaire, "Trois tablettes cunéiformes à onomastique ouest-sémitique (collection Sh. Moussaïeff)," *Transeuphratène* 17 (1999), 17–34.
2 The most important variants are *ia-(a-)ḫu-u*, *ia-ku-ú* and *ia-ʾ-ú*.
3 The most important variants are *ia-ma* and *iá-a-ma*.
4 For instance, *ʾabī-ia-a-ma*, *ʾaḫī-ia-a-ma*, *banā-ia-a-ma*, *barak-ia-a-ma*, *barīk-ia-a-ma*, *gadal-ia-a-ma*, *ḥanan-ia-a-ma*, *yigdal-ia-a-ma*, *yadaʿ-ia-a-ma*, *mīka-ia-a-ma*, *mantan-ia-a-ma*, *ʿaqab-ia-a-ma*, *pa-da-a-ma* and *nērī-ia-a-ma*.
5 F.M. Cross, "Yahweh and the God of the Patriarchs," *HThR* 55 (1962), 225–259.
6 The phonetic value wa_6 for the sign MA is mentioned in the pertinent sign lists and syllabaries and can also be detected in genuinely Akkadian word forms from the Late Babylonian period on (e.g., in the royal inscriptions of Nabonidus); see Coogan, *West Semitic Personal Names* (see n. 1), 63, n. 69 and M. Weippert, Art. "Jahwe," *RlA* V (1977), 249.

DOI 10.1515/9783110448221-001

is most relevant to the dating of the original form of the divine name "Yahwe," it has thus far not received adequate scholarly attention.[7]

2. The interpretation of the writing *ia-a-wa₆* as /yaw/ and its identification with the alphabetical *yw* entails several problematic aspects. First of all, it should be noted that "Yahwe" as the second element in alphabetically recorded personal names of that period – also in Aramaic inscriptions to Akkadian texts – appears mostly as *-yhw* or *-yh* and only rarely as *-yw*.[8] Weippert (1977, 249) tried to tackle this problem by proposing that *ia-a-wa₆* "wenigstens z.T. nur konventionelle (aber auf *Jaw zurückgehende) Schreibung des isr. Gottesnamens als 2. Element von Personennamen ist, hinter der sich, jedenfalls in der Achämenidenzeit, unterschiedliche phonetische Realitäten verbergen." But what convention should the writing *ia-a-wa₆* follow? Why do we find consistently *-a* at the end of the word? And why is this writing encountered only in the second position of the personal name? These questions still lack no convincing answers.

3. It is quite noteworthy in this context that in two recently published texts in the collection Sh. Moussaïeff, Joannès – Lemaire (1999) have discovered the name ¹*ab-du-*ᵈ*ia/iá-a-ḫu-ú* (text 1, line 12 and 21)[9] or ¹*ab-da-ia-ḫu-ú* (text 2, lines 1) = /ʿabdu-yahû/ "servant of Yahweh" (cf. the alphabetical spellings ʿ*bdyh* and ʿ*bdyhw* in Aramaic texts, as well as the Hebrew ʿ*obadyāh*). These are the first instances of names containing "Yahwe" with spelling *ia-a-ḫu-ú* in the second position. They violate the seemingly fixed rule that *ia-a-ḫu-ú* is always in the first position and *ia-a-wa₆* always in the second. Joannès – Lemaire (1999, 20) have suggested that the (Babylonian) composers used the writing *ia-a-ḫu-ú* because they recognized this element as a divine name due to its clear name structure (following *ʿabd) and consequently prefixed the determinative "dingir." In their view, the Babylonian scribes would not have viewed the element *ia-a-wa₆* as a general divine name. This assumption is obviously relativized by the fact that we do not find the "dingir" determinative in the form ¹*ab-da-ia-ḫu-ú* (text 2), and that *ia-a-wa₆* is attested with determinative also in other texts (though rarely). Due to the fact that *ia-a-wa₆* and *ia-a-ḫu-ú* could change (in the second name position), Joannès and Lemaire (1999, 21) have expressed doubt – similar to Weippert (1977) – that *ia-a-wa₆* is to be identified with alphabetical *yw*. However, this finding could just as well be interpreted in another way; by differ-

---

7 This writing is not mentioned under the tetragrammaton YHWH in W. Gesenius, *Hebräisches und Aramäisches Handwörterbuch über das Alte Testament*, neu bearbeitet von R. Meyer und H. Donner unter Mitarbeit von U. Rüterswörden (Berlin ¹⁸1987 ff.), 446–447.

8 See Coogan, *West Semitic Personal Names* (see n. 1), 53.

9 This text is of particular interest because it mentions in l. 23 a city in Babylon named URU *ia-a-ḫu-du* (Joannès – Lemaire (see n. 1): "la ville de Juda").

ent pronunciation variants of ia-a-wa₆ and ia-a-ḫu-ú, precisely because orthographies change and the position of the name is not the only factor to have caused this change, unlike previously assumed. Consequently, the writing ia-a-wa₆ could stand for the form of the divine name with a final vowel /a/.

4. The assumption that the writing ia-a-wa₆ attests to a specific final vowel is, from the outset, no less improbable than the view that the ending /a/ has no phonological justification. Although short vowels were no longer consistently differentiated in genuinely Akkadian word forms during the Late Babylonian period, they were yet predominantly still written, and, surprisingly, in many cases even in a historically correct manner.[10] A view most commonly held in earlier Assyriology scholarship and based on (relatively late) Greek transcriptions is that all short vowels of the Late Babylonian period, whether (correctly) written or not,[11] were no longer spoken. This view is hardly found in more recent scholarship. Instead, Aro (1975, 12)[12] estimates "dass bevor ein weitgehender Abfall der Auslautvokale eingetreten ist, diese Vokale nur abgeschwächt wurden und allerlei Assimilationen unterlagen." In fact, this is the only way the high number of correct spellings and the wide range of orthographical variants can be explained.

With this regard, and yet to be treated separately, the question of the principles for rendering non-Akkadian word forms or proper names in the Late Babylonian period needs to be tackled. Given the large variability of writings there are only relatively few certain findings. The Babylonian scribes in these cases would have certainly been more oriented towards phonetics, as is generally common practice in the case of foreign words and proper names. Because the "Yahweh" element is consistently attested – well over 100 times[13] – in the second name position as ia-a-wa₆ written with the unchangeable -a in the final syllable, it is most likely that this word form indeed had a final vowel /a/.[14]

Are there further details in the Late Babylonian "Yahwe"-writings that can be outlined? The consistent plene-writing (ia-a) ia-a-wa₆ could speak for a long vowel in the first syllable, i.e. /yâwa/ (vowel lengthening as a result of diminution or loss of /h/), or for a pronunciation with /h/, i.e. /yahwa/. The writing ia-a-ḫu-ú should, on the other hand, be vocalized as /yahû/ or – because of

---

10 For documentation see J.P. Hyatt, *The Treatment of Final Vowels in Early Neo-Babylonian* (YOAR 23; New Haven 1941), 13–20.

11 See for example Hyatt, *Treatment* (see n. 10), esp. p. 23 und p. 28; cf. also GAG § 13c.

12 J. Aro, "Der Abfall der kurzen Auslautvokale im Spätbabylonischen und seine Einwirkung auf die Formenlehre," *Studia Orientalia* 46 (1975), 11–20.

13 Zadok, *Jews ins Babylonia* (see n. 1), 8, has already enumerated 111 examples of this writing.

14 This view is not new and has already been advanced by S. Mowinckel, "The Name of the God of Moses" (*HUCA 32*; 1961), 129. Mowinckel, however, traced *yahwa* back to an older *ya-huwa*.

the frequent *plene*-writing – as /yāhû/ (with secondary lengthening of the tone syllable) and most likely stands for **yahw* (word stem without an ending).[15]

5. But how can the final vowel /a/ of the postulated form /ya(h)wa/ be explained? It cannot be due to the inflection vowel of the accusative case, because this element never stands syntactically in the accusative in the attested personal names. Besides, singular nouns were certainly no longer declined triptotically in the Hebrew of that day. An possible solution may be found in ancient West Semitic personal names, especially Amorite names.

5.1 The nominal components of Amorite names have an ending -*u*, -*i* or -*a* or are completely without an ending.[16] Thus, one speaks of the *u*-, *i*-, *a*- or Ø-cases. These cases are distributed as follows[17]: the *u*-case functions as subject or (nominal) predicate. The *i*-case is only attested in the genitive, and exclusively in the second name-element. The *a*-case and Ø-case, respectively, are far more frequent than the *u*- and *i*-case and are attested in all syntactical functions. Adjectives prefer the Ø-case, but show also the *a*-case when they function clearly as predicatives.[18] While the *u*-case and *i*-case are sporadically expanded by the mimation (endings -*um* or -*im*), the *a*-case never has a mimation (a further indication that the *a*-case is not the accusative). Of course, the Ø-case, too, never has a mimation. It is clear from what has been said that the *a*-case and Ø-case are functionally closely related. This impression is further confirmed by the fact that forms with consonant gemination in the final stem sound never take the Ø-case, but instead usually take the *a*-case (e. g., the divine names "Hadda," "Jamma" and "Kakka"), and sometimes the *u*-case (e. g., the divine name "'Ammu").

When comparing the *u*- and *a*-cases to each other in their subject and predicate function, the following picture emerges: the *u*-case is predominantly in the first name-element (usually the subject); in the second element it is regulary present, only when it is lengthened by the emphasizing enclitic particle -*ma* (mostly it concerns the emphasized subject). The *a*-case, on the other hand, is attested mainly in the second name-element; it only stands in the first position if it has a clearly predicative function. For example, the element **il* ("God")

---

15 Concerning the development of *yahw* > *yāhû* see BL § 20s. Theoretically, *yāhû* could also have originated from the nominative form **yahwu*.

16 Here, only name endings which are not attributed to context inflection (inflection of the name as a whole according to the requirements of the syntactic context) are considered.

17 See M.P. Streck, *Das amurritische Onomastikon der altbabylonischen Zeit. Die Amurriter: Die onomastische Forschung. Orthographie und Phonologie. Nominalmorphologie* (AOAT 271/1; Münster 2000), §§ 3.40 – 3.43.

18 Adjectives are rarely found in the *a*-case, and never in the *i*-case.

serves as a subject only in the second position in the a-case (u-case only before an enclitic -ma).[19] Below are some examples of two-part names with a-case:

- a-bi-ia-ma /ʾabī-yamma/ (Nr. 91)[20] "(My) father is Yammu" [Subject]
- zi-im-ri-e-id-da /ḏimrī-hedda/ (Nr. 6501) "(My) protection is Haddu" [Subject]
- zi-im-ri-ḫa-na-ta /ḏimrī-ʿanata/ (Nr. 6507) "(My) protection is ʿAnatu" [Subject]
- ḫa-an-ni-i-la /ḥann(i)-ʾila/ (Nr. 1938) "God is merciful" [Subject]
- ia-wi-i-la /yaḥwī-ila/ (ARM 16/1, 237) "God has proved himself to be alive" [Subject following the PC[21] short form]
- iš-me-eḫ-ba-la /yišmaʿ-baʿla/ (Nr. 3816) "The Lord/Baʿlu has listened" [Subject following the PC short form]
- i-la-nu-nu (Nr. 2540) "Nunu is God" [Predicate]
- i-la-sa-lim (Nr. 2544) "Salim is God" [Predicate]
- zi-id-qa-ᵈIM /ṣidqa-haddV/ (Nr. 6461) "Haddu is righteousness" [Predicate]
- am-mi-za-du-ga /ʿammī-ṣaduqa/ (Nr. 753) "(My) father-brother is righteous" [Predicate]
- ḫa-an-naᵈi-dur-me-er (Nr. 1934) "Iturmer is merciful" [Predicate]
- su-mu-ba-la /šumu-baʿla/ (Nr. 5624) "Name/offspring of the Lord/Baʿlu" [Genitive]
- ḫa-ab-du-ba-aḫ-la /ʿabdu-baʿla/ (Nr. 1838) "Servant of the Lord/Baʿlu" [Genitive]

5.2 The a-case is also attested in cuneiform syllabic personal names of younger periods and is still widespread in West Semitic / Canaanite personal names of the Amarna letters, significantly primarily in the second position and commonly in association with divine names. Within the corpus of names collected by Hess (1993) which can be classified as West Semitic, the following two-part names with elements in the a-case (without contextual inflection) can be found.

Certain attestations:

- am-mu-ni-ra /ʿAmmu-nīra/ (EA 136:29; 1.141:3) "ʿAmmu is light" [Predicate][22]
- zi-im-ri-da /ḏimrī-(ha)dda/ (EA 83:26 u. ö.) "Haddu is (my) protection" [Subject]
- ia-aḫ-zi-ba-da /yaʿḏib-(h)adda/(?) (EA 275:4; 276:4) "Haddu has restored(?)" [Subject following the short form of the PC]

---

19 See Streck, *Das amurritische Onomastikon* (see n. 17), § 3.43. *il is more commonly found in the Ø-case.

20 The numbers refer to the "Index of Names" in I.J. Gelb, *Computer-Aided Analysis of Amorite* (Chicago 1980), 552–653.

21 PC = prefix conjugation, with two formal variants, the short form *yaqtul (= preterite or jussive) and the long form *yaqtulu (= imperfect).

22 Alongside this also ḫa-mu-ni-ri "ʿAmmu is my(?) light" (EA 137:15).

- *ia-ap-ti-ḫa-da* /yaptiḥ-(h)adda/ (EA 335:9) "Haddu has opened" [Subject following the short form of the prefix conjugation]
- *šu(-u)m-ad-da* /šum-(h)adda/ (EA 8:18 u.ö.) "Name/offspring of Haddu" [Genitive][23]
- ÌR-*a-ši-ir-ta* /ʿabd(V)-ʾaṯirta/ (EA 71:17 u.ö.) or ÌR-*aš-ra-ta* (EA 94:11; 102:23) "Servant of Ashera" [Genitive][24]
- DUMU-*a-na* /bin(V)-ʿana/ (EA 170:37) "Son of (the god) ʿAnu" [Genitive]
- *ri-ib-ad-da* /rīb-(h)adda/ (EA 73:2 u.ö.) "Litigation of Haddu" [Genitive][25]
- Further possible attestations are:
- *ši-ip-ṭú-ri-a* /šipṭu-rēṣa/(?) (EA 226:3) "the court/judgment is help(?)" [Predicate]
- *níq-ma-*ᵈIM /niqma-haddV/ (EA 49:2) "Haddu is (my) revenge" [Predicate][26]
- *ṣú-ra-šar* /ṣūr(a)-ašar/ (EA 319:4) "Ašar is a rock" [Predicative]
- ÌR-*ri-ša* /ʿabdV-riša/(?) (EA 363:3) [Genitive]
- *pu-ba-aḫ-la* /pû-baʿla/ (EA 104:7)[27] "Mouth/Command of Baʿlu" [Genitive]
- ÌR-*i-ra-ma* (EA 123:36) "...(?) is sublime(?)" [most likely predicate; alternatively: genitive]

In addition, monadic short names are also attested in the *a*-case (not conditioned by contextual syntax), for example, *a-zi-ra* "helper (?)" (continuously in EA 55, 59, 149 and 151)[28] and *ia-ma* "Yammu" (EA 230: 2).

5.3 It should be noted that finite PC verbal forms (always in the short form) normally do not have a specific (nominal) ending when functioning as a component of personal names. Hypocoristic names that consist only of the verbal element, however, can be nominalized and – depending on the syntactic context – be declined triptotically, i.e. they may bear the endings -*u(m)*, -*i(m)* or -*a(m)*, e.g. *ia-an-ḫa-mu/i/a* (nominative/genitive/accusative), literally, "he consoles."

6. Regarding the linguistic-historical explanation of this *a*-case, which occurs in personal names, there is no consensus in biblical scholarship. In the author's opinion it is to be interpreted as the ending of the "absolutive case," in use only in early Semitic. The functions of this case correspond to those of the so-called "status absolutus" in Akkadian, which probably can be traced back to the early Semitic absolutive case. It functions, among other things, as a predicative, vocative and (isolated)

---

23 In EA 97:1, however, *šu-mu-ḫa-d*[i] (if properly restored).
24 Alongside this, forms with *i*- und *u*-cases are also found (more seldom).
25 But more common are variants with the *i*-case, i.e. *ri-ib-(ḫa)-ad-di* (among others).
26 Alternative: "Revenge of Haddu."
27 Reading is unclear; see R.S. Hess, *Amarna Personal Names* (ASORDS 9; Winona Lake 1993), 126f.
28 In other texts the name is usually encountered in the *u*- or *i*-case.

citation form[29] of the noun, and is furthermore used when the case distinction is neutralized.[30] This case may be regarded as a relic of an older ergative-absolutive syntax in Semitic, in which the absolutive case (ending with -a) covered all the syntactic core functions with the exception of the identification of the agent of transitive verbs (i.e. the "ergative," ending with -u).[31]

The absolutive case could have persisted in proper names for two reasons: a) because proper names often have preserved linguistically archaic features that otherwise have become obsolete; b) because many nominal elements in proper names are encountered in the syntactic environment typical for the absolutive case (predicate function, case neutralization, citation form). Since names are grammatically conservative, remnants of the a-case are also to be expected in (West Semitic) proper names of the 1st millennium BCE, especially in theophoric elements.

7. Returning to the subject of the "Yahwe"-bearing names in Late Babylonian texts: the above mentioned line of arguments supports the assumption that the writing ia-a-ḫu-ú stands for the unexpanded form of the divine name in the Ø-case, i.e. for /yāḫû/ < *yahw, and the writing ia-a-wa₆ in turn for the divine name in the a-case, i.e. for /ya(h)wa/. The case rules presented above offer for the first time a plausible explanation as to why the element ia-a-ḫu-ú – with one exception – always appears in the first position and the element ia-a-wa₆ always in the second position. And, indeed, with regard to the findings concerning the a-case, presented in §6 – particularly in connection with the divine name – is to be expected primarily in the second position. Even the only exception in the form of ab-du/a-ᵈia/iá-a-ḫu-ú, "servant of Yahweh," mentioned in §3, is consistent with the findings concerning ancient West Semitic names. Here the divine name clearly has a genitive function. And in this function the i- or Ø- case is used more frequently than the a-case in older names.[32]

---

29 This is probably the reason why early West Semitic loanwords in Akkadian (e.g. kumra "priest") and also a large part (over 70%) of Semitic loanwords in Egyptian sources of the New Kingdom have an a-ending (cf. J.E. Hoch, Semitic Words in Egyptian Texts of the New Kingdom and Third Intermediate Period (Princeton 1994), 454.

30 Concerning this see Streck, Das amurritische Onomastikon (see n. 17), §§ 3.51–52, J. Tropper, "Die Endungen der semitischen Suffixkonjugation und der Absolutivkasus," JSS 44 (1999), esp. pp. 187–191 and H.-J. Sasse, "Case in Cushitic, Semitic and Berber," in Current Progress in Afro-Asiatic Linguistics. Papers of the Third International Hamito-Semitic Congress, (ed. J. Bynon; Amsterdam and Philadelphia 1984), who reconstructs an absolutive case in -a (with comparable functions) for Proto Cushitic and Proto Berber.

31 C.H.P. Müller, "Ergative Constructions in Early Semitic Languages," JNES 54 (1995), esp. 264 f.

32 See Streck, Das amurritische Onomastikon (see n. 17), §§ 3.14 and 3.18. The writing ᵈia/iá-a-ḫu-ú stands for the divine name in the Ø-case (see § 4).

The preserved *a*-case may perhaps also be the reason why the "dingir"-determinative is almost never found before the name element *ia-a-wa$_6$*. As in these cases the determinative is more dispensable than in the form of the divine name without an ending, because the *a*-ending itself (and probably also the second position in the name) indirectly indicates that a divine name is present. At any rate, it is not to be concluded from the absence of the determinative that the writer would not have recognized "Yahwe" as a divine name. In syllabically attested older Semitic personal names, too, the theophoric element predominantly appears without the "dingir"-determinative.

8. The syllabically discernable variants */yāhû/* vs. */ya(h)wa/* probably also have a rough equivalent in alphabetical spellings of personal names, although the distribution of the variants is not directly comparable. For example, the "Yahwe"-element in epigraphically attested earlier Judean personal names is predominantly written *yhw*, while in contemporary (northern) Israelite personal names it was usually *yw*,[33] most of them attested in the second name position. Furthermore, in Judah a diachronic development can be observed: in the pre-exilic period, almost exclusively names with the *yhw*-element occur, whereas in the post-exilic period names with the *yh*-element predominate.[34]

The "Judean" writing *yhw* probably stands for */yāhû/* and thus corresponds to the syllabic variant *ia-a-ḫu-ú*.[35] The writing *yh*, which prevails in later times, reflects a phonetic reduction revealing the loss of the final vowel (*/yāh/* < **yāhû*). This is a consequence of the strong emphasis on the first syllable producing a lengthening of this syllables's vowel, of which the syllabic *plene*-writing (*ia-a-*) also testifies.

The so-called "Israelite" writing *yw*, which is clearly not limited to northern Palestine only, but also appears in Juda, particularly in ancient times – for instance in Kuntillet ʿAjrud (several names with *yw*-element in the second position), and sometimes also in later Aramaic texts of the Achaemenid period (among other spellings) – has been until now vocalized as */yaw/* and interpreted as having developed from **yahw* or **yahû* due to the diminution of */h/*. Such an interpretation is possible, but not mandatory. It is important to bear two things in mind: on the one hand, the postulated */yaw/*-pronunciation would be a phonetically very advanced form of the divine name and typologically clearly young-

---

33 See D.N. Freedman and M. O'Connor, Art. "JHWH," *ThWAT III* (Stuttgart *et al.* 1980), 539 f. and Weippert, Jahwe (see n. 6), 247 f.

34 See J. Renz, *Die Althebräischen Inschriften, Bd. II/1: Zusammenfassende Erörterungen, Paläographie und Glossar* (Darmstadt 1995), 90; cf. also G.R. Driver, "The Original Form of the Name 'Yahweh': Evidence and Conclusions," *ZAW 46* (1928), 18 f.

35 Theoretically, the writing *yhw* could also stand for */yahwa/* (name in the *a*-case).

er than the "Judean" /yắhû/; on the other hand, particularly in the Northern Kingdom, we would expect a monophthongization of the form to *yô (< *yaw), whose vowel should be at least sporadically written with h-grapheme.

Given the very early attestation of the names with the yw-element, an alternative explanation should be considered: The writing yw could stand for /yâwa/ < *yahwa and thus represent the form of the divine name in the (Early Semitic) a-case.[36] This theory has several advantages over the traditional explanation: a) The loss of /h/ in the original syllable-closing position, which would be assumed to be present, would be here phonetically very obvious (and similar to the phenomenon of Aleph quiescens). b) The form would not be typologically younger than the /yãhû/-form which prevailed in Judah. c) The form would directly correspond to the syllabic writing ia-a-wa₆ = /ya(h)wa/, which would otherwise be isolated. d) By assuming different basic shapes of the "Yahwe"-name, the theory would for the first time provide an explanation for why this element has taken such various phonetic developments within a very small geographical area.

9. It follows from the foregoing considerations that the divine name "Yahwe" (basic form *yahw) – at least in the Late Babylonian period – is syntactically treated as a nominal word form, and, more precisely, as a qatl-pattern analogous to many other divine names such as Baʻl(u), Hadd(u) and Yamm(u). In particular, the writing ia-a-wa₆ rules out an interpretation of the name as a verbal prefix conjugation (= PC), since PC-forms never show the specific a-case in ancient Semitic names.

This result is diametrically opposed to the dominant and long-held opinion in Hebrew Studies, according to which the name "Yahwe" is to be analyzed formally as a PC-form of the root √hwy (which, only sencondarily, would have been nominalized). This view can be found in recent contributions regarding the "Yahwe"-name, including encyclopedias[37] and relevant dictionaries (KBL³ und Ges¹⁸), explicitly in Knauf (1988, 43) in particular: "YHWH repräsentiert altes /YvHWv:/ oder /YvHWv/; Versuche, darin etwas anderes als eine Imperfektform zu erkennen, sind als gescheitert zu betrachten." If this is true, our considerations would be invalid. But how firm is the foundation on which this "verbal theory" is based? Below, weak points of this theory are stated:

---

36 The final vowel /a/ could of course have been dropped in the course of the language's history, in the context caof the general diminution of short vowels. But the starting point of the genesis of the yw-writing is the basic form *yahwa (a-case).

37 M. Görg, Art. "Jahwe," NBL, Bd. II (Zürich and Düsseldorf 1992), 260–266; Freedman and O'Connor, JHWH (see n. 33); K. van der Toorn, Art. "Yahweh" in DDD, (ed. K. van der Toorn et al.; Leiden. 1995), 1711–1730.

a) Divine names that exist formally (only) from a PC-form are very rare in ancient Semitic cultures (whereas personal names of this type are common), cf. the name ^{d}Ikšudum (from Mari) and the divine bynames ya'ūq "he protects" and yaġūṯ "he helps,"[38] attested in ancient North Arabia.

b) The greatest weakness of the verbal theory lies in the fact that it has to assume the long form of the PC (i. e. the imperfect tense) of the root √hwy to explain spellings of the tetragrammaton with h and Greek renderings of the name with /e/ in the final syllable; see for instance Knauf (1988, 43, note 206.): "Der Name geht eher auf ein Lang- als ein Kurzimperfekt zurück, er hat beschreibenden Charakter." Against this interpretation it is to be said that not a single reliable PC long form (type yaqtulu) can be detected in ancient West Semitic names, including the Amarna names. Even the previously mentioned Arabic divine bynames refer to the short form of the PC. A basic form /yahwī/ and not /yahwē/ (or similar) would therefore be expected for the "Yahweh"-name.

c) The repeatedly postulated linking of the "Yahwe"-name with the verbal element ia-(aḫ-)wi (for instance ia-wi-DINGIR, ia-wi-i-la, ia-wi-um and ia-aḫ-wi-um),[39] attested in Amorite personal names, is refuted. The element ia-(aḫ-)wi is to be derived not from √hwy, but instead from √ḥwy "live" (PC short form /yaḥwī/: "[The god NN] has proved to be alive").[40]

d) Moreover, the /a/-vocalism of the postulated prefix-syllable presents a problem. According to Hebrew morphonology, an /i/-vocalism (in the Qal) would be expected.[41] The /a/-vocalism would only be justified if the name had a pre-Hebrew origin (and would not have been changed subsequently) or could be assigned to the causative stem (√hwy Hifʿil). If a causative stem is postulated, one could point to even fewer formal parallels to the "Yahwe"-name. An additional consideration is that no causative stem is attested to the root √hwy "be," with which the "Yahwe"-name is primarily associated.[42]

---

38 C.E.A. Knauf, "Yahwe," VT 34 (1984), 468; id. Midian. Untersuchungen zur Geschichte Palästinas und Nordarabiens am Ende des 2. Jahrtausends v. Chr. (Wiesbaden 1988), 44 f.

39 For proponents of this view see M.P. Streck, "Der Gottesname 'Jahwe' und das amurritische Onomastikon," WO 30 (1999), 35–38. Of enduring influence has been W. von Soden, "Jahwe 'Er ist, Er erweist sich,'" WO 3 (1966), 177–187, who derived ia-aḫ-wi and ia-wi from the Verb √hwy "to be" and explained the forms as being so-called "präfigierende Stative" with the meaning "he is" = "he proves to be" (ibid. p. 183).

40 See Streck, Gottesname (see n. 39); cf. also Knauf, "Yahwe" (see n. 38), 467.

41 See Freedman, "JHWH" (see n. 33), 545.

42 See for instance Görg, "Jahwe" (see n. 37), 261.

e) Similarly, the /w/ can not be expected as a second radical assuming a southern Canaanite origin of the divine name (one expects /y/). The name would have to be of Aramaic or northern Arabic provenance.

f) To date, representatives of the verbal theory cannot present a truly plausible etymology for the postulated PC-form *yahwē, even when all etymological possibilities for √hwy that Semitic dictionaries have to offer have been exhausted (e.g. "be;" "fall;" "blow;" "desire, love;" "speak").[43]

g) Starting from a basic form *yahwē (PC long form), the attested shortenings of the "Yahwe"-name, for instance the variants *yahû and *yah, cannot be explained. *yahû could at best be attributed to a PC short form, such as Weippert (1977, 252) has suggested: "Jāhū (< *Jáhū < *Jáhw < *Jáhwî)." But if a PC short form were the underlying basis, this would have to be found at least somewhere in the form of a writing *yhwy for /yahwî/. It is also hard to imagine (and not supported by parallels) that the short and long form of the PC would coexist beside each other from the beginning as equal or dialectal variants of one name, the more so as the meanings of the short and long form are diametrically opposed to each other.

In summary, it should be noted that verbal theories to explain the "Yahwe"-name raise serious problems and leave many questions unanswered. And in no case they are so compelling that they would eliminate other explanations.

10. If the divine name "Yahwe" was indeed considered a nominal word form, then it is unlikely that the "Yahwe"-name is derived from a root √hwy, since nominal yVqtVl-formations are extremly rare in Semitic. If the spellings testified a qatl-pattern – as pointed out above – then this deduction would be completely ruled out. Regarding the etymology, in this case only the roots √yhw/y or √whw/y[44] (and theoretically also √w/yhh) would be possible. Roots with this radical sequence are not very frequent in Semitic languages, but still sporadically detectable. The Arabic lexicon offers several such roots with different meanings, listed e.g. in Cohen (1996, 505–508).[45] However, none of these meanings seems appropriate for a divine name. Therefore, the etymology of the "Yahwe"-name must still remain open. It will, maybe, never be resolved with certainty, the more so as a non-Semitic origin cannot be excluded. As is well-known, many other divine names of Semitic Panthea, too, have no certain etymology, e.g. Aṯirat, ʿAnat und Dagān.

In this context, we also have to consider the possibility that the variants of the "Yahwe"-element found in personal names do not match the basic form of the in-

---

43 See Weippert, "Jahwe" (see n. 6), 251f.
44 Forms I-w became I-y in Northwest Semitic.
45 D. Cohen, *Dictionnaire des racines sémitiques ou attestées dans les langues sémitiques*, Fasc. 6 (Leuven 1996).

dependent divine name. Theoretically, all these variants could represent abbreviations of the name. The (independent) divine name "Yahwe" could be traced back, for example, to a reduplication form of a biradical base *wah: *wah-wah- > yahwah- (w > y in initial sound). The tetragrammaton would then testify to a complete reduplication of this basis, and the element *yahw, which is found in personal names, to an incomplete reduplication. And, lastly, the additionally attested name variant yāh (or yah) would correspond with the non-reduplicated base.[46]

11. But the basic form of the (independent) divine name "Yahwe" could very well have been *yahwa (divine name with a-case). First of all, it should be noted that the ancient Greek transcriptions of the divine name do not rule out this hypothesis in any way. The transcriptions in question show predominantly an ε in the final position (ιαουε, ιαβε [etc.]), and also αι (ιαουαι). It is indisputable that the Greek ε can reflect Semitic /a/ in a stressed closed syllable.[47] Likewise, ε is also used to transcribe an unstressed vowel /a/ or long /ā/ in an open final syllable. It is to be further noted that from the first century AD on, the Greek αι was pronounced as an (lengthened) ε and therefore presupposes neither a diphthong nor an /i/-vocalism in the final sound of the "Yahwe"-name.

Particularly instructive in this context are the Septuagint renderings of the Old Testament personal name šammā(h) in the form of σομμε, σομε, σαμαι and the like (e.g. σαμ(μ)α), because here an unstressed final vowel /-ā/ – however it may be explained grammatically[48] (it could be a secondary lengthened case vowel) – is transliterated with ε and αι.

Given this finding, the Greek ιαουε (and similar) can unproblematically reflect a name form *yahwa or (with secondary lengthening of the final vowel) *yahwā. The transliterations mentioned above would imply that the divine name was stressed on the first syllable, as expected. With a stress on the second syllable, rather a transcription with α in final position is to be expected, especially considering that Hebrew word forms with a feminine ending (St. abs.) are often transliterated in this way.[49]

As is well known, there are also transcriptions of the "Yahwe"-name as (Greek) ιαω or (Latin) iaho, which is particularly widespread in the writings of syncretistic Gnostic circles and in the context of personal names with the

---

46 This explanation of the divine name could be supported by the repetition of the yāh-element (instead of the tetragrammaton) in Isa 38:11, although this is debated by text critics.

47 In Origen's *Secunda* this phenomenon is very common; see G. Janssens, *Studies in Hebrew Historical Linguistics Based on Origen's Secunda* (OrGand 9; Leuven 1982), 67–75.

48 Cf. KBL[3], 1437b ("die Erkl[ärung] des PN ist fraglich") and Ges[18], 1376a ("Etym[ologie] uns[icher] ... wobei nicht alle fünf Belege v. derselben Wz. stammen müssen").

49 See Janssens, *Studies in Hebrew* (see n. 47), 150–153.

"Yahwe"-element.[50] These writings clearly reflect the short form of the divine name without the *a*-extension, i.e. they stand for *yahû* or *yaw*. In any case the coexistence of the orthographies ιαουε and ιαω (or *iaho*) proves that a short and long form of the divine name existed alongside each other in Hebrew. The first is to be identified as *yahû* < *yahw* (name without case ending), whereas the latter seems to be based on the form *yahwa* (name with case ending -*a*).

12. However, the Hebrew tetragrammaton *yhwh* as well as *yhwh*-spellings of the (independent) divine name in earlier epigraphic texts (e.g. in the Kuntillet ʿAjrud inscriptions and the Moabite Mesha-inscription, line 18) seem to argue against a basic form *yahwa*, because a short /*a*/-final vowel is not to be expected to be written *plene*. Here, however, we must warn against jumping to conclusions.

First of all, it should be noted that the divine name is written often, but not always, *plene* in early Hebrew inscriptions.[51] For instance, in the inscription from Kuntillet ʿAjrud (KAǧr) 10:1,[52] which dates from the 9th century, one encounters the spelling *yhw* (*w-ntn lh yhw k-lbbh*), while in the immediately following line of the same inscription we find *yhwh* (*l-yhwh htmn w-l-ʾšrth*).

Furthermore, it can be expected that the ancient Hebrew speakers wanted to consciously preserve the /*a*/-final vowel in the divine name to give it an archaic sound, and thus counteracted the impending loss by a secondary lengthening of this vowel: *yahwa* > /*yahwā*/. Special phonetic variations of word forms with a numinous meaning can also be observed elsewhere in Semitic.[53] On the other hand, according to Hebrew writing, a long final vowel /-*ā*/ could already have been written *plene* using *h* in the 9th century BCE,[54] especially considering that *plene* writing is to be expected in proper names rather than in other word forms.[55]

---

50 An excellent overview of the ancient transcriptions of the divine name in the patristic literature is offered by M. Rose, *Jahwe. Zum Streit um den alttestamentlichen Gottesnamen* (Theologische Studien 122; Zürich 1978), 6–16.

51 See Renz, *Inschriften II/1* (see n. 34), 89.

52 Abbreviations (sigla) and numbering of ancient Hebrew inscriptions according to Renz, *Inschriften II/1* (see n.32).

53 One may think of the Arabic pronunciation of the divine name with [ḷ] (Aḷḷāh), a phoneme that does not exist elsewhere in the language, or of Akkadian word forms with so-called numinous gemination (e.g. *ziqqurratum* "ziggurat, temple tower" or *namurrum* "awe-inspiringly radiant" [see GAG § 55p-q]).

54 The opinion of Renz, *Inschriften II/1* (see n. 34), 92 that the unstressed /*ā*/ is written consistently defective in pre-exilic Hebrew inscriptions in general, and in particular in the (early) inscriptions of Kuntillet ʿAjrud, is not tenable in this form. Regarding Kuntillet ʿAjrud, J. Renz, *Die Althebräischen Inschriften, Bd. I: Text und Kommentar* (Darmstadt 1995), 52 can only claim that the pronominal suffix 2.m.sg. -*k* and the adverb ʿ*t* "now" are not written *plene*. In both cases, however, there is no guarantee that long vowels are actually present (from the perspective of his-

But is the here postulated *plene* spelling of a secondary lengthened case vowel -*a* in the divine name "Yahwe" really an isolated phenomenon? The subsequent observations will show that this is not the case. Also in several other (Hebrew and Moabite) word forms, a case vowel -*a* can be written *plene*. Significant in this context are particularly feminine word forms with the letters -*th* in the final position, since the *h* here cannot be feminine marker:

a) In ancient Hebrew poetry we repeatedly encounter feminine nouns in the status absolutus ending -*ātā(h)* instead of -*ā(h)*, e.g. *yᵉšûʿātā(h)* "salvation" (Ps 3:3). These forms have been interpreted in older grammars (GK § 90f and BL § 65 t) as archaic (solidified) "locatives" (i.e. forms with *he* locale) or archaic accusatives, in which it was presupposed that these two cases were historically of the same origin. We know today, mainly due to Ugaritic, that this assumption is not correct.[56] With these word forms a "locative" is syntactically highly implausible because no clear information about direction or location is intended. Thus there remains only the possibility of an accusative. If we examine more closely the syntactical context of these word forms, however, it appears that the accusative case would be justified only in certain instances. The situation is different, however, if one starts from the absolutive case, which in the singular formally coincides with the accusative singular. This assumption is especially supported by the fact that the word forms in question are repeatedly found in predicative use, a central domain of the absolutive case, for example subsequent to *ʾên* "there is not," *loʾ* "(it is) not" (in a nominal clause) or the auxiliary verb √*hyh* "to be (something)."[57] Here are some examples: *ʾên yᵉšûʾātā(h)-llô be(ʾ)lohîm* "there is no salvation in God for him" (Ps 3:3); *kî hāyîtā*

---

torical linguistics, rather short vowels form the basis!). On the other hand, it is observed that the Kuntillet ʿAjrud inscriptions do contain *plene* spellings in end position of words, e.g. in the (masculine) personal names *ywʿśh* /*yaw(a)-ʿaśâ*/ "Yahweh has done" (KAgr 8:1) and *ʿdnh* (KAgr 3:1). The latter name, which corresponds to the biblical *ʿadnā(h/ʾ)*, could be based on *ʿi/adna* (lexeme *ʿi/adn* "pleasance" in the *a*-case). In more recent pre-exilic inscriptions (Lachish), even the ending /-*tā*/ of the "perfect" tense (2.m.sg.) could be written *plene* as -*th* (see S. Gogel, *A Grammar of Epigraphic Hebrew* [SBLRBS 23; Atlanta 1998], 84–87).

55 It is interesting in this context that in Geʿez (Ethiopian), a specific accusative marker -*hā* is found (only) for proper names, while the accusative case is otherwise denoted by -*a* (see CDG, 213a). Although the derivation of the morpheme -*hā* is unclear, an etymological relation with the case morpheme -*a* is very likely.

56 Cf. Ugaritic *arṣh* = /ʾarṣah/ "to the earth" (directional [terminative] case) versus accusative *arṣ* = /ʾarṣa/.

57 In Classical Arabic the predicate following *kāna* "to be," *laysa* "be not" and *lā* as an expression of general denial stands formally in the accusative case. From a diachronic point of view this correlates to the functions of the ancient absolutive case (concerning this reasoning, see J. Tropper, "Kasusverhältnisse in arabischen Ausnahmesätzen: Absolutiv nach ʾillā," *ZAL* 37 (1999), 27f.

ʿæzrātā(h)-llî "for you are my help" (Ps 63:8); wᵉloʾ-ʿawlātā(h)-bbô (Qere) "there is no unrighteousness in him" (Ps 92:16); lûlê YHWH ʿæzrātāh llî "If Yahweh were not my help" (Ps 94:17).[58]

Forms with the ending -ātā(h) are found in poetry also in a subject function (such as ʾêmātā(h) in Exod 15:16) or following the preposition b (e.g. Ps 12:1; 125:3). Assuming an absolute case and considering the broad syntactic use of the a-case in ancient Semitic personal names, these syntagmas do not get completely out of the line.

b) In Old Testament prose texts there are numerous geographical names with the ending -āh. Of particular importance are, again, feminine lexemes ending in -ātā(h) (with clear penultimate stress), e.g. timnātā(h) "Ti/amna" (Josh 19:43 and passim). In earlier research, these forms were interpreted as archaic "locatives." But this is contradicted by the fact that many of these names are attested in the genitive function, after prepositions as well as after a nomen regens. A different interpretation was proposed by Segert (1988),[59] who assumed a diptotic inflection of this name (nominative -u, genitive/accusative -a). However, also this solution is not always applicable. In cannot explain, for example, why in Josh 19:43, as part of a list-like enumeration of place names (i.e. nominative function), the form timnātā(h) is present. Yet when considering the word forms in question as attestations of a (preserved) absolute case, this problem disappears, since the absolute as a "citation form" is expected exactly in a syntactically isolated position. Whichever of the two solutions is favored, it remains a fact that here an originally short case vowel /a/ is written plene.[60]

c) In a Hebrew ostracon of the Moussaieff collection from the 7ᵗʰ/6ᵗʰ centuries BCE (D. / H. No. 79/4), published by German – Heltzer (1995) and updated by Lehmann (1998), a personal name ʾḥmlkh (bn yhwʾr) is found in line 4 which is likely to be equated with ᵃʾḥîmælæk and (epigraphic) ʾḥmlk ("[My] brother is Malk/king") respectively, despite the writing with h. This assumption is supported primarily by the seal WSS 58, where the same name (written ʾḥmlk) is encountered with the same patronym (yhwʾr): l ʾḥmlk yhwʾr. Therefore, it is obvious that

---

58 Note that in each case the initial consonant of the (following) preposition is geminated (doubled). Apparently, the preceding case vowel was pronounced shortly, despite the plene writing.

59 S. Segert, "Diptotic Geographical Feminine Names in the Hebrew Bible," ZAH 1/1 (Probeheft 1988), 34–37.

60 From the perspective of historical linguistics, the two aforementioned explanations do not contradict each other at all. The phenomenon of diptosy – primarily attested in connection with proper names – reflects an older ergative case system, in which two main cases (a-case and u-case) are in opposition to each other (see § 6).

the element *mlkh* in *'ḥmlkh* stands for /*malkā*/ < **mal(i)ka* (divine name "Mal (i)k" in the secondary lengthened *a*-case).[61]

d) Also, several of the numerous masculine personal names found in the Old Testament with the ending /-*ā*/ (written *plene* with *h* or *'*)[62] probably reflect a preserved (and secondarily lengthened) *a*-case, especially since there are obviously also names with a preserved *u*-case (nominative) exhibiting a (lengthened) ending /-*ō*/.[63] The following names come into consideration: *'abdā(')* (alongside *'æbæd* [cf. *'æbæd* "servant"]); *'adnā(h/')* (alongside *'edæn* [cf. *'edæn* "delight"]; *'uzzā('/h)* (cf. *'oz* "protection"); *'îrā(')* (alongside *'îr*, *'îrû* und *'îrî* [cf. *'îr* "donkey foal"]) *ṣibyā(')* (cf. *ṣᵉbî* "gazelle"); cf. also *šammā(h)* (cf. § 11) and *šim'ā('/h)*.[64]

e) The tribal name "Judah," i.e. *yᵉhûdā(h)*, can also be explained as a masculine word form in the *a*-case for various reasons: firstly, as a tribal name, "Judah" has a masculine gender and also refers to the (male) ancestor "Judah"; secondly, the Old Testament also contains an ending-less place name *yᵉhud* (Josh 19:45); and thirdly, the name "Judah" appears in neighboring languages and cultures in the masculine form, e.g. cuneiform **ia-(a-ḫ)u-du* (and similar), Biblical Aramaic *yᵉhûd*[65] and Arabic *yahūd*.

f) Clearly a number of particle-like word forms, which have been passed down in biblical Hebrew with an ending -*ā(h)* or -*o(h)*, attest to an (lengthened) case ending -*a*. Particularly significant are particles which are found alongside each other with or without a corresponding ending, such as *'ôyā(h)* "woe!" (alongside *'êk*), *'êkāh* "how?" (alongside *'êk*) and *ko(h)* "here, so" (alongside *kākāh* "so"). We may also point to the adverb *'attā(h)* "now, currently" (*'et* "(point in) time" in the *a*-case), which in earlier times epigraphically appeared (still) defectively as *'t*. Sometimes it cannot be decided with certainty whether

---

61 For other explanations – emendation of *'ḥmlky* or assumption of a female theophoric element corresponding to the Phoenician (*')ḥmlkt* – see R.G. Lehmann, "Typologie und Signatur. Studien zu einem Listenostrakon aus der Sammlung Moussaieff," *UF* 30 (1998), 433.

62 A list of such names is given by R. Zadok, *The Pre-Hellenistic Israelite Anthroponymy and Prosopography* (OLA 28; Leuven 1988), 155f.

63 See Zadok, *Anthroponymy* (see n. 62), 158 with supporting attestations (including the name *dôdô*).

64 The ending /-*ā*/ may, of course, be due to another morpheme. But, that they may also represent a case ending has been largely overlooked in previous research; Zadok, *Anthroponymy* (see n. 62), 154–156 did not consider this possibility.

65 In BLA § 51n Aramaic *yᵉhûd* is explained – following C. Brockelmann, *Grundriß der vergleichenden Grammatik der semitischen Sprachen, I: Laut- und Formenlehre* (Berlin 1908), 398, n. 1 – as a secondary back-formation of the nisbe form *yᵉhûdāy* ("Judaean"). This explanation would only be convincing if "der alte Stammesname verschollen war," as Brockelmann has suspected. This assumption, however, is historically implausible.

an *a*-case or a "locative" ending is the base, for example with *hennā(h)* "here," *'ānāh* "where(?)" (alongside *'ān*), *šammāh* "there" (alongside *šām*). In Biblical Aramaic, on the other hand, similar adverbs exhibit the endings *-ā(')* or *-ā(h)*, for example *kā(h)* "so," *ṭammā(h)* "there," *kollā(')* "entirely," *yattîrā(h)* "very, excessively," *'ellā(')* "above," *'ar'ā(')* "below" (cf. BLA §§ 55 and 68b).

g) As already mentioned, the Israelite divine name "Yahwe" is attested in the Moabite Mesha inscription (l. 18) spelled out as *yhwh*. According to our analysis, this is a *plene* writing of **yahwa*. Significantly, the same inscription testifies to a second divine name according to the same orthographic principle: namely the name "Dawda" in the form of the writing *dwdh* (l. 12). The context is: *w-'šb mšm 't 'r'l dwdh* "And I brought back from there the cultic hearth(?) of Dawda."[66] "Dawda" is to be identified either with the name of a local Moabite deity or – as Na'aman (1997, 88 f.)[67] has suggested – with the name of the deified founder of the Hauronen dynasty. The name is most easily interpreted as a nominal *qatl*-pattern of the root √*dwd* (with a preserved diphthong) according to the Hebrew divine name *dod* < **dawd* (Amos 8,14 [cj.]) and the Hebrew personal name *dôdô* (2 Sam 23:9, 24 // 1 Chr 11:12, 26), which stems from **dawdu*.[68] The writing with *h* indicates the preserved and possibly secondarily lengthened *a*-case (absolute).[69] The Moabite "tetragrammaton" *dwdh* thus stands for /*dawdā*/ just as the Israelite tetragrammaton *yhwh* stands for /*yahwā*/.

h) In earlier Hebrew inscriptions, the divine name "Yahwe" appears mostly as *yhwh*. In addition, however, the writing *yhw* occurs (indisputably in Kuntillet 'Ajrud [KAgr] 10:1; possibly in KAgr 3:1), which in the (later) Aramaic texts from Elephantine (alongside the rarer *yhh*) is the normal writing for "Yahwe." According to our interpretation *yhwh* stands for the name in the (preserved) *a*-case, while *yhw* stands for the name in the Ø-case (without a final vowel) and thus

---

66 Cf. line 17 f. (parallel structure): *w-'qḥ mšm '[t k]ly yhwh* "And I took from there [the cultic] tools/vessels(?) of Yahwe."

67 N. Na'aman, "King Mesha and the Foundation of the Moabite Monarchy," *IEJ* 47 (1997), 83–92.

68 A *qatl* pattern with preserved and secondarily lengthened nominative ending *-u*; cf. Ges[18] (see n. 7), 244.

69 Thus contradicting L. Delekat, "Yahō-Yahwáe und die alttestamentlichen Gottesnamenkorrekturen," in *Tradition und Glaube. Festgabe für K.G. Kuhn* (ed. G. Jeremias et al. Göttingen 1971), 66 f. and Rose, Jahwe (see n. 50), 28 f., who interpret the *-h* in *dwdh* (l. 12) and *yhwh* (l.18) as divine names with a pronominal suffix 3.m.sg. (/-ō/). Both authors were convinced that the *yhwh*-writing (i.e. the tetragrammaton) were epigraphically of relatively late origin. The inscriptions of Kuntillet 'Ajrud, published in 1978, have refuted that assumption, however (see J.A. Emerton, "New Light on Israelite Religion. The Implications of the Inscriptions from Kuntillet 'Ajrud," *ZAW* 94 [1982], 5 f.).

for a typologically later form. The diachronic distribution of the orthographic variants supports this thesis.

It is worth noting that in at least four early inscriptions, the name of the goddess "Asherah," written ʾšrth, appears directly adjacent to "Yahweh" in the form of yhwh: Kuntillet ʿAjrud (KAgr) 8:2, 9:6, 10:2; Khirbet el-Kom (Kom) 3:3.5.6.[70] In the above-named Kuntillet ʿAjrud inscriptions there is a direct parallelization of Yahweh and Asherah, e.g. KAgr 8:1–2: brkt ʾtkm l-yhwh šmrn w-l-ʾšrth. This turn is translated by the great majority of interpreters roughly as follows: "I bless you on behalf of (=in the name of) Yahwe of Samaria and on behalf of his Asherah."[71] This means that it is generally believed that the Asherah-name was extended by a pronominal suffix (3.m.sg.), by which Ashera would be assigned, as well as subordinated, to Yahwe as his Parhedra. However, there is no suffix to be expected with a proper name, which is self-determinative.[72] In order to explain the suffix more easily, some authors have considered seeing behind Ashera not the goddess, but instead the cultic object associated with her, i.e. a pole or pillar – an interpretation which entails significant problems. On the one hand, the asherah-pole is not Yahwe's, but Asherah's cultic symbol, and on the other, the deity and not the cultic object is to be expected as part of a blessing formula.[73] In addition, it has also been attempted to interpret the h in ʾšrth as a he-locale[74] or as a second feminine morpheme alongside -t (doubled feminine marker).[75] These proposals, however, have received very little approval.

---

70 See additionally the writing ʾšrt [ ] in KAgr 6, fragment B (cf. Renz, *Inschriften I* [see n. 54], 58).
71 See Renz, *Inschriften I* (see n. 54), 61 and others; for the discussion cf. especially Emerton, *New Light* (see n. 69), 13–18.
72 See for instance S.A. Wiggins, *A Reassessment of 'Asherah'* (AOAT 235; Kevelaer 1993), 188.
73 See Renz, *Inschriften I* (see n. 54), 92 and M. Köckert, "Von einem zum einzigen Gott. Zur Diskussion der Religionsgeschichte Israels," *BThZ* 15 (1998), 165 ["Schließlich wird die Segensquelle mit der Präposition *l* eingeführt, was im AT sonst stets bei einer göttlichen Person, nicht aber bei anderen Größen als Segensquelle geschieht."].
74 See T. Binger, Asherah. *Godesses in Ugarit, Israel and the Old Testament* (JSOTSS 232; Sheffield 1997), 107 f., who also explains the yhwh-writing (as opposed to yhw-writing) in this way – as "he-locale or a locative-accusative ending" – and postulats that the -h would function to link a deity with a particular place. Her reasoning, however, is syntactically unsatisfactory.
75 See for instance A. Angerstorfer, "Ašerah als 'consort of Jahwe' oder Aširtah?," *BN 17* (1982), esp. 11), who vocalizes ʾšrth as "ʾAširtāh" and would like to directly associate it with syllabic writings of the "Aširta"-name (the /-a/ in the syllabic "Ašira" spellings is certainly not a feminine marker, however!). A similar view was expressed also Zevit, Z., "The Khirbet el-Qôm Inscription Mentioning a Goddess," *BASOR 255* [1984] ["double feminization"]). For criticism see Wiggins, *Reassesment* (see n. 72), 170–171; P. Merlo, "L'Ašerah di YHWH a Kuntillet ʿAjrud. Rassegna critica degli studi e delle interpretazioni," *Studi Epigrafici e Linguistici 11* (1994), 32 and Renz, *Inschriften II/1* (see n. 34), 92.

Based on our considerations on the writing *yhwh*, however, another solution suggests itself which until now has obviously not been reckoned with. If the (second) *h* in *yhwh* stands for a case ending (as has been argued above), then this grapheme can also have precisely the same function in the form *'šrth*. In other words: *'šrth* stands for /ʾašir(a)tā/ and is nothing else than the (archaic) full form of the name of the goddess in the (lengthened) *a*-case, which appears continuously in the Old Testament without case ending as *ᵃšerā(h)* (epigraphically, however, the writing **'šrh* is never attested!). The phrase *l-yhwh ... w-l-'šrth* thus simply means "in relation to the Lord ... and in relation to Asherah (more precisely Ashir(a)ta)." Yahwe and Asherah are designated by this formula as a pair of gods without expressing the formal subordination of Asherah.[76] Concerning the writing of the *a*-case for feminine word forms by means -*th*, compare the remarks in paragraphs (a) and (b). The assumption of a basic form **'ašir(a)ta* for Asherah is obvious in the light of the proper name "'Abdu-'Aširta" (i.e. Servant of Asherah), which is very frequently attested in the Amarna letters (and elsewhere as well), where the theophoric element predominantly appears in the *a*-case – in 67 of a total of 95 documents (ÌR-*a-ši-ir-ta* or ÌR-*aš-ra-ta*; cf. § 5.2).[77] The epigraphically attested parallelization of *l yhwh* and *l 'šrth* strongly supports the interpretation of the "Yahwe"-name favored here, since the relationship of the orthographies *yhw* vs. *yhwh* can be explained in the same way as the orthographies **'šrh* (Biblical Hebrew *ᵃšerā(h)*) vs. *'šrth*.[78]

This new interpretation of the writing *'šrth* also allows the textually difficult grave inscription Khirbet el-Kom Nr. 3 (8th century BCE)[79] to appear in a new light. In this inscription the term *l-'šrth* is attested a total of three times (lines 3, 5 and 6), without being directly attached to the expression *l-yhwh*. This fact speaks from the outset against the view that *l-'šrth* contains a pronominal suffix. Probably *l-'šrth* should be regarded in lines 5 and 6 as a separate dedication formula: "(dedicated/consecrated) to the Ashir(a)ta." *l-'šrth* would thus be considered the same as the term *l-'šrt*, which is attested in two vessel inscriptions from

---

76 However, a subordination is to be deduced from the consistent position of the goddess Asherah behind Yahwe, as well as the fact that in KAgr 9:6ff. – after mentioning both deities, Yahwe and Asherah -Yahwe alone is the subject of the blessing and the protection (*ybrk* [l. 6–7] can only mean "may he bless you"; a form 3.m.pl. would have to be spelled **ybrkk*).
77 See Hess, *Amarna* (see n. 27), 7–9.
78 Of particular interest in this context is the already mentioned inscription KAgr 10, where in l. 1 the short form of the "Yahwe"-name is attested (*yhw*), whereas in l. 2, in the formula "dedicated to the Yahwe of Têman and to Ashir(a)ta" (*l-yhwh htmn w-l-'šrth*), it is the long form (*yhwh*).
79 Renz, *Inschriften I* (see n. 54), 202–211.

Tel Miqne (Ekron) (7th century BCE).[80] The spelling *'šrt* follows Phoenician orthography and can stand for /*'aširat*/ (name without case ending) or for /*'ašir (a)ta*/ (name in *a*-case).

In summary, we may maintain that the phenomenon of a *plene* spelling of a secondary lengthened case marker *-a* with {h} is observable with nouns in poetic texts of the Old Testament, as well as in several biblically attested particles and finally in numerous biblically as well as epigraphically attested proper names, including the names of the gods "Dauda" (*dwdh* [Mesha-Inschrift]) and "Ašir (a)ta" (*'šrth*). All these phenomena speak in favour of explaining the tetragrammaton *yhwh* in the sense of /*yahwā*/ < **yahwa*.

This closes the line of argumentation of this investigation which started with syllabically attested Jewish personal names of the Late Babylonian period with formation element *ia-a-wa₆*: the Israelite divine name "Yahwe" is of a nominal nature (*qatl*-pattern). Its ending-less basic form is **yahw* (> *yahû*). Alongside this existed a name-form with a preserved case ending *-a*, namely **yahwa*, on which tetragrammaton-writing is based.

Conclusion

Starting from personal names with the theophoric element *ia-a-wa₆* in Late Babylonian texts, it is argued in this paper that the divine name "Yahwe" is a nominal lexeme of the *qatl*-pattern. While its basic form is **yahw* (> *yahû*), there also existed an elongated form with case marker *-a*, written with {h} as a *mater lectionis* (i. e. the tetragrammaton YHWH). In support of this view other material is presented showing the preservation of a case maker *-a* in early 1st millenium B.C.E. Hebrew and Moabite. In this regard, the form *'šrth* (for "Asherah") as attested in several early Hebrew inscriptions (e. g. Kuntillet 'Ajrud) is analysed in the same way, with {h} representing the case marker *-a*. The formula *l-yhwh ... w-l-'šrth* is thus translated as "(I bless you)

---

80 For the inscriptions in question see S. Gitin, "Seventh Century BCE Cultic Elements at Ekron," *Biblical Archaeology Today* (Jerusalem 1990), 250–253, Wiggins, Reassessment (see n. 72), 181 f.; T. Dothan and S. Gitin, "Tel Miqne/Ekron: The Rise and Fall of a Philistine City," *Qadmoniot* 105–106 (1994), 2–28 (Hebrew); C. Frevel, *Aschera und der Ausschließlichkeitsanspruch YHWHs. Beiträge zu literarischen, religionsgeschichtlichen und ikonographischen Aspekten der Ascheradiskussion*, 2 Bde. (Bonner Biblische Beiträge 94; Weinheim 1995), 989, and S. Ahituv, *Echoes from the Past. Hebrew and Cognate Inscriptions from the Biblical World* (Jerusalem 2008), 342f. In one of these inscriptions we find the phrase *qdš / l-'šrt* "devotement(?) to Ashirat," provided that the two word forms belong together semantically (they are placed opposite each other on the same pitcher).

to (= in the name of) Yahwe ... and Ashirta." The preserved ending -a is interpreted as the marker of the absolutive case. It is demonstrated that this case is very common in early West Semitic proper names, especially within syllabically attested (Amorite and Amarna) personal names.

Mark S. Smith
YHWH's Original Character:
Questions about an Unknown God

The question of YHWH's original character characteristically proceeds from efforts to recover the oldest texts attesting to YHWH and then to examine the profile exhibited in such texts. This essay largely follows suit, while recognizing that in the end it is impossible to answer the question adequately given the lack of relevant primary sources.

This study is divided into four parts. Part 1 briefly reviews putative Egyptian evidence for the name of YHWH. Part 2 locates this evidence in conjunction with biblical evidence. Part 3 focuses on Judg 5:4–5 and Ps 68:8–9, thought to be the oldest texts about YHWH in the Hebrew Bible. Part 4 is devoted to the question of YHWH's original profile.

1 Putative Egyptian Evidence

Standing in a long line of scholarship,[1] a 2008 survey of the Egyptian evidence for the name of YHWH opens with the claim: "It has become a commonly accepted view both in Egyptology and Biblical Studies that the name of the later god YHWH – the tetragrammaton YHWH – makes an early appearance in Egyptian topographical lists of the New Kingdom, where it is closely associated with a provenance that is characteristic to statements about YHWH's origins in the Old Testament."[2] The author, the Egyptologist Thomas Schneider, is referring

---

1 For example, S. Aḥituv, *Canaanite Toponyms in Ancient Egyptian Documents* (Jerusalem 1984), 121–122; L.E. Axelsson, *The Lord Rose Up from Seir: Studies in the History and Traditions of the Negev and Southern Judah* (ConBOT 25; Stockholm 1987), 48–59; J. Leclant, "Le 'Tétragramme' à l'époque d'Aménophis III," in *Near Eastern Studies dedicated to H. I. H. Prince Takahito Mikasa on the Occasion of His Seventy-Fifth Birthday* (Wiesbaden 1991), 215–219; M. Görg, "Jahwe," *NBL* 2 (1992), 265, and "YHWH als Toponym? – Weitere Perspektiven," *BN* 101 (2000), 8–12; D.B. Redford, *Egypt, Canaan, and Israel in Ancient Times* (Princeton 1992), 272–273; M. Weippert, *Jahwe und die anderen Götter: Studien zur Religionsgeschichte des antiken Israel in ihrem syrisch-palästinischen Kontext* (FAT 18; Tübingen 1997), 40 and 97; F. Moore Cross, *From Epic to Canon: History and Literature in Ancient Israel* (Baltimore 1998), 67 n. 51; and K. van der Toorn, "Yahweh," in *DDD*² (ed. K. van der Toorn *et al.*; Leiden ²1999), 911–912; and F. Adrom and M. Müller, "Das Tetragramm in ägyptischen Quellen," *BThZ 30/1* (2013), 120–141, here 123–131.
2 T. Schneider, "The First Documented Occurrence of the God Yahweh? (Book of the Dead Princeton 'Roll 5')," *JANER 7/2* (2008), 113–120, here 113. See also Schneider, "Zur Interpretation

DOI 10.1515/9783110448221-002

to the much-cited fifteen-century list of places produced under Amenophis III at a temple in Soleb and a later compilation of place-names under Ramesses II at Amara-West, both located north of the third cataract of the Nile in Nubia (today in Sudan). These records list places belonging to Shasu-nomads located in the southern Transjordan in proximity to Edom. These entries include *t3 š3św yhw3*, which Schneiders renders "the Shasu-land, (more precisely:) Yhw3."[3] The Amara-West version of the list also locates in the "Shasu-land" a place called *sa-'-r-ir*, thought to be related to biblical Seir.[4] Schneider accepts the commonly cited opinion that this "would be a mountainous region linked to the worship of a god named YHWH after the place of worship."[5] This place-name in these Egyptian sources has been discussed in conjunction with the divine name since 1947, when it was proposed first by Bernard Grdseloff.[6] What has given this evidence its particular appeal to biblical scholars is the combination of the place name, which looks quite similar to the biblical divine name, and its location, which dovetails with the southern locales given for the biblical tradition enshrined especially in Judg 5:4.

While Schneider's presentation may give the impression that consensus has been reached in the matter, scepticism has been expressed about whether this place is to be associated with YHWH (in any form), for example, by Hans Goedicke and Gösta W. Ahlström.[7] Questions have also been raised about the geo-

---

des Eigennamens des Papyrus-Besitzers," in *Der Totenbuch-Papyrus Princeton Pharaonic Roll 5* (ed. B. Lüscher; BAÄ 2; Basel 2008), 102–110.

3 For further discussion with hieroglyphs represented and transliterated, see R. Giveon, *Les bédouines Shosou des documents egyptiens* (Leiden 1971), 26–28, no. 6a, and 74–77 no. 16a, with reading corrected by M. Weippert, "Semitische Nomaden des zweiten Jahrausends," *Bib* 55 (1974), 265–280 and 427–433, here 427, 430; and Adrom and Müller, "Das Tetragramm in ägyptischen Quellen" (see n. 1), 124, 126. Their article surveys other possible Egyptian cases that appear less convincing.

4 Noted by Redford among others; see Redford, *Egypt, Canaan, and Israel* (see n. 1), 272. Critics also note the irregular spelling; see Cross, *From Epic to Canon* (see n. 1), 67 n. 51. As a result some reject the identification; see J.C. de Moor, *The Rise of Yahwism: The Roots of Israelite Monotheism* (revised and enlarged edition; BETL XCI; Leuven 1997), 124.

5 Schneider, "The First Documented Occurrence of the God Yahweh?" (see n. 2), 114.

6 Grdseloff, "Edôm d'après les sources égpytiennes," *Revue de l'histoire Juive en Egypte* 1 (1947), 69–70.

7 Goedicke, "The Tetragram in Egyptian?" *Society for the Study of Egyptian Antiquities* 24 (1994), 24–27; Ahlström, *Who Were the Israelites?* (Winona Lake 1986), 57–60. See also the cautious position taken by Cross, *From Epic to Canon* (see n. 1), 67 n. 51; and Adrom and Müller, "Das Tetragramm in ägyptischen Quellen" (see n. 1), 120–141.

graphical location of the place.[8] Sixty years after the initial proposal by Grdseloff, Schneiders has identified what he believes to be another possible reference to YHWH, this time in the name of the owner of a papyrus of the Egyptian Book of the Dead, housed in the Princeton University Library (Pharaonic Roll 5).[9] The papyrus dates to the late 18th or the 19th dynasty (ca. 1330–1230). According to Schneider, the name of the owner most commonly rendered *j:-t-w-n-j₂-rʿ3-y-h*, is to be understood as **'adoni-roʿe-yah,*" "my lord is the shepherd of Yah," which would reflect the idea of the god as the shepherd of the region called Yah (YHWH).[10] Schneiders would see the person in question as an acculturated foreigner and member of Egyptian elite society who owned this copy of the Book of the Dead.

2 The Convergences of Egyptian and Biblical Evidence

While the Egyptian evidence for YHWH does not seem particularly strong, it appears consonant with the biblical tradition of YHWH attached to southern locale known by various names: Edom (Judg 5:4; cf. Num 24:18) and Seir (Deut 33:2; Judg 5:4; cf. Num 24:18)[11]; Teman (Hab 3:3; cf. "YHWH of Teman," *yhwh tmn/ tymn*, in the Kuntillet ʿAjrud inscriptions[12]); Paran (Deut 33:2; Hab 3:3); and

---

8 See M. Astour, "Yahweh in Egyptian Topographic Lists," in *Festschrift Elmer Edel: 12 März 1979* (ed. M. Görg and E. Pusch; Bamberg 1979), 17–33; and G.W. Ahlström, *The History of Ancient Palestine* (Minneapolis 1993), 276–277.

9 Schneider, "The First Documented Occurrence" (see n. 2), 113–120 and "Zur Interpretation des Eigennamens" (see n. 2), 102–110.

10 The more common interpretation, *'aduni-raʿiyu-hu*, "(my) lord is his shepherd," encounters orthographic, phonological and onomastic difficulties, according to Schneiders.

11 Note Edom and Seir not only paired together in Judg 5:4 and Ps 68:8, but also identified in Gen 25:4 (see also 36:8, 21; cf. Isa 21:11; Ezek 35:15).

12 For *yhwh tmn* on Pithos B, see S. Aḥituv *et al.*, in Z. Meshel, *Kuntillet ʿAjrud (Horvat Teman): An Iron Age II Religious Site on the Judah-Sinai Border* (Jerusalem 2012), 92–97, Inscription 3.5. See also F.W. Dobbs-Allsopp *et al.*, *Hebrew Inscriptions: Texts from the Biblical Period of the Monarchy with Concordance* (New Haven 2005), 293–296; and J. Hutton, "Local Manifestations of Yahweh and Worship in the Interstices: A Note on Kuntillet ʿAjrud," *JANER* 10 (2010), 177–210, esp. 189. For *yhwh tymn* on a plaster inscription found in the "bench room," see Meshel, *Kuntillet ʿAjrud (Horvat Teman)*, 105–107, Inscription 4.1.1; and Dobbs-Allsopp *et al.*, *Hebrew Inscriptions*, 285–286. For *yhwh tymn* on a plaster inscription found in the "bench room," see Meshel, *Kuntillet ʿAjrud (Horvat Teman)*, 105–107, Inscription 4.1.1; and Dobbs-Allsopp *et al.*, *Hebrew Inscriptions*, 285–286. Note also the synthesis in O. Keel and C. Uehlinger, *Gods, Goddesses, and Images of God in Ancient Israel* (trans. T.H. Trapp; Minneapolis 1998), 226–228.

the best-known of these locales, Sinai, attested both as a place-name (Ps 68:18; Deut 33:2) and as part of a divine title, "the One of Sinai" (Judg 5:4; Ps 68:8).[13] We may also note the names of Cushan and Midian in Hab 3:7.[14] Scholars have emphasized three aspects of these passages: the high antiquity of their tradition (despite some protests); YHWH's southern locale in Edom, or as perhaps Gal 4:25 says of Sinai, "a mountain in Arabia" (NABRE)[15]; and the representation of this deity as a warrior figure associated with the rainstorm.

Building on these basic features, three related points come into focus. First, from the perspective of the poems and the putative Egyptian evidence, YHWH is grounded in a place outside of Israel. By the thirteenth century, Israel is known to be in the land, as seen not only in the Merneptah stele (ca. 1208), but also possibly earlier, as recently claimed for an Egyptian inscription (Berlin Statue Pedestal Relief 21687) dating to the reign of Ramesses II (reigned ca. 1279 – 1218).[16]

Second, the evidence presently known gives reason to entertain a more complex form of what has been come to be known as the "Midianite hypothesis" or the "Kenite hypothesis."[17] According to this approach, either the Midianites or the Kenites transmitted the cult of YHWH to Israel. As noted above, Midian is

---

13 These names and these texts that contain them are studied by many scholars, including F. M. Cross, *Canaanite Myth and Hebrew Epic: Studies in the History of the Religion of Israel* (Cambridge 1973), 100 – 103; Axelsson, *The Lord Rose Up from Seir* (see n. 1), 48 – 55; and H. Pfeiffer, *Jahwes Kommen von Süden: Jdc 5; Hab 3; Dtn 33 und Ps 68 in ihrem literatur- und theologiegeschichtlichen Umfeld* (FRLANT 211; Göttingen 2005).

14 For discussion, see T. Hiebert, *God of My Victory: The Ancient Hymn in Habakkuk 3* (HSM 38; Atlanta 1986); S. Aḥituv, "The Sinai Theophany in the Psalm of Habakkuk," in *Birkat Shalom: Studies in the Bible, Ancient Near Eastern Literature, and Postbiblical Judaism Presented to Shalom M. Paul on the Occasion of his Seventieth Birthday* (ed. C. Cohen *et al.*; two vols.; Winona Lake 2008), 1225 – 1232; G.T.M. Prinsloo, "Yahweh the Warrior: An Intertextual Reading of Habakkuk 3," *Old Testament Essays* 14 (2001), 475 – 493; N. Shupak, "The God from Teman and the Egyptian Sun God: A Reconsideration of Habakkuk 3, 3 – 7," *JANES* 28 (2002), 97 – 116; and J.E. Anderson, "Awaiting an Answered Prayer: The Development and Reinterpretation of Habakkuk 3 in its Contexts," *ZAW* 123 (2011), 57 – 71.

15 To be sure, this usage of "Arabia" need not be far understood as the far south (i. e., northwestern Saudi Arabia today), since in the time of Paul it would denote "the area or east of Damascus under the control of the Nabatean native kings," according to W.A. Meeks, *The First Urban Christians: The Social World of the Apostle Paul* (New Haven 1983), 40. Still it may denote a more southern locale and not the Sinai peninsula.

16 See P. van der Veen *et al.*, "Israel in Canaan (Long) Before Pharaoh Merenptah? A Fresh Look at Berlin Statue Pedestal Relief 21687," *JAEI* 2/4 (2010), 15 – 25.

17 See Cross, *From Epic to Canon* (see n. 1), 66 – 70; van der Toorn, "Yahweh" (see n. 1), 911 – 913. Note also J. Blenkinsopp, "The Midianite-Kenite Hypothesis Revisited and the Origins of Judah," *JSOT* 33 (2008), 131 – 153; and J.E. Dunn, "A God of Volcanoes: Did Yahwism Take Root in Volcanic Ashes?" *JSOT* 38 (2014), 387 – 424.

one of the old names for the southern site of YHWH (Hab 3:7). The Kenites are the tribe that Moses' father-in-law is said to come from (Judg 4:11). The biblical prose story in effect "narrativized" the ancient tradition of YHWH's origins in the south, the setting of Yahwistic cult among a southern people other than Israel, and the secondary contact of Israel with this god. That there seems to be some antiquity to these rather difficult traditions may be suggested by references to Kenites in Israel's older literary traditions (e.g., Judg 5:24; cf. the old tradition underlying Jethro especially in Exodus 18).

Both the Midianites and the Kenites are known from the Bible, but they are not associated in the Egyptian evidence with the divine name. Instead, the name is associated in Egyptian sources with the Shasu, an Egyptian term applied to "semi-nomadic groups" in a number of different regions.[18] They are occasionally associated in Egyptian texts with Edom and Seir, the two locations named in Judg 5:4 (and Num 24:18).[19] Above it is noted that the Shasu of *yhw3* and of Seir appear in one of the lists. Such Shasu are associated with Seir in other texts. A thirteenth century text of Ramesses II mentions "the land of the Shosu" and "Mount Seir."[20] An eleventh century boast of Ramesses III mentions the Shasu in conjunction with Seir: "I brought about the destruction of Seir among the Shosu tribes. I laid waste their tents with their people, their belongings, and likewise their cattle without number."[21] The "Shasu of Edom" are attested in an thirteenth century Egyptian model letter: "Another information for my lord that we have just let the Shasu tribes of Edom pass the Fortress of Merneptah-Hetephermaat."[22] The mention of the Shasu in connection with Edom

---

18 K. Kitchen, "Karnak, Campaign from Sile to Pa-Canaan, Year 1," *COS* 2.23 n. 1. Shasu are known also considerably further north, for example in K. Kitchen, "Karnak, Campaign from Sile to Pa-Canaan, Year 1," *COS* 2.24, and "The Battle of Qadesh – The 'Bulletin' Text," *COS* 2.38; and J.P. Allen, "The Craft of the Scribe" (Papyrus Anastasi I), *COS* 2.12–13.

19 See Redford, *Egypt, Canaan, and Israel* (see n. 1), 273; de Moor, *The Rise of Yahwism* (see n. 4), 124–126; E. Lipiński, *On the Skirts of Canaan in the Iron Age: Historical and Topographical Researches* (OLA 153; Leuven 2006), 364–366. See the listing in Aḥituv, *Canaanite Toponyms* (see n. 1), 169. Seir has been identified with Akkadian Sheru in EA 288:26, as discussed by J.R. Bartlett, *Edom and the Edomites* (JSOTSup 77; JSOT/PEF Monograph series 1; Sheffield 1989), 41; there the place is represented as a far southern locale from the perspective of a Middle Bronze ruler of Jerusalem.

20 See Bartlett, *Edom and the Edomites* (see n. 18), 42–43; and Redford, *Egypt, Canaan, and Israel* (see n. 1), 272 n. 70.

21 See *ANET* 262. The translation follows Bartlett, *Edom and the Edomites* (see n. 18), 42 (*ANET* uses "Bedouin tribes" for "Shasu-tribes").

22 So J.P. Allen, "A Report of Bedouin" (Papyrus Anastasi VI), *COS* 3.16. The text is called in *ANET* 259 "The Report of a Frontier Official." See also Aḥituv, *Canaanite Toponyms* (see n. 1),

and Seir in these Egyptian texts is congruent with the same two place-names in the old poetic tradition of YHWH's southern site in Judg 5:4 (cf. Num 24:18). It is to be noted at this juncture that the names, Edom and Seir, shared by the Shasu (perhaps including the Shasu of *yhw3*) and Judg 5:4, is suggestive for the high antiquity of the motif in this particular biblical passage, compared with Ps 68:8 (or the other exemplars of the old poetic tradition), which we will examine below.

The association of the Shasu with the *yhw3*-land in Egyptian sources coupled with the lack of the name of the Shasu in the Bible suggests a secondary mediation of YHWH cult to Midianites or Kenites, perhaps via the Shasu of Seir or perhaps Edom. Accordingly, it may be preferable to posit a Shasu of Seir-Edom/Midianite-Kenite hypothesis. It is possible to imagine (at least) two stages for this hypothesis. The Shasu of the *yhw3-land* seem to be the best candidate presently for the old context of YHWH -cult. Such Shasu may not have been in contact with early Israel, and thus they may not have provided a direct point of transmission of the cult of YHWH to Israel.[23] Instead, a further cultural conduit perhaps via the Shasu of Seir and/or Edom may have mediated the cult of YHWH more broadly to Midianites or Kenites, peoples that biblical memory recalled as the southerners that Israel knew. If so, biblical tradition did not preserve the memory of the earlier people among whom its deity had earlier enjoyed cultic devotion.

A third and related point concerns the distance between the Egyptian and biblical evidence in terms of both time and geography. In terms of time-frame, the Egyptian evidence would suggest at least a fifteenth century date for the cult of YHWH if not earlier, while the biblical references even in the most optimistic scenario would not date prior to the twelfth century. Hence there are several centuries between the Egyptian evidence and the biblical record. With respect to geographical markers for this tradition, the Egyptian evidence associating *yhw3* with the Shasu of Seir, links more closely with Judg 5:4 (and Num 24:18), with its reference to Seir (also Deut 33:2) and Edom (cf. the Shasu of Edom, noted above), in contrast with the other locations mentioned in the poetic sources noted above, Paran, Teman, and Sinai.

90; Redford, *Egypt, Canaan, and Israel* (see n. 1), 228 and 272 n. 70; and Bartlett, *Edom and the Edomites* (see n. 18), 42.

23 Cf. the view of early Israel as Shasu or at least one Shasu group by Redford, *Egypt, Canaan, and Israel* (see n. 1), 275–280, and by A. Faust, *Israel's Ethnogenesis: Settlement, Interaction, Expansion and Resistance* (Approaches to Anthropological Archaeology; London 2007), 177, 183, 186–187 (with citation of earlier scholars who espouse this view). The emphasis on the Shasu as the original basis for ancient Israel is somewhat belied by the absence of the name of the Shasu in the biblical record compared with the Kenites or Midianites.

In noting the distance between the Egyptian evidence and the biblical evidence, the Israelites who composed these relatively early pieces worked with a certain ignorance of their own about the original profile of their God. At the same time, their understanding of God, which may have included a lack of knowledge of the old profile of their God, would seem to have been sufficient for them. It may have been the very mystery about these old depictions that made them all the more attractive to later tradition. Moreover, for the biblical composers the present understanding of God was presumed to be consonant with this prior profile, whatever was known of it. The early biblical tradition formulated its understanding of this old inherited tradition in terms of its own concerns, as seen in the Bible's oldest fragments about God in Judges 5 and Psalm 68.

3 Early Fragments of Yнwн in Judges 5:4 – 5 and Psalm 68:8 – 9

The two oldest exemplars of the divine march appear in Judg 5:4 – 5 and Ps 68:8 – 9. These two pieces are so close in wording that scholars have understood them to be an independent set piece or motif that the authors of Judges 5 and Psalm 68 inherited and used.[24] In other words, the earliest manifestation of

---

24 In view of the shared language, some scholars see literary dependence between the two passages. For example, M. Fishbane (*Biblical Interpretation in Ancient Israel* [Oxford 1985], 54 – 55, 75 n. 30] sees Judg 5:4 – 5 as a quotation of Ps 68:8 – 9, while H. Niehr ("He-of-the-Sinai," *in DDD²* [ed. K. van der Toorn *et al.* Leiden ²1999], 387) views Ps 68:8 – 9 as the quotation of Judg 5:4 – 5. Judg 5:4 – 5 and Ps 68:8 – 9 exhibit differences and perhaps one was not copied from the other. The theory of copying does not provide sufficient explanation about the motivation for altering the place-names. Some scholars view the relationship in terms of "reworking." Thus M.D. Coogan posits Judg 5:4 – 5 as the source for Ps 68:8 – 9. See Coogan, "A Structural and Literary Analysis of the Song of Deborah," *CBQ* 40 (1978), 143 – 166, here 161 – 162, and in particular the list of common elements. Coogan suggests a theory of direct literary relationship "quite possibly in written form." A. Rofé similarly understands Ps 68:8 – 9 as an "Elohistic" reworking of Judges 5:4 – 5. See Rofé, *Introduction to the Literature of the Hebrew Bible* (Jerusalem Bible Studies 9; Jerusalem 2009), 445. Following another line of scholarship, Israel Knohl has proposed seeing the influence working in the opposite direction, based mostly on the expansion in Judges 5:4 – 5 relative to Psalm 68:8 – 9. See Knohl, "Pharaoh's War on the Israelites: The Untold Story," *AZURE* 41 (Summer 2010) http://www.azure.org.il/article.php?id=543 (accessed April 23, 2011). Knohl believes that Ps 68:5 – 33 (demarcated by an *inclusio*) is older than Judg 5:2 – 30. For a survey of views, see J.H. Charlesworth, "Bashan, Symbology, Haplography, and Theology in Psalm 68," in *David and Zion: Biblical Studies in Honor of J.J.M. Roberts* (ed. B.F. Batto and K.L. Roberts; Winona Lake 2004), 351 – 372. Like the theory of scribal copying, the theory of reworking in either direction suffers, as it provides little explanation for minor differences. For example, the

God survives only in poetic fragments; it was received and re-interpreted by later authors. The poetic lines of these two biblical contexts describe the divine march and its effects[25]:

	Judges 5:4–5	Psalm 68:8–9
i.	YHWH, when you went out from Seir,	God, when you went out before your people
ii.	when you marched from the region of Edom,	when you marched through the wilderness
iii.	the earth trembled,	the earth trembled,
iv.	also the heavens poured,	also the heavens poured,
v.	the clouds indeed poured water,	
vi.	the mountains quaked,	
vii.	before YHWH, the One of Sinai, [26]	before God, the One of Sinai,
viii.	before YHWH, the god of Israel.	Before God,[27] the god of Israel.

---

second line ii show the variation of *gam* and *'ap*. These are semantic variants; see C.H.J. van der Merwe, "The Biblical Hebrew Particle *'ap*," *VT* 59 (2009), 266–283. Neither would have been copied from the other. This case fits F.M. Cross' theory of "ancient oral variants" (*Canaanite Myth* [see n. 13], 101 n. 35) and the notion of "memory variants" espoused by D.M. Carr, *The Formation of the Hebrew Bible: A New Reconstruction* (Oxford 2011), 14–18, 25–34, 41–42, 54–55, 57–65, and 98–100. Other differences of a very minor sort also do not fit well with a theory of reworking.

25 See also the layout and discussion of the two passages by W. Groß, *Richter: Übersetzt und ausgelegt* (HThKAT; Freiburg 2009), 306.

26 The phrase *zeh sînay* in Judg 5:5 is often regarded as a secondary gloss introduced from Ps 68:9. See G.F. Moore, *A Critical and Exegetical Commentary on Judges* (ICC; Edinburgh 1895), 142; C.F. Burney, *The Book of Judges* (London 1918), 113; *GKC* 137d note 2; C. Levin, "Das Alter des Deboralieds," in his *Fortschreibungen: Gesammelte Studien zum Alten Testament* (BZAW 316; Berlin 2003), 132–135, with older references. This approach assumed that in Judg 5:5 *hārîm nāzĕlû mippĕnê yhwh zeh sînay* was overloaded and thus the title *zeh sînay* must be extra. However, this reading of the lines of the two poems in tandem hardly appears necessary, as the layout here suggests. Some scholars take it as a gloss on the name of the deity ("the One of Sinai"), while others, such as Fishbane, argued for *zeh sînay* after the reference to the deity as a gloss meaning "this is Sinai," pertaining to the preceding reference to mountains (*hārîm*). See Fishbane, *Biblical Interpretation in Ancient Israel* (see n. 24), 54–55, 75 n. 30. Again, the layout of lines as understood above, shows *zeh sînay* in parallelism with *'ĕlōhê yiśrā'ēl*. Also problematic for Fishbane's view, the gloss identifies a singular, while the word putatively glossed, "mountains," is plural; so, too, is the verb. It also does not serve Fishbane's case that the gloss does not follow the word that it is supposed to gloss, namely "mountains." To obviate these problems, Fishbane reads the gloss as "this (refers to the event at) Mount Sinai." This explanation is not persuasive.

27 This is missing from LXX A and so BHS suggests its deletion. However, it works well with the poetic length of lines and parallelism in context. In addition, it has a precise correspondence with the divine name in Judg 5:5.

As commentators have long noted, the precise language shared by the two passages is remarkable. Each bicolon is addressed in turn, highlighting some of their differences. In lines i-ii, both poems show the same verbal forms, with the same preposition fronted and the same second person masculine suffix. The deity heads line i in both passages, but how the deity is referenced differs. The first uses the specific name of the deity, with no poetic resonance. The second uses the general word for the divinity, with some alliteration with /m/ in *'ammekā* ("your people") and *bîšîmôn* ("the wilderness"). In combination with the same fronted preposition and the same suffix appended to them, the two verbal forms *běṣē'těkā* ("when you went out") and *běṣa'děkā* ("when you marched") enjoy considerable sonant parallelism. The first verb, **yṣ'*, might denote in itself departure from a place, but the parallel verb, **ṣ'd*, denotes the march of the god. In context, the first may be read as no less a verb of marching, in accordance with its common military usage. The first verb also shows the same form on the human level for going to battle in 2 Sam 11:1: "It was at the turn of the year, the time when kings go out (*ṣē't*) [to battle]."[28] The second root in this usage for the deity has been compared by Aloysius Fitzgerald with "the sound of the march" (*qwl ṣ'd*) of YHWH in the wind rustling in the trees in 2 Sam 5:24 = 1 Chr 14:15.[29] This usage also fits three Ugaritic attestations, all predicated of gods: (i) "Baal marched," *b'l yṣġd* in KTU 1.10 III 7, preceding Baal's ascent to his mountain (in lines 11–12); (ii) "he marched to the shore of the Deep," *yṣġd gp thm* in KTU 1.23.30, used to describe El's proceeding to the shore; and (iii) "he marched," *'il yṣġd* in KTU 1.174.1, perhaps involving El.[30] It is the first of these passages about Baal marching that seems contextually proximate to the march

---

28 Compare the full idiom, *ṣā̌ṣē't lammilḥāmâ* in Jud 20:14, 20, 28; for the idiom, see also 2 Sam 21:17. For discussion, see Shalom E. Holtz, "The Case for Adverbial *yaḥad*," *VT* 59 (2009), 211–221, here 211–212.

29 Fitzgerald, *The Lord of the East Wind* (CBQMS 34; Washington 2002), 86 n. 31. See also the root in Hab 3:12. For the expression of the deity going before the people in Ps 68:8, cf. Exod 13:22, etc.; see *DCH* 4.558.

30 There is *prima facie* a philological difficulty in the comparison between the Ugaritic and Hebrew roots, since the Arabic cognate is *ṣ'd* and not *ṣġd*; see G. del Olmo Lete and J. Sanmartín, *A Dictionary of the Ugaritic Language in the Alphabetic Tradition* (trans. W.G.E. Watson; HdO I/112; Leiden ³2015), 769. There are examples of this irregular correspondence, e. g., Ugaritic **n'm*, "to sing," compared with Arabic **nġm*. See J.A. Emerton, "Some Notes on the Ugaritic Counterpart of the Arabic *ghain*," in *Studies in Philology in Honour of Ronald James Williams* (ed. G.E. Kadish and G.E. Freeman; Toronto 1982), 31–50; and Cross, *From Epic to Canon* (see n. 1), 140 n. 15.

of Yhwh with quaking mountains in Judg 5:4 and Ps 68:8. Baal's march from his mountain in the Baal Cycle is also to be noted in this context.[31]

Lines i-ii in the two texts also differ as to spatial horizons. Judg 5:4 contains place-names referring to the south. By contrast, Ps 68:8 does not reference a name; instead, it has a standard expression of the deity going in battle before the "people (*'am). The second line of Ps 68:8 instead has a term for a sort of region ("waste-land" or the like). Judges 5 is far more concerned with space, in providing two clear geographical references, while by comparison Psalm 68 focuses on "the people." It has been common to lump these descriptions of under the rubric of God as the divine warrior,[32] and in view of the later exemplars of the motif especially in Deut 33:2–5 as well as other parallel texts, this is not an unreasonable approach.[33] However, what needs to be noted in the cases of both Judg 5:4–5 and Ps 68:8–9 is that the divine march involves a great demonstration of power in shaking the heavens and earth, but it engages no enemies, divine or human. These lines in Psalm 68 do not show this God as a violent divine warrior fighting enemies, but a powerful God marching "before your people." In other words, the picture in Psalm 68 may involve divine protection of the people, while Judges 5 by comparison is open-ended. While these passages have been received and fitted into the larger military contexts of Judges 5 and Psalm 68 (and perhaps even belonged to a military context in an older setting), the military is hardly what is stressed here; instead, the first biblical glimpses of God show divine power and protection without reference to battle or violence.

In lines iii-iv, both poems have the same words describing attendant effects of the earth trembling and the heavens flowing. The usual categories of historical versus mythic do not apply very well to this description. If anything, the motif here seems only slightly mythic. Despite the clear meteorological effects of the deity, both passages are fairly terrestrial in that the representations are tied to earthly locations.[34] It is also important to note that the suffix forms of the

---

31 KTU 1.4 VII 7–13, in M.S. Smith, "The Baal Cycle," in *Ugaritic Narrative Poetry* (ed. S.B. Parker; SBLWAW 9; Atlanta 1997), 135–36. For discussion, see M.S. Smith and W.T. Pitard, *The Ugaritic Baal Cycle: Volume 2. Introduction with Text, Translation and Commentary of KTU 1.3–1.4* (SVT 114; Leiden 2009), 647, 649, 651–652, and 660–666.

32 For example, Cross, *Canaanite Myth* (see n. 13), 157; and P.D. Miller, Jr., *The Divine Warrior in Early Israel* (Cambridge 1973; repr. ed., Atlanta 2006), 91, 107. Cross (*Canaanite Myth* [see n. 13], 100) also sees "heavenly armies" in these passages, but the motif as represented in these two texts is not explicit on this score.

33 These are addressed by Miller, *The Divine Warrior* (see n. 32), inter alia.

34 Cf. the terrestrial march of Baal mentioned above. See also the comparison of Seti I: "He is like Baal (as) he treads the mountains"; see K. Tazawa, *Syro-Palestinian Deities in New Kingdom Egypt: The Hermeneutics of Their Existence* (BAR 1965; Oxford 2009), 28, document #62. Cf.

verbs in lines iii-iv set the divine march in the past. Given the location of the motif relative to the rest of the poems, it would appear that this divine victory was regarded as prior to the time of the victories to which the poems are primarily devoted.

In lines v-vi, Judg 5:4 expands the description. The result is a chiastic structure that balances "earth" with "mountains" and "heavens" with "clouds." There is not a considerable addition in information, but the fact of the addition is not insignificant. As we will see, the exemplars of the motif were open to addition. In the case of Judg 5:4–5, it is inserted the motif; in the other cases such as Deut 33:2–5, it follows as material added to the motif. Expansion and elaboration are integral to the tradition process in these passages.

In lines vii-viii, the natural effects are from before the deity, named in both passages as "the one of Sinai" and "the god of Israel." Thus in the earliest biblical glimpses of the deity, this deity is represented in association with earthly space of Sinai and with Israel. With these earthly locations, some cultural distance from our Egyptian sources is evident: neither Sinai nor Israel is known from the specific Egyptian sources that we noted earlier. For the early tradition that produced this motif, this god was the god of the people of Israel, and at the same time this god was associated with a place outside of the land of Israel. We will return to this core point.

Before doing so, it is important also to note that neither passages provides much specific information about the site from which the god marches. While scholars have assumed that the southern home of Yнwн entailed a mountain,[35] this is not entirely clear and it is also not known if a sanctuary or temple was involved. While it is reasonable to suppose that such was the case, it is an important to observe that neither of the two biblical poems offers an explicit depiction along these lines. Finally, there seems to be an ongoing tradition that celebrated Yнwн of Teman, as seen in the Kuntillet 'Ajrud inscriptions and in Habakkuk 3.[36]

In the final bicolon in lines vii-viii, the divine referent in line i in each poem, Yнwн (*yhwh*) for Judges 5 and *'ĕlōhîm* ("God") for Psalm 68, re-appears. In ad-

---

"When he [Ramessess III] is sent storming like unto Baal, the lands burn up in their land for terror of him," in Tazawa, *Syro-Palestinian Deities in New Kingdom Egypt*, 32, document #79; "His Majesty is like the Baal upon the mountain tops," in Tazawa, *Syro-Palestinian Deities in New Kingdom Egypt*, 33, document #83.

35 This would be especially the case if *miśśĕdēh* in Judg 5:4 is read as "from the highlands" (so Cross, *Canaanite Myth* [see n. 13], 101). See also W.H.C. Propp, "On Hebrew *śāde(h)*, 'Highland,'" *VT* 37 (1987), 230–236. That a mountain was thought later in Israelite tradition to be entailed might be thought to be suggested by 1 Kgs 19:8.

36 See above n. 14 for references.

dition, *mippĕnê*, literally "from before," in lines vii-viii links back with *lipnê*, "before," in line i in Psalm 68. Indeed, it might be thought that the use of *mippĕnê* in vii-viii might have inspired the composer of that poem to use the hardly uncommon construction, **lipnê 'amm-*, "before the people," in line i.

The motif of the divine march in the two poems was fitted within and adapted to their contexts. The authors have issues with which they are concerned, and they show their own mode of reflection. In Psalm 68, the motif in vv. 8 – 9 follows a hymnic introduction in vv. 5 – 7. It is not well integrated into the preceding context. By contrast with Judg 5:4 – 5, Psalm 68 expands on the motif at the end, in vv. 10 – 11, in commenting further on the rain provided to the land and the benefit it provides for the people. This focus is missing from the other exemplars of the motif. The larger context for the motif in Psalm 68 adds a further focus, with the reiteration of Sinai in v. 18. Here the poem picks up on "the One of Sinai" (*zeh sînay*), as seen in v. 9. At first glance, the reference to Sinai seems to name the location of the divine retinue. Sinai seems to be the mountain mentioned in v. 17 that God "desired for his dwelling." The syntax in v. 18b requires some attention; this line may be translated as follows: "The Lord is among them, at Sinai, among the holy (host)/in the holy place" (*'ădōnāy bām sînay baqqōdeš*). The internal rhyme of *'ădōnāy* and *sînay* is notable, as is the internal parallelism of *bām* and *baqqōdeš*. Still, the line remains difficult. The first prepositional phrase, "among them" (*bām*) seems to refer back to the thousands and myriads of the divine retinue, while Sinai (*sînay*) may be an adverbial accusative ("at Sinai"), in apposition to "among the holy (host)/in the holy place" (*baqqōdeš*), which may refer a descriptor for the divine mountain, as it is used for Baal's mountain.[37] Or, it could be a descriptor for the divine retinue (cf. *qōdeš* in Deut 33:2, discussed in the following section). In this case, the line might be rendered, "The Lord is among them, at Sinai among the holy (ones)."[38] The mountain of Sinai is contrasted with Bashan.

The motif in Psalm 68 is particularly notable for its lack of geographical referencing. The question is why Psalm 68 departs from the tradition of the motif as seen in both Judges 5 and, to some degree, in its later exemplars in Deuteronomy 33 and Habakkuk 3. An answer informed by the larger context of the poem has been suggested by a number of scholars. For example, Alexander Rofé suggests that Edom drops out of the picture in Ps 68:9 as a conscious effort on the part of the "Elohistic reworking," in Rofé's words, "to eradicate the original connection

---

37 KTU 1.3 III 30, in Smith, "The Baal Cycle" (see n. 31), 110.
38 Knohl ("Pharaoh's War on the Israelites" [see n. 24]) regards Sinai as a divine name, on the basis of reading the line in terms of internal parallelism.

between YHWH God of Israel and the field of Edom; God's abode is in Jerusalem (vs. 30)."[39] The notion that Edom was the original home of Israel's deity might not suit later conflict between Edom and Israel. In this context, Edom might have dropped out perhaps not so much as a deliberate reworking but because of a perceived lack of applicability in context.[40]

As in Psalm 68, the larger poetic context in Judges 5 shows both the reception of the motif as well as the larger role that it exercises in context. The poem in Judges 5 contains a double introduction (vv. 2–13) that is quite extraordinary compared with other introductions, both for its length and for its uneven parts.[41] Within this introduction, the motif is but one piece that serves to invoke praise of the deity. In Judges 5, it follows a hymnic invocation of the deity in v. 2 and a first person hymnic address in v. 3, and it is followed in vv. 6–9 by a second hymnic address that provides the context for the conflict. Thus the context to which the motif belongs is not a single, integrated piece. It is also to be noted that the geographical locations named in v. 4 stand at a considerable distance from the location of the battle in the Jezreel valley described in the body of the poem of Judges 5. Thus it is not without reason that scholars have seen the motif here as something of a poetic fragment not related originally to the report of the battle.

Given the independent attestation of the motif in early Hebrew poetry, it seems to have been known to and used by the composer of the poem, as we have it now, in order to introduce the themes of the body of the poem, which runs from v. 14 onwards.[42] The purpose of the introduction (vv. 2–13) seems to be to offer a view of the events in the poem's body, as showing YHWH as Israel's god and Israel as the overarching social unit, even though the poem's body (vv. 14–30) hardly mentions YHWH (only in the fragmentary v. 23), and it does not even mention Israel. Thus the introduction sounds thematic notes that are

---

39 Rofé, *Introduction to the Literature of the Hebrew Bible* (see n. 24), 445.

40 The association of Edom and Seir in Judah's prose storytelling tradition informs the wordplay in Gen 26:25's introduction of the newborn Esau as 'admônî kullô kĕ'adderet śē'ār, "red, like a hairy mantle all over" (NJPS), as commonly noted by commentators, e.g., Y. Zakovitch, *Jacob: Unexpected Patriarch* (trans. V. Zakovitch; New Haven 2012), 17. Esau is located in Seir-Edom in Gen 32:4. In Gen 36:8 Esau is said to settle in Seir and is then identified as Edom.

41 For a recent discussion, see M.S. Smith, *Poetic Heroes: Literary Commemorations of Warriors and Warrior Culture in the Early Biblical World* (Grand Rapids 2014), 234–266, especially 251–252, 254, and 257–258.

42 For this proposal, see M.S. Smith, "What is Prologue is Past: Composing Israelite Identity in Judges 5," in *Thus Says the Lord: Essays on the Former and Latter Prophets in Honor of Robert R. Wilson* (ed. J.J. Ahn and S.L. Cook; LHBOTS 502; New York 2009), 43–58. See also Smith, *Poetic Heroes* (see n. 41), 234–266.

interpretative for the body of the poem. The poem's body lays claim to YHWH as a military god in the central hill-country in the pre-monarchic period. In terms of the coordination between the representation of YHWH in the introduction and in the body, we might say that the tradition of the southern sanctuary in v. 4 has come north.[43]

There may be a further interpretive purpose to adding the motif to the poem's introduction. Arguably importantly for the shape of Israelite polytheism at the time, the stars are said in v. 20 to fight: "The stars, in their courses, they fought; they fought with Sisera." The perception is not simply a heavenly one; these stars are said to fight with Sisera. V. 21 relates how the river Kishon swept "them" ("the kings of Canaan" of v. 19) away. Thus the divine action is manifest on earth. These stars are, in other words, the heavenly host, the divine army, that because of vv. 4–5 is presumed to being led by Israel's divine warrior. In other words, vv. 4–5 arguably provides the explicit interpretive lens for understanding the divine army of v. 20.

In the case of both Judges 5 and Psalm 68, the larger context of the poems affects the sense of the motif, and the motif provides an interpretive lens for the poems' larger context. Within the larger contexts of the poems, the motif provides an antecedent for the divine victory for Israel celebrated in the body of the poems. As a result, both poems construct a genealogy of a tradition of divine victory, and define this tradition specifically in terms of YHWH for Israel. For Psalm 68, Sinai of the past and Jerusalem of the present signal the coordination of space and time as a single, continuous reality of divine aid and acknowledgement. For Judges 5, the motif, which originally had nothing to do with the account of battle in the Jezreel valley, became a central element in the composer's larger assertion about the battle in the past, namely that it was all about God and Israel. In the literary construction of Judges 5, two different past events, the past event of the motif with the divine march of the south and the past event of the battle in the Jezreel, became interrelated parts of a single past. For the biblical composer, the order of experience as separate events is not the order of reality as an ultimately related whole.

---

43 I remain open to the theory that trade from the south via the Jordan valley might have been the mechanism for the southern god, YHWH, becoming established in the central highlands. See J.D. Schloen, "Caravans, Kenites, and Casus Belli: Enmity and Alliance in the Song of Deborah," *CBQ* 55 (1993), 18–38.

4 Proposals for the Original Profile of Yнwн

The old poetic texts surveyed thus far point to Yнwн as a divine warrior providing precipitation. Scholars compare Yнwн as seen in these texts with other West Semitic gods, but not with West Semitic goddesses. Although the goddesses Anat and Astarte are important divine warriors, they are not manifest in the rainstorm in any of the texts noted in the preceding section. For this reason, these goddesses have not been included in the scholarly discussion of this question.[44] There are currently a number of proposals that may be noted.

First, Yнwн was originally a stormy divine warrior[45] like Baal. The evident storm language in the earliest available biblical witnesses as well as the representation of Yнwн's march in these sources corresponds to Baal's character as a divine warrior manifest in the rainstorm that marches against terrestrial enemies. Yнwн's march is from the south,[46] while Baal's is manifest from Mount Sapan in the Ugaritic texts. Given that Edom is given as one of the names of the region from which Yнwн comes in the old poetic sources, it may be worth noting that the name of Baal is thought to be attested as Edomite.[47] Moreover, the name of Yнwн has been derived from *hwh, "to blow" (Syriac hawwē, "wind").[48] To be sure, many proposals for the etymology of Yнwн's name have been offered, and the issue remains *sub iudice* (we will return to the ques-

---

44 Some caution is warranted on this point, as goddesses could assume masculine epithets. For example, see the case of the goddess *ḏt Ṣntm* who bears the male titles, *mr* ("lord") and *bʿl* ("master"), in A. Avanzini, *Corpus of South Arabian Inscriptions I-III: Qatabanic, Marginal Qatabanic, Awsanite Inscriptions* (Arabica Antica 2; Pisa 2004), 179 (see line 7).

45 See K. Budde, *Religion of Israel to the Exile* (New York 1899), 27–28; H. Ringgren, *Israelite Religion* (trans. D. Green; Philadelphia 1966), 45–46; T.N.D. Mettinger, "The Elusive Essence: YHWH, El and Baal and the Distinctiveness of Israelite Faith," in *Die Hebräische Bibel und ihre zweifache Nachgeschichte. Festschrift für Rolf Rendtorff zum 65. Geburstag* (ed. E. Blum *et al.*; Neukirchen-Vluyn 1990), 393–417, here 409–410; E.A. Knauf, "Yahwe," VT 34 (1984), 467–472.

46 Judg 5:5, discussed in Cross, *Canaanite Myth* (see n. 13), 100. It is to be noted that the old poetic texts never refers to Yнwн's southern mountain as such. Cross (*Canaanite Myth* [see n. 13], 103) included Exodus 15 in this constellation of ancient poetry (and hence the divine mountain in v. 17), but this poem is rather different in character from either Judges 5 or Psalm 68, and I do not include it in this discussion. I also cannot affirm Cross' high dating for Exodus 15; see Smith, *Poetic Heroes* (see n. 41), 211–220.

47 Bartlett (*Edom and the Edomites* [see n. 18], 99, 194, 196) points to the name Baal-hanan in Gen 36:38–39 and possibly the name of Baal on a seal from Petra and on an ostracon from Tell el-Kheleifeh "though here the names may be Phoenician" (p. 196).

48 See van der Toorn, "Yahweh" (see n. 1), 915–916.

tion below).[49] Generally, the evidence for YHWH as a storm god is quite strong in biblical sources.[50] Moreover, it is sometimes thought that YHWH and Baal are regarded as incompatible later in the biblical tradition precisely because they had similar profiles. Yet, at this point it is important to note the vast majority of biblical witnesses date to the monarchic period or later, when features associated with El, Baal and other deities were manifest in representations of YHWH (in what I have called "the convergence" of divinity in this divine figure).[51] Indeed, some texts such as Psalm 29 show particular influence of the tradition of Baal manifest in the rainstorm that moves eastward across the Mediterranean and strikes the coast of Lebanon. Accordingly, much of the imagery for YHWH also associated with Baal may have been appropriated secondarily.[52] Yet early in the tradition (in the texts noted in the preceding section), YHWH does appear to be a stormy warrior god. Despite the issues noted here, the threads of evidence presently available to scholars arguably offer the greatest support for this sort of profile for YHWH.

Second, YHWH is believed to be originally the god El.[53] There are indeed several old traditions about YHWH that do correspond to El's features.[54] Moreover, the name of El is attested in Edomite sources.[55] As support for the "El hypothesis," Frank Moore Cross following W. F. Albright took YHWH's name as the causative of the verb "to be" (*hwy),[56] which would be suitable for El as a creator of

---

49 *HALOT* 395; R. Albertz, *A History of Israelite Religion in the Old Testament Period: Volume I: From the Beginnings to the End of the Monarchy* (trans. J. Bowden; OTL; Louisville1994), 50; van der Toorn, "Yahweh" (see n. 1), 915–916.

50 See R. Müller, *Jahwe als Wettergott: Studien zur althebräischen Kultlyrik anhand ausgewählter Psalmen* (BZAW 387; Berlin 2011).

51 M.S. Smith, *The Early History of God: Yahweh and the Other Deities in Ancient Israel* (BRS; Grand Rapids ²2002), xxii, xxxvi, 7–9, 11, 54–59, 184, 195–202.

52 See the survey of J. Day, *Yahweh and the Gods and Goddesses of Canaan* (JSOTSup 265; Sheffield 2000), 91–127.

53 J. Wellhausen, *Prolegomena to the History of Israel* (trans. J.S. Black and A. Menzies; Edinburgh 1855; repr. Gloucester 1973), 433 n. 1; Cross, *Canaanite Myth* (see n. 13), 60–75; de Moor, *The Rise of Yahwism* (see n. 4), 102, 108, 163, 188, 274, 298, 323–335. De Moor (*The Rise of Yahwism*, 244) further suggests YHWH was originally "a divine ancestor," a view that has been criticized (see van der Toorn, "Yahweh" [see n 1], 914). See also H. Niehr, *Der höchste Gott* (BZAW 190; Berlin 1990), 4–5.

54 For summaries, see Cross, *Canaanite Myth* (see n. 13), 60–75; and Smith, *The Early History of God* (see n. 47), 32–43.

55 Bartlett (*Edom and the Edomites* [see n. 18], 196, 214–215) points to the name Magdiel in Gen 36:43 as well as a seal bearing the name, *šm'l*.

56 Albright, *Yahweh and the Gods of Canaan: A Historical Analysis of Two Contrasting Faiths* (Winona Lake; originally published in 1968), 168–172; Cross, *Canaanite Myth* (see n. 13), 62–

the earth, as attested in his titular. Cross compared Amorite PNs consisting of DN and the prefix indicative of *hwy and suggested that the title yhwh ṣb'wt was originally a title of El pointing to his creator role as "the one who brought the armies into being." John Day has strongly criticized the proposal ("this is pure speculation").[57] He also thinks that the lack of the causative stem of this root in Hebrew constitutes an impediment to this theory.[58] Johannes de Moor instead proposes that the name of Yнwн derives from the qal (G-stem) as a hypocoristic of El meaning "may he (El) be present (as helper)."[59] This proposal is quite sensible from a grammatical perspective and arguably from a semantic one as well. Indeed, Cross himself cites two South Arabian deities which exhibit the G-stem imperfect formations: yagūr, "He brings aid," and ḏū yahriq, "he (the star) who sets" (the god Athtar as the evening star).[60] Cross further suggests that Yнwн may have been El's epithet as patron deity of the Midianite league in the south.[61] However, the theories of Cross and de Moor that El was the missing deity behind the name suffers from a lack of evidence. (If this approach to the name of Yнwн were correct, there is no theoretical reason why it could not be another deity, such as Baal or Athtar, or perhaps a lesser known Midianite, Edomite or other pre-Islamic Arabian deity.[62]) In any case, Karel van der Toorn criticizes either theory that the name of Yнwн developed from a hypocoristic plus verbal form, as it lacks a basis in the history of West Semitic religion.[63]

A difficulty of a different sort, the evidence for El as a divine warrior is weak.[64] In neither the Ugaritic texts nor the Hebrew Bible is El presented in battle or marching to battle. Nor in these sources is El manifest in the storm,[65] or nor is he angry or violent like Yнwн.[66] Patrick D. Miller, Jr., recognizing the difficulty

---

65. See also D.N. Freedman, "The Name of the God of Moses," *JBL* 79 (1960), 151–156; and more recently P.D. Miller, *The Religion of Ancient Israel* (LAI; London 2000), 2.

57 Day, *Yahweh* (see n. 48), 14. For further criticism, see A. Gibson, *Biblical Semantic Logic: A Preliminary Analysis* (The Biblical Seminar 75; London 2001), 71–74, 159–164.

58 Day, *Yahweh* (see n. 48), 14.

59 De Moor, *The Rise of Yahwism* (see n. 49), 237–239.

60 Cross, *Canaanite Myth* (see n.13), 68.

61 Cross, *Canaanite Myth* (see n.13), 71.

62 Albertz compares the Akkadian PN ᵈIkšudum (cf. PN ᵈIk-šu-da in *CAD* K:278), as well as Arabic names consisting of the prefix indicative verbal forms. See Albertz, *A History of Israelite Religion* (see n. 47), 259 n. 41.

63 Van der Toorn, "Yahweh" (see n. 1), 915.

64 Note the case made by P.D. Miller, Jr., "El the Warrior," *HTR* 60 (1967), 411–431.

65 See Day, *Yahweh* (see n. 48), 113–114. See also R.S. Hess, *Israelite Religions: An Archaeological and Biblical Survey* (Grand Rapids 2007), 98.

66 See Day, *Yahweh* (see n. 48), 1. See Hess, *Israelite Religions* (see n. 52), 98.

here, hypothesized that the warlike trait of El was preserved for the most part among the less urbanized population of southern Canaan and thus not in the Ugaritic texts.[67] Responding to this proposal, J. J. M. Roberts remarks: "Even its prominence there, however, may be the result of a partial coalescence of 'El, the creator and clan leader, who as such would be characterized by love for the clan and the zeal to defend it, with Baal, the cosmogonic creator, and cosmic warrior."[68] In defense of his El hypothesis, Miller appeals also to the title *'ēl gibbôr* in Isa 9:5.[69] Yet even if this title were to be understood as an El reference, by the time of Isa 9:5 (whenever the verse is to be dated), this could represent a feature attributed secondarily to this god. It is also to be noted that the old El traditions in the Hebrew Bible do not appear in the early texts about YHWH discussed in the preceding section. Moreover, there are several texts that seem to recognize El on his own without being identified with YHWH (e.g., El as the god of the Exodus in Num 23:22 and 24:8; El and perhaps Asherah in Gen 49:25–26).[70] In view of these considerations, YHWH in the oldest poetic sources noted above does not resemble El. Accordingly, it may be judged that the El hypothesis is weaker in terms of evidence than the Baal hypothesis.

Third, I proposed the possibility that YHWH was a figure resembling the god Athtar,[71] best known from the Ugaritic texts, Aramaic sources and South Arabian inscriptions.[72] This hypothesis has found no acceptance, as far as I am aware. Athtar is a divine warrior who generates precipitation, though not clearly in the rainstorm unlike Baal or YHWH. Like YHWH, he is also an inland deity. Athtar is further associated with the evening star, a feature that does not accord particularly well with any presently known information about YHWH. At the same time, there is some astral imagery associated with YHWH. Many scholars take

---

67 Miller, "El the Warrior" (see n. 64), 431.

68 Roberts, *The Earliest Semitic Pantheon: A Study of the Semitic Deities Attested in Mesopotamia before Ur III* (Baltimore 1972), 96. The characterization of Baal as "cosmogonic creator" is problematic.

69 See Miller, *The Divine Warrior* (see n. 32), 56. The other so-called evidence cited by Miller (48–63) never represents El as a warrior as such.

70 For the former, see M.S. Smith, *The Origins of Biblical Monotheism: Israel's Polytheistic Background and the Ugaritic Texts* (Oxford 2001), 146–147. For the latter, see Smith, *The Early History of God* (see n. 47), 48–49.

71 Smith, *The Origins of Biblical Monotheism* (see n. 63), 146.

72 For a summary of Athtar, see M.S. Smith, "The God Athtar in the Ancient Near East and His Place in KTU 1.6 I," in *Solving Riddles and Untying Knots: Biblical, Epigraphic, and Semitic Studies Presented to Jonas C. Greenfield* (ed. Z. Zevit et al.; Winona Lake 1995), 627–640.

the stars in Judg 5:20 as evidence,[73] and YHWH as the head of the heavenly or astral armies would comport with this view.[74] The hypothesis that YHWH may be comparable to Athtar depends on an argument either that the profiles of these two gods differed slightly or that early in biblical tradition some features associated with YHWH were lost or shifted, as YHWH "acclimated" to the hill country of Israel. The rainstorm imagery attested for YHWH in the earliest biblical sources would already reflect this hypothetical shift. YHWH could be have "baal-ized" by the time of the early poetic sources under discussion above.

Fourth, YHWH has been thought to have solar features,[75] based on biblical verses such as Deut 33:2, Hab 3:3, as well as one of plaster inscriptions from the Kuntillet 'Ajrud: "and when God/El shone forth."[76] While these features have been long noted,[77] no scholar presently holds that YHWH was originally a sun god.[78] Others hold that YHWH's solar features, while secondary, were nevertheless quite old.[79]

Fifth and finally, it has been suggested that YHWH would not match the profile of any other particular god.[80] Given the lack of firm evidence, this position is understandable. Some scholars, such as John Day, J. Andrew Dearman, Richard S. Hess, and Karel van der Toorn, do not take a position on the issue.[81] André Lemaire offers a minimal portrait (e. g., YHWH as a "mountain god").[82] Some dis-

---

73 Cf. the scholars cited in this vein along with some cautionary comments by Smith, *Poetic Heroes* (see n. 41), 230 – 231.

74 J.G. Taylor, *Yahweh and the Sun: Biblical and Archaeological Evidence for Sun Worship in Ancient Israel* (JSOTSup 111; Sheffield 1993), 99 – 107, 259 – 260.

75 See the listing of scholars by Day, *Yahweh* (see n. 48), 156.

76 Aḥituv et al., in Meshel, *Kuntillet 'Ajrud (Ḥorvat Teman)* (see n. 12), 110; KAjr 15 in Dobbs-Allsopp et al., *Hebrew Inscriptions* (see n. 12), 287. See Van der Toorn, "Yahweh" (see n. 1), 917.

77 Taylor, *Yahweh and the Sun* (see n. 67); M.S. Smith, "The Near Eastern Background of Solar Language for Yahweh," *JBL* 109 (2990), 29 – 39, and *The Early History of God* (see n. 47), 148 – 159.

78 Taylor, *Yahweh and the Sun* (see n. 55), 264: "should Yahweh be viewed as a 'sun god'? Certainly not."

79 See de Moor, *The Rise of Yahwism* (see n. 4), 163 – 164. Van der Toorn ("Yahweh" [see n. 1], 917) traces solar features of YHWH back to El ("only with great caution").

80 For thoughtful comments on the larger issue, see E.L. Greenstein, "The God of Israel and the Gods of Canaan: How Different Were They?" in *The Bible and Its World: Proceedings of the Twelfth World Congress of Jewish Studies Jerusalem, July 29 – August 5, 1997. Division A* (ed. R. Margolin; Jerusalem 1999), 47*–58*.

81 Day, *Yahweh* (see n. 51), 1; Dearman, *Religion & Culture in Ancient Israel* (Hendrickson, 1992), 20; Hess, *Israelite Religions* (see n. 52), 98; van der Toorn, "Yahweh" (see n. 1).

82 A. Lemaire, *The Birth of Monotheism: The Rise and Disappearance of Yahwism* (Washington 2007), 26.

cussions dismiss the notion that Yнwн was a "nature god."[83] Others emphasize socio-religious traits associated with Yнwн, such as "cultic aloofness,"[84] covenant,[85] or liberation.[86] There is a good deal to recommend covenant (and perhaps other traits connected with it). It would also have been associated with other West Semitic deities.[87] Indeed, one of the oldest prose sources in the Hebrew Bible, Judges 9, associates covenant with the names of both El and Baal, but not Yнwн (see vv. 4 and 46).[88] It is to be noted that several studies in this vein do not explain why such a comparative approach is incongruent with associating traits such as covenant with Yнwн.

As this brief survey of views shows, the current scholarly consensus on the issue of Yнwн's original profile holds that this deity was a divine warrior from the southern region associated with Seir, Edom, Paran and Teman. Otherwise, scholars are divided over the question. While the original god of Israel may have been El, Yнwн does not appear to have been originally identified with El. While the strongest profile for comparison with Yнwн may be Baal, some differences have been noted, and as with El, some features of Baal assigned also to Yнwн may be secondary. The similarities of Yнwн with Athtar serve to highlight some of the weaknesses inherent in the comparison with Baal (or with El for that matter). Moreover, this proposal also raises a methodological difficulty: the original profile of Yнwн apart from the details of his southern abode and his warrior nature may be lost, a point that includes the divine name, as Rainer Albertz remarks: "It is highly improbable that Israel was still aware of the meaning of the

---

83 G. Fohrer, *History of Israelite Religion* (trans. D.E. Green; New York 1972), 79; W. Baumgartner, *Geschichte der israelitischen Religion* (Baslter Vorträge notiert von D. Karasszon; Debrecen 2004), 53.

84 R.P. Gordon, "Introducing the God of Israel," in *The God of Israel* (ed. R.P. Gordon; UCOP 64; Cambridge 2007), 5.

85 See Fohrer, *History of Israelite Religion* (see n. 75), 75–79; Cross, *From Epic to Canon* (see n. 1), 3–21; Miller, *The Religion of Ancient Israel* (see n. 55), 4–5. Note also S.L. Cook, *The Social Roots of Biblical Yahwism* (StBL 8; Atlanta 2004), 20–44.

86 Albertz, *A History of Israelite Religion* (see n. 47), 49–52. To be clear, Albertz does not attribute liberation to the pre-Mosaic group, only that Yнwн's origins outside of any state system helped to make this deity amenable as a divine emblem of liberation.

87 See T.J. Lewis, "Covenant and Blood Rituals: Understanding Exodus 24:3–8 in Its Ancient Near Eastern Context," in *Confronting the Past: Archaeological and Historical Essays on Ancient Israel in Honor of William G. Dever* (ed. S. Gitin et al.; Winona Lake 2006), 341–350.

88 Judg 8:33 represents a later interpretive take on the deity by the same title in 9:4. About its date, Groß (*Richter* [see n. 25], 388) views the verse as post-deuteronomistic. See also J. Pakkala, "Deuteronomy and 1–2 Kings in the Redaction of the Pentateuch and Former Prophets," in *Deuteronomy in the Pentateuch, Hexateuch, and the Deuteronomistic History* (ed. K. Schmid and R.F. Person, Jr.; FAT 2/56; Tübingen 2012), 150–151.

name Yʜᴡʜ."[89] The same may be said for some of the other features associated with Yʜᴡʜ. This deity may have exhibited any number of early traits and associations that failed to transfer from "the Shasu tribes"[90] into the Hebrew Bible or other records from ancient Israel.

Largely because the biblical evidence is so sparse for early Israel, scholars take recourse to other sources as seems coherent with what is known of West Semitic religion. The fact of the matter is that the earliest record for Yʜᴡʜ locates this deity at a periphery of West Semitic religion and culture, perhaps in a rather isolated context to which there is little or no access at the level of primary evidence. It has been sometimes emphasized that the original location of Yʜᴡʜ situates this deity in an early Midianite, Edomite or pre-Islamic Arab context.[91] In view of the Egyptian evidence noted in the first part of this essay, the timeframe involved may reach back to the Late Bronze Age. If any weight may be put on the poetic, fragmentary memories about Yʜᴡʜ in Judges 5 and Psalm 68 for the deity's older background, then the military dimension of the deity remains evident. It may in turn point to the sort of human setting that championed this deity, namely a group that this deity championed in the form of divine protection in warfare.[92] In any case, given how little is known of the religion of this region in the Late Bronze Age or early Iron Age, it is to be expected that there is some amount of information – perhaps even a considerable amount – about Yʜᴡʜ that is unknown in this early period. Yʜᴡʜ known to ancient Israel may not have been the same Yʜᴡʜ as known before biblical tradition.

---

89 Albertz, *A History of Israelite Religion* (see n. 47), 50–51. Albertz also comments (p. 52): "We hardly know what characteristics were attributed to Yahweh before he became the god of the Moses group."

90 J.P. Allen, "A Report of Bedouin," *COS* 3.16. See above in Part Two of this essay.

91 See Knauf, "Yahwe," (see n. 45), and Midian, *Untersuchungen zur Geschichte Palästinas und Nordarabiens am Ende des Jahrtausends v. Chr.* (Wiesbaden 1988), 48–114. See also comments made by van der Toorn, "Yahweh" (see n. 1), 915–916.

92 As heuristic comparisons, see any number of military texts, including the Mesha Stele (KAI 181) and South Arabian inscriptions, which thank the deity for protection in battle. For example, see the protection afforded by the deities Athtar and ʿm in Avanzini, *Corpus of South Arabian Inscriptions I-III* (see n. 44), 167–168.

Manfred Krebernik
The Beginnings of Yahwism from an Assyriological Perspective

1 The cultural background

The Old Testament is the only continuous tradition based on word and writing which reaches from the Ancient Near East into our modern world. It conveys, however, a perception of the Ancient Near Easter as a background for the history of the "chosen people" and the revelation of their god. The whole Ancient Near East world is seen, so to speak, from the perspective of Jerusalem. Other perspectives have been opening since, in the 19th century, the Egyptian and cuneiform writing systems were deciphered, and archaeological excavations brought to light an increasing number of textual and material witnesses. The evolution of Ancient Near Eastern archaeology and philology was paralleled by the evolution of an "archaeology of scripture," i.e. the observation of textual "layers" in the Old Testament and the historical reconstruction of its formation which turned out to have been a long-lasting and complex process.

The area in which the kingdoms of Judah and Israel came into existence and vanished, and where the origins of the YHWH religion are to be sought, is situated in a border zone between the cultural spheres of Egypt and Mesopotamia. From a geographical viewpoint, this area is more fragmented than Egypt and Mesopotamia with their large watercourses. Both Egypt and Mesopotamia offered more favorable preconditions for the evolution and continuity of powerful empires. In this context may also be seen the creation of the two earliest writing systems. They appear more or less simultaneously towards the end of the 4th millennium BC, in Egypt and Mesopotamia, and they remained in use for more than three thousand years as one of the most characteristic features of the two respective cultures. During the 3rd and 2nd millennium, the cuneiform script spread from Southern Mesopotamia to large parts of the Ancient Near East serving as a medium for a number of different language: Sumerian, Akkadian, Elamite, Hurrian, Hittite, and Urartian, to mention only the most important in chronological order. At the time of its largest expansion, during the 14th and 13th centuries BC, "cuneiform culture" stretched from Baḥrain in the Persian Gulf to the Mediterranean, and from Anatolia to Egypt, while Akkadian, the Semitic language of Mesopotamia (in its Babylonian variety), served as a *lingua franca* in this vast area. In contrast to cuneiform, the Egyptian script (in its varieties hieroglyphic, hieratic and finally demotic) remained almost entirely limited

DOI 10.1515/9783110448221-003

to the Nile valley and the Egyptian language. In the Middle and Southern Levant, especially in the area of (later) Judah and Israel, political and cultural influences from Egypt prevailed from the late 3rd millennium down to the 8th century BC. The population spoke Central and Northwest Semitic vernaculars, i.e. predecessors of North Arabic, Hebrew-Phoenician, and Aramaic. Presumably for one or some of these Semitic languages, the alphabet had been created after the model of the Egyptian script, perhaps as early as in the 19th century BC. Apart from the small corpus of "Proto-Sinaitic" inscriptions detected on the Southern Sinai peninsula in the vicinity of Egyptian mines and settlements (and recently also in Egypt), early witnesses are extremely rare. The first large alphabetic corpus comes from Ugarit in the Northern Levant and dates between 1400 and 1290 approximately. The texts owe their preservation to the circumstance that they were written on clay tablets in the Mesopotamian cuneiform writing technique (Mesopotamian cuneiform was used in Ugarit at the same time). Since longer texts in "linear" alphabetic script – like their Egyptian counterparts – were normally written on perishable material (leather, papyrus), alphabetic documents remain scarce throughout in comparison to cuneiform sources even after the alphabet started to replace cuneiform. Abecedaria from Ugarit testify for the first time not only the sequence of letters familiar to us from Hebrew, Greek and Latin, but also to the South Semitic letter order otherwise known only from much later sources. Interestingly, a clay tablet displaying a South Semitic alphabet written in the cuneiform writing technique known from Ugarit and dating roughly from the period of the Ugarit texts was found at Bet Shemesh in the vicinity of Jerusalem.

2 The religious background: Ancient Near Eastern polytheism

Textual sources in different scripts and languages, complemented by archaeological data, provide a vast historico-cultural panorama in which the origin and beginnings of the YHWH religion can by sought. The wide range and complementarity of the entire material should be kept in mind when we now foreground the cuneiform sources and the cultural space which they define. In accordance with our topic, we focus chronologically on the 2nd and early first millennium BC. Subsequent developments, e.g. the possible impact of Assyrian state religion on the shaping of Biblical monotheism, remain out of consideration.

The cuneiform sources reflect for the Ancient Near East in general a complex polytheistic world-view. The texts mention the names of thousands of deities, they illustrate the history, character, and cults of many of them, and they pass down myths involving many of them. The Ancient Near Eastern religious landscape can be subdivided geographically, ethnically and socially, but at least its areal subdivisions are not separated by sharp borderlines. Transitions and adaptations are quite common. During the periods covered by the cuneiform documentation, we can observe the disappearance of older deities and the entrance of new ones. Thus, Nabû (older form Nabium), a god of scribal art and wisdom who played a major role in the 1st millennium, is first attested in the beginning of the 2nd millennium, around 800 years after the scribes began to compose comprehensive god-lists. Regarding individual deities, we can distinguish universal features from more specific traits which may be typical of geographical areas and places, ethnicities, social groups or particular responsibilities. The most important general features are the following:

(1) Deities represent cosmic or cultural entities and their powers, and they own characteristic traits and functions corresponding to those entities.
(2) They are conceived like human persons (which includes gender).
(3) They have anthropomorphic and non-anthropomorphic manifestations (e.g. heavenly bodies, mountains and rivers, animals, mixed creatures, and artificial objects like parts of buildings or musical instruments).
(4) Deities (at least the most important ones) are associated with symbolic animals, objects or numbers which may either function as attributes accompanying them or emblems representing them.
(5) Deities are not isolated "personalities," but interconnected in many different ways (e.g. cosmology, genealogy, family, office and function).
(6) Most deities are arranged in couples.
(7) Deities have local ties. Cities are normally associated with one main deity.
(8) The principal deities together with their divine families and households are worshipped in "temples" on which (official) religious life centers. Temples are usually cult places and economic institutions at the same time.
(9) The organization of the pantheon as a whole and in its local varieties parallels society and particularly kingship as the common form of rule in the Ancient Near East. The basic structure of a pantheon is that of a royal household. The head of the pantheon varied according to "religious areas" and historical periods. Thus, *An* and *Enlil* were the supreme gods in Sumer and Babylonia, the latter being succeeded by Marduk towards the end of the 2nd millennium, whereas *Dagan* held the same position in Upper Mesopotamia, *Assur* in Assyria, and *El* at Ugarit.
(10) Human kings were ascribed a particular affinity to the divine realm. In Babylonia several kings (beginning with Narām-Sîn of Akkade, 23th century

BC) claimed the rank of a "god" at their lifetimes, while Assyrian kings regarded themselves as representatives or vice-regents of the god Assur.

(11) Deities of similar character could easily be identified with each other or even merged, but this did not imply that their names or local cults were reduced to one.

(12) Many deities, especially the most important ones, are referred to by several different names, some of them common, some learned and rare. They can mostly be explained either as names of originally distinct deities or as frozen titles and epithets.

In its final form, the Old Testament constitutes a counter-concept to the Ancient Near Eastern polytheistic model, promulgating one single and universal god who revealed himself to Moses under the name of YHWH. The Biblical texts are, however, the product of long-lasting mental and textual processes the traces of which can be glimpsed in the texts themselves and in documents from their periphery. It seems reasonable to assume that the divine figure in the focus of this development originally shared some aspects with other Ancient Near Eastern deities and adopted some from them. A most obvious candidate for both is the Canaanite storm-god "Baal" whom the OT presents as YHWH's most powerful rival.

In order to approach the origins and early development of Yahwism, we shall try to combine the textual evidence in and around the Bible with our knowledge about the general Ancient Near Eastern background as sketched above. This method involves, however, two elements of uncertainty:

(1) Our model of polytheism is substantially based on the urban milieu of Mesopotamian city-states and empires, whereas Yahwism probably originated (in accordance with the Biblical tradition) in a non-sedentary ambiente;

(2) from and for the presumed area and time of its origin, contemporaneous written sources are rare.

3 YHWH's affinities to other Ancient Near Eastern deities

If one looks, with Ancient Near Eastern prototypes in mind, at the manifestations of YHWH as described in the OT, his associations with the sky, with storm, thunder and mountains (Sinai, Horeb, Nebo, Garizim, Zion) as well as his warlike aspects remind immediately of some Ancient Near Eastern deities. The closest parallels are generally seen in the weather-god Baal and his father El as they occur in mythological texts form Ugarit.

In the mountainous areas stretching from Anatolia to Canaan, the weal and woe of men and kingdoms depended mainly on the benevolence of the weather-god, who fertilized the soil with his rain, manifesting himself most impressively with storm, thunder, lightning and hail. It seems natural that the weather-god in various regional manifestations, often associated with mountains, played a dominating role in these areas, whereas in regions like Babylonia, where agriculture was based on artificial irrigation, the most important and mythologically active deities were of different types. Nevertheless, the weather-god was an important figure also of the Mesopotamian pantheon. His Semitic proper name was *Hadad* (> Akkadian *Adad*) or (with inflectional ending) *Haddu*, but in Syria and the Levant he was more often simply called *Ba'lu* (> Hebrew *Ba'al*, Baal) "the Lord."

Another deity to whom YHWH partially resembles is the head of the Ugaritic pantheon, *'Ilu* (often rendered in the Hebrew form *El*). His name is nothing else than the common Semitic word for "god." Its use as a proper name can either be explained in the sense of "the god" *par excellence* or it could go back to an original epithet or title. In this case, the full form could be preserved in a fragmentary Hittite myth [1] of Levantine origin were El appears under the name Elkunirsa which obviously represents Northwest Semitic *'il(u) qōni 'arṣ(i)* "the god who created the earth," surviving as Palmyrene *'lq(w)nr'* and Greek Κόνναρος.

Like many other Ancient Near Eastern deities, *Haddu*/Baal and El are associated with an animal. This is in both cases the bull, a paragon of strength and fertility. For the weather-god, the association is mainly documented iconographically, while El is explicitly called "bull" in Ugaritic texts. Incidentally it should be noted that the bull, according to a tradition probably at home in Sumer/Babylonia, was also associated with the moon-god, the crescent being his "horns" and the stars his herd of cows.

Baal and El occur as protagonists of Ugaritic myths. The largest mythological composition from Ugarit, the so-called "Baal Cycle,"[2] narrates the deeds of Baal and his "sister" (consort) Anat. The first episode, Baal's victorious struggle against the sea-god Yammu, is indirectly attested by an allusion already in an

---

1 For Hittite texts we refer generally to the "Hethitologie-Portal" where up-to-date translations and bibliographies can be found: http://www.hethport.uni-wuerzburg.de.
2 For a German translation with introduction and commentary see M. Dietrich and O. Loretz in *TUAT III/6* (1997), 1091–1198. A monumental new edition has been undertaken by M.S. Smith, *The Ugaritic Baal Cycle* (Leiden 1996/2009). Ugaritic Texts are mostly quoted after the comprehensive edition (in transcription) by M. Dietrich *et al.*, *The Cuneiform Alphabetic Texts from Ugarit, Ras Ibn Hani and Other Places. Third, Enlarged edition* (AOAT 360/1; Münster 2013). Abbr.: KTU³.

Old Babylonian letter from Mari.[3] The old motif is still noticeable in the OT, where YHWH is praised as the lord of the sea with its monsters.[4] In the second episode of the Baal Cycle, Baal achieves El's approval for building a palace of his own which he finally erects on Mount Ṣapā/ūnu (Hittite Ḫazzi, Greek Kasios). The Ugaritic name of the mountain has a Hebrew equivalent ṣāpōn with the general meaning "North," which in Ps 48:3 it is still recognizable as the name of a mountain associated with YHWH. The last episode of the Baal Cycle deals with the conflict between Baal and Mot, "Death"; Baal succumbs first, but finally defeats his enemy. This motif, too, is echoed in the OT.[5] The Ugaritic text is only partially preserved, and the plot cannot be reconstructed entirely and with certainty. In any case, two female deities, the sun-goddess Šapšu and his consort Anat are involved in Baal's retrieval and revival, and for leaving the realm of Death, he has to provide seven gods (whom he had engendered himself in the netherworld?) as substitutes. Baal thus represents the widespread type of a dying and resurrecting deity. He stands not only for the rain of the winter season but also for the vegetation resulting from it, in particular wine and grain. His role as a vegetation deity is matched by the names of his two servants, Gapnu "Grape" and Ugāru "(Fertile) Field." Similar deities are known from Anatolia and Mesopotamia. In a famous Sumero-Babylonian myth, the goddess Inanna/ Ištar descends to the Netherworld, ruled here by the goddess Ereškigal, and has to promise her a substitute for being allowed to return. Tragically, she surrenders her lover, the shepherd Dumuzi/Tammuz, but his sister shares his lot so that he can return each year for some months form the netherworld. The myth was reenacted in rite, and Ezekiel in one of his visions sees women bewailing Tammuz even in the temple of Jerusalem. But let us return to Baal. The mythology connected with him determined in all likelihood the cultic year in Ugarit as well as in Canaan. The major feast marking the turn of the year seems to have been Baal's resurrection when wine and grain were harvested. The later Jewish calendar (whose month names are of Babylonian provenience) still reflects such a cultic year. With the eighth month, Tishri, starts the New Year, and in the same month are celebrated the important festivals of Yom Kippur and Sukkot, which followed the vintage according to Deut 16:13.

---

3 See J. M. Durand, "Le mythologème du combat entre le dieu de l'Orage et la Mer en Mésopotamie," *MARI* 7 (1993), 41–61.
4 See J. Day, *God's Conflict with the Dragon and the Sea. Echoes of a Canaanite Myth in the Old Testament* (Cambridge 1985).
5 See W. Herrmann, "Jahwes Triumph über Mot," *UF* 11 (1979), 371–377.

El is, according to the Ugaritic myths, the father of the gods and the head of the pantheon. The gods are called the "sons of El," and we are explicitly told how El engendered the gods *Šaḥaru* "Dawn" and *Šalimu* "Dusk." El's abode is situated "at the spring of the (two) rivers, at the source of the (two) oceans." On the other hand, he is also associated, like Baal, with a mountain, in this case of the name *Kas(s)u*. The mythological concept underlying El's abode is still a matter of discussion,[6] but it seems likely that it has something to do with the ideas of creation connected with him, and if so, the motif could be related to the separation of the primeval waters in Gen 1:6. As chief of the pantheon, El presides the "Assembly of the Gods," which gathers amid an opulent meal on a mountain called *Lullu*. El's wife is *'Aṯiratu*, her name corresponds exactly to Hebrew Asherah, an issue which we shall address later.

To the Ugaritic El roughly correspond the gods Dagan in Upper Mesopotamia and Enlil in Babylonia. The first equation is confirmed in the Baal Cycle, where Baal is explicitly called "son of Dagan," and Dagan is equated with Enlil in Mesopotamian god lists. Enlil and Dagan are ultimately gods of earth, agriculture and especially grain. Enlil's background is best visible in his family ties: his wife Ninlil is the daughter of the grain goddess, his first-born son Ninurta carries a term for "earth" in his name (*urta*), and his emblem is the plough. As to Dagan's name, one could speculate that it is related with a proto-Indo-European word for earth preserved as *tekan* in Hittite and χθών in Greek. The Hebrew term *dāgān* "grain" obviously goes back to a metonymic use of the theonym Dagan; the same phenomenon can be observed in Mesopotamia, where the name of the grain goddess Ašnan was used metonymically for "grain." Possibly also the god of the Amorites, nomadic tribes form North-Eastern Syria who immigrated into Mesopotamia in the late 3rd and early 2nd millennia BC, is to be identified with El. His name, spelled logographically in cuneiform as (AN.)AN.-MAR.TU, is probably to be read Amurru(m) or Il Amurri(m), and the name of his wife, given as Ašratum in cuneiform sources, can be identified with Aṯiratu/Asherah. Also with the Hurrians, a people who entered Upper Mesopotamia from the Zagros mountains and founded there the powerful kingdom of Mittani, we find two deities corresponding to Baal and El, called Teššub and Kumarbi, respectively. A Hurrian cycle of myths, containing also Babylonian elements and handed down in Hittite, deals with their struggle for hegemony.

---

6 See, e.g., M.S. Smith, *Baal Cycle I* (see n. 2), 225–234; H. Niehr, "Die Wohnsitze des Gottes El nach den Mythen aus Ugarit. Ein Beitrag zu ihrer Lokalisierung," in *Das biblische Weltbild und seine altorientalischen Kontexte* (ed. B. Janowski and B. Ego; FAT 32; Tübingen 2001), 325–360.

Myths like those mentioned above were of course incompatible with later Biblical monotheism, but certain affinities of YHWH with the protagonists of the ancient myths are still noticeable in some passages of the OT. One of the most impressive and best-known witnesses for YHWH 's character as a storm-god is Psalm 29; its core passage describes his manifestation as a thunderstrom:

(3) The voice of YHWH (is) above the waters, [...]
     YHWH (is) above the great waters,
(4) the voice of YHWH with power,
     the voice of YHWH with splendour!
(5) The voice of YHWH breaks cedar trees, [...]
(7) the voice of YHWH lights flames of fire,
(8) the voice of YHWH makes the desert tremble,
(9) the voice of YHWH shakes oak trees![7]

The "voice of YHWH" is evidently the thunder which can be called with an analogous expression *rigim Adad* "the voice of (the storm-god) Adad" in Akkadian.

Somewhat less concrete are the traits of YHWH connecting him with El.[8] The most obvious link is his role as creator of the world. As already mentioned above, the separation of the primeval waters in Gen 1:6 could reflect the same myth as the description of El's cosmic abode "at the spring of the (two) rivers" in Ugarit. There is also a faint possibility that the creation of heaven and earth was originally conceived as an act of separation like in Mesopotamia where this idea is first connected with Enlil (who separates heaven and earth) and later also with Marduk (who splits the body of Tiamat). This suspicion is raised by the verb *bārā(')* "he created" (root b-r-') in Gen 1:1 in view of a similar root b-r-y meaning "to separate, discern," from which the Akkadian term *birīt-* "(space in) between" is derived. Several passages in the OT seem to indicate that YHWH has adopted El's position as father of the gods, head of the pantheon and head of the assembly of the gods. Thus, at the beginning of Psalm 29 (already quoted above), the *bnê 'ilîm* "Sons of Gods" are addressed: "Give to YHWH, Sons of Gods, give to YHWH glory and might!" Similarly, the "divine" frame story of the book of Job opens with the arrival of the *bnê hā-'ælōhîm* "Sons of God" (among them Satan), presumably in the heavenly court or assembly (Job 1:6). The two expressions, usually understood in the sense of "angels," could well go back to **banū 'Ili(-ma)* "the sons of El," attested as a general designation for the gods in Ugarit, and refer to the gods taking part in the assembly.

---

7 Textual analysis after U. Becker (Jena), who treated Psalm in the course of a joint seminary in 2011.
8 See, e. g., O. Eissfeldt, "El and Yahweh," *JSS* 1 (1956), 25–37.

An assembly of the gods, in which the creation of man is decided, could be postulated as the former background of Gen 1:26, where "Let us make man in our image" is commonly interpreted as a *pluralis maiestatis*. The most explicit passage is Psalm 82:1[9]: "God (Elohim) has arisen in the divine assembly (or: the assembly of El), he is judging among the gods." Finally, the title YHWH *ṣəbāʾôt* "Lord of hosts" should be mentioned in this connection since "hosts/ troops" certainly referred once to gods (not necessarily only warriors).[10]

Reminiscent of the bull-aspect of El and Baal are the proverbial "Golden Calf" of Exod 32:1–20 and the two golden calf images which Jerobeam had put up in Bethel and Dan according to 1 Kings 28–30. In spite (or because) of the polemic in the OT, one can surmise that this specific theriomorphic aspect was once ascribed also to a predecessor of YHWH.

YHWH has his affinity to mountains in common with Baal, El, and other Ancient Near Eastern deities, in particular those at home in the mountainous regions of the North.[11] In Northern Syria and Upper Mesopatamia we find even a number of deified mountains: *Ǧebel Sinǧār* (in cuneiform sources Sangar, Saggar) und *Ǧebel ʿAbd al-ʿAzīz* (in cuneiform sources De/ipar) in Northern Syria, *Ǧebel Bišrī*[12] between Palmyra and Euphrates, *Ǧebel Ḥaʾimrīn* (in cuneiform sources Ebiḫ) to the North of Bagdad. Assur, the god of the city of the same name, and later state god of the Assyrian empire started his career most probably as a local mountain god associated with the mountain on which the city was founded. A peculiar trait of YHWH, which cannot be explained as a simple concomitant phenomenon of his association with lightning, is his affinity to fire. During Israel's journey through the wilderness, he leads them "by day in a pillar of cloud, and by night in a pillar of fire" (Exod 13:21–22), and on Mount Sinai he appears amidst thunder and clouds while smoke rises from the mountain as from a melting furnace (Exod 19:16–19). These descriptions seem to be derived from impressions of a volcano and could thus – either as a fiction or as a historical reminiscence – point to a Northeast Arabian background. In this connection, O. Keel has drawn attention to another aspect which speaks against an all too close relationship between YHWH and the "Northern" gods: "Die gern wiederholte Behauptung, JHWH sei ein Wettergott vom Typ Hadads oder Baals gewe-

---

9 For a comprehensive study of Psalm 82 see P. Machinist, "How Gods Die, Biblically and Otherwise: A Problem of Cosmic Restructuring," in *Reconsidering the Concept of Revolutionary Monotheism* (ed. B. Pongratz-Leisten; Winona Lake 2011), 189–240.
10 See, e. g., T. Mettinger, "Yahweh Zebaoth," *DDD²* 920–924; H. Niehr, "Host of Heaven," *DDD²* 428–430.
11 Cf., e. g., V. Haas, *Hethitische Berggötter und hurritische Steindämonen* (Mainz 1982).
12 To be understood as a theonym e. g. in the Amorite personal name Mut-Bišir "Man of Bišir."

sen, ignoriert erstens die originellen, nur mit ihm verbundenen Elemente. Zweitens trägt sie der Tatsache nicht Rechnung, dass die Ägypter während ihrer drei Jahrhunderte lang während Herrschaft über die südliche Levante den kanaanäischen Wettergott in einer interkulturellen Ligatur mit ihrem eher unheimlichen, aggressiven und gewalttätigen Gott der Fremde, mit Seth, verbunden haben (Keel 2009). Dieser Baal-Seth war zwar ein Sturm- und Kriegs-, aber kein Fruchtbarkeitsgott."[13]

4 Traces of Yʜᴡʜ 's entourage

Considering the general structure of Ancient Near Eastern polytheism as sketched above, we should expect that Yʜᴡʜ initially was not isolated but linked somehow to other deities, the most likely type of entourage being a family and servants. Traces of his "sons" were already mentioned above. A female deity connected with Yʜᴡʜ is clearly attested in extra-Biblical sources of a relatively late date: Aramaic documents from a Jewish military colony in Elephantine (Egypt) dating approximately to 400 BC witness to the existence of a Yʜᴡʜ-temple in which beside Yʜᴡʜ himself (*Yhw* and rarely *Yhh*, pronounced Yahô) the deities Ešem-Bayt-El (*'šmbyt'l*) "Name of the (god?) Bayt-El" and ʿAnat-Bayt-El (*'ntbyt'l*) "Anat of the (god?) Bayt-El" were worshipped. Bayt-El, litterally "House of the god(s)" is either a place name ("Bethel") or much more likely a god, the deified "standing-stone" (Greek *baitylos*). ʿAnat-Baitʾel seems to be identical with ʿAnat-Jahô (*'ntyhw*) "ʿAnat Jahôs" attested in the same corpus of texts. ʿAnat is the goddess known from the Ugaritic myths as Baals consort. ʿAnat-Bayt-El is attested in cuneiform together with Bayt-El among the oath-deities in a contract concluded in 675/4 BC by Asarhaddon with Baal I of Tyre: ᵈBa-a-a-ti-DINGIR.MEŠ ᵈA-na-ti-ba-a-[a-ti-DING]IR.MEŠ. However, the form of both theonyms points to an Aramaic (and not Phoenician) origin. In the temple of Elephantine, Jahô, ʿAnat-Bayt-El and Ešem-Bayt-El represented perhaps a divine family consisting of father, mother and child[14]. The historical background of the evidence from Elephantine and its implications for the history of Yahwism are not yet fully understood. First, we do not know with certainty when the Jewish colony in Elephantine was founded, under Psammetichus I (664–610) or II (595–589)? Sec-

---

13 O. Keel, *Jerusalem und der eine Gott. Eine Religionsgeschichte* (Göttingen 2011), 51. The reference within the quotation is to: O. Keel, "Seth-Baal und Seth-Baal-Jahweh – interkulturelle Ligaturen," in *Jerusalem und die Länder. Ikonographie – Topographie – Theologie. Festschrift für Max Küchler zum 65. Geburtstag* (ed. I.J. Theißen *et al.*; NTOA 70; Göttingen 2009), 87–107.
14 W. Röllig, *"Bethel," DDD²* 173f.

ond, there are earlier indications that YHWH once was associated with another goddess: Hebrew inscriptions from *Kuntillet 'Ajrud* (around 800 BC) und *Khirbet el-Kom* (end of 8th century BC)[15] speak of "YHWH and his Asherah ('šrth)." This expression has been much discussed since the first publication of the inscriptions in 1978 and 1970, respectively. It is tempting to recognize here the name of El's consort attested in Ugarit as 'Aṭiratu, which seems to be by now the *communis opinio*. Previously, the term 'ašērā(h), which is attested more than 40 times in the OT and mostly occurs in connection with Baal, had been understood as a wooden cultic object. This is indeed the meaning required most often by the context. A new look at the material stimulated by the epigraphic finds makes it seem plausible that, at least for some passages, originally the name of the goddess was meant[16]. As far as the epigraphic evidence is concerned, the commonly accepted interpretation as YHWH's consort remains problematic in spite of several philological attempts to prove it. Admittedly, proper names specified by possessive pronouns or genitive attributes do occur in Ancient Near Eastern languages – e. g. "YHWH of Teman" and "YHWH of Samaria" in the aforementioned inscriptions or "my Damu" (with a hypocoristic-expressive undertone) in Sumerian cult songs – but neither divine nor human couples are introduced by constructions of the type "YHWH and his Asherah," which are possible, e. g., in colloquial German ("Fritz und seine Susi"). I would maintain therefore that 'šrt is here a common noun designating an emblem (like in the OT), which in turn could refer to the deity it represents.[17] This ambivalent semantics of emblems is well known from Mesopotamia.[18] One possible conclusion is that proposed by M. Weippert who suggests that we are dealing in Elephantine with "das Überbleibsel einer lokalen Variante (Bethel?) der israelitischen Religion [...], in der 'Ānāt-Yahō, die ,Anat Yahōs', die Gemahlin Yahōs gewesen ist – in Juda, genauer, in Jerusalem, war in vorexilischer Zeit bereits Aschera in diese Rolle eingerückt."

In accordance with the general structure of Ancient Near Eastern polytheism, we should expect that YHWH had initially not only a wife (and other family members) but also a "royal court" comprising servants and messengers who are

---

15 M. Weippert, *Historisches Textbuch zum Alten Testament* (GAT 10; Göttingen 2010), Nr. 216, 217 and 220, respectively.
16 J.M. Hadley, *The Cult of Asherah in Ancient Israel and Judah. Evidence for a Hebrew Goddess* (Cambridge 2000).
17 For this interpretation see J.M. Hadley, "Yahweh and "His Asherah" – Archaeological and Textual Evidence for the Cult of the Goddess," in *Ein Gott allein* (ed. W. Dietrich and M.A. Klopfenstein; OBO 139; 1994), 235.
18 See, e. g., B. Pongratz-Leisten, in *Reconsidering the Concept of Revolutionary Monotheism* (ed. Eadem; Winona Lake 2011), 141–142 and 148–151.

attested in Mesopotamia for all major deities and in Ugarit for Baal[19] and Asherah[20]. As a matter of fact, remnants of a "royal court" survive in the Old Testament in the guise of angels. Several "officials" are discernible, among them guardians like the snake-shaped Seraphim and the sphinx-shaped Cherubim, who surround YHWH 's throne, and "messengers" called *mal'ak* in Hebrew. The term was translated into Greek as ἄγγελος, which was rendered as *angelus* in Latin. The Latin word was in turn borrowed as a religious term into a variety of modern languages including English *angel*, French *ange* and German *Engel*. A peculiar role in YHWH 's court was played by Satan, who was later to become his antagonist. In the earliest attestations (Job 1:6; Zech 3:1) he appears as a kind of warden and prosecutor. In this function, he may be compared to subordinate Mesopotamian deities ensuring law and order as judges, bailiffs, prison guards or policemen. These deities show particular affinities to the sungod as the supreme judge, but also to the netherworld.[21]

5 YHWH's provenience: cult-geographical and linguistic aspects

Stable relations between cities and deities – some of them documented through thousands of years – are a characteristic feature of Ancient Near Eastern (and also Ancient Egyptian) religion. Cuneiform sources document, in particular for Mesopotamia and its periphery, many such pairings. This may be illustrated by the following alphabetical list of important cities (of different periods) and their deities: Adab – Ninmaḫ (mother goddess), Arbela (Erbil) – Ištar (Venus, sexuality and war); Assur – Assur (local mountain and city god, later state god of the Assyrian empire and identified with Enlil), Babylon – Marduk (city god of Babylon, magic and incantations, identified with Asalluḫi, a son of Enki/Ea), Borsippa – Nabium/Nabû (scribal art and wisdom, later regarded as a son of Marduk), Dilbat – Uraš (earth god identifed with Ninurta), Ebla –

---

19 Gapnu wa Ugāru.

20 *Qudšu wa 'Amrāru* (vocalization in some points uncertain).

21 Mesopotamian deities of this type are gathered in M. Krebernik, "Richtergott(heiten)," *RlA* 11/5–6, 354–361. For the prison goddess Nungal and her circle see A. Cavigneaux and M. Krebernik, "Nungal," *RlA* 9/7–8, 615–620. The closest similarities with Satan are shown perhaps by the sinister herald and psychopompos called Ḫendursaĝa in Sumerian and Išum in Akkadian, for whom see P. Attinger and M. Krebernik, "L'hymne à Ḫendursaĝa (Ḫendursaĝa A)," in *Von Sumer bis Homer. Festschrift für Manfred Schretter zum 60. Geburtstag am 25. Ferbruar 2004* (ed. R. Rollinger; AOAT 325; Münster 2004), 21–104, particularly 32f.

Kura (probably a netherworld god), Eridu – Enki/Ea (water, fertility and creativity, crafts), Ĝirsu – Ninĝirsu/Ninurta (agriculture, war-like defender of the civilized world); Ḫalab (Aleppo) – Haddu (storm-god), Ḫarran – Sîn (moon), Isin – Ninisina/Gula (healing), Keš – Dingirmaḫ/Ninmaḫ (mother-goddess), Lagaš – Gatumdug (city goddess), Larsa – Utu/Šamaš (sun), Niniveh – Ištar, Nippur – Enlil (creator, agriculture, kingship, head of Sumerian pantheon), Sippar – Utu/Šamaš (sun), Šuruppak (Fāra) – Sud (city goddess, identidied with Ninlil), Terqa – Dagan (earth and agriculture, identified with Enlil), Tuttul – Dagan, Umma – Šara (warlike sun of Inanna), Ugarit – El, Ur – Nanna/Sîn (moon), Zabalam – Inanna/Ištar. A few cities had two principal deities: thus in Uruk, the largest city of the Ancient Near East, the main deities were Inanna/Ištar and An (heaven), whereas Inanna/Ištar and Zababa (a local warrior-god identified with Ninurta) were the main deities of Kiš. The reason for this is in both cases that two formerly distinct settlements had grown together. Cases like Mari where the hierarchy of the local pantheon is less clear are rare. Stable links existed not only between single cities and deities, but also between (city) states and deities. Discontinuities in this respect are exceptional and need individual explanations, which are not always easy to find. Thus, e. g., Nabium/Nabû, a god of unknown (most probably Amorite) origin, superimposed (but did not completely replace) Tutu as city god of Borsippa. The main deity of a city resides – in the form his/her cult image – together with his/her family and court in the (main) temple. He/she stands in the focus of the local cult, but at the same time, he/she is part of a wider, cosmologically, genealogically and hierarchically structured pantheon. As illustrated by the above list, some deities (especially those representing elementary natural entities and powers) have more than one cult center (important exceptions are Enlil und Assur). In larger political units, the main deity of the capital played an important role, which could collide with that of other deities. In conflict situations like this, we can observe polytheistic theology operating. Its elementary strategies are identification (mostly not in an absolute sense), integration (of deities and features) and myth. Perhaps the most obvious examples are the rise of the local Babylonian god Marduk to the supreme position in the Babylonian pantheon (formerly held by Enlil) during the 2nd millennium BC and a similar rise of the city and state god Assur, who was not a member of the traditional Babylonian pantheon.[22] The major deities are present in many places, often beside the local

---

22 The theology of Marduk's rise to universal power is elaborated in form of a mythological narrative in the so-called Babylonian "Epic of Creation" *Enūma eliš*. See most recently R. Kämmerer and K. Metzler (ed.), *Das babylonische Weltschöpfungsepos Enūma eliš* (AOAT 375; Münster 2012); W.G. Lambert, *Babylonian Creation Myths* (Mesopotamian Civilizations 16; Winona Lake 2013), 1–

main deity. Their local manifestations are usually denoted in the form divine name + place name in the genitive, e. g., "Dagan of Terqa" or, "Ištar of Niniveh." Alternatively, they can be designated by relational adjectives derived from place names; this applies mostly to female deities of the Inanna/Ištar type, e. g. *Urkītu* "the one (female) of Uruk" = Inanna/Ištar of Uruk.

If we turn now, with this background in mind, to the question of YHWH's provenience, the first interesting observation is that he was obviously not the ancient city god of Jerusalem.

Furthermore, a circumstance very familiar to us, namely that the two neighboring kingdoms of Judah and Israel had the same state god YHWH, seems somewhat anomalous against this background since state deities – be it Milkom, Kemosh and Qaus in the surrounding small states of Ammon, Moab and Edom or be it Marduk in Babylonia and Assur in Assyria – were the patrons of rulers and guarantors of national identity. The duplication resulted, according to the Biblical narratives, from the split of the dynasty, and one would expect that the two new dynasties tried to differentiate also their state deities. Biblical reproaches mainly against the northern kingdom of Israel because of its closeness to the "pagan" Baal cult might indeed be taken as indications for that. On the other hand, one could speculate how far this duplication may have contributed to the universalization of YHWH. The later centralization of his cult in Jerusalem could have been influenced by the cult of the Assyrian state god Assur, which was also restricted to the capital (Assur).

According to Biblical tradition, David introduced YHWH in Jerusalem after he had conquered the city, whereas the building of his temple is ascribed to his son Solomon. The place name "Jerusalem" occurs already in cuneiform sources from the 14th century BC as Uru-Salim (*Ú-ru-sa-lim*).[23] It seems to indicate that the former city god was Šalim, known from the Ugarit texts as god of the dusk sired by El along with his brother Šaḫar "Dawn." The etymological interpretation of the toponym as "foundation of Šalim" is, however, not absolutely sure, since the in-

---

144; and G. Gabriel, enūma eliš – Weg zu einer globalen Weltordnung (ORA 12; Tübingen 2014). – For the rise of Assur and its theology, see, e. g., V. Chamaza, *Die Omnipotenz Aššurs. Entwicklungen in der Aššur-Theologie unter den Sargoniden Sargon II., Sanherib und Asarhaddon* (AOAT 295; Münster 2002); B. Pongratz-Leisten, "Divine Agency and Astralization of the Gods," in *Reconsidering the Concept of Revolutionary Monotheism* (ed. Eadem; Winona Lake 2011), 137–187, especially 162–181.

23 See A. Rainey, *The El-Amarna Correspondence* (HdO 110/1; Leiden 2015), 1109–1125, EA 287: 25, 46, 61, 63; EA 289: 14, 29; EA 290: 15. KUR URU *Ú-ru-sa-lim* (EA 287: 25, 46). KUR *Ú-ru-sa-lim* (EA 287: 61). KUR.ḪI.A URU *Ú-ru-sa-lim* (EA 287: 63). URU *Ú-ru-sa-lim*ki (EA 289: 14, 29). URU KUR *Ú-ru-sa-lim* (EA 290:15)

ital element is unique and contrasts with similar placenames formed with *bayt/ bēt* "house" (also in the sense of "temple"). To this type belongs, e. g., *Bēt-Šæmæš* in the vicinity of Jerusalem, which was obviously named after the sun-god(dess?) *Šamš*. Possible indications of a former cult of the Sun in this region might also be contained in the names of two legendary kings of Jerusalem mentioned in the Bible, *'Adônî-Șædæq* and *Malkî-Șædæq* (Melchizedek) "my lord/ king is *Șædæq*." They seem to refer to a god *Șidq(u)* "Justice,"[24] whom we can compare with Mesopotamian deities bearing semantically related names and belonging to the circle of the sun-god Utu/Šamaš, the divine judge:[25] *Kīttum* "Righteousness" and *Mišārum* "Justice" as well as their Sumerian equivalents *Nig̃-gina* und *Nig̃-sisa*. Biblical and extra-biblical sources associate the early cult of YHWH with several other places than Jerusalem. The most important Biblical evidence points to Bethel ("House/Temple of El"), where according to Judges 1:27 the Ark of the Covenant stood at that time. Around 840 BC, king Mesha of Moab (his name is better to be reconstructed as *Mōšiʿ*) reports on his famous stele that he carried off cult objects of YHWH from Nebo after he had captured the town.[26] The inscriptions from *Kuntillet ʿAjrud* (around 800 BC) mention a "YHWH of Samaria" and a "YHWH of Teman"[27]. The latter toponym (litterally "South") is in the OT attestations a part or an equivalent of Edom. However, by analogy with "YHWH of Samaria" and many other expressions of this kind, one would rather expect that it refers to a concrete cult place. This geographical designation can be connected with hieroglyphic-luwian *ta-i-ma-ni-ti-ha*(URBS) in an inscription of king Yariris of Carchemish (8th century BC)[28] where it designates the last of the four different scripts Yariris claims to master. The common assumption that the Aramaic alphabet is meant[29] seems unlikely to me. As suggested by J.C. Greenfield,[30] it rather refers to the South Arabian script which was used in several local variants in the oasis of North Arabia. In this case, one could

---

24 See B.F. Batto, "Zedeq," *DDD*[2] 929 – 934.

25 Cf. M. Krebernik, "Sonnengott. A. I. In Mesopotamien. Philologisch," *RlA* 12/7 – 8, 599 – 611, especially § 3.1.

26 See M. Weippert, *Textbuch* (see n. 15), Nr. 105: 18.

27 See M. Weippert, *Textbuch* (see n. 15), Nr. 216 and 217.

28 J.D. Hawkins, *Corpus of Hieroglyphic Luwian Inscriptions, Vol. I: Inscriptions of the Iron Age* (Berlin and New York 2000), Nr. 24, § 20.

29 F. Starke, "Sprachen und Schriften in Karkamiš," in *Ana šadî Labnāni lū allik. Beiträge zu altorientalischen und mittelmeerischen Kulturen. Festschrift für Wolfgang Röllig* (ed. B. Pongratz-Leisten et al.; AOAT 247; Neukirchen-Vluyn 1997), 381 – 395, here 382f. und 388.

30 J.C. Greenfield, "Of Scribes, Scripts and Languages," in *Phoinikeia Grammata. Lire et écrire en Méditerranée* (ed. C. Baurain et al.; Namur 1991), 173 – 185, here 179.

think of Taimā' as a possible candidate for the Teman of the *Kuntillet 'Ajrud* inscriptions, but the two placenames cannot easily be identified with each other.[31]

Evidently, the worship of YHWH was not linked to one central cult place or city when it was established in Juda and Israel. If one tries to trace it further back, one has to dissect possible historical reminiscences in Biblical texts[32] and to look for external written evidence. The earliest possible Egyptian evidence consists in the name of a settlement similar to or identical with "YHWH" and associated with the Asiatic Shasu-nomades.[33]

In cuneiform texts, YHWH is well attested as an element of Jewish personal names.[34] The identification of possible earlier attestations is hampered by several problems: (1) the theonym is relatively short; (2) it had at least two variants, roughly Yahwe and Yahu/o; (3) it consists of "weak" consonants only which could not be expressed unambiguously in cuneiform[35]; and (4) there was a wide-spread ending -*aya/u* or the like for abbreviated, hypocoristic names which at least in writing is hard to distinguish from the theonym. Partially due to these difficulties, the cuneiform evidence for the beginnings of Yahwism is almost entirely negative.

---

31 The name of the oasis ended originally in -*ā(')* whereas forms with final -*n(y)* represent adjectives derived from it. The earliest cuneiform attestation is an Akkadian adjective based on a form without -*n*: An inscription by Ninurta-kudurrī-uṣur of Sūḫi (mid-8th century BC) mentions Temanites along with Sabaens (LÚ *te-ma-'-a-a* LÚ *šá-ba-'-a-a*), see G. Frame, *Rulers of Babylonia* (RIMB 2; Toronto 1995), 300, S.0.1002.2: 27'.

32 According to O. Keel, *Jerusalem* (see n. 13), 47 f., they seem to reflect two different ways of reception: "Der YHWH-Kult dürfte schon zur Zeit Davids in Palästina in zwei verschiedenen Formen existiert haben, die auf verschiedenen Wegen dahin gekommen waren. Eine Form dürfte etwas früher von Süden her mit den Kenitern über die Senke zwischen dem Roten und dem Toten Meer in den Negev und nach Juda Eingang gefunden haben (vgl. Gen 4,26; Ri 1:16). Eine etwas jüngere Form gelangte aus der gleichen Gegend mit den Midianitern über Transjordanien von Osten her nach Mittelpalästina."

33 First attested in inscriptions of Amenophis III. See M. Görg, "Jahwe – ein Toponym?," *BN* 1 (1976), 7 – 14; re-published with additions in *Beiträge zur Zeitgeschichte der Anfänge Israels* (ÄAT 2; Wiesbaden 1989), 180 – 187; A. Knauf, Midian. *Untersuchungen zur Geschichte Palästinas und Nordarabiens am Ende des 2. Jahrtausends v. Chr.* (Wiesbaden 1988), 46 – 48; M. Weippert, Textbuch (see n. 15), Nr. 75.

34 Attestations and spellings are treated in detail by M. Weippert, "Jahwe," *RlA* 5/3 – 4, 246 – 253. For additional material see most recently L.E. Pearce and C. Wunsch, *Documents of Judean Exiles and West Semites in Babylonia in the Collection of David Sofer* (CUSAS 28; Bethesda 2014), 308 – 311.

35 There was no special sign for *h* at all, and the expression of *y* and *w* varied. Initial y- became non-phonemic and was lost in Akkadian since ca. 2200 BC.

When in 1974/5 large cuneiform archives from the 24th century BC came to light in the royal palace G of Syrian Ebla, they raised much hope to throw new light on the prehistory of the Holy Land, and wishful thinking lead to some premature conclusions. As we know today, the geographical horizon of the Ebla archives is mainly orientated in the direction of Mesopotamia and does not reach beyond Hama in the South. Alleged attestations for Jerusalem and other Biblical sites turned out to be wrong, and this applies also to "YHWH" as an element of personal names.[36]

Similar conclusions were reached with regard to Amorite personal names (end of 3rd to first half of 2nd millennium BC) allegedly containing "YHWH" as an initial element: instead, an interpretation as a verbal form *yaḥwī from the root ḥ-w-y "to live" is much more likely as M.P. Streck has demonstrated.[37]

S. Dalley has, however, recently drawn attention to three personal names from Babylonia dating around 1500 BC in which she recognizes the element "YHWH" in spite of the difficulties detailed above: ÌR-ia-ú "Servant of Yau" (Arad-Yau) , Ì-lí-ia-ú "Yau is my god" (Yau-ilī), and Ia-ú-ba-ni "Yau creates" (Yau-bāni) or "Yau is beautiful" (Yau-bani).[38] S. Dalley refutes other possibilities, namely a hypocoristic ending and Akkadian iā'u "mine, My One."[39] If she is correct, this would be the earliest attestations of YHWH whom she identifies with "Yau." She concludes that it is "apparent that men who acknowledged the cult of Yau lived in lower Mesopotamia during the sixteenth/early fifteenth centures BC and suggests "a link between the Sealand dynasty and people of the

---

36 See already H.-P. Müller, "Gab es in Ebla einen Gottesnamen Ja?," *ZA* 70 (1981), 70 – 92. Müller eliminated all but 4 names in which the cuneiform sign NI(-a) according to a suggestion by G. Pettinato was read ià(-a) and interpreted as a short form of YHWH. Systematic studies of the Eblaite syllabary have indeed shown that the syllabic value ià does not exist in Ebla, and that the names are to be interpreted differently. In most of them, NI = ì represents 'il(u) "god" (or probably also "El"), either as an abbreviation or implying a sound change typical of Ebla, the so-called "l-reduction." For the 4 names retained by Müller as possible, but uncertain instances of YHWH-names, *Su-mi-a-ù* (= *Su-mi-a*), NI-*a*-BE, NI-*a*-du-ud and En-nu-NI-*a*, other explanations are possible and preferable.

37 M.P. Streck, "Der Gottesname "Jahwe" und das amurritische Onomastikon," *WO* 30 (1999), 35 – 46.

38 S. Dalley, "Gods from north-eastern and northwestern Arabia in cuneiform texts from the First Sealand Dynasty, and a cuneiform inscription from Tell en-Naṣbeh, c. 1500 BC," *Arabian Archaeology and Epigraphy* 25 (2013), 177 – 185. The names occur partly on cuneiform tablets from illicit diggings (ÌR-ia-ú, Ì-lí-ia-ú) and partly on tablets excavated in Nippur (ÌR-ia-ú, Ia-ú-ba-ni). The former date in the reign of Ayadaragalama, a king of the First Sealand dynasty who ruled between ca. 1560 and 1480, the Nippur were written ca. 100 years later.

39 As suggested earlier by M. Hölscher, *Die Personennamen der kassitischen Texte aus Nippur* (Münster 1996).

land later known as Midian, corresponding to southern Jordan and north-west Saudi Arabia" from where the cult would have been introduced to Babylonia. The names are, apart from the element "Yau," Akkadian; for one of the name bearers, even an Akkadian patronym is attested. S. Dalley explains this by the assumption that the "Yau"-worshippers "were thouroughly assimilated to Sealand society." In spite of S. Dalley's detailed argumentation, her interpretation of the three names seems doubtful for the following reasons: (1) The cuneiform "determinative" (classifier) for deities, which in principle should precede the divine name "Yau," is lacking in all attestations; this is, however, only a weak argument, since the classifier is often omitted with less common or foreign deities. (2) I would not categorically deny the possibility of an (admittedly unusual) hypocoristic ending in the first two names: *Ardiyā'u* or *Ardiyû*, *Iliyā'u* or *Iliyû* (as mentioned by S. Dalley, the syllabogram *ia* can also be read *iù*). If so, we are dealing with abbreviations for names of the very common types Arad-... "Servant of (a deity or cult object/place)" and Ilī-... "My god is ..." Alternatively, at least in the second name, *yā'u* "mine" is possible, since the same combination occurs also in reverse order, see below. (3) The third name certainly represents the common name type DN (= divine name) + *bāni* "... is/was the creator (of the child)" or DN + *bani* "... is beautiful," and Akkadian personal names containing the names of foreign deities are well attested, as pointed out by S. Dalley. But these deities are usually at home in neighboring areas (Elam, Dilmun) were Babylonian culture had spread. The name in question would be, however, the first and hitherto unique evidence for the presence in Southern Babylonia of fully assimilated immigrants from northwest Saudi Arabia, something which seems *per se* not very likely in this period. If the names indeed witness to the worship of an early form of YHWH in Southern Babylonia already around 1500 BC, this would raise the question if his origins have to be sought in this direction rather than in the South. Rather, M. Hölscher's[40] interpretation of the element *ia-ú* (or *iù-ú*) in the third name as "the mine one" should be maintained in spite of S. Dalley's counter-argument that "it has no parallels in names of similar formation." An element commonly interpreted as *yā'um >yû* "mine" does occur, albeit rarely, in personal names. Thus, *Li-pu-uš-i-a-um* is the name of a female musician from the time of Narām-Suen; it was interpreted by I.J. Gelb as "may mine (i.e. my child) breathe."[41] In Old Babylonian texts, the names Iā(w)um-il(um)

---

40 See n. 39.

41 For the inscription mentioning her see D.R. Frayne, *Sargonic and Gutian Periods The Royal Inscriptions of Mesopotamia* (Early Periods Volume 2; Toronto 1993), 159f., E2.1.54. For the interpretation see I.J. Gelb, *Glossary of Old Akkadian* (Materials for the Akkadian Dictionary No. 3; Chicago 1957), 1 s.v. 'ⱼiaum "mine" (in the reference, DC II, "Pl. LII" is an error for Pl. LVII).

"Mine is the god" and Iā'u-kûm "Thine is Mine" are found.[42] In the case of *Ia-ú-ba-ni*, an element *yā'u* or *yû* "mine" would make sense, referring either to the personal deity of the name giver (he is the "creator" of the child) or to the child (it is "beautiful").

The oldest cuneiform finds in Canaan[43] date in the Middle Bronze Age, i.e. slightly earlier than the Babylonian personal names discussed above. Most of the MBA finds come from Hazor, others from Bet Šean, Shechem, Hebron, Bet Mirsim und Jemmeh. For Late Bronze Age Canaan, we have not only local text finds, but also part of the cuneiform correspondence of Canaanite rulers with their Egyptian overlord found in 1887 (and followings years) by villagers in Tell el-Amarna, the royal residence of Amenophis IV.[44] The Canaanite cities, where cuneiform tablets have been found, and those represented by letters from or to their rulers in the Amarna archive, constitute a relatively dense network between Ugarit in the North and Jurṣa in the South[45], including Jerusalem: the Amarna corpus contains 6 letters from the local ruler to the pharaoh. A small fragment from the same period has recently been found in Jerusalem itself[46]. Cuneiform texts (most of them in Akkadian) and texts in Ugaritic script and language offer much information on the Syro-Palestine city-states of the 14th/13th century BC. They also preserve many theonyms, occurring independently or as elements of personal and place names. Thus, the name of the ruler of Jerusalem was ʿAbdi-Ḫepa "Servant of Ḫepa." The goddess Ḫeb/pa(t) was originally the spouse of the storm-god of Ḫalab (Aleppo). Her cult was widespread in Northern Syria and Anatolia, where she constituted a triad together with the Hurrian storm-god Teššub and their son Šarruma. Her name survived as Ἵππα in Greek

---

Note that the two other attestations quoted there are, *I-a-um* MAR.TU and *Ià-a-um* MAR.TU "I., the Amorite" are wrongly analysed as personal names composed of *Ia/Ià-a-um* + divine name in AHw. I, 413 s.v. *jā'u(m)*.

42 T. Pinches, Berens 101:1f.: *Ia-wu-um*-DINGIR; Ungnad BB (VAB 6), 217 = Frankena, aBB 2, 94: 3: *Ia-ú-um*-DINGIR.

43 See W. Horowitz, *Cuneiform in Canaan. Cuneiform Sources from the Land of Israel in Ancient Times* (Jerusalem 2006).

44 Most recent editions: W.L. Moran, *The Amarna Letters. Edited and Translated* (Baltimore and London 1992); A.F. Rainey Z"L, *The El-Amarna Correspondence. A New Edition of the Cuneiform Letters from the Site of El-Amarna based on Collations of the Extant Texts* (ed. W. Schniedewind and Z. Cochavi-Rainey; HdO 110; Leiden and Boston 2015).

45 For an overview, see, e.g., D.O. Edzard, "Amarna und die Archive seiner Korrespondenten zwischen Ugarit und Gaza," in *Biblical Archaeology Today. Proceedings of the International Congress on Biblical Archaeology* (ed. J. Amitai; Jerusalem 1984/1985), 248–259.

46 E. Mazar, "A Cuneiform Tablet from the Ophel in Jerusalem," *IEJ* 60 (2010), 4–21.

sources.[47] Other deities attested by place-names in the later core territory of Yahwism include the sun-god(dess) Šamš(u) (see above), El (Beth-El "House/Temple of El") and ʿAnat (Beth-ʿAnath, Beth-ʿAnoth, ʿAnathoth). A cuneiform letter from El-Amarna mentions along with Jerusalem a place written É-ᵈNIN.URTA "House/Temple of NINURTA";[48] the Sumerian theonym ᵈNIN.URTA is used here as a logogram for the local name of a god unknown to us.

For the period and area in question, sources in cuneiform and Ugaritic script have yielded so far no clear evidence of Yhwh[49]. In view of the wide range of possible sources (even if they are not as dense as one could wish for), this *nil return* is of significance for the historical reconstruction. Since the north is generally better "illuminated" by the written sources than the south[50], the search for Yhwh's origins has to focus on the southern limits of cuneiform documentation and beyond it. However, even if the texts do not offer direct evidence, they may contain valuable background information. Thus, they indicate that the linguistic situation did not change drastically between the age of the Amarna texts and the beginning of the 1st millennium BC. This speaks against a military conquest of Canaan by non-Canaanite (i.e. Israelite) tribes as reported in the Old Testament. On the other hand, the name of "Yhwh" shows non-Hebrew traits[51] pointing to a

---

47 M.-C. Trémouille, ᵈ*Ḫébat. Une divinité syro-anatolienne* (Eothen 7; Firenze 1997); F. Graf, "Hipta," *DNP 5* (1998), 611. The hypothesis advanced by E. Forrer and B. Hrozny, that Hebrew *Ḥawwāh* (Eve) goes back to the theonym, is highly problematic for phonetical and geographical reasons, see J. Danmanville, "Ḫepat," *RlA* 4 (1972), 326–329, in particular 329; cf. also O. Keel, *Jerusalem* (see n. 13), 43. The name of ʿAbdi-Ḫepa alone is not sufficient to prove the existence of a cult of the goddess Ḫepa(t) in Jerusalem, we do not even know if the ruler had local roots.
48 EA 290:16, see A. Rainey, *El-Amarna* (see n. 23), 1124.
49 A very similar theonym is *Yw* (to be vocalized most probably *Yawwu*), the former name of the sea-god Yammu according to the Ugaritic Baal cycle (CAT 1.1 iv 14). *Yw* has been connected with Yhwh and with "Ieuo" mentioned by Philo of Byblos, s. M.S. Smith, *Baal Cycle I* (see n. 2), 151 f. Phonetically, relationship with Yhwh is not completely excluded, since Ugaritic *h* is assimilated elsewhere to a following voiced consonant, see J. Tropper, *Ugaritische Grammatik* (AOAT 273; Münster ²2012), 160. From a mythological and historical point of view, however, connecting this isolated passage with Yhwh seems problematic as long as no missing link is detected. Later cuneiform evidence, referring to persons from Israel and Juda whose names contain " Yhwh ," is not relevant for our purpose. This applies also to the interesting case of a ruler of Hamath whose name is attested in two variants, *Ya(h)ū-bi'dī* and *'Ilu-bi'dī* " Yhwh/El is my support," see S. Dalley, "Yahweh in Hamath in the 8th Century BC," *VT* 40 (1990) 21–32, and A. Fuchs and S. Parpola, "Iaū-bi'di," in *Prosopography of the nea-Assyrian Empire, Vol. 2, Part I* (ed. S. Parpola and H. Baker; Helsinki 2000), 497.
50 In the northern periphery, larger Middle and Late Bronze Age text corpora were found at Ugarit, Qatna, Alalaḫ (Syria/Levant) and Emar, Ekalte, Tuttul, Terqa, Mari (Euphrates valley).
51 For the linguistic aspects see M. Weippert, "Jahwe" (see n. 34), 246–253; E.A. Knauf, "Yahweh," *VT* 34 (1984), 467–472; K. van der Toorn, "Yahweh," *DDD²* 910–919. The etymologizing

foreign origin. The two diverging aspects of the problem can be reconciled if we connect them with another piece of evidence contained in cuneiform texts from Amarna (and elsewhere): they witness to the existence of non-sedentary and multi-ethnic groups called Ḫab/piru in cuneiform texts, who made life hard for the sedentary population and their kinglets (among them ʿAbdi-Ḫepa of Jerusalem) who often hired them as mercenaries. The early "wild years" of king David as described in the Old Testament are strongly reminiscent of their way of life. Their name possibly survives as ʿIbrî "Hebrew,"[52] and it seems not unlikely that the first worshippers of YHWH who spread his cult in Canaan were among the Ḫab/piru people.

---

explanation of the name in Exod 3:14 based on the verb for "to be," implicitly presupposes a root-variant h-w-y (in contrast to genuine Hebrew h-y-y) as attested, e. g., in Aramaic. Presently, the most accepted hypothesis, matching with YHWH's character as an original strom-god, is the derivation of his name from a homophonous root h-w-y "to blow" attested in Arabic.

52 The cuneiform spelling Ḫab/piru reflects ʿab/pir-, evidence for the second consonant as *p* comes from the Egyptian rendering of the term, which is, however, not compelling. The most recent monograph is O. Loretz, *Habiru-Hebräer. Eine sozio-linguistische Studie über die Herkunft des Gentiliziums ʿibrî vom Appellativum ḫabiru* (BZAW 160; Berlin 1984). Important additional evidence is a long list of Ḫab/piru individuals published in M. Salvini, *The Ḫabiru Prism of King Tunip-Teššup of Tikunani* (Documenta Asiana 3; Roma 1996); their names indicate that they were not a homogeneous ethnic group. See also W. Zwickel, "Der Beitrag der Ḫabiru zur Entstehung des Königtums," *UF* 28 (1996), 751–766; V. Haas and I. Wegner, "Betrachtungen zu den Ḫabiru," in *Munuscula Mesopotamica. Festschrift für Johannes Renger* (ed. B. Böck et al.; AOAT 267; München 1999), 197–200; N. Naʾaman, "Ḫabiru-like Bands in the Assyrian Empire and Bands in Biblical Historiography," *JAOS* 120 (2000), 621–624; A. Bemporad, "I Habiru nella documentazione ittita," *SMEA* 51 (2009), 71–93; M. Guichard, "Un David raté ou une histoire de habiru à l'époque amorrite. Vie et mort de Samsi-Eraḫ, chef de guerre et homme du peuple," in *Le jeune héros* (ed. J.-M. Durand et al.; OBO 250; Fribourg 2011), 29–93.

Angelika Berlejung

The Origins and Beginnings of the Worship of Yhwh: The Iconographic Evidence

1 Introduction

The attempt to reach back to the origins and beginnings of the worship of Yhwh iconographically is destined to fail if one approaches the problem by seeking visual material from Israel/Palestine that clearly depicts Yhwh (or depicts him for the first time). During the entire span of time from the beginnings of the worship of Yhwh through the Hellenistic period, there are no depictions of deities that can interpreted beyond doubt as pictorial representations of Yhwh.

While there is certainly a large number of representations of autochthonous male and female deities from Israel/Palestine from the second and first millennia B.C.E., so far no attempt to identify a *specific* iconography of Yhwh has succeeded, and thus none of these images has been securely assigned to Yhwh. This state of affairs can either be evaluated as merely a problem for the modern observer, who is not in a position to recognize an image of Yhwh even if it lays before her, or it can be interpreted as indicating that there were no images of Yhwh. Before assuming too hastily that the aniconicity of Yhwh and the prohibition of images as propagated in the Hebrew Bible were observed from the beginning, it should be kept in mind that there is a large number of deities known by name from Israel/Palestine whose specific iconography is unknown or of whom no clear representations are known, yet which are not immediately connected to aniconism. Conversely, numerous representations are attested that cannot be associated securely with the names of deities from antiquity. Thus, the problem that arises from the lack of clear images of Yhwh or the lack of a specific iconography of Yhwh is not unique but rather is part of the larger problem of correlating ancient textual and visual sources: the names of deities attested in textual sources and the deities represented in ancient Near Eastern visual sources cannot always be identified with each other clearly. The present situation in which no clear image of Yhwh or iconographic characteristics of Yhwh can currently be identified does not mean that such images did not exist.

The iconographic evidence relating to deities from Israel/Palestine can be easily profiled. Accordingly, male deities in anthropomorphic form are represented primarily in two different poses assigned to two different types – the Baal/Hadad type and the El type – without the specific deities Baal/Hadad and El necessarily being intended. The two poses represent a typology whose simplicity in-

DOI 10.1515/9783110448221-004

dicates that the world of Palestinian deities and its iconography is not as differentiated as in Egypt or Mesopotamia. Thus, if there were anthropomorphic images of YHWH, they would have to be subsumed under representations of the Baal/Hadad- or El type. Theriomorphic representations of deities are also possible and are well attested in the archaeological record of Palestine. In light of Exod 32; 1 Kgs 12:26 ff. and Hos 8:5 f.; 13:2, the bull has been discussed in particular as a possible figural manifestation of YHWH. In recent years, some scholars have considered whether certain symbols can be connected to YHWH or whether YHWH is represented by *maṣṣebot*, more or less creatively modified standing stones.

The association of YHWH with the archaeologically attested representations of deities in the style of (1) the anthropomorphic Baal/Hadad- or El type, (2) bovine types, (3) symbols, or (4) standing stones was and is undertaken in very different ways among scholars. The guiding principle for attempts to correlate YHWH with individual depictions of deities is that YHWH's particular theological profile would also be translated iconographically. Thus, the preliminary decisions regarding which theological profile one assigns to YHWH's earliest nature, as well as how one (re-)constructs these origins along with later developments, are decisive. In this respect, the various proposals for whether YHWH could have been represented *materially* reflect religio-historical but also exegetical hypotheses (for example, the delineation of the most basic material within – and the dating of – Judg 5; 1 Kgs 12; Exod 32; and Hos 8; 13).

The iconographic evidence from the Iron Age in Israel/Palestine can itself be divided into different types of divine representations (see above), be sketched within certain diachronic developments, and seldom be correlated to deities known by name. Regarding the origins of the worship of YHWH, it may be asked how YHWH, who reached the land from the south[1] during the Iron I

---

1 Since the worship of YHWH is not attested in Syro-Palestinian sources outside of Israel/Judah, it is normally concluded that YHWH did not belong to the traditional pantheon of deities in the region. Extrabiblical attestations from Egypt dating to the 14th/13th c. B.C.E. mention a "Yahu [used as a place name] in the land of the Shasu-Nomads" and point to the northwest of the Arabian Peninsula. Since otherwise there are no extrabiblical sources for the history of YHWH prior to his encounter with "Israel," on the basis of the biblical theophany texts and the epithet "the one of Sinai" YHWH place of origin is usually located in the desert to the south of Palestine (an exception is H. Pfeiffer, who advocates an origin in the north). YHWH is usually also connected with Sinai—the mountain of God—the location of which, however, is debated (i. e., whether it is located in the Sinai Peninsula or the Arabian Peninsula); see O. Keel, *Die Geschichte Jerusalems und die Entstehung des Monotheismus* (OLB IV.1; Göttingen 2007), § 236 f. (with a detailed refutation of Pfeiffer's thesis). For a different perspective see R. Müller, *Jahwe als Wettergott: Studien zur althebräischen Kultlyrik anhand ausgewählter Psalmen* (BZAW 387; Berlin 2008), 243 f., who

(1200/1150 – 1000 B.C.E.), relates to the autochthonous predecessor deities and contemporaries and whether the iconography of the Iron Age[2] in Cisjordan/central Palestine (the territories of the later states of Israel and Judah) reflects innovations that may be traced back to Yнwн's arrival on the scene. A number of proposals have been made in prior scholarship in this area, and individual representations have been interpreted as images of Yнwн, although none of these has led to a real consensus.

Yet many questions remain open even after the point at which Yнwн became the god of the tribes of the south and north of central Palestine. The history of Yнwн during the Iron IIA (during the 10th c. B.C.E.) in "Israel" and Judah, which are currently described by historians in terms of a disparate and only loosely centralized tribal society, turns out to be completely different from the biblical representation, which speaks of an imageless Yнwн as the exclusive focus of the official temple cult of an organized Davidic-Solomonic state with its capital in Jerusalem. According to the biblical depiction, Yнwн was invisibly enthroned as the highest god in the Jerusalem temple on the empty cherubim throne under which the ark stood (1 Kgs 8:6) since the time of Solomon. This picture of things is not shared by current scholarship, which concludes instead that a deity by the name of Yнwн (together with the other local deities) was worshiped as a tribal deity or as the deity of a confederation of tribes at a variety of local tribal sanctuaries and later became associated with major ruling families and their urban residences and was integrated into preexisting forms of worship. During the Iron IIB (926/900 – 722/700 B.C.E.), with the development of state structures, the transition from formerly local deities of individual clans or tribes into dynastic, temple-based deities of territorial states was complete, so that parallel to Milcom of Ammon, Kemosh of Moab, and Qos/Qaus of Edom, so too did Yнwн of Israel/Samaria and Yнwн of Judah/Jerusalem become the highest god in the pantheon of each territorial state.

It can no longer be determined which deities were worshiped in the individual urban centers, villages, and thus local sanctuaries of Palestine before Yнwн; whether Yнwн was placed at the top of the respective preexisting pantheons from the beginning or originally held a lower place; and where or how (including

---

suggests that Yнwн did not come from outside of Palestine and is an "autochthonous manifestation of a type of deity that resided in the Levant from time immemorial."

2 Epigraphically, the tetragrammaton Yнwн (with unknown vocalization) is attested beginning with the inscription of the Moabite king Mesha (9th c.) and from Kuntillet 'Ajrud (8th c.) and is also well attested during the centuries that followed, such as at Khirbet el-Kom (8th c.), on ostraca from Arad and Lachish (8th–6th c.), in inscriptions from Khirbet Beit Lei (7th c.), and on the amulets from Ketef Hinnom (5th/4th c.).

in which visual form) he was integrated into the local forms of worship. It seems that YHWH, who was originally a bachelor, only took on a divine partner (Asherah) during the course of his rise to becoming the highest god; whether or not this partnership resulted in offspring is unclear. With the establishment of the northern kingdom of Israel and the southern kingdom of Judah, YHWH, as the national and dynastic god (beginning in the 9th c.), was in any event the highest god (but not the only one!) of both states and their royal dynasties. According to extra-biblical and biblical sources, the cultic reality was polytheistic (Baal, Asherah, Bes, and Horus[3]) and poly-Yahwistic and included a wide variety of local manifestations, of which only a few are known: YHWH of Samaria with his Asherah (Kuntillet 'Ajrud, 8th c.), YHWH of Teman with his Asherah (Kuntillet 'Ajrud, 8th c.), YHWH the god of Jerusalem with his claim to the hill country of Judah and the entire land (Khirbet Beit Layy, 7th c.[4]), YHWH of Zion (Ps 99:2) and of Hebron (2 Sam 15:7), thus various regional forms of YHWH whose iconographies sometimes differed (see below).

2 General remarks on the iconography of deities

In ancient Near Eastern and thus also in Palestinian iconography, deities represented anthropomorphically are recognizable—and distinguishable from representations of kings or princes—by their wearing a horned headdress. Deities of the El type are usually depicted seated with a long robe (static), while deities of the Baal/Hadad type[5] are depicted standing upright with a short skirt in a striding posture and a raised arm with a weapon in hand (dynamic). Identifying the image of a deity by name (if lacking a caption) is often not possible, since the deities could only be distinguished (1) by clear emblems, insignia, weapons, plants, animals, or symbols in their hand or on the pedestal or throne of the image, or (2) by the archaeological context, and often both are lacking, particularly for figurines and plaques. Sometimes representations on seals can be helpful here, since they depict the deities with their equipment in particular contexts and constellations. Goddesses are also difficult to identify by name and are divided into broad types, being differentiated according to whether they are seated or standing, dressed or nude. Deities can also be represented by their symbolic

---

3 Baal and both Egyptian gods are attested in the Samaria Ostraca.
4 J. Renz and W. Röllig, *Handbuch der althebräischen Epigraphik I: Die althebräischen Inschriften, Teil 1. Text und Kommentar* (Darmstadt 1995), BLay(7):1.
5 On the typology of the "El type" and "Baal type" and the problems involved cf. C. Uehlinger, "Götterbild," *NBL 1.* 871–892, here 879f.

animal with which they share a particular characteristic, which led to a certain affinity of the strong and aggressive Baal/Hadad with the bull, although El and the moon-god can also be associated with the bull. Symbols that represent a particular deity are very well documented. Thus, sun disks, Venus stars, Pleiades, or crescents are attested for solar, astral, or lunar deities. Combinations of anthropomorphic, theriomorphic, and symbolic elements are also possible. For example, the god of the city gate in et-Tell (whose name is not known) is represented with the head of a bull, crescent-shaped horns, and a schematized body bearing a weapon. (*Fig. 1*).[6]

Sacred stones (baetyli, standing stones, stelae) were erected either alone or in groups. During the Iron Age they were usually considered as markers of a deity's presence but could also represent ancestors (especially prior to the Iron Age). The stones could be hewn (e.g., the bull stela at the gate of et-Tell), painted, or left largely in their natural state, and they often have the great advantage of being found still *in situ* in excavations.

The iconography of Palestinian deities and ancestors attests to the fact that Palestine and Syria shared the same types of gods (including the use of anthropomorphic and theriomorphic representations, symbols, and standing stones), even if a strong influence of Egyptian symbolism can be also seen, particularly in southern Palestine, along the coast, and in Egyptian-dominated urban centers. Located at the threshold between Egypt and Syria-Mesopotamia, Palestine not only adopted genuinely Egyptian or Syro-Mesopotamian deities; it also adopted preexisting Egyptian or Mesopotamian motifs, such that autochthonous Palestinian deities are represented in an Egyptianizing or Syrianizing fashion or even both together. All of this makes the correlation of the deities depicted with particular names of gods difficult; moreover, the use of analogy runs the risk of either flattening local idiosyncracies and diachronic developments or (precisely the opposite) of reading these into the material evidence. The optimal case would be to find a representation of a deity bearing an inscription with the deity's name. Whether such a case from Israel/Palestine and for YHWH is attested is a matter of debate. The only potential case of this is a drawing on a pithos from Kuntillet 'Ajrud (Pithos A), which attests to YHWH of Samaria (and Asherah) epigraphically[7] and which can fortunately be dated quite precisely (between 795 and ca. 730/720 B.C.E.).

---

6 M. Bernett and O. Keel, *Mond, Stier und der Kult am Stadttor: Die Stele von Betsaida (et-Tell)* (OBO 161; Fribourg and Göttingen 1998).

7 On the inscription on Pithos A see Renz and Röllig, *Handbuch* (see n. 4), 59 – 61; O. Keel and C. Uehlinger, *Göttinnen, Götter und Gottessymbole: Neue Erkenntnisse zur Religionsgeschichte Kanaans und Israels aufgrund bislang unerschlossener ikonographischer Quellen* (4th ed.; QD 134;

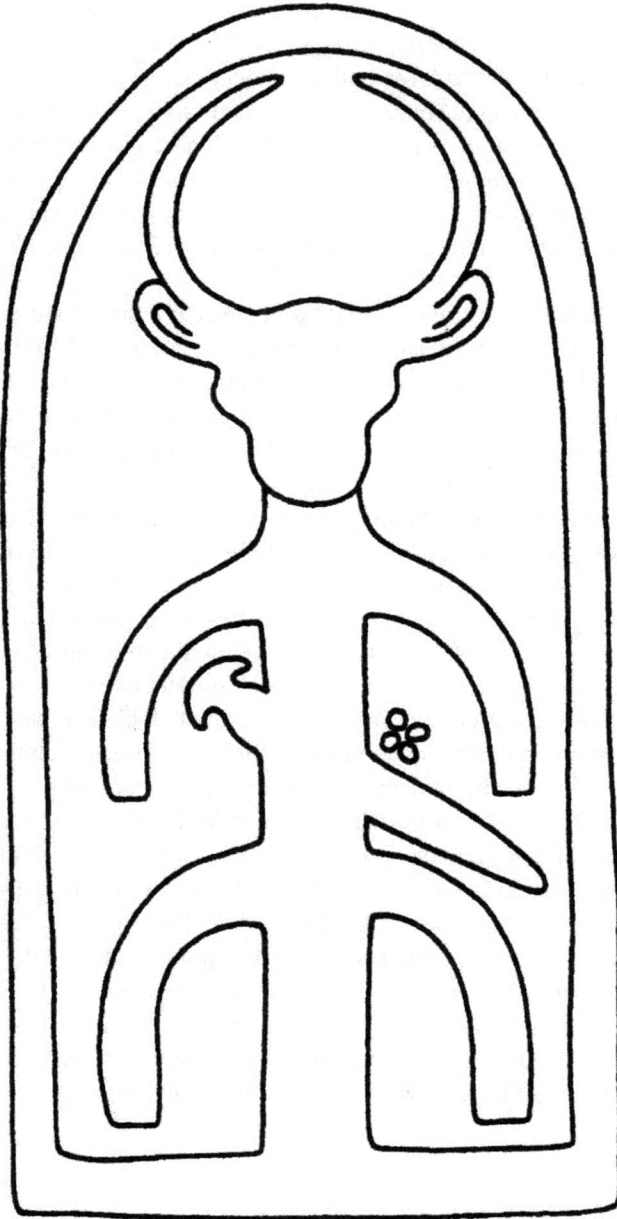

Fig. 1: Stone stela; god of the city gate in et-Tell, represented with the head of a bull, crescent horns, schematized body and weapon. Keel and Uehlinger, *Göttinen, Götter und Gottessymbole* (see n. 7), Abb. 394. p. 552.

Fig. 2: Pithos drawing from Kuntillet ʿAjrud (Pithos A). Keel and Uelinger, *Gods, Goddesses, and Images of God in Ancient Israel* (see n. 7), fig. 220, p. 213.

Both of the male figures in the drawing (*Fig. 2*) are hybrid forms with theriomorphic elements, possibly Bes[8] or (more probably) lion-faced creatures (the left one, according to the new photographs, with a lion's tail [not a penis] between the legs), indicating that they were hardly intended to be a representation

---

Freiburg *et al.* 1997), § 134; English translation: Gods, Goddesses, and Images of God in Ancient Israel (trans. T.H. Trapp; Minneapolis 1998), § 134; M. Weippert, *Historisches Textbuch zum Alten Testament* (GAT 10; Göttingen 2010), No. 216; A. Berlejung, "Die Inschriften von Kuntillet ʿAjrud," in *Texte aus der Umwelt des Alten Testaments, Neue Folge 6. Grab-, Sarg-, Bau- und Votivinschriften* (ed. B. Janowski and D. Schwemer; Gütersloh 2011), 314–319: 2.1; S. Ahituv *et al.*, "The Inscriptions," in *Kuntillet ʿAjrud (Horvat Teman): An Iron Age II Religious Site on the Judah-Sinai Border* (ed. Z. Meshel; Jerusalem 2012), 73–142, esp. inscription 3.1; for a photo of the drawings see fig. 5.25.

8 For a detailed discussion see C. Uehlinger, "Anthropomorphic Cult Statuary in Iron Age Palestine and the Search for Yahweh's Cult Images," in *The Image and the Book: Iconic Cults, Aniconism, and the Rise of Book Religion in Israel and the Ancient Near East* (ed. K. van der Toorn; CBET 21; Leuven 1997), 97–155, here 142–146; and arguing again for Bes: P. Beck, "The Drawings and Decorative Designs," in *Kuntillet ʿAjrud (Horvat Teman): An Iron Age II Religious Site on the Judah-Sinai Border* (ed. Z. Meshel 2012), 143–203, here 165–173 and esp. fig. 6.20a.

of Yhwh of Samaria.[9] Moreover, a synchronic and intentional relationship between the drawings and the inscriptions on the pithos cannot be drawn unproblematically and beyond doubt. Rather, certain considerations suggest that the drawings and the inscriptions were applied at different times and independently of each other (for example, there are three figures in the image but only two deities in the blessing formula of the inscription, and the inscription overlaps with the drawing). Additional representations of animals decorate the vessel, of which harnessed horses, a (suckling) cow-and-calf combination, and the well-known motif of caprids by the tree of life are particularly noteworthy. Here too there are no connections to the inscription, which contains the following much-discussed text:

1. Message of '[...]w the [...]: Say to Yehal[y] and to Yo'asha and to [...]: I bless you (pl.) 2. by Yhwh of Samaria and by his Asherah.

3 Yhwh and images

While the identification of a divine representation with a deity known by name on the basis of a theological profile and area of activity as derived from textual evidence is often the normal way of identifying images of deities, such a procedure is not free of problems. This is particularly true in the case of Yhwh, since the dating of the biblical texts is debated and Yhwh's original profile is still not clearly defined and apparently developed considerably over the course of Israel's and Judah's religious history. If Yhwh successively took on the theological traits, competencies, and epithets of other deities over the course of the first millennium B.C.E., as is assumed by a majority of scholars and can also be deduced from the Hebrew Bible, this would at least raise the possibility that Yhwh also did this in relation to these deities' iconographies, paraphernalia, attributes, and symbolism. Since, however, we do not know with certainty what comprised Yhwh's original characteristics, iconography, paraphernalia, attributes, and symbols (which possibly included the Baal/Hadad type, the El type, bull iconography, symbols, and/or standing stones), it is not possible to (re-)construct this diachronic development. Thus, currently the point of departure consists of two different theories that stand side by side: those which see in Yhwh a storm

---

9 For a different view see, for example, B.B. Schmidt, "The Aniconic Tradition: On Reading Images and Viewing Texts," in *The Triumph of Elohim: From Yahwisms to Judaisms* (ed. D.V. Edelman; CBET 13; Kampen 1995), 75–105, here 103f., who assumes that Yhwh has the form of a hybrid creature on the basis of the well-known drawing (and in his view its caption) from Pithos A from Kuntillet 'Ajrud.

god who was later identified with El and those which see an El-type god who was later identified with the weather god. Both of these approaches are able to draw on bull iconography in their support (see below).

The original imagelessness of Yʜᴡʜ would also be an option (even if the biblical texts on this topic all clearly originated after the Iron I/IIA), which can neither be proven nor refuted on the basis of the iconographic sources that are currently available. In addition to this is the possibility that the Yʜᴡʜs of the north, of Jerusalem, of Transjordan, and of the south each underwent different developments in tandem with political events and possible acculturation, such that Yʜᴡʜ (even at a synchronic level) need not have looked the same everywhere.

3.1 Yʜᴡʜ, an anthropomorphic deity of the Baal/Hadad or El type?

The metal statues of the Iron I (and II), which are much less frequently attested than in the Late Bronze Age, almost without exception show male deities of the enthroned El type or of the smiting Baal/Hadad type (*Fig. 3*).[10] Within the scholarly literature, these representations have been associated with Yʜᴡʜ in a wide variety of ways. What is ultimately decisive is which theological profile one assigns to Yʜᴡʜ's earliest origins. Those who regard Yʜᴡʜ as a local manifestation of a weather god of the "Baal/Hadad type"[11] decide correspondingly in Yʜᴡʜ's iconographic identification. In this context, Yʜᴡʜ's theological profile is described in such a way that Yʜᴡʜ appears as an aggressive and mighty war-

---

10 For an overview see A. Berlejung, *Die Theologie der Bilder: Das Kultbild in Mesopotamien und die alttestamentliche Bilderpolemik unter besonderer Berücksichtigung der Herstellung und Einweihung der Statuen* (OBO 162; Fribourg and Göttingen 1998) and Uehlinger, "Cult Statuary" (see n. 8).

11 So, for example, M. Weippert, "Synkretismus und Monotheismus: Religionsinterne Konfliktbewältigung im alten Israel," in *Kultur und Konflikt* (ed. J. Assmann and D. Harth; Frankfurt 1990), 143–179 (reproduced in idem, *Jahwe und die anderen Götter: Studien zur Religionsgeschichte des antiken Israel in ihrem syrisch-palästinischen Kontext* [FAT 18; Tübingen 1997], 1–24), 157 f. and H. Niehr, *Der höchste Gott: Alttestamentlicher JHWH-Glaube im Kontext syrisch-kanaanäischer Religion des 1. Jahrtausends v. Chr.* (BZAW 190; Berlin 1990), 43. On the history of research see Müller, *Jahwe* (see n. 1), 13–16, who opts for a "royal weather god" in Jerusalem during the monarchic period, i. e., a reshaping of the weather god in light of royal theology (ibid., 17, 244–248). The derivation of the name Yʜᴡʜ from the root "to blow" as well as biblical texts that describe storm-phenomena in the context of theophanies seem to point in the direction of a storm god; for a critique see Keel, *Geschichte* (see n. 1), § 238 f.

rior in the storm, defeats mythical enemies, provides rain to the earth, and is thus responsible for the ability to reproduce and for life. In this scenario, divine representations of YHWH would look no different from representations of the deities Baal or Hadad. In addition to anthropomorphic representations of striding warrior deities, theriomorphic forms are also conceivable (with the symbolism of aggression and strength), particularly the bull.[12]

Fig. 3a and **3b:** Metal figurines from Iron I (and II): male deities of the enthroned El type or the smiting Baal/Hadad type. Keel and Uelinger, Gods, Goddesses, and Images of God in Ancient Israel (see n. 7), figs. 139 + 141, p. 117.

---

12 For a brief history of research on bull iconography see J.S. Bray, *Sacred Dan: Religious Tradition and Cultic Practice in Judges 17–18* (LHBOTS 449; New York and London 2006), 71–80, who himself adheres to the theory of YHWH as a storm god whose worship included bull images (in the north).

Those who regard YHWH in his origins or in particular local manifestations (attached to place names such as Bethel) instead as a deity of the "El type"[13] tend to identify YHWH in iconographic attestations of enthroned deities, where the bull also remains a possibility.[14] In this case, kingship and the capacity to create would have been among YHWH's original competencies.

Since the time of his arrival in Palestine – on this point there is widespread agreement – YHWH successively took on different functions from a variety of autochthonous deities, such that deities of the Baal/Hadad type and El type, among others, were combined in him.[15] This was not a singular occurrence, since deities in the ancient Near East often (and especially in the context of their "rise" to the position of highest god) took over attributes (and iconographic traits) of one or several other deities and thus attained greater reverence in an increased area of influence. In the case of YHWH, this process would have caused YHWH's iconography to change correspondingly over time – something which is no longer conceivable to us but was probably not regarded as problematic by those who experienced it at the time. Since the viewer is significantly involved in recognizing images,[16] it is reasonable to assume that YHWH -worshipers during the Iron Age (who shared the same cultural background and symbol system) were able to recognize representations of their deity as such.

---

13 For Bethel and Beersheba this is assumed by Weippert, "Synkretismus" (see n. 11), 155 f. In contrast, F.M. Cross, *Canaanite Myth and Hebrew Epic: Essays in the History of the Religion of Israel* (Cambridge 1973), 44–75; R.S. Hendel, "The Social Origins of the Aniconic Tradition in Early Israel," *CBQ* 50 (1988), 365–382, here 377 f.; M. Dijkstra, "El, the God of Israel – Israel the People of YHWH: On the Origins of Ancient Israelite Yahwism," in *Only One God? Monotheism in Ancient Israel and the Veneration of the Goddess Asherah* (ed. B. Becking; Sheffield 2001), 81–126, here 102–107, presuppose that YHWH is an El-type deity. M.S. Smith, *The Memoirs of God: History, Memory, and the Experience of the Divine in Ancient Israel* (Minneapolis 2004), 106–114 constructs several levels connected to this. According to Smith, the premonarchic Israelite pantheon consisted of El with Asherah (level 1), Baal, Astarte, Shahar, Shalim, Reshef, Dever, YHWH (as a new arrival from the south) (level 2), and early monarchic Israel already identified YHWH with El, who achieved level 1 and also received Asherah as his partner. Thus, for the subsequent periods, Smith only speaks of YHWH – El.

14 So, for example, J.F. Gomes, *The Sanctuary of Bethel and the Configuration of Israelite Identity* (BZAW 368; Berlin 2006), 25–28.

15 On the combination of both types of gods in YHWH see T.N.D. Mettinger, "The Elusive Essence: YHWH, El and Baal and the Distinctiveness of Israelite Faith," in *Die Hebräische Bibel und ihre zweifache Nachgeschichte. Festschrift für Rolf Rendtorff zum 65. Geburtstag* (ed. E. Blum et al.; Neukirchen-Vluyn 1990), 393–417, here 411.

16 On the role of the observer in recognizing images cf. E.H. Gombrich, *Art and Illusion: A Study in the Psychology of Pictorial Representation* (5th ed.; Oxford 1977): 250 ff. 273–275. 426–428 [S.G.: these are the German page numbers] and passim.

3.2 Yhwh as a bull?

Bull iconography is attested from earliest times in Palestine.[17] During the Late Bronze Age and Iron I, bulls could be associated with the weather god as well as with El. Bronze bull figurines (e.g., from Tell Dotan) are rare during the Iron Age and should be regarded as the symbolic animal of deities of the Baal/Hadad type (*Fig. 4*).

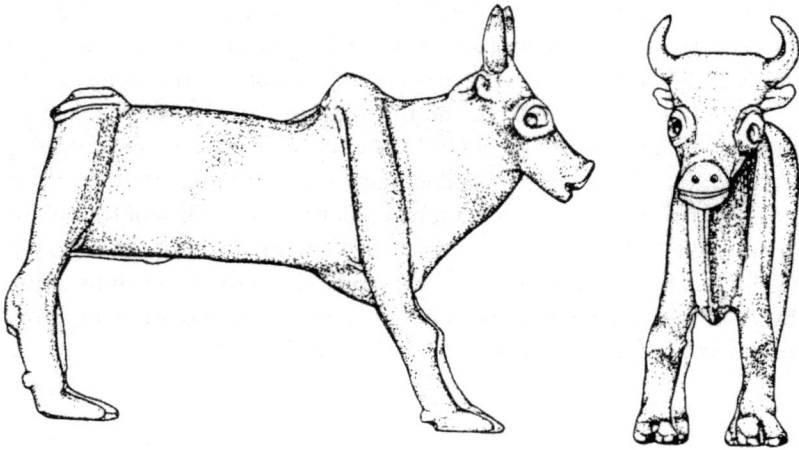

Fig. 4: Bronze bull figurines (Tell Dotan) as the symbolic animal of male deities of the Baal/Hadad type. Keel and Uelinger, *Gods, Goddesses, and Images of God in Ancient Israel* (see n. 7), fig. 142, p. 119.

The majority of finds of cultic objects from this period are not from costly metals, however, but rather from clay as the cheaper substitute. In the iconography of these terra cotta objects there are representations of bulls (e.g., from Shiloh), although anthropomorphic goddesses predominate. Bovines are attested throughout Palestine and are thus not particular to the cult of the north, even though biblical texts could suggest this (see below). For northern Palestine and the later northern kingdom of Israel, however, another factor should be taken into consideration, namely, the presence of the Arameans in northern Palestine beginning around 1200 B.C.E. and more tangibly in the 10th and 9th c., es-

---

17 For early examples see O. Keel and S. Schroer, *Die Ikonographie Palästinas/Israels und der Alte Orient: Eine Religionsgeschichte in Bildern, Band 1. Vom ausgehenden Mesolithikum bis zur Frühbronzezeit* (Fribourg 2005), nos. 11 (Neolithic, Kilwa) and 121 (EB I, Megiddo). Further examples (beginning in the Middle Bronze Age) are found in Berlejung, *Theologie* (see n. 10), 288 f.

pecially around the Sea of Galilee. The Arameans brought the moon-god Sin of Harran (in northwestern Mesopotamia) to Palestine (first in the north, followed later by the south), whose symbolism included bovine iconography in addition to his crescent standard adorned with small bells. Whether Yʜwʜ was reconceived as a bull at this time is debated.

According to 1 Kgs 12:26 ff.; Hos 8:5 f.; 10:5; and 13:2, bull cults existed in Samaria, Bethel, and Dan, and the Exodus formula in 1 Kgs 12:28 demonstrates that the bulls were understood as representations of Yʜwʜ and not merely as animals on which he sat or stood.[18] Thus, whoever regards the biblical exodus credo as a cornerstone of the early worship of Yʜwʜ could find in a calf a possible, albeit biblically proscribed, representation of Yʜwʜ. The historical value of these texts, however, is widely disputed, and their evaluation spans the full range of possibilities, from the assumption of their historical factuality to that of their fictitiousness. Whether Yʜwʜ was actually worshiped in the form of a bull or whether the aforementioned texts merely seek to discredit the cult of the northern kingdom (from the later Jerusalemite perspective) can no longer be determined in light of the redaction-critical problems posed by 1 Kgs 12 and by the book of Hosea. In any case, 1 Kgs 12 in particular seems to retroject the political and religious conditions under Jeroboam II (785 – 745 B.C.E.) onto the time of Jeroboam I[19] and thus says nothing about the early worship of Yʜwʜ in the northern kingdom. The Hebrew Bible refers to the bull as a divine image exclusively in polemical contexts, such that, in my view, it can hardly be taken as an "original" form of representing Yʜwʜ. Perhaps only at a later time (during the 8th c.?) and during the process of Yʜwʜ's rise to becoming the highest god of two states did a debate arise as to whether images of bulls could be associated with him.

3.3 Yʜwʜ, the ark, and solar symbolism?

As a liberator god of a mobile and martial nature, battle standards as well as the ark[20] were deemed appropriate to the god of the exodus, since both standards

---

18 On this debate see Berlejung, *Theologie* (see n. 10), 328 f.

19 A. Berlejung, "Twisting Traditions: Programmatic Absence-Theology for the Northern Kingdom in 1 Kgs 12:26 – 33* (the 'Sin of Jeroboam')," *JNSL* 35/2 (2009), 1 – 42. For an approach that closely follows the biblical account see M. Tilly and W. Zwickel, *Religionsgeschichte Israels: Von der Vorzeit bis zu den Anfängen des Christentums* (Darmstadt 2011), 90 – 92.

20 On the ark see T. Staubli, *Das Image der Nomaden im Alten Israel und in der Ikonographie seiner sesshaften Nachbarn* (CBO 107; Fribourg and Göttingen 1991), 222 – 229, Keel, *Geschichte* (see n. 1), § 247 – 249. For a different view see Tilly and Zwickel, *Religionsgeschichte*, 81 f., accord-

and chest-shrines are attested in the ancient Near East and in ancient Egypt.[21] Archaeologically speaking, so far nothing has been found from Israel/Palestine that could connect to or support this supposition. Although within biblical narratives the ark is referred to positively as a representation of YHWH, these narratives provide no specific information on the iconography of YHWH or the possible contents of the ark. Even if it was considered already in early scholarship that the ark contained a bull image of YHWH, a stone idol, or baetyli,[22] this cannot be verified. The only thing that is clear is that the ark relates to YHWH's mobile, dynamic, and martial characteristics and thus envisions him functioning as a warrior god who acts with his warriors. Consequently, the divine designation YHWH ṣeba'ot (YHWH of hosts) seems to be connected to the ark. With the bringing of the ark to Jerusalem by Abiathar/David and its later placement in the temple of Solomon, the majority of biblical scholars connect YHWH's entry into the city to his identification with the preexisting city god of Jerusalem,[23] whose precise profile is also debated. Othmar Keel proposes that there was a solar deity in pre-Davidic Jerusalem[24] who was at first worshiped alongside the newer god YHWH until the latter was identified with the sun god. Precisely when YHWH's identification with the sun god took place remains an open question, although there are a variety of considerations that point to the late 8th c. B.C.E. Beginning at this time, religious solar symbolism bearing an Egyptian influence is well attested in Jerusalem and in Judah as a whole (e.g., the pharaoh as a sun god,

---

ing to whom the ark was originally connected to the god El and his processional pedestal. In my view, the biblical emphasis on the martial aspects of the ark speaks against the notion that it belonged to El and his processions (which are pure constructions).

21 See Keel, *Geschichte* (see n. 1), § 249f.

22 Staubli, *Image* (see n. 20), 131f., 224f. and Keel, *Geschichte* (see n. 1), § 250 assume the existence of baetyli, followed by T.N.D. Mettinger, "Israelite Aniconism: Developments and Origins," in *The Image and the Book: Iconic Cults, Aniconism, and the Rise of Book Religion in Israel and the Ancient Near East* (ed. K. van der Toorn; CBET 21; Leuven 1997), 173–204, here 198. H. Gressmann, *Die Lade Jahves und das Allerheiligste des Salomonischen Tempels* (BWAT NF 1; Berlin 1920), 26–28 and S. Mowinckel, "Wann wurde der Jahwäkultus in Jerusalem offiziell bildlos?" *AcOr* 8 (1930), 257–279, here 259, 272f. (only the first ark in Jerusalem prior to Sheshonk's plundering of the temple; in his view the second ark contained stone idols, see ibid., 276–279) argued for a bull image (of YHWH). On further hypotheses regarding the contents of the ark see H.-J. Zobel, ארון, *TWAT* 1:391–404, here 400f. and K. van der Toorn, "The Iconic Book: Analogies between the Babylonian Cult of Images and the Veneration of the Torah," in *The Image and the Book, Iconic Cults, Aniconism, and the Rise of Book Religion in Israel and the Ancient Near East* (ed. K. van der Toorn; CBET 21; Leuven 1997), 229–248, here 242.

23 See Keel, *Geschichte* (see n. 1), § 254–256.

24 Keel, *Geschichte* (see n. 1), § 332–343. Tilly and Zwickel, *Religionsgeschichte* (see n. 19), 81 follow older research in favor of Shalim and Zedek.

winged scarab, or sun disk). Beginning in the second half of the 8th c., this symbolism also had an influence on the seals of Judahite functionaries and the royal *lmlk* sealings of Hezekiah, which display the winged sun disk or the four-winged scarab. As the name "Yhw is resplendent"[25] on an aniconic bulla dating to around 700 B.C.E. indicates, YHWH of Jerusalem bore clear solar attributes at this time, which also come to expression or are further developed in texts such as Deut 33:2; Hab 3:3 ff; Zeph 3:5; Ps 46; 72; 84:12; Isa 1:26; 18:4; 59:9; 60:1–3; and Mal 3:20. Here it should be emphasized that the Hebrew Bible has a tendency to receive the attributes of the ancient Near Eastern sun god that relate to the deity's punishing/judging (using the key words "law and justice"), delivering, and salvific actions. YHWH's identification with the sun god of/in Jerusalem would have resulted in the adoption of solar iconography, at least locally, which is perhaps alluded to in the reference to the "chariots of the sun" in 2 Kgs 23:11. Whether elements of solar symbolism on image-bearing objects from Jerusalem beginning in the 8th/7th c. B.C.E. are representations of YHWH remains a possibility; in my view, an association with YHWH cannot be ruled out. However, the possibility that this solar symbolism belonged to YHWH *from the beginning* – like his cherubim throne, which was likewise only acquired in Jerusalem – is generally (and rightly) regarded as rather unlikely.

3.4 YHWH as a standing stone or as invisible?

Since the Hebrew Bible includes YHWH's imageless and formless nature among his most important characteristics, this state of affairs should be discussed against the background of the attested material culture. If YHWH's imagelessness was one of the basic statements made about YHWH from the beginning, then it would indeed be expected that there were no images of YHWH, insofar as or as long as everyone maintained such a perspective. In this case, the archaeologically attested images discussed above would all reflect other deities and polytheistic cults.

The fact that the Hebrew Bible repeatedly attests to cultic and legal activities "before God" raises the question of the concrete point of reference for these actions. In this context, standing stones[26] as "material aniconism" as well as empty

---

25 Keel and Uehlinger, *Gods* (see n. 7), § 162.
26 On standing stones see T.N.D. Mettinger, *No Graven Image? Israelite Aniconism in its Ancient Near Eastern Context* (CBOT 42; Stockholm 1995), 32–35, 140–191; idem, "The Roots of Aniconism: An Israelite Phenomenon in Comparative Perspective," in *Congress Volume Cambridge 1995*

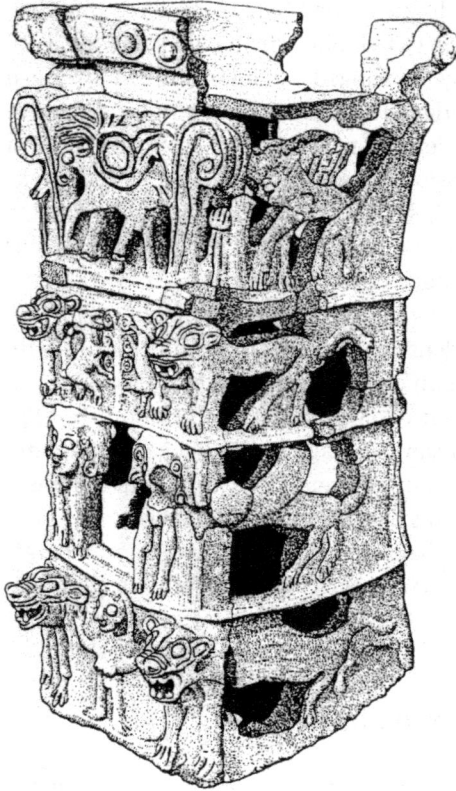

Fig. 5: Cultic stand from Taanach, panel 2: the open space between the sphinxes. Keel and Uelinger, *Gods, Goddesses, and Images of God in Ancient Israel* (see n. 7), fig. 184, p. 159.

thrones or even empty pictorial surfaces on otherwise image-bearing objects (e.g., the cultic stand from Taanach [*Fig. 5*],[27] panel 2: the open space between two sphinxes[28]) as "empty space aniconism" are both discussed as early, image-

(ed. J.A. Emerton; VTSup 66; Leiden 1997), 219–233, here 226–228; and J.C. de Moor, "Standing Stones and Ancestor Worship," *UF* 27 (1995), 1–20.

27 Keel and Uehlinger, *Gods* (see n. 7), § 98 fig. 184.

28 On this thesis (drawing on J.G. Taylor), see (once again) R.S. Hess, *Israelite Religions: An Archaeological and Biblical Survey* (Grand Rapids 2007), 323 f., who argues that panel 4 would then also necessarily represent YHWH. Thus, in his view, the empty space between the sphinxes (panel 2) and the bull with the winged sun disk (panel 4) a possibly typical northern iconography of YHWH. If the animal in panel 4 were a horse, which is also possible, then in his view this

less representations of Yʜwʜ at the center of his cult.[29] Forms of argumentation that postulate Yʜwʜ's original imagelessness and then correspondingly interpret the archaeological evidence from a particular site are highly problematic, since they inevitably involve the premature conclusion that if no iconic material is found at a cultic site, then such a site is associated with the Israelite cult or with Yʜwʜ (thus recently for Khirbet Qeiyafa).[30] Yet one is at the fringes of academic honesty if one withholds the figurines (as at Arad, see below) or the iconic material (e. g., the iconically-formed terra cotta shrine at Khirbet Qeiyafa) from cultic sites that are securely associated with Yʜwʜ.

In principle, the sharp distinction between the iconism (e. g., the use of an anthropomorphic or theriomorphic cultic image) and aniconism (e. g., the use of a standing stone, stela, or baetylus) of a deity disregards the cultic reality in antiquity, according to which the function of a marker of divine presence was more important than its visual appearance.[31] What was significant for the cult was that the god's presence was realized performatively, which could be ensured in equal measure by symbols, standards, standing stones, natural forma-

---

could also be interpreted as Yʜwʜ (with reference to 2 Kgs 23:11). Thus, for Hess, the Taanach cult stand (dated to the 10th c.) contains an aniconic (panel 2) and a theriomorphic-solar (panel 4) representation of Yʜwʜ and his Asherah (in panels 1 and 3). For a critique of Taylor, see already Keel and Uehlinger, *Gods* (see n. 7), § 98, who regard the empty space as a (guarded) entry, see a horse as the symbolic animal of Anat-Astarte in panel 4, and regard the winged sun disk as a general sign for the heavenly realm.

29 On the terminology see Mettinger, *No Graven Image?* (see n. 26), 30, 201f.); idem, "Roots" (see n. 26), passim.

30 So Y. Garfinkel in an interview with Israel Today Magazine from May 15, 2012 (http://www.israeltoday.co.il/NewsItem/tabid/178/nid/23224/language/en-US/Default.aspx) (accessed May 16, 2012). The decorated terra cotta cultic shrines that were discovered at the site, however, suggest otherwise.

31 Thus, a Hittite text allows people to choose whether to represent a deity as a pithos, *huwaši*-stone, or a divine image; see M. Popko, "Anikonische Götterdarstellungen in der altanatolischen Religion," in *Ritual and Sacrifice in the Ancient Near East: Proceedings of the International Conference organized by the Katholieke Universiteit Leuven from the 17th to the 20th of April 1991* (ed. J. Quaegebeur; OLA 55; Leuven 1993), 319–327, here 325. Here, *huwaši* indicates the function (bearer of numinous qualities) rather than the appearance; it could be a worked or unworked cultic stone, the sanctuary surrounding the cultic stone, the larger area and possibly even the natural rock formation (with or without an image carved into the rock); see D. Schwemer, "Das hethitische Reichspantheon: Überlegungen zu Struktur und Genese," in *Götterbilder, Gottesbilder, Weltbilder, Band 1: Ägypten, Mesopotamien, Persien, Kleinasien, Syrien, Palästina* (ed. R.G. Kratz and H. Spieckermann; FAT II/17; Tübingen 2006), 241–265, here 263f. On the equivalence of stelae and cultic images (and symbols) in terms of their function and performative presencing of the deity see also V. Haas, *Geschichte der Hethitischen Religion* (HO I/15; Leiden 1994), 507–509.

tions, and cultic images (of various forms and technical quality). Even vessels could serve this purpose: there is a well-known case from the Hittite cultural sphere in which a vessel which was made for the cult of a particular deity also served to represent the deity[32] – a notion that deserves further investigation in light of the evidence of iconically-formed vessels from Palestine.[33]

In earlier research, the possibility was hardly considered that putting on a mask could always change an aniconic cultic object into an iconic one. There are impressive examples from Syria and from northern Transjordan (et-Tell, see *Fig. 1*) that figurative and non-figurative elements could be combined: an aniconic stand or pole could be transformed by placing the head of a bull on top of it. This connection need not have always existed, since the stand or pole could also be displayed without the head (and probably also vice-versa)[34] without creating any ambiguity for the ancient viewer.

The main question is to what extent a cultic stone or pole as a material representation of a deity is actually aniconic – in other words, where "imageness" begins and ends. Standing stones, stelae, and baetyli could already invoke something object-like or could even be worked or painted.[35] They were erected in buildings, at gates, and also in open-air sanctuaries, both within and outside of settlements, and they give no indication of the social structure of their worshipers – they can certainly not be evaluated as evidence of nomadism.[36] It is

---

32 Examples are found in Haas, *Geschichte* (see n. 31), 520–523.

33 See, for example, Y. Garfinkel and C. Epstein, *Neolithic and Chalcolithic Pottery of the Southern Levant* (Jerusalem 1999), 261 (bull- and bird-shaped vessels); S. Schroer, *Die Ikonographie Palästinas/Israels und der Alte Orient: Eine Religionsgeschichte in Bildern, Band 2. Die Mittelbronzezeit* (Fribourg 2008), no. 473 (bull-shaped); as well as the finds from Horvat Qitmit; on the latter see P. Beck, "Catalogue of Cult Objects and Study of the Iconography," in *Horvat Qitmit: An Edomite Shrine in the Biblical Negev* (ed. I. Beit-Arieh; Monograph Series of the Institute of Archaeology Tel Aviv University 11; Tel Aviv 1995), 27–197.

34 For a discussion and examples see Bernett and Keel, *Mond* (see n. 6), 22–27, to be supplemented with S.J. Wimmer and K. Janaydeh, "Eine Mondgottstele aus eṭ-Ṭurra/Jordanien," *ZDPV* 127 (2011), 135–141. For masks on poles in the Greek cult of Dionysos see also I. Jenkins, "The Masks of Dionysos/Pan – Osiris – Apis," *Jahrbuch des Deutschen Archäologischen Instituts* 109 (1994), 273–299. The topic of masks in the Hebrew Bible will be discussed in A. Berlejung, "Masks in the Old Testament?" in *The Physicality of the Other: Masks as a Means of Encounter* (ed. A. Berlejung and J. Filitz; ORA; Tübingen 2016).

35 As is the case for the Nabatean baetyli, which could nevertheless be provided with human eyes, noses, and mouths (for examples see Mettinger, *No Graven Image?* [see n. 26], 63), and for the sculpted standing stones from Tell Kittan and ʻEn Ḥaṣeva; see C. Uehlinger, "Israelite Aniconism in Context: Review of T.N.D. Mettinger, No Graven Image?" *Biblica* 77 (1996), 540–549, here 544. On the stela from et-Tell see above.

36 Against Tilly and Zwickel, *Religionsgeschichte* (see n. 19), 81.

also not possible to (re-)construct an aniconic west Semitic tradition from the well-documented and widespread use of standing stones in Syria-Palestine from which the biblical prohibition against images can be derived.[37] Some standing stones and cultic poles are similar in appearance to cultic images and symbols and are in no way inferior to them in function. They represented the (respective) deity whose presence and effect was so performatively present that it was included or could be provided in this form in rituals.[38]

Blank pictorial surfaces cannot bear the burden of proof for the claim that they represented an aniconic god. On the aforementioned cultic stand from Taanach (*Fig. 5*), the open space between the sphinxes could also serve purely pragmatic grounds; besides, "window holes" on cultic stands are nothing out of the ordinary.[39] In the end, a gap must be able to remain simply a gap.

The notion that Yʜwʜ was enthroned on an empty cherubim/sphinx throne in Jerusalem at the time of Solomon appears rather improbable, since *empty* (cherubim/sphinx) thrones for deities are only attested beginning in the 7th/6th c. (in Phoenicia) (*Fig. 6a*).[40] The "Solomonic" cherubim throne was first developed retrospectively from this for the Jerusalem temple and (if one combines the biblical text with the iconographic evidence) its ascription to Solomon during the 10th c. B.C.E. represents a biblical anachronism.[41] In any case, it could not

---

37 This is the thesis of Mettinger, *No Graven Image?* (see n. 26). For counterarguments see already Berlejung, *Theologie* (see n. 10), 74f. with n. 428 and Uehlinger, "Aniconism" (see n. 35).

38 For examples see Berlejung, *Theologie* (see n. 10), 72–75.

39 See the second cult stand from Taanach, discussed in Keel and Uehlinger, *Gods* (see n. 7), § 97 fig. 182a.

40 Keel, *Geschichte* (see n. 1), § 356. It can be doubted to what extent the bulla impression from Jerusalem (*Fig. 6b*) dating to the 9th/8th c. (see O. Keel, "Paraphernalia of Jerusalem Sanctuaries and Their Relation to Deities Worshiped Therein during the Iron Age IIA–C," in *Temple Building and Temple Cult: Architecture and Cultic Paraphernalia of Temples in the Levant (2.–1. Mill. B.C.E.). Proceedings of a Conference on the Occasion of the 50th Anniversary of the Institute of Biblical Archaeology at the University of Tübingen (28–30 May 2010)* [ed. J. Kamlah; ADPV 41; Wiesbaden 2012], 317–342, here fig. 95* with pp. 331f.) really depicts a completely empty throne. Directly in front of the throne is a standard topped by a winged disc. Both the throne and the standard together form a cultic unit of divine representation. Perhaps the standard was placed slightly in front of the throne and not directly on its seat due to technical reasons of composition and perspective. In any event, this singular piece cannot constitute proof of a genuinely aniconic cult of the city god of Jerusalem or any relation to Yʜwʜ.

41 Tilly and Zwickel, *Religionsgeschichte* (see n. 19), 86–89 have recently returned to following this anachronism; only the cherub/sphinx throne as an *occupied royal throne* is older (see the Ahiram sarcophagus). A pair of gods on a sphinx throne can be seen on a terra cotta acquired through the antiquities trade and which supposedly originated from Tell Beit Mirsim (late 8th/

Fig. 6a: Empty (cherubim/sphinx-) throne for deities (Phoenicia). M. Metzger, "Jahwe, der Kerubenthroner," in idem, *Vorderorientalische Ikonographie und das Alte Testament: Gesammelte Aufsätze* (Münster 2004), 112–123, here fig. 157.

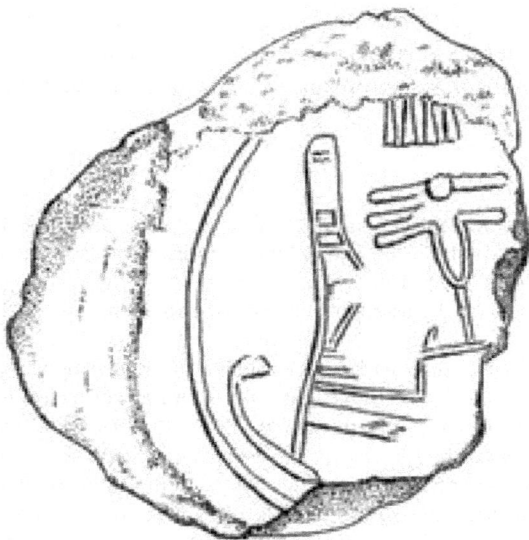

Fig. 6b: Bulla from Jerusalem (9th/8th c. B.C.E.). O. Keel, *Geschichte* (see n. 1), fig. 191.

early 7th c. B.C.E.). Christoph Uehlinger ("Cult Statuary" [see n. 8], 149–152) proposed to identify Yhwh and Asherah in the pair, although few scholars have found this proposal convincing.

have belonged to the original iconography of Yhwh, since it was only after Yhwh's move to Jerusalem that he took up residence in the temple there and obtained royal qualities and a throne.

Fig. 7: A standing stone (or two) and incense altars in the Arad temple in the Negev (cf. p. ###). Photo from W. Zwickel, *Der salomonische Tempel* (Mainz 1999).

The potential variety and the lack of exclusivity in cultic matters is illustrated by the later sanctuary (late 8th c. B.C.E.) in the Arad fortress in the Negev. There, pillar figurines of goddesses, which were typical for Judah and belong in the realm of local production and private piety,[42] were found on the surrounding deposit benches of the sacrificial altar in the courtyard. These clay figurines originated during the second half of the 8th c. and found great appeal during the 7th c. They display a goddess who is not identifiable by name (Asherah?) in a bell-shaped skirt who supports her breasts. In the niche of the temple there stood a

---

42 See Keel and Uehlinger, *Gods* (see n. 7), § 190 – 195; E. Darby, *Interpreting Judean Pillar Figurines: Gender and Empire in Judean Apotropaic Ritual* (FAT II/69; Tübingen 2014).

standing stone (or perhaps two of them[43]) and two incense altars (*Fig. 7*). The standing stone(s) and the pillar indicate that multiple deities in different forms (as a standing stone, anthropomorphically as a goddess supporting her breasts, and also zoomorphically[44]) were represented at the temple of Arad, which must be regarded as a local temple of YHWH during that time. In any case, the figurines speak against generalized conclusions about the aniconic character of the religion of Judah during the monarchic period.[45]

Since standing stones, stelae, and baetyli for different deities (and ancestors) are attested from earliest times in Syria-Palestine, YHWH could very well have been imagined in this form during the Iron Age. In this respect, however, a typical form of "Yahwism" does not exist, since only preexisting forms of cultic representation would have been adopted. Whether a typical (e. g., distinctly formed or painted) sort of YHWH-standing stone or stela existed (e. g., analogous to the stela at et-Tell) is beyond our present state of knowledge.

4 Regional forms of YHWH?

With reference to Mic 1:4; Exod 19; Judg 5; a plaster wall inscription from Kuntillet 'Ajrud;[46] and the pillar of cloud and fire from the book of Exodus, Othmar Keel has recently argued for a connection between YHWH (or his original home in the south) and mountains or volcanoes. Without associating YHWH with a particular, identifiable volcano, YHWH's volcanic phenomena, according to Keel, encode the "completely different" nature of YHWH's power, "which was experienced above all in the deliverance from one's enemies."[47] Thus, at least in the south, YHWH was not a variant of the Syrian weather god of the Baal/Hadad-type but rather a deity whose most basic appearance involves volcanism, earthquakes, and mountains. At the same time, Keel draws a connection to the iconographic motif of the "lord of the ostriches" (*Fig. 8*), which he propos-

---

43 On this problem see Mettinger, *No Graven Image?* (see n. 26), 143–149.

44 R. Kletter, *The Judean Pillar-Figurines and the Archaeology of Asherah* (BAR International Series 636; Oxford 1996), nos. 442, 446 and 448. See also Kletter's overview of the finds in the fortress in fig. 35.

45 Arad is often used as a parade example of aniconic religious practice or even the application of prohibition against images; see, for example, Beck, "Catalogue" (see n. 33), 182; similarly Mettinger, "Israelite Aniconism" (see n. 22), 203.

46 On the inscription see Renz and Röllig, *Handbuch I* (see n. 4), 59 (fragment 3), Keel and Uehlinger, *Gods* (see n. 7), § 144; Berlejung, "Inschriften" (see n. 7), 2.3; Ahituv *et al.*, "Inscriptions" (see n. 7), 4.2.

47 Keel, *Geschichte* (see n. 1), § 239.

es as a possible represer.tation of the southern Yʜwʜ,[48] even though this motif cannot be easily connected to volcanic mountains but rather has connections with steppes and wilderness (and possibly even with the "Kenite hypothesis"). In principle, Keel's notion that the Yʜwʜ of the south should be differentiated from the Yʜwʜ of the north both in terms of his areas of competency as well as in his iconography is convincing.

Fig. 8: Seal. Motif of the "lord of the ostriches." Keel and Uelinger, *Gods, Goddesses, and Images of God in Ancient Israel* (see n. 7), figs. 162a-162d, p. 139.

Whether an early identification of Yʜwʜ with Baal-Seth for the south[49] and an identification with Baal-shamem for the north is debatable. The latter was proposed by Herbert Niehr,[50] drawing on the earlier work of Otto Eissfeldt. Taking Phoenician religion beginning in the 10th c. B.C.E. as a starting point, in which neither Baal nor El but rather Baal-shamem (the Baal/lord of heaven) – as the protective deity cf the king, the weather god of the sky, and the highest god – was worshiped or was identified with the local highest god, Niehr noted that the tendency toward uranization was true not only of the Phoenician or the Aramean Baal/Hadad but also of the northern Israelite Yʜwʜ of the Omrides (and thus of the official cult), such that Yʜwʜ in Samaria was supposedly imagined as a celestial-solar Baal-shamem. Thus, Yʜwʜ would have been engaged in this role and adopted solar and celestial symbolism, which itself originated in Egypt but only became known to the north through Phoenician mediation.

As a result of these hypotheses that reckon with regional forms of Yʜwʜ (poly-Yahwism), the iconography of Yʜwʜ in the south would thus have had a stronger Egyptian influence, while that in the north would have had a stronger Syro-Phoenician influence (yet indirectly also Egyptianizing).[51] This could have

---

48 Keel, *Geschichte* (see n. 1), § 240f.

49 So Keel, *Geschichte* (see n. 1), § 241.

50 H. Niehr, "JHWH in der Rolle des Baalšamem," in *Ein Gott allein? JHWH-Verehrung und biblischer Monotheismus im Kontext der israelitischen und altorientalischen Religionsgeschichte* (ed. W. Dietrich and M. A. Klopfenstein; OBO 139; Fribourg and Göttingen 1994), 307–326.

51 As shown in the Nimrud Prism of Sargon II (TUAT I/4, 382), there were anthropomorphic cult statues in the local temple of Yʜwʜ of Samaria at least during the 8th c., which were carried off

also led to a characteristic regional differentiation for YHWH's symbolic animals, since Baal-Seth tends to be identified with the lion[52] and with the horned viper, while Baal-shamem tends to be connected to the bull. No matter how attractive this notion is, particularly in terms of its correlation with biblical texts that locate the bull in the north (see above) and a snake symbol (2 Kgs 18:4) and lion iconography (1 Kgs 7; yet where there is also bull symbolism) in the Jerusalem temple, ultimately it remains unprovable.

5 Summary

YHWH seems to have migrated to Palestine during the Iron I as a mountain-, storm-, and war god and to have been worshiped by various tribes there. During the course of state formation in Cisjordan, he became established as the highest god of the tribes or confederations of tribes in the north and south and later as their state and dynastic god. This first result of development is attested extrabiblically in the Mesha Stele of the 9th c., in which YHWH is known to the Moabites as the god of Israel, a known entity who is capable of having (subordinate) religious and military-political relations with Kemosh, the god of the Moabites. Precisely how YHWH was conceived of theologically and rendered iconographically at the beginning of his rise to prominence cannot be decided with confidence. Thus far, it has not been possible to identify a specific and unique iconography of YHWH. Nevertheless, various autochthonous divine iconographies in Palestine are known, which YHWH could have adopted upon his arrival and over the course of his identification with local gods (and could have possibly combined with his original iconic elements). Regional differentiations in the anthropomorphic, theriomorphic, or symbolic form of representation between the

---

by the Assyrian king. Nothing can be known of the appearance of these statues and thereby of YHWH of Samaria and his Ashera (and possibly the deity Ašimah; see Amos 8:14 cj). On this topic see C. Uehlinger, "'... und wo sind die Götter von Samarien?' Die Wegführung syrisch-palästinischer Kultstatuen auf einem Relief Sargons II. in Ḫorṣābād/Dūr-Šarrukīn," in *"Und Mose schrieb dieses Lied auf..." Festschrift O. Loretz* (ed. M. Dietrich and I. Kottsieper; AOAT 250; Münster 1998), 739–776, here 765–771; B. Becking, "The Gods in Whom They Trusted ... Assyrian Evidence for Iconic Polytheism in Ancient Israel?" in *Only One God? Monotheism in Ancient Israel and the Veneration of the Goddess Asherah* (ed. B. Becking et al.; Sheffield 2001), 151–163, here 159–163.

52 The lion, however, belongs to the entourage of a variety of goddesses; thus, B.A. Strawn, *What is Stronger than a Lion?*, *Leonine Image and Metaphor in the Hebrew Bible and the Ancient Near East* (OBO 212; Fribourg and Göttingen 2005), 252–268 regards both Ishtar and Sekhmet as having influenced "Yahweh's leonine profile" (265).

Yнwн of the northern tribes (and the later kingdom of Israel) and the tribes of the south (and the later kingdom of Judah) would thus also be possible, as were standing stones, which were hardly regarded as problematic for the cult of Yнwн in the pre-Deuteronomistic period (this only changes with Deut 16:22; 2 Kgs 18:4; and Mic 5:12).

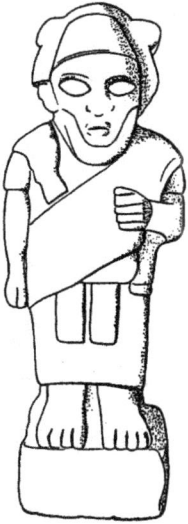

Fig. 9: Statue. National and dynastic gods as bearded males with Egyptian Atef-crown in long dress (Tell Jawa south; Amman citadel). Uehlinger, "Cult Statuary" (see n. 8), p. 118, fig. 30.

Since the national and dynastic gods of Transjordan during the Iron IIB (926/ 900 – 722/700 B.C.E.) were apparently depicted as bearded males with Egyptian Atef-crowns (Tell Jawa south; Amman citadel) in a long dress (*Fig. 9*) and their female partners were depicted as dressed rulers who expressed their nurturing aspects by holding their breasts,[53] beginning in the monarchic period one could imagine by analogy something similar for Yнwн and his partner Asherah, who had been placed alongside him in the meantime, even if this cannot be known with certainty.

Many questions must remain open, but it is at least clear that Yнwн's arrival during Iron I did not mark an end to the autochthonous divine iconographies of Palestine and the tradition that developed there to adopt and combine Syro-Egyptian elements. The origins of a hostility toward images as propagated in the biblical prohibition against images or in the prophetic polemic against images can by no means be retrojected into the Iron I or IIA, whose iconographic

---

53 Uehlinger, "Cult Statuary" (see n. 8), 112–123.

material attests to the continuation of traditional motifs (enthroned and smiting deities, goddesses supporting their breasts, goddesses with child, bulls) as well as the emergence of new motifs (e. g., the "lord of the ostriches"). On the whole, the evidence does not indicate that there were any reservations against the representation of deities in an anthropomorphic form during the Iron IIA in Palestine,[54] a time in which the traditional diversity in divine representations (e. g., theriomorphic, symbolic, and as standing stones) persisted. The 10th c. B.C.E. is *not* characterized by a reduction in the world of gods or dramatic shifts in cultic paradigms (e. g., aniconism, monotheism, or the end of goddess worship), such that YHWH's arrival in Palestine – at least from an iconographic perspective – is invisible and imperceptible to us.

---

54 Against Keel and Uehlinger, *Gods* (see n. 7), § 109.

Faried Adrom and Matthias Müller

The Tetragrammaton in Egyptian Sources – Facts and Fiction

1 Background of scholarly history

Ever since the first identification of the Tetragrammaton (YHWH) within the onomastics of the texts from Ugarit in the 1930s, all available text corpora of the 2nd
and 1st millennium BCE have been scrutinized for pre- or extra-biblical attestations of the Israelite divine name, YHWH.[1] The rich source of foreign names attested in Egyptian script attracted attention, especially in light of the biblical
Exodus-narrative with its connection to Egypt.

Appearing in 1947, Bernhard Grdseloff's[2] paper "Édôm, d'après les sources
égyptiennes" introduced a first hieroglyphically written pretender for the Tetragrammaton into the discussion. Until 1964, the hieroglyphic writings of names
Grdseloff had collected within a so-called *Fremdvölkerliste* in the Nubian temple
at Amarah-West were the only secure attestation of an Egyptian representation of
the Tetragrammaton. Then, after the publication of initial reports and copies of
inscriptions from the Nubian temple of Soleb, by a comparison of the Soleb-lists
with those in the temple at Amarah Raphael Giveon was able to add two further
attestations. In addition, Giveon identified three further possible candidates: He
introduced an attestation from the early 2nd millennium into the discussion and
pointed at two lists with names of foreign peoples and toponyms at the Ramesside temple at Medinet Habu (dated into the reign of Ramses' III.). The Egyptian
evidence is insofar interesting as it antedates the second earliest attestation of
the Tetragrammaton, i. e., that on the Moabite Mesha-stela, by at least 350 years.

Even though all involved authors usually point out the often rather speculative character of the YHWH-discussion, even the most bizarre localisation and
etymological attempts always find a grateful audience in the neighbouring scien-
tific disciplines. In recent times, one has to observe that the debate on the origins
of the YHWH-cult has moved from referring to the primary Egyptian sources to
quoting secondary literature of often doubtful standards.[3] The present paper at-

---

1 R. S. Hess, "The Divine Name Yahweh in Late Bronze Age Sources," *UF* 23 (1991), 181–188.
2 B. Grdseloff, "Édôm, d'après les sources égyptiennes," *Revue del l'histoire juive en Égypte* 1
(1947), 69–99.
3 Thus paving the way for "parallel discussion," cf. K. Koch *et al.*, *Der Gott Israels und die Götter
des Orients: Religionsgeschichtliche Studien* II (FRLANT 216; Göttingen 2007), 441.

DOI 10.1515/9783110448221-005

tempts to supply the interested non-specialist reader with the current state of the art of the sources as well as of the research trying to elucidate the various and at times quite contrary opinions on them.

2 Egyptian attestations of names associated with the Tetragrammaton

2.1 Biography of Khety (11th dynasty)

Within the archaeological season of 1913–14, the excavators of the Theban tomb[4] of a man called Khety, an overseer of the quarries,[5] discovered three stelae at the tomb's outer front that were part of the external decoration.[6] When Sir Alan H. Gardiner published a preliminary study of the texts in 1917, he addressed, among other details, a word he identified as a toponym, which he read "*Ihuiu*," and which he declared to be of "unknown" location. The respective passage of Khety's biography runs as follows:

> "[1.9] (...) I returned in peace to his (the king's) palace (*ʿḥ=f*) and brought him the best of the foreign lands in new metal from Bau(t) (𓄿𓏏), [1.10] shining (*psḏ*) metal from Ihuiu (𓇋𓂝𓅱𓏭𓈉), hard metal from Menkau (𓏠𓎡); turquoise from Hererut (𓉔𓂋𓂋𓏏𓈉) and lapis lazuli from Tefreret (𓏏𓆑𓂋𓂋𓏏), [1.11] best Saherut from the mountains, Khetauau from the mountain of Hesa/Heset (𓎛𓊃𓏏𓈉); Ranetjet from Baq-[1.12] Desheret (𓃀𓄿𓈎𓂧𓈙𓂋𓏏𓈉), staffs (*mdw.w*?) from Rashaut (𓂋𓄿𓈙𓄿𓅱𓏏) and Mesdjemet from Kehebu (𓎡𓃀𓏤)."

The mention of the "mine-country" (*bj3*, 𓃀𓇋𓄿𓈉) makes it probable to locate Khety's expedition in the Sinai.[7] Since Khety mentions that he delivers the commodities from Ihuiu to the "palace of Pharaoh" without giving any details whence and how he obtained these, any deliberations about the location of Ihuiu as well as the

---

4 According to Carnarvon's numbering tomb No. 65.

5 For the title *jmy-r š* see W. A. Ward, *Index of Egyptian administrative and religious titles of the Middle Kingdom* (Beirut 1982), 47 No. 369.

6 A. H. Gardiner, "The Tomb of a Much-Travelled Theban Official," *JEA* 4 (1917), 29. For the architecture and especially the stela of Khety see A. Hermann, *Die Stelen der thebanischen Felsgräber der 18. Dynastie* (ÄF 11; Glückstadt 1940), 40 as well as F. Kampp, *Die Thebanische Nekropole zum Wandel des Grabgedankens von der XVIII. bis zur XX. Dynastie* (Theben XIII/1–2; Mayence 1996), 108–109 with note 517; according to Gardiner the stelae were on storage in the Cairo Museum at the time of his study.

7 E. Graefe, *Untersuchungen zur Wortfamilie bj3-*, Diss. phil. (Köln 1971), 35; M. Görg, "Jahwe – ein Toponym?," *BN* 1 (1976), 182.

other mentioned toponyms are mere speculations.[8] Since then, no further attestations have been adduced that might help to locate the names of the mining areas, or the places of origin of the bartered commodities. Thus, for the toponym in question, i. e. Ihuiu, "eine Lokalisation im südpalästinischen (transjordanischen) Gebiet kann nur als möglich, keineswegs als bewiesen gelten."[9]

Based on comparative phonology, the land designated as *ʾ-h-ʾ* COUNTRY in the biography of Khety can easily be eliminated from the discussion.[10] Even though Egyptological conventions transcribe the initial sign by *j*, this sign does not represent a glide (i. e. /j/), but – especially in combination with the sign A2 of Gardiner's *Signlist*[11] as in our case – the (epi)-glottal plosive /ʾ/ (i. e. the glottal stop or *Aleph*).[12] According to James Hoch's system of transcription,[13] the whole word should be transcribed as *ʾa-hu-ʾu* COUNTRY. The representation of the vowel quality, however, should be considered with utter caution.[14] Previously, Edel,[15] Görg,[16] and Astour[17] had already pointed to this fact and the equation has been rejected for other reasons by Aḥituv[18] and Leclant.[19] Even so, Axelsson[20] and Goedicke[21] have reintroduced the toponym into the discussion quite unnecessarily.

---

8 S. Aḥituv, *Canaanite Toponyms in Ancient Egyptian Documents* (Jerusalem 1984), actually does not exclude a connection to the Tetragrammaton, but only with the forms of the name in the Medinet Habu texts.

9 Görg, "Jahwe – ein Toponym?" (see n. 7), 182.

10 Gardiner, "Tomb" (see n. 6), 28–38, especially 36 and pl. VIII.

11 A. H. Gardiner, *Egyptian Grammar, Being an Introduction to the Study of Hieroglyphs* (Oxford ³1957), 442.

12 Cf. J. E. Hoch, *Semitic Words in Egyptian Texts of the New Kingdom and Third Intermediate Period* (Princeton 1994), 503. The reasoning of E. A. Knauf is hence obsolete, cf E. A. Knauf, *Midian: Untersuchungen zur Geschichte Palästinas und Nordarabiens am Ende des 2. Jahrtausends v. Chr.* (ADPV; Wiesbaden 1988), 46 note 225.

13 Hoch, *Semitic Words* (see n. 12), 487–504.

14 See W. A. Ward, "A New Look at Semitic Personal Names and Loanwords in Egyptian," *CÉg* 71 (1996), 41–47.

15 E. Edel, *Die Ortsnamenlisten aus dem Totentempel Amenophis III* (BBB 25; Bonn 1966), 64.

16 Görg, "Jahwe – ein Toponym?" (see n. 8), 7–9, as well as idem, "YHWH – ein Toponym? Weitere Perspektiven," *BN* 101 (2000), 12.

17 M. C. Astour, "Yahweh in Egyptian Topographical Lists," in *Festschrift Elmar Edel* (ed. M. Görg and E. Pusch; ÄAT 1; Bamberg 1979), 17–34, here 18 note 10.

18 Aḥituv, *Canaanite Toponyms* (see n. 7), 122 note 295.

19 J. Leclant, "Le " tétragramme " à l'époque d'Aménophis III," in *Near Eastern Studies dedicated to H. I. H. Prince Takahito Mikasa on the Occasion of His Seventy-Fifth Birthday* (ed. M. Mori et al.; Wiesbaden 1991), 215–219, here 216 note 12.

20 L. E. Axelsson, *The Lord rose up from Seir. Studies in the History and Traditions of the Negev and Southern Judah* (CB.OT 25; Stockholm 1987), 60.

2.2 The Soleb-lists

In the Nubian temples at Soleb and Amarah-West, a total of three lists with names of foreign places and peoples survived, containing names that have been connected with the Tetragrammaton. The oldest two attestations survived in the temple of Amenhotep III. at Soleb, dedicated to the god Amun and celebrating the so-called 'Sed festival' (Heb Sed) of the king.[22] The temple's ruins were excavated between the years 1957 and 1977 by a French-Italian expedition headed by Michela Schiff Giorgini. The epigraphic documentation resided with Jean Leclant, who published parts of the names in the lists through drawings and photographs in various preliminary reports and papers.[23]

The first instance at Soleb is attested within a heavily destroyed list[24] upon an isolated block (Sb. 69: *T3 š3sw Y-h-w*[...]).[25] Another fragment of the same list is Sb. 79 and shows the remains of [*T*]*3 š3sw P-y-s-p*[...].[26]

The second instance of the Tetragrammaton at Soleb is found in the hypostyle hall (sector IV) upon column IV N4.[27] The individual columns of the hypostyle hall each carry eight to ten names and each represents a specific geographic or geopolitical area of the Egyptian map of the world.

Writings of column N4 (left half →):

---

21 H. Goedicke, "The Tetragram in Egyptian?," *The Journal of the Society for the Study of Egyptian Antiquities* 24 (1994), 24–27, here 26.

22 E. B. Porter and R. L. B. Moss, *Topographical Bibliography of Ancient Egyptian Hieroglyphic Texts, Reliefs, and Paintings VII: Nubia, the Deserts, and Outside Egypt* (Oxford 1995), 169–171; I. Hein, *Die ramessidische Bautätigkeit in Nubien* (GOF.B 22; Wiesbaden 1991), 60–61.

23 J. Leclant, "Fouilles et travaux en Égypte et au Soudan, 1961–1962," *Or.* 32 (1963), 184–219, here 202–204, idem, "Fouilles et travaux en Égypte et au Soudan, 1962–1963," *Or.* 33 (1964), 337–404, here 383–385, idem, "Les fouilles de Soleb (Nubie soudanaise), quelques remarques sur les écussons des peuples envoûtés de la salle hypostyle du secteur IV," in: *Göttinger Vorträge* (NAWG.PH 13; Göttingen 1965), 205–216.

24 M. Schiff Giorgini and C. Robichon, *Soleb 3: Le temple—description*; préparé et éd. par Nathalie Beaux (Bibliothèque générale 23; Cairo: 2002), 179 sowie M. Schiff Giorginia and C. Robichon, *Soleb 5: Le temple—bas-reliefs et inscriptions*; préparé et éd. par Nathalie Beaux (Bibliothèque générale 19; Cairo 1998), pl. 206–207.

25 Leclant, "Fouilles et travaux 1961–62," (see n. 23), 203 note 3.

26 The initial publication of Leclant, "Les fouilles de Soleb" (see n. 23), 215 fig. f, shows still the probably correct sign form with the rectangular *p*-seat (Gardiner, Sign-List: Q3) and the head of the alighting duck. In the later publications of the block the sign has been altered in such a way that it now resembles the *g*-jar stand (Gardiner, Sign-List: W11). Also the form of the back wing of the *p3*-bird has been deformed in such a way that it looks like a logographic stroke.

27 Schiff Giorgini and Robichon, *Soleb 5* (see n. 24), pl. 221.

α1   𓈖𓏲𓃀𓅱𓏤𓂋𓏤   *T3 š3sw T-r-b-r*

α2   𓈖𓏤𓇋𓇋𓅱𓀭𓅱   *T3 š3sw Y-h-w*[28]

α3   𓈖𓏤𓊃𓅓𓏏𓏏   *T3 š3sw Ś-m-t*[29]

α4–... destroyed   (destroyed)

Writings of column N4 (right half ←):

β1   𓃀𓏏𓂝𓈖𓆑▨   *B-t-ᶜ-n/f* [?][...]

β2–... destroyed   (destroyed)

Due to the extensive gaps in the list, owing to its preservation and its different sequence of names compared to other lists, the internal organisation of the Soleb-list could so far not be cleared.[30] The picture is complicated by the fact that each column contains two mirrored partial lists resulting in various mistakes of the sculptors during the transfer from the template onto the correct side of the column. Therefore, the original sequence of the place names has been disturbed[31] and thus the Soleb-list, even though closer to the "Urliste", must make way for the later lists at Amarah-West and Aksha in reconstructing the sequence. Already in one in his preliminary papers Leclant made aware of the parallelism between these lists (treated in the following section) and the Soleb one.[32]

---

28 Represented erroneously with the Aleph-vulture in Aḥituv, *Canaanite Toponyms* (see n. 8), 121. The initial copy of Leclant, "Les fouilles de Soleb" (see n. 23), Fig. c. shows distinctly the quail-chick as lowermost sign (thus, also in R. Giveon, *Les Bédouins Shosou des documents Égyptiens* [DMOA 18; Leiden 1971]. 26 Doc. 6a).

29 The representation (with D37 of Gardiner, Sign-List) in Aḥituv, *Canaanite Toponyms* (see n. 8), 177 has to be corrected accordingly (cf. Schiff Giorgini and Robichon, *Soleb* 5 (see n. 24), pl. 221).

30 Cf. the reconstruction in W. Helck, *Die Beziehungen Ägyptens zu Vorderasien im 3. und 2. Jahrtausend v. Chr.* (ÄA 5; Wiesbaden ²1971), 264–266 and E. Edel, "Die Ortsnamenlisten in den Tempeln von Aksha, Amarah und Soleb im Sudan," *BN* 11 (1980), 64 (with schematic representation). Helck's hypothesis that the position of column N IV was the last within the sequence of the northern half of the hypostyle hall is based solely on the assumption the names it contains must belong to the "desert of southern Palestine" (266).

31 Cf. N.-C. Grimal, *Civilisation pharaonique: archéologie, philologie, histoire. Les Egyptiens et la géographie du monde* (online publication; Paris 2003), 721, 723.

32 J. Leclant, "Fouilles et travaux en Égypte et au Soudan, 1960–1961," *Or.* 31 (1962), 328 n. 4 and "Fouilles et travaux 1961–1962" (see n. 23), 203 note 2; for earlier literature see cf R. Giveon, "Toponymes ouest-asiatiques à Soleb," *VT* 14 (1964), 239–255, here 239, Note 1.

2.3 The lists of Amarah-West

Approximately 50 km north of Soleb lie the settlement and its adjacent temple of Amarah-West.[33] The temple of Ramesses II. had been excavated by the English archaeologist Herbert Fairman on behalf of the Egypt Exploration Fund in the years 1938 and 1939, as well as between 1947 and 1950, and was the topic of various preliminary reports. The inner walls of the eastern half of the temple's peristyle is decorated in the lower part with an extensive list of northern peoples and place names.

Even though the first volume of the Amarah-West edition (The architectural report) contains a large amount of results as well as images taken from Fairman's legacy,[34] the proper epigraphic documentation and publication is still lacking. So far, the texts are available only in Kenneth A. Kitchen's handwritten copies in his "Ramesside Inscriptions."[35]

Hieroglyphic writings (northern wall, east of the gate ←):

93   *T3 š3sw Š-ʿ-r-r*

94   *T3 š3sw R-b-n*

95   *T3 š3sw P-y-s-p-y-s*

96   *T3 š3sw Š-m-t*

97   *T3 š3sw Y-h-w*[36]

98   *T3 š3sw <T>-r-b-r*[37]

---

33 Hein, *Ramessidische Bautätigkeit* (see n. 22), 51–52, Tafel 17.

34 P. Spencer, *Amara West I: The architectural report. With contributions by P.L. Shinnie, F.C. Fraser and H.W. Parker* (MEES 63; London 1997).

35 Porter/Moss, *Topographical Bibliography VII* (see n. 22), 161 (24)–(27) as well as (29)–(31); K. A. Kitchen, *Ramesside Inscriptions* II (Oxford 1979), 215–217.

36 See Kitchen, *Ramesside Inscriptions* II (see n. 37), 217 (10). The assumed change from the sign *w3* to the sign actually read as *rwḏ/3r/3j* can be easily explained as a copy error from a hieratic template, see Görg, "Jahwe – ein Toponym?" (see n. 7), 185. The Soleb-list shows a quail chick (read *w*) at the end of the name instead of a vulture (read *3*) but an alike emendation seems easily possible. Görg, "Jahwe – ein Toponym?" (see n. 7), 185, considered this as unlikely since the scribe of the Amarah-list otherwise displays no difficulties in discriminating between the Aleph-sign and the *w*-quail chicken. In Görg, "YHWH – ein Toponym?" (see n. 7 and 16), 11 Görg refers to an opinion expressed by Elmar Edel: Edel transferred his analysis of the scribal mistakes in the list of African place names of Thutmosis III. to our list and concluded that "natürliche Lesung *Y-h-w3-3* anzusetzen sei" (the natural reading should be *Y-h-w3-3*).

Commentary:

(93) The starting point of all identification and localisation attempts made hitherto for the Shasu-names, especially the *Y-h-w* one, is the first name of the Shasu sequence at Amarah-West: *Š-ʿ-r-r*.[38] Assuming that this equates with the otherwise also in New Kingdom texts attested "Sëir," we would at least be able to recognize one name of the Shasu sequence. Proceeding from there, i.e. that Egyptian *Š-ʿ-r-r* is identical with the Old Testament place name Sëir (or Mount Sëir), one might further assume that the whole Shasu sequence can be located in southern Palestine or the Edomite realm.[39]

As later researchers[40] pointed out correctly, this line of argument developed by Grdseloff is circular: Since Yʜwʜ's origin is, according to the Old Testament, in the Kenite-Edomite area, the *Š-ʿ-r-r* of the Amarah-list must be identical with the biblical Sëir. The mention of Sëir on the other hand proves Yʜwʜ's descent from the southern Palestine area (Edom).[41] To establish the identification be-

---

37 Giveon, "*Toponymes,*" (see n. 32), 244 refers to the reading of B. Grdseloff and corrects the latter's *irbir* to *twrbir*, since in the list ETL XXVII (Medinet Habu) the number 116 (*T-w-r*) appears next to *Y-h-ꜣ* (No. 115).
38 At first in Grdseloff, "Édôm" (see n. 2), 79–80; M. Weippert, *Edom. Studien und Materialien zur Geschichte der Edomiter auf Grund schriftlicher und archäologischer Quellen* (Diss. Tübingen 1971), 31; idem, "Semitische Nomaden des zweiten Jahrtausends. Über die Šꜣśw der ägyptischen Quellen," *Biblica* 55 (1974), 265–280, here 270–271; M. Görg, "Jahwe – ein Toponym?" (see n. 7), 12–13 Anm. 34; E. A. Knauf, *Midian* (see n. 12), 50–51.
39 See for instance K.A. Kitchen, "The Egyptian Evidence on Ancient Jordan," in *Early Edom and Moab. The Beginning of the Iron Age in Southern Jordan* (ed. P. Bienkowski; SAM 7; Sheffield 1992), Fig. 3.2. The majority of the more recent biblical scholarly/exegetic literature adheres to this line of reasoning (see e.g. J. Day, *In search of pre-exilic Israel. Proceedings of the Oxford Old Testament seminar* [JSOT S 406; London et al. 2006], 50–51). The basic assumption is that the first name in the sequence works as a headline (Leittoponym) for the following place names, a system to be seen in the lists on the statue bases from Kom el-Hettân (see E.Edel and M. Görg, *Die Ortsnamenlisten im nördlichen Säulenhof des Totentempels Amenophis' III.* [ÄAT 50; Wiesbaden 2005], 45).
40 At first in Astour, "Yahweh in Egyptian Topographical Lists" (see n. 17), 21.
41 Similarly S. Herrmann, "Der alttestamentliche Gottesname," in *Gesammelte Studien zur Geschichte und Theologie des Alten Testaments* (ed. S. Herrmann; TB 75; München 1986), 76–88 and more recently T. Schneider, "The first documented occurence of the God Yahweh? (Book of the Dead Princeton "Roll 5")," *JANE* 7 (2008), 113–120, here 114 as well as M. Leuenberger, "Jhwhs Herkunft aus dem Süden. Archäologische Befunde – biblische Überlieferungen – historische Korrelationen," *ZAW* 122 (2010). 1–19, here 4–8 reprinted in: M. Leuenberger, *Gott in Bewegung. Religions- und theologiegeschichtliche Beiträge zu Gottesvorstellungen im alten Israel* (FAT 76; Tübingen 2011), 14–22.

tween *Š-ʿ-r-r* and Sëir, Grdseloff and those scholars following him,[42] have to explain the hieroglyphic writing of the name in the Amarah-West list as an error for *Š-ʿ-r* or as "common" duplication of the *r*.[43]

While the identification of the single graphemes with the assumed phonemes poses no problem at all (Egyptian <*s*> = Semitic *š* /s/; Egyptian <ʿ> = Semitic /ʿ/; Egyptian <*r*> = Semitic /r/[44]), the equation of the whole complex carries the problem that <*r*> appears graphically twice. Grdseloff[45] emended this to *s-ʿ-r* based on Ramesside inscriptions and texts mentioning a tribe/people called *s-ʿ-r*[46] or a similarly written place name.[47] He assumed the first <*r*> to be a mistake for the sign ꜡ʒ of the hieratic template. Weippert[48] used a similar explanation by identifying the supposedly wrongly written sign as an original book roll sign. Görg[49] finally reasoned that the whole double <*r*>-writing should be considered a graphic peculiarity of the Ramesside writing system showing this feature more often. The latter is indeed a well-known phenomenon[50] and is usually expressed by two <*r*>-graphemes positioned one above the other, with the lower marked in addition by an ideographic stroke. The whole group serves to express graphically the fact that the rhotic sound was retained.[51] In our case, however, the last group consists of a combination of a double stroke, an <*r*> and a stroke. This group is typically used if a syllable final rhotic sound had to be expressed. According to

---

42 M. Weippert, "Semitische Nomaden des zweiten Jahrtausends" (see n. 38), 271 note 1.

43 See Görg, "Jahwe – ein Toponym?," (see n. 7), 185 note 34 with instances supposedly proving his interpretation as duplication.

44 Which rhotic phoneme actually is represented by the sign is irrelevant for our question; Egyptian might have had at least two different rhotic sounds, cf. M. Müller, "Ägyptische Phonologie? Möglichkeiten und Grenzen linguistischer Modelle bei der Beschreibung des Lautsystems einer extinkten Sprache," in *Methodik und Didaktik in der Ägyptologie. Herausforderungen eines kulturwissenschaftlichen Paradigmenwechsels in den Altertumswissenschaften* (ed. A. Verbovsek et al.; Ägyptologie und Kulturwissenschaften IV; München 2011), 509–531, here 519.

45 Grdseloff, "Édôm," (see n. 2), 79–80.

46 Thus, for instance in the Great Harris Papyrus (pHarris I 76,9–10): "I smote the *Š-ʿ-r* from the Shasu tribe" cf. P. Grandet, *Le Papyrus Harris I* (BEt 109; Kairo ²2005), 337 (vol. I) and 243–245 (vol. II).

47 As *ḏw n-Š-ʿ-r* in an epithet of Ramesses II. upon a column at Tanis ("savage wild lion who seized the Shasu and hacked up the mountain of *Š-ʿ-r* with his strong arm/sword"), see Kitchen, *Ramesside Inscriptions II* (see n. 36), 408,16–409,1.

48 Weippert, "Semitische Nomaden des zweiten Jahrtausends" (see n. 38), 271 note 1.

49 Görg, "Jahwe – ein Toponym?" (see n. 7), 12 note 34.

50 See e.g. A. Erman, *Neuägyptische Grammatik* (Leipzig ²1933), §§48–51; F. Junge, *Neuägyptisch. Einführung in die Grammatik* (Wiesbaden ³2008), 34–35.

51 The rhotic approximant /ɹ/ of Egyptian disappears in syllable final position. If /ɹ/ is retained in the onset of the syllable this fact is marked graphically via the mentioned double writing.

the evidence gathered by Hoch, this group does *always* represent an actually realised rhotic phoneme.[52] Thus, the assumption of a double graphic representation would be highly redundant.

Graphemic problems result also from the other explanations and emenda-
tions. Even though the complementation of bi- or tri-consonantal signs is rather
common in the Egyptian writing system, but – especially with ꜥꜣ[53] – in Ramesside
times, rather by the succeeding than the preceding consonant. In those cases in
which the initial consonants appear, it follows the sign ꜣ.[54] Therefore, Grdseloff's[55] emendation would result in a combination which – to put it positively –
would be unusual and hence, would be no real improvement compared to the
actual writing.

Similar problems arise from Weippert's[56] emendation of the book roll sign
beneath the sign <ꜥ>: Even though attested as the graphemic complement of
ꜣ, within the system of group writing, simple <ꜥ> is not used alone,[57] and appears
only with complementing on <y> or <w>. Thus again, the emendation results in
no improvement compared to the actual writing.

Hence, one cannot but state that the list at Amarah contains a place name
with the consonants *Š-ꜥ-r-r*, definitely more than necessary for an equation
with the Mount Sëir. If one would insist on this equation, one would have to
look for an emendation that would reduce the amount of rhotic graphemes. Otherwise, one cannot but look for a place name that suits the attested writing better
(see Astour's suggestion below).

(94) According to Grdseloff, the name *R-b-n* should be equated with the
Transjordanian Laban (Deut 1:1) = Libnah (Num 33:20 – 21).[58] Giveon refers to "Libona, l'actuel Khirbet el Libben, au sud d'Amman." Ahituv[59] and Wilson[60] sug-

---

52 Hoch, *Semitic Words* (see n. 12), 509; see also the latter's analysis Hoch, *Semitic Words* (see n.
12), 407.
53 Also with other horizontally arranged bi- or tri-consonantal signs. The use of initial consonants is more common with vertically arranged signs.
54 See the writings of the various lemmata ꜣ (and derivations) in *Wörterbuch der aegyptischen
Sprache* I (ed. A. Erman and H. Grapow; Berlin 1926), 161 – 168; see also the use of ꜣ in the system
of group writing in Th. Schneider, *Asiatische Personennamen in ägyptischen Quellen des Neuen
Reiches* (OBO 114; Fribourg and Göttingen 1992), 370.
55 Grdseloff, "Édôm" (see n. 2), 79 – 80.
56 Weippert, "Semitische Nomaden des zweiten Jahrtausends" (see n. 38), 271 note 1.
57 See Th. Schneider, *Asiatische Personennamen* (see n. 54), 369 – 370.
58 Grdseloff, "Édôm" (see n. 2), 80. Cf. Ahituv, *Canaanite Toponyms* (see n. 8), 129.
59 Ahituv, *Canaanite Toponyms* (see n. 8), 129.
60 K.A. Wilson, *The Campaign of Pharaoh Shoshenq I into Palestine* (FAT 9/II; Tübigen 2005), 133.

gested Tell Abu Seleimeh behind esh-Sheikh Zuweid. From the phonological point of view nothing speaks against the equation with Laban nor with Libona.

(95) Görg suggested for the name *P-y-s-p-y-s* a connection to the name *Nāpiš*, a son Ismael's (Gen 25:15; 1 Chr 5:19).[61] He furthermore suggested, confirmed by Edel,[62] that the duplicated writing of an absolutely used possessive pronoun, had been used to represent the place name.Thus, the name could have been vocalized as Paspas. Grdseloff assumed a connection to Semitic *bisbâs* "muscadier" or to the meaning "coloured" which he connected with the Beduin habit to colour their tents.

(96) Grdseloff saw in the name *Š-m-t* a "gentilice" (designation of a race) which he equated with the Biblical Shimatites (1 Chr 2:55). These he identified with the Kenites and hence part of the nomadic groups of the Arabah (biblical Sëir).[63] Weippert assumed to identify them as the tribe Šammāh (Gen 36:13, 17).[64] However, as Anson F. Rainey's pointed out, the Egyptian grapheme <s> is never used to represent the Semitic post-alveolar fricative / ʃ / in secure equations.[65]

(97) According to Grdseloff, this represents "*incontestably*" the name "Jahwă." He felt confirmed in the reading of the first two signs by the Late Period instance *pȝ-tȝ-(n)-yht* (stele Berlin 1107), which he interprets as "la terre de Jahoud."[66] He assumed an Edomite locality but confessed that "*il nous manque encore tous les éléments*" for a specific localisation. Yet based on the biblical context he is rather confident that this "*ville de Jahwă*" must have been a "*centre ḳénite*" ("*il n'y a pas de doute que notre localité édômite portait d'après notre source qui date du règne de Ramsès II (...) le nom sacré du dieu des Israélites*").[67] Giveon followed Grdseloff in that issue and read "*Yahwe en terre de Shosou.*" For

---

61 Görg, "Jahwe – ein Toponym?," (see n. 7), 186 assumed a "*eine reduplizierte Bildung des Stamnes NPŠ ("zahlreich sein")*." Thus suggestion has been rejected by Aḥituv, *Canaanite Toponyms* (see n. 8), 155 without further discussion.

62 Edel, "Die Ortsnamenlisten" (see n. 30), 78.

63 Giveon, "Toponymes ouest-asiatiques à Soleb" (see n. 32), 244 refers to the place name *Š-m-y* in the list ETL XXVII, 39 (Ramesses III.), although without drawing any further conclusions: "*Samat et Pyspys sont inconnus*" (Giveon, "Toponymes ouest-asiatiques à Soleb" [see n. 32], 245).

64 See Weippert, "Semitische Nomaden des zweiten Jahrtausends" (see n. 38), 271.

65 A. Rainey, "Review of Hoch, Semitic Words," *IOS* 18 (1998), 431–453, here 452.

66 Grdseloff, "Édôm" (see n. 2), 81. This goes back to Sethe who, however, has not been able to substantiate his assumption further, see K. Sethe, *Spuren der Perserherrschaft in der späteren ägyptischen Sprache* (NGWG.PH; Berlin 1916), 128–129.

67 Grdseloff, "Édôm" (see n. 2), 82.

him the identity of the place name written in Egyptian and the name of the Israelite deity is certain: "*Le nom est le tétragramme.*"[68]

(98) Grdseloff knew only the defective writing from Soleb and identified the place hence with Arbela, a place to the east of the Tigris river (ancient Urbilum, nowadays Irbil/Arbil). In addition, he suggested a place called Irbid in Transjordan (Beth-Arbel).[69] Giveon corrected Grdseloff's *W-r-b-r* to *<T>-r-b-r*, since the list ETL XXVII (Medinet Habu) shows under #116 the name *T-w-r* close to the name *Y-h-ꜣ* (#115).[70]

In his analysis of the lists at Soleb, Amarah-West, and Akscha, Edel[71] was able to show that, despite their different direct templates, all three of these lists go back to a single "Urliste", the sequence of which can be reconstructed according to the sequence of the Amarah-list.[72] Confronting the Soleb- with the Amarah-list (see table 1), shows that the scribe of the Soleb-list placed the Shasu-sequence in reversed order, and that his template must have contained at least one further name (β1 Beth-Anath?) which was omitted at Amarah-West.

Despite the considerable uncertainties in the identification and localisation of the names in the Soleb- and Amarah-lists, and the numerous premises necessary to assume localities in southern Palestine or the Transjordan area, most scholars accept the southern location based on the identification of Sëir (Amarah-list #92).[73] However, this interpretation is not without alternative, as a further list with names shows, in which the Tetragrammaton is assumed to appear.

2.4 The Medinet Habu-lists (20th dynasty)

As early as 1964, Giveon referred to possible parallels of the writings of the Shasu-sequence at Soleb and Amarah-West in the great list of Ramesses III. at

---

68 Giveon, *Bédouins Shosou* (see n. 28), 26–27; similarly in W. Helck, "Die Bedrohung Palästinas durch einwandernde Gruppen am Ende der 18. und am Anfang der 19. Dynastie," *VT* 18 (1968), 472–480, here 477–478. ("Die Lokalisierung dieser einzelnen Landschaften ist bisher nicht möglich, was besonders wegen der Landschaft Jahwe wichtig wäre, weil doch sicherlich ihr Gott von den Israeliten zu ihrem Gott gemacht worden ist").

69 Grdseloff, "Édôm" (see n. 2), 82–83.

70 Giveon, "Toponymes ouest-asiatiques à Soleb" (see n. 32), 244.

71 Since the list at Aksha (Ramesses II.) ends with #29, it cannot be used in this issue (thus also Edel, "Die Ortsnamenlisten" [see n. 30], 64).

72 See Edel, "Die Ortsnamenlisten" (see n. 30).

73 See Görg, "Jahwe – ein Toponym?" (see n. 7), 185: "Mit einem gewissen Grad an Wahrscheinlichkeit lassen sich die Namen in Transjordanien und Südpalästina lokalisieren."

the 1st pylon at Medinet Habu.[74] This list at the southern tower of the 1st pylon preserves 125 cartouches with names. These names are divided according to their geographic distribution and their sources into three groups.[75] Group I consists of the names 1–69 with names from northern Mesopotamia from the Transtigris area.[76] According to Michael Astour, this list can be traced back to a list of Thutmosis III. Group II with the names 76–94 and 98–110 is a copy of a list of Ramesses II. at Karnak, only with their order reversed.[77] Group III with the numbers 70–75 and 111–121 should be traced back, according to Astour, to a nowadays lost list of Ramesses II. Within this third group, one finds as number 115 the place name *Y-h* [hieroglyphs],[78] which Giveon originally connected with the *Y-h-w-* writings at Amarah-West and Soleb.[79]

The identification and localisation of the names of this third group in which the supposed Tetragrammaton-writing *Y-h* appears is difficult, in want of parallels. Giveon suggests for #116 a connection to the *T-r-b-r* of the Soleb-list.[80] Görg wanted to connect "at least the names 111–112" with places in southern Palestine,[81] and posed the question whether two separate names might hide behind the writing *T-w-r-b-r* in the Soleb- and the Amarah-list. For this, he refers to #112 (list XXVII) naming a place *B-w-r/B-r* that could be complemented with #116 *T-w-r* to yield the Soleb-name. Görg thought to identify in #112 the element *br* "well." In addition, he suggested to associate *T-w-r* (#116) with the Itureans.[82]

---

74 Giveon connected Soleb N IV α1 *T-r-b-r* with ETL XXVII #116, Soleb N IV α2 *Y-h-w* with ETL XXVII, #115 and XXIX, #13 (*Y-h*). Soleb N IV α3 *Š-m-t* with ETL XXVII, #39.

75 Astour, "Yahweh in Egyptian Topographical Lists" (see n. 17), 24.

76 M.C. Astour, "Mesopotamian and Transtigridian Place Names in the Medinet Habu Lists of Ramses III," *JAOS* 88 (1968), 733–752, here 733–734.

77 Helck, *Beziehungen* (see n. 30), 237

78 J. Leclant's refusal of this additional possible instance of the Tetragrammaton is left without explanation (cf Leclant, "Le "tetragramme"" [see n. 19], 216 with note 12).

79 Giveon, "Toponymes ouest-asiatiques à Soleb" (see n. 32), 244. The sign Z4 (Gardiner, Sign-List) has according to Görg, "Jahwe – ein Toponym?" (see n. 7), 186 "lediglich ornamentale Funktion" (merely ornamental function). Also the Aleph-sign of the final group is considered by Görg as "entwertet/indifferent" (devalued/indifferent) in its vocalic reference. The identical writing reappears in a short list at the 1st pylon of Medinet Habu (J. J. Simons, *Handbook for the Study of Egyptian Topographical Lists relating to Western Asia* [Leiden 1937], list XXIX, #13). However, as the latter list seems nothing but a random collection of names taken from the larger list, the latter reference is of no relevance in the present discussion.

80 Giveon, "Toponymes ouest-asiatiques à Soleb" (see n. 32), 244.

81 Görg, "Jahwe – ein Toponym?" (see n. 7).

82 Sons of Ismael according to the OT tradition (Gen 25:15; 1 Chr 1:31); see Görg, "Jahwe – ein Toponym?" (see n. 7), 186–187. Görg carries on with additional prosopographic identifications: Thus he wants to recognize in #111 (*rwjr*) the biblical name Reüel, a son of Esau (1 Chr 1:35, 37)

A completely different track was followed in Michael C. Astour's work of 1964:[83] Ignoring the conceived wisdom of the Sëir-identification, seeing *Y-h* neutral as a geographical name, and disregarding the Old Testament tradition of a southern origin of the YΞWH cult, he extended the geographic realm of possible candidates into the whole Syrian-Palestinian area. Thus, Astour was able to present identifications with topo- or oronymes in the northern Palestinian and Lebanese area for most of the names in the third group of the Medinet Habu-list.

Further confirmation to Astour's reconstruction is possibly added by the Solebname β1, which is positioned in opposite direction to the Shasu-sequence on the column N IV, and which can be reconstructed with Edel as Beth-Anath.[84] The close proximity of this name with a list of southern Palestinian mountain areas seems of limited plausibility. The same must be said for the mention of Ginti-Kirmil (Amarah-list #98) directly following the Shasu-sequence. Both place names, disregarded by the majority of scholars dealing with the Shasu-sequence, do speak in favour of Astour's suggestions, particularly since the place Ginti-Kirmil is connected to Sëir in another context (EA 288,26; 289,18).[85]

The identification of the name 'Ain Shasu in a list of Amenhotep III. at Kom el-Hettân,[86] and the Palestine-list of Thutmosis III.[87] at Karnak by Rainey[88] and

(see also Weippert's suggestion to connect *smt* with Shamma, the son of Reüel, in: Weippert, "Semitische Nomaden des zweiten Jahrtausends" [see n. 38], 271–272). The #122 (*krn*) reminded him of Kerān (Gen 36:26; 1 Chr 1:41), also connected to Sëir. A similar genealogical connection Görg proposed already for the name *Pyspys* by connecting it to *Nāpiš*, being in turn a son of Ismael (see above).

83 Astour, "Mesopotamian and Transtigridian Place Names" (see n. 76).

84 The reading is refused by Aḥituv, *Canaanite Toponyms* (see n. 8), 75 Anm. 105a. Instead the name should be read as *Beth-'fy*(?). And indeed the copy in Schiff Giorgini and Robichon, *Soleb 5* (see n. 24), pl. 221 shows instead of the expected *n* the head of a *f*-viper. Our photographic documentation did not confirm this though since the surface is severely damaged in this area. Elusive is also the description of Schiff Giorgini and Robichon, *Soleb 3* (see n. 24), 123 of the cartouche as *"presque intact,"* even though the lower third is destroyed. Our images show traces in the lower part of the cartouche that might have been part of the throw-stick-sign typically used to mark foreign place names (Gardiner, Sign-List: N25) which have not been noted in the publication. The inaccuracy of the drawings of the Soleb-list (in Schiff Giorgini and Robichon, *Soleb 5* [see n. 24]) is as deplorable as the fact that damages and breaks are never properly marked.

85 For the reading and identification see Edel, "Die Ortsnamenlisten," (see n. 30), 78.

86 Edel, *Ortsnamenlisten* (see n. 15), 25 as well as Edel and Görg, *Ortsnamenlisten* (see n. 39), 106.

87 Simons, *Handbook* (see n. 79), 111 (Liste I, 5).

Weippert,[89] proved that the Shasu-groups operated also far to the north within northern Palestinian territory. The mentioned 'Ain Shasu can be located with all probability in the Lebanese Biqā, which in return adds further weight to Astour's suggestions.[90]

ETL I (T III.)	Soleb (A. III.)	Amarah-West (R. II.)	ETL XXVII (R. III.)	Identification acc. to Astour (1979)
(337) Š-ʿ-r-r	–	(92) Š-ʿ-r-r	–	Šeḫlal (?)
–	–	–	(70) H-r-n-m	Hirmil (at Orontes)
(10) R-b-n	–	(93) R-b-n	(71) R-b-n-t	Labana
–	–	–	(72) B-t-d-q-n	Daqqun/Dqun
–	–	–	(73) Q-r-b-q	'Ayn al-Baqq
–	–	–	(74) K-r-m-y-m	not identified
(73) Š-b-t-n	–	–	(75) Š-b-d-n	Riblah
	P-y-s-p[...][91]	(94) P-y-s-p-y-s	–	'Ayn Fišfiš
	α3 Š-m-t	(95) Š-m-t	–[92]	Šāmāt
–	–	–	(111) R-w-j-r	Lawiyah/Galmidun
–	–	–	(112)	see below
–	–	–	(113) Q-m-q	Ḍahr/Wadi al-Ǧimmāqah
–	–	–	(114) Q-b-r-ʿ	Ḍuhūr Qaʿbūrā
	α2 Y-h-w	(96) Y-h-ȝ	(115) Y-h	not identified
	α1 T-r-b-r	(97) <T>w-r-b-r	(116)+(112) T-r B-r	(Gabal) Turbul
–	–	–	(117) Š-n-n-r	Sanir
–	–	–	(118) M-n-d-r	Mandarah
–	–	–	(119) Ḍ-b-b	Dabbābīyah

---

88 A. F. Rainey, ²*EAT.S*, 91; idem, "El-ʿAmarna Notes," *UF* 6 (1974), 297; idem, "Toponymic Problems," *Tel Aviv* 2 (1975), 13–14.

89 M. Weippert, "Die Nomadenquelle. Ein Beitrag zur Topographie der Biqāʾ im 2. Jahrtausend v. Chr.," in *Archäologie und Altes Testament. Festschrift für Kurt Galling zum 8. Januar 1970* (ed. A. Kuschke and E. Kutsch; Tübingen 1970), 259–272, here 263–265; Weippert, "Semitische Nomaden des zweiten Jahrtausends" (see n. 38), 273.

90 A further possible case has been described in M. Görg, "Thutmosis III. und die šȝsw-Region," *JNES* 38 (1979), 199–202, here 201–202. Against this identification and localisation of the "well of the nomads" E. Lipiński, *On the skirts of Canaan in the Iron Age: historical and topographical researches* (OLA 153; Leuven et al. 2006), 362–363, raised some rather weak and altogether unconvincing counterarguments. Astour's reconstruction has been accepted by J. C. de Moor, *The Rise of Yahwism: The Roots of Israelite Monotheism* (BEThL XCI; Leuven 1990), 112 with note 51. The northern localisation of the place names was dismissed out of hand rather *ex cathedra* by Axelsson, *The Lord rose up* (see n. 20) and Knauf, *Midian* (see n. 12), 46–47.

91 Attested in Sb.II 69.

92 Giveon, "Toponymes ouest-asiatiques à Soleb" (see n. 32), 244 refers here to Š-m-y (#39) of the list ETL XXVII (Medinet Habu).

Continued

ETL I (T III.)	Soleb (A. III.)	Amarah-West (R. II.)	ETL XXVII (R. III.)	Identification acc. to Astour (1979)
(122) *ʾI-m-t*	–	–	(120) *ʾI-m-t*	Hamath (Ḥamāh)
–	–	–	(121) *D̲-w-r*	Tyrus
(97) *B-t-i-n-t*	β1 *B-t ʿ-[n-t]*	–	–	Beth Anath
–	β2 [	(98) *Q-n-t-k-ʾ-m-r*	–	–
–	β3 [	(99) *Q-ʿ-s*	–	–
–	β4 [	(100) *M-t-ʿ-w*	–	–

table 1: Sequences of names discussed from the lists of Thutmosis III. (ETL I), Amenhotep III. (Soleb), Ramesses II. (Amarah-West), and Ramesses III. (Theben-West, Medinet Habu) in synopsis with the respective identifications (after M.C. Astour, in: FS. Edel (see n. 18), 17 – 34)

Astour's suggestions to locate the place names of the Shasu-sequence from the Soleb- and Amarah-lists in northern Palestine do not exclude their presence in the southern (biblical Edomite) area in the 18th dynasty. The Shasu's sphere of action is just extended significantly to the north to achieve a better consistency with the information supplied by the contemporary Egyptian sources. Thus, Görg's suggested localisation of the place name *T3ʾ š3ʾsw P3-wnw* in the Amarah-list (#45) retains a certain plausibility, as both Edel and Görg showed convincingly that the name hides behind the rather peculiar writing. Whether this toponym actually belongs – despite its position in the list – to the Shasu-sequence (Amarah-West #93–97), and thus to the same geographical horizon, still remains uncertain at present. Görg opted for a connection with the Edomite mining centre פוּנֹן Punon (modern Feinan).[93]

Recently, Manfred Görg introduced a further interpretation of the "Egyptian" Shasu-names by connecting them with (Hebrew) designations of animals or colour terms, suggesting to consider these as tribal names.[94]

Unlike with the above discussed and dismissed instance from the 11th dynasty biography of Kheti, no grapho-phonetic obstacles speak against an identifica-

---

93 M. Görg, "Punon – ein weiterer Distrikt der š3św-Beduinen?," *BN* 19 (1982), 15–21, here 19.
94 Görg, "YHWH – ein Toponym?" (see n. 7 and 16). Sëir would then not only be a place name but also the designation of the he-goat, the Shasu-name *P-y-s-p-y-s* was connected by Görg with the Akkadian *paspasu* "duck," and for *R-b-n* he referred to Hebrew *laban* "white," probably connected to the colour of an animal's hide. Accordingly, he connected *Ś-m-t* with the Akkadian word *sāmtu* "redness." Görg suggested also for *T-r-b-r* a connection to animals (*srbl* "cock's comb").

tion of the writing *y-h-w*, that is attested in Soleb und elsewhere, with the Hebrew form of the name of God. One might consider the missing final <*h*>, but this may not have been considered as distinctive, since it is positioned in the absolute final position. Similar phenomena are attested with the representation of other words.[95] The plausibility of Manfred Görg's[96] suggested etymology from the name of a bird (of prey) must be valued by scholars of Hebrew.

2.5 Additional attestations of the Tetragrammaton in Egyptian sources

Kurt Sethe, in his study on "traces of the Persian rule," translated the place name *p3-t3 Y-h-t* of the stele Berlin 1107 as "the land of the Jews."[97] Henri Gauthier included it without further discussion as the possible writing of *Y-h* = Jahwe (YHWH) into his *Dictionnaire Géographique*,[98] and Jean Leclant quoted it in 1963 as a parallel for the "*Y-h-w*" of the Soleb-lists.[99]

Recently, Thomas Schneider referred to the personal name (𓃾𓏤𓈖𓏤𓆑) in an Egyptian Book of the Dead papyrus (BD Princeton "Roll 5," 18th or early 19th dyn.). According to Schneider, the owner's name is a theophoric sentence-name in Egyptian transcription designating "My lord is the shepherd of Yah." Schneider considers Yah to be an abbreviated form of the Tetragrammaton and it is connected by him with the writings in the Shasu-sequence at Soleb and Amarah-West.[100] However, his presuppositions in connection to the Soleb- and Amarah-instances, as well as his conclusions thereof, seem dubious from a methodo-

---

95 See for instance Hoch, *Semitic Words* (see n. 12), No. 7, No. 34, No. 38 or No. 41 (the written *t* in the Egyptian form can be ignored as any *t* still pronounced should have been written as the combination *t+w* or by the sign *tj*). The instances given contain only examples considered absolutely sure by Hoch.

96 Görg, "YHWH – ein Toponym" (see n. 7 and 16), 13–14.

97 However, Sethe, who pointed out that writing, was unable to substantiate this claim any further, see Sethe, *Perserherrschaft* (see n. 66), 128–129.

98 H. Gauthier, *Dictionnaire des noms géographiques contenus dans les textes hiéroglyphiques* I (Cairo 1925), 171 (Stele Berlin #1107). See also H. Schäfer, "Ein Phönizier auf einem ägyptischen Grabstein der Ptolemäerzeit," *ZÄS* 40 (1902–03), 32, Taf. 1 as well as K. Sethe, *UÄA* II: *Hieroglyphische Urkunden der griechisch-römischen Zeit* (Leipzig 1904), 164 (12).

99 Leclant, "Fouilles et travaux 1961–1962" (see n. 23), 203 note 3.

100 Schneider, "The first documented occurrence" (see n. 41), 114 reasons that "*yhw3*" would be a mountainous region linked to the worship of a god named Yahweh after the place of worship. This is in agreement with passages from the Old Testament where Yahweh is said to have risen up from Seir (Edom)." The writing in Soleb/Amarah-West would thus refer not directly to the divine name but to "a place associated with his cult."

logical point of view. Especially since his interpretation of the Soleb- and Amarah-instances follows the biblical tradition verbatim, as well as the fact that he is compelled to assume, for the sake of his argument, that the Shasu-sequence' *Y-h-w* was a divine name transferred into a toponym, for which there is no evidence.[101]

Karl-Theodor Zauzich compiled additional (partly unpublished) attestations from Demotic sources in the expression *rmṯ jhw(3)* which he interprets as 'man from Juda.'[102] However, the construction is used in Demotic word formation with toponyms (designating a place of origin, such as *rmṯ-kmy* 'man-Egypt' > 'Egyptian'), divine names (designating a devotion to or a connection with a deity, such as *rmṯ-inp* 'man-Anubis' > 'person dedicated to Anubis'), infinitives (designating a profession, such as *rmṯ-ḥn* 'man-row' > 'oarsman, rower') as well as 'adjectives' (designating a characteristic or virtue, such as *rmṯ-swg* 'man-stupid' > 'idiot').[103] Zauzich, however, assumes the word formation *rmṯ* to equate an otherwise unrecognized suffix *=da* in the word 'Judah,' thus *rmṯ-jhw* = Jud-ean = Ju=da. Be that as it may, the data do not help to settle the question whether *jhw(3)* designates a toponym or a divine name.

Purely into the realm of imagination belongs De Moor's idea of the identity of the Egyptian chancellor Beja (Bay) with the Biblical figure of Moses.[104] He extends on Knauf's idea that the Asian Beja (Bay) had used the political unrest in the aftermath of the Sea peoples' raid to flee with a group of loyal subjects to Egypt.[105] According to de Moor, the final syllable –ja in Beja's (Bay's) name would represent a shortened form of the Israelite name of God.

---

101 Schneider, "The first documented occurrence" (see n. 41), 119 concluded "Yah would thus be the use of the later divine name as a toponym which, in its long form, is attested in Egyptian toponym lists."

102 K.-T. Zauzich, "Der ägyptische Name der Juden," in: *In the Shadow of Bezalel. Aramaic, Biblical, and Ancient Near Eastern Studies in Honor of Bezalel Porten* (ed. A. Botta; CHANE 60; Leiden and Boston 2013), 409–416, here 412–413.

103 See W. Spiegelberg, *Demotische Grammatik* (Heidelberg 1925), §28, augmented by W. Erichsen, *Demotisches Glossar* (Copenhagen 1945), 247–248.

104 Similarly also A.F. Rainey in his review of de Moor, "Rise of Yahwism," *JNES* 60 (2001), 148 "one is confronted with impossible assumptions based on flimsy and often untenable interpretations of archaeological or philological evidence." A critical assessment of the sources on the Siptah-Beja-problem has been presented by T. Schneider, "Siptah und Beja: Neubeurteilung einer historischen Konstellation," *ZÄS* 130 (2003), 134–146.

105 An overview of de Moor's argumentation as well as some counter arguments can be found in Hess, "The Divine Name" (see n. 1), 182.

3 Town, land or mountain? Topographical consideration about the Egyptian evidence

All scholars who have studied the Shasu-sequence have agreed so far in considering the first two elements (i.e. *t3 š3sw*) as an ethno-geographical instead of a political designation, with the element "land" (i.e. *t3*) referring to the vast and infinite conception of nomadic space.[106] The problems arise when turning to the respective specification that follows *T3 š3sw*. As in none of the instances a determinative (such as one for a tribe, one to discriminate between an alien or a cultivated country, etc.) follows the specification, any learned speculation about an Egyptian understanding of the individual designations is moot.

The motivations for designations are specific to a given culture and are thus rather variegated. Prerequisite for the reconstruction of the history of designations of a specific name, would be an exact and continuous knowledge about the decisive factors of that culture's practice of appointing terms to things and concepts. From what is known about Egypt, the Levant, and Mesopotamia, the Shasu-names (and thus also *Y-h-w*) might have been derived from divine, personal, group or tribal, place, scenic, mountain, or homestead names. In addition, it seems possible that certain names lost their original designative background due to the exodus/expulsion of the group that appointed the designation, and thus gave way for a change of meaning or popular etymologies.[107] The toponomastic (not topographical) possibilities of interpretation the sparse Egyptian data allow for, are much too limited for far-reaching conclusions on the history of names, or on the religious and settlement history.

Most non-Egyptological scholars assume tacitly that the Egyptian writing *Y-h-w* represents the Israelite name of God, rather than the designating of a place name, as in the present case.[108] Since any indicators in favour of an interpretation as a divine name are lacking, scholars have tried to avoid the resulting pit-

---

106 See Goedicke, "The tetragramm in Egyptian?" (see n. 21), 24 ("It denotes in a rather general fashion, land inhabited by wandering people without implying borders or social structures").
107 Similarly in Herrmann, "Gottesname" (see n. 41), 83–84 in connection to the "history of designation" of the "Shasu Jahwe".
108 Grdseloff, "Édôm" (see n. 2), 81–82 speaks of "l'existence d'une ville Jahwa en territoire kénite, ce qui rend l'origine kénite du culte de Jahwa encore plus probable." and Giveon, "Toponymes ouest-asiatiques à Soleb" (see n. 32), 28 assumed that the name should be interpreted as "Beth Yahwe, la maison de Yahwe," which in return designates "une ville avec un sanctuaire dans la meme region."

falls by postulating an identification of a divine and settlement or terrain name (town, area or mountain name), for which again no proof has been presented.

Grdseloff connected the attestation of the word *Y-h-w* in the hieroglyphically written Shasu-sequences with the Israelite name of God, and concluded that it stood for a settlement or cult centre of a clan of YHWH-devotees.[109] Instead Görg wavered undecided between considering it a "regional or a tribal name" not dismissing the third option, to derive the Egyptian *Y-h-w* from the Israelite name of God, paralleling it with the attested use of the name Assur as a tribal, country, and divine name.[110] Jean Leclant attributes only a *"qualité de nom de lieu"* (YHWH) to the name hieroglyphically attested at Soleb and Amarah-West.[111]

A more detailed picture was envisaged by M. Astour assuming that "(t)he Shasu districts of Soleb-ʿAmarah must be understood as areas inside the cultivated territory of Syria, in which nomads were permitted to establish permanent or seasonal camps." Thus, the Shasu-designations would have been derived from places or settlements that were – as regional centres – located near these "seasonal camps." A derivation from natural landmarks such as wells, etc. would then also be possible. Unanswered, not only in Astour's case, remains the question whether the Shasu-names are indigenous or foreign designations. Especially with Astour's suggested identification (see above), one would assume a sedentary group to designate a pasture that was temporarily provided to nomadic tribes.[112]

4 Conclusion

Even after decades of heated debates about the identification and localisation of the instances discussed above, scholarship has not advanced much further than where it was after Astour's and Herrmann's critical evaluations of the evidence:

- Despite the phonologically possible match between the hieroglyphic *Y-h-w* in Soleb and Amarah-West, and what one might expect as rendition of the Tetra-grammaton in hieroglyphs. The attribution to possible "(proto-)Israelites" re-

---

109 This rather imaginative notion is also the base of in Aḥituv's explanation in *Canaanite Toponyms* (see n. 8), 122 according to him "(t)he *šśsw*-land of Jahu (Yāhū) is the wandering area of the clan of the worshippers of Yāhū, the God of Israel. It most probably pertains to the region of Kadesh-barnea and Jebel Hilāl, which might be the sacred Mt. Sinai."
110 Görg, "Jahwe – ein Toponym?" (see n. 7), 187.
111 Leclant, "Le "tétragramme"" (see n. 19), 217.
112 de Moor, *Rise of Yahwism* (see n. 89).

mains hypothetical, since reliable facts about the historical linguistic and cultural background for *Y-h-w* at Soleb and Amarah-West are not available.[113]

- The Egyptian instances cannot be exploited for the question of YHWH's origin in the south, as the geographical context, and especially the ordering principle of the geographical list that contains them, are not clarified.[114]
- In addition, it remains unclear whether *Y-h-w* (as well as the other Shasu-names) designates a tribe, an area/region or a settlement. Similarly, no clear indication for the derivation from the divine name (and vice versa), and the assumption that the divine name should be considered also as a tribal or settlement name (sanctuary or shrine), as with the above mentioned Assur, have come to the fore.[115]
- The spatial connection of the Shasu-names at Soleb and Amarah-West into a continuous territory is purely speculative. Neither the extension of the Shasu-areas nor their respective locations to each other can be identified based on the Egyptian lists. It is possible, but cannot be proven, that the Shasu-names that follow in the Amarah-West-list after the place name identified as Sëir, are subordinate to the latter.[116]
- Finally, the localisation of Sëir ($\acute{S}$-^{c}-r-r), that is essentially connected to *Y-h-w*, is not without difficulties. Thus, the location of the Sëir-lands in the 18th dynasty still needs to be clarified.[117]

Many scholars' euphoria and their associated expectations often hampered a critical evaluation of the Egyptian attestations. The interpretation of the sources was adjusted to an event horizon based on a predisposition influenced by the

---

113 See S. H. Horn, "Jericho in a Topographical List of Ramesses II," *JNES* 12 (1953), 201–203, here 201: "Whether one of the Edomite tribal names bearing the name Yahweh (…) implies that Edomites were followers of the god Yahweh, or whether the name of the tribe has only a curious coincidence with the name of the Israelite god, is still undecided;" similarly sceptical is also K. A. Kitchen, *Ramesside inscriptions. Translated & Annotated. Notes and Comments 2* (Oxford 1999), 128–129.

114 Thus also H. Pfeiffer, *Jahwes Kommen von Süden, Jdc 5, Hab 3, Dtn 33 und Ps 68 in ihrem literatur- und theologiegeschichtlichen Umfeld* (FRLANT 211; Göttingen 2005), 261.

115 In addition, it cannot be excluded that the Egyptian writing refers to the divine name – for a different view see M. Weippert, *Jahwe und die anderen Götter: Studien zur Religionsgeschichte des antiken Israel in ihrem syrisch-palästinischen Kontext* (FAT 18; Tübingen 1997), 40–41. Weippert considered it as definite that it must be "eine geographische und/oder ethnische Bezeichnung."

116 Unclear as well is the connection of the Shasu-names at Soleb and Amarah-West to the "lands of Sëir" in EA 288, 26; see M. Köckert, "Wandlungen Gottes im antiken Israel," *BThZ* 22 (2005), 20 note 43.

117 See Köckert, "Wandlungen Gottes im antiken Israel" (see n. 115), 3–36, here 20 note 43.

Old Testament tradition, and was thus made fit into the topography transmitted in the Old Testament for the existing biblical scholarly narrative.

Also, the historiographic utilization of the Egyptian attestation calls for utter care. Various detail studies of the lists attested in Egyptian temples showed that the majority of the names in the Ramesside-lists, and presumably also a part of the Nubian-lists at Soleb and Amarah-West/Aksha, go back to templates of the early or middle 18th dynasty.[118] Considering the far-ranging conclusions that have been, and are drawn, based on the few *Y-h-w*-attestations that have been summarized above, the chronology of the Egyptian evidence and its transmission history should be focused upon in the future.

---

118 The question of the date of the template or the "Urliste" of the lists at Soleb, Amarah-West, and Medinet Habu should be considered for the issue at hand here. Doubts about the authorship of Amenhotep III. for the lists at Soleb and Amarah-West have been uttered already by H.W. Fairman, "Review of Simons, Handbook," *JEA* 26 (1940), 165 and Horn, "Jericho in a Topographical List of Ramesses II" (see n. 112), 202. Also Giveon, "Toponymes ouest-asiatiques à Soleb" (see n. 32), 254–255, opted for a redaction under Thutmosis III. or Amenhotep II. (maybe even Thutmosis I.) based on historical and graphemic considerations. A similar opinion was expressed by Helck, "Die Bedrohung Palästinas" (see n. 68), 478: "Diese Liste ist sicher nicht aus der Zeit Amenophis' III., sondern älter und mag auf einen früheren Feldzug zurückgehen, etwa auf Thutmosis' II. (Urk. IV 36, 13) oder den Thutmosis' III. in seinem 39. Jahr (Urk. IV 721, 12)."

Henrik Pfeiffer
The Origin of Yʜᴡʜ and its Attestation*

Like no other theological discipline, scholarship of the Hebrew Bible is currently experiencing radical changes. The reappraisal of the literary origin of large parts of the biblical writings, the continuing archaeological development of the Southern Levant, the systematic analysis of epigraphic and iconographic sources as well as the now common interdisciplinary cooperation with neighbouring historical and philological disciplines resulted in a widespread scepticism towards familiar scholarly positions. The reconstructions of the history and religious history of ancient Israel continue to depart increasingly from the biblical portrait. The Hebrew Bible has long lost its undisputed role as a key witness for the reconstruction of the (religious) history of ancient Israel. This is especially the case for the early period, which the Hebrew Bible links to the stories of the Patriarchs, the Exodus from Egypt, Sinai and the conquest of the land.

However, the notion of an origin of Yʜᴡʜ in a Southern marginal region of the Palestinian cultivated land remained largely unaffected by these criticisms. Until today, most scholars regard such a view close to the biblical portrait as a kind of secured minimum of the religious history of Israel. Such certainty is based on a correlation of the biblical material from various parts with epigraphic evidence – a methodology that suggests from the outset a high accuracy toward the formation of a hypothesis. Nevertheless, this consensus, too, is becoming more fragile. Christoph Levin in his 1996 inaugural lecture delivered at Gießen tersely states in regard to the religious historical question of the origin of Yʜᴡʜ:

> "According to the oldest attestations, namely the Psalms, Yʜᴡʜ, the God of Israel, represents the same type as a Syrian storm-god. It is highly unlikely that he was imported into Palestine from the outside."[1]

Because of an increasing scepticism towards the traditional view,[2] this proposal, originally ignored by scholars, has recently triggered vehement reactions.[3] The

---

* Revised version of an article originally published in BThZ 30 (2013). I thank Anselm C. Hagedorn (Humboldt-Universität zu Berlin) for his help with the English translation.
1 Cf. C. Levin, "Das vorstaatliche Israel," in *Fortschreibungen. Gesammelte Studien zum Alten Testament* (ed. C. Levin; BZAW 316; Berlin 2003), 142–157, here 146.
2 See M. Köckert, "Wandlungen Gottes im antiken Israel," *BThZ* 22 (2005), 3–36, here 20, n. 43; H. Pfeiffer, *Jahwes Kommen von Süden. Jdc 5; Hab 3; Dtn 33 und Ps 68 in ihrem literatur- und traditionsgeschichtlichen Umfeld* (FRLANT 211; Göttingen 2001); R. Müller, *Jahwe als Wettergott. Studien zur althebräischen Kultlyrik anhand ausgewählter Psalmen* (BZAW 387; Berlin 2008), 243 f.

DOI 10.1515/9783110448221-006

relevant textual witnesses on which the argument for an origin of YHWH in the South is based are still the same: The Sinai tradition of the Pentateuch and its assumed precursors in those texts that describe a theophany (Judg 5:4–5, Hab 3:3.7, Deut 33:2 and Ps 68:8–9), the tradition of the Exodus, texts that seem to attest to Midianite hypothesis as well as the inscriptions from Kuntillet 'Ajrud and from the temples of Amenophis III and Ramses II at Soleb and Amara-West. The reliability of the biblical evidence, however, rests upon literary- and tradition-historical assumptions that are rather problematic when subjected to scrutiny. The epigraphic sources, too, are by no means undisputed. To provide some orientation in the debate it seems appropriate to review the individual witnesses.

1

The notion that the roots of the worship of YHWH have to be situated in the regions South of Palestine seems to find support in the monumental entity of the Sinai pericope (Exod 19:1–Num 10:10).[4] Nowhere else in the Hebrew Bible is YHWH associated to such an extent with the South. If one reads closely, however, the Sinai pericope does not localize the *God* YHWH at Sinai but only the unparalleled *revelation* of his will which manifests itself in the legal texts and cultic stipulations as well as in the concept of a covenant that finally transforms Israel into the people of YHWH. It is not the text of the Hebrew Bible but its tradition-historical reconstruction that connects Sinai to the problem of YHWH's origin. Such assumption can already be found in the work of Julius Wellhausen:

---

3 See e.g. O. Keel, *Die Geschichte Jerusalems und die Entstehung des Monotheismus. Teil 1* (Orte und Landschaften der Bibel 4,1; Göttingen 2007), 199–202; M. Leuenberger, "Jahwes Herkunft aus dem Süden. Archäologische Befunde – biblische Überlieferungen – historische Korrelationen," *ZAW* 122 (2010), 1–19; E. Blum, "Der historische Mose und die Frühgeschichte Israels," *HeBAI* 1 (2012), 37–63.

4 For a history of scholarship see W. Oswald, *Israel am Gottesberg. Eine Untersuchung zur Literargeschichte der vorderen Sinaiperikope Exod 19–24 und deren historischem Hintergrund* (OBO 159; Fribourg 1998) 1–21; K. Schmid, "Israel am Sinai. Etappen der Forschungsgeschichte zu Exod 32–34 in seinen Kontexten," in *Gottes Volk am Sinai. Untersuchungen zu Exod 32–34 und Dtn 9–10* (ed. M. Köckert and E. Blum; VWGTh Theologie 18; Gütersloh 2001), 9–40; Pfeiffer, Kommen (see n. 2), 262–265.

"The true and original significance of Sinai is quite independent of the legislation. It was the seat of the Deity, the sacred mountain, doubtless not only for the Israelites, but generally for all the Hebrew and Cainite (Kenite) tribes of the surrounding region."[5]

This assumption, which Wellhausen relates to the pre-literary tradition, clashes with his own literary-historical assessment of the Sinai pericope:

"In the Jehovist, one form of the tradition may still be discerned, according to which the Israelites on crossing the Red Sea at once proceeded towards Kadesh, without making the detour to Sinai. We only get to Sinai in Exodus xix., but in Exodus xvii. we are already at Massah and Meribah, i.e., on the ground of Kadesh ... Hence the narratives which are told before the arrival at Sinai are repeated after the departure from it, because the locality is the same before and after, namely, the wilderness of Kadesh, the true scene of the Mosaic history ... In other words, the Israelites arrived at Kadesh, the original object of their wanderings, not after the digression to Sinai but immediately after the Exodus, and they spent there the forty years of their residence in the wilderness."[6]

In other words: The Sinai pericope as a whole is a *literary insertion* into an older context of the Exodus, wandering in the desert, and the conquest of the land. The "Jehovist" working during the later period of the monarchy is responsible for this insertion and he is not only a redactor here but has to be regarded as the original author of the passages about the giving of the law at Sinai.[7] J. Wellhausen, then, understands the Sinai pericope as a late addition which could nevertheless draw on knowledge as old as the hills. Curiously enough he does not derive this knowledge from the text of the Sinai pericope itself but rather by looking at the allegedly old Song of Deborah (Judg 5) and the anterior frame of Deut 33.[8] Gerhard von Rad, the virtuoso of tradition-historical reconstruction, reasons in similar fashion:

---

5 J. Wellhausen, *Prolegomena to a History of Israel. With a Reprint of the Article 'Israel' from the Encyclopaedia Britannica* (Cambridge Library Collection; Cambridge 2013), 343.

6 Wellhausen, *Prolegomena* (see n. 5), 342–343.

7 Cf. J. Wellhausen, *Die Composition des Hexateuchs und der historischen Bücher des Alten Testaments*, (Berlin ⁴1963), 94 f.

8 "There [i.e. on Sinai], to the Israelites, Jehovah still dwelt long after they had settled in Palestine; in the song of Deborah He is summoned to come from Sinai to succour His oppressed people and to place Himself at the head of His warriors. According to the view of the poet of Deuteronomy xxxiii. the Israelites did not go to Jehovah to Sinai, but the converse; He came to them from Sinai to Kadesh: 'Jehovah came from Sinai and shone from Seir unto them; He lightened from Mount Paran and came to Meribath Kadesh.'" (Wellhausen, *Prolegomena* [see n. 5], 344; on texts like Judg 5; Deut 33; Hab 3, and Ps 68 see below II).

"It is thus obvious that the Sinai tradition has been secondarily inserted into already extant traditions concerning the Wanderings in the Wilderness."[9]

In contrast to Wellhausen, G. v. Rad no longer argued that the "Jehovist" inserted the Sinai pericope but attributed this process to the earlier Yahwist whom he dated to the Solomonic period. In doing so he was able to close the gap between the assumed pre-literary Sinai tradition and its first literary attestation. Because of the form-critical and tradition-historical approach favoured by G. v. Rad, the old tradition grew in richness and extent when he ascribed not only the theophany but also the Decalogue to it. Additionally he charcterized the literary tradition as a "sacral tradition" serving already in the pre-monarchic period as a foundation legend for a festival of a renewal of the covenant at Shechem.[10] Finally, the substance of the tradition is traced back to Midian, where YHWH was worshipped before the Israelites encountered him.[11]

This fairly optimistic view has been rightly criticised. It became obvious that the festival of a renewal of the covenant at Shechem was the product of theological desk-work. As a result the institutional anchor of the Sinai tradition within the earliest history of Israel was lost.[12] Furthermore, additional literary-historical analyses of the non-P text of the Sinai pericope led to doubts about the fairly extensive substance of tradition postulated by v. Rad. Here, the detailed study by L. Perlitt was a milestone in the interpretation of the literary evidence.[13] Perlitt maintains that the base layer of the Sinai pericope has to be attributed to the

---

9 G. v. Rad, *Old Testament Theology. Volume I: The Theology of Israel's Historical Traditions* (OTL; Louisville 2001), 187; comp. G. v. Rad, "Das formgeschichtliche Problem des Hexateuch," in *Gesammelte Studien zum Alten Testament* (ed. G. v. Rad; TB 8; München 1958), 9–86 (originally published in 1938), here 20–27; see already H. Gressmann, *Mose und seine Zeit. Ein Kommentar zu den Mose-Sagen* (FRLANT 18; Göttingen 1913), *passim*; E. Meyer, *Die Israeliten und ihre Nachbarstämme. Alttestamentliche Untersuchungen. Mit Beiträgen von B. Luther* (Halle 1906), 60–71.
10 See v. Rad, "Problem" (see n. 9), 28–48; v. Rad, *Theology I* (see n. 9), 192f.. Already E. Meyer had argued – assuming old age for Joshua 24 – for an affinity of the Sinai tradition with Shechem (E. Meyer, *Israeliten* [see n. 9], 550). M. Noth finally gave this theory its break (see M. Noth, *Überlieferungsgeschichte des Pentateuch* [Stuttgart 1948], 48–67).
11 See v. Rad, *Theology I* (see n. 9), 9; on the so-called Midianite theory see IV below.
12 The problem was already recognised by S. Mowinckel. He nevertheless maintained a cultic interpretation of the Sinai tradition but no longer connected it to an imaginary festival at Shechem. Instead he proposed a connection to a new year's festival in Jerusalem. As a result no only was the old age of the Sinai tradition questioned but also situating it before the origin of the cult. The tradition of Sinai is now formed within the context of the cult at Jerusalem (!); see S. Mowinckel, *Le décalogue* (EhPhR 16; Paris 1927), 120 f.
13 L. Perlitt, *Bundestheologie im Alten Testament* (WMANT 36; Neukirchen-Vluyn 1969).

Yahwist.[14] But he argues for an extensive reworking of the P material by deuteronomistic authors so that only the elements theophany and cult (Exod 19*; 24*)
remain as a pre-deuteronomistic kernel. Unfortunately the kernel is not analysed
further by Perlitt.[15] He, too, keeps assuming that we have older knowledge of
Y~HWH~'s origin in the Southern regions of Palestine. L. Perlitt, however, does
not find this knowledge in the Yahwistic texts but in those parts of the Hebrew
Bible that announce Y~HWH~'s coming from the South (Judg 5; Deut 33; Hab 3; Ps
68).[16] According to this analysis the Sinai pericope has to be excluded from the
list of witnesses for an origin of Y~HWH~ from the South.

Finally, C. Levin completely removes the basis for the assumption of a pre-
literary tradition of the Sinai pericope.[17] He follows those scholars who argue
that the Sinai pericope is a literary parenthesis and he localizes it between the
two itinerary notes (*Itinerarnotizen*) Exod 19:2a and Num 10:12a.[18] The layer of
these notes has to be dated to the period of the monarchy. The original form
of the (later) Sinai pericope is thus reduced to the moment of Moses' divine encounter as the archetype of a cultic rapprochement (Exod 19:2b–3a; 24:18b).[19] Everything else is the product of later expansions during the various processes of
Fortschreibung. The "wilderness of Sinai" (Exod 19:2a) of the older literary tradition is first supplemented by the "mountain" in the "wilderness of Sinai" (Exod
19:2b) and later tradition, then, unites both statements and speaks of "Mount

---

14 But he too assumes that the Sinai pericope is a later addition: "Die Sinaiperikope erweckt
selbst in ihrer jüngsten Gestalt den Eindruck eines gewaltigen Einschubs" (Perlitt, *Bundestheologie* [see n. 13], 156).

15 The proposal to reduce of the base layer of the Sinai pericope to theophany and cult (Exod
19* and 24*) has several prominent followers and we will only mention J. Jeremias, *Theophanie.
Die Geschichte einer alttestamentlichen Gattung* (WMANT 10; Neukirchen-Vluyn ²1977) here. The
current trend to keep the law (in whatever form) as part of the base layer of the Sinai pericope
only intensifies the problems when searching for an older Sinai (see e.g. Oswald, *Israel* [see n.
4], 102–113).

16 See. L. Perlitt, "Sinai und Horeb," in *Beiträge zur alttestamentlichen Theologie* (ed. H. Donner, R. Hanhart and R. Smend; Göttingen 1977), 302–322.

17 See. C. Levin, "Der Dekalog am Sinai," in *Fortschreibungen* (see n. 1), 60–80 (originally published in 1985); C. Levin, *Der Jahwist* (FRLANT 157; Göttingen 1993), bes. 362–369.

18 See already – *mutatis mutandis* –J. Vermeylen, "Les sections narratives de Deut 5–11 et leur
relation à Exod 19–34," in *Das Deuteronomium. Entstehung, Gestalt und Botschaft* (ed. N. Lohfink; BEThL 68; Leuven 1985), 174–207, here 176, and references to other scholarship in Schmid,
"Israel" (see n. 4), 18f

19 Levin, *Jahwist* (see n. 17), 364.

Sinai" (19:11, 18, 20 etc.). If Levin is correct, the Sinai pericope was never anything else than the product of literary *Fortschreibung*.[20]

In fact, to explain the origin of the Sinai pericope on the basis of purely literary activity of *Fortschreibung* has proven very useful.[21] Against this background it becomes superfluous to continue to look for a pre-literary tradition of Sinai.[22] As a result the Sinai pericope can no longer serve as a reliable witness for the religion-historical quest for the origin of YHWH. This leaves the question about the status of the other texts that – openly or covertly – tend to bear the burden of proof: the Song of Deborah (Judg 5); the frame of the Song of Moses (Deut 33:2–5, 26–29); Habakkuk 3 and Psalm 68.

---

20 In contrast to Levin's position, E. Blum, "Mose" (see n. 3), 61 f. argues for a an originally independent Sinai pericope composed of an older form of the Covenant Code and a pre- Covenant Code etiology (Exod 19:...[3a.]10 – 13.14 – 19a; 20:18.21b[.22aα]; 20:24 ff; 21:1 – 23:19 + 24:3[?]). Blum's decision is based on the duplicate 20:18bβ/20:21a and his observation of a late literary bridge in 20:19 f (+ 22.23) which transforms 20:21a into a resumption of 20:18bβ. Whether this is evidence for the existence of a (fragmentary) "Pre-Covenant-Code-composition" remains unclear. If Blum is correct, however, such a composition would not only presume the existence of a base layer of the Covenant Code in the monarchic period but also of "Mount Sinai." This would imply that the addition of Exod 19:2b and thus the archetype of the Sinai pericope would have existed in the context of a pre-priestly composition of the Hexateuch.

21 See e. g. Oswald, *Israel* (see n. 4) who argues for an older Exodus narrative in Exod 1–15 which was expanded by the Sinai pericope during post-monarchic period, and R. G. Kratz, *The Composition of the Narrative Books of the Old Testament* (London 2005), 136 – 140.282 – 283, who proposes that the Sinai pericope interrupts an older connection of Exod 15:22 with Num 20:1aβ.b.

22 This impression is reinforced when one continues to date the base layer of the Sinai pericope later rather than earlier. C. Levin proposes a date during the period of the monarchy while W. Oswald, *Israel* (see n. 4), esp. 125 – 149 describes it as a manifesto of a body politic during the time of Gedaliah. For a dater after 587 BCE see furthermore Pfeiffer, *Kommen* (see n. 2), 267 – 268. The charge against Pfeiffer, *ibid.* that such a proposal overrates the creativity of tradition literature (*Traditionsliteratur*) like the Hebrew Bible (O. Keel, *Geschichte* [see n. 3], 201 and repeated by M. Leuenberger, "Herkunft" [see n. 3], 14 – 15) appears strange because the Hebrew Bible as such is a representative of a literature that originates via interpretation. Additionally, according to Pfeiffer, *ibid.* it was never the intention of the redactors to create a secondary home or a refuge in the wilderness for YHWH (thus the accusations found in O. Keel, *ibid.*). Rather, the redactors create a mythical foundation of an encounter with God that will constitute the relationship between Israel and YHWH and will thus be able to survive the destruction of the sanctuary. This attempt at a theological clarification has nothing to do with the withdrawal of deities in the context of the destructions of temples, which Keel uses as a counterargument.

2

These four texts are united by their poetic character, distinguishing them from the prose narrative of the Sinai pericope, as well as by the common topic: Yʜᴡʜ arrives from the Southern fringes of Palestine to help, in one way or the other, his people. The crucial passages are:[23]

Judg 5:4 – 5.31
4 Yʜᴡʜ, when you came forth from Seir,
  advanced from the climes of Edom
  the earth trembled, the heavens dripped.
5 Mountains streamed before Yʜᴡʜ [him of Sinai],
  before Yʜᴡʜ, the God of Israel.

  ....

31a Thus may all your enemies perish, Yʜᴡʜ,
  but those who love him,
  may be as the sun rising in might.

Hab 3:3 – 4.7*
3 God is coming from Teman
  and the Holy One from Mount Paran. *Selah*
  His majesty covers the skies,
  and his splendour fills the earth.
4 Brightness is like light,
  and horns project from his hand.
7 [...] The tents of Cushan quiver,
  the curtains of the land of Midian.

Deut 33:2*
  Yʜᴡʜ came from Sinai;
  he shone upon them from Seir;
  He appeared from Mount Paran;
  and he approached from the myriads of holy ones.

Ps 68:8 – 9
8 God, when you went at the head of your people,
  when you marched through the desert
9   the earth trembled
  the sky rained,
  because of God, (him) of Sinai,
  because of God, the God of Israel.

---

23 Limited space does not allow discussing the manifold philological and interpretive problems of the texts. On the history of scholarship as well as on individual problems see Pfeiffer, *Kommen* (see n. 2). On Judges 5 see now (albeit with different results) W. Groß, *Richter. Übersetzt und ausgelegt von Walter Groß. Mit Karten von Erasmus Gaß* (HTHK.AT; Freiburg 2009).

Already J. Wellhausen based his interpretation of "[t]he true and original Sinai" as "the seat of the Deity" less on the Sinai tradition of the Hexateuchal narrative than on Judges 5 and Deuteronomy 33.[24] Until today Judges 5, Deuteronomy 33, Habakkuk 3, and Psalm 68 serve as the undisputed witnesses for an original home of YHWH in the arid zones of the South.[25] This amazing confidence into the reliability of the tradition rests on three factors: Firstly, the context of texts like Judges 5 and Deuteronomy 33 (pre-monarchic period) suggests a certain antiquity of the tradition. The same was said about the Sinai pericope but the detailed literary-critical analysis quickly showed that the opposite is the case. Such detailed analysis of the above-mentioned texts was long missing. Secondly, the distribution of the same topic of knowledge over quite separate textual realms suggests a multiple tradition of the topic. Finally, two of the places from where YHWH sets off are reminiscent of the Sinai tradition (cf. "Sinai" in Deut 33:2; Judg 5:5; "Mount Paran" in Deut 33:2; Hab 3:3). For the other three toponyms it is difficult to find a connection to the Pentateuchal narrative ("Edom/Seir" in Judg 5:4; "Teman" in Hab 3:3). The variation of the place names signals an uncertainty which invites the reader to interpret the names against the background of archaic knowledge used by the later Sinai tradition. Such an understanding of the four texts describing a theophany seemed at first to be confirmed by a form-critical and linguistic analysis:

Jörg Jeremias, for example, discovered a *Gattung* within the texts describing a theophany in the Hebrew Bible.[26] The oldest form is found in Judg 5:4f. and Ps 68:8f. and consists of the "approach of YHWH" and the "turmoil of nature."[27] While there are manifold tradition-historical parallels from the Ancient Near East for the element "turmoil of nature," the approach of the deity remains unique to ancient Israel. Its earliest attestation can be found in those texts that describe YHWH as coming from Sinai (Judg 5:4f.; Deut 33:2; Hab 3:3; Ps

---

24 J. Wellhausen, *Prolegomena* (see n. 5), 343.

25 See e.g. J. Jeremias, *Theophanie* (see n. 15); Perlitt, "Sinai und Horeb" (see n. 16); L.E. Axelsson, *The Lord Rose up From Seir: Studies in the History and Traditions of the Negev and Southern Judah* (CB.OTS 25; Stockholm 1987); J. Van Seters, *The Life of Moses. The Yahwist as Historian in Exodus–Numbers* (CBET 10; Kampen 1994), 287; Oswald, *Israel* (see n. 4), 250; Keel, *Geschichte* (see n. 3), 200; Leuenberger, "Herkunft" (see n. 3); Blum, "Mose" (see n. 3).

26 See Jeremias, *Thephanie* (see n. 15). Older form-critical explanation can be found in A. Weiser, "Zur Frage nach den Beziehungen der Psalmen zum Kult. Die Darstellung der Theophanie in den Psalmen und im Festkult," in *Festschrift Alfred Bertholet zum 80. Geburtstag* (ed. W. Baumgartner; Tübingen 1950), 513–531, and C. Westermann, *Das Loben Gottes in den Psalmen* (Berlin 1953 [reprinted.]), 69–76.

27 See Jeremias, *Theophanie* (see n. 15), esp. 7–16 with reference to Isa 63:19b; Am 1:2; Mi 1:3f. and Ps 46:7.

68:9.18b).[28] According to this interpretation this group of texts conserves at least in part the oldest *Gestalt* of a description of a theophany as well as archaic traditions about Sinai. Furthermore, Jeremias states: "Wenn [...] die Theophanieschilderungen in ihrer ältesten Gestalt von einem Kommen oder Aufbrechen Jahwes vom Sinai sprachen, war es dann nicht ganz selbstverständlich gegeben, daß sie seine Offenbarung am Sinai mit im Blick hatten? War nicht schon in der Vorstellung, daß Jahwe am Sinai wohnte, jenes so bedeutsame Erscheinen Jahwes am Sinai implizit enthalten?"[29] Judg 5:4f.; Deut 33:2; Hab 3:3; Ps 68:9.18b serve at the same time as the guarantor of the tradition-historical bed-rock of the Sinai tradition as found in the narrative of the Pentateuch.

William F. Albright[30] and his pupils David Noel Freedman and Frank Moore Cross[31] on the other hand offer linguistic reasons for dating the passages to the 13th – 10th century BCE. Within this strand of scholarship the four texts under scrutiny are part of a "corpus of ancient Yahwistic poetry."[32] This is not the place to describe in detail the arguments for such a characterization. Orthography, linguistic aspects such as metre, morphology, syntax, and lexicography are used to show the old age of the texts. In retrospective, D. N. Freedman and F. M. Cross remain sceptical about the punch of such arguments: "The attempt to date a document by survivals of archaic orthographies is a precarious enterprise, and orthographic analysis at best may confirm other typological evidence, linguistic, prosodic etc."[33] Archaic orthography is indeed hardly a plausible criterion for an early date of biblical texts. Even if we cannot discuss the problems of a "linguistic dating" of biblical texts here it is apparent that the imagination or archaic modes of writing that remain in existence over centuries is quite problematic. Additionally we have to allow for artificial archaisms during later times as the

---

28 See Jeremias, *Theophanie* (see n. 15), 155.
29 Jeremias, *Theophanie* (see n. 15), 155.
30 See esp. W.F. Albright, *Yahweh and the Gods of Canaan. A Historical Analyses of two Contrasting Faiths* (London 1968), 1–46.
31 Cf. D.N. Freedman, "Archaic Forms In Early Hebrew Poetry," *ZAW* 72 (1960), 101–107; idem, "Pottery, Poetry, and Prophecy. An Essay on biblical Poetry," in *Pottery, Poetry, and Prophecy. Studies in Early Hebrew Poetry* (ed. D.N. Freedman; Winona Lake 1980), 1–22 (originally published 1977); idem, "Early Israelite History in the Light of Early Israelite Poetry," in idem, Pottery, 131–166 (originally published 1975); idem, *Early Israelite Poetry and Historical Reconstructions*, in idem, Pottery, 167–178 (originally published 1979); F.M. Cross, *Canaanite Myth and Hebrew Epic. Essays in the History of the Religion of Israel* (Cambridge 1973); idem and D.N. Freedman, *Studies in Ancient Yahwistic Poetry* (Grand Rapids 1997).
32 See Cross and Freedman, *Studies* (see n. 31), 5–8. The assumed corpus of texts is supplemented by Exod 15; Deut 32; Ps 18 (= II Sam 22); 29 etc.
33 Cross and Freedman, *Studies* (see n. 31), 183 ("Postscript" from 1975).

Qumran scrolls show. Finally the climactic parallelism so often used to date a text early is also attested in late text from the Hebrew Bible (Ps 77:17[34]; 92:10).[35]

If one scrutinizes the methodologies of such explanations, it becomes obvious that they all refrain from a detailed literary-critical analysis of the individual texts. At the same time there are many exegetical attempts that do precisely this and they unearth astonishing results: None of the four texts is dated early.[36] For all texts we find detailed analyses that argue for a multi-layered process of literary origin. This in turn poses the question where to place the passages describing YHWH's epiphany within Israel's literary history. Finally, there are century old proposals arguing for literary interdependencies between the texts that make it difficult to see them as different forms of a similar tradition.[37] Be it as it

---

34 Sometimes Ps 77:17–20 is described as an older piece of tradition. The literary contacts of Ps 77:17 with Exod 15:5.8 and of Ps 77:20 with Isa 43:16 f.; 51:9 f. speak against such an assumption.
35 On the proposal by E.A. Knauf to date the theophany of Judg 5:4 f. to the 10th/9th century BCE (E.A. Knauf, "Deborah's Language. Judges ch. 5 in its Hebrew and Semitic Context," in *Studia Semitica et Semitohamitica, FS R. Voigt* [ed. B. Burtea et al.; AOAT 317; Münster 2005], 167–182), which is used by Keel, *Geschichte* (see n. 3), 200, and Leuenberger, "Herkunft" (see n. 3), 15 f., see already Groß, *Richter* (see n. 23), 296. The linguistic arguments for a date between the 4th century BCE and the 1st century CE put forth in M. Waltisberg, "Zum Alter der Sprache des Deboraliedes Ri 5*," *ZAH* 13 (2000), 218–232, and B. Diebner, "Wann sang Deborah ihr Lied? Überlegungen zu zwei der ältesten Texte des TNK (Ri 4 und 5)," ACEBT (1995), 105–130, for a date between the 4th century BCE and the 1st century CE, remain equally vague.
36 As far as the Song of Deborah (Judg 5) is concerned U. Bechmann, *Das Deboralied zwischen Geschichte und Fiktion. Eine exegetische Untersuchung zu Richter 5* (Diss.T 33; St. Ottilien 1989) argues for a date between 722 and 587 while C. Levin proposes an origin sometime between the 5th and the 3rd century BCE (C. Levin, "Das Alter des Deboraliedes," in *Fortschreibungen* [see n. 1], 124–141). M. Witte, "Orakel und Gebete im Buch Habakuk," in *Orakel und Gebete. Interdisziplinäre Studien zur Sprache der Religion in Ägypten, Vorderasien und Griechenland in hellenistischer Zeit* (ed. J. Diehl and M. Witte; FAT 2,38; Tübingen 2009), 67–91 dates the Book of Habakkuk (including the Psalm in Hab 3) to the Hellenistic period. The frame of Deut 33 is assigned to the post-monarchic period by U. Schorn, *Ruben und das System der zwölf Stämme Israels. Redaktionsgeschichtliche Untersuchungen zur Bedeutung des Erstgeborenen Jakobs* (BZAW 248; Berlin 1997), 105–109, or E. Otto, *Das Deuteronomium im Pentateuch und Hexateuch. Studien zur Literaturgeschichte von Pentateuch und Hexateuch im Lichte des Deuteronomiumrahmens* (FAT 30; Tübingen 2000), 189. As far as Psalm 68 is concerned, scholarship of the 19th and early 20th century recognized its anthology like character and opted for an origin during Persian or Hellenistic times (see the references in Pfeiffer, *Kommen* [see n. 2], 205). Only later did the cultic interpretation again argue for an early date.
37 W. Nowack, *Richter – Ruth übersetzt und erklärt* (HK 1/4.1; Göttingen 1900), 43, for example, saw Judg 5:4 f. as the source of Deut 33:2 f.; Hab 3 and Ps 68:8 f. while F. Delitzsch, *Biblischer Commentar über die Psalmen* (BC 4,1; Leipzig [5]1894), 448, stated in regard to Ps 68: "Er wiederholt in V8 f. Worte Debora's Richt. 5,4 f. und die Worte dieser gehen auf Dtn 33,2 vgl. Exod 19,15 ff. zurück; für Hab. c. 3 ist hinwieder unser Ps. Original."

may the diverging positions in regard to the origin of the texts makes it necessary to look in detail into the literary-critical development. This is especially the case as the texts mentioned above are still used as main witnesses for an origin of YHWH in the South.

I have proposed elsewhere that the texts are the product of a multi-layered process of origin and that during this process we can detect quite an extensive degree of mutual influence and interaction.[38] Here, the Song of Deborah integrates the oldest traditions. The kernel of the history of origin is an epic song from the 9th or 8th century BCE.[39] Its contents – making use of knowledge of the early history of Israel[40] – describes an unexpected victory of the tribes of Sebulon and Naphtali (v. 18) under their leaders Deborah and Barak (v. 12) over Sisera and the "kings of Canaan" (v. 19 – 21a.22). In the base layer it is not YHWH who fights for his people; rather the stars (numinous entities in Ancient Near Eastern world view) come to the aid of the tribes of Naphtali and Sebulon.

The song was reworked several times in the post-monarchic period. When it was integrated in the book of Judges a hymnic prelude (v. 2.10 – 11a) was added which allocates the events to the "gracious acts of YHWH" (v. 11a). The verses – important to our enterprise – that describe a coming of YHWH from Edom/Seir (v. 3.4 – 5) were then constructed (together with v. 31a) as a frame around the song itself. Here the addition זה סיני[41] in v. 5, which interrupts the poetic structure, is still missing.[42] These editions force the stars (v. 20) to join the ranks of YHWH's entourage. On this level of redaction the fight of YHWH is not only against the "kings of Canaan" (v. 19) but also against "*all* enemies of YHWH" (v. 31a) – a statement that seems to include inner-Jewish adversaries as well as can be established from the mentioning of "those who love him" (v. 31a). Judg 5:3–*5.31a seem to be aware of the inner-Jewish distinction between the pious and the wicked, which does not appear before the 5th century BCE. The addition זה סיני points to an even later stage and explains the strange Edom theophany in v. 4–*5 in the light of the canonical Sinai theophany of Exod 19[43] and thus presupposes it.[44]

---

38 Pfeiffer, *Kommen* (see n. 2).

39 Jdc 5,12*(minus דברי שיר).13a.18/19 – 21a.22/24*(minus חבר הקיני).25.26*(minus אשת ומחצה)–27/ 28*(minus ותיבב).29 – 30.

40 It is possibly a local tradition situated at Tanaach (v. 19).

41 On the difficulties of translating the phrase see Pfeiffer, *Kommen* (see n. 2), 35.

42 For details see Pfeiffer, *Kommen* (see n. 2) 41–44.

43 See esp. Exod 19:16.18 – Leuenberger, however, regards the evidence for a late origin (which he rejects, of course) as secondary for a reconstruction of the tradition history and argues that the move from the literary- and redaction-history to the tradition-history is shortsighted and

The genesis of the Song of Deborah proposed here[45] does not really invite the solution to explain the rather *young* concept of a theophany in Edom in Judg 5:4–*5 with *oldest* knowledge of the God YHWH. Rather, it is methodologically far sounder to interpret it by using contemporary texts. Here the texts that connect Edom in various ways with YHWH's judgement suggest themselves.[46] The historical background for these texts is the conquest of Edom by Nabonid (552 BCE) as well as the raids of the Edomite territory by proto-Arabic tribes during the first half of the 5th century BCE. These Edom-texts interpret the historical realities as YHWH's judgement on the Edomites. At the same time they articulate a hostility towards Edom that is normally connected to an Edomite occupation of the Southern Negev since the 7th century BCE. Later text will regard Edom – like Babylon – as God's enemy per se. Isa. 63:1–6* is clearly one of the most prominent texts in this group:[47]

1   Who is this coming from Edom,
        in crimson garments from Bozrah?
    This person, majestic in attire,
        stooping in the greatness of his strength?
    I am speaking in justice,
        strong to deliver.
2   Why is your garment so red,
        your clothes like someone treading in a wine trough?
3   I trod out a vintage – alone
        and from the people there was no one with me [...]
4   For I planned a day of vengeance,
        and my year of redemption arrived.

---

methodologically questionable (Leuenberger, "Herkunft" [see n. 3], 15). The opposite is the case unless a subjunctive should be regarded as an argument.

44 The description of distress and guilt in v. 6–8 (including the literary bridge to the hymnic frame in verse 9), the expansion of verse 18 which creates a list of ten tribes (v. 14–17) and several smaller additions (v.11b.12*[only דברי שיר].21b.23.24aβ[only אשת חבר הקיני]. 26bβ*[only ומחצה] and ותיבב in v.28) are even later.

45 Groß, *Richter* (see n. 23) rejects our interpretation and several scholars follow him in doing so (see Leuenberger, "Herkunft" [see n. 3], 13–17; Blum, "Mose" [see n. 3], 54, n. 65). W. Groß, too, recognizes several ruptures in the literary consistency but he does not explain them by assuming several levels of redactions (only v. 31 is an addition for him). Instead he assumes a larger fundus of traditions with different accentuations (340). It remains doubtful whether the assumption of pre-literary *Vorlagen* of unclear provenance has more advantages than a literary-critical solution. Additionally, to separate v. 31a (a verse that refers to Ps 92:10) from v 4–*5 appears artificial; for the connection of v. 4–*5.31a see Pfeiffer, *Kommen* (see n. 2), 40.78–90.

46 Isa 34; 63:1–6; Jer 49:7–22; Ez 25:12–14; 32:29; 35; Jl 4:19; Am 1:11 f.; Ob 10–14; Mal 1:2–5 as well as Ps 137:7; Lam 4:21 f.

47 Isa. 63:1 f.3aα.4.5b.

5   [...] So my own arm has effected deliverance for me,
       and my own rage was my aid.

The text appears to be a dialogue between an anonymous person, maybe a watchmen or a sentinel at the gate of Jerusalem, and Yʜwʜ who is "stooping in the greatness of his strength" and "strong to deliver" (v. 1). He is described as someone treading in a wine trough who is coming (בא) from Edom (מאדום) robed in a garment red (אדם) from the blood of the Edomites.[48] The base layer of the text only describes the judgment as a judgement against Edom; a later redactor, however, expands the horizon by adding v. 3aβ.b.5a.6. The judgement of Edom is now the prelude to a universal judgment of the nations:[49]

I will (?) trample nations in may anger,
   and I will (?) make them drunk in my rage
      and hurl their glory to the ground (Isa 63:6).

Isa 34[50] and Ob 15 connect the judgment of Edom in a similar way with the judgement of the nations.

If we connect Judg 5:4–*5 with the Edom text of the post-monarchic period, the God who comes from Edom is inevitably the warlike and victorious God.[51] For the author of Judg 5:4–*5.31, too, the judgment of Edom, which was already a topos of the theological tradition and became the link for more universal statements, will not stand alone. In Judg 5, Yʜwʜ as the warlike and victorious God sets off from Edom to fight against the "kings of Canaan" (v. 19 f.) who are already part of the base layer. They serve – on a literary level of Judg 5:3–*5.31a – as a model for "all your enemies" (v. 31a).

It is, therefore, not very difficult to explain the epiphany of Yʜwʜ from Edom in Judg 5:4 f.* in the light of other contemporary Edom texts. To explain it by reference to archaic knowledge is hardly the better option, especially as we do not know whether such knowledge has ever existed.

---

48 Isa 34:5–7 describes in a similar way the judgment on Edom as bloody slaughter.
49 The assessment of the passages as a later redaction is triggered by the change in the tendency of the text (judgment of the nations instead of Edom alone) and by the change of the tenses. The question of translation (see the remarks in E. Blum, "Mose" [see n.3], 55 n.68) is independent from the literary-critical decisions. If one follows BHS and changes to the narrative tense here one has to explain the intention of the masoretic vocalization.
50 Cf. Isa 34:2 where even the cosmos is affected by the judgment.
51 In a similar way to Judg 5:4 phrases using יצא and a divine subject in general imply the annihilation of the enemies of Israel or Yʜwʜ; see F. Schnutenhaus, "Das Kommen und Erscheinen Jahwes im Alten Testament," *ZAW* 76 (1974), 1–21, here 2f.

The same has to be said of the parallels Hab 3; Deut 33 and Ps 68. As far as the origin of these texts is concerned they have to be interpreted in the light of the Song of Deborah. The core of the Habakkuk-Psalm (Hab 3*)[52] was added after the prophetic book was joined with the preceding Book of Nahum and the subsequent Book of Zephaniah.[53] The Psalm outlines a universal judgement of the nations (v. 12) and thus cannot be earlier than the Hellenistic period. For the core it is impossible to trace a literary dependence on Judg 5. Because of the late origin, however, it is entirely possible that the text was written in knowledge of the Song of Deborah. It remains unclear which geographical idea is represented by the names "Teman" and "Mount Paran" (Hab 3:3), which serve as place of origin of the theophany. As far as "Paran" is concerned a connection to Wadi Feran on the Southern Sinai Peninsula might be possible. If that is the case, "Mount Paran" would then be located in the region West to the Arabah. In the Hebrew Bible, "Teman" generally describes the South but also Edom, a certain region of Edom[54] or an Edomite place (Am 1:12).[55] If we connect "Teman" in Hab 3:3 to Edomite localities, the place of origin of the theophany would be in the regions East and West of the Arabah. The theophany from Edom/Seir (Judg 5:4 f.*) would then have changed into an Epiphany of Yhwh from the South (cf. Isa 21:1; Zech 9:14). If one interprets "Teman" as describing the South and assumes that "Mount Paran" specifies it, we would be in the Western regions of the Arabah. However, as part of a purely contextual interpretation a reference to the Negev would also be possible.[56] In comparison to Judg 5 the theophany of Hab 3* shifts its starting point to the West or expands it to include the South as well. As a result, Edom – so prominent in Judg 5:4 f.* – appears in Hab 3* only in an attenuated form.

As far as the literary dependence is concerned things are clearer when looking at Deut 33 and Ps 68. Deut 33 obviously uses Judg 5 and Hab 3.[57] This can be seen by the simple evidence (quoted above) that a coming of Yhwh from *Seir* and *Sinai* is otherwise only attested in Judg 5:4 and the expression "Mount Paran" only appears in Hab 3:3. In other words: Deut 33 accumulates the toponyms of the other two texts. It is much more difficult to argue that Judg 5:4 and

---

52 Hab 3:3.4a.5–6a.7aβ*(minus ראיתי).b/8*.9.10.11*(minus ירד).12.

53 See Pfeiffer, *Kommen* (see n. 2), 117–177.

54 See E.A. Knauf, "Teman," in: M. Bauks and K. Koenen (ed.), *Das wissenschaftliche Bibellexikon im Internet*, www.wibilex.de (last accessed December 6, 2015).

55 Cf. Z. Meshel (ed.), *Kuntillet 'Ajrud (Ḥorvat Teman). An Iron Age II Religious Site on the Judah-Sinai Border* (Jerusalem 2012), 96.

56 Cf. Knauf, "Teman" (see n. 54).

57 See Pfeiffer, *Kommen* (see n. 2), 178–203.

Hab 3 each make selective use of Deut 33. It has long been recognised that Psalm 68 as a whole is an anthological text that uses – next to Judg 5 and Deut 33 – a variety of other sources.[53] As a result of this quick survey we have to acknowledge that Judg 5; Hab 3; Deut 33 and Ps 68 cannot bear the burden of proof.

3

The Exodus tradition is a further component of a hypothesis of an origin of Yhwh in the South.[59] Already the biblical portrait of the early history of Israel connects the Exodus with the question of the beginning of the worship of Yhwh.[60] Scholarship tends to move in the wake of this representation when it tries to uncover the oldest Israelite concept of Yhwh.[61]

But here too, the historical inquiry is not very productive: As it is well known the extra-biblical sources of the late Bronze and early Iron Age are silent about an Israelite sojourn in Egypt. From what we know Israel never immigrated from the outside to Canaan. Rather it originated as a result of inner-Canaanite changes during the transition from the late Bronze to the early Iron Age.

Until about 1200 BCE the Ancient Near East was ruled by a system of various empires with centres in Egypt, Mesopotamia and central Anatolia. During the second half of the 2nd millennium BCE Canaan was an Egyptian province. We are informed about the affairs in Palestine by Egyptian sources, mainly the Amarna correspondence. Politically, the Canaanites were organised in city-states situated mainly at the coast and in the lowlands. Next to the residents we encounter several nomadic tribes, a group called Hapiru of possibly lower social status and stray gangs that often put pressure on the cities. Already during the Bronze Age can we observe first attempts at state building in middle Palestine (Jerusalem, Shechem).[62] Around 1200 BCE the system of empires collapses leading to a political instability of the region. Egypt was no longer able to exercise its hegemony over Palestine/Canaan and this quickened the collapse of the city-states. The coming of the "sea people" contributed further to the decline. The

---

58 See the evidence in Pfeiffer, *Kommen* (see n. 2), 204–257.
59 See the essay of C. Berner in the current volume as well as U. Becker, "Das Exodus-Credo. Historischer Haftpunkt und Geschichte einer alttestamentlichen Glaubensformel," in *Das Alte Testament – Ein Geschichtsbuch?! Geschichtsschreibung oder Geschichtsüberlieferung im antiken Israel* (ed. U. Becker and J. van Oorschot; ABG 17; Leipzig 2005), 81–100.
60 Cf. Hos 10:12; 13:4.
61 See recently Leuenberger, "Herkunft" (see n. 3) and Blum, "Mose" (see n. 3).
62 See Levin, "Israel" (see n. 1), 142–156: 151.

inhabitants of the cities who were no longer able to survive in their ancestral dwelling places started to develop new areas of settlements, mainly in the middle part of the central mountain region. The patterns of settlements now show villages and an agrarian lifestyle. At he the same time the nomads who had previously formed a close symbiosis with the residents were forced to settle down. The Hapiru, too, whose affinity to the Hebrews has long been recognised, also seem to have integrated themselves into the new village structure. As far as the cultural history is concerned this shift marks the end of the Bronze Age and the beginning of the Iron Age. During this period we have the first epigraphic attestation of Israel. It is found on the victory stele of Pharaoh Merenptah, the successor of Rameses II, from the year 1209 BCE.[63] The "Israel" mentioned here describes a group of people, maybe a tribe or a small group of tribes, who settled in middle Palestine. There is some evidence that this Israel should be identified with the new settlers of the early Iron Age. The next mentioning of "Israel" is then found in Assyrian and Moabite sources as a term for the Northern Kingdom.

The negative findings of the sources correspond to the fact that the biblical texts describing an Exodus from Egypt are several centuries younger than the assumed event. Already the fathers of the New Documentary Hypothesis proposed a date during the 9th and 8th century BCE for the pre-priestly sources of the Exodus (J and E). Today one generally favours a 7th century date for the oldest traceable core of the narrative.[64] It is a myth of origin of the Northern Kingdom that wants – after the fall of the monarchy (720 BCE) – to provide a new religious identity as the people of Yʜᴡʜ.

It may be possible to find the oldest traces of the Exodus tradition in the official theology of the Northern Kingdom (1 Kings 12:28) and in the corresponding sayings of the Book of Hosea.[65] If that is the case, we have to note that these traditions do not say anything more than that Yʜᴡʜ brought Israel up from the land of Egypt. It remains open what detailed notions were associated with these formulae. Be it as it may, the literary evidence for an Exodus from Egypt

---

63 *CoS II*, 40 – 41.

64 See D.B. Redford, *Egypt, Canaan and Israel in Ancient Times* (Princeton 1992), 98 – 122; R.G. Kratz, *Composition* (see n. 21), 303 – 306; Blum, "Mose" (see n. 3), 62; E. Otto, *Mose. Geschichte und Legende* (München 2006); K. Schmid, *The Old Testament. A Literary History* (Minneapolis 2012), 87 – 92; J.C. Gertz, "The Literature of the Old Testament: Torah and Former Prophets," in *T&T Clark Handbook of the Old Testament. An Introduction to the Literature, Religion and History of the Old Testament* (ed. J.C. Gertz et al.; London 2012), 235 – 382: 356 – 360; C. Berner, *Die Exoduserzählung. Das literarische Werden einer Ursprungslegende Israels* (FAT 73; Tübingen 2010).

65 See H. Pfeiffer, *Das Heiligtum von Bethel im Spiegel des Hoseabuches* (FRLANT 183; Göttingen 1999). The so-called Song of Miriam (Exod 15:21) cannot be used as an ancient source fort he Exodus; see Kratz, *Composition* (see n. 21), 284.

is hardly older than the period of the monarchy. Any quest for historical events that are centuries older leads into the realm of speculation. If one does not want to abandon speculation, the popular explanation that not Israel as a whole but only an Exodus-group came from Egypt seems to be the best solution. Neither the Hebrew Bible, nor the extra-biblical sources, however, are aware of such a *group*.[66] Additionally one has to explain how a particular experience of an alleged group could be transformed into a notion that *all Israel* had an Egyptian past.[67] On the basis of the sources, the model, then, appears rather intricate.

Other attempts to correlate the tradition of Israel's Egyptian past with Egypt's hegemony over late Bronze Age Canaan are more promising as they take the historical data available into account. Here, the origin of the tradition is not Egypt as the geographical place but rather as *political* entity. Angelika Berlejung states:

> "It is possible, however, that the Egypt of the exodus did not in fact refer to Egypt in the geographical sense, but rather to Egypt in a political sense, so that a migration from southern Palestinian city-states could be interpreted as an exodus from Egypt."[68]

Indeed, from a Hittite perspective "Egypt" could denote the Canaanite territory as well.[69] The local rulers, too, who simply use the title *ḫazannu* ("mayor") in

---

66 The identification of an assumed "Exodus-group" with Edomites or other Shasu known from the Egyptian sources (as proposed by Leuenberger, "Herkunft" [see n. 3], 8–11) already presupposes the correctness of the assumption of an Exodus-group.

67 This problem was only partly solved by M. Noth's theory of an amphictyony and by the revolutionary model proposed by G.E. Mendenhall and N.K. Gottwald (see the overview in H. Donner, *Geschichte des Volkes Israel und seiner Nachbarn in Grundzügen I* [GAT 4,1; Göttingen 1984], 124–126).

68 A. Berlejung, "History and Religion of Ancient Israel," in *T&T Clark Handbook* (see n. 62), 59–234, here 108; cf. *ead.*, "Exodus," *HGANT*, 176–178, here 177; M. Köckert, "YHWH in the Northern and Southern Kingdom," in *One God – One Cult – One Nation. Archaeological and Biblical Perspectives* (ed. R.G. Kratz and H. Spieckermann; BZAW 405; Berlin 2010), 357–394, here 370.

69 See CTH 378.II ("Mursili's 'Second' Plague Prayer to the Storm-god of Hatti"); English translation in I. Singer, *Hittite Prayers* (SBLWAW 11; Atlanta 2002), 57–60. On the cuneiform text see A. Goetze, "Die Pestgebete des Muršiliš," in *Kleinasiatische Forschungen* [ed. F. Sommer and H. Ehelolf; Weimar 1929], 161–251, here 208–211 and 224–227). In the proposed resettlement to Egypt agreed to in the Kurustamma treaty (on the complex sources see D. Sürenhagen, *Paritätische Staatsverträge aus hethitischer Sicht* [StMed 5; Pavia 1985]), Egypt (*I-NA* KUR ^{URU}*Mi-iz-ri*) does not mean the country by the Nile but Canaan (see H. Cancik, "Das ganze Land Ḫet," in *Die Hethiter und ihr Reich. Das Volk der 1000 Götter* [ed. Kunst- uns Ausstellungshalle der Bundesrepublik Deutschland GmbH; Stuttgart 2002], 30–33, here 32). In a similar way the land of Amka (between Lebanon and anti-Lebanon) belongs to the borderland of Egypt.

their correspondence with Egypt,[70] do not tire to remind Pharaoh of his responsibility for the land/the cities/the fields of the king.[71] Next to the diplomatic correspondence, the material culture of late Bronze Age Canaan, too, displays various degrees of Egyptian influence.[72] Against this background it is not surprising that the anthropomorphic geography of the Table of Nations (P) presents Canaan as the son of Ham and the brother of Mizraim (Gen 10:6). If one looks for the origin of the Exodus tradition not in Egypt as a country but as representing the Egyptian province of Canaan, then Israel comes indeed out of "Egypt." As far as the Bible is concerned this would imply a secondary process of theologisation of the Exodus tradition and a change in the perception of Egypt, now referring to the land by the Nile.[73]

Either way the nature of the sources of the Exodus do not allow to argue for an Israel in Egypt that would then become the carrier of a YHWH tradition originally located in the South.

4

Finally, in our quest for the possibility of an origin of YHWH in the South we have to look at those non-priestly parts of the narrative that connect Moses, the Midianites or Kenites, and YHWH (Exod 2:15–20; 3:1–4:17, 18–20.24–26; 18; Num 10:29–32; [12;] Judg 1:16; 4:11). The texts gave rise to the so-called Midianite hypothesis, i.e. a theory placing the origins of the worship of YHWH in Midian.[74] According to the theory, Moses – related by marriage to the Midianites – serves as the mediator of YHWH worship to Israel. Even the most optimistic assessment of the tradition-historical circumstances has to admit that the circumstances are not that clear. W. H. Schmidt for example states that the different reports of Exod

---

70 See M. Weippert, *Historisches Textbuch zum Alten Testament* (GAT 10; Göttingen), 139 n. 384.
71 See EA 244; 250; 287; 288 (English translation in W.L. Moran, *The Armana Letters* [Baltimore 1992]).
72 On the iconography see O. Keel and C. Uehlinger, *Gods, Goddesses, and Images of God in Ancient Israel* (Edinburgh 1998), 49–108.
73 E. Blum ("Mose" [see n. 3], 46–48) does not subscribe to this view but nevertheless combines the classic view of an Exodus group with the proposal above: "Falls die ägyptische Herrschaft [...] tatsächlich prägende Erinnerungsspuren bei der früh-israelitischen Bevölkerung hinterlassen haben sollte, bildeten diese einen Resonanzboden, der die Identifikation mit einer 'von außen' vermittelten Exodustradition nicht unerheblich zu fördern vermochte" (48).
74 See the overview in W. H. Schmidt, *Alttestamentlicher Glaube* (Neukirchen–Vluyn ⁸1996), 86–93 and the major trends in the history of scholarship in W. H. Schmidt, *Exodus, Sinai und Mose* (EdF 191; Darmstadt ³1995), 124–130.

2–3 and Exod 18 do not indicate beyond doubt that the Midianties worshipped
Yʜwʜ.[75] As a result he is forced to concede that the Midianite hypothesis cannot
be proven beyond reasonable doubt.[76]

Like all the other texts discussed above, the Midianite hypothesis has the
genesis of the text against itself. The central text is Exod 18:1–12. Here we
read of a joint sacrifice of Moses and his Midianite relatives (v. 12) led by "Jethro,
priest of Midian, Moses' father-in-law" (v. 1). The sacrifice is later followed by a
solemn avowal of Jethro (v. 10). Already the founders of the New Documentary
Hypothesis assumed that we have a passage here that cannot be older than
the Elohistic source. Recent exegesis, however, has shown that the pericope is
fairly late and may be a post-priestly addition,[77] later updated by Exod 18:13–27.

Exod 2:11–4:20a, too, cannot support a Midianite hypothesis. The literary
core is as follows:

> (2:11) One day, when Moses had grown up, he went out to his people [...][78] and he saw an
> Egyptian beating a Hebrew, one of his people. (12) He looked this way and that, and seeing
> no one he killed the Egyptian and hid him in the sand. (13) When he went out the next day,
> behold, two Hebrews were struggling together; and he said to the man that did the wrong,
> "Why do you strike your fellow?" (14) He answered, "Who made you a prince and a judge
> over us? Do you mean to kill me as you killed the Egyptian?" Then Moses was afraid, and
> thought, "Surely the thing is known." (15) When Pharaoh heard of it, he sought to kill
> Moses. But Moses fled from Pharaoh, and stayed in the land of Midian [...].[79]
> (3:1) Now Moses was keeping the flock of his father-in-law, Jethro [...][80] and he led his
> flock to the west side of the steppe, and came [...][81] into the wilderness[82] (2) [...][83] and he

---

75 "Die verschiedenen Berichte (in Exod 2f; 18) über Beziehungen Israels zu den Midianitern
bezeugen nicht ausdrücklich, daß diese – und mit ihnen Moses Schwiegervater, der ‚Priester
von Midian' – Jahwe verehrten" (W.H. Schmidt, *Glaube* [see n. 74], 90).

76 "Die sog. Midiniter- oder Keniterhypothese läßt sich [...] nicht eindeutig erweisen" (W.H.
Schmidt, *Glaube* [see n. 74], 93 who then, nevertheless, refuses to give up the theory).

77 See Blum, *Studien zur Komposition des Pentateuch* (BZAW 189; Berlin 1990), 158–163; Blum,
"Mose" (see n. 3), 51 f.; V. Haarmann, *JHWH-Verehrer der Völker. Die Hinwendung von Nichtisrae-
liten zum Gott Israels in alttestamentlichen Überlieferungen* (AThANT 91; Zürich 2008), 59–94;
Berner, *Exoduserzählung* (see n. 64), 406–426.

78 Cf. Berner, *Exoduserzählung* (see n. 64), 53.

79 The tensions in 2:15bβ₂–22 (change of name of Moses' father-in-law [2:18; 3:1; 4:18]; number of
Moses' children [2:22; 4:20aʾ]) are of a literary nature as the double use of שׁוב in 2:15 indicates.
The parallel motif in Gen 24 and Gen 29 rather points to a (pre-priestly) addition (see Kratz, *Com-
position* [see n. 21], 284–285) than to a "pre-Yahwistic source" (Levin, *Jahwist* [see n. 17], 323 f.);
2:23aβ–25 belong to P (M. Noth, *Überlieferungsgeschichte* [see n. 10], 18) and 2:23aα is part of the
Pentateuchal redaction (Kratz, *Composition* [see n. 21], 285).

80 Cf. 2:16 and see n. 79.

81 Cf. Schmidt, *Exodus* (see n. 74), 136; Levin, *Jahwist* (see n. 17), 331.

82 Cf. Levin, *Jahwist* (see n. 17), 331.

looked and a bush[84] was burning, yet it was not consumed. (3) And Moses said, "I will turn aside and see this great sight" [...][85] When YHWH saw that he turned aside to see, God[86] called to him out of the bush, "Moses, Moses!" And he said, "Here am I." (5) Then he said, "Do not come near; put off your sandals from your feet, for the place on which you are standing is holy ground." (6) [...][87] And Moses hid his face, for he was afraid to look at God. (7) Then YHWH said, "I have seen the affliction of my people [...], and have heard their cry [...] (8) and I have come down to deliver them out of the hand of the Egyptians, and to bring them up out of that land to a good and broad land [...] Go and gather the elders of Israel together, and say to them, 'YHWH, the God of your fathers, [...] has appeared to me, saying, [...] (17) [...] I will bring you up out of the affliction of Egypt [...] (21) And I will give this people favour in the sight of the Egyptians; and when you go, you shall not go empty. (22) Each woman shall ask of her neighbour, and of her who sojourns in her house, jewellery of silver and of gold, and clothing, and you shall put them on your sons and on your daughters; thus you shall despoil the Egyptians'" [...] (4:18) Moses went back to Jethro his father-in-law and said to him, "Let me go back, I pray, to my kinsmen in Egypt and see whether they are still alive." And Jethro said to Moses, "Go in peace." [...][88] (20a) So Moses took his wife and his sons and set them on an ass, and went back to the land of Egypt.

The passage is part of the older Exodus narrative from the 7th century BCE. It hardly gives raise to further tradition-historical queries. At best, the scene of the burning bush in Exod 3:1–6*, reconstructed here, may display such signs. Mentioning Moses' father in-law[89] indirectly and by name (cf. 4:18) appears quite abrupt after the note of his flight in 2:15 where Midianite relatives of

---

83 Cf. Schmidt, *Exodus* (see n. 74), 112 f.; Levin, *Jahwist* (see n. 17), 326; J.C. Gertz, *Tradition und Redaktion in der Exoduserzählung. Untersuchungen zur Endredaktion des Pentateuch* (FRLANT 186; Göttingen 2000), 266 f.

84 On the determination see GK[28] §126 q–r.

85 3:3b is a dogmatic correction that – on the basis of v. 6b – aims to avoid the misunderstanding that the "great sight" is God himself.

86 The repetition of the subject while changing the designation for God in 3:4a and 3:4b appears motiveless (see the changes in LXX and Sam.) and – in the new documentary hypothesis – is generally used as an indication to separate the text in two different sources (see e.g. L. Schmidt, "Die Berufung des Mose in Exodus 3 als Beispiel für Jahwist [J] und Elohist [E]," *ZAW* 85 [2014], 339–357). Alternatively one could argue for a tradition-historical solution; then 3:1–6* would integrate a tradition already known to the oldest composition of the Exodus narrative (see below); if that is correct, v. 4b and v. 6b ("Elohim") would be part of the tradition while v. 4a and v. 7 ("YHWH") can be attributed to the composition (cf. v. 6; Levin, *Jahwist* [see n. 17], 329; differently Gertz, *Tradition* [see n. 83], 270).

87 Cf. Gertz, *Tradition* (see n. 83), 270 f. For a further reconstruction of the core in 3:1–4:17 see Gertz, *Tradition* (see n. 83), 281–327.

88 On 4:19 see Wellhausen, *Composition* (see n. 7), 71; Kratz, *Composition* (see n. 21), 284–285.

89 If this mentioning is indeed part of the original story; for a different assumption see Berner, *Exoduserzählung* (see n. 64), 68 ff.

Moses are not mentioned. In contrast to the announcement in 3:7–8* and 3:16–17* that Yʜᴡʜ will deliver his people from Egypt, 3:1–6* can be interpreted as an independent story describing the discovery of a sacred place. Against this background, the conventional hypothesis that Exod 3:1–6* integrates parts of an older cultic etiology is worth considering.[90]

If our hypothesis is correct, the assumed piece of tradition would be crucial for a tradition-historical enterprise. Especially so if one realizes that – beyond Exod 3:1–6* – it is more than difficult to argue for a pre-literary tradition of Moses. Even more striking is the fact that neither "Yʜᴡʜ" nor "Midian" are part of the tradition. The scene is simply a "burning bush"[91] in an unknown wasteland beyond some steppe. Only in the literary form of the Exodus narrative will this place be localized in Midian (Exod 2:15*).[92] As a result, Moses Midianite relatives are part of a late literary process. The deity who appears in the burning bush is called "Elohim" by the assumed tradition. Only the authors of the Exodus narrative identify this God with Yʜᴡʜ. Against this background it is impossible to pose religion-historical queries about the origin of Yʜᴡʜ here.[93]

In passing it should be noted that the literary core of the Exodus narrative by no means gives the impression that Yʜᴡʜ belongs to Midianite realms. According to Exod 3:16 he presents himself as being "the God of your fathers,"[94] i.e. a deity that is already known to the Israelites although Moses only discovers the sacred place in the Midianite wasteland. The encounter with Yʜᴡʜ as such is neither new for Moses nor for the Israelites. What is new is Yʜᴡʜ's appearance and promise for deliverance at this precise place. The epiphany of Yʜᴡʜ in a burning bush of the Midianite desert is due to the geographical realities of the

---

90 Cf. Noth, *Überlieferungsgeschichte* (see n. 10), 221 n. 547; Schmidt, *Exoduserzählung* (see n. 74), 110–122; Levin, *Jahwist* (see n. 17), 329; contrast Berner, *Exoduserzählung*, (see n. 64), 75.
91 For religious-historical parallels see Gressmann, *Mose* (see n. 9), 25–31.
92 That the Midianite relatives of Moses will be a problem for later traditions (cf. Exod 4:24–26; 18; Num 12 [?]; Judg 1:16; 4:18) is not necessarily and argument against such a view. In the Hebrew Bible the Midianites are not simply known as enemies of Israel: Gen 37:28.36 and Bar 3:13 mention Midianite merchants. Still in the post-monarchic period in texts like Gen 25:1–4 the Midianites are genealogically linked to Abraham and Keturah und thus part of the (extended) relatives of Israel (cf. 1 Chr 1:32f.). Conversely, the text that display an open enmity with Midian are probably younger than the Exodus narrative (Num 22:4.7; 25; 31; Jos 13:21; Isa 9:3; Ps 83). Only the core of the Gideon narrative (Judg 6–9*) may reflect an older local conflict between Manassites and Midianites.
93 Thus already Levin, "Israel" (see n. 11), 146. Even if the name Yʜᴡʜ would be part of the original core in Exod 3* this would only provide limited information since the *Gattung* of a cultic etiology does not necessarily allow for conclusions about the origin of the deity.
94 Equivalent to the "God of your ancestors" (*Gott eurer Vorfahren*) in the Neue Zürcher Bibel.

narrative and it fits very well with the theological style of the Exodus narrative. It provides a response to the downfall of the monarchy in Israel by dissolving the religious symbiosis of God, kingship and people. Instead of such a symbiosis the narrative creates the notion of a people of Yhwh (Exod 3:7), which is not in cultic continuity to the official sanctuaries of the cultivated land. Since *this* Israel originates from the void of Egyptian hardship, it is only logical that its God will appear in the void of the Midinanite desert to announce deliverance to his people.[95]

Within this frame it is also possible to explain the integration of the figure of Moses into the Exodus narrative.[96] The name of Moses is reminiscent of Egyptian royal names (Thutmoses, Ramses) and thus of kingship (cf. Exod 2:1–10) – but not of Israelite kingship, which is theologically absent in the Exodus narrative. On the other hand it was possible to create a Hebrew meaning for the Egyptian name and connect it to the narrative of deliverance (Exod 2:10). Both aspects provide good conditions to outline a leader figure for the defunct monarchy – especially so as the abbreviated form of the name keeps the distance to Egyptian royal names. Lastly, the tradition in Exod 3:1–6* did already know of a special relationship of Moses to God, which could be easily transferred to Yhwh.

We can neglect the other passages that connect Moses to Midian. Exod 4:24–26 and Num 10:29–32 presuppose the Midianite relatives of Moses and also belong to late parts of the Pentateuch.[97] A growing uneasiness with the Midianite relatives of Moses[98] during the post-monarchic period is responsible for connecting him with the Kenites in Judg 1:16 and 4:11.[99] These passages cannot clarify the question of the origin of Yhwh anyway.

---

95 Cf. Kratz, *Composition* (see n. 21), 284–286.

96 The conjecture that Moses was added later to the tradition of the Exodus is not new: cf. already Noth, *Überlieferungsgeschichte* (see n. 10), 178–180. – Hos 12:14 does not represent a conscious new accentuation by Hosea during the 8th century (thus Blum, "Mose" [see n. 3], 42f. but rather presupposes the deuteronomistic portrait of Moses as a prophet (Deut 18:15.18) and tutor of Israel. This finds support in the otherwise opaque and indirect formulations: "By a prophet Yhwh brought Israel up from Egypt, and by a prophet it [sc. Israel] was preserved." On the literary origin of Hosea 12 see M. Schott, "Die Jakobpassagen in Hosea 12," *ZThK* 112 (2015), 1–26.

97 See e.g. Levin, *Jahwist* (see n. 17), 332f.370f.

98 Cf. Blum, "Mose" (see n. 3), 50.

99 Judg 1:16 is part of the late frame of the Book of Judges. The information "father-in-law of Moses" is a gloss following Judg 4:11 – a passage that is not part of the core of Judg 4 and that presupposes Judg 1:16* (minus "father-in-law of Moses").

5

The repertoire of arguments for an origin of YHWH in the South also includes epi-graphic sources from Palestine and Egypt. These are the inscriptions from the southern Palestinian site of Kuntillet 'Ajrud as well as the Egyptian list of place names found at Soleb and its younger copy from Amara-West.[100]

As far as Kuntillet 'Ajrud is concerned, for our investigation the designations for God – normally rendered as "YHWH of Samaria" and "YHWH of Teman/the South" – are of importance. In contrast to the expression "YHWH of Samaria" the phrase "YHWH of Teman/the South" is regarded as evidence for the tradi-tion-historical origin of the worship of YHWH.[101] Specifically, the evidence comes from a site excavated by Z. Meshel in 1975/76 and situated on a hill rough-ly 15 km west from the road between Gaza and Elat (*Darb el Ghazza*) and 50 km south of Kadesh Barnea. The site is dated to the 8th century BCE.[102] The inscrip-tions with the designations for God come from a building whose layout resem-bles a fortification ("Building A"). A second building belonging to the site ("Building B") is thus far without parallel in the archaeology of Palestine.[103] Shortly after the discovery a broad discussion of the finds developed. A final re-port of the excavations including photographs and an edition of the texts was published in 2012.[104]

Architecture, epigraphy, and iconography convey, altogether, a unique char-acter; this makes statements about their function quite difficult. Current scholar-ship describes the site either as a caravanserai or as a sanctuary (including a school).[105] It is argued that inscriptions and iconography point to a Northern ori-gin of the site.[106]

---

100 See the essay by F. Adrom and M. Müller in this volume.
101 See Judg 5:4f; Hab 3:3 (!).7; Deut 33:2 and Ps 68:8.
102 Cf. Meshel, *Kuntillet 'Ajrud* (see n. 55), 3–9.61–63.
103 Cf. Meshel, *Kuntillet 'Ajrud* (see n. 55), 11–59.
104 Cf. Meshel, *Kuntillet 'Ajrud* (see n. 55).
105 For the dominating interpretation as a caravanserai see recently E. Blum, "Die Wandins-chriften 4.2 und 4.6 sowie die Pithos-Inschrift 3.9 aus Kuntillet 'Aǧrūd," *ZDPV* 129 (2013), 22–54; for the interpretation as a sanctuary on the basis of the Mazzebas in the entry to Building A see N. Na'aman and N. Lissovsky, "Kuntillet 'Ajrud. Sacred Trees and the Ashera," *Tel Aviv* 35 (2008), 186–208. The interpretation as a school (cf. A. Lemaire, *Les écoles et la formation de la Bible dans L'ancient Israel* [OBO 39; Fribourg 1981], 25–32) regards the inscriptions on the storage jars as a scribal exercise of pupils but cannot explain the remote location. H. Weip-pert, *Palästina in vorhellenistischer Zeit. Mit einem Beitrag von L. Mildenberg* (HdArch. Vordera-sien 2,1; München 1988), 618, und Meshel, *Kuntillet 'Ajrud* (see n. 55), 65–69 argues for a sanc-tuary that included a school.

The relevant inscriptions were applied with red and black ink to storage jars (Pithoi) and walls. The designations for God appear in the context of blessings, letters[107] and epistolary formulae.[108] The "pragmatics" of the texts, which can only be discussed in the context of an overall discussion of the site, remains vague. Possible interpretations are the context of a school[109] or so-called "stationary" letters[110] left behind by travellers. According to the transliteration of the *editio princeps* the designations for God are as follows:[111] *yhwh. šmrn* (Pithos–inscription 3.1, line 2 [Pithos A]), *yhwh tmn* (Pithos–inscription 3.6, line 5–6 ["Pithos B"]), *yhwh.htmn* (Pithos–inscription 3.9, line 1 ["Pithos B"]), []*hwh[.]tymn* (Wall–inscription 4.11, line 1) and *yhwh,htj[mn ...]* (Wall–inscription 4.1.1, line 2).

As far as one can discern from the photographs of the *editio princeps* the epigraphic evidence is not as clear as sometimes assumed:[112]

–   In inscription 3.6[113] there is a significant gap between *hwh* and the rest of the next sign. According to the photograph it is difficult to identify it as *taw*. The sign before the *nun* can be interpreted as a *mem* but *kaph* or *nun* are equally possible,

–   In inscription 3.9[114] we can only identify for certain the *he* and maybe the *yod* of the assumed Tetragrammaton. Of the sequence of letters generally read as *htmn* only *he* and *taw* are legible. It is followed by a slightly curved downstroke and maybe the letter *nun*.[115]

---

106 Cf. Meshel, *Kuntillet 'Ajrud* (see n. 55), 65–69.

107 Cf. Blum, "Die Wandinschriften" (see n. 105), esp. 48–50.

108 Cf. J. Renz, *Die althebräischen Inschriften. Teil 1: Text und Kommentar* (Handbuch der althebräischen Epigraphik 1; Darmstadt 1995), 47–64; J. Renz, *Die althebräischen Inschriften. Teil 2: Zusammenfassende Erörterungen, Paläographie und Glossar* (Handbuch der althebräischen Epigraphik 2; Darmstadt 1995), 24.

109 See n. 105. We cannot debate here how possible scribal exercises of pupils can be used in a discussion about the origin of Yhwh.

110 See Blum, "Wandinschriften" (see n. 105), esp. 48–50.

111 See Meshel, *Kuntillet 'Ajrud* (see n. 55), 86–100.105–107 (transliteration here in square script). The numbering follows the editions of Meshel.

112 My sincere thanks to Prof. Dr. Josef Tropper (Humboldt-Universität zu Berlin) for his help with the epigraphic problems as well as for stimulating discussion of the evidence.

113 Meshel, *Kuntillet 'Ajrud* (see n. 55), fig. 5.38 and fig. 5.39.

114 Meshel, *Kuntillet 'Ajrud* (see n. 55), fig. 5.42a. and fig. 5.42b.

115 An alternative reading to *htm?n* could be *htn?n* ("who gives us") – interpreting it as ptc. q. act with suff. 1st pers. pl. of *tnh* (by-form to *ntn*, cf. Hos 8:9, 10); the same should then be contemplated for inscription 3.6.

– The reading []*hwh*[.]*tymn* – possibly written in Phoenician – in the wall inscription 4.1.1 (line 1)[116] harbours several uncertainties due to the strong fragmentation. The rest of the Tetragrammaton and the assumed *tymn* are found on different fragments that cannot be connected seamlessly. The same has to be said of the following fragment preserving *'šrt*. There are only traces of the *taw* of *tymn*. In line 2 only the *yod* of *hty*[*mn* ...] can be identified with certainty.

According to the above the attestation of a "Yʜwʜ (ha-)Teman" is likely for the wall inscription 4.1.1 although not certain. The same interpretation is possible for the Pithos-inscriptions 3.6 and 3.9 but there are other alternative readings too. Here we have to note that the orthography of the wall inscription appears to be of Judean provenance while the two Pithos-inscriptions reveal Israelite writing.[117] The phrase "Yʜwʜ (ha-)Teman" would then be attested with some certainty by a hand of a Judean and possibly, too, by an Israelite. The evidence limits all attempts to understand the phrase "Yʜwʜ (ha-)Teman" in the light of *yhwh.šmrn*.[118] Additionally we have to note that the reading of *šmrn* (Pithos-inscription 3.1, line 2) as "Samaria" is only one possibility – especially so as former interpretations have drawn attention to the possibility that the epithet may simply mean "our guardian"[119] (*šmr* ptc. q. act. m. sg. with suff. 1st pers. pl.).[120]

In all, it remains unclear why the phrase "Yʜwʜ (ha-) Teman" should provide information about the original home of the God Yʜwʜ. As is shown by comparative evidence from the Ancient Near East, the construction "name of the deity + toponym" is used to connect the godhead with its cultic places or prominent geographic realities (e. g. "Haddah of Chalab"; "Ishtar of Nineveh"; "Baal Zaphon"). Designations of this kind point to certain geographic or cultic manifestations of the deities but never to their *origin*.

It is further unclear which geographical reality "(ha-)Teman" refers to and how "(ha-)Teman" at Kuntillet 'Ajrud relates to the far from conclusive evidence

---

116 Meshel, *Kuntillet 'Ajrud* (see n. 55), fig. 5.49.

117 Meshel, *Kuntillet 'Ajrud* (see n. 55).

118 See e. g. Blum, "Mose" (see n. 3), 57 who argues that the travellers resting at Kuntillet 'Ajrud use both phrases to indicate their lace of origin (Samaria) and their destination (Teman): "Hält man sich die Situation der Fernreisenden vor Augen, liegen die Gründe gerade für diese Gottesbezeichnungen auf der Hand: Sie benennen innerhalb der Segenswünsche die Gottheit entweder aus der Perspektive ihrer Herkunft (JHWH von Samaria) oder in der Perspektive ihres Reiseziels (JHWH von Teman). Beide Male wird JHWH nicht nach einem einzelnen Kultort, sondern nach einer Region näher bestimmt."

119 Cf. Renz, *Handbuch I* (see n. 108), 61 n. 2.

120 For a use of *šmr* in the context of a blessing see the inscription 3.6, line 1.

of Teman in the Hebrew Bible.[121] Against the background of Ancient Near Eastern designations for gods an interpretation as a cultic place[122] (in or outside Edom) could be as likely as a regional interpretation.[123] The expression "YHWH (ha-)Teman" does not provide any more information about his origin than the phrase "Ishtar of Nineveh" does about the one of Ishtar.

A list of Egyptian place names from the temple of Amenophis III (1402–1364 BCE) at Nubian Soleb is often used as a further evidence for an original home of YHWH in the South. To this is added a further list from the temple of Rameses II (1290–1224 BCE) at Amara-West, which is usually regarded as a copy of the list from Soleb.[124] S. Herrmann, especially, has utilized these lists for a Southern origin of YHWH.[125] More recently, M. Leuenberger has again defended this view.[126]

The list of Soleb is part of the inscriptions on the pillars of the hypostyle hall of the temple. These inscriptions mention territories, cities, and groups of people. The pillars to the North of the East-West axis are covered with entries referring to the Asiatic region, while the Southern pillars are inscribed with African names. On pillar 4 of the Northern row three of originally six entries are preserved. Each entry begins with the phrase "land of the Shasu (-nomads)" or "Shasu-land" followed by a proper name which one generally interprets as the name of the respective country:

4 a 1 Š3św-Land *T-w'-b-ï-r'*
4 a 2 Š3św-Land *Y-h-w3*
4 a 3 Š3św-Land *Š3-m-t'*

The list from Amara-West contains six entries; here the last three names seem to include the Soleb list in reverse order. There are, however, two variants in No 96 and No 97 that can be explained as scribal errors:

92   Š3św-Land *Š3-'-r- ï- r'*

---

121 See above p. 128.
122 For the appelative sense of personal names and the possibility of determination see GK[28] §125 c–e; Meshel, *Kuntillet 'Ajrud* (see n. 55), 100.
123 I am not aware of any Ancient Near Eastern evidence that connects a deity's name with a region or a designation for a territory. If the interpretation of *yhwh šmrn* as "YHWH of Samaria" is correct, I would argue here too for an explanation of *šmrn* as a cultic place rather than a region. Bethel and Dan (1 Kings 12:29) only became state sanctuaries during the 8th century BCE.
124 See Weippert, *Handbuch* (see n. 63), No. 075, 183 f. The quotes from the lists follow this edition.
125 S. Herrmann, "Der alttestamentliche Gottesname," in *Gesammelte Studien zur Geschichte und Theologie des Alten Testaments* (ed. S. Hermann; ThB 75; München 1986), 76–88.
126 See Leuenberger, "Herkunft," (see n. 3), esp. 4–8.

93 Š3św-Land R'-b3-n-3
94 Š3św-Land P-y-s- p3-y-ś
95 Š3św-Land Š3-m-t'
96 Š3św-Land Y-h-*w3
97 Š3św-Land W-r'-ï-b-r'

For our investigation, the name of the Shasu land Y-h-w3 in the list from Soleb is important as it suggests – on the basis of the same consonants – a relationship to the divine name.[127] Additionally it is believed that one can extrapolate the geographical location of the Shasu land from the list – though not from the Soleb list itself but rather from the list from Amara-West as here too – after an emendation in No 96 – appears the toponym "Yhw(h)."[128] The relevant paragraph of the latter list opens with the entry "Shasu land Š3-'-r- ï- r'" (No 92), usually identified with the Edomite Seir of the Hebrew Bible.[129] It is further argued that the entry also serves as a heading for the passage as a whole[130] so that all other Shasu lands of the list – including the "Shasu land *Yhw(h)" – have to be located in the vicinity of Seir. Takening all this together, then, would attest to an affinity of the God Yʜwʜ to the region of Edom-Seir during the late Bronze Age.

This interpretation can – at best – be described as ambitious. The correlation of toponym and divine name is pure conjecture[131] – even though the possibility of such a connection in principal could exist. The same has to be said of the rather speculative proposal to interpret entry No 92 of the list from Amara-West as a heading. To point only to the fact that *other* lists display such phenomenon is hardly enough.[132] There is a reason why M. Weippert, for example, does not repeat this argument in his recent edition of the lists.[133] Furthermore, to describe the function of the Š3-'-r- ï- r'-entry as heading would only fit for the younger list (Amara-West) because in the list from Soleb, Š3-'-r- ï- r' would be expected in sixth position and in any case after Y-h-w3. This prompts the further question

---

127 See esp. M. Görg, "Jahwe – ein Toponym?," *BN* 1 (1976), 7–14.
128 Weippert, *Textbuch* (see n. 63), 184 n. 39.
129 E.g. Leuenberger, "Herkunft" (see n. 3), 7.
130 See M. Weippert, "Edom und Israel," *TRE* 9.291–299, here 292; and recently Leuenberger, "Herkunft" (see n. 3), 7.
131 Already in 1972 did M. Weippert dismiss such a correlation (see M. Weippert, "'Heiliger Krieg' in Israel und Assyrien. Kritische Anmerkungen zu Gerhard von Rads Konzept des 'Heiligen Krieges in Israel,'" *ZAW* 84 [1972], 460–493, here 491, n. 144); for a critique from Egyptology see H. Goedicke, "The Tetragramm in Egyptian?," *SSEA.J* 24 (1997), 24–27.
132 See Leuenberger, "Herkunft" (see n. 3), 7.
133 Cf. Weippert, *Textbuch* (see n. 63), 183f.

of the reasons for such an arraying interest of the copyist who otherwise were not even able to reproduce the names of the list from Soleb correctly.

We can thus only discern the sequence "Land of the Shasu"/"Shasu-land" as a pattern of order. The decision whether the toponyms point to one and the same region presupposes the previous identification of the places mentioned. Here we encounter the actual *crux interpretum* of the lists. Thus far, none of the toponyms mentioned have been identified beyond doubt. In a strict sense this has to be said of *Š3-ʿ-r- ï- r'* (Amara-West, No 92) too as the usual identification with (Edomite) Seir is based on an emendation (*Š3-ʿ ï- r*).[134] In the light of frequent dittographies in Egyptian as well as numerous other scribal errors in the list from Amara-West such an emendation may be possible. Every solution, however, that operates without such auxiliary assumption is methodological preferable. Maybe an older proposal by M. C. Astour who identified *Š3-ʿ-r- ï- r'* with Middle-Assyrian Šeḫlal should be reconsidered.[135] That this interpretation has not been widely received is surprising – especially so as it could provide an explanation for the name used by Ramses II.[136] M.C. Astour's explanation has the further advantage that it allows to connect the other toponyms to the Middle-Assyrian realm.[137] If that is correct, the "Shasu-Land Yhw(h)" would then not be Edom-Seir but located somewhere in the Northern regions. Such a localisation would tally well with the continuation of the list from Amara-West, which mentions Gintikirmil in the Carmel region (No 98) and Bet-Anat (Soleb, No 4 b 1) in Northern (?) Palestine.[138] Even if one continues to read "Seir" in the list from Amara-West (No. 92), the geographical relationship between the Shasu-land (*) Yhw(h) and the "Shasu-land *Seir" remains unclear and equally a relation of the toponym "Yhw(h)" to the deity YHWH remains a mere postulate. It is, therefore, not possible to use the lists as a subsistent witness for the origin of the worship of YHWH in the region of Edom-Seir.

The review of the evidence generally used to argue for a home of YHWH in the Southern regions of the cultivated land of Palestine arrives at a sobering result: When looking at the texts individually none of the credentials supports such a view. The Sinai pericope is a late insertion into the pre-priestly story of Exodus and conquest of the land. The texts describing a theophany, which are

---

134 Weippert, *Textbuch* (see n. 63), 183 f.
135 Writing ⟨r⟩ for /l/; see M.C. Astour, "Yahweh in Egyptian Topographic Lists," in *FS E. Edel* (ed. M. Görg and E. Pusch; ÄAT 1; Bamberg 1979), 17–33: 22 (vgl. EAT 62,11.16.20.31.32.46; 371,19).
136 M. Weippert, *Textbuch* (see n. 63), 183.
137 For details see the identifications in Astour, "Yahweh" (see n. 135).
138 Cf. E. Edel, "Die Ortsnamenlisten in den Tempeln von Aksha, Amarah und Soleb im Sudan," *BN* 11 (1980), 63–79, here 68; Müller, *Wettergott* (see n. 2), 243 f., n. 50.

usually regarded as tradition-historical precursors of the Sinai tradition, are either dependent on the Sinai pericope or can be explained by other tradition-historical contexts. Only the Exodus-Moses narrative of the 7th century BCE connects Yʜwʜ, Moses, and Midian. As a result, this literary process cannot support any Midianite antecedents of Yʜwʜ. Additionally, there are alternatives to the common explanation that the Exodus tradition is connected to an "Exodus-group" which served as a carrier of allochthonous traditions of Yʜwʜ. Finally, the evidence from Kuntillet 'Ajrud and Soleb/Amara-West is inconclusive at best. It remains puzzling[139] how these findings shall provide "cumulative evidence."[140]

Only the cultic songs of the monarchic period – according to current scholarship most likely the oldest texts in the Hebrew Bible – preserved in the Psalter provide a secure tradition-historical basis. These texts depict Yʜwʜ as a storm-god analogous to the type of Baal-Hadad attested in Syria-Palestine.[141] The core of Ps 29 is an old litany of the thunderous voice of Yʜwʜ. This voice is accompanied by the classic elements of a theophany of a storm-god: storm (v. 5.9), earthquake (v. 6.8) and fire (v. 7). Its power surpasses the power of the chaotic sea as the notorious adversary of the Syrian storm-god (v. 3 f.):

3 The voice of Yʜwʜ is upon the waters [...]
   Yʜwʜ upon many waters.
4 The voice of Yʜwʜ is powerful,
   the voice of Yʜwʜ is full of majesty.
5 The voice of Yʜwʜ breaks cedars,
   Yʜwʜ breaks the cedars of Lebanon.
6 He makes[142] Lebanon skip like a calf,
   and Sir'ion like a young wild ox.
7 The voice of Yʜwʜ strikes sparks.[143]
8 The voice of Yʜwʜ shakes the wilderness,
   Yʜwʜ shakes the 'holy" wilderness.[144]
9a The voice of Yʜwʜ makes the 'oaks'[145] whirl,
   and strips[146] the forests bare.

---

139 As a result, I would answer the query who is guided by which bias differently than O. Keel, *Geschichte* (see n. 3), 201 f.
140 Cf. Leuenberger, "Herkunft" (see n. 3), 18.
141 See C. Levin (above) and the detailed study by Müller, *Wettergott* (see n. 2) as well as the essay in this volume.
142 See H. Spieckermann, *Heilsgegenwart. Eine Theologie der Psalmen* (FRLANT 148; Göttingen 1989), 168.
143 See Spieckermann, *Heilsgegenwart* (see n. 142), 166.175.
144 Spieckermann, *Heilsgegenwart* (see n. 142), 166.176.
145 Cf. BHS.
146 Spieckermann, *Heilsgegenwart* (see n. 142), 168.

YHWHs profile as a storm-god is already present in the oldest biblical texts and remains remarkably stable though other profiles join it. It is hardly surprising then that several scholars assume that YHWH was originally a storm-god.[147] In support of such a view Psalm 29 does not localize the epiphany of YHWH's thunderous voice in North-West Arabia but in the regions of Lebanon and Anti-Lebanon (Sir'ion) as v. 5 f. shows.[148] A similar picture emerges from a piece of tradition (v. 9–15) now incorporated in Psalm 89; here YHWH is connected with Zaphon, Amanus (?), Tabor and Hermon (v. 13).[149] Here, the visible traditions place YHWH's actions in those regions which have always been seen as the home of the Syrian-Canaanite storm-god[150], while up to now, attempts to uncover an older prehistory of YHWH in the South remain highly speculative.

---

147 See the discussion in Müller, *Wettergott* (see n. 2), 13–16.

148 "The Holy wilderness" (v. 8) is a topos of mythical geography (cf. KTU 1.23 Rs. 65; Spieckermann, *Heilsgegenwart* [see n. 142], 166. 176) and cannot be localized.

149 See Köckert, "YHWH" (see n. 68), 375.

150 Cf. also the place names and divine epithets like Baal Zaphon (e. g. KTU 1.16 I 6–7), Baal Libanon (KAI 31, 1–2) or Baal Hermon (Judg 3:3).

Jörg Jeremias
Three Theses on the Early History of Israel

In the biblical memories of the early history of Israel and of the origins of its relationship to its deity, there are a number of blind spots that can only be filled
now by way of reconstruction. Whether background knowledge was expected of
readers in antiquity or whether the biblical authors simply had no interest in
clarifying the questions that were raised can no longer be determined.

1

"Yhwh (is) the God of Israel" is one of the earliest—if not the earliest—expressions of Israel's relationship to its deity in the Hebrew Bible. Nevertheless, it
is striking that the two elements of this statement are incongruent with each
other insofar as "Israel" contains a divine name other than that of Yhwh, namely, El.[1] This incongruence is all the more noteworthy in view of the fact that at
least one biblical text attests the congruent expression "El (is) the God of
Isra–El" (Gen 33:20).[2]

1.1 Consequently, it seems possible that the congruent statement "El (is) the
God of Israel" could mark an earlier stage in Israel's relationship to its deity that
preceded the statement "Yhwh (is) the God of Israel." This stage may possibly
apply to the "Israel" that is named in the well–known victory stele of Pharaoh
Merenptah at the end of the 13th c. B.C.E.[3] and of whose size, area of settlement,
and nature we know nothing further.

1.2 This possibility finds support in the observation that in Syria–Palestine
there are no attested place names with the theophoric element Yhwh (or a
short form such as Yh),[4] while there are a number of place names with the theophoric element El. It appears that the worship of Yhwh did not originate in
Syria–Palestine but came to Palestine through the migration of new groups to
the area.

---

1 Cf. the tribal names of the Ishmaelites, Othnielites, Jerahmeelites, etc.
2 Cf. R. Smend, *Die Bundesformel* (ThSt 68; Zürich 1963), 14f.; reproduced in id., *Die Mitte des
Alten Testaments* (Tübingen 2002), 11f.
3 Cf., for example, M. Weippert, *Historisches Textbuch zum Alten Testament* (GAT 10; Göttingen
2010), 168–171.
4 This is noted, for example, in C. Levin, "Integrativer Monotheismus im Alten Testament,"
ZThK 109 (2012), 153–175; here 155.

DOI 10.1515/9783110448221-007

1.3 This assumption is supported by the three well-known theophany texts (Judg 5:4 f.; Deut 33:2; Hab 3:3) that announce YHWH's help for his people by describing his arrival from southern regions. This issue will be taken up in more detail below.

1.4 The aforementioned indications that YHWH was not originally a deity of the land of Palestine correspond to biblical reports that Moses first learned of the divine name YHWH in the desert to the east of the Nile Delta, specifically in the settlement area of the Midianites, to whom he had fled under personal distress. There, Moses married a Midianite woman (Exod 2:15 ff.; 4:18 f.; 18:1 ff.; Num 10:29; in Judg 1:16; 4:11 she is described as a Kenite and in Num 12:1 as a Cushite). This information should be regarded as a particularly reliable core element of the tradition, since later tradition found it quite problematic. The late text of Num 25:6 ff. states in Moses' name that relations between an Israelite and a Midianite constitute an offense punishable by death, and Num 31:1 ff. depicts Moses as leading a brutal war of divine retribution against the Midianites. Wars between Israel and the Midianites are already attested in the period of the Judges; the Midianites were capable of rapid, predatory attacks through the use of camels (Judg 6 ff.)

1.5 Moses' marriage to a Midianite (or Kenite) and the location of his learning of the divine name YHWH in Midianite territory have long led many exegetes to assume the so-called "Midianite (or Kenite) Hypothesis," that is, the notion that Israelite groups adopted the worship of YHWH (in whatever form) from the Midianites or Kenites.[5] Among the exceptional notices that have led to this thesis are the following: the Israelite elders' ritual celebration with the Midianites at the mountain of God "in the wilderness," in which Moses' father-in-law served as priest (Exod 18:12), the sparing of the Kenites in Israel's war against the hated Amalekites (1 Sam 15:6), and the heroic deed of Jael the Kenite in the battle against Sisera (Judg 4:11, 17; 5:24 ff.).[6] Gen 4:26 could indicate that the Kenites were the first to invoke the name of YHWH, although according to Gen 4:16 they lived "away from the presence of YHWH." Even though these scattered reports do not provide a clear and coherent picture and the juxtaposition of the Kenites and Midianites in particular is now opaque to us, they are unusual enough to gather more from them than simply friendly contacts between (pre-)Israelite groups with Kenites and Midianites.

---

5 A detailed list of references is found in W.H. Schmidt, *Alttestamentlicher Glaube* (Neukirchen-Vluyn [11]2011), 83–90; cf. also A. Lemaire, *The Birth of Monotheism* (Washington 2007), 25–27.
6 Cf. also 1 Sam 27:10 and 30:29, where the Kenites are counted among the Judahites.

1.6 The attestation of two different divine names in Israel's earliest religious history corresponds on a sociological level to the attestation of two different female ancestors from whom the later Israelite tribes would descend (if, for the sake of simplicity, one sets aside the fact that according to Gen 30 some of the tribes are also descended from Jacob's other wives). Unlike the two female ancestors of the Edomites in Gen 36:10 – 14, these two female ancestors are not placed on equal footing; rather, they are differentiated as the older and less beloved (Leah) and the younger and much sought–after (Rachel). From the beginning, Jacob's true longing was for the younger sister, Rachel: "He loved Rachel more than Leah" (Gen 29:30). This raises the possibility that the differentiation between an older and a younger female ancestor of the Israelite tribes, one less beloved and one more, is connected to an older worship of El by the older (Leah) tribes and the more recent worship of YHWH by the younger (Rachel) tribes, whereby the contrast between the two female ancestors in the manner described here is only conceivable from the perspective of the Rachel tribes. Thus, the older Leah tribes would have worshiped El as their deity, while the Rachel tribes (or, rather, at first only some of them) would have worshiped YHWH.

1.7 Our conjecture finds support in the observation that by far the most reports in the Hebrew Bible that relate to Israel's existence in the land prior to the monarchy come from the area of the two "younger" Rachel tribes of Joseph and Benjamin. This is true in several respects:

1.7.1 The conquest report in the book of Joshua that has all Israel settle the land at the same time selects a route through Benjamin with stops in Jericho, Gilgal, and Ai as a means of giving narrative shape to the confession that YHWH has given the land to Israel.

1.7.2 In contrast, the narratives in the book of Judges are characterized largely by the experiences of the house of Joseph. The great deeds of the charismatic heroes of the early period in Judg 3 – 12 take place exclusively in central Palestine: the first hero, Ehud, is a Benjaminite (ch. 3); the most prominent female figure of the period, Deborah, performs her function in Ephraim (chs. 4 – 5); the most significant of the so–called "great judges," Gideon, was an Ephraimite (chs. 6 – 8); and Jephthah, who is controversial on account of his lineage, is associated with Gilead in Transjordan, which is counted as a settlement area of the tribe of Manasseh (chs. 10 – 12). Only Samson, who stands apart from the other judges in every respect on account of his peculiar behavior (chs. 13 – 16), is a Danite.

1.7.3 A comparable picture is provided by the prosaic lists of the so–called "minor judges," for whom we only know names, places of activity, and places of burial (Judg 10:1 – 5; 12:7 – 15). Regardless of the size of their area of administration, they are said—in stereotypical fashion—to have "judged Israel." Two such judges performed their function in Ephraim (one, Tola, descended from Issachar but was active in Ephraim), two were active in Gilead in Transjordan (associated with Manasseh), and only one "minor judge" is associated with the south (Bethlehem) and the north (Zebulon) respectively.

1.7.4 Finally, the shrines that are associated with the early period in biblical texts reflect a clear preference for the Rachel tribes. While only two shrines located at some distance from each other are attested for both the north and the south of Palestine—in the north, Tabor as the border shrine for Issachar, Zebulon, and Naphtali, and the shrine of the northernmost tribe, Dan; in the south, the two shrines of the ancestors Abraham and Isaac, Mamre near Hebron and Beersheba—, in south–central Palestine a number of shrines are attested within a very small area: Shechem, Shiloh, Ophrah, Bethel, Mizpah, Gilgal, and Gibeon, to name only the most important.

1.7.5 The jealousy of Joseph's brothers regarding his dreams also has a background in the historical relations between the tribes, and it is no coincidence that it is the other Rachel tribe, Benjamin, who is set apart in this respect.

1.7.6 Archaeology has provided an impressive confirmation of the Hebrew Bible's focus on the Rachel tribes and particularly on the house of Joseph. The archaeological surveys of the 1970s and 1980s revealed, in general terms, a surprising tripartite division of the land during the transition from the Late Bronze age to Iron I. While cities maintained a high degree of cultural continuity despite a reduction in population size,[7] in the hill country both in the south (i.e., south of Jerusalem but also in the area of Benjamin) as well as in the north (i.e., north of the Jezreel Valley) there was modest population growth of up to 20% in existing settlements. In contrast, in central Palestine this growth was explosive, both to the east (biblical "Gilead") and to the west of the Jordan. Based on the new technological ability to seal cisterns and to construct terraces, the number of settlements in this region grew up to four or five times in relation to the previous period.[8] For comparison: in Judah, 10 Iron I settlements are known, in Benjamin 12, in Ephraim 120, and in Manasseh around 140 west and 70 east of the Jordan.[9]

---

7 Judg 1:27 also knows of such continuity for the Jezreel Valley.

8 See esp. I. Finkelstein, *The Archaeology of the Israelite Settlement* (Jerusalem 1988).

9 Finkelstein, ibid., 353; V. Fritz, *Die Entstehung Israels im 12. und 11. Jahrhundert v. Chr.* (BE 2; Stuttgart 1996), 75–79; E. Gaß, "Das Gebirge Manasse zwischen Bronze- und Eisenzeit," *ThQ* 186 (2006), 96–117; 103f. On the basis of the surveys, Finkelstein estimates that during the Iron I more than two-thirds of the Israelite population lived in central Palestine, that is, in the area of the house of Joseph (332f.).

1.8 Even if the thesis in no. 6 above must remain unproven, one thing is certain: the "younger" central Palestinian Rachel tribes, and the greater house of Joseph in particular, constituted the most historically significant Israelite groups during the premonarchic period (archaeologically speaking, the Iron I). Thus, it should hardly be considered a coincidence that a number of elements within the Moses– and Joshua traditions show a close connection to the house of Joseph and probably originated there. No other tribe is as closely connected to Egypt as (the house of) Joseph, and Joshua, Moses' successor who already bears a Yahwistic name, is described as an Ephraimite (Josh 24:30). The same is also true of the Jacob tradition, which, in addition to the aforementioned connection to the female ancestor Rachel, is also indicated in the geographical setting of the narratives (Penuel, Mahanaim, Bethel, and Shechem).[10] This tradition will be discussed under thesis 2.

2

A second significant gap in Israel's memories of its early history is found in the statement—attested more than once—that the Edomites are a "brother" nation to the Israelites. This notion is found both in prophetic texts (Amos 1:11; Obad 10, 12; Mal 1:2) as well as in predominately late texts within the Pentateuch (Num 20:14; Deut 2:4–5; 23:8) but above all in the narratives of the Jacob–Esau cycle (Gen 25; 27; 32–33), which are among the oldest narratives relating to Israel's ancestors. In these texts, Esau is even awarded the position of the (older) twin brother, that is, the closest conceivable relationship to the ancestor Jacob within the genealogical system of relations used in the ancestral narratives[11] and at the same time a privileged position over him.

2.1 This description of such a close relationship between Israel and Edom is completely incomprehensible from the perspective of the history of Israel as it is described in the Hebrew Bible. Rather, the Bible presents a picture of a permanent and growing enmity between the two peoples. This enmity begins with David's subjugation of the Edomites following his victory in battle in the "Valley of Salt" (2 Sam 8:13–14), which probably persisted up to the reign of Jehoram (2 Kgs 8:20); it reaches its peak after decades of coexistence largely without contact

---

10 Further important grounds for this connection are discussed in E. Blum, "The Jacob Tradition," in *The Book of Genesis: Composition, Reception, and Interpretation* (ed. C.A. Evans *et al.*; Leiden 2012), 181–211; here 208–210.
11 On this system cf. E. Blum, *Die Komposition der Vätergeschichte* (WMANT 57; Neukirchen-Vluyn 1984), 481 ff.

under Assyrian rule, during which time the Edomites established state structures,[12] in the so–called "hatred of the Edomites," which is attested in a number of prophetic books (Isa 34; 63:1–6; Jer 49:7 ff.; Ezek 25:12 f.; 35:1–15; Joel 4:19; Obad 8 ff.; Mal 1:2; cf. Ps 137:7). Whatever role the Edomites played in the siege and conquest of Jerusalem by the Babylonians (described in Obad 10–14 in highly charged language), it cannot be denied that the Edomites profited significantly from the destruction of Jerusalem inasmuch as they came to possess the southern territory of the former Judahite state during the exilic and post–exilic period and thereby became Judah's archenemies. As far as we are able to see, from the time of David onwards the origin of the tradition of a fraternal relationship between Israel and Edom becomes inexplicable.[13]

2.2 On the other hand, the notion sometimes proposed by earlier exegetes that "Esau" in the Jacob narratives was not originally a cipher for Edom[14] (in which case the secondary connection to Edom in the biblical attestations would also need to be explained) can be ruled out. Even though the geographical terms "Seir" and "Edom" are attested for the area to the east of the *wādi el–ʿarabah* prior to the name "Esau," the word play with the names "Seir" and "Edom" in the narratives about the beginning of the conflict between the twin brothers Jacob and Esau (Gen 25:25; 27:11, 16, 21–23) as well as the resolution of the conflict using the same terms, only now as geographical concepts (Gen 32:4; 33:16), leave no doubt that Esau was regarded as the ancestor of the Edomites from the outset.[15] Numerous passages in the Hebrew Bible use the name "Esau" in a geographical sense to designate Edom (e. g. Jer 49:8, 10; Obad 6 ; cf. esp. the phrase "the hill country of Esau" in Obad 9). In addition to this is the fact that Deut 2:4 locates the area of settlement for the "children of Esau" in Seir. L. Perlitt has shown that here the name "Esau" is used in order to avoid referring to "Edom" explicitly.[16]

2.3 Thus, the concept of Israel's close relationship to Edom in terms of lineage stands in tension with the feeling of bitter enmity that was the reality. In light of our knowledge of history, the latter is easily explainable, while the former is not. And yet this notion proves to be deeply rooted in the texts, making it dif-

---

12 For a more detailed discussion see M. Weippert, "Edom und Israel," *TRE* IX, 291–299; here 295 and esp. J. R. Bartlett, *Edom and the Edomites* (JSOT.S 77; Sheffield 1989), 145 ff.

13 For older theories trying in vain to explain Israel's brotherhood to Edom from the time of David or even later see J.R. Bartlett, "The brotherhood of Edom," *JSOT* 4 (1977), 2–27.

14 This notion is still held by B. Dicou, *Edom, Israel's Brother and Antagonist* (JSOT.S 169; Sheffield 1994), 137 ff.

15 Cf. esp. Blum, *Komposition* (see n. 11), 86 ff.

16 L. Perlitt, *Deuteronomium* (BK V/2; Neukirchen-Vluyn 1991), 153 f.

ficult to understand as a later construct – on whatever grounds. Not only do the texts repeatedly express Israelites' incomprehension that the brother nation of the Edomites could be capable of such bitter hostility (Amos 1:11; Obad 10, 12; Mal 1:2f.), but the Israelites' own early history under Moses in the Pentateuch was later reworked in order to cast the Edomites in the most positive light possible (cf. Num 20:14–21 with Deut 2:4f.).[17] The "hatred of the Edomites" found in other texts runs completely counter to this trend and cannot be explained by it.

2.4 Even after the foregoing observations, the most significant influence of the concept of Israel's fraternal relationship with Edom remains to be discussed. The so–called "law of the congregation" in Deut 23:2–9 evaluates the Edomites fundamentally differently from Israel's other Transjordanian neighbors, the Moabites and the Ammonites. In a context that deals with the purity of the congregation, the Moabites and Ammonites are excluded (along with emasculated and castrated men) from the possibility of becoming members of the community, perhaps originally with reference to the act of incest from which they descended (Gen 19:30–38). The Edomites are treated in a different manner: If they wish to become members of the congregation, they should not be turned away – at least up to the third generation, as the addition in v. 9 decrees–, and this only on account of Edom's fraternal relationship with Israel. Regardless of when the "law of the congregation" was created – and here opinions vary widely[18]—it must have been in effect during the decades or centuries characterized by the "hatred of the Edomites." In an addition to the so–called Nehemiah Memoir, the ordinances of the law of the congregation are explicitly stated to be binding (Neh 13:1–3), although this text is not interested in the exceptional position of the Edomites.

2.5 It can also hardly be coincidental that such a complex genealogical list about the Edomites has been handed down in Gen 36, which is without analogue for any of Israel's other neighbors. Within this text, the list of "kings who ruled in the land of Edom" (vv. 31–39) stands out and was probably originally a list of

---

17 The fact that Deut 2:4f. intentionally corrects Num 20:14–21 has been shown particularly by S. Mittmann, *Deuteronomium 1,1–6,3 literarkritisch und traditionsgeschichtlich untersucht* (BZAW 139; Berlin 1975), 72–79, who is followed by L. Perlitt, *Deuteronomium* (see n. 16), 147ff.

18 Following K. Galling, "Das Gemeindegesetz in Deuteronomium 23," in *Festschrift Alfred Bertholet* (ed. W. Baumgartner et al.; Tübingen 1950), 176–191, some exegetes regard Dtn 23,2–9* as very old, while others regard it as relatively late. Representative of the difficulty in dating the text is E. Otto; while in 1999 he followed U. Kellermann in dating the core of the text as pre-exilic (*Das Deuteronomium*; BZAW 284, Berlin 231f.), a year later he followed H.-D. Preuss and O. Kaiser in dating it to the post-exilic period (*Das Deuteronomium im Pentateuch und Hexateuch;* FAT 30; Tübingen 2000, 203f.).

local rulers who were secondarily arranged into a schema of succession.[19] Yet the division of the "children of Esau" into two tribes and their descent from two female ancestors (vv. 10–14, 20–28) probably also draws on old material.[20] However, it is less the age of the core of the lists that is noteworthy but rather the intensive engagement with the material, which is shown through numerous additions and particularly in the construction of the Priestly Writing. Just as striking is how such a prominent place – more than any other non–Israelite nation – is ascribed to the "children of Esau" in the presentation of the Israelites' family tree in 1 Chr 1 through a long quotation of Gen 36. "The reasons for this lie more in the evaluation of Edom by the biblical tradition than in the events of the Chronicler's own time."[21]

2.6 This biblical tradition becomes even more understandable considering that there were clans that are introduced as Edomite in Gen 36 but that are counted as Judahite or Simeonite elsewhere in the Hebrew Bible.[22]

2.7 Thus, the following conclusion drawn by M. Weippert remains valid: "The historical anchor for this strongly contradictory attitude in the history of both nations since the time of David ... could perhaps best be sought in a shared prehistory of population groups that merged into Edom and Israel (Judah?), respectively."[23] Israel's "brotherhood" with Edom thus underlies the history known to us to the same extent as Israel's (and YHWH's) "age–old" enmity with the Amalekites (Exod 17:16). Here it should be taken into account that Israel knew very well that the Amalekites, for their part, were "related" to the Edomites (Gen 36:12).

2.8 Thus, the sequence of events that forms the basis of the Jacob–and–Esau cycle (too) must have a historical basis, namely, that Esau was the firstborn of the twin brothers. Genesis 36:31 in particular indicates that the Edomites were of greater historical significance in the pre–monarchic period, noting that "kings" ruled in Edom earlier than in Israel. However the area of control of these "kings" is to be understood, who, like the aforementioned so–called

---

19 Cf., for example, Weippert, Edom (see n. 12), 293; J.R. Bartlett, "Edom," *ABD* 2, 288.

20 So at least Weippert, ibid., 293; differently Bartlett, ibid., 289.

21 T. Willi, *Chronik, I. Teilband* (BK XXIV/1; Neukirchen-Vluyn 2009), 26: "Die Gründe dafür liegen mehr in der Wertung Edoms durch die biblische Tradition als in der Zeitgeschichte des Chronisten."

22 This is true for the clan of Kenaz (cf. Gen 36:11, 15, 42 with Josh 14:6, 14; 15:17) and the clan of Zerah (cf. Gen 36:13, 33 with Num 26:13); cf. H. Gese, *Alttestamentliche Studien* (Tübingen 1991), 50.

23 Weippert, Edom (see n. 12), 297: "Der historische Ansatzpunkt dieser der Geschichte beider Völker seit David aufs schärfste widersprechenden Haltung [...] dürfte am ehesten in einer gemeinsamen Vorgeschichte von Bevölkerungsgruppen zu suchen sein, die in Edom bzw. Israel (Juda?) aufgegangen sind."

"minor judges" (Judg 10:1–5; 12:7–15), ruled without dynastic succession and whose duration of rule is not mentioned – they were probably "local petty lords" (Weippert) – , what is important to the biblical text is the fact that in "Israel" during the same period there was nothing comparable. It is possible that the Jacob–and–Esau narrative preserves a reflex of Edom's earlier predominance in its description of Jacob's reconciliation with Esau: not only did all of Jacob's wives and children bow down before Esau, but Jacob himself bowed before his twin brother "seven times" (Gen 33:3).

3

Should the two theses discussed thus far be joined, indicating that Israel – more precisely, some of the groups belonging to the Rachel–tribes – adopted the worship of YHWH from its "brother nation," the Edomites?

3.1 Such a conclusion is suggested upon an initial reading of the three well–known theophany texts that describe YHWH as coming to the aid of his people from his southern abode (Judg 5:4f.; Deut 33:2; Hab 3:3). All three texts refer to areas in Edom as the place from which the divine presence appeared or will appear: in Judg 5:4 and Deut 33:2 it is "Seir" (with an additional reference to the "plains of Edom" in Judg 5:4), while in Hab 3:3 it is "Teman." Within the Hebrew Bible, "Seir" is almost always used with reference to "Edom," while "Teman" is a term that can indicate the "south" generally but is also used for a specific part of Edom (Ezek 25:13) and more frequently *pars pro toto* for Edom as a whole (e. g., Jer 49:20; Amos 1:12; Obad 9).

3.2 On the other hand, there are no indications in the biblical text that Israel was connected to Edom through a common faith.[24] Edom's national deity was called Qaus (or later Qôs), and this name is widely attested in the Iron II and Iron III, particularly in personal names. The Israelites and Edomites were only related in terms of religion insofar as the Edomites, like the Moabites and Ammonites, did not have a pantheon but rather worshiped their national deity in a monolatrous fashion.

3.3 At the same time, it is noteworthy that the three aforementioned theophany texts that describe YHWH arriving from the distant south not only mention geographical regions within Edom (and which represent Edom) but also those

---

24 The assumption of a common worship of YHWH by early Edomite and Israelite groups (J. Gray, *VT* 4, 1954, 148–154; M.Rose, *JSOT* 4, 1977, 28–34; R.J. Barlett, *JSOT* 5, 1978, 29–38) is pure speculation.

that go beyond Edom's borders.[25] Thus, the reference to "Sinai" alone in Deut 33:2 is apparently not meant as a mountain or mountainous region (such as the "hill country of Paran," see below) but rather as a region or desert south of Edom, as L. Perlitt already showed several decades ago.[26] Likewise, the region called the "hill country of Paran" in Deut 33:2 and Hab 3:3, which is only attested in these two passages, is otherwise referred to as the "wilderness of Paran" (six times, preferred in the Priestly Writing) or as "Paran" alone (Deut 1:1; 1 Kgs 18:11). The "wilderness of Paran" is described as the territory of the Ishmaelites (Gen 21:21). On account of the name, several scholars have attempted to locate Paran near *wādi fērān* in the south of the Sinai Peninsula,[27] but this area with its lush oasis lies too far south for the biblical texts. In the Priestly Writing, the "wilderness of Paran" is the point of departure for the spies, who reach the hill country of Judah by travelling north from there through the Negev (Num 13:3, 17, 26). The older report placed this point of departure in Kadesh, ca. 75 km south of Beersheba, and both places are identified with each other in Num 13:26. Thus, the region in view here is the extreme south of Palestine, connecting to the Negev.[28]

3.4 It is striking that while YHWH's arrival "from the hill country of Paran" in Hab 3:3 unsurprisingly causes a reaction of terror from both nature and humans, here the Cushites and Midianites are mentioned as those who are affected first by this terror (v. 7), apparently because they live closest to the place from which YHWH comes. We learn nothing further of the Cushites (who here are clearly not Ethiopians, as is meant in many other passages) apart from the fact that Moses' wife, who is normally described as a Midianite, is called a Cushite in Num 12:1. The territory of the Midianites is connected directly to the south of Edom, southeast of the Gulf of Aqaba. This can be deduced particularly from 1 Kgs 11:18, which reports that the Edomite prince Hadad fled to Egypt: "They

---

25 This has been noted by E.A. Knauf, *Midian: Untersuchungen zur Geschichte Palästinas und Nordarabiens am Ende des 2. Jahrtausends* (ADPV; Wiesbaden 1988), 51 ff.

26 L. Perlitt, "Sinai und Horeb," in *Beiträge zur alttestamentlichen Theologie, Festschrift W. Zimmerli* (ed. H. Donner *et al.*; Göttingen 1977), 302–322; here 303 f.; reproduced in id., *Deuteronomium-Studien* (FAT 8; Tübingen 1994), 32–49; here 33 f. One should also recall the old divine name זה סיני "the one from Sinai" in Judg 5:5 and Ps 68:9, which, however, is regarded by some authors as a gloss.

27 For example, M. Noth, *Das vierte Buch Mose. Numeri* (ATD 7; Göttingen 1966), 69 and in more detail S. Timm, "Gott kommt von Teman, der Heilige vom Berg Paran" (Habakuk 3:3) – und archäologisch Neues aus dem äußersten Süden (Tell el-Meharret)," *OTE N.S.* 9,2 (1996), 308–333; here 316 ff.

28 Cf. J.M. Hamilton, "Paran," *ABD* 5,162.

set out from Midian and came to Paran," which is named as the only stopover. Thus, the prince first fled southward and then westward.

3.5 The inscriptions on the large pithoi from Kuntillet ʿAjrud dating to the 9th/ 8th c. B.C.E. have played a major role recently in evaluating the problems discussed thus far. When "YHWH of Teman" is invoked alongside the national deity "YHWH of Samaria" in the blessing formulae,[29] presumably this means "YHWH from the south" or "YHWH the southerner," since *tmn* is used in this context both with and without the article, which would be unusual for the name of a region. Kuntillet ʿAjrud lies deep in the south of the Negev, some 50 km south of Kadesh–Barnea; the name "YHWH from the south" presumably refers to some area still further to the south. At least into the 9th/8th c., YHWH remained connected to the region in which former groups of Israel encountered him for the first time.

3.6 Thus, in using the Edomite regional names "Seir" and "Teman," the three aforementioned theophany texts do not seek to specify the precise place from which YHWH came or will come to the aid of his people but rather the direction from which he comes. His point of departure lay further south than Edom.

3.7 For the early history of Israel that can be traced and reconstructed behind the texts, it is apparently necessary to differentiate between the history of groups (belonging to the Rachel tribes) which was shared with the "twin brother" groups of the later Edomites and decisive religious impulses (to which the theophany texts indirectly attest) that spread from the Midianites (and related groups) to other members of these groups; their leader, Moses, was related to the Midianites through marriage.[30] It is also probable that the divine name YHWH is of northwest Arabian origin.[31]

In any event, it is remarkable that in the biblical texts that describe the "historical," post–Mosaic period, both the Midianites and the Edomites appear as Israel's enemies, the Midianites even in premonarchic time.[32]

---

[29] Cf. J.A. Emerton, "New Light on Israelite Religion: The Implications from Kuntillet ʿAjrud," *ZAW* 94 (1982), 2–20; here 9 f. On newer readings of the divine names cf. O. Keel, *Die Geschichte Jerusalems und die Entstehung des Monotheismus* (Göttingen 2007), 201.

[30] Recently E. Blum, "Der historische Mose und die Frühgeschichte Israels," *Hebrew Bible and Ancient Israel* 1 (2012), 37–63. 58 f. has demonstrated convincingly that the oldest Moses-stories as well as the early Jacob-stories as well as the oldest theophany traditions and also the inscriptions of Kuntillet ʿAjrud stem from traditions of the realm of the Rachel-tribes. Cf. id., "The Jacob tradition," (see no.10).

[31] Cf. E.A. Knauf, "Yahwe," *VT* 34 (1984), 467–472.

[32] Cf. especially K.L. Sparks, "Israel and the Nomads of Ancient Palestine," in *Community Identity in Judean Historiography* (ed. G.N. Knoppers and K.A. Ristau; Winona Lake 2009), 9–26; here 12–17.

3.8 Almost nothing can be said with certainty about the nature of Yʜwʜ during this early period. On the other hand, if the hypotheses presented above are correct, then the various traces of polytheism contained in the Hebrew Bible (such as in Deut 32:8 f.; Ps 29; 82) should be traced back to the worship of El by the older Leah tribes.

Additional note

H. Pfeiffer's conclusion that the three theophany texts are postexilic constructs relies on two assumptions: 1. Pfeiffer completely avoids the texts treated above that describe Israel's special relationship to Edom. 2. He derives Judg 5:4 f. as the oldest theophany text from Isa 63:1–6, since this late text is "the only parallel for an arrival of Yʜwʜ from the south apart from Hab 3 and Deut 33:2;" for Pfeiffer in Isa 63 Edom is "a sort of model enemy."[33] If Pfeiffer were correct, then the differentiated geographical information found in the three theophany texts would need to allow for reconstructions that simply had "Edom" as their *Vorlage*—a rather far-fetched notion. Additionally, Yʜwʜ in Isa 63 comes from Edom because he had to punish it, while in Judg 5:4 f.; Deut 33:2, and Hab 3 the region of Edom and south of it is noted as the realm of his dominion. O. Keel and especially M. Leuenberger have offered detailed critiques of Pfeiffer's theses, both of whom rightly emphasize the early traditio–historical date of the three theophany texts.[34] Pfeiffer argues from a purely literary–critical perspective and does not account for the possibility that literarily later texts such as Hab 3 could intentionally employ archaizing motifs that readers would recognize as ancient conceptions.[35]

Since both Keel and Leuenberger discuss in detail the extrabiblical material that supports the notion of Yʜwʜ's origins in the south—the Egyptian lists from the temple of Amen–Hotep III in Soleb and from the Temple of Ramesses II in Amara–West referring to "Yhw(h) nomads" (šȝśw yhwȝ[–w]) and the Egyptian papyri and temple inscriptions that refer to nomads (šȝśw) from Edom and Seir—, I have foregone a discussion of these texts here.

---

33 H. Pfeiffer, *Jahwes Kommen von Süden* (FRLANT 211; Göttingen 2005), 82, 86.

34 Keel, *Geschichte Jerusalems* (see n. 29), 200–202; M. Leuenberger, *Gott in Bewegung* (FAT 76; Tübingen 2011), 10–33. Cf. also the important new Judges commentary by W. Groß: *Richter* (HThKAT; Freiburg–Basel–Wien 2009), 305–311.

35 So, for example, L.A. Axelsson, *The Lord Rose up from Seir* (CB.OTS 25; Lund 1987), 53.

Martin Leuenberger

YHWH's Provenance from the South

A New Evaluation of the Arguments pro and contra*

1 Introduction: The Problem

The problems regarding the 'beginnings and origins'[1] of the Biblical god YHWH are as multifaceted as they are complex, comprising a wide range of topics, sources and methods which are often interrelated and therefore need meticulous and transparent exploration. Within the context of recent research (s. below II.), the present article specifically focuses on the *religious-historical question of YHWH's origin and provenance:* Where and when does YHWH enter the 'light of history'? The answer I will elaborate in this article is based on a critical evaluation of all sources presently available (including the external evidence of the relevant primary sources as well as the secondary Biblical sources' pertinent traditions).

The traditional model argues for *YHWH's provenance from the south* 'outside of the land' (referring to the region of the Canaanite province of the Late Bronze Age and the territorial states Israel and Juda of the Iron Age II), i.e. from the South Palestinian-Edomite area of the Araba, where he emerges in the Late Bronze Age. In contrast, the so-called Berlin antithesis which has been developed since the turn of the millennium, favours *a northern origin of YHWH* – be it in the Levant north of Canaan/Israel or (with smooth transitions) in the land itself – in the course of the Late Bronze or Iron I Age. In conjunction with these diverging hypotheses, the oldest identifiable type, position and functions of the deity 'YHWH' also differ significantly, resulting finally in varying reconstructions of the early history of YHWH (roughly up to the late 8th century) on the whole.

In what follows, I shall first provide a short overview of the recent history of research in order to clarify the dynamic of the current debate and the big picture

* I wish to sincerely thank David Ray (Melbourne/Tuebingen) for his help in polishing this article.

1 S. the representative title of the relevant issue of the BThZ 1/2013 ("Anfänge und Ursprünge der Jahwe-Verehrung") which the present volume integrates und expands. In what follows, I use both terms, together with 'provenance,' in a similar sense although at times they may set different accents (s. F. Hartenstein, "The Beginnings of YHWH and 'Longing for the Origin.' A Historico-Hermeneutical Query," in this volume 283–307; s. BThZ 30 [2013], 166–192).

DOI 10.1515/9783110448221-003

implied therein (2.). This allows us to then evaluate all the main arguments for southern and northern provenances of YHWH (3.). Finally, after summarising the results, a short consideration on the implications (of the differing models) for the early history of YHWH will help to sharpen perspectives on further religious- and theological-historical research on the conceptions of YHWH in ancient Israel (4.).

2 History of Research: The Recent Debate

YHWH's religious-historical provenance and origin have been much debated over the past decade; the discussion was initiated in German-speaking research but has recently spread into an international context, which helps in advancing a well-balanced overall evaluation (s. below 2.3 with n. 16).

2.1 YHWH's Origin in the South

The core hypothesis, assuming that YHWH's *religious-historical* origin is to be found *in the Araba of the Late Bronze Age*, evolved during the 19th century in a distinct pre-Wellhausenian period of research, and Wellhausen adopted it without problematizing any important aspect.[2] This model then controlled the dominant theories during the 20th century, including notably the period after the (relatively early) discovery of the Ugaritic texts (since 1928) and other primary sources concerning Canaan/Israel (such as the Amarna correspondence [1887] or the Taanach archive [1904]).[3] Hence, the external evidence was considered important in this field of research from early on: Despite the well founded abandonment of the classical paradigm of a 'nomadic god'[4] and the equally well ar-

---

2 It remains a desideratum to write this chapter of the history of research; for now s. my hints (M. Leuenberger, *Gott in Bewegung. Religions- und theologiegeschichtliche Beiträge zu Gottesvorstellungen im alten Israel* [FAT 76; Tübingen 2011], 10 ff) and more extensive O. Kaiser, *Glaube und Geschichte im Alten Testament. Das neue Bild der Vor- und Frühgeschichte Israels und das Problem der Heilsgeschichte* (BThSt 150; Neukirchen-Vluyn 2014), 3–8.
3 For the impact of Ugarit s. already W.H. Schmidt, *Das Königtum Gottes in Ugarit und Israel. Zur Herkunft der Königsprädikation Jahwes* (BZAW 60; Berlin ²1966).
4 For the critique of Alt's god of the father, Noth's amphictyony and the early dating of the small historical credo by v.Rad and others, s. e. g. M. Köckert, *Vätergott und Väterverheißungen. Eine Auseinandersetzung mit Albrecht Alt und seinen Erben* (FRLANT 142; Göttingen 1988); R. Albertz, *Religionsgeschichte Israels in alttestamentlicher Zeit, 1. Von den Anfängen bis zum Ende der Königszeit* (GAT 8/I–II; Göttingen 1992), 127 ff and J.C. Gertz, "Die Stellung des kleinen geschichtlichen Credos in der Redaktionsgeschichte von Deuteronomium und Pentateuch," in *Liebe und*

gued fundamental changes in the models for the pre- and early-monarchic history of 'Israel,'[5] Yhwh's southern origins and beginnings outside the land were – and presently still are – maintained with good reason.

2.2 Yhwh's Origin in the North

Against this long standing consensus, the Berlin antithesis favours Yhwh's provenance *from the north, i.e. from the land of Canaan/Israel itself or the Levant north of it,*[6] where he emerges in the pre-monarchic era (Late Bronze or Iron I Age) or the early-state period. The model comprises a religious-historical and a literary-historical component and has been proposed since 2001 by scholars such as Matthias Köckert and Henrik Pfeiffer.

Matthias Köckert argued in 2001 that the theophany tradition (esp. Judg 5:4f; Dtn 33:2; Ps 68:8f) is rooted in the Jerusalemite temple theology and was only later transferred from Zion to Sinai.[7] That means: "Der Gott Jahwe betritt, historisch greifbar, erst im 1. Jt. v.Chr. die Bühne der Geschichte,"[8] and this stance corresponds with "einer mittelpalästinischen Lokalisierung" of Yhwh.[9] With regard

---

Gebot. Studien zum Deuteronomium. FS zum 70. Geburtstag von L. Perlitt (ed. R.G. Kratz and H. Spieckermann; FRLANT 190; Göttingen 2000), 30 – 45. S. also Leuenberger, *Gott* (see n. 2), 10f (with further references).

5 S. the most recent overview by J.-L. Ska, "Questions of the 'History of Israel' in Recent Research," in *Hebrew Bible/Old Testament. The History of its Interpretation. Vol. III: From Modernism to Post-Modernism (The Nineteenth and Twentieth Centuries). Part 2: The Twentieth Century – From Modernism to Post-Modernism* (ed. M. Sæbø; Göttingen 2015), 391 – 432: here 403ff and concerning the so-called Midianite-Kenite hypothesis E. Blum, "Der historische Mose und die Frühgeschichte Israels," *HEBAI* 1 (2012), 37 – 63: here 49ff.52ff.

6 For the last option s. already H.-P. Müller's cautious considerations from 1981 (H.-P. Müller, "Der Jahwename und seine Deutung Ex 3:14 im Licht der Textpublikationen aus Ebla," *Bib.* 62 [1981], 305 – 327: here 325f).

7 S. M. Köckert, "Die Theophanie des Wettergottes in Psalm 18," in *Kulturgeschichten. Altorientalische Studien für Volkert Haas zum 65. Geburtstag* (ed. T. Richter *et al.*; Saarbrücken 2001), 209 – 226: here 226: "Die Theophanieüberlieferung kommt nicht von Seir ..., sondern stammt aus der Tempeltheologie." This contrasts both with the traditional view he still presented in 1998 (s. Leuenberger, *Gott* [see n. 2], 173) and the passing on of the theophany texts Judg 5 and Deut 33 in the north (s. below 3.3.e[2.d] with n. 62 – 64).

8 M. Köckert, "Wandlungen Gottes im antiken Israel," *BThZ* 22 (2005), 3 – 36: here 20; s. his recent synthesis: M. Köckert, "YHWH in the Northern and Southern Kingdom," in, *One God – One Cult – One Nation. Archaeological and Biblical Perspectives* (ed. R.G. Kratz and H. Spieckermann; BZAW 405; Berlin *et al.* 2010), 357 – 394.

9 Köckert, "Wandlungen" (see n. 8), 20 Anm. 43; s. also id., "Psalm 18" (see n. 7), 212f.226; H. Pfeiffer, *Jahwes Kommen von Süden. Jdc 5; Hab 3; Dtn 33 und Ps 68 in ihrem literatur- und theo-*

to the literary history, Köckert's student *Henrik Pfeiffer* has disputed that the theophany texts (Judg 5 etc.) can bear any significance for Yhwh in the pre-state period; he also claims that the epigraphic documents "letztlich nichts für einen Ursprung Jahwes im Süden abwerfen."[10]

Sharing this view, *Reinhard Müller* chooses another line of argumentation: Ignoring the Biblical theophany texts[11] he focuses on the oldest Psalms where he – convincingly – sees Yhwh portrayed as a royal weather-god of the North Levantine and Syriac Adad-Baal type.[12]

Most recently, *Markus Witte* has summarised the question of Yhwh's original provenance, which he initially judges to be undecidable due to the state of our source material.[13] Then however – shifting Yhwh's profile significantly with regard to time and societal context – he continues: "Einiges deutet aber darauf hin, dass die Verehrung Jhwhs als eines Wettergottes im Kulturland ihren Anfang genommen hat."[14]

2.3 The Differences and the Current State of Research

This short overview may suffice to outline the problem of Yhwh's provenance and the main religious-historical models: They differ not only in what concerns

---

logiegeschichtlichen Umfeld (FRLANT 211; Göttingen 2005), 261; M. Dijkstra, "El, the God of Israel – Israel, the People of Yhwh: On the Origins of Ancient Israelite Yahwism," in *Only One God? Monotheism in Ancient Israel and the Veneration of the Goddess Asherah* (ed. B. Becking *et al.*; BiSe 77; Sheffield 2001), 81–126: here 101f (combining it with a southern origin, s. 83) and C. Levin, "Das vorstaatliche Israel," *ZThK* 97 (2000), 385–403, according to whom Yhwh belongs to the "Typus des syrischen Wettergottes. Daß er von außen nach Palästina eingewandert sei, ist eher unwahrscheinlich" (390).

10 Pfeiffer, *Kommen* (see n. 9), 261; s. also id., "The Origin of YHWH and its Attestation," in this volume 115–144; s. *BThZ* 30 (2013), 11–43.

11 According to him, we deal here with a "brüchigen alttestamentlichen Überlieferung" (R. Müller, *Jahwe als Wettergott. Studien zur althebräischen Kultlyrik anhand ausgewählter Psalmen* [BZAW 387; Berlin *et al.* 2008], 243; s. below 3.1.d[2] with n. 28).

12 S. R. Müller, "The Origins of YHWH in Light of the Earliest Psalms," in this volume 207–236; s. *BThZ* 30 (2013), 89–119; id., *Wettergott* (see n. 11), esp. 243f. S. to it below 3.1.d.

13 S. M. Witte, Jesus Christus im Alten Testament. Eine biblisch-theologische Skizze (SEThV 4; Münster *et al.* 2013), 23.

14 Witte, *Jesus Christus* (see n. 13). For a critical evaluation s. M. Leuenberger, "Noch einmal: Jhwh aus dem Süden. Methodische und religionsgeschichtliche Überlegungen in der jüngsten Debatte," in *Gott und Geschichte* (ed. M. Meyer-Blanck; Veröffentlichungen der Wissenschaftlichen Gesellschaft für Theologie 44; Leipzig 2015), 268f.

the space and time of YHWH's emergence, but also with regard to the *relevant sources and the corresponding profile of YHWH.*

To make and keep all of these aspects transparent is therefore imperative when formulating religious-historical hypotheses in the present context of research. In my view, the main weakness of the northern-provenance-hypothesis – although understandable it may be considering the research history – consists in its argumentative structure: In a first step, the conclusiveness of the indications for a southern provenance are contested. Then, in a second step, an argumentum a contrario takes effect without actually furnishing positive evidence from the sources for a northern origin. Thus, Henrik Pfeiffer concludes the religious-historical outlook of his pioneering work: "Eindeutige epigrafische Zeugnisse für eine Verhaftung [sc. of YHWH, M.L.] im Norden fehlen zwar. Doch spricht angesichts des durch und durch negativen Befundes für eine Beheimatung im Süden das Wettergott-Profil Jahwes für sein Kommen von Norden."[15]

Despite the growing acceptance of the thesis of YHWH's northern provenance, the advocates for a southern origin have maintained and – most recently in reaction to the opposing point of view – strengthened their position.[16] There-

---

15 Pfeiffer, *Kommen* (see n. 9), 267. Recently, he has repeated this conclusion after negatively evaluating the sources indicating a southern origin (s. Pfeiffer, "Origin" [see n. 10], 129]).

16 S. for the classical position in the anglophone field instead of many Mark Smith's solid argumentation (M.S. Smith, *The Early History of God. Yahweh and the Other Deities in Ancient Israel* [New York et al. 2²002], esp. XVIIff.5 ff.32 f.81 ff.145 f.182 ff; id., *God in Translation. Deities in Cross-Cultural Discourese in the Biblical World* [FAT 57; Tübingen 2008], 96–98) and the recent contributions of N. Na'aman, "The Exodus Story. Between Historical Memory and Historiographical Composition," *JANER* 11 (2011). 59–69: here 66 f and D. Miano, "Art. Yahweh," in *The Encyclopedia of Ancient History* (ed. R.S. Bagnall et al.; Chichester 2013), 7156–7158.

In the German speaking literature, the voices responding to the Berlin thesis also have increased, s. in particular O. Keel, *Die Geschichte Jerusalems und die Entstehung des Monotheismus, Teil 1–2* (OLB 4/1–2; Göttingen 2007), 199 ff; Blum, "Mose" (see n. 5), 52 ff; F. Hartenstein, "Die Geschichte JHWHs im Spiegel seiner Namen," in *Gott Nennen. Gottes Namen und Gott als Name* (ed. I.U. Dalferth and P. Stoellger; Tübingen 2008), here 76 f; H. Niehr, *Religionen in Israels Umwelt. Einführung in die nordwestsemitischen Religionen Syrien-Palästinas* (NEB.Erg 5; Würzburg 1998), 237; B. Janowski, "Art. Gottesvorstellungen," *HGANT*, 25; C. Frevel, "Grundriss der Geschichte Israels," in *Einleitung in das Alte Testament*, Stuttgart (ed. E. Zenger et al.; KStTh 1/1; Stuttgart et al. ⁷2008), 602; U. Berges, *Die dunklen Seiten des guten Gottes. Zu Ambiguitäten im Gottesbild JHWHs aus religions- und theologiegeschichtlicher Perspektive*, Paderborn 2013, 18 f; and in this volume (expanding *BThZ* 30 [1/2013]) the essays of M. Krebernik, "The Beginnings of Yahwism from an Assyriological Perspective," esp. 53 f.60.64 (s. *BThZ* 30 [2013], 52.58.60 f), A. Berlejung, "The Origins and Beginnings of the Worship of YHWH: The Iconographic Evidence," esp. 68 f.88–90 and Hartenstein, "Query" (see n. 1).

It is remarkable that also in the francophone research, the votes against a northern origin and for a southern origin most recently have gained prominence, s. notably T. C. Römer, *L'invention*

fore, in what follows I will present an exhaustive evaluation of all the relevant arguments.

3 Evaluation: The Arguments pro and contra Northern and Southern Provenances of Yhwh

In a religious- and theological-historical perspective, the undisputed starting point is that Yhwh is venerated from the very beginning as the national god of both the territorial states of Israel and Judah, which take shape from the 10th century. Thus, *Yhwh must have older origins and beginnings in the pre-state period of the Iron I or Late Bronze Age*, be it initially in the land itself or be it outside the land and subsequently immigrating into it (s. above 1.2 with n. 6). Both scenarios, however, agree that Yhwh very likely first emerges and

---

de Dieu (Paris 2014), 51 ff; id., "Le Baal d'Ougarit et le Yahvé biblique," in *Les écritures mises au jour sur le site antique d'Ougarit (Syrie) et leur déchiffrement* (ed. P. Bordreuil *et al.* Paris 2013), here 34 f.35 f; id., "The Revelation of the Divine Name to Moses and the Construction of a Memory about the Origins of the Encounter between Yhwh and Israel, " in *Israel's Exodus in Transdisciplinary Perspective. Text, Archaeology, Culture, and Geoscience* (ed. T.E. Levy and T. Schneider and W.H.C. Propp; Heidelberg 2015), 305–315: here 313 and F. Pfitzmann, "Le 'maître des autruches' parmi le représentations de YHWH au Sud," in *Représenter dieux et hommes* (ed. T. C. Römer; Paris 2016), esp. the introduction and ch. IV.a (in preparation).
Further, s. also for the Israeli literature N. Amzallag, "Some Implications of the Volcanic Theophany of YHWH on his Primeval Identity," *Antiguo Oriente* 12 (2014), 11–38: here 21.
And finally, for the same position from an Archaeological point of view s. e.g. A. Faust, "The Emergence of Israel: On Origins and Habitus," in *Israel's Exodus in Transdisciplinary Perspective. Text, Archaeology, Culture, and Geoscience* (ed. T.E. Levy *et al.*; Heidelberg, 2015), 467–482: here 473 ff; 477 n. 12.
This increasing number of firmly decided positions – the volume edited by Levy, Schneider and Propp just mentioned most recently documents remarkably convergent votes for a southern origin of Yhwh (s. esp. the articles of M. Bietak, "On the Historicity of the Exodus: What Egyptology Today Can Contribute to Assessing the Biblical Account of the Sojourn in Egypt,"; 19–37: 19 f; T.C. Römer, "The Revelation of the Divine Name to Moses and the Construction of a Memory About the Origins of the Encounter Between Yhwh and Israel," 305–315: here 312–314; N. Na'aman, "Out of Egypt or Out of Canaan? The Exodus Story Between Memory and Historical Reality," in *Israel's Exodus in Transdisciplinary Perspective. Text, Archaeology, Culture, and Geoscience* [ed. T. E. Levy et al.; Heidelberg 2015] 527–533: here 529 f) – seems to indicate the importance of the debate as well as the critical evaluation of the northern hypothesis; the following chapter intends to summarise and evaluate carefully the main arguments pro and contra in order to bring out the prevailing evidence for Yhwh's southern provenance.

gains relevance in the land during the Iron I Age.[17] This state of affairs leads directly to the crucial question: *Where and when* can YHWH's initial origin and provenance be located?

In order to engage the problem of YHWH's southern or northern provenance in a methodologically transparent way, an evaluation of all presently known (textual)[18] sources is required. Given the limited and accidental state of our source material, we may also need to adopt a polycausal explanatory model, which takes into account aspects of both hypotheses (s. below 3.2).

3.1 Evidence for YHWH's Provenance from the North?

Since it is methodologically not at all convincing to deduce a northern provenance simply by denying the evidence for a southern origin, it is imperative to verify potential positive clues. Five issues require evaluation: Place names, personal names, deity names, more general religious-historical constellations, and YHWH's solitary character. Having treated the material evidence and its evaluation for all of these issues elsewhere,[19] it suffices here to summarise the results beyond dispute and to briefly discuss the controversial aspects.

Concerning the theophoric toponyms, personal names, and deity names in sources for Canaan in the Late Bronze and Iron I Age, an extensive survey simply produces a negative result with regard to YHWH: YHWH is not attested at all.

a) Toponyms

There is no Yahwistic toponym from Palestine at all,[20] which contrasts sharply with nearly all other regionally important gods (esp. El, Baal, Schamasch, Schalem, Astarte) and indicates that YHWH does not belong to the land's indigenous gods.

---

17 According to the famous stele of Merenptah (1209 BCE) providing the earliest evidence for "Israel" (*jj-s-r-j-3-r* = *ysrj3r*), El was the eponymous reference-god for this collective, which initially evolved towards the end of the Late Bronze Age.

18 I.e. Biblical and epigraphic evidence. It is obvious that archaeological and iconographic sources in the narrower sense fail to produce results in this regard.

19 S. hereto in detail my article Leuenberger, "Debatte" (see n. 14), 270–280 (with further literature).

20 S. Leuenberger, "Debatte" (see n. 14), n. 15 and Keel, *Geschichte* (see n. 16), 199: "Ein palästinischer Ortsname, der mit JHWH zusammengesetzt wäre, ist nicht bekannt."

b) Personal Names

The less persistent personal names from the Late Bronze and Iron I Age-Canaan and the Levant north of it[21] also do not attest to YHWH, although the more comprehensive corpora such as the Amarna correspondence and the Taanach archive feature quite tangible panthea. Despite varying regionally and temporally, prominent names include El, Adad, Baal, Heba(t), Anat, Astarte, Asherah and others – YHWH however is missing, and this holds true also for the Eblaite and Amurrite onomasticon.[22] Extra-Biblical sources attest Yahwistic personal names only for the Israelite and Judahite state period (complemented by cuneiform documents following the middle of the 9th century). Considering the large number and the high adaptability of personal names compared to toponyms, these circumstances render a Late Bronze Age provenance of YHWH from the land or from the Levant north of it most improbable: In this case, at least some reflections in the relatively close-meshed sources for the Late Bronze and Iron I Age-Canaan and the territories north of it would be expected (as is the case for the south despite the unequally poorer state of sources [s. below 3.3]). An origin in the land during the Iron I Age is not strictly excluded, but nor is it positively indicated.

c) Independent Deity Names

Further, the independent deity names (not integrated in toponyms and personal names), which are documented in lists of gods and/or sacrifices, in letters, prayers, treaties etc. from the Levant and the West Semitic territory of the 2nd millennium, do not provide any reference to YHWH.[23] Again, this fact argues against a

---

21 Only extra-Biblical sources from the relevant periods are taken into account here, whereas the Biblical personal names are left due to their highly uncertain dating (s. Leuenberger, "Debatte" [see n. 14], n. 19).

22 Neither letter 154 from Amarna ("troops against Yawa [(ʾ)ia-wa]") nor the ending 'NI = yaʾ' in personal names from Ebla (the ending is also attested in toponyms and represents a hypocoristic name or a short form of ili: "my god") nor the element 'ia-aḫ-wi/ia-wi' attested in the Amurrite onomasticon (being a verbal form of auf ḥwy: "to live" and not a theophoric parameter) can be connected to the tetragrammaton or any form of YHWH (s. Leuenberger, "Debatte" [see n. 14], n. 23 ff).

23 For this wide consensus s. Pfeiffer, Kommen (see n. 9), 267; Leuenberger, "Debatte" (see n. 14), n. 31 ff. Notably, this holds true also for the Ugaritic Baal myth: The god name Yawwu (yw) which Ilu changes to Yammu (ym) in KTU 1.1 IV,14 f, has no connection with the tetragramm-

northern provenance of YHWH during the Late Bronze Age, as Manfred Krebernik has emphasized: "For the period and area in question, sources in cuneiform and Ugaritic script have yielded so far no clear evidence of YHWH. In view of the wide range of possible sources (even if they are not as dense as one could wish for), this *nil return* is of significance for the historical reconstruction."[24] Thus, Angelika Berlejung has convincingly summarised that YHWH "did not belong to the traditional pantheon of deities in the region [sc. of Syro-Palestine, M.L.]."[25]

d) The Religious-Historical Constellation

The most important argument for a northern provenance of YHWH draws on the more general religious-historical constellation, according to which *YHWH belongs to the North Levantine-Syriac type of the kingly weather-god Adad-Baal*. Recently, Reinhard Müller has demonstrated that "the oldest psalms depict the Ancient Hebrew deity YHWH as a storm-god" and that "[i]n the early days of YHWH worship, this deity seems to have been conceived similarly to storm-gods of neighboring cultures."[26]

In contrast to the negative evidence in the sources discussed above, the Adad-Baal profile of YHWH constitutes *the only positive indication for a northern provenance*. This is, therefore, important evidence which has to be considered within any model – notably within the hypothesis postulating a southern origin of YHWH.

(1) Before doing that, nevertheless, it is worth noting that the relevant evidence pointing to a northern provenance is based (solely) on *Biblical source material*, whereas extra-Biblical primary sources are lacking.

(2) More concretely, the evidence is based on important *old Psalms and early Psalm material* which present YHWH as a kingly weather-god. This indeed constitutes, in my view too, YHWH's core profile in the early Judahite monarchy. The decisive point, however, is that YHWH's profile is *not* comprehensively and exhaustively represented in this material: Dealing with a range of (indeed important) older Psalms, Müller then subtly shifts the argument by referring to "Jahwe *der* ältesten Psalmen" and speaking of the profile visible "in *den* ältesten

---

aton, but probably reflects the middle Babylonian change $w > m$ (s. S. TUAT 3/6, 1113f n. 97; Römer, *Dieu* [see n. 16], 53f).

24 Krebernik, "Beginnings" (see n. 16), 165.

25 Berlejung, in this volume, 68 n. 1.

26 Müller, in this volume, 208 (s. *BThZ* 30 [2013], 90: this early YHWH worship was "in ihrem Umfeld, dem nordwestsemitischen Kulturkreis, kein Fremdkörper").

Psalmen."[27] In contrast, YHWH's profile actually comprises several other functions as is demonstrated not only by the older Psalms ('Jerusalemite temple theology') but notably also by the early traditions of YHWH's theophany (s. below 3.3.d): Neither with regard to method nor from a thematic point of view is it convincing to qualify these theophany texts with the label of a "brüchigen alttestamentlichen Überlieferung."[28]

(3) The artificial restriction to the older Psalms mentioned presents a perspective which obviously is *limited to the state period of the 1st millennium with regard to time and to the southern kingdom of Judah with regard to space.*[29] Methodologically, such a restriction is highly problematic, although substantiating concrete pre-state traditions (even of North Israelite origins) also proves to be difficult.

(4) *If* one focuses exclusively on 'state' circumstances and corresponding texts from a Jerusalemite context of the 1st millennium, it is of course no surprise to detect *exact and substantial analogies to the cultural and religious environment of the Levant.* Nor is it astonishing that such texts provide "keinerlei Hinweise darauf, dass die Jahweverehrung außerhalb des palästinischen Kulturlandes entstanden ist."[30] However, this fact by no means justifies the religious-historical conclusion (reaching back in the pre-state period) which understands YHWH as a "im althebräischen Sprachraum verwurzelte und autochthone Manifestation

---

27 Müller, *BThZ* 30 (2013), 90 (emphasis mine; s. in this volume 208 slightly reforumaleted to "the early YHWH" and "the oldest psalms"). In the same way, Witte, *Jesus Christus* (see n. 13), 22 focuses on a few Psalms (along the same lines) he designates as the "mutmaßlich ältesten Texte[.] der israelitischen Kultlyrik." S.a. Pfeiffer, in this volume, 143: "Only the cultic songs of the monarchic period – according to current scholarship most likely the oldest texts in the Hebrew Bible – preserved in the Psalter provide a secure tradition-historical basis. These texts depict YHWH as a storm-god analogous to the type of Baal-Hadad attested in Syria-Palestine" (s. id. *BThZ* 30 [2013], 41: "Traditionsgeschichtlich sichereres Terrain [sc. compared to the sources for YHWH's southern origin, M.L.] betritt man erst mit den königszeitlichen Kultliedern des Psalters, die ... zu den ältesten Texten des Alten Testaments gehören und Jahwe als einen Wettergott vom Typ des syrisch-kanaanäischen Baal-Hadad zeichnen").

28 Müller, *Wettergott* (see n. 11), 243. S. similar Berner, "'I am YHWH your God, who brought you out of the land of Egypt' (Exod 20:2). Reflections on the Status of the Exodus Creed in the History of Israel and the Literary History of the Hebrew Bible," in this volume, 189, who refers to Pfeiffer, but does not substantiate the claim that "there are good reasons for the assumption that the passages in question [sc. in the theophany texts Judg 5 etc., M.L.] only originated in post-exilic times."

29 S. Müller, *Wettergott* (see n. 11), 244 (Jerusalemite temple); id., in this volume, 207: "probably composed for cultic settings of the monarchic age."

30 Müller, *Wettergott* (see n. 11), 243.

eines Göttertypus, der in der Levante seit alters beheimatet war,"[31] nor does it indicate "that the veneration of this deity originated somewhere in Palestine or its surroundings."[32]

(5) But if YHWH indeed has his roots in a pre-state milieu of the Late Bronze or Iron I Age (be it in the north or in the south), all religious-historical probability suggests that *YHWH's original profile* differs distinctively from the later transformations under the conditions of an evolving state. The important task, then consists in scrutinising on the basis of *all* sources whether and how far these transformation processes can still be reconstructed.

In summary, the pertinent Psalm traditions provide important evidence for YHWH's profile as a kingly weather-god during the early Judahite monarchy, but do not provide conclusive evidence for YHWH's pre-state period beginnings and origins, nor do they represent the exclusive or most important basis for reconstructing the oldest recognisable profile(s) of YHWH.

e) The Solitary Character of the Earliest YHWH

Finally, the solitary character of the earliest YHWH, which is widely acknowledged due to the unanimous testimony of the Biblical and epigraphic sources,[33] is hardly compatible with a northern origin in the rather complex and stratified structures of society; on the contrary, it connects excellently with the South Palestine-Edomite Araba, where at least groups such as the Shasu and the Hapiru were not integrated into institutionalised social orders. For such circles it makes sense to assume a self-contained god who functionally and typologically covers all the most important areas of life and to that extent functions as an autonomous god.

---

31 Müller, *Wettergott* (see n. 11), 243, s. 120; s.a. id., in this volume, 208.

32 Müller, in this volume, 208 (s. *BThZ* 30 [2013], 91: "einen lokalen, irgendwo in Palästina gelegenen Herkunftsort") following Levin, "Israel" (see n. 9), 390; s.a. Dijkstra, "Origins" (see n. 9), 101f.

33 S. for Details Leuenberger, "Debatte" (see n. 14), n. 50ff; id., *Gott* (see n. 2), 29–33. The most important exceptions are YHWH's assignment to the sons of god (s. בני אלוהים Deu 32:8 according to 4QDtn[j]) and the pair 'YHWH and his Asherah.' Both aspects genuinely stick with El and most probably represent implications of YHWH's inculturation in the land.

3.2 Brief Summary

Despite the comparatively close-meshed sources for Canaan and the adjoining Levant north of it, neither theophoric toponyms and personal names nor independent deity names from the second half of the 2nd millennium furnish one single piece of evidence which positively indicates a genuine origin and provenance of YHWH from Canaan or farther north. The religious-historical constellations there have been absorbed to some extent by (Psalm) texts dating from the earlier periods of the Judahite monarchy in Jerusalem. But with regard both to method and content, these adoptions do not allow to extrapolate to YHWH's original profile under pre-state conditions. Notably, YHWH's solitary character is diametrically opposed to the hypothesis of a northern origin.

This state of affairs makes clear that positive indications, which could corroborate the argument from silence for a northern provenance of YHWH adduced up to now, are still completely lacking at present. On the whole, all religious-historical probability based on the current state of sources contradicts the hypothesis of YHWH's original provenance from the north.

At this point, it is worth returning to the *polycausal model* mentioned above: It ponders whether YHWH (when and wherever he has his origin) would have emerged, as far as we can recognise, more or less at the same time and independently in the south *and* in the north. If on general grounds, the reliability of sources is assessed much more sceptically, it would be necessary to refrain from any proposition about YHWH's origins and beginnings in the pre-state period and the religious-historical (re-)construction would have to take the literary tradition, beginning in the early state period, as a starting point.[34] In my view however, the material state of our (Biblical and extra-Biblical) sources allows for a critical as well as careful and meticulous reconstruction of YHWH's history, which inches its way back to the origins and beginnings in the pre-state period. Evaluating all the sources presently at our disposal leads most probably to an origin and provenance of YHWH in the South Palestine-Edomite Araba during the Late Bronze Age, as the following analyses of the relevant sources will positively substantiate.

---

34 The same logic then should apply notably to the question about the historical Mose (s. J.C. Gertz, "Mose und die Anfänge der jüdischen Religion," *ZThK* 99 [2002], 3–20: here 10f.; id., Mose [2008], www.wibilex.de [05/26/2015], Kap. 4), where the source basis obviously is restricted to the Biblical texts (s. on the topic Blum, "Mose" [see n. 5]).

Of course, a paradigm of this sort would also have severe implications on the established literary- and redaction-historical models, whose hypothetical degree is at least equal to that of the religious-historical reconstruction elaborated here.

3.3 Evidence for YHWH's Provenance from the South!

Opposed to the negative findings for a northern origin of YHWH stands, in fact, the evidence for an original provenance of YHWH from the south, which evidence is by no means thoroughly negative and 'brittle,'[35] but indeed rather positive, although narrow, with regard to the Biblical and extra-Biblical texts. Following older and more recent studies, the crucial extra-Biblical (III.3.a–c) and Biblical (III.3.d) evidence (which I have treated elsewhere more elaborately[36]) is shortly set out below.

a) YHWH Shasu in Late Bronze Age Lists of Foreign Names from Egypt

I begin with the Late Bronze Age lists of foreign names from Egypt, which are the oldest epigraphic sources for the name of YHWH: Two long lists of geographically ordered foreign names from temples in Soleb (Amenhotep III, ca. 1370) and Amara-West (Ramses II, ca. 1250) contain sections listing a set of Shasu territories.[37] For our purpose, the crucial passage is the mentioning of *t3 š3św yhw3* (Soleb, IV N 4 α; also on rock block II 69) resp. *t3 š3św yhw3* (< *y-h-3r-3*) (Amara-West, # 96): "the land of the Shasu of YHWH" or " YHWH in the land of the Shasu."

(1) Philologically, the identification of the term '*yhw3*' with the Hebrew tetragrammaton '*yhwh*' is undisputed[38] (and remains independent of a vocal or consonantal interpretation of the final *w*-complement); within the syntactic construction, the apposition '*yhwh*' qualifies the preceding genitive more precisely.

(2) With regard to meaning, '*yhwh*' first of all designates a specific territory, but then, as they gradually overlap, probably also refers to the population group

---

35 S. above n. 11.28.

36 S. on that Leuenberger, *Gott* (see n. 2), 10–33 (expanding the article from *ZAW* 122 [2010], 1–19) and most recently Leuenberger, "Debatte" (see n. 14), 282–285.

37 The often mentioned documents need to be evaluated in their proper context which happens only rarely, s. as exceptions esp. Görg, M., "Jahwe – ein Toponym?," in *Ägypten und Altes Testament. Studien zu Geschichte, Kultur und Religion Ägyptens* (ed. M. Görg; ÄAT 2; Wiesbaden 1989), 180–187; M. Weippert, *Historisches Textbuch zum Alten Testament. Mit Beiträgen von J.F. Quack, B.U. Schipper und S.J. Wimmer* (GAT 10; Göttingen 2010), 183f; Leuenberger, *Gott* (see n. 2), 14ff and now F. Adrom and M. Müller, "The Tetragrammaton in Egyptian Sources – Facts and Fiction," in this volume, 96–103.

38 S. below n. 40.

living there. Further, the later history of Yʜwʜ may even suggest an additional understanding as a god name,[39] but this point can be left undecided here.

(3) Most recently, Faried Adrom and Matthias Müller also support the identification with Yʜwʜ,[40] but following Michael C. Astour,[41] they deny a geographic localisation in the South Palestine-Edomite zone and favour a North Palestine localisation, implying that "nothing in the Egyptian data proves itself of any value with relation to the place of origin of the deity in question [sc. Y-h-w, M.L.]."[42]

This argumentation, however, is not persuasive due to three points of weakness:[43] (a) Despite the not unproblematic equation 'š-ʿ-r-r = Seir', critically discussed by Adrom and Müller (s. in this volume, 99–101.112f), the most probable solution in the light of several misspellings and multiple records of Seir (š-ʿ-r) still assumes a writing peculiarity for Seir. (b) It is true that the position of exactly this 'Seir' (š-ʿ-r-r) in the list from Amara-West can not prove its function as a superscription for the whole Shasu group (although the group obviously constitutes a unit that begins with š-ʿ-r-r in # 92 and ends with # 97). But regardless of this issue, Seir effects in any case a geographic localisation in the South Palestine-Edomite Araba.[44] (c) In contrast, Adrom and Müller favour a North Palestine-Lebanese positioning (in this volume, 105). For this alternative however, they have to fall back on the North Palestinian interpretation of the younger list of Ramses II from Medinet Habu by Astour, which is (to say the least) contentious, and then to postulate an analogue setting for the Soleb and Amara West lists. Compared to the internal analyses advocated above, however, this seems unfavourable with respect to both methodology and content.

On the whole, the presented understanding of the Yʜwʜ Shasu land in the Egyptian lists (independent from the Biblical texts and therefore not to be denigrated as a circular argument [see n. 44]) amounts to a localisation of the territory, the population and (only here taking the later Biblical evidence into ac-

---

39 So e.g. Görg, "Jahwe" (see n. 37), 187 and Römer, "Revelation" (see n. 16), 313; s. further Leuenberger, *Gott* (see n. 2), 16 n. 34.

40 Adrom and Müller, in this volume, 110–113. S. also my references for this consensus Leuenberger, *Gott* (see n. 2), 15 n. 31.

41 S. M.C. Astour, "Yahweh in Egyptian Topographic Lists," in *Festschrift Elmar Edel, 12. März 1979* (ed. M. Görg and E. Pusch; ÄAT 1; Bamberg 1979), 24–30.

42 Adrom and Müller, *BThZ* 30 (2013), 141 in their summary (which is lacking in the present volume).

43 S. Leuenberger, "Debatte" (see n. 14), 282–284.

44 S. for the relevant extra-Biblical sources Weippert, "Textbuch" (see n. 37), 179ff. Since they allow for an independent localisation of Seir, the accusation of a circular argument (so Adrom and Müller, "Tetragramm" [see n. 37], 127 with regard to Grdseloff) is void.

count) possibly also the god 'Yнwн' in the South Palestine-Edomite Araba during the Late Bronze Age. Being the oldest reference group for Yнwн (*yhw3*) this external, extra-Biblical evidence is in terms of time, space and religious history of central importance for the earliest Yнwн as he is historically recognisable in our sources.[45]

b) Shasu in the Araba

Pursuing the close connection of Yнwн with Shasu groups (*š3św*) in the lists of foreign names, the *Shasu in the Araba* as a whole come into focus. Here, a few remarks on the most important results and implications must suffice: Shasu people are rather well-documented in the epigraphic, iconographic and archaeological sources, mainly from Egypt.[46] The term – although referring to Semitic people – does not so much designate an ethnic entity as indicate the population group's semi-nomadic status, not being integrated into the established society but existing in opposition to the institutionalised social orders. In the present context, the most important aspect is the localisation of several Shasu groups in Edom and Seir according to textual and iconographic sources from Egypt (14th–12th century); there, they have regular contact with the Egyptian power, the relationships being at times amiable and including trade, but often also growing discordant and hostile. It is in this field of tension that their involvement with the (Egyptian controlled) copper mining in Timna and Faynan-Punon has to be understood. The important role Shasu groups were playing there can be deduced by the locally produced Negev ceramic, the correlation with Ramesses' III security measures and the *[t3 š3-]św p3-wnw/pwnw:* "[the land of the S]hasu of Puno(n)/Punon in [the land of the S]hasu" attested in the above treated Amara-West list (# 45).

---

45 Of course, this appraisal has at the same time to respect the specific character of the sources expressing Egyptian royal ideology, but the sources nevertheless have a reference to reality and therefore express factual ethno-geographic knowledge (s. on that Leuenberger, *Gott* [see n. 2], 18).

46 S. for the texts Weippert, "Textbuch" (see n. 37), 181 ff (Lit.), for the Iconography T. Staubli, *Das Image der Nomaden im Alten Israel und in der Ikonographie seiner sesshaften Nachbarn* (OBO 107; Fribourg 1991); s. to the whole Leuenberger, *Gott* [see n. 2], 19 ff (Lit.) and most recently Römer, "Revelation" (see n. 16), 314; M. Bietak, "On the Historicity of the Exodus: What Egyptology today can contribute to Assessing the Biblical Account of the Sojourn in Egypt," in *Israel's Exodus in Transdisciplinary Perspective. Text, Archaeology, Culture, and Geoscience* (ed. T.E. Levy et al.; Heidelberg 2015), 17–37: here 18 ff.

These sources substantiate the important role which certain Shasu groups played in southern Palestine during the 13th and 12th centuries. Widening the focus, they can be firstly identified as one of the transmitting group(s) of the earliest YHWH beliefs as far as our sources allow for a conclusion. Secondly, their intensive and often conflictual relation to the Egyptian suzerainty allows for a religious-historical correlation with the Exodus tradition (which issue we may let rest for now). And thirdly, they possess a central function in the constitutive phase of Israel in the land, as is widely acknowledged. Taken together, these wide ranging sources shed light on the historical, political and social situation of the Shasu in the Late Bronze Age Araba and hence serve to plausibly contextualise the Egyptian evidence of YHWH.

d) YHWH from Teman in Kuntillet ʿAjrud

Another major set of evidence is provided by the famous Kuntillet ʿAjrud inscriptions from the early 8th century, which have been discussed intensively with regard to other issues but also provide instructive clues for this topic: North Israelites mostly[47] make use of blessing formulas in a traditional way. These blessings not only refer to YHWH and his Asherah, but also specify YHWH in two ways: as *yhwh šmrn:* "YHWH from Samaria" and as *yhwh (h)t(y)mn:* "YHWH from Teman/ the south."[48] Even if one does not want to accept old (north) Israelite traditions but prefers to reckon with contemporary knowledge of a corresponding YHWH veneration around 800 BCE in Teman, far outside the Israelite-Judean sphere of influence, one can not avoid supposing YHWH's religious-historical origins and beginnings in the pre-state period outside the land (since postulating migrations of YHWH venerating Israelites to Teman during the 10th or 9th century is hardly a convincing alternative). The inscriptions from Kuntillet ʿAjrud therefore offer a further positive, although indirect clue for a southern provenance of

---

47 The wall inscription 4.1 with the written diphtong form *yhwh (h)tymn* : "YHWH from Teman" (l.1f) provides also an example for the Jewish dialect, and is, additionally, not written in the typical North Israelite script (s. Z. Meshel, *Kuntillet ʿAjrud (Ḥorvat Teman). An Iron Age II Religious Site on the Judah-Sinai Border* [Jerusalem 2012], 105–107; E. Blum, "Die Wandinschriften 4.2 und 4.6 sowie die Pithos-Inschrift 3.9 aus Kuntillet ʿAǧrūd," *ZDPV* 125 [2013], 49 with n. 123). This might be evidence for a Judean tradition of YHWH's southern provenance, but how viable this conclusion is, needs to be evaluated more extensively.

48 S. in detail beside 4.1,1f. (*yhwh [h]tymn*) the variants in 3.6,5f. (*yhwh tmn*) and 3.9,1 (*yhwh htmn*), whose legibility is unproblematic.

YHWH and thus add considerable strength to the extra-Biblical evidence, as Erhard Blum rightly has emphasised.[49]

e) The Biblical Theophany Texts (Judg 5:4 f; Ps 68:8 f; Deut 33:2; Hab 3:3)

The group of Biblical theophany texts in Judg 5; Ps 68; Hab 3 and Deut 33 also deserves consideration. That we deal with a connected group here is clearly indicated by the topos of YHWH's coming from the south, which is singular in the Hebrew Bible (s. e. g. his title זֶה סִינַי: "the one of Sinai" Judg 5:5; Ps 68:9; s.a. מִסִּינַי Deut 33:2) and which links exactly these texts; conversely, all these passages are only loosely incorporated into their respective contexts, indicating independent entities. In a first step, to be sure, the examination proceeds independently from the above results based on the extra-Biblical evidence; it is only in a second step that more comprehensive correlations can be developed.

Based on philological (e. g. W.F. Albright; F.M. Cross; D.N. Freedman), form-critical (esp. J. Jeremias) and tradition-historical (P.D. Miller and others) studies, this text-group has long been judged as containing old traditions of YHWH ideas; however, Pfeiffer's literary-historical investigation has questioned this understanding.[50] A new evaluation is therefore required, and in what follows, I will outline the key arguments provided by an analysis of the four texts.

(1) According to a solid consensus shared also by Pfeiffer, the song of Deborah in *Judg 5* constitutes the basic text: On the one hand, it is almost certain that Ps 68:8 f with the title זֶה סִינַי: "the one of Sinai" literarily depends on and explicitely cites Judg 5:4 f.[51] On the other hand, Deut 33:2 and Hab 3:3 probably are also younger, but in contrast to Ps 68 they do not evidence similar indications of literary dependency,[52] despite exhibiting tradition-historical commonalities (s. below).

---

49 S. Blum, "Mose" (see n. 5), 55–58; s. also my short argument Leuenberger, "Debatte" (see n. 14), 284 f; id., *Gott* (see n. 2), 29 n. 92.

50 S. my brief report Leuenberger, *Gott* (see n. 2), 23 f and 24 ff for the following argumentation.

51 S. e. g. E.A. Knauf, *Midian. Untersuchungen zur Geschichte Palästinas und Nordarabiens am Ende des 2. Jahrtausends v. Chr.* (ADPV 10; Wiesbaden 1988), 49; W. Groß, *Richter. Übersetzt und ausgelegt. Mit Karten von E. Gaß* (HThK; Freiburg 2009), 305 ff; Pfeiffer, who additionally assumes a literary dependency also for Hab 3, Deut 33 and Ps 68, which he judges – in this sequence – as Hellenistic texts (s. the summary Kommen [see n. 9], 258 f).

52 For Deut 33:2 s. Leuenberger, *Gott* (see n. 2), 23 n. 59; 50 f; id., *Segen und Segenstheologien im alten Israel. Untersuchungen zu ihren religions- und theologiegeschichtlichen Konstellationen und Transformationen* (AThANT 90; Zürich 2008), 351 f. In the present context, Hab 3:3 is of secon-

בְּצֵאתְךָ מִשֵּׂעִיר	יְהוָה	4 YHWH, when you went out *from Seir*,
בְּצַעְדְּךָ מִשְּׂדֵה אֱדוֹם		when you marched *from the field of Edom*,
רָעָשָׁה	אֶרֶץ	the earth quaked,
נָטְפוּ	גַּם־שָׁמַיִם	also, the heavens poured,
נָטְפוּ מָיִם	גַּם־עָבִים	also, the clouds poured water.
נָזְלוּ מִפְּנֵי יְהוָה זֶה סִינַי	הָרִים	5 The mountains trembled before YHWH,
		the *one from Sinai*,
מִפְּנֵי יְהוָה אֱלֹהֵי יִשְׂרָאֵל		before YHWH, the god of Israel.

Axel Knauf has argued on philological grounds for a core layer (including V.4 f) from the 10th or 9th century, which later was revised: "The resulting impression is that of a non-standard text incompletely standardized rather than that of a sub-standard text, i.e. a text produced by someone only semi-literate in SBH."[53]

(2) In this perspective, *four main arguments* for an early, i.e. a pre-monarchic (and, more precisely, 13th or 12th century) dating of the idea that YHWH is coming from the south emerge:

(a) With regard to Judg 5:4f, Knauf's analysis makes a relatively early date for the *literary* core of Judg 5 together with V.4 f very probable, placing it in the early monarchic period.[54]

---

dary importance, s. only W. Dietrich, *Nahum, Habakuk, Zephanja* (IEKAT; Stuttgart 2014), 168 ff, esp. 170 f.

53 E.A. Knauf, "Deborah's Language. Judges Ch. 5 in its Hebrew and Semitic Context," in *Studia Semitica et Semitohamitica. FS für R. Voigt anläßlich seines 60. Geburtstages am 17. Januar 2004* (ed. B. Burtea and J. Tropper and H. Younansardaroud; AOAT 317; Münster 2005), 167–182, here 176, s. 171 ff; a similar result is justified also by Groß, *Richter* (see n. 51), 296 f; s. further the hints of R. Tadiello, "Il canto di Debora (Gdc 5): studio poetico e testuale," *RivBib* 61 (2013), 331–373: esp. 337.

From a theological-historical perspective, the missing Exodus tradition also seems to be significant, the construction of which would be very surprising in a post-exilic text (s. e.g. the analogue process of adding solar traditions in Deut 33:2 and Hab 3:4, probably reflecting monarchic developments in Jerusalem [s. Leuenberger, *Gott* (see n. 2), 50]).

This middle-position implies a critique both of the classical corpus of 'early Israelite poetry' and of a late dating into the postexilic or even Hellenistic era (s. the references in Leuenberger, *Gott* [see n. 2], 27 n. 85 and recently S. Frolov, "How old is the song of Deborah?," *JSOT* 36 [2011], 163–184: here 165, who himself opts for a late pre-exilic, exilic or early post-exilic date between ca. 700 and 450). For the latter opts also Pfeiffer, *Kommen* [see n. 9], 40 ff.69 f, seeing V.4 f as a postexilic addition in 'Psalm style' to the war epos in 'ballad style' from the 9th or 8th century.

54 Whether YHWH's title זֶה סִינַי is original does not matter in the present context, although it fits in the context as show Jeremias' structural analysis and Knauf's interpretation of זֶה as a relative pronoun, which have corroborated this (s. Leuenberger, *Gott* [see n. 2], 25 with n. 74).

(b) The *tradition* of YHWH's southern provenance, which forms the basis of Judg 5 and the other theophany texts, must be even older, as a tradition-historical examination of these texts demonstrates. From a methodological point of view, it is therefore important to distinguish properly between literary and tradition history: Even a literary-critical elimination of V.4f by itself indicates little about the age of the conception! Yet, exactly this connection is implied, when Pfeiffer maintains that "[t]raditionsgeschichtlich hohes Alter kann damit definitiv ausgeschlossen werden."[55] This knee-jerk conclusion from the literary and redaction history on the tradition-historical origin is highly problematic and must be avoided.

If one compares the specific propositions on the helpfulness of YHWH's coming from the south, telling variances in the formulations can be observed: YHWH is approaching his venerators from different territories in southern Palestine: from Seir and the field of Edom (מִשְׂעִיר; אֱדוֹם מִשְׂדֵה Judg 5:4; s. מִשֵּׂעִיר Deut 33:2; s. already *ś'rr* in the Amara West list # 92), from Teman (i.e. the south) and from Mount Paran (מִתֵּימָן; מֵהַר־פָּארָן Hab 3:3; s. מֵהַר פָּארָן and מְרִיבַת קָדֵשׁ [cj., s. above n. 52] Deut 33:2). The term *yhwh (h)t(y)mn*: "YHWH from the south" in the inscriptions from Kuntillet 'Ajrud [56] bundles these ideas, as does the expression "from his [sc. YHWH's] south (מִימִינוֹ)" in Deut 33:2 (if that is indeed the correct reading[57]).

On the basis of this survey, it becomes obvious, that a theological-historical reconstruction of this topos – YHWH's coming from the south – combining the philological, form-critical, tradition-historical and literary-historical approach, as mentioned above, is an urgent desideratum. Yet, even the elementary evidence just reviewed, provides two further basic arguments:

(c) The *variances in the designation of YHWH's place of origin* can not be explained by a model based on literary dependencies alone (which holds true in the first place for Hab 3:3 and in the second place for Deut 33:2), especially since the variations are not owed to the different contexts, as a detailed analysis clearly shows. On the contrary, YHWH's coming from Edom, Seir, Teman and Paran points to a common tradition-historical background, localising YHWH's region of origin in the south.[58] On the grounds of the above considerations one can exclude an overall postexilic formation of the topos: The evidence positively

---

55 Pfeiffer, *Kommen* (see n. 9), 90.

56 S. above 3.3.c with n. 48.

57 So e.g. with S. Beyerle, *Der Mosesegen im Deuteronomium. Eine text-, kompositions- und formkritische Studie zu Deuteronomium 33* (BZAW 250; Berlin 1997), 16ff and A. Lemaire, *The Birth of Monotheism. The Rise and Disappearance of Yahwism* (Washington 2007), 21f.

58 Leuenberger, *Gott* (see n. 2), 28 and now Blum, "Mose" (see n. 5), 58.

points to a pre-monarchic origin and beginning (possibly even connected with a residence on a mountain).

(d) To this pluriformity of geographic localisations fits the fact *that the specific territory of Yhwh's origin only plays a marginal role in all four texts* compared to his earth-shaking, yet for his venerators helpful theophany. This speaks against intended redactional *Fortschreibungen*; rather, it pleads for old substrates. For the same reason, Pfeiffer's reductionist explanation – according to which all the differing local designations constitute illustrations but for one and the same programmatic (post-exilic) equation of "'Edom' als Chiffre für das Gericht"[59] – is not at all convincing.

On a larger scale, Pfeiffer presents an observation of great importance:[60] That Yhwh's coming from the south fundamentally competes with the idea of Yhwh sitting enthroned on Zion, which idea dominates the official Judahite state religion. But in that a postexilic invention of Yhwh's southern provenance is virtually impossible, the competition with the Zion tradition in fact again boils down to a pre-monarchic origin: Just like Yhwh's coming from the south constitutes a basic paradigm in the pre-state period, Yhwh's dwelling on Zion represents monarchic Judah's official religion. The formulas of 'Yhwh from the south' and 'Yhwh on Zion' each represent a different system of symbols, and with Hartmut Gese the transformational process can be abbreviated to a movement from "Sinai to Zion."[61] This theological-historical model then can be readily combined with a regional differentiation during the monarchic period,[62] since at least the theophany texts Judg 5 and Deut 33 clearly have their "Heimat im Nordreich Israel"[63]. During the state era, Yhwh's epithet "סני שכני" bildet demnach das nördliche Gegenstück zum Jerusalemer השכן בהר ציון (Jes 8:18)."[64]

In this context, to be sure, 'Sinai' is broadly understood and – subsequent to Judg 5:5 – simply refers to Yhwh's coming from the south as described in the theophany texts. There, 'Sinai'

---

59 Pfeiffer, *Kommen* (see n. 9), 258; s.a. 69ff.80ff.90f, admitting that one "wird die Edom-Begrifflichkeit in Jdc 5:4 vielleicht nicht im präzisen Sinn dechiffrieren können" (86).

60 Pfeiffer, *Kommen* (see n. 9), 90f.267f.

61 S. the title of his collected essays: H. Gese, *Vom Sinai zum Zion. Alttestamentliche Beiträge zur biblischen Theologie* (BEvTh 64; Tübingen ²1984).

62 In my view, the differing conceptions of time – Yhwh's help coming from the south *in specific instances* vs. Yhwh's *permanent* presence on Zion securing kingdom and providing steady auspiciousness – advocate against an exclusively regional explanation as two strictly contemporary 'counter-concepts' from the state period, much as the first could be (re)used under monarchic conditions in Israel.

63 Blum, "Mose" (see n. 5), 59.

64 Blum, "Mose" (see n. 5), 60.

might be original and would then designate YHWH's residence on the mount Sinai (whose original location though is not to be equated with the later traditions).[65] But whatever might be the case here, the Biblical Sinai tradition in its proper sense elaborates a distinct concept in which YHWH indeed is visited by the Israelites at the mountain of god (Ex 19 ff, whereas in Judg 5 etc. YHWH comes, as mentioned, from the Sinai or the like to his venerators) – and not in Jerusalem.

However, Pfeiffer's interpretation of the complete *Sinai tradition as an exilic invention*, developed for the first time in a situation, "in der die Möglichkeit des Gotteskontaktes im Lande grundsätzlich nicht mehr gegeben war," is much too one-sided:[66] Firstly, the literary history is much more complex and includes older, in part much older, material;[67] the explanation that the redactors had YHWH's "Verortung [sc. at Sinai, M.L.] auf halbem Wege zwischen Ägypten und Kanaan ausdrücklich gewollt," seems to be construed rather artificially. Secondly, from a religious-historical perspective, the interpretation of the formative Sinai tradition as an exilic reaction to the Zion tradition would also prinicipally compete with the prominent retreat of YHWH into heaven (notably also within the Deuteronomistic tradition).[68] Thirdly, the model overrates the creativity of Israelite traditional literature ('Traditionsliteratur'), which does not just construe completely free-handedly, as e.g. a comparison of the Deuteronomistic and the Chronistic history demonstrates.

(3) Taking these arguments into account, the Biblical theophany texts corroborate and substantiate the extra-Biblical evidence: With regard to the literary history, Judg 5 leads into the early monarchic phase; with regard to the tradition and religious history, even an early, i.e. pre-monarchic (and, more precisely, 13th or 12th century) origin of the idea of YHWH's coming from the south can positively be reconstructed.

4 Summary and Implications: YHWH's Origin and the Early History of YHWH

Having evaluated all relevant extra-Biblical and Biblical sources with regard to YHWH's northern or southern origin and provenance, the results give clear reasons to support the latter option: Neither specific theophoric toponyms, personal names, independent deity names nor YHWH's solitary character, nor even more general religious-historical constellations in Canaan provide any positive evidence for a northern origin and beginning of YHWH (whether it in the land itself

---

65 Leuenberger, *Gott* (see n. 2), 30 f with n. 96 and the religious-historical analogies Krebernik mentions (in this volume, 53).

66 S. for the following my more detailed argumentation Leuenberger, *Gott* (see n. 2), 25 f.

67 S. e. g. the nuanced summary of W. Oswald, *Israel am Gottesberg. Eine Untersuchung zur Literargeschichte der vorderen Sinaiperikope Ex 19–24 und deren historischem Hintergrund* (OBO 159; Freiburg et al. 1998), 241 f. 247 ff.

68 S. esp. Keel, *Geschichte* (see n. 16), 201.

or north of it) during the second half of the 2nd millennium (s. 3.1 and the brief summary in 3.2). In contrast, the Late Bronze Age lists from Egypt with foreign names mentioning YHWH Shasu, combined with a socio-economic contextualization of the corresponding Shasu groups, as well as "YHWH from Teman" in the Kuntillet 'Ajrud inscriptions from ca. 800, provide positive, though narrow extra-Biblical evidence for a southern provenance and origin of YHWH in the Late Bronze Age. Finally, this reconstruction is further supported by the Biblical theophany texts in Judg 5 etc.

In my view, the verdict is rather clear: The extra-Biblical and the Biblical evidence substantiates YHWH's origin in respectively provenance from the south, i.e. in respectively from the South Palestine-Edomite Araba during the Late Bronze Age, as a majority of exegetes still advocates (s. above the references in n. 16). This model is further able to explain the findings in the sources discussed with regard to a northern origin (esp. in 3.1.d), which is not only very important from a methodological point of view, but also renders unnecessary a polycausal hypothesis, which combines both origins in one way or another (s. 1.2).

In a next step, a detailed religious-historical comparison and correlation of the extra-Biblical and the Biblical evidence is methodologically compelling: First, this procedure could elaborate in detail on convergences and divergences in the different sources and traditions; secondly, it could add overall 'cumulative evidence'[69] to YHWH's origin in the Late Bronze Age Araba, as far as we can see based on all source material presently available, and in so doing it could further enhance the usefulness of religious-historical modelling.[70]

Obviously, this religious-historical thesis has *implications for the early history of YHWH as a whole*, but reciprocally also gains a higher plausibility within this larger horizon. Central issues deserving further investigation are the 'transportation' of YHWH into the land (the so-called Midianite-Kenite hypothesis), the Exodus tradition(s) and YHWH's inculturation and his ascent in the land.[71]

The present article, however, has focused on the religious-historical question of YHWH's origin and provenance. Ultimately, in my view it is all about "a

---

69 S. on the one hand Leuenberger, *Gott* (see n. 2), 32; id., "Debatte" (see n. 14), 285 with n. 70 and Krebernik's argumentation (in this volume, 64 f), on the other hand the critical query of Pfeiffer (in this volume, 143).

70 Recently, Römer, *Dieu* (see n. 16), 69 f has hinted at a further piece of evidence which needs further analysis: In an unedited papyrus from the 18th dynasty (again connected to Shasu people) a mountain "Laban" in Edom is mentioned.

71 S. N. Amzallag, "Yahweh, the Canaanite God of Metallurgy?," *JSOT* 33 (2009), 387–404; Faust, "Emergence" (see n. 16), 476 f and my provisional outline Leuenberger, "Debatte" (see n. 14), 285 f.

deeper *historical understanding* of the unique character of Israel and its religion," including its god:[72] How can we (re)construct the origins and beginnings of YHWH and his subsequent history in a hermeneutically reflected and religious-historically well-founded way?

To me, the evidence presented and evaluated here, confirms and, in certain ways, modifies the old hypothesis of YHWH's southern provenance by including older and newer extra-Biblical source material: It provides a decisive increase in data and therefore advances the argumentative base of the religious-historical reconstruction. This broadening of source material essentially adds to the "integrierenden Zusammenschau … der Anfänge des Jhwhglaubens," which still is "ein bleibendes Postulat."[73] The religious-historical reconstruction of YHWH's origin, provenance and oldest profile under the pre-state conditions of the Late Bronze and Iron I Age Araba is the indispensable first step in reconstructing the history of YHWH, the Biblical god.

---

72 Hartenstein, in this volume 306 (emphasis mine, following the German version).
73 Görg, "Art. Jahwe," *NBL* 2 (1995), 260–266: here 264, who pioneered work on this complex field.

Christoph Berner

"I am Yнwн your God, who brought you out of the land of Egypt" (Exod 20:2)

Reflections on the Status of the Exodus Creed in the History of Israel and the Literary History of the Hebrew Bible*

1 Introduction

According to the Hebrew Bible, there is a simple answer to the question as to when the Israelites started worshipping Yнwн. The origins of their Yнwн worship lie with their exodus out of Egypt; or, to be more precise, with their being led out of the land by Yнwн. Having grown into a people in Egypt and then having been enslaved by the Egyptians, the Israelites are eventually freed by Yнwн and enter into a covenant with him at Sinai. This is in any case the situation – simplified, of course – according to the testimony of Exod 1–24, in which the mentioned events find their most elaborate narrative development within the Old Testament. However, outside of these chapters there is certainly no silence concerning the exodus. Allusions to the exodus events, particularly to the experience of liberation in Exod 1–15, pervade virtually the entire Hebrew Bible and – despite their clear predominance in the Pentateuch and the former prophets (Joshua – 2 Kings), – they can be found also in the prophetic books and the Psalter. Moreover, many references to the exodus resemble each other in that they follow a particular formulaic tradition which is attested in a prominent position in the introduction of the Decalogue: "I am Yнwн your God, who brought you out of the land of Egypt, out of the house of slavery" (Exod 20:2; cf. Deut 5:6).

In light of the frequent occurrence of this so-called *Herausführungsformel* (and its variants[1]) in the Hebrew Bible, Martin Noth formulated a position with wide-reaching religious- and literary-historical implications:

---

* This article is a slightly revised and expanded version of my 2013 German article "Mein Gott von Ägypten her." My cordial thanks go to the translator Stephen Hamilton and to Dr. Anja Klein who did the proofreading.

1 W. Groß, "Die Herausführungsformel – Zum Verhältnis von Formel und Syntax," *ZAW 86* (1974), 425–453. Cf. also the extensive study by I. Schulmeister, *Israels Befreiung aus Ägypten: Eine Formeluntersuchung zur Theologie des Deuteronomiums* (ÖBS 36; Frankfurt a.M. 2010).

DOI 10.1515/9783110448221-009

> "In the case of the 'guidance out of Egypt' we are dealing with a *primary confession (Urbekkenntnis) of Israel* [...] and at the same time with *the kernel of the whole subsequent Pentateuchal tradition*. Although we know very little about the inner life of ancient Israel, we have here – unless we are completely mistaken – a *common* confession of *all* Israel."[2]

Noth does not postulate that all of Israel participated in the exodus experience, but he assumes that an exodus group integrated itself into the clans involved in the conquest of Canaan and imparted its beliefs. He thus finds the biblical portrayal to be fundamentally confirmed: according to Noth, the beginnings of Israel's YHWH worship are inseparably tied with the exodus experience.

This perspective of Noth is determined by two crucial premises. Firstly, he presupposes the paradigm of the documentary hypothesis ("Neuere Urkundenhypothese"), according to which substantial parts in the Pentateuchal narrative were already in writing in the early monarchic period. Secondly, he assumes that these early literary testimonies were themselves preceded by a longer phase of oral tradition, which bridges the divide between the historical events and the earliest literary reports thereof. Recent Old Testament scholarship in Continental Europe, however, has shown that these premises are highly problematic. Today, the earliest literary version of the Pentateuchal narrative is generally assigned a much later date, and the idea that its text necessarily presupposes an oral tradition is met with increasing skepticism. Rather, it can be shown frequently that Old Testament texts are scribal products, which from their very beginning were conceived for a particular context and never had an oral pre-stage.[3]

This new orientation in scholarship has had significant consequences for determining the relationship between the history of Old Testament literature and Israelite religion. While Noth and his contemporaries assumed to have obtained a direct view into the early history of Israel by way of the postulated oral tradition, this path is now closed to contemporary scholarship. Instead of speculating about possible oral pre-stages, it is first and foremost important to read biblical texts as literary documents. If therefore a large number of texts from various phases of literary history reflect the conviction that the origins of YHWH worship are related to the exodus, then this discovery initially shows only that, over the course of the literary growth of the Hebrew Bible, the exodus creed developed into a central interpretive category which was used in the attempt to comprehend God's relationship to Israel. To put it pointedly, we have no first-hand informa-

---

2 M. Noth, *A History of Pentateuchal Traditions* (trans. B.W. Anderson; Chico (CA) 1981), 49. Similarly already G. von Rad, "Das formgeschichtliche Problem des Hexateuchs," in *Gesammelte Studien zum Alten Testament* (TB 8; München ⁴1971), 9 – 86.
3 See below, section *3.1.*

tion about ancient Israel's religious history, but instead primarily a view into the theological history of an emerging Judaism which reflected theologically on its own origins through the successive redactional continuation (*Fortschreibung*) of the biblical text.

To shed more light on the particular phases of this literary development is the task of redaction criticism, which analyzes the content and theology of the various layers, determines their relative chronology, and thereby traces the dynamics that were active during the process of *Fortschreibung*. Only in a second step – on the basis of a solid redaction historical model and with all necessary caution –, can we inquire both into the historical background and the specific traditions which may have influenced a particular stage of literary development. When applied to the question of possible lines of connection between the exodus creed and the beginnings of YHWH worship in Israel, this entails identifying the earliest layers of text in order to obtain a sound basis for historical inquiry.

This outlined approach will be applied in the following, focusing on two points. Firstly, it will be asked whether a point in time in the monarchic period can be identified, at which the exodus creed (notwithstanding its actual origins) could claim official status (2.). Here, it is imperative to investigate if – as has often been assumed – the exodus creed was the rallying cry of Jeroboam and the Northern Tribes in their rebellion against Solomonic forced labor, which later developed into the official state ideology of the Northern Kingdom. Secondly, we will pursue the question of the historical background and the possible religious-historical implications of the actual creedal content (3.). Here we must clarify whether it is possible to infer back into the historical origins of the exodus tradition and identify its religious-historical implications from the earliest literary layers of the book of Exodus.

2 The Status of the Exodus Creed in the History of the Northern Kingdom of Israel

2.1 The Exodus Creed as Rallying Cry of Jeroboam's Rebellion?

It has been demonstrated on various occasions that the record of Jeroboam's revolt and the division of the Solomonic kingdom (1 Kgs 11:26 – 12:24) shows noticeable parallels to the content of the Exodus story (Exod 1–15). Rainer Albertz summarizes these parallels thus:

"[L]ike Jeroboam, Moses too is depicted as a man from royal circles who shows solidarity with his hard-pressed fellow countrymen and ventures to rebel by striking an Egyptian overseer (Exod2.11–15, cf. I Kings 11.26–28). Both times the attempted revolt fails; like Jeroboam, Moses has to flee abroad to escape the punishment of the king (Exod 2.15; cf. I Kings 11.40). Both return to their fellow-countrymen only after the death of the king (Exod 2.23aα + 4.19, 20a, cf. I Kings 11.40; 12.2cj, 20). In both cases there are negotiations with the king's successor to ease the burden, but these end with a heightening of the demands (Exod 5.3–19; I Kings 12.3b–15) [...]. Finally, both times the liberation from forced labour takes place in a comparable way by departure from the sphere of power of the oppressive potentate (Exod 14.5a; I Kings 12.16, 19)."[4]

But how are these parallels to be interpreted? Albertz suggests the following model: The rebellion of Jeroboam and the Northern tribes against the Solomonic system of forced labor was conducted in reference to the Exodus tradition, and "these old religious reminiscences took their first narrative form from the contemporary experiences of Jeroboam's revolt."[5] Albertz thus estimates a three-layered process: in the beginning is the unwritten Exodus tradition, which then is used by the rebels under Jeroboam as a theological motto for the fight against Solomon's forced labor, finally to be given literary shape in light of the insurrection's successful outcome. A text such as the story of the intensification of compulsory labor (Exod 5:3–19) is according to this theory the direct expression of the Northern tribes' propaganda against the labor imposed on them by Solomon and his son Rehoboam.[6]

With these far-reaching (literary-)historical reconstructions, Albertz clearly lacks the required distance to the Old Testament texts which he consults. The historical circumstances of Jeroboam's rebellion and the division of the kingdom are not critically reconstructed, but instead are ultimately deduced from a mere retelling of the biblical record in 1 Kgs 11. It is clear that such an approach is highly problematic. 1 Kgs 11–12 cannot be read like an entry from a royal archive, but the chapters are part of the so-called Deuteronomistic History (DtrH), which narrates the history of the monarchy in Israel and Judah from a Judaean perspective and with clear theological evaluation. Moreover, the composition of the DtrH

---

4 R. Albertz, *From the Beginnings to the End of the Monarchy. Vol. 1, A History of Israelite Religion in the Old Testament Period* (trans. J. Bowden; OTL; London 1994), 141–142.
5 R. Albertz, *History I* (see n. 4), 142. Cf. also F. Crüsemann, *Der Widerstand gegen das Königtum: Die antiköniglichen Texte des Alten Testaments und der Kampf um den frühen israelitischen Staat* (WMANT 49; Neukirchen-Vluyn 1978), 167–180.
6 Cf. also the study of P. Särkiö, *Exodus und Salomo. Erwägungen zur verdeckten Salomokritik anhand von Ex 1–2; 5; 14 und 32* (SESJ 71; Helsinki and Göttingen 1988), which reads Exodus 5 and further Exodus texts as testimonies of "hidden criticism of Solomon" ("[einer] verdeckten Salomokritik").

did not take place prior to the 6th century BCE and thus is to be dated about 400 years after the events reported in 1 Kgs 11–12.[7] Finally, it must be considered that at best only parts of 1 Kgs 11–12 can be attributed to the earliest version of the DtrH. Much of the text only accrued during a long process of *Fortschreibung* and reveals nothing about the historical circumstances in the time of Solomon or Rehoboam, but instead shows how the events in question were later envisioned.

If we allow for all the necessary literary-historical differentiations within 1 Kgs 11–12, then Albertz' thesis that Jeroboam's rebellion was fought under the banner of the Exodus tradition is significantly weakened. It relies primarily on two texts (1 Kgs 11:27–28; 12:1–19) which in their literary context clearly prove to be later additions. That 1 Kgs 12:1–19 is a secondary expansion, influenced by the wisdom tradition, has been convincingly demonstrated by Uwe Becker and Alexander Rofé.[8] The verses address Rehoboam's foolishness in not reducing the workload of the Northern tribes – as was the advice of the elders – but instead intensifying it and ultimately causing the secession. Rehoboam is in this manner made jointly liable for the division of the kingdoms, with the motive of forced labor functioning merely as a narrative instrument. There can be no inferences to the historical events in Rehoboam's time.

Exactly the same must be said of 1 Kgs 11:27–28. Both verses interrupt the original textual sequence between 11:26b ("*and he [sc. Jeroboam] lifted up his hand against the king*") and 11:40 ("*and Solomon sought to kill Jeroboam*")[9] and subsequently explicate the exact circumstances under which Jeroboam revolted against Solomon (11:27a: "*and this was the cause that he lifted up his hand against the king*"): Jeroboam was among the corvée workers of the northern tribes and due to his impressive abilities was given charge by Solomon over the forced labor of the House of Joseph (11:27b–28). That this narrative thread is not continued has been frequently explained by a supposed missing textual installment which was suppressed or simply lost.[10] This, however, is hardly probable. Much more likely is the hypothesis that there was never an additional textual installment and 1 Kgs 11:27–28 simply reflects the endeavor to illuminate

---

7 For the most recent discussion of the DtrH, cf. e. g. T. Römer, *The So-Called Deuteronomistic History: A Sociological, Historical and Literary Introduction* (London 2007).
8 Cf. U. Becker, "Die Reichsteilung in I Reg 12," *ZAW* 112 (2000), 210–229; A. Rofé, "Elders or Youngsters? Critical Remarks on 1 Kings 12," in *One God – One Cult – One Nation: Archaeological and Biblical Perspectives* (ed. R. G. Kratz and H. Spieckermann; BZAW 405; Berlin 2010), 78–79.
9 Also the confrontation in 1 Kgs 11:29–39 between Jeroboam and the prophet Ahijah of Silo is in this textual context a later development. Cf. M. Köhlmoos, *Bet-El – Erinnerungen an eine Stadt* (FAT 49; Tübingen 2006), 154–163.
10 Cf. R. Albertz, *History I* (see n. 4), 140.

the background of the revolt in light of verses 12:1–19. As Rehoboam is portrayed there as a foolish taskmaster, the author of 11:27–28 is attempting retrospectively to reference the theme of forced labor in Jeroboam's biography as well.[11] Yet this has nothing to do with the historical Jeroboam and the reasons for his rebellion against Solomon.

If the references to forced labor in 1 Kgs 11:27–28 and 12:1–19 prove to be motivated by the narrative interests of later Deuteronomists, then the textual basis for the thesis that Jeroboam and the Northern tribes led their revolt inspired by the exodus creed is completely removed. There are no indications that the exodus tradition played any role in the division of the kingdoms – assuming that this event itself is not to be seen as the construction of the DtrH.[12] At most, one might ask whether *literary* paradigms from the exodus narrative influenced the narrative arrangement of the references to the forced labor in 1 Kgs 11:27–28 and 12:1–19 (or *vice versa*). Yet, also in this respect the findings are sobering. The parallels between Exod 5:3–19 and 1 Kgs 12:1–9, emphasized by Albertz and others, are limited to both texts reporting an intensification of forced labor. Specific lexemic correspondence or an analogous narrative intention, however, cannot be shown; therefore there is not sufficient evidence to justify the hypothesis of literary dependency.[13]

An influence of the exodus tradition on Jeroboam's rebellion and the division of the kingdom is thus unsustainable on historical as well as literary grounds. This also means that Albertz' theory, namely that the Northern tribes elevated the exodus creed to a state ideology in remembrance of their struggle for liberation, cannot be accepted. To completely dismiss it, however, would be premature. In 1 Kgs 12:28 we find an important quotation that appears, at least on the surface, to support the exodus creed's status as a charter myth of the Northern Kingdom, and which has in the past repeatedly been interpreted in this way.[14] This interpretation shall be critically examined in the following.

---

11 Cf. U. Becker, "Reichsteilung" (see n. 8), 221; C. Berner, "The Egyptian Bondage and Solomon's Forced Labor. Literary Connections between Exod 1–15 and 1 Kgs 1–12," in *Pentateuch, Hexateuch or Enneateuch? Identifying Literary Works in Genesis through Kings* (ed. T.B. Dozeman et al.; AIL 8; Atlanta (GA) 2011), 236–237.

12 See the discussion in R. G. Kratz, and H. Spieckermann, *One God – One Cult – One Nation: Archaological and Biblical Perspectives* (BZAW 405; Berlin 2010), 3–78.

13 Cf. C. Berner, "Egyptian Bondage" (see n. 11), 211–240.

14 Cf. R. Albertz, *History I* (see n. 4), 138–146; K. van der Toorn, "The Exodus as Charter Myth," in *Religious Identity and the Invention of Tradition* (ed. J.W. van Henten and A. Houtepen; STAR 3; Assen 2001), 113–127; M. Köckert, "YHWH in the Northern and Southern Kingdom," in *One God – One Cult – One Nation: Archaological and Biblical Perspectives* (ed. R.G. Kratz and H. Spieckermann; BZAW 405; Berlin 2010), 357–394.

2.2 The Exodus Creed as Charter Myth of the Northern Kingdom?

1 Kings 12:28 reports that Jeroboam has two golden calves made as one of the first acts of his reign, which he then presents to his people with the following words: "*Behold your gods, O Israel, who brought you up out of the land of Egypt!*" Although the interpretation that Jeroboam elevated the exodus creed from a motto during the war for independence into a state ideology can be ruled out according to section *2.1.* of this study, it is still possible that 1 Kgs 12:28 reflects a situation in the kingdom's later history which was projected on the founder of the dynasty. The probability of this view, however, depends on the analysis of 1 Kgs 12:28, which must first and foremost be interpreted as part of the DtrH. The verse is, after all, not isolated, but it is embedded in a portrayal which sharply polemicizes against Jeroboam's cultic misconduct. Even Albertz emphasizes this when he points out that "almost everything in this description is polemical: the calves in the plural are meant to emphasize the charge of polytheism or poly-Yahwism, the interpretation of them as divine images to raise the charge of idolatry, and the disrespectful designation of them as 'calf, heifer' (*'egel*) to discredit the whole enterprise."[15]

Although the whole passage on the (alleged) measures of Jeroboam (1 Kgs 12:25 – 33) is overwhelmingly marked by Deuteronomistic polemics, Albertz and many others with him believe that the very exodus-formula passed down in 1 Kgs 12:28bβγ represents a largely unadulterated record. To be sure, Albertz acknowledges a certain polemical character (manifest in the plural "your gods"), but according to him the formula's original structure is still easily recognizable: "*Behold your god, O Israel, who brought you up out of the land of Egypt!*" According to Albertz, it represents none other than the "cultic cry with which the cultic image was presented to the assembled community in the temple of Bethel."[16]

Admittedly, there is no doubt that 1 Kgs 12:28bβγ provides a presentation formula, yet this does not mean that this formula should be attributed a reality beyond its literary context. As the formula is unattested in pre-Deuteronomistic texts,[17] it seems preferable to interpret it from the outset as a Deuteronomistic construct intended to express the very polemics against the religious policy which is the particular context of 1 Kgs 12:25 – 33 as a whole. The structure of

---

15 R. Albertz, *History I* (see n. 4), 144.
16 R. Albertz, *History I* (see n. 4), 145. Cf. also the recent study by E. Blum, "Der historische Mose und die Frühgeschichte Israels," *HeBAI 1* (2012), 43 – 44.
17 The references in Exod 32:4, 8 and Neh 9:18 are literarily dependent on 1 Kgs 12:28.

the presentation formula in 1 Kgs 12:28bα can be explained without any difficulty as a purposeful allusion to the preamble of the Decalogue in Exod 20:2 and Deut 5:6, in which Yнwн introduces himself to Israel as *"your God, who brought you out of the land of Egypt."* The author, it should be assumed, had Jeroboam cite this text during the presentation of the two calves as a deliberate allusion to the Decalogue, the central commandments of which he was so glaringly violating. By using this literary means, he put into the king's mouth words of open revolt against the divine commandment.[18]

One might object that 1 Kgs 12:28bβγ deviates from the widespread form of the exodus-formula also found in Exod 20:2 and Deut 5:6, as it does not speak of "bringing out of" (*yṣ'* Hiphil) but instead of "bringing up" (*'lh* Hiphil). Yet, this deviation only apparently contradicts the thesis of this paper and, when examined more closely, rather seems to support it. The deviation can be easily explained as an intentional adjustment to the immediately preceding context in 1 Kgs 12:28bα, which further strengthens the impression that the presentation-formula is not a piece of old tradition but instead from the outset a context-dependent creation of the Deuteronomists. While Jeroboam initially proclaims to his people in 12:28bα that they have *"gone up to Jerusalem* long enough," he introduces to them in 12:28bβγ the alternative cultic sites in the North. Their legitimacy is obviously justified by the fact that here, in the image of two calves, the two gods can be worshipped which once *brought* the people *out of* Egypt – i.e., as is obviously presumed, *to the sites in question.* The presentation-formula in 12:28bβγ is therefore, in its very wording, interwoven in the previous context and is intended to reveal Jeroboam's outrageous political calculation. Of all possible ways to justify the departure from the one legitimate cultic site and the introduction of banned cultic practices, Jeroboam uses the exodus experience, to which, according to the Deuteronomistic position, Israel owes its liberation to true worship.

The advantages of interpreting the presentation-formula in 1 Kgs 12:28bβγ as a Deutoronomistic creation are obvious. They become even clearer when one considers that it is highly questionable whether 1 Kgs 12:28 was part of the chapter from the very beginning. For instance, Reinhard G. Kratz and and Melanie Köhlmoos consider the presentation-formula to be a later addition,[19] while Juha Pakkala argues that the mention of the two calves along with the formula which identifies them (1 Kgs 12:28aβ–30) represents an appendage.[20] A further

---

18 Similarly R.G. Kratz, *The Composition of the Narrative Books of the Old Testament* (trans. J. Bowden; London 2005), 155.
19 Cf. R.G. Kratz, *Composition* (see n. 18), 165; Köhlmoos, *Bet-El* (see n. 9), 155–156.
20 Cf. J. Pakkala, "Jeroboam without Bulls," *ZAW* 120 (2008), 501–525.

option to be considered is that Jeroboam's reflections in 12:26–28aα together with the subsequent presentation of the two calves in 12:28bα.βγ might be a secondary addition to an earlier version of the narrative which reported only the making (12:28aβ) and erecting (12:29) of the two images of the calves. In any case, 1 Kgs 12:29 connects much more smoothly to 12:28aβ than to its present context. Furthermore, 1 Kgs 12:28aβ shares the more sober style of the construction memo in 12:25. Thus, 1 Kgs 12:28aβ could very well have immediately followed this.[21]

If the presentation-formula in 1 Kgs 12:28bβγ can not only be easily explained as a Deuteronomistic creation, but is also to be considered with great certainty as a literary expansion within the DtrH, then the assumption that it reflects the traditional cultic cry from Bethel becomes significantly less feasible. As a result, the evidence does not allow for the conclusion that the exodus creed once functioned as charter myth of the Northern Kingdom. With this in mind, even the specific references to the exodus in the books of Hosea and Amos do not change the overall picture.[22] Although one can assume that both prophets were active in the Northern Kingdom during the 8th century BCE, this does not say anything about the literary history of the books attributed to them. The books of Hosea and Amos were updated over a long period of time, and there are good reasons to assume that the exodus-references in both books successively accrued in this later process. It may be that the consensus for this opinion is stronger in the case of Amos than of Hosea,[23] yet it is hard to believe that the theologically charged references to the exodus in Hosea should represent a particularly old stage of the tradition. Divine predications like *"your god from the land of Egypt"* (Hos 12:10; 13:4), the description of Israel's election as the adoption of a beloved son (Hos 12:4), or the motif of "bringing up" Israel through a prophet (Hos 12:14) are not the sources of the portrayal in the books of Exodus – Joshua. Rather, they are based on this literary composition and further condense its theological message.[24]

---

21 Cf. H. Pfeiffer, *Das Heiligtum von Bethel im Spiegel des Hoseabuches* (FRLANT 183; Göttingen 1999), 29 (note, however, that he considers the exodus formula in 1 Kgs 12:28bβγ as original).
22 Cf. Hos 2:17; 11:1; 12:10, 14; 13:4–5; Am. 2:10–11; 3:1; 9:7
23 Cf. on Amos, W.H. Schmidt. "Die deuteronomisitsche Redaktion des Amosbuches," *ZAW* 77 (1965), 168–193; On Hosea, cf. R.G. Kratz, "Erkenntnis Gottes im Hosebuch," *ZThK* 94 (1997), 1–24; S. Rudnig-Zelt, *Hoseastudien: Redaktionskritische Untersuchungen zur Genese des Hoseabuches* (FRLANT 213; Göttingen 2005), 275–278; R.Vielhauer, *Das Werden des Buches Hosea. Eine redaktionsgeschichtliche Untersuchung* (BZAW 349; Berlin 2007), 225–229.
24 Differently e.g. Y. Hoffman, "A North Israelite Typological Myth and a Judaean Historical Tradition: the Exodus in Hosea and Amos," *VT* 39 (1989), 169–182; Blum, "Mose" (see n. 16), 42–44.

2.3 Results

After all this, what then can be said about the often postulated connection between the exodus tradition and the Northern Kingdom? With our literary findings in 1 Kgs 11–12, as well as in Hosea and Amos in mind, the conclusion is sobering. The widespread claim that the exodus tradition played an official role in monarchic Israel cannot be corroborated on the basis of the (in any case meagre) Old Testament reference texts. YHWH of Samaria was worshipped as a dynasty god, but not verifiably as the God of the exodus. As a result, this also excludes the possibility of deducing from the Northern Kingdom's history a *terminus ante quem* for the emergence of the exodus tradition and the (religious-)historical situation it reflects. Instead, concerning these questions one is completely dependent on the analysis of the pertinent texts in the book of Exodus. These will be considered in the following.

3 The Book of Exodus and the Origins of the Exodus Tradition

3.1 Introductory Remarks: The Book of Exodus in Contemporary Pentateuchal Research

It has already been pointed out above that Old Testament scholarship since the days of Martin Noth has changed significantly. The paradigm of the documentary hypothesis, according to which the text of the Tetrateuch (Genesis through Numbers) can be divided up among three previously independent sources (Yahwist, Elohist, and Priestly Code), has experienced serious damage.[25] The sections of text classically attributed to the Jahwist (J) and the Elohist (E) are now classified much more cautiously as "non-priestly," which reflects what little can be said for

---

25 This applies at least to significant parts of Continental European scholarship. In contrast, one can observe a surprising revival of the Documentary hypothesis among the socalled "Neo-Documentarians" in Israel and the United States (cf. e. g. J.S. Baden, *J, E, and the Redaction of the Pentateuch* (FAT 68; Tübingen 2009), who, oblivious to the developments of recent decades, practice a radical form of source division. For the present state of the Pentateuch debate, cf. the contributions in T.B. Dozeman, and K. Schmid (ed.), *A Farewell to the Yahwist? The Composition of the Pentateuch in Recent European Interpretation*, SBLSymS 34 (Atlanta (GA) 2006); Ibid. et al. (ed.), *The Pentateuch: International Perspectives on Current Research* (FAT 78; Tübingen 2011); F. Hartenstein, and K. Schmid (ed.), *Abschied von der Priesterschrift? Zum Stand der Pentateuchdebatte* (VWGTh 40; Leipzig 2015)).

certain: they are not part of the priestly text, the delineation of which is still a wide scholarly consensus. In a way, the Priestly text has developed into the Archimedean point of Pentateuchal criticism, from which the non-priestly material can be classified: one distinguishes between pre- and post-priestly sections, i.e. texts on the one hand which chronologically predate the Priestly writings (pre-P), and on the other those which already assume the literary connection between Priestly and pre-priestly writings (post-P). As a further result of this paradigmatic change, it has become more and more apparent that the amount of post-priestly material is considerable; it reflects an intensive activity of *Fortschreibung* in Persian and early Hellenistic periods (6th–4th centuries BCE), to which the Pentateuch owes large parts of its present form.[26]

Applied to the book of Exodus,[27] this means that large sections of the narrative are of post-priestly origin, which in turn makes them irrelevant for historical inquiries into the background of the exodus tradition. Information about this background can only be given – if at all – by the pre-priestly text, which is chronologically closest to the experiences (or traditions) which were recorded here. The pre-priestly parts of the book of Exodus are presently found in an exodus account which begins with the birth of Moses and, according to widespread opinion, spans at least to the report of the miracle at the sea in Exod 14(–15).[28] Yet, it is debated whether this caesura also marks the original conclusion of the pre-priestly exodus account. Some scholars have rightly pointed out that the narrative thread found in Exod 2–14(15) can be further followed over a series of itinerary notes within the Pentateuch. Therefore, the narrative could have from the very beginning spanned from Exod 2 as far as into the Book of Joshua, where the exodus from Egypt reaches its ultimate goal with the conquest of Canaan.[29]

Irrespective of whether one presumes the existence of an original pre-priestly exodus-conquest narrative, or supposes further intermediate stages of devel-

---

26 Cf. Kratz, *Composition* (see n. 18), passim; C. Levin, *Das Alte Testament* (München 2006), 81–85; K. Schmid, *The Old Testament: A Literary History* (trans. L.M. Maloney; Minneapolis 2012), 141–182; D.M. Carr, *The Formation of the Hebrew Bible: A New Reconstruction* (Oxford 2011), 153–224.

27 For the most recent discussion on the Book of Exodus, cf. the contributions in T.B. Dozeman and K. Schmid (ed.), *The Book of Exodus: Composition, Reception, and Interpretation* (VT.S 164; Leiden 2014); T.E. Levy et al. (ed.), *Israel's Exodus in Transdisciplinary Perspective: Text, Archaeology, Culture, and Geoscience* (Heidelberg 2015).

28 Cf. Schmid, *Old Testament* (see n. 26), 79–84. See also the general reflections by D.M. Carr, "The Moses Story: Literary Historical Reflections," *HeBAI* 1 (2012), 7–36.

29 Cf. Kratz, *Composition* (see n. 18), 300–308; J.C. Gertz, "Mose und die Anfänge der jüdischen Religion," *ZThK* 99 (2002), 7–10.

opment,[30] the challenge arises to define which sections of the present text can be considered elements of the pre-priestly text and which originated only later. In the following, this very question will be considered using the example of the topoi and narrative threads which in the past were repeatedly interpreted as early pieces of tradition, and which served as the basis for inquiry into the religious-historical background of the exodus tradition (3.3.). In doing so, it will become clear that these apparently archaic pieces of tradition generally do not belong to the pre-priestly text, but instead are to be attributed to significantly later stages of development. What this yields for the question of the origins of the religious- and theological-historical implications of the exodus tradition will be asked subsequently (3.3).

3.2 Allegedly Ancient Elements of the Exodus Tradition and their Literary Horizon in the Book of Exodus

3.2.1 Moses, the Midianites and the Mountain of God

In the portrayal of the book of Exodus, the Israelites' exodus under the leadership of Moses is tightly interwoven with the beginnings of YHWH worship at the mountain of God. Already at the burning bush, YHWH does not only reveal his intention to lead the Israelites out of Egypt "*to a good and broad land*" (Exod 3:8); he also makes known to Moses that the latter's mission as the people's leader will only find its goal and fulfilment when the Israelites "*will worship God on this mountain*" (Exod 3:12). Apparently, the verse posits an explicit relation between the scene at the burning bush, situated at the mountain of God in Exod 3:1, and the beginning of the Sinai pericope in Exod 19. It thus indicates a compository arch the profile of which is further accentuated by a number of passages in the immediate context of the two chapters.[31] Of central importance is the scene in Exod 18:1–12, which functions as a macro-contextual counterpart to the announcement in 3:12: In the Israelites' camp at the foot of the mountain of God, Jethro, Moses' father in law, praises the greatness of the God of the exodus, YHWH, and arranges a sacrifice.

---

30 Cf. for instance W. Oswald, *Israel am Gottesberg: Eine Untersuchung zur Literargeschichte der vorderen Sinaiperikope Ex 19–24 und deren historischem Hintergrund* (OBO 159; Freiburg (CH) 1998), 119–125, who believes there to be an expansion of the original exodus narrative (Exod 1–15*) into a exodus-mountain of God narrative (Exod 1–24*).
31 Cf. the references to the mountain of God in Exod 4:18, 27; 5:22; 17:6; 18:5.

Now this would all be far less noteworthy if it were only about Jethro as Moses' father-in-law. However, Jethro is also repeatedly described as a religious official, namely, *"the priest of Midian."*[32] In the context of the religious and sacrificial ceremony depicted in Exod 18:1–12, this title has led to wide speculation about the origins of YHWH worship in Israel. The diverse theories can be summed up in the so-called "Midianite hypothesis,"[33] which essentially claims that Moses and the Israelites led by him adopted YHWH worship from the Midianites. After the exodus from Egypt, according to this theory, they travelled through the territory of Midian and here (at the mountain of God) for the first time came into contact with the God YHWH. Only after this did they recognize him and confessed him to be the God of the exodus event. In consequence, Moses is perceived as a religious founder, who was pivotal in mediating the YHWH-religion of his Medianite relatives.

The persuasiveness of the "Midianite hypothesis" stands or falls with the resilience of its foundational sources, which have never been particularly strong[34] and which, moreover, recent scholarship has shown to be downright fragile. This is particularly the case with respect to the scene in Exod 18:1–12, which establishes the only explicit relation between Moses' Midianite relatives and the worship of YHWH, and hence must carry the most significant burden of proof. The text can hardly be considered an ancient piece of tradition, but rather represents a late post-priestly manifesto.[35] This manifesto does not reflect the origins of Israel's YHWH worship, but instead tries to illustrate its radiant success beyond Israel's borders. In clear opposition to Pharaoh (Exod 5:2: *"Who is* YHWH, *that I should heed him and let Israel go? I do not know* YHWH, *and I will not let Israel go"*), the Midianite Jethro is presented as the prototype of a pagan YHWH worshipper (Exod 18:11: *"Now I know that* YHWH *is greater than all gods"*). Also the sacrificial and cultic meal organized by Jethro in the subsequent verse is an articulation of this confession and cannot be isolated from its previous context. Thus Exod 18:12 does not preserve an ancient piece of tradition, but instead

---

32 Exod 3:1; 18:1; cf. 2:16.

33 Cf. amongst others E. Meyer, *Die Israeliten und ihre Nachbarstämme: Alttestamentliche Untersuchungen* (Halle 1906); H. Greßmann, *Mose und seine Zeit: Ein Kommentar zu den Mose-Sagen* (FRLANT 18; Göttingen 1913), 431–448. A research-historical overview is offered by W.H. Schmidt, *Exodus, Sinai und Mose* (EdF 191; Darmstadt ³1995), 124–130.

34 Exod 2:15–22; 3:1; 4:24–26; 18:1–27; Num 10:29–32; 12:1; Judg 1:16; 4:11.

35 Cf. Kratz, *Composition* (see n. 18), 291; E. Otto, *Das Deuteronomium im Pentateuch und Hexateuch: Studien zur Literargeschichte von Pentateuch und Hexateuch im Lichte des Deuteronomiumsrahmens* (FAT 30; Tübingen 2000), 131; Blum, "Mose" (see n. 16), 51–52; as well as V. Haarmann, *JHWH-Verehrer der Völker: die Hinwendung von Nichtisraeliten zum Gott Israels in alttestamentlichen Überlieferungen* (AThANT 91; Zürich 2008), 59–94.

was from the outset conceived as the conclusion of a theological program. In some respect, it is reminiscent of the Melchizedek-scene in Gen 14:18–20, which has been similarly classified as a very late redactional insertion.[36]

The post-priestly dating of Exod 18:1–12 has consequences not only for the genesis of the chapter in question, but also for the Midian texts in the book of Exodus as a whole. On the one hand, the judicial reform initiated by Jethro (18:13–27) proves to be an even later expansion of the basic layer of Exod 18.[37] On the other hand, the report of the cordial meeting between Moses and his father-in-law, his wife, and his two sons (18:2–6), is so tightly interwoven with the references to Midian in Moses "biography" (2:15–22; 3:1; 4:18, 20, 24–26) that one easily gets the impression that the entire material is fairly late. That this is the case for 4:18, 20, 24–26 and the mention of Jethro in 3:1 has already been demonstrated at length elsewhere[38] and would have to be examined once again separately concerning the report in 2:15–22 of Moses' flight to Midian and his marriage into the family of the local priest.

In the context of the Pentateuchal Moses tradition, the narrative in Exod 2:15–22 is not only completely singular; it also exhibits – as Rabbinical exegetes have already noted (cf. ExR I, 32) – striking similarities to the motives of the Jacob-Laban narrative in Gen 27–29. Therefore, one has to consider the possibility that Exod 2:15–22 was from its very beginning composed as a means of conferring the figure of Moses a certain patriarchal character. It would thus not reflect a particularly authentic element of the (pre-literary) Moses tradition, but instead be the result of the attempt to fit the once separate patriarchal and exodus (-conquest) narratives to each other in their narrative substance.[39]

The widespread claim for the authenticity of the Midian references in Moses' "biography" is mainly based on two reasons. First, particular discrepancies in detail (concerning the names of Moses father-in-law and the number of his sons) are interpreted as an indicator for the high age of the tradition. Second, it is argued that it would be hard to imagine why Moses of all people would have been associated with the Midianites, as they are portrayed in a very negative fashion in a number of biblical texts.[40] Yet, these two reasons are

---

36 On this subject, cf. G. Granerød, *Abraham and Melchizedek: Scribal Activity of Second Temple Times in Genesis 14 and Psalm 110* (BZAW 406; Berlin 2010); C. Berner, "Abraham amidst Kings, Coalitions and Military Campaigns: Reflections on the Redaction History of Gen 14 and its Early Rewritings," in *The Reception of Biblical War Legislation in Narrative Contexts* (ed. C. Berner and H. Samuel; BZAW 460; Berlin 2015), 44–47.

37 Cf. C. Berner, *Die Exoduserzählung: Das literarische Werden einer Ursprungslegende Israels* (FAT 73; Tübingen 2010), 406–429.

38 Cf. Berner, *Exoduserzählung* (see n. 37), 106–136.

39 A counterpart in the partriarchal narrative would be Gen 12:10–20, which has Abraham undergo an exodus experience after just having reached Canaan. He thus anticipates prototypically the fate of his Israelite descendants.

40 Cf. most recently Blum, "Mose" (see n. 16), 49 f.

not persuasive. As elsewhere, the said discrepancies can just as easily be attributed to a longer process of *Fortschreibung*. Moreover, a text such as Exod 18 shows exactly that even at a fairly late stage in the formation of the Hebrew Bible, it was obviously no problem to portray Midian in a markedly positive fashion (cf. Num 10:29–32). The fact that there are Midian-critical voices in other sections (cf. Num 25:1–5), and that in Num 12:1aβb Moses' marriage is perhaps problematized in retrospect, does not in principle conflict with this thesis.

Irrespective of whether the documented references to Midian in Exod 2–18 are to be considered completely or only partially post-priestly, it must be held that there is no evidence in the book of Exodus for the perspective of the "Midianite hypothesis" that the beginnings of Yʜᴡʜ worship in Israel were due to the contact of Israel, or an exodus-group, with the Midianites.

A defence of the essential correctness of the "Midianite hypothesis" has been recently attempted by Erhard Blum with reference to further biblical and epigraphic evidence. He refers on the one hand to the well-known references to Yʜᴡʜ in Egyptian registers of Šasu-lands (14th/13th centuries BCE) which according to Blum indicate Yʜᴡʜ worshippers in Southern Palestine.[41] A comparable situation, he argues, is found expressed in the poetic and theophanic portrayals in Judg 5:4–5, Hab. 3:3, 7, and Deut 33:2, which describe Yʜᴡʜ's arrival in a southern mountainous region and are to be seen as the background of the biblical tradition of the mountain of God. Finally, Blum points to inscriptions from Kuntillet 'Ajrud (8th century BCE) in which the designation "Yʜᴡʜ of Samaria" and "Yʜᴡʜ of Teman" or rather "Yʜᴡʜ of ha-Teman/ Yʜᴡʜ of the South" are attested.

Because the inscriptions as well as the above-mentioned theophany texts bear a northern Israelite imprint, Blum believes it should be concluded that the tradition of a "home of Yʜᴡʜ 'in the South'" ("Heimat JHWHs ,im Süden'") was especially treasured in the North (besides the exodus tradition).[42] This in turn, he argues, would support the localisation of the "the Šasu land Yʜᴡʜ" mentioned in Egyptian registers in southern Palestine. The complete evidence, according to Blum, speaks strongly "for an origin of Yʜᴡʜ worship from the regions of Midian/Edom adjacent to southern Canaan" ("für eine Herkunft der JHWH-Verehrung aus den an das südliche Kanaan angrenzenden Regionen von Midian/Edom"). Therefore, also "the hypothesis [holds] strong plausibility that this Yʜᴡʜ-cult was mediated through an 'exodus group' ... to the Israel which was about to constitute itself in Canaan. The same can be said for the hypothesis that a leader named 'Moses' played a central role in this exodus-groups story of its origins" (die Hypothese eine hohe Plausibilität [behalte], dass dieser JHWH-Kult durch eine ,Exodus-Gruppe' [...] an das sich in Kanaan konstituierende Israel vermittelt wurde. Das gleiche gilt für die Annahme, dass eine Führungsgestalt

---

41 Cf. Blum, "Mose" (see n. 16). 52–53. Also M. Leuenberger, "Jhwhs Herkunft aus dem Süden: Archäologische Befunde – biblische Überlieferungen – historische Korrelationen," *ZAW* 122 (2010), 4–11 (with an overview of the the epigraphic evidence).
42 Blum, "Mose" (see n. 16), 59.

namens ‚Mose' in der Ursprungsgeschichte dieser Exodus-Gruppe eine zentrale Rolle spielte.").[43]

Blum's case for the "Midianite hypothesis" suggests an unambiguousness which cannot be claimed in view of the source material. Already the localization of the "Šasu land YHWH" is not uncontroversial,[44] yet it is Blum's interpretation of the theophany texts Judg 5:4–5, Hab. 3:3, 7, and Deut 33:2 which is most problematic. As Henrik Pfeiffer has convincingly shown, there are good reasons for the assumption that the passages in question only originated in post-exilic times.[45] Their estimation as ancient elements of tradition is thus extremely questionable, and the same goes for the conclusion that the tradition of the mountain of God is the expression of an ancient tradition of YHWH worship in the south. Instead, it appears doubtful whether there was ever something like an independent tradition of the mountain of God, and whether the motive cannot be better explained as the result of the transfer of Jerusalem temple-theology to an imaginary desert mountain after Judah's downfall.[46] Thus, Blum's hypothesis that the tradition of YHWH's origins in the South was preserved especially in the Northern Kingdom proves highly questionable. The inscriptions from Kuntillet ʿAjrud do not change the overall picture, as their significance is rather limited in this context.[47] In sum, the sources consulted by Blum reveal, even when interpreted optimistically, at best vague references to YHWH worshippers in southern Palestine. They are unable to carry the burden of proof for such far-reaching religious-historical reconstructions as implied by the "Midianite hypothesis."

3.2.2 Festal Traditions within the Exodus Narrative

The present text of Exod 12:1–13:16 is determined by a complex network of ritual stipulations which are essentially dealing with the festival of Passover (Pessaḥ) and the closely related festival of Unleavened Bread (Maṣṣot).[48] Hence the impression arises that we are dealing, with a single festal celebration with two subsequent parts: the night-time Passover meal, which involves the eating of a lamb

---

43 Blum, "Mose" (see n. 16), 60. Also E. Otto, *Mose: Geschichte und Legende* (München 2006), 31–33.

44 Cf. M. Köckert, "Wandlungen Gottes im antiken Israel," *BThZ* 22 (2005), 20; Pfeiffer, *Jahwes Kommen* (see n. 45), 261, who argue for a location in central Palestine.

45 Cf. H. Pfeiffer, *Jahwes Kommen von Süden: Jdc 5, Hab 3, Dtn 33 und Ps 68 in ihrem literatur- und theologiegeschichtlichen Umfeld* (FRLANT 211; Göttingen 2005), 19–203.

46 Cf. Oswald, *Israel* (see n. 30), 247–254; M. Köckert, "Die Theophanie des Wettergottes in Psalm 18," in *Kulturgeschichten: Altorientalische Studien für Volkert Haas zum 65. Geburtstag* (ed. T. Richter *et al.*; Saarbrücken 2001), 225–226.

47 Cf. A. Berlejung, "Geschichte und Religionsgeschichte des antiken Israel," in *Grundinformation Altes Testament* (ed. J.C. Gertz *et al.*; 59–192. Göttingen ³2009), 128, footnote 137, who emphasizes that the texts belong to the context of private piety. As a result, it is problematic to infer from here on the 'official cult' in the Northern Kingdom.

48 Exod 13:1–2, 11–16 passes down, in a kind of appendix, stipulations on the sacrifice of the firstborn.

in the family circle, is followed by the seven days of the Maṣṣot week, in which nothing is to be consumed which uses leaven in its production. However, in biblical scholarship there has been a long-held consensus that this dual form of the festival has not existed since time immemorial, but instead reflects the amalgamation of two previously independent festivals which apparently were both celebrated in springtime. While the festival of Passover can be originally placed in the context of cattle breeders, the festival of Unleavened Bread assumes an agricultural community, which practiced the respective rite annually during the harvesting of their spring crops (cf. Exod 23:15).[49]

Especially the festival of Passover has been repeatedly associated with the historical events at the time of the exodus. While according to some it represents a rite which was already practiced by the Israelites in Egypt,[50] Eckart Otto has argued that the Passover tradition served as the contact point for a still pre-literary connection between Moses and the exodus events: "The Passover was celebrated through the centuries in Israel and Judah and with it the memory of the Exodus as Israel's foundational narrative [...]. Moses had become the leader of his people with the Passover celebration, which he had founded in the night prior to the exodus to protect the people. Literary Moses narratives could be [...] connected to this." ("Das Passa wurde durch die Jahrhunderte hindurch in Israel und Juda gefeiert und mit ihm die Erinnerung an den Exodus als Ursprungserzählung Israels [...]. Mose war mit der Passafeier, die er in der Nacht vor dem Auszug zum Schutz des Volkes gestiftet habe, zum Führer dieses Volkes geworden. Daran konnten schriftlich abgefasste Mose-Erzählungen [...] anknüpfen.").[51]

It certainly cannot be denied that the portrayal of the Passover as an apotropaic ritual of protection shows archaic elements which could indicate a long tradition. But with this it has not yet been proven that the respective ritual practices stand in an organic relation to the exodus tradition. To provide sufficient evidence for this, there needs to be a significant proof-text, which is usually found in Exod 12:21–23. These verses, which are classically regarded as the core of the Yahwist's Passover ordinance,[52] report of how Moses gathered the elders of Israel and ordered them to slaughter a lamb and smear its blood on the doorposts of the houses. In the night, when Yʜᴡʜ moves through Egypt to kill

---

49 For theories concerning the early history of the two festivals cf. the overview by Schmidt, *Exodus* (see n. 33), 55–60, as well as the extensive treatment by J.B. Segal, *The Hebrew Passover: From Earliest Times to A.D. 70* (LOS 12; London 1963).
50 Cf. for instance P. Laaf, *Die Pascha-Feier Israels: eine literar- und überlieferungsgeschichtliche Studie* (BBB 36; Bonn 1970), 147.
51 Otto, *Mose* (see n. 43), 34.
52 Cf. Schmidt, *Exodus* (see n. 33), 59.

the first-born, he will spare the marked houses and prevent the destroyer from entering.

Especially the reference to the "destroyer" – obviously an evil demon – has repeatedly been taken as a strong piece of evidence for the claim that Exod 12:21–23 represents an early stage in the development of the Passover tradition. The deviation in the priestly text which does not mention the "blow of the destroyer," but rather speaks of a "blow of destruction" (12:13), is frequently interpreted as the result of a dogmatic correction. The priestly writer, it is argued, wanted to avoid the offensive idea of the involvement of a demonic force, and therefore pointed out that it was YHWH himself who killed the firstborn of Egypt.[53]

However plausible this purported relationship between the Yahwistic (non-priestly) and the Priestly text might seem at first glance, it proves nevertheless to be unsound upon further examination. Pertinent examples elsewhere show that there was a tendency in later times to conceive of YHWH's action no longer as direct but instead mediated through a divine being.[54] In light of this discovery, the mention of the destroyer in Exod 12:23 can be read precisely as a correction of the Priestly portrayal which in 12:13 views YHWH himself as acting. As a result, Exod 12:21–23 would not have to be classified as pre-, but instead as post-priestly. A host of other details shows that this conclusion is ultimately without serious alternative. Thus 12:21–23 presupposes the Priestly Passover ordinance in 12:1–13 not only as a connecting link with the preceding context, but also on a thematic level, for the purpose of the Passover, whose slaughter is abruptly called by Moses, is found only in 12:6–11 P. Exod 12:21–23 is thus to be classified as a later expansion of the Passover ordinance found in the Priestly text, in which further particulars of the rite are specified, and which culminates in the explicit demand in 12:25 to continue the rite after the conquest of the land.[55]

The above observations on the literary history of Exod 12 lead to the conclusion that there was no organic relation between the Passover and the exodus tradition. In its pre-priestly form, the exodus narrative only narrates the killing of the firstborns (12:29–33*) without using this event to establish a particular religious practice. The earliest festival etiology is introduced in the Priestly text which connects the Passover rite to the protection of the Israelite homes (12:1–

---

53 Cf. E. Otto, "פסח," *ThWAT* 6, 659–682; S. Gesundheit, *Three Times a Year: Studies on Festival Legislation in the Pentateuch* (FAT 82; Tübingen 2012), 67–73.

54 Cf. for instance the redactional addition of the the angel in the revelation scene at the burning bush (Exod 3:2a) and in the report of the parting of the sea (Exod 14:19a) as well as the introduction of Satan in the retelling of 2 Sam 24:1 in 1 Chr 21:1.

55 Cf. Berner, *Exoduserzählung* (see n. 37), 286–293.

13*.28). As a result, the earliest etiology of the Maṣṣot Festival in 12:34, 39 and 13:3–10*[56] is already of post-priestly origin. Neither of these festival etiologies in Exod 12–13, which in their aftermath came to be literarily entangled with one another in various ways, allows for any kind of inferences to the historical origins of this festal practice or a possible connection to the exodus event. Rather, they express the steadily growing importance of the exodus within the literary history of the Hebrew Bible. In this process, the exodus increasingly developed into a central key-event from which post-exilic Israel defined its religious identity and practice.[57]

Another issue which is thematically related to the festal ordinances from Exod 12–13 is the motif of a sacrifice or pilgrimage festival in the desert, which in certain passages is the subject of the negotiations with Pharaoh.[58] Here scholars have on various occasions claimed to find references to an ancient desert festival tradition, or have attempted to establish a relation to the origins of the Passover ritual.[59] Yet such tradition historical speculations once again completely lack any foundation. The exodus negotiations in their entirety belong to the post-priestly stages in the development of the plague cycle and are therefore not part of an underlying tradition, but originate with the literary development of the exodus narrative itself. They reflect the attempt to specify the fundamental demand found in the pre-priestly stratum of the plague cycle, namely that the Israelites are to be freed in order to worship Yʜwʜ.[60] This idea of worshipping Yʜwʜ was only later specified by a post-priestly editor who interpreted it as a reference to a pilgrimage festival to which the entire people, including the cattle, must set forth.[61]

The theme of the pilgrimage festival was then taken up by another post-priestly editor and reconfigured into a pure pretence to confuse Pharaoh from the very beginning about the true intentions of Yʜwʜ and the Israelites: Now they claim that they merely want to spend three days journeying into the wilder-

---

56 The etiology deduces the custom of eating unleavened bread from the fact that in the hurry of the exodus there was not enough time to leaven the bread.

57 Also the references to the exodus in the festival calendars of the Covenant Code (Exod 23:15) and Deuteronomy (Deut 16:1) already pressupose the etiologies from Exod 12–13.

58 Exod 3:16–20; 5:1–4; 8:4b, 21b–24a.

59 Cf. for instance Laaf, *Pascha-Feier* (see n. 50), 116–125 (with further lit.).

60 Exod 7:16, 26; 8:16. For the presupposed literary-critical decisions here and in the following, cf. Berner, *Exoduserzählung* (see n. 37), 168–266.

61 The corresponding negotiations stretch over three scenes in total (Exod 10:7–11; 10:21a, 22, 24–29; 12:31–32), the final of which reports Pharaoh's complete relenting. Now, the departure of the entire people, reported in 12:37–38, secondarily receives the Pharaonic blessing.

ness in order to sacrifice to YHWH.[62] This pretence is completely developed from within the literary context of the exodus narrative. It strengthens the profiling of YHWH and his representatives at the expense of Pharaoh, a notion characteristic of the post-priestly layers of the plague cycle where the King of Egypt is no longer taken seriously as negotiating partner. These later narrative embellishments reveal as little about the religious-historical background of the exodus tradition as the priestly and post-priestly festival etiologies in Exod 12–13.

3.2.3 The Miracle at the Sea

It is one of the few points of consensus in Pentateuchal criticism that in Exod 14 two different representations of the miracle at the sea are overlapping and that this connection is not original.[63] While the Priestly version reports the Israelites passing through the parted sea and the Egyptian pursuers meeting their end when the two towering water-walls crash down upon them, the non-priestly version depicts a completely different course of events: here, YHWH first drives the water back through a strong wind and consequently sets the Egyptian army into panic, so that they rush toward the returning waters and drown.

According to widespread opinion, the non-priestly version was from the beginning an essential component of the exodus narrative, which was already part of its pre-priestly form.[64] Only with the experience of deliverance at the Sea of Reeds, argues Wolfgang Oswald, did the theme of liberation from Egypt reach its target point.[65] Under the presupposition that this literary-historical reconstruction is valid,[66] crucial implications arise for the inquiry into the exodus tradition's historical background. In contrast to the themes and motifs discussed up to now, the sea miracle could not be assumed to be the result of scribal speculation from the start; instead, one would have to deal with the possibility that it possibly represents an ancient element of tradition which could shed light on the origins of the exodus tradition.

---

62 Exod 3:18b, 19a, 20; 5:3–4*; 8:4b; 8:21b–24a, 25b.
63 Cf. Schmidt, *Exodus* (see n. 33), 60–70. It need not be decided here whether the connection is due to the combination of two originally independent reports or rather the result of a heavy editorial reworking of one basic narrative.
64 Cf. J.C. Gertz, *Tradition und Redaktion in der Exoduserzählung: Studien zur Endredaktion des Pentateuch* (FRLANT 186; Göttingen 2000), 206–232.
65 Cf. H. Utzschneider and W. Oswald, *Exodus 1–15* (IEKAT; Stuttgart 2013), 44–46.
66 That it is hardly as certain as generally assumed can here only be mentioned in passing. Cf. C. Berner, "Gab es einen vorpriesterlichen Meerwunderbericht?" *Bib* 95 (2014).

It is therefore not surprising that the scholarly literature contains a myriad of conjectures on the geographical and historical parameters of the miracle at the sea, which sometimes go hand in hand with ambitious speculations about the beginnings of Israel's YHWH worship. Already Hugo Greßmann, for instance, is of the opinion that only Israel's experience of deliverance at the Sea of Reeds led to their beginning to worship YHWH as their God: "What a powerful God that must have been, who could perform this action and subdue the sea! From the leaders or from the residents of this area, the Midianites, one learned the name of the God who had revealed himself in such an imposing manner: YHWH" ("Was für ein mächtiger Gott mußte das sein, der diese Tat vollbracht hatte und dem das Meer untertan war! Von den Führern oder von den Bewohnern jener Gegend, den Midianitern, erfuhr man den Namen des Gottes, der sich in so imposanter Weise geoffenbart hatte: Jahve.").[67]

At this point, it would already suffice to recall our above observations in section *3.2.1.* in order to clarify that also this particular version of the "Midianite hypothesis" must be rejected. That this is the case, however, becomes even clearer when we consider that the biblical portrayal itself leaves no doubt that it was YHWH who was viewed as the origin of the deliverance at the Sea of Reeds from the very beginning. This not only applies to the presumably pre-priestly version of the sea miracle in Exod 14*, but also to the praise given by the prophetess Miriam in 15:21: "*Sing to YHWH, for he has triumphed gloriously; horse and rider he has thrown into the sea.*" The song of Miriam is particularly interesting because it not only serves as the model for the song of Moses (Exod 15:1–19),[68] but also because – according to some – it is even older than the prose report in Exod 14*. As Christoph Levin argues, it is a hymnic piece which was already available to the composer of the pre-priestly exodus narrative and was integrated into his narrative as the conclusion to the report of the miracle at the sea.[69]

---

67 Greßmann, *Mose* (see n. 33), 445.
68 On the poetic pieces in Exod 15 cf. A. Klein, "Hymn and History in Exod 15," *ZAW* 124 (2012). The still widespread early dating of the song of the Sea, particularly in Anglo-American scholarship (most recently R. Hendel, "The Exodus as Cultural Memory: Egyptian Bondage and the Song of the Sea," in *Israel's Exodus in Transdisciplinary Perspective: Text, Archaeology, Culture, and Geoscience* [ed. T.E. Levy et al., 65–77. Heidelberg 2015], 65–77), is not supported by the literary evidence: The song of Moses contains a number of evident references to the prose account in Exod (1–)14 and makes use of both priestly and non-priestly material. Therefore, it must be seen as a literary creation for its present context. Cf. Berner, *Exoduserzählung* (see n. 37), 386–402, as well as A. Klein, *Geschichte und Gebet: die Rezeption der biblischen Geschichte in den Psalmen des Alten Testaments* (FAT 94; Tübingen 2014), 16–49.
69 Cf. C. Levin, *Der Jahwist* (FRLANT 157; Göttingen 1993), 342–343.

Now the short hymn delivered in Exod 15:21 underlines not only that deliverance which it praises has always been connected to Yhwh. According to Reinhard G. Kratz, it also shows that originally, there was no necessary relation of this experience to the exodus. In itself the song of Miriam "is merely about the victory of Yhwh over some horses and riders whom he has at one point thrown 'into the sea.'"[70] Also with respect to form-critical considerations, such praise has fairly little to do with the situational context in which the author of the Exodus story presents it. As Jan Christian Gertz has pointed out, the song of Miriam does not represent a spontaneous song of victory, but rather a short hymn which originally "belongs to the Yhwh cult in cultivated land" ("in den Jahwekult im Kulturland gehört")[71] and therefore comes from the monarchic period. In good ancient near eastern tradition, the song praises the dynasty god for the triumph over an enemy force.

Although these form-critical and tradition-historical observations are without question accurate, it does not necessarily follow that the song of Miriam must be a piece of tradition from monarchic times that was first applied to the Israelites' exodus by the author of the pre-priestly narrative to serve as a template for the prose report in Exod 14. The opposite position is also conceivable, namely that Exod 15:21 was only composed late (post-priestly) for the present context and the author thereby made use of certain elements of the hymn genre.[72] This question need not be decided here. In any case, it is crucial that the song of Miriam does not permit conclusions about the origins of Yhwh worship: the short hymn in Exod 15:21 served to assure the presupposed relationship to Yhwh, whether as a monarchic victory song without genuine connection to the exodus, or as a late literary creation for the context of the exodus story. The same applies as seen to the post-priestly song of Moses (Exod 15:1–19) and the preceding prose report in Exod 14, regardless of whether parts of it are pre-priestly or not.

In sum, our discussion of the portrayal of the miracle at the sea in Exod 14–15 ultimately yields the same results as our previous analysis of the references to Midian and the festival etiologies: the text provides a starting point for the reconstruction of literary and theological developments within the horizon of the written exodus narrative, but it is no reliable basis for (religious-)historical inquiry.

---

70 Kratz, *Composition* (see n. 18), 284.

71 Gertz, "Mose" (see n. 29), 9. As well as H. Spieckermann, *Heilsgegenwart: Eine Theologie der Psalmen* (FRLANT 148; Göttingen 1989), 102.

72 Cf. P. Weimar, *Die Meerwundererzählung: eine redaktionskritische Analyse von Ex 13,17–14,31* (ÄAT 9; Wiesbaden 1985), 107, footnote 2. As well as recently Utzschneider and Oswald, *Exodus 1–15* (see n. 65), 343.

Or in other words: it gives insight into the literary self-portrayal of biblical Israel, but not into the origins of historical Israel and its early religious history.[73] Within which historical framework and with which theological objective this literary self-presentation began will be outlined below briefly.

3.3 The Pre-Priestly Exodus Narrative and the Redefinition of Israel's Identity as Yhwh's People

While the earliest literary version of the Exodus narrative was traditionally considered part of the Yahwistic source from the time of Solomon (10th century BCE), there has been in recent Pentateuchal scholarship a growing tendency of dating the earliest (pre-priestly) version of the exodus(-conquest) narrative in the Neo-Assyrian period (7th century BCE).[74] This is, on the one hand, based on references to the propaganda of the Neo-Assyrian Empire in the childhood story of Moses (Exod 2:1–10).[75] On the other hand, it has to do with fundamental considerations relating to the theological-historical context of the narrative. It is apparent, namely, that the exodus(-conquest) narrative decidedly avoids elements of royal ideology, which is most easily explained by assuming a post-monarchic situation, or more precisely: a situation after the conquest of the Northern Kingdom of Israel by the Assyrians (722 BCE). This event meant not just a political defeat, but also and above all a religious-theological crisis because it ultimately took the ground from under the traditional conviction that the dynasty god Yhwh safeguarded the existence of the small state of Israel and the welfare of its population through the king as his earthly representative.

From the ruins of this conviction left by the Assyrians emerged something completely new in the pre-priestly exodus(-conquest) narrative. Here, Israel's relationship to God received a salvation-historical foundation with the exodus, which no historical tremors, irrespective of how massive they might be, could jeopardize any longer: Israel owes its identity to the god who once freed it from the Egyptian bondage and thus established a divine relationship, which no longer requires the intermediary figure of the king. While Israel developed from a small Syro-Palestinian state into the people of Yhwh, Yhwh transformed

---

73 Concerning this distinction cf. R.G. Kratz, *Historical and Biblical Israel: The History, Tradition, and Archives of Israel and Judah* (trans. P.M. Kurtz; Oxford forthcoming).
74 Cf. for instance Kratz, *Composition* (see n. 18), 309–316; Schmid, *Old Testament* (see n. 26), 78–84; Blum, "Mose" (see n. 16), 62; Carr, *Formation* (see n. 36), 313–314.
75 Cf. Otto, *Mose* (2006) (see n. 43), 35–42.

from the dynasty god worshipped in Samaria into the God of his chosen people.[76] The exodus as the key event in the new accentuation of Israel's relationship to God is, from the outset, so strongly interwoven into the salvation-historical concept of the pre-priestly exodus narrative that already here, on the oldest attainable level of literary tradition, the historical events dissolve into this theology of history. One can therefore say that the exodus, from the beginning of biblical literary history, was more a meta-historical than a historical event.

This is not to say that no real events underlie the pre-priestly exodus narrative. That the exodus experience has a historical point-of-contact – and did not in its entirety merely spring into the imagination of the author of the pre-priestly exodus narrative – should be considered very probable. After all, the attempt to establish Israel's identity anew from the exodus experience is only conceivable under the presupposition that the exodus had a particular significance in the circles, in which the pre-priestly exodus narrative emerged. The question of what this significance was based on, however, is largely open. Although it might appear natural that the author of the pre-priestly exodus narrative inherited an official confession of the defunct Northern Kingdom, this possibility can be ruled out in light of the conclusions reached in section 2.

This of course in no way precludes the possibility that there still may have been an old Exodus tradition, but it proves impossible to precisely reconstruct its original historical context. Attempts to identify the historical Moses and assign him his place in Egyptian history should be considered a failure,[77] and even the few elements of the exodus narrative which traditionally serve as the basis of historical reconstruction turn out in this regard to be hardly sound: the information about the forced labor of the Israelites is owed mainly (if not exclusively) to later literary expansions,[78] and even the reference to the construction of the store cities Pithom and Rameses (Exod 1:11b) – itself very difficult to classify literary-historically – does not allow the conclusion that Israelites were forced to work at the construction sites of Ramesses II.[79] At the earliest, Exod 1:11b reflects circumstances of the 7th century BCE.[80] As with the childhood

---

76 Cf. R.G. Kratz, "Israel als Staat und als Volk," *ZThK* 97 (2000), 1–17.

77 Concerning this, cf. the contributions in E. Otto (ed.), *Mose: Ägypten und das Alte Testament* (SBS 189; Stuttgart 2000).

78 Cf. Berner, "Egyptian Bondage" (see n. 11), 213–224.

79 Concerning this classic view, cf. for instance Schmidt, *Exodus* (see n. 33), 26–28; J.K. Hoffmeier, *Israel in Egypt: The Evidence for the Authenticity of the Exodus Tradition* (New York 1996), 116–122.

80 The Hebrew term for store cities (ערי מסכנות) is an Akkadian loan word. Moreover, a city called Pithom in the northeastern Nile Delta cannot be verified archeologically prior to the 7th

story of Moses (Exod 2:1–10), the literary evidence for the Israelites' forced labor does not provide access to any events prior to the Neo-Assyrian period in which the pre-priestly Exodus narrative was written.

If the author of the pre-priestly exodus narrative had fallen back upon an ancient exodus tradition, he would have consequently transformed it in such a way that its original historical contact point was ultimately unrecognizable. Only the connection with Egypt appears to be associated from the outset with the exodus theme,[81] but this must not necessarily indicate conditions of the second millennium BCE.[82] In light of the literary findings one must ask whether the exodus tradition could not be rooted in events of the Neo-Assyrian period, or at least be strongly influenced by these. One could think about the (deliverance) experiences of refugees from the Northern Kingdom or prisoners of war in Egypt who interpreted these events either already in the light of a passed-down exodus tradition, or molded them for the first time into a distinct exodus theology while grappling with the traditional imperial and royal ideology.[83]

To sum up, there is a variety of conceivable historical scenarios, all of which are to some degree plausible but none of which provable with any certainty.[84] The historical background of the biblical exodus tradition largely eludes our grasp, yet this is ultimately of little significance for our understanding of it. After all, the exodus tradition is first and foremost an aspect of the history of bib-

---

century BCE. Cf. D.B. Redford. "Exodus I 11," *VT* 13 (1963), 401–418. 401–418; E.A. Knauf, *Midian: Untersuchungen zur Geschichte Palästinas und Nordarabiens am Ende des 2. Jahrtausends v. Chr* (ADPV 10; Wiesbaden 1988), 104–105; N.P. Lemche, *Die Vorgeschichte Israels: Von den Anfängen bis zum Ausgang des 13. Jahrhunderts v. Chr* (BE 1; Stuttgart *et al.* 1996), 63–65; B.U. Schipper, "Raamses, Pithom, and the Exodus: A Critical Evaluation of Exod 1:11," *VT* 65 (2015), 276–282.

81 This is supported not least by the Egyptian-influenced name Moses (derived from *mśj* = to birth/sire; cf. for instance Thutmose), whose figure is firmly interwoven with the exodus tradition. Cf. most recently Blum, "Mose" (see n. 16), 38–42 (with further lit.).

82 In this context one must mention the recent attempts to interpret the exodus tradition figuratively as a reflection on the Egyptian dominance over the Syro-Palestinian land-bridge in the 2nd millennium BCE; cf. M. Köckert, "YHWH in the Northern and Southern Kingdom," in *One God – One Cult – One Nation: Archaeological and Biblical Perspectives* (ed. R.G. Kratz and H. Spieckermann; BZAW 405; Berlin 2010), 370; N. Naaman, "The Exodus Story: Between Historical Memory and Historiographical Composition," *JNER* 11 (2011), 39–69. Although this is theoretically conceivable, it seems not very likely in light of the Old Testament evidence.

83 In light of recent scholarship, even a connection with the reign of Necho II (610–595 BCE) should seriously be considered. After all, it seems quite likely that the literary exodus tradition was at least updated against this backround; cf. Lemche, *Vorgeschichte* (see n. 80), 63; Utzschneider and Oswald, *Exodus 1–15* (see n. 65), 74; Schipper, "Raamses," (see n. 80), 276–283.

84 For the most recent discussion cf. the contributions in Levy (ed.), *Exodus* (see n. 27), 3–344.

lical literature and theology, and its main lines of development can be traced, regardless of their historical roots, in the development of the biblical text itself.

4 Conclusions

The starting point of the preceding reflections was the observation that the exodus creed occupies a central position within the Hebrew Bible, and the idea of Martin Noth's that this has to do with an ancient confession of Israel. The examination of this thesis on the basis of the relevant texts, however, has brought a sobering result. That the exodus creed found use as a parole in the struggle for liberation of the northern tribes, or even functioned as a state ideology of the Northern Kingdom, cannot be verified. In general, there is no evidence for a special status of the confession during the monarchic period. The earliest literary evidence for the exodus, the pre-priestly exodus narrative, dates in all likelihood from the time after the collapse of the Northern Kingdom (7th century BCE) and uses the exodus to establish a salvation-historical identity of Israel in order to provide an alternative to the failed royal ideology. In this respect, one can at least say that the origins of exodus literature are related to the post-history of the Northern Kingdom from where it eventually found its way to Judah/Yehud.[85] Yet, it remains an open question whether the author of the pre-priestly exodus narrative referred to a given exodus tradition, or events in the recent past, or even a combination of both.

In no case, however, is there a reliable basis for the assumption that the YHWH worship of Israel historically took its beginning with the exodus from Egypt. The idea does not belong to the religious-historical presupposition of the exodus story, but rather represents its central theological accomplishment which should be taken up and developed further in the course of the ensuing literary history of the biblical writings. Credo texts like the preamble of the Decalogue (Exod 20:5; Deut 5:6) which point to the exodus as origin of Israel's covenantal relationship with YHWH have to be interpreted in the context of this literary process. They reveal nothing about the religious history of ancient Israel, but rather belong to the realm of the history of the theology of nascent biblical Judaism, which saw its relationship with God as decisively determined by the exodus.

---

85 Cf. Hoffman, "Typological Myth," (see n. 24), 181–182.

Reinhard Müller
The Origins of Yhwh in Light of the Earliest Psalms

Remnants of Ancient Hebrew literature attesting the early veneration of Yhwh are found more often in the book of Psalms than in any other book of the Old Testament. From the perspective of literary history, the Psalter can be perceived as a literary cathedral[1] or temple[2] that was gradually erected in the centuries following the downfall of the Judean kingdom,[3] built upon a fundament of hymns and prayers that originated in much earlier periods.

The textual remains of early Hebrew religious poetry that are embedded in the Psalter were probably composed for cultic settings of the monarchic age.[4] Since it is evident that the earliest pieces of Hebrew psalmody were edited and reworked in later times,[5] we have to assume that only fragments of the oldest cultic poetry survived in the final edition of the Psalter. It is nevertheless possible to discern the contours of this poetry in the Psalter. Early hymns and prayers contain peculiar poetic forms, and they depict the Ancient Hebrew deity in a way that differs conspicuously from theological concepts of later periods.

Furthermore, several forms and motifs in these poems have parallels in Ancient Near Eastern hymns, prayers, and other genres of religious literature. Although many sources containing such parallels have been known for decades, scholars have not yet understood how early Hebrew psalmody is related to comparable Ancient Near Eastern religious literature; some enigmatic expressions of the Psalms have only recently been clarified by help of Ancient Near Eastern par-

---

1 This metaphor is borrowed from U. Becker, *Exegese des Alten Testaments* (Tübingen ³2011), 1–2, who convincingly compares the entire Old Testament with a cathedral that was built during several centuries.
2 See E. Zenger, "Der Psalter als Buch: Beobachtungen zu seiner Entstehung, Komposition und Funktion," in *Der Psalter in Judentum und Christentum* (HBS 18; Freiburg 1998), 1–57, here 35–48.
3 Psalms 74, 79, 137, among others, look back on the Babylonian conquest of Jerusalem in the early sixth century B.C.E., irrespective of their precise historical origins.
4 See H. Spieckermann, *Heilsgegenwart: Eine Theologie der Psalmen* (FRLANT 148; Göttingen 1989), 9–10, and R. Müller, *Jahwe als Wettergott: Studien zur althebräischen Kultlyrik anhand ausgewählter Psalmen* (BZAW 387; Berlin 2008), 240.
5 See the case study on Ps 108 in R. Müller *et al.*, *Evidence of Editing: Growth and Change of Texts in the Hebrew Bible* (SBLRBS 75; Atlanta 2014), 159–177.

DOI 10.1515/9783110448221-010

allels.[6] In addition, there is the vast treasure of Ancient Near Eastern iconography. Reading the Psalms in light of Ancient Near Eastern pictorial and glyptic art provides us with a better understanding of the early Hebrew concepts of God, world, and human life.[7]

The way God is depicted in the early psalms points to a type of deity that has been venerated not only in Ancient Israel but also in several neighboring cultures. In most areas of the Levant, of northern Mesopotamia, and of Asia Minor where rainfed cultivation was practiced, a storm-god played a dominant role in the local pantheon,[8] and the oldest psalms depict the Ancient Hebrew deity YHWH as a storm-god.[9] In the early days of YHWH worship, this deity seems to have been conceived in a similar way to storm-gods of neighboring cultures.

This does not mean that the early YHWH was imagined as identical or interchangeable with the storm-gods of adjacent regions like the Phoenician Ba'al Shamem—"the Lord of Heavens"[10]—or the Aramean Hadad of Damascus.[11] De-

---

6 A case in point is given by F. Hartenstein, *Das Angesicht JHWHs: Studien zu seinem höfischen und kultischen Bedeutungshintergrund in den Psalmen und in Exodus 32–34* (FAT 55; Tübingen 2008), 111–118, who gathers new insights on the term נעם יהוה "the delightfulness of YHWH" (Ps 27:4) from well-known Phoenician inscriptions.

7 See the groundbreaking contribution of O. Keel, *The Symbolism of the Biblical World: Near Eastern Iconography and the Book of Psalms* (trans. T.J. Hallett; Winona Lake, IN 1997). Additional methodological considerations and important insights into iconographic backgrounds of the Biblical concept of an audience before the divine king are given by Hartenstein, *Das Angesicht JHWHs* (see n. 6), 10–52, 116–125.

8 A comprehensive overview on Ancient-Near Eastern storm-gods is given by D. Schwemer, "The Storm-Gods of the Ancient Near East: Summary, Synthesis, Recent Studies," Part I, *JANER* 7 (2008), 121–168; Part II, *JANER* 8 (2008), 1–44; see also Schwemer's monumental monograph *Die Wettergottgestalten Mesopotamiens und Nordsyriens im Zeitalter der Keilschriftkulturen: Materialien und Studien nach den schriftlichen Quellen* (Wiesbaden 2001).

9 Cf., e. g., E.A. Knauf, *Midian: Untersuchungen zur Geschichte Palästinas und Nordarabiens am Ende des 2. Jahrtausends v. Chr.* (ADPV 10; Wiesbaden 1988), 48–60; M. Weippert, "Synkretismus und Monotheismus," in *Jahwe und die anderen Götter* (FAT 18; Tübingen 1997), 1–24, here 17; C. Levin, "Altes Testament und Rechtfertigung," in *Fortschreibungen: Gesammelte Studien zum Alten Testament* (BZAW 316; Berlin 2003), 9–22, here 13–14; R.G. Kratz, "Reste hebräischen Heidentums am Beispiel der Psalmen," in *Mythos und Geschichte: Kleine Schriften III* (FAT 102; Tübingen 2015), 156–189, esp. 160–164; M. Köckert, "Wandlungen Gottes im antiken Israel," *BTZ* 22 (2005), 3–36, here 20–21; F. Hartenstein, "Wettergott – Schöpfergott – Einziger," in *JHWH und die Götter der Völker: Symposium zum 80. Geburtstag von Klaus Koch* (ed. F. Hartenstein and M. Rösel; Neukirchen-Vluyn 2009), 77–97, here 84–91; Müller, *Jahwe als Wettergott* (see n. 4), 237–244.

10 On the history of this deity cf. H. Niehr, *Ba'alšamem: Studien zu Herkunft, Geschichte und Rezeptionsgeschichte eines phönizischen Gottes* (OLA 123 = StudPhoen 17; Leuven 2003).

spite all similarities, the deity name Yʜwʜ attests a strong concept of divine individuality.[12] This name is only rarely attested in neighboring regions of Israel and Judah,[13] and it seems that the veneration of this deity originated somewhere in Palestine or its surroundings.[14] However, the oldest psalms nevertheless indicate that Yʜwʜ, in spite of his individual name, shared essential characteristics with the storm-gods of neighboring regions. This fits well with the old theory according to which the deity name Yʜwʜ ("Yahweh") originally meant something like "He blows"[15]—a theory that to date gives the best etymological explanation of the divine name.[16]

Another notable phenomenon is the mention of other deities besides Yʜwʜ in the earliest pieces of psalmody, although the texts do not indicate that these deities played more than a marginal role compared to the storm-god and divine king Yʜwʜ. Some early psalms speak of "gods" (אלים or אלהים) or "sons of gods" (בני אלים) who submissively pay homage to Yʜwʜ (Ps 29:1–2; 97:7), and other

---

11 On the sources witnessing the veneration of this deity cf. Schwemer, *Die Wettergottgestalten Mesopotamiens* (see n. 8), 623–624.

12 See *below no. 2* on the proclamation of the name "Yʜwʜ" in Ps 24:8, 10 and the expression כבוד שמו "the honor of his name" in Ps 29:2.

13 See the contribution of M. Krebernik to the present volume.

14 The question in which region of Palestine or its near surroundings the veneration of Yʜwʜ originated is intensely debated in recent scholarship. The classic theory according to which the cult of Yʜwʜ was brought to central Palestine from regions in the south or south-east of central Palestine (e. g., J. Wellhausen, *Prolegomena to the History of Ancient Israel* [New York 1957], 343–344), has been recently defended particularly by O. Keel, *Die Geschichte Jerusalems und die Entstehung des Monotheismus* (OLB 4.1; Göttingen 2007), 1:202–12, M. Leuenberger, "Jhwhs Herkunft aus dem Süden: Archäologische Befunde – biblische Überlieferungen – historische Korrelation," in *Gott in Bewegung: Religions- und theologiegeschichtliche Beiträge zu Gottesvorstellungen im alten Israel* (FAT 76; Tübingen 2011), 10–33, and E. Blum, "Der historische Mose und die Frühgeschichte Israels," *HeBAI* 1 (2012), 37–63, here 52–61. An alternative model according to which the cult of Yʜwʜ originated in central or northern Palestine has been proposed by M. Köckert, "Wandlungen Gottes im antiken Israel," *BTZ* 22 (2005), 3–36, here 20 n. 43, and H. Pfeiffer, *Jahwes Kommen von Süden: Jdc 5; Hab 3; Dtn 33 und Ps 68 in ihrem literatur- und theologiegeschichtlichen Umfeld* (FRLANT 211; Göttingen 2005), esp. 261; see the contribution of H. Pfeiffer to the present volume. The probable Egyptian attestations of the name Yʜwʜ from the 14th and 13th centuries B.C.E. that are usually taken as corroborating the origins of the Yʜwʜ cult in Edomite regions are highly difficult to interpret, see Müller, *Jahwe als Wettergott* (see n. 4), 243–244 n. 50 (with bibliographical references), and the contribution of F. Adrom and M. Müller to the present volume.

15 J. Wellhausen, *Israelitische und jüdische Geschichte* (Berlin ⁷1914), 23 n. 1.

16 See E.A. Knauf, "Yahwe," *VT* 34 (1984), 467–472.

psalms praise YHWH's incomparability among the gods (Ex 15:11; Ps 89:7),[17] but the extant hymns and prayers do not clearly focus on individual deities besides YHWH.[18] Passages with more explicit polytheistic content may have been blurred or omitted during the long process of textual transmission,[19] but the oldest texts in the Psalter suggest that YHWH worship had a monolatrous tendency from its beginnings. Similar monolatries seem to have emerged in the official cults of the Eastern Jordanian kingdoms of Ammon, Moab, and Edom.[20] During the 9th century B.C.E., YHWH probably became the patron deity of the ruling dynasties of the kingdoms of Israel and Judah, as can be inferred particularly from the names of the Israelite and Judahite kings.[21] Since this period, YHWH and the divine kings of the neighboring states in the east, particularly Chemosh of Moab and Milcom of the Ammonite kingdom, seem to have taken on similar functions in the official cults, and each of them was imagined as guaranteeing the existence of his kingdom and defending it against its enemies.

In the following, a selection of early psalms will be interpreted. The image of God depicted in these poems was part of a highly differentiated concept of the world, the complex logic of which can only be reconstructed in modern terminology by approximation.

---

17 See R. Müller, "Der unvergleichliche Gott: Zur Umformung einer polytheistischen Redeweise im Alten Testament," in *Gott – Götter – Götzen: XIV. Europäischer Kongress für Theologie* (ed. C. Schwöbel; VWGT 38; Leipzig 2013), 304–319.

18 Entities like אור "light," אש "fire," אמת "truth," צדק "righteousness," חסד "lovingkindness," and שלום "peace" are sometimes mentioned as YHWH's heavenly entourage (Ps 43:3; 85:11–14; 97:3; 104:4), but the texts do not unequivocally depict these entities as individual deities; in the cases of צדק "righteousness" and אש "fire" it is however evident that in some North-West Semitic traditions they were in fact conceived as deities, see B.F. Batto, "Zedeq צדק," *DDD²*, 929–934, and W.G.E. Watson, "Fire אש," *DDD²*, 331–332. The same holds true for entities like ים "Sea," מים רבים "great waters," נהרות "rivers," and תהום "deep sea" that belong to the sphere of YHWH's cosmic adversaries (esp. Ps 24:2; 29:3; 93:3–4). It is evident that at least some of these entities were regarded as deities in some North-West Semitic traditions, see F. Stolz, "Sea ים," *DDD²*, 737–742; id., "River נהר," *DDD²*, 707–709. The fact that the extant remnants of early psalmody do not explicitly refer to their deified character does not imply that this dimension is completely absent in the texts and that these entities became strictly "naturalized" in the Ancient Hebrew context. This can be particularly inferred from the deity list of the Sfire treaty Sf I (= KAI 222) that mentions שמי[ן] וארק ... מצ[לה] ומעינן ... יום ולילה "Heav[en and Earth ..., A]byss and Springs, ... Day and Night" (A I 11–12 = J.A. Fitzmyer, *The Aramaic Inscriptions of Sefire* (BibOr 19/A; rev. ed.; Rome 1995, 42–43).

19 A well-known case in point is Deut 32:8–9 MT, see BHS and BHQ.

20 On this functional monolatry see H.P. Müller, "Chemosh," *DDD²*,186–189, here 188.

21 C. Levin, "Integrativer Monotheismus im Alten Testament," *ZTK* 109 (2012), 153–175, here 157.

1 Divine Epiphanies in a Thunderstorm

Conspicuous pieces of early cultic poetry are the so-called theophanies, poetic descriptions of a divine epiphany in a thunderstorm.[22] A most impressive example is found in Psalm 29, whose early origin is widely acknowledged.[23] The middle part of the psalm praises the powerful voice of Yнwн:[24]

(3) The voice of Yнwн is over the waters,
   Yнwн is over great waters!

(4) The voice of Yнwн is powerful,
   the voice of Yнwн is full of majesty!

(5*) The voice of Yнwн breaks cedars,
(7) the voice of Yнwн cleaves flames of fire!

(8) The voice of Yнwн causes wilderness to go into labor,
   Yнwн causes <holy> wilderness to go into labor!

(9) The voice of Yнwн causes hinds to calve
   and <causes> chamois (?) to give birth quickly (?)![25]

The opening of the poem describes how the divine voice is heard in the distance "over" the "great waters" (מים רבים) above the skies. This sound attests to the power and majesty of the god, who is approaching quickly. After that, the poem depicts the effects of a thunderstorm on the extra-human nature. Yнwн's voice breaks cedars, cleaves rocks and emits sparks, and causes the wilderness and hinds, i. e. female deer, to go into labor. The monotonous sevenfold repetition of the words "the voice of Yнwн" (קול יהוה) sounds like a litany or magic incantation that tries to evoke the crashing sound of thunder.

---

22 On the complex history of this genre see J. Jeremias, *Theophanie: Die Geschichte einer alttestamentlichen Gattung* (WMANT 10; Neukirchen-Vluyn ²1977); A. Scriba, *Die Geschichte des Motivkomplexes Theophanie: Seine Elemente, Einbindung in Geschehensabläufe und Verwendungsweisen in altisraelitischer, frühjüdischer und frühchristlicher Literatur* (FRLANT 167; Göttingen 1995); on its origins Müller, *Jahwe als Wettergott* (see n. 4), 237–244.

23 See, e. g., J. Goldingay, *Psalms I: 1–41* (Baker Commentary on the Old Testament; Grand Rapids, Mich 2006), 413–414.

24 This reconstruction of the original core of Ps 29 is similar to the model proposed by U. Becker, quoted in the contribution of M. Krebernik to the present volume; in contrast to my reconstruction in *Jahwe als Wettergott* (see n. 4), 107–122, I attribute vv. 5b.6 here to the secondarily added framework (vv. 1*, 2, 9*, 10) that praises Yнwн as divine king (*see below no. 2*).

25 On text and translation of this difficult verse see Müller, *Jahwe als Wettergott* (see n. 4), 103–113.

We can fairly assume that this song belonged to a related ritual. Its *Sitz im Leben* may have been the ancient Israelite festival of the New Year, celebrated around the beginning of the autumnal rains that end the summer drought.[26] The crashes of thunder in the autumnal storms were evidently identified with a divine voice. The same is attested for the storm-god of the late bronze-age kingdom of Ugarit:[27]

> His holy voice made the earth tremble,
> the saying of his lips the mountains.

It is notable that Psalm 29* envisages peripheral regions of the cosmos. The poem mentions the heavenly bodies of water, the mountainous and rocky regions where cedars grow, and the wilderness (מדבר). The latter is called "holy," presumably because it was perceived as a liminal sphere in relation to the human world. The "holy wilderness" – an expression also found in a mythologic poem from Ugarit[28] – was known to be inhabited by untamable beasts, while humans were unable to live in these regions; the wilderness was therefore seen as a border between the human world and divine spheres. When YHWH appears in the thunderstorm, he even "causes" this usually dry region "to go into labor," which implies that, in spite of his threatening voice, he provides fertility and new life to the entire world. A close parallel can be found in a prayer to the North-Mesopotamian storm-god, Adad:[29]

> [...] who irrigates the [hea]t, pours out [fertili]ty,
> because of his voice people are deathly still,
> meadowlands are broken up, steppes come into labor [...].

These texts refer to the ambivalence of the divine activity. When the storm-god approaches, threatening phenomena occur. YHWH, when he appears in the thunderstorm, smashes the proud cedars, splits rocks, and ignites fire on the earth. Yet the thunderstorm also brings abundant rain (1 Kgs 18:44 – 45); although Psalm 29* does not explicitly mention the rain, the poem alludes to the divine

---

26 See Müller, *Jahwe als Wettergott* (see n. 4), 36.
27 CAT 1.4 VII 31– 37, in my own translation, and see Müller, *Jahwe als Wettergott* (see n. 4), 30.
28 CAT 1.23:65, and see M.S. Smith, *The Rituals and Myths of the FEAST OF THE GOODLY GODS of KTU/CAT 1.23: Royal Constructions of Opposition, Intersection, Integration, and Domination* (SBLRBS 51; Atlanta 2006), 117.
29 Adad 1a (Schwemer, *Die Wettergottgestalten Mesopotamiens* [see n. 8], 671– 674), in my own translation.

gift of fertility through the ambivalent imagery of labor-pains that beset the wilderness when Yнwн approaches.

A shorter theophany, probably also of ancient origin, is embedded in Psalm 97:[30]

(2*)	Clouds and thick darkness are around him,
(3)	fire goes before him,
	and scorches his adversaries round about.

(4)	His flashes of lightning have lighted up the world,
	the earth saw it and came into labor.

(5*)	Mountains melt like wax
	before the lord of all the earth.

This poem reveals the ambivalent character of the Ancient Hebrew storm-god through images similar to those found in Psalm 29*.[31] The motif of labor-pains besetting the earth implies that the storm-god has fertilized the earth with his flashes of lighting (v. 4). At the same time, the poem highlights the aggressive power of the god. He is hidden in dark clouds, and "fire," acting as his life guard, repulses "his adversaries"—presumably hostile deities—who challenge the god's supremacy (v. 3). He even makes the numinous mountains "melt like wax,"—an impressive hyperbole depicting the god's unstoppable power. The theophany concludes by calling the storm-god "lord of all the earth" (אדן כל הארץ). Similar epithets can be found in North-West Semitic inscriptions.[32]

Another dramatic theophany can be found in Ps 18:8–16*. This poem reads like a section of a larger epic:[33]

(8*)	And the earth shook and trembled,
	so that the foundations of the mountains quaked.

---

30 E. Lipiński, *La Royauté de Yahwé dans la poesie et la culte de l'ancien Israël* (Brüssel 1965), 219–241; C. Levin, "Das Gebetbuch der Gerechten," in *Fortschreibungen: Gesammelte Studien zum Alten Testament* (BZAW 316; Berlin 2003), 291–313; here 299–300; Kratz, *Reste hebräischen Heidentums* (see n. 9), 177–178; M. Leuenberger, *Konzeptionen des Königtums Gottes im Psalter: Untersuchungen zu Komposition und Redaktion der theokratischen Bücher IV-V im Psalter* (ATANT 83; Zürich 2004), 158 n. 107; Müller, *Jahwe als Wettergott* (see n. 4), 93–98.
31 It seems that the oldest version of this poem did not contain a deity name; poetological observations indicate that the phrase מלפני יהוה "before Yнwн" has been secondarily inserted into v. 5 (Müller, *Jahwe als Wettergott* [see n. 4], 92). The אדן "lord" of Ps 97* has nevertheless the same characteristics as the Yнwн of Ps 29*.
32 See Müller, *Jahwe als Wettergott* (see n. 4), 98.
33 On text and translation see Müller, *Jahwe als Wettergott* (see n. 4), 18–29.

(9*) Smoke went up at his nostrils,
and fire out of his mouth devoured.

(10) And he spread the heavens and came down,
and thick darkness was under his feet.

(11) And he rode upon a cherub, and did fly,
he swooped down upon the wings of the wind.

(12*) He made darkness his hiding place,
round about him was darkness of waters, thick clouds of the skies.

(13*) Before him his thick clouds passed,
hailstones and coals of fire.

(15) And he sent out his arrows, and he scattered them,
and flashes of lightning manifold, and he confused them.

(16) Then the beds of <the Sea> appeared,
<> the foundations of the world were laid bare.

The verbal forms indicate that this highly poetic description relates an event from a mythic past. This suggests that the recurrent phenomena of the thunderstorm were perceived as echoes of a primeval divine battle.

This text also focuses on the frightening aspects of the divine epiphany. The earth and its foundations tremble, and a furious god is hidden in the clouds. It is notable that he has anthropomorphic traits; by referring to his nose, mouth and feet, the text adumbrates the notion of a human-like divine body.[34] But the anthropomorphism is also broken by dragon-like characteristics: Smoke is emanating from the deity's nose, and a devouring fire burns from his mouth.

After spreading the dark clouds like a black tent, the god descends (v. 10a); similarly Adad is called "the one who climbed down from the skies."[35] The deity of Psalm 18* descends from the skies riding on a cherub (v. 11), a sphinx-like hybrid creature symbolizing power and speed. The cherub *per se* belongs to the sphere of life-threatening powers, which can be illustrated with a neo-Assyrian cylinder-seal showing how a winged divine archer repulses a cherub from the sphere of vegetation (fig. 1).

Yet, cherubs were also imagined as being tamed and forced into servitude by the gods, which is illustrated by the monumental sphinxes that were protecting

---

34 See Hartenstein, *Das Angesicht JHWHs* (see n. 6), 15–52, on the "symbol of the divine 'body.'"

35 Schwemer, *Die Wettergottgestalten Mesopotamiens* (see n. 8), 714.

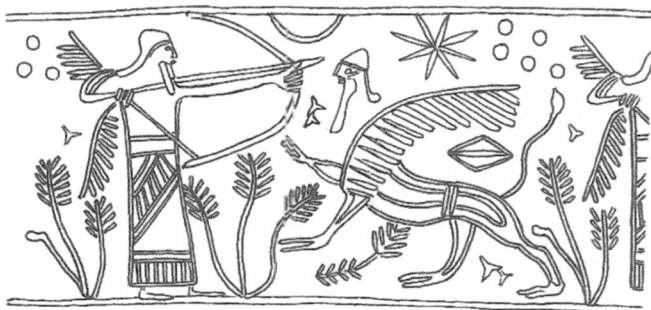

Fig. 1: Neo-Assyrian cylinder seal (8th to 7th century B.C.E.). Drawing by H. Keel-Leu, in *Die Geschichte Jerusalems und die Entstehung des Monotheismus: Teil 1* (OLB 4.1; Göttingen 2007), fig. 178 on p. 297 (cf. H. Keel-Leu and B. Teissier, Die vorderasiatischen Rollsiegel der Sammlung "Bibel + Orient" der Universität Freiburg Schweiz [OBO 200; Fribourg 2004], fig. 167).

the gates of the neo-Assyrian palaces.[36] The storm-god of Psalm 18* has trained a cherub to ride on it through the thunderstorm. From the back of this swift mount he shoots flashes of lightning as his arrows (v. 15). The text does not explicitly state whom the god is fighting against. Yet it is probable that he is defeating divine adversaries that belong to the sphere of chaotic powers.[37] According to the conclusion of the poem (v. 16*), "the Sea" (ים) is driven away from the pillars of the earth, which seems to allude to the old North-West Semitic myth of a divine victory over the sea.[38]

In Ps 77:17–20 we find a song of praise that uses a conspicuous poetic form: the archaic tricolon or staircase parallelism, a threefold *parallelismus membrorum*. The song praises Yнwн for his victorious combat against chaotic floods:[39]

(17)   The waters saw you, < Yнwн >,
     the waters saw you, they came into labor,
     yea, the floods trembled.

---

36 See S. Maul, "Der Sieg über die Mächte des Bösen: Götterkampf, Triumphrituale und Torarchitektur in Assyrien," in *Gegenwelten zu den Kulturen Griechenlands und Roms in der Antike* (ed. T. Hölscher; Leipzig 2000), 19–46.

37 On the term "chaos" as a heuristic concept, see T. Podella, "Der 'Chaoskampfmythos' im Alten Testament: Eine Problemanzeige," in *Mesopotamica – Ugaritica – Biblica* (ed. M. Dietrich and O. Loretz; AOAT 232; Kevelaer 1993), 283–329.

38 On this myth see Schwemer, "The Storm-Gods of the Ancient Near East," Part II, 24–27; N. Ayali-Darshan, "The Other Version of the Story of the Storm-god's Combat with the Sea in Light of Egyptian, Ugaritic, and Hurro-Hittite Texts," *JANER* 15 (2015), 20–51.

39 On text and translation see Müller, *Jahwe als Wettergott* (see n. 4), 43, 51–53.

(18) The clouds poured out water,
the skies gave their voice,
yea, your arrows went abroad.

(19) The voice of your thunder sounded at the wheel,
flashes of lightning illumined the world,
the earth trembled and shook.

(20) Your way was in the sea
and your <paths> in great waters,
and your tracks were not known.

In the context of Psalm 77, these verses are associated with Israel's crossing of the sea (vv. 14–16, 21). Yet the four tricola of vv. 17–20 do not contain any reference to the delivery of God's people. The archaic song depicts the waters themselves as YHWH's cosmic adversaries, and the motif of YHWH taking his path through their midst (v. 20) is not necessarily an allusion to Israel's crossing of the sea but can also be understood as an act of triumph after the defeat of the cosmic floods.[40]

The waters in the skies (מים רבים), the primeval floods (תהמות) and the sea (ים) belong to the same sphere. When the divine warrior appears, the waters and floods start to tremble (v. 17), and the clouds pour out torrents of rain (v. 18). Yet it seems that YHWH does not aim at annihilating the floods but rather at taming them. By overcoming their destructive force, he makes the vital rain coming down abundantly.

Like in Psalm 18*, the divine warrior is imagined as an archer (v. 18). The crashes of thunder are, unlike in Psalm 29*, caused by the "wheel" (v. 19) which alludes to the chariot on which YHWH rumbles through the thunderstorm. This can be illustrated by a beautiful relief from the recently unearthed temple of the storm-god of Aleppo (fig. 2) that shows a pair of wheels *pars pro toto* for the divine chariot.

---

40 C.A. Briggs and E.G. Briggs, *The Book of Psalms* (ICC; Edinburgh 1909), 2:175–176; H. Simian-Yofre, "La teodicea del Deuteroisaías," *Bib* 62 (1981), 55–72, here 58–9; O. Loretz, *Ugarit-Texte und Thronbesteigungspsalmen: Die Metamorphose des Regenspenders Baal-Jahwe (Ps 24,7–10; 29; 47; 93; 95–100 sowie Ps 77,17–20; 114)* (UBL 7; Münster 1988), 392; E.J. Waschke, "תְּהוֹם tᵉhôm," in *ThWAT* 8:563–571, here 569; C. Levin, "Old Testament Religion: Conflict and Peace," in *Re-Reading the Scriptures: Essays on the Literary History of the Old Testament* (FAT 87; Tübingen 2013), 165–181, here 171; Müller, *Jahwe als Wettergott* (see n. 4), 58.

Fig. 2: Relief from the temple of the storm-god of Aleppo. Drawing by H. Keel-Leu, in *Die Geschichte Jerusalems und die Entstehung des Monotheismus: Teil 1* (OLB 4.1; Göttingen 2007), fig. 265 on p. 382 (cf. K. Kohlmeyer, *Der Tempel des Wettergottes von Aleppo* [Münster 2000], pl. 16 and 17).

An ancient song of praise quoted in Psalm 65 celebrates the storm-god's gift of fertility to the earth.[41] Here we find another allusion to the divine chariot (v. 12):

(10*) You visited the land and watered it,
  you greatly enriched it,
  yea, thus you established it.

(11) Its furrows saturating,
  settling its ridges,
  you soften it with showers,
  you bless its growth.

(12) You crowned the year of your goodness,
  and your wagon-tracks drip with fatness.

(13) The pastures of the wilderness drip,
  and the hills gird themselves with rejoicing.

(14*) The meadows have clothed themselves with flocks,
  and the valleys cover themselves with grain.

The poem looks back, as if in fast-forward, upon the entire agricultural year. During the rainy season the praised god "visited" the land, he blessed its fertility,

---

41 S. Schroer, "Psalm 65 – Zeugnis eines integrativen JHWH-Glaubens?," *UF* 22 (1990), 285 – 301; Müller, *Jahwe als Wettergott* (see n. 4), 133 – 146.

provided the livestock with rich pastures, and finally made the grain ripen. He "crowned" the year with his gifts (v. 12)—which suggests that this song was sung at harvest celebrations at the end of the agricultural year.

The pieces that depict the Ancient Hebrew storm-god reveal a distinct ambivalence that is of great theological importance. The early YHWH is at the same time perceived as an aggressive warrior and as a giver of life. With his irresistible power he defeats the floods that are trying to destroy the earth, and pours them out as rain. Yet Psalm 29*, Psalm 97*, Psalm 18*, and Psalm 77* focus primarily on the aggressive aspects of the divine epiphany. This indicates indirectly that the cult of the storm-god YHWH possessed a distinct political dimension from the outset.

2 The Divine King

The closing verses of Psalm 24, the early origin of which is undisputed, contain a key text for the theology of divine kingship:[42]

(7) "Raise, O gates, your heads,
     and lift up yourselves, O eternal doors,'
     so that the king of honor may come in!"

(8) "Who is this, the king of honor?"
     "YHWH, a strong one and a warrior,
     YHWH, a battle warrior!"

(9) "Raise, O gates, your heads,
     and <lift up yourselves>, O eternal doors,
     so that the king of honor may come in!"

(10*) "Who, then, is this, the king of honor?"
     "YHWH of hosts,
     he is the king of honor!"

This is a liturgical dialogue between two speakers, and we can fairly assume that it was part of a corresponding ritual. The first speaker stands outside the gates. He takes the role of a messenger who, after having hurried ahead of the approaching YHWH, addresses the gates: "Raise, O gates, your heads ...!" The second speaker assumes the role of the gates themselves: "Who is this, the king of

---

42 See Müller, *Jahwe als Wettergott* (see n. 4), 147–167.

honor?" The scene corresponds to the dialogue between the warden of the city gate and the one who demands to be let in.[43]

Yнwн's messenger addresses the gates as "eternal doors," which hints at their mythic dimension; they participate in the sphere of the eternal gods. The call "Raise your heads!" indicates that the gates have lowered their heads in a gesture of mourning, since the city is threatened by enemies. The divine warrior has left his residency to fight them off.

A close parallel can be found in the Ugaritic Ba'al epic that narrates the conflict between the storm-god Ba'al and the sea-god Yamm (KTU/CAT 1.1–1.2). When the assembly of the gods receives messengers of Yamm, requesting to deliver Ba'al into his power, the horrified gods lower their heads. But the fearless Ba'al rebukes them—and the rhythm of his first words sounds strikingly similar to the call of Yнwн's messenger (Ps 24:7, 9: "Raise, O gates, your heads"):

"Raise, O gods, your heads,
from the tops of your knees,
from your royal thrones!

And I myself will answer Yamm's messengers,
the legation of Judge River."

The gods raise their heads
from the tops of their knees,
from their royal thrones.[44]

In the ensuing combat, Ba'al kills Yamm, and the gods acclaim Ba'al's kingship.[45] Psalm 24* seems related to a similar tale. The liturgy looks back on the victory of Yнwн, which implies the notion of a divine combat. Yнwн, "the king of honor" (מלך הכבוד), demands from the gates of his city to be let in to

---

43 M.I. Gruber, *Aspects of Nonverbal Communication in the Ancient Near East* (trans. M.S. Smith; Studia Pohl 12/I–II; Rome 1980), 600. Usually the liturgy is explained as referring to the gate of the temple. However, this cannot be deduced from vv. 7–10, only from vv. 3–6 which are clearly of later origin. When the Hebrew Bible mentions "gates" and "doors," this refers usually to the city gate; here the warrior who returned from battle was welcomed back (cf. Judg 11:34; 1 Sam 18:6).

44 CAT 1.2 I 27–29 (translation according to S.B. Parker (ed.), *Ugaritic Narrative Poetry* [SBLWAW 9; Atlanta 1997], 100); see Müller, *Jahwe als Wettergott* (see n. 4), 151.

45 See M. Dietrich and O. Loretz, "Mythen und Epen in ugaritischer Sprache," in *TUAT III/6* (ed. Otto Kaiser et al.; Gütersloh 1987), 1091–1316, here 1121–1134; H. Niehr, "Mythen und Epen aus Ugarit," in *TUAT.NF VIII* (ed. B. Janowski and D. Schwemer et al.; Gütersloh 2015), 177–301, here 190–202.

take up his residency again. The gates however have to check his identity: "Who is this, the king of honor?" It is possible that a foreign and hostile god prevailed on the battlefield. This may be either a cosmic adversary of the storm-god, like the sea-god Yamm, or a patron deity of a neighboring kingdom; these deities fought against YHWH time and again, as illustrated by the famous stele of the Moabite king Mesha that connects Mesha's victory over the Israelite kingdom with the supremacy of the Moabite patron deity Chemosh over the Israelite YHWH.[46] From the perspective of the Yahwistic cult, such divine enemies of YHWH must have been perceived as exponents of defeat, destruction and chaos.

YHWH's messenger answers the gates by proclaiming the name of the approaching king, adding a series of martial epithets: "a strong one and a warrior," "a battle warrior." As a climax, he proclaims the divine name "YHWH of hosts" (יהוה צבאות) in which YHWH's martial nature seems condensed. Psalm 24:10* is in all likelihood the earliest attestation of this famous divine name.[47] It is notable that the name "YHWH of hosts" closely corresponds to a political title of the Hittite storm-god—one of the main deities of the Hittite empire—, namely "Storm-god of the army"[48] that persisted in the neo-Hittite deity name "Tarhunza of the army"[49]; in addition, "YHWH of hosts" also resembles the name of the divine warrior "Reshef of host" that is attested in Ugarit.[50] All these names seem to imply that a divine warrior is leading an earthly army into battle. In this context, the divine individuality that is contained in the name "YHWH" must have become decisive.

The liturgy illustrates that the term "honor" (כבוד) was foundational for the Ancient Hebrew concept of divine kingship. The victorious YHWH claimed to be "the king of honor" (מלך הכבוד). What is meant by "honor" can be deduced from the framing passages in Psalm 29* that were secondarily added to the incantation about YHWH's voice:

---

46 See the recent edition in M. Weippert, *Historisches Textbuch zum Alten Testament* (GAT 10; Göttingen 2010), 242–248.

47 Thus R. Smend, "Jahwekrieg und Stämmebund: Erwägungen zur ältesten Geschichte Israels," in *Zur ältesten Geschichte Israels: Gesammelte Studien 2* (München 1987), 116–199, here 166.

48 See V. Haas and H. Koch, *Religionen des Alten Orients Teil 1: Hethiter und Iran* (GAT 1,1; Göttingen 2011), 223.

49 TELL AHMAR 6 § 23 (G. Bunnens, *A New Luwian Stele and the Cult of the Storm-God at Til Barsib-Masuwari* [Publication de la Mission archéologique de'l Université de Liège en Syrie: Tell Ahmar 2; Leuven 2006], 15).

50 See Keel, *Die Geschichte Jerusalems* (see n. 14), 214.

(1*) *Bestow on* YHWH, *sons of gods,*
bestow on YHWH *honor and strength,*

(2) *bestow on* YHWH *the honor of his name,*
prostrate yourself to YHWH *in holy ornaments!*

(3) The voice of YHWH is over the waters,
the god of honor has thundered,
YHWH is over great waters!

(4) The voice of YHWH is powerful,
the voice of YHWH is full of majesty!

(5) The voice of YHWH breaks cedars!

And YHWH *shattered the cedars of the Lebanon,*
(6) *and he made Lebanon*[51] *skip like a calf*
and Sirion like a young wild-ox.

(7) The voice of YHWH cleaves flames of fire!

(8) The voice of YHWH makes wilderness to go into labor,
YHWH makes <holy> wilderness to go into labor!

(9) The voice of YHWH makes hinds to calve
and *made* chamois (?) to give birth quickly (?),[52]
and in his palace each one of it says: "Honor!"

(10) YHWH took his seat on the flood,
yea, YHWH took his seat as king forever!

The framework of the theophany depicts a scene in YHWH's divine "palace" (v. 9). After having taken up his place on his throne (cf. v. 10), YHWH receives homage and tribute from "sons of gods" (vv. 1*–2). They bestow on him "honor and strength" and prostrate themselves before him, and this act of submission demonstrates how overwhelming the "honor of his name" is. The honor of the divine king is therefore nothing other than his supremacy over the gods, and this supremacy becomes the essence of his name.

A similar concept can be found in the praise of YHWH's incomparability that has close parallels in several Ancient Near Eastern hymns about divine kings.[53]

---

51 Against the Masoretic interpretation of the verse that was defended by me in *Jahwe als Wettergott* (see n. 4), 111–112, it is more probable that the *mem* of וירקידם was originally no suffix but an enclitic "-*ma*," see R. Meyer, *Hebräische Grammatik* (Berlin 1992), 2:180–181.
52 See n. 25.
53 See C.J. Labuschange, *The Incomparability of Yahweh in the Old Testament* (POS V; Leiden 1966), 33–45; R. Müller, "Der unvergleichliche Gott: Zur Umformung einer polytheistischen Re-

According to Ps 89:7*–8, YHWH is called incomparable since he is intensely feared by the divine council:

(7*) Who in the clouds can be compared to YHWH,
be like YHWH among the sons of gods?

(8) A god (אל), feared in the council of the holy ones,
<great is he> and awesome above all that are around him!

Because of this fear, the gods submissively pay tribute to YHWH (Ps 29:1*–2; cf. Ps 97:7b).

It should not be overlooked that Psalm 29* does not simply describe what takes place in YHWH's palace. Instead, the psalm opens with hymnic calls addressed to the gods: "Bestow on YHWH, sons of gods, / bestow on YHWH honor and strength ...!" The cultic singing of this psalm, which probably took place in the temple or the sacred precinct, was perceived as part of the events in the divine palace. The singer of the initial hymnic call (cf. Exod 15:21) takes the role of a lord steward who calls the entering subjects to pay homage to the king and to prostrate themselves before him. The visible temple and the invisible divine palace touch each other, and this can be experienced through the singing of the psalm.

At the same time, the framed theophany relates the cultic present to the mythic past. The theophany itself refers to a present thunderstorm, but in combination with the framework it is expanded by retrospective references to primeval events. YHWH, "the god" or "El of honor (אל הכבוד) has thundered" in the primeval past (v. 3bα), and he shattered the cedars of Lebanon and made Lebanon and Sirion (Anti-Lebanon) skip—possibly an echo of an old Levantine myth depicting how this enormous mountain range split into two.[54]

The conclusion of the framework looks back on YHWH's ascension to the throne (v. 10): "YHWH took his seat on the flood, / yea, YHWH took his seat forever!" This implies that YHWH continuously masters "the flood" (מבול) after his ascension to the throne. It is linguistically ambiguous whether the text means that YHWH is enthroned "*upon* the flood" so that the flood itself becomes his

---

deweise im Alten Testament," in *Gott – Götter – Götzen: XIV. Europäischer Kongress für Theologie* (ed. Christoph Schwöbel; Veröffentlichungen der Wissenschaftlichen Gesellschaft für Theologie 38; Leipzig 2013), 304–319, here 309–311.

54 Thus A.R. George, "The Day the Earth Divided: A Geological Aetiology in the Babylonian Gilgameš Epic," *ZA* 80 (1990), 214–219.

throne, or that YHWH sits "*in front of* the flood" in order to master it[55]; the second option may be connected with the "molten sea" that was placed in front of the temple (1 Kgs 7:23–26) and seems to have symbolized the tamed primeval floods.[56] The motif of divine control over the flood is also found in traditions of other storm-gods; for example, the North-Mesopotamian Adad could be called "lord of the flood."[57]

Another poem on YHWH's kingship, the early origin of which is widely accepted, is Psalm 93. It shows how foundational the idea of divinely tamed floods was for the Ancient Hebrew perception of the world:

(1) *YHWH has become king,*
    with majesty he has clothed himself,
    YHWH has clothed himself,
    he has girded himself with strength!

    Yea, the world is established,
    it cannot totter.

(2) *your throne is established from of old,*
    you are there from primeval times.

(3) The rivers have lifted up, YHWH,
    the rivers have lifted up their voice,
    the rivers lift up their roaring.

(4) More than the voices of great waters,
    <mightier than> the breakers of the sea,
    mighty is YHWH on high,
(5*) YHWH for evermore!

The psalm begins with a herald's call proclaiming YHWH's ascension to the throne (v. 1a).[58] After that, the psalm describes a foundational cosmological idea. The "world" (תבל), that is, the habitable surface of the earth, "cannot totter" (v. 1b), for YHWH's throne has been established since primeval times when

---

55 Thus F. Hartenstein, *Die Unzugänglichkeit Gottes im Heiligtum: Jesaja 6 und der Wohnort JHWHs in der Jerusalemer Kulttradition* (WMANT 75; Neukirchen-Vluyn 1997), 59–60 n. 117.
56 See Keel, *Die Geschichte Jerusalems* (see n. 14), 320–322, according to whom the rim of this basin, which was formed like a lotus, referred at the same time to the Egyptian idea of the primeval ocean.
57 See Schwemer, *Die Wettergottgestalten Mesopotamiens* (see n. 8), 706.
58 Several scholars suggested that in Ps 93:1a the original dynamic and ingressive concept of ascension to the throne has been transformed into a static concept of divine kingship, but this theory cannot be substantiated for grammatical and motif critical reasons, see Müller, *Jahwe als Wettergott* (see n. 4), 75–81.

he took his seat on it (v. 2). It is conspicuous that the psalm unfolds this idea in the meter of lamentation, the Qînā (vv. 1b, 2). This may allude to the contrasting fact that from time to time earthquakes occurred in Palestine,[59] and these were thought to be caused by the floods underneath the earth (Ps 46:3). Psalm 93:1b–2 may be an indirect echo of laments about such earthquakes, but here the lament has turned into praise; the divine throne provides the earth with permanent stability.

The second part of the psalm (vv. 3–5*), which may be slightly older than the first,[60] unfolds a similar idea in relation to the chaotic floods that endanger the inhabited world. This part begins with a dramatic lamentation[61] that uses the archaic poetic form of a triple staircase parallelism (v. 3). It describes in impressive monotony and partly in onomatopoeic style[62] how the rivers are rising up against YHWH's supremacy. The ensuing tetracolon (vv. 4, 5b), an elaborately extended comparative, gradually reveals that YHWH "on high" is incomparably mightier than the great waters, and will remain so "for evermore."

It is undeniable that the deity praised by Psalm 93* is related to other Ancient Near Eastern and particularly North-West Semitic storm-gods and divine kings. The topos of divine enthronement, the epithet "mighty" (אדיר), and the phrases "on high" (במרום) and "for evermore" (לארך ימים) have distinct parallels in Israel's neighboring cultures.[63] The central idea of a divinely established and consolidated world is also very old, but hitherto no clear parallels for the connection of this idea to a storm-god have been found. It is possible that this was a singular concept in the early theology of YHWH.[64]

A poem that is closely comparable to Psalm 93* can be found in Psalm 97*. Here the theophany of the storm-god with the title "lord of all the earth" (Ps 97:2–5*) was secondarily framed, like in Psalm 29*, with motifs of divine kingship:

---

59 See, e.g., W. Zwickel, *Einführung in die biblische Landes- und Altertumskunde* (Darmstadt 2002), 73.
60 See Müller, *Jahwe als Wettergott* (see n. 4), 68–71.
61 See R. Mosis, "'Ströme erheben, Jahwe, ihr Tosen …': Beobachtungen zu Ps 93," in *Ein Gott, eine Offenbarung: Beiträge zur biblischen Exegese, Theologie und Spiritualität* (ed. F.V. Reiterer; Würzburg 1991), 223–255, here 241–242.
62 Particularly the word דכים *dåkjām* "their roaring" imitates the pounding sound of the waves.
63 Müller, *Jahwe als Wettergott* (see n. 4), 73–75.
64 Müller, *Jahwe als Wettergott* (see n. 4), 82–83, 143, 156–161; Hartenstein, "Wettergott – Schöpfergott – Einziger" (see n. 9), 84–91.

(1)   *YHWH has become king,*
       let the earth rejoice,
       let the many coasts be glad!

(2)   Clouds and thick darkness are around him,
       righteousness and justice are the foundation of his throne.

(3)   Fire goes before him,
       and scorches his adversaries round about.

(4)   His flashes of lightning have lighted up the world,
       the earth saw it and came into labor.

(5*)   Mountains melt like wax
       before the lord of all the earth.

(6*)   *The heavens have declared his righteousness,*
(7*)   *all gods have prostrated themselves before him.*

This is another song that also celebrates YHWH's primeval ascension to the throne. The song begins by proclaiming YHWH's kingship and calling upon the whole earth to rejoice. YHWH's royal power is illustrated with the storm-god's epiphany in the thunderstorm. Together with the framing passages, a reference to the divine throne was inserted into the theophany (v. 2b). YHWH's throne is erected on "foundations" (Hebr. מכון, from the root כון "to be firm") of "righteousness and justice." This alludes to the fact that the divine kingdom provides order and stability to the world; the word-pair "righteousness and justice" has distinct parallels in North-West Semitic and Mesopotamian concepts of world order. The motif of the throne's fundament, however, seems to be of Egyptian origin.[65] Egyptian depictions showed Pharaoh's throne standing on the hieroglyph of the goddess Ma'at who was imagined as providing harmonious order to the process of the world.[66] Following the theophany, the psalm tells how the world came to notice YHWH's righteousness (v. 6a). "The heavens"—in the role of divine heralds—"have declared" it to the earth. The song concludes with a final look at the divine sphere; all gods have prostrated themselves before the divine king.

---

65 See F.L. Hossfeld and E. Zenger, *Psalmen 51–100: Übersetzt und ausgelegt* (HTKAT; Freiburg i. B ²2000), 679–680.
66 See J. Assmann, *Ma'at: Gerechtigkeit und Unsterblichkeit im Alten Ägypten* (Munich ²1995), esp. 34–35.

The hymn that forms the second half of Psalm 98 belongs to the same context:[67]

(4)   Shout to Yʜᴡʜ, all the earth,
      break forth and jubilate and make melody,

(5)   make melody to Yʜᴡʜ with the lyre,
      with the lyre and the sound of melody,

(6*)   with trumpets and the sound of the horn,
      shout before the king!

(7)   Let the Sea thunder and its fullness,
      the world and those who dwell therein,

(8)   let the Rivers clap their hands,
      together let the mountains jubilate,

(9)   before Yʜᴡʜ, for he has come
      to rule the earth,

      he will rule the world with righteousness
      and the peoples with equity!

The cultic background of this hymn is evident. The musical instruments mentioned probably referred to the real music of the temple cult. It is however decisive to note that the text attributes a cosmic dimension to this kind of music.[68] Psalm 98* calls upon the whole earth to jubilate and make melody. The music of the temple service echoes in the world-wide rejoicing before the divine king. It is certainly no coincidence that the series in which the musical instruments are mentioned points at a *crescendo*; the playing of the lyre is drowned out by trumpets, and the climax is the sound of the horn (שׁופר) which also had a crucial function in the human king's ritual ascension to the throne (cf. 1 Kgs 1:39; 2 Kgs 9:13). According to the second part of the hymn, all inhabitants of the earth, even the numinous mountains and the chaotic entities Sea and Rivers, are called to participate in the ritual joy by jubilating and clapping hands (cf. 2 Kgs 11:12). In this context, a conspicuous pun is formulated; the Sea is

---

67 Vv. 4–9 originated earlier than the initial vv. 1–3 that are influenced by Deutero-Isaiah, see Kratz, "Reste hebräischen Heidentums" (see n. 9), 175; Müller, *Jahwe als Wettergott* (see n. 4), 169–172.

68 See F. Hartenstein, "'Wach auf, Harfe und Leier, ich will wecken das Morgenrot' (Psalm 57,9): Musikinstrumente als Medien des Gotteskontakts im Alten Orient und im Alten Testament," in *Musik, Tanz und Gott: Tonspuren durch das Alte Testament* (ed. M. Geiger and R. Kessler; SBS 207; Stuttgart 2007), 101–127.

called to "thunder" (רעם) which implies that YHWH's thundering voice (cf. Ps 29:3 – 9) echoes in the roaring of his tamed adversary. The song ends by proclaiming the advent of the divine king. YHWH has approached the earth to rule it with "righteousness and equity." The divine king's ascension to the throne, which is the outcome of his victory over chaotic and destructive powers, leads to the establishment of a "righteous" world order. "Righteousness" (צדק) in this context is no *iustitia distributiva* but rather the measure upon which a stable order of the supra-human cosmos and human society has to be founded.

An ancient song, quoted in a much younger context in Psalm 85,[69] indicates that "righteousness" was in fact imagined as an entity of divine origin.

[11] Grace and Faithfulness have met together,
Righteousness and Peace have kissed each other.

[12] Faithfulness sprouts forth from the earth,
and Righteousness looks down from heaven.

[13] Yea, YHWH gives what is good,
and our land yields its increase.

[14] Righteousness goes before him
and sets (the heart) on the path of his steps.

The divine attributes "Grace" (חסד), "Faithfulness" (אמת), "Righteousness" (צדק), and "Peace" (שלום) are personified as divine courtiers. This brings to mind North-West Semitic evidence that attests to the veneration of a deity called צדק "Righteousness."[70] All four attributes mentioned here are closely connected with the idea of divine kingship. "Grace" is the divine king's commitment to his subjects and his kind affection for them, his "Faithfulness" protects the world from chaos and makes life possible, "Peace / Shalom" is the perfection and equilibrium of the divine world order. A beautiful series of metaphors depicts how the four entities cooperate. They "have met together" and "kissed each other"—horizontal moves supplemented by the vertical moves of "Faithfulness sprouting forth from the earth" and "Righteousness looking down from heaven," like from a window of the royal palace. However, like the fire in Ps 97:3 that is consuming the storm-god's adversaries, "Righteousness" also goes before YHWH to protect the divine king whose main activity is providing fertility to the earth.

---

69 See H. Spieckermann, "Schöpfung, Gerechtigkeit und Heil als Horizont alttestamentlicher Theologie," *ZTK* 100 (2003), 399 – 419, here 406.
70 See B.F. Batto, "Zedeq צדק," in *DDD²*, 929 – 934.

The middle part of Psalm 36 praises Yнwн's overwhelming majesty and affection for his subjects:

(6)   *Yнwн, your grace stands in the heavens,*
      your faithful deed extends to the clouds.

(7)   *Your righteous deed is like the mountains of El,*
      your judgment <like> the great Flood

      You deliver human being and cattle.

      Yнwн, (8) how precious is your grace,
      gods and human beings
      take refuge in the shadow of your wings.

(9)   They are abundantly satisfied with the fat of your house,
      and you make them drink of the brook of your pleasures.

(10) For with you is the fountain of life,
      in your light we see light.

The song probably originated in two stages.[71] The second and older part (vv. 7*, 8–10) praises the abundance of Yнwн's royal grace by which he provides refuge to both "gods and human beings." The mention of the divine wings refers to the protective sphere of the divine throne room.[72] To be there – in the audience before the divine king – means to be protected from chaotic powers. Such an audience becomes a feast in which the divine king hosts his subjects, and this was imagined as the invisible background of the sacrificial meals in the temple. A close parallel for this imagery can be found in the Ugaritic Ba'al cycle. After the completion of his temple, the storm-god Ba'al boasts:

> I am the only one who rules as king over the gods,
> who fattens gods and human beings,
> who satis[fies] the multitudes of the earth.[73]

Psalm 36* concludes with two impressive images for the life-giving sphere of the divine king. "With Yнwн," that is, in his palace, is "the fountain of life"—which refers to the Ancient Near Eastern image of a stream of water emanating from the temple (cf. Ezek 47:1–12). And in Yнwн's light, that is, in the light of his face

---

71 See Müller, *Jahwe als Wettergott* (see n. 4), 204–205.
72 See Hartenstein, *Das Angesicht JHWHs* (see n. 6), 179–182 with n. 107.
73 CAT 1.4 VII 49–52; own translation, see Müller, *Jahwe als Wettergott* (see n. 4), 206, and see M.S. Smith and W.T. Pitard, *The Ugaritic Baal Cycle, vol. II: Introduction with Text, Translation and Commentary of KTU/CAT 1.3–1.4* (VTSup 114; Leiden 2009), 691–694.

which illuminates the eyes of his subject in the audience (Ps 13:4), the congregation sees the essence of the cosmic light that illuminates the world (cf. Gen 1:3–4).

The first part of Psalm 36* (vv. 6, 7*) depicts the cosmic dimensions of Yʜwʜ's royal characteristics and deeds. His "grace" fills the skies, his "faithful deed" extends to the clouds, and his "righteous deed" is comparable with the mountainous seat of the North-West Semitic divine king El who is here imagined as residing in the background of the world, like in the Ugaritic texts[74]; Yʜwʜ's "judgment" is as mighty as "the great Flood" (תהום רבה). Against this cosmic background, the psalm praises Yʜwʜ for "delivering human being and cattle." Human beings and their animal companions always depend on being protected and rescued from life threatening dangers, and only a god who is mighty enough can provide them with such protection.

In the Judean kingdom with its capital Jerusalem, the temple on Mount Zion was imagined as the center of the world. Psalm 48* praises the divine presence on this mountain:[75]

(2)   Great is Yhwh
   and highly to be praised!

   His holy mountain,
(3)   beautiful in elevation,
   joy of the whole earth!

   Mount Zion,
   peak of the Northern Mountain,
   city of a great king!
(4)   < Yʜwʜ > is in her citadels,
   he has shown himself as a fortress.

(9*)   < Yʜwʜ > may establish her forever!

In contrast to geography, Zion is depicted as the peak of the whole earth, the object of world-wide ritual joy. At the same time, Zion is identified with the "Northern Mountain," that is, with Mount Zaphon (צפן) on the north Syrian coast (*Djebel el-Aqra*) which in the second millennium was venerated as the seat of the

---

74 On the veneration of El in the first millenium B.C.E., see I. Kottsieper, "El – ferner oder naher Gott? Zur Bedeutung einer semitischen Gottheit in verschiedenen sozialen Kontexten im 1. Jtsd. v. Chr.," in *Religion und Gesellschaft: Studien zu ihrer Wechselbeziehung in den Kulturen des Antiken Vorderen Orients* (ed. R. Albertz and S. Otto; AOAT 248; Münster 1997), 25–74.
75 On the reconstruction of this song see Müller, *Jahwe als Wettergott* (see n. 4), 183–192.

Ugaritic Baʿal.[76] Yhwh of Zion seems to have been imagined in a similar way to the North-West Semitic Baʿal of Zaphon, although the individual deity name "Yhwh" became inseparably associated with the singular place name "Zion."[77] This was the origin of the so-called Zion theology.

Psalm 48* depicts not only the peak of the world but also the city lying upon it—which mirrors Jerusalem on Mount Zion. Yhwh, the "great king" (מלך רב), is present "in her citadels." The divine kingship finds an earthly mirror in the Jerusalemite kingdom. The statement that Yhwh "has shown himself as a fortress" belongs to this context, since it alludes to situations of besiegement. It is Yhwh who delivers the city from being conquered. The original psalm ends by wishing that this will remain so forever. Like the divine throne that has been established by Yhwh's everlasting kingship (Ps 93:1–2), Yhwh may establish his city forever.

3 Divine and Human Kingship

The divine kingship was regarded as the source of human political power. The earthly king was imagined as being appointed by Yhwh. Ancient Hebrew theology shared this idea with the entire Ancient Near East.[78] Remnants of this concept can be found in the oldest royal psalms.[79]

Psalm 21* was probably composed for the human king's ritual ascension to the throne, perhaps also for the anniversary of his coronation:[80]

(2) Yhwh, in your strength the king is glad,
and in your victorious deed he <rejoices> greatly!

(3*) You have given him his heart's desire,
and the request of his lips you have not withheld.

---

76 The holiness of Mount Zaphon was not forgotten after the downfall of Ugarit in c. 1185 B.C.E., and many sources of the first millenium refer to the Zaphon, see H. Niehr, "Zaphon צפון," *DDD*², 927–929.

77 In this context, it should however not be overlooked that Yhwh of Zion was not the only manifestation of Yhwh in Palestine. Politically and culturally more important seems to have been initially "Yhwh of Samaria," attested by the inscriptions from *Kuntillet ʿAjrud*, although we do not know much about his cult. Some of the earliest psalms, particularly Psalm 29*, may have originated in the Northern Kingdom and only later been imported to the Jerusalemite cult.

78 Cf. the groundbreaking study of H. Frankfort, *Kingship and the Gods: A Study of Ancient Near Eastern Religion as the Integration of Society and Nature* (Chicago 1948).

79 Probably Ps 18*; 21*; 45*; 72*, perhaps also Ps 101*.

80 See Spieckermann, *Heilsgegenwart* (see n. 4), 216.

(4) For you go to meet him with blessings of good,
you set on his head a diadem of gold.

(5) Life he has asked from you, you gave it to him,
length of days forever and ever.

(6) His honor is great in your victorious deed,
splendor and majesty you put on him.

(7) For you make him an abundant blessing forever,
you gladden him with joy at your face.

The king rejoices ritually in Yʜwʜ's "victorious deed" (v. 2) to which he owes his "honor" (כבוד in v. 6). The term "victorious deed" (ישועה) could refer to Yʜwʜ's triumph over superhuman chaotic forces by which he delivered the world from destruction (cf. Ps 93*). Yʜwʜ has crowned the king and given him everlasting life—which points at the supra-individual dimension of dynastic kingship. The human king has received all his power and majesty from the divine king. He is Yʜwʜ's earthly vassal and a mediator of the divine blessing.

His most important task is defending the kingdom from its earthly enemies. This is the topic of the second part of Psalm 21*, which addresses the king himself and promises him victory:[81]

(9) Your hand will find all your enemies,
your right hand will find all those who hate you!

(10*) You will make them like a furnace of fire,
(11) their offspring you will destroy from the earth
and their seed from among humankind!

(13) For you will make them turn their shoulder in flight,
with your bowstrings you will aim against their face.

It is probable that the king's enemies were seen as earthly emissaries of superhuman chaotic powers. By annihilating his human foes, the king completes Yʜwʜ's "victorious deed."

The second half of Ps 18* contains a song of victory that can be interpreted as the king's response to the promise of victory in Ps 21*:

(33) The god who has girded me with strength
and made my way perfect

---

81 Spieckermann, *Heilsgegenwart* (see n. 4), 215.

(34)   made my feet like hinds
        and set me on my high places.

(35*)   He teaches my hands for war,
        and my arms bend the bow.

(38)   I pursue my enemies and I overtake them,
        and I do not return until they are consumed.

(39)   I smite them so that they are not able to rise,
        they fall under my feet.

The singer of this song owes his god all his strength. YHWH, who "has girded himself with strength" when he ascended to the throne (Ps 93:1), girds the royal warrior for the battle. He sets his feet on the high places of his empire as if he himself is striding on the high places of the earth (Deut 33:29; Am 4:13; Mic 1:3) and the sea (Job 9:8). He even teaches the king how to use the bow—which is illustrated by an impressive Egyptian depiction of the war-god Month supporting the Pharaoh in the battle (fig. 3). The song ends by proclaiming complete victory. The king's enemies are not able to rise again; the promise of victory in Ps 21:9 – 13* has been fullfilled.

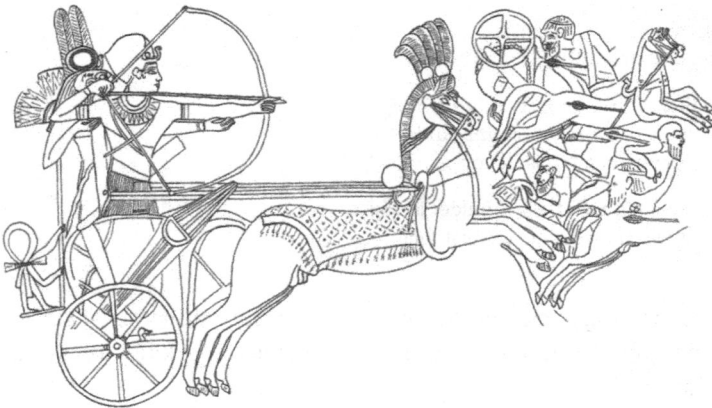

Fig. 3: Wood covered with linen and stucco, from the tomb of Thutmose IV. (1422 – 1413). Drawing by H. Keel-Leu, in O. Keel, *The Symbolism of the Biblical World: Near Eastern Iconography and the Book of Psalms* (trans. T. J. Hallett; Winona Lake, Ind. 1997), fig. 357 on p. 265.

It is certainly no coincidence that the ancient song of victory in the second half of Psalm 18* was placed after the storm-god's theophany in the first half of the psalm in which the fighting storm-god is depicted as an archer (*see above no. 1*). His fight against the chaotic powers is mirrored in the human king's fight against his enemies. In other words, the earthly archer cooperates with the divine archer. This is illustrated by a neo-Assyrian depiction from the 9th century B.C.E. (fig. 4) which shows how a winged storm-god surrounded by flames is flying in the midst of rainy clouds and shooting arrows; below an earthly battle is taking place.[82] The divine arrows seem to have been directed against the human king's enemies.

Fig. 4: Enameled seal from Assur with inscription of Tukulti-Ninurta II. (888–884). Drawing by O. Keel, in Idem, *The Symbolism of the Biblical World*, fig. 295 on p. 216.

This synergism was foundational for the Ancient Hebrew theology of divine and human kingship, but it did not pay too much attention to the ambivalence of the storm-god's deeds. The threatening effects of the storm-god's epiphany that made the earth tremble (Ps 18:8; 29:5–7; 77:19; 97:4) seem to have been interpreted as being directed exclusively against the enemies of the human king. But when the neo-Assyrian expansion endangered the political sovereignty of Israel and Judah, these aspects of the divine became evident in a new way. The early prophecy of doom, which reacted to the political threats and catastrophic events, focused on the eerie and threatening aspects of the divine and referred several times to the ancient theophany tradition.[83]

---

82 See H. Greßmann, *Altorientalische Bilder zum Alten Testament* (Berlin ²1927), 95.

83 E.g., by the motif of "the day of YHWH" which belongs to this tradition, see Jeremias, *Theophanie* (see n. 22), 97–100, and R. Müller, "Der finstere Tag Jahwes: Zum kultischen Hintergrund von Am 5,18–20," *ZAW* 122 (2010), 576–592; or by the motif of the storm-god's "overflowing scourge" in Isa 28:14–18*, see R. Müller, "Adad's Overflowing Scourge and the Weather God

4 Early Soteriology

The theophany of Psalm 18* is framed with a prayer that shows basic aspects of an early soteriology. In the framing passages, a supplicant narrates how he was rescued by YHWH from mortal peril:

(4)   *As the one to be praised, I call on YHWH,*
      and from my enemies I am delivered:

(5)   *The ropes of Death encompassed me,*
      and the torrents of Belial overwhelmed me.

(6)   *The ropes of Sheol encircled me,*
      The snares of Death came to meet me.

(7)   *In my distress I called upon YHWH,*
      and to my god I cried for help.

      From his palace he heard my voice,
      and my cry for help came <> to his ears.

(8)   And the earth shook and trembled,
      so that the foundations of the mountains quaked,
      and they shook because he burned with anger.

(9*) Smoke went up at his nostrils,
      and fire out of his mouth devoured.

(10) And he spread the heavens and came down,
      and thick darkness was under his feet.

(11) And he rode upon a cherub, and did fly,
      he swooped down upon the wings of the wind.

(12) *He made darkness his hiding place,*
      round about him was his booth,
      darkness of waters, thick clouds of the skies.
(13*) *Before him his thick clouds passed,*
      hailstones and coals of fire.

(15) *And he sent out his arrows, and he scattered them,*
      and flashes of lightning manifold, and he confused them.

(16) *Then the beds of <the Sea> appeared,*
      <> the foundations of the world were laid bare.

---

of Zion: Observations on Motif History in Isa 28:14–18," in *Thinking of Water in the Early Second Temple Period* (ed. E. Ben Zvi and C. Levin; BZAW 461; Berlin 2014), 257–277.

(17) *He reaches from on high, he takes me,*
      he draws me out of great waters.

(18) *He rescues me from my strong enemy*
      and from those who hate me for they are stronger than me.

(19) *They come to meet me in the day of my calamity,*
      but Yʜwʜ became a support to me.

(20) *And he brought me out into the wide place,*
      he delivers me because he took pleasure in me.

The forces that threatened the suffering individual belong to the sphere of chaos and destruction; "torrents" and "great waters" (vv. 5, 17) are mentioned together with "Death" (מות), "Sheol" (שאול)—the netherworld as Death's dominion—and "Belial/Wickedness" (בליעל). But the supplicant's cry for help reaches Yʜwʜ's ears in his palace, and the furious Yʜwʜ fights back against the forces of death (vv. 8–16*). He reaches out of his sphere "on high" (v. 17; cf. Ps 93:4) to rescue the supplicant from the devouring floods and to protect him from strong earthly foes. Finally he "brings him out into the wide place"—which combines a horizontal move with the vertical act of deliverance from the raging waters.

The framework of the theophany, which refers explicitly to the divine palace (v. 7), is reminiscent of Psalm 29* and Psalm 97*. In all these psalms, a theophany of the storm-god is combined with the imagery of the enthroned divine king. In this context, the theophany of Psalm 18* was expanded with a crucial motif of the theology of the temple. The dark clouds in which the storm-god hides were identified with "his booth" (v. 12) which refers to the protective sphere of the divine throne room (cf. Ps 27:5; 31:21).[84]

As in all individual psalms, the supplicant of Ps 18:4–20* is stylized with supra-individual traits. On the one hand, the praying "I" cannot be clearly separated from the image of a king. Particularly the "strong enemy" (v. 18) may be imagined as a hostile ruler. On the other hand, this song of thanksgiving does not stress the royal character of the supplicant. In contrast to the song of victory in the second half of Psalm 18 (*see above no. 3*), the supplicant is depicted as a suffering human being. Such a prayer can be spoken in manifold situations, and also individuals who are not kings can pray using these words. This supra-individual dimension is deepened by the imagery of superhuman chaotic forces that threaten all human beings. Just as Yʜwʜ is constantly protecting the world

---

84 On this motif see Hartenstein, *Das Angesicht JHWHs* (see n. 6), 161–170, esp. 168–169 on Ps 18:12.

against these forces, he can also deliver the suffering human being who is threatened to be devoured by them.

The individual human being therefore becomes a mirror of the endangered cosmos. This foundational idea is most impressively explicated in Psalm 57*[85]:

(2) Be gracious to me, < Yhwh >, be gracious to me!
     For in you I have taken refuge,
     and in the shadow of your wings I seek refuge,
     until the destroying forces pass by.

(5*) I am in the midst of lions,
     I must lie down among those who devour,
     whose teeth are spears and arrows
     and whose tongue is a sharp sword.

(7) They set a net for my feet,
     my soul <was bowed down>,
     they dug before me a pit,
     they fell into its midst.

(8) My heart is fixed, < Yhwh >,
     my heart is fixed,
     I will sing and make melody!

(9) Awake, my glory,
     awake, lyre and zither,
     I will awake the Dawn!

(12) Be exalted above the heavens, < Yhwh >,
     let your glory be over all the earth!

The supplicant is threatened by "destroying forces" that materialize in a nightmarish series of images as devouring lions, a besieging army bristling with weapons, and hunters and trappers. But the image of the pit dug by the enemies reminds the supplicant of the sapiential experience that those who try to destroy others sooner or later destroy themselves (Prov 26:27). This experience is based on the idea of a divinely established just order of the world.[86] The individual of Psalm 57* evokes this order with these words of prayer. Initially, the supplicant takes refuge in Yhwh's throne room to await the passing of the mortal peril (v. 2), and immediately before the morning comes, the supplicant's heart "is fixed" to

---

85 See R. Müller, "Das befestigte Herz: Psalm 57 und die kosmologische Dimension der althebräischen Anthropologie," in *Die kleine Biblia: Beiträge zur Theologie der Psalmen und des Psalters* (Biblisch-Theologische Studien 148; Neukirchen Vluyn 2014), 59–82.
86 Hossfeld and Zenger, *Psalmen 51–100* (see n. 65), 128.

make music of praise. This corresponds to the cosmologic idea that the earth is established against chaotic floods by the divine throne (Ps 93:1–2; cf. 24:2; 48:9*; 65:7–8). The praying heart that focuses on Yhwh's kingship participates in the divinely-given stability of the cosmos.[87]

5 The Early Theology of Yhwh in the Architecture of the Psalter

In the literary cathedral of the Psalter, the early Hebrew cultic poetry has been reshaped by added verses and stanzas and many new psalms. These additions changed the theological profile of the psalms, since the new texts present an image of God, the world and human beings that differs in many aspects from the ancient theology.[88] But the ancient theology remained foundational also in later periods. Metaphorically speaking, the early pieces of cultic poetry became the literary and theological pillars of the Psalter. For example, Psalm 18 and Psalm 29 have a key position in their immediate literary contexts in the Psalter, and Psalm 93, Psalm 97 and Psalm 98 became the pillars of the so-called theocratic Psalter (Ps 93–100). In addition, psalms of later origin often quote early poems or modify the ancient theology. Psalm 77 and Psalm 114 relate the divine triumph over the floods with the miracle at the sea (Exod 14–15), Psalm 148 amalgamates Yhwh's power over weather phenomena with a theology of the creative divine word (cf. Gen 1), and several late psalms renew the ancient theology of divine and human kingship in the context of hope for a restituted monarchy (e.g., Ps 20; 132; 144).

The conceptional changes that result from the literary growth of the Psalter are accompanied by an impressive theological continuity. Its center is the idea of the divine king. This idea seems to have originated in rather early stages of Yhwh worship (Ps 29; 93), but psalms of late origin still also refer to the related imagery (e.g., Ps 149; 150). A theology of the Psalter can therefore only be written if sufficient attention is paid to its most ancient fundaments and their contexts in religious history.

---

87 H. Spieckermann, "Der theologische Kosmos des Psalters," *BTZ* 21 (2004), 61–79, here 78.
88 The ancient image is changed particularly by extensive references to Israel's history, "eschatological" perspectives, and the idea of a special relationship of the "righteous ones" (צדיקים) to Yhwh.

Images

I thank Othmar Keel and Hildi Keel-Leu for the permission to print these images.

Ronald Hendel
God and the Gods in the Tetrateuch

> Fire
> God of Abraham, God of Isaac, God of Jacob.
> not of the philosophers and the scholars.
> – Pascal[1]

On November 23, 1654, Blaise Pascal experienced a divine revelation, his "night of fire," whose poetic description he kept in his coat lining until his dying day. In his description, Pascal alludes to several biblical passages in order to articulate the content of his experience. His description begins with the word "Fire," evoking the burning bush and other biblical instances of revelatory fire (e.g., Exod 3:2; Jer 20:9; Acts 2:1–4; 9:3–9). His text continues: "God of Abraham, God of Isaac, God of Jacob." This quotes the divine self-revelation at the burning bush, where God says to Moses: "I am the God of your fathers, God of Abraham, God of Isaac, and God of Jacob" (Exod 3:6, cf. 3:13–15). Pascal is describing his own experience through the lens of this key biblical event, illuminated by the fire that burns but does not consume. Through this tissue of biblical allusions (and there are others in his description), Pascal articulates the meaning of his revelation.[2]

There is also a polemical element in Pascal's text. The God who revealed himself to Pascal is *not* the God of the philosophers and scholars. Who are these philosophers and learned men? A conflict of interpretations circulates in the background of this text. From Pascal's other writings we learn that his adversaries are the Jesuit theologians of Paris, whose views Pascal (himself a devoted Jansenist) excoriated. On the basis of his experience of divine revelation, Pascal negates the reality of the God of his opponents.

From this brief Pascalian reflection, we can draw out some general principles of descriptions of divine revelations that hold true for many revelations in the Hebrew Bible. First, the language used to describe God is in dialogue with previous descriptions, either to affirm them (Exod 3:6) or to deny them (Jesuit

---

1 B. Pascal, "Mémorial": "Feu / Dieu d'Abraham, Dieu d'Isaac, Dieu de Jacob, / non des philosophes et des savants." An earlier version of this essay appeared as "Dios y los dioses en el Tetrateuco," in *Los rostros de Dios: Imágenes y experiencias de lo divino en la Biblia* (ed. C. Bernabé Estella 2013), 43–66.
2 On the elucidation of these lines in *Penseés* fragment 449, see D. Wetsel, *Pascal and Disbelief: Catechesis and Conversion in the Pensées* (Washington 1994), 283–284, and the photo of the "Mémorial" on 344 (pl. XIV).

DOI 10.1515/9783110448221-011

treatises). Second, in this implicit dialogue, social and institutional conflicts are not far from the surface (Jansenists vs. Jesuits). Third, the description focuses on personal experience and cultural memory (viz. past events narrated in the Bible), not rational arguments. That is to say, the text narrates what Pascal calls the reasons of the heart, which are resistant to rational inquiry. In the Bible too, religion is a loose system of practices and beliefs, rooted in collective and personal memories, which in turn are subject to contestation and revision. The truth-claims of religion are persuasive because of reasons of the heart, not because of rational demonstration or systematic theology. In order to take seriously biblical discourses about God, these features need to be taken into account. The representations of revelation are dialogical, critical, and rooted in a dialectic of cultural memory and personal experience. Like Pascal's text, biblical revelations are colored by allusion and resonance more than by exposition.

With these principles in mind, I will address a series of key descriptions of divine revelation in Genesis and Exodus. When viewed in their narrative sequence, these descriptions articulate what we may call native Israelite histories of religion. Each of these sequences – corresponding to the conventional Pentateuchal sources: J, E, and P – represents a distinctive history of religion, including different concepts of God and his relationship to other gods. In a sense, they are alternative memories of the origins of monotheism. However, since the term "monotheism" has its own modern history and theological entailments, it is arguably too blunt an instrument to draw out the nuances of these ancient histories of religion.[3] We need a finer set of analytic tools.

I will be utilizing a scholarly model of the literary history of the Pentateuch – what I call the Standard Model – that has been hotly contested in recent years, mostly within European biblical scholarship.[4] I have elsewhere criticized the assumptions and arguments of the newer European model regarding the non-

---

3 B. Pongratz-Leisten, "A New Agenda for the Study of the Rise of Monotheism," in *Reconsidering the Concept of Revolutionary Monotheism* (ed. B. Pongratz-Leisten; Winona Lake 2011), 1–40, esp. 12–16.
4 I prescind from burdening the reader with a full bibliography, but I note that I accept many of the modifications of the Standard Model by the neo-Documentarian school; see J.S. Baden, *J, E, and the Redaction of the Pentateuch* (Tübingen 2009); idem, *The Composition of the Pentateuch: Renewing the Documentary Hypothesis* (New Haven 2012); B.J. Schwartz, "The Torah: Its Five Books and Four Documents," in *The Literature of the Hebrew Bible: Introduction and Studies* (ed. Z. Talshir; 2 vols.; Jerusalem 2011), 1. 161–226 (in Hebrew); J. Stackert, *A Prophet Like Moses: Prophecy, Law, and Israelite Religion* (New York 2014). However, since aspects of the neo-Documentary methodology are unnecessarily restrictive – e.g. the avoidance of literary criticism (including the central issue of literary style) and historical linguistics – I regard myself as a paleo-Documentarian.

Priestly sources in Genesis, focusing on the continuity of the J source in the primeval and patriarchal narratives.[5] My discussion below will involve the continuity of the J, E, and P sources in Genesis and Exodus, which has also been contested for the non-Priestly sources.[6] I will show that the distinctive native histories of religion involve webs of allusion, argument, and fore- and backshadowing that highlight literary continuities across these books. The source-critical implications of these observations cannot be fully treated here, but I will address them more fully in another study.[7]

This essay is part of a larger project involving cultural memory in the Hebrew Bible. Too often scholars dismiss or ignore the native histories in the Bible in favor of reconstructing an empirically oriented and accurate history of religion. But the histories of religion in the Bible are not just incorrect histories. They are better described as cultural memories, that is, a group's (or authoritative interpreter's) representation of the past with present relevance. The J, E, and P histories of religion portray a collective past that is relevant to the interests of these authors and the social groups to which they belong. Subsequently, the composite text becomes authoritative to other groups, who reinterpret these native histories in ways that retain or regenerate contemporary relevance. This is why the native histories need to be the objects of our study, and not simply rejected as unhistorical or sieved for historically accurate details. It is the task of the scholar as cultural historian to explore the meanings of ancient histories, and not limit oneself to the *realia* of ancient history.

But it is also important to relate these ancient histories to our modern models of the history of Israelite religion. Both kinds of history – the native and the scholarly – are logically intertwined, since in our hermeneutical practices each is an epistemological condition for understanding the other. That is, there is a historical dialectic between the native and the scholarly representations of the history of Israelite religion. A nuanced understanding needs to attend to their reciprocal influences. This reflective task involves the dialectic between the imagined and the actual histories of religion.

---

5 R. Hendel, "Is the 'J' Primeval Narrative an Independent Composition? A Critique of Crüsemann's 'Die Eigenständigkeit der Urgeschichte,'" in *The Pentateuch: International Perspectives on Current Research* (eds. T. B. Dozeman *et al.*; Tübingen 2011), pp. 181–205.

6 See K. Schmid, *Genesis and the Moses Story: Israel's Dual Origins in the Hebrew Bible* (Winona Lake 2010); and the review of scholarship in T. Römer, "Zwischen Urkunden, Fragmenten und Ergänzungen: Zum Stand der Pentateuchforschung," *ZAW* 125 (2013), 2–24.

7 R. Hendel, *"Literaturkritik and Literary Criticism of the Pentateuch,"* forthcoming.

1 God and the Gods in E

The most detailed of the native histories of religion in the Tetrateuch belongs to the E source.[8] I will begin with the event that figured centrally for Pascal: God's revelation to Moses in Exodus 3:4–6:[9]

וַיִּקְרָא אֵלָיו אֱלֹהִים ... וַיֹּאמֶר מֹשֶׁה מֹשֶׁה וַיֹּאמֶר הִנֵּנִי ... וַיֹּאמֶר אָנֹכִי אֱלֹהֵי אָבִיךָ אֱלֹהֵי אַבְרָהָם אֱלֹהֵי יִצְחָק וֵאלֹהֵי יַעֲקֹב וַיַּסְתֵּר מֹשֶׁה פָּנָיו כִּי יָרֵא מֵהַבִּיט אֶל־הָאֱלֹהִים:

God called out to him ... and said, "Moses, Moses." And he said, "Here am I"... And He said, "I am the God of your father, God of Abraham, God of Isaac, and god of Jacob." And Moses hid his face, for he was afraid to look at God. (Exod 3:4–6)

This revelation takes place on the mountain where Moses is commanded to bring the Israelites after the Exodus: "When you lead the people out of Egypt, you will worship God on this mountain" (Exod 3:12). Moses is afraid to look at God, because of the tradition that no one may see God and live (e.g. Gen 32:31). Later at this mountain the people are afraid even to hear God, "lest we die" (Exod 20:16). These details in the revelation to Moses in Exodus 3 motivate and foreshadow the more expansive divine revelation to Israel at Mt. Horeb.

---

8 See above, n. 3. In my view the incompleteness of this source is not a sufficient reason to argue for its nonexistence. The degree of narrative connectivity warrants the hypothesis of E as a once-continuous source. One must infer that portions of E did not survive the redactor's combinatory work. Against this view, see recently J.C. Gertz, "The Miracle at the Sea: Remarks on the Recent Discussion about Origin and Composition of the Exodus Narrative," in *The Book of Exodus: Composition, Reception, and Interpretation* (eds. T.B. Dozeman *et al.*; Leiden 2014), 93–95.
9 On the source analysis of this passage in the (modified) Standard Model, see W. H. C. Propp, *Exodus 1–18* (New York 1999), 192; Stackert, *Moses* (see n. 4), 56–57. The intervening phrase, מִתּוֹךְ הַסְּנֶה ("from the midst of the bush"), is arguably, as many commentators have noted, a redactional insertion that harmonizes the J and E versions of the scene; see Baden, *Redaction* (see n. 4), 269–270; and see below on the word-play between סְנֶה ("bush") and סִינַי (Sinai). For criticisms of the criticisms of the two-source analysis of Exodus 3, see E. Blum, *Studien zur Komposition des Pentateuch* (Berlin 1990), 22–27; idem, "The Literary Connection between the Books of Genesis and Exodus and the End of the Book of Joshua," in *A Farewell to the Yahwist? The Composition of the Pentateuch in Recent European Interpretation* (eds. T.B Dozeman and K. Schmid; Atlanta 2006), 91–96; and Schmid, *Moses Story* (see n. 6), 172–181, both of whom argue that Exodus 3 (at least) is a single unified composition. For additional strata, see J.C. Gertz, *Tradition und Redaktion in der Exoduserzählung: Untersuchungen zur Endredaktion des Pentateuch* (Göttingen 2000), 268–281, 394; and J. Jeon, *The Call of Moses and the Exodus Story: A Redaction-Critical Study* (Tübingen 2013), 87–92.

This revelation also explicitly and implicitly recalls prior revelations in Genesis – a literary technique that Gary Morson calls "back-shadowing."[10] The revelation explicitly recalls Genesis through the terms of God's self-identification: "I am the God of your father, God of Abraham, God of Isaac, and God of Jacob." The initial term, אֱלֹהֵי אָבִיךָ ("God of your father"), has a deliberate ambiguity, since it most naturally refers to Moses' father, but can also refer to a paternal ancestor (or family patriarch) whose personal god has been passed down through the generations. In the rhetoric of the verse, the meaning of the term seems to shift and disambiguate from the first meaning to the second – or more precisely, to a fusion of both – as "God of your father" is identified as "God of Abraham, God of Isaac, and God of Jacob." This shift of focus identifies the God of Moses' immediate lineage with the God of the patriarchs. In God's instructions to Moses later in the chapter, this rhetorical linkage repeats on a collective level: "Thus you shall say to the children of Israel: 'YHWH, the God of your fathers, God of Abraham, God of Isaac, and God of Jacob, sent me to you'" (Exod 3:15). Here the term אֱלֹהֵי אֲבֹתֵיכֶם ("God of your fathers") neatly merges the God of the contemporary Israelite households with the God of the patriarchs. This genealogical link is subtly anticipated in semantics of the name "Israel" – which can signify the patriarch and/or the collective polity – in the command, "say to the children of Israel."[11] The potential polysemy of the phrase "God of your father(s)" is, I suggest, deliberately activated in the rhetoric of these verses.[12]

This backward look identifies the newly revealed God with the God of the patriarchs, thereby establishing a history of religion from Abraham to Moses. In ancient Israel, the identity of an individual is defined by one's place within the patrilineal genealogy; so too here the identity of God is defined by his relationship to the patrilineal genealogy in the *longue durée* of "the children of Israel." The present, as so often in the Bible, is constituted by the shadows and relationships of the past.

In addition to this linkage to patriarchal religion, an implicit back-shadowing of previous divine revelations in Genesis is produced by the resonant word-

---

10 G.S. Morson, *Narrative and Freedom: The Shadows of Time* (New Haven 1994), 234–243.
11 To be more precise, it can mean "descendants of (the patriarch) Israel" and/or "members of (the collective polity) Israel." These are overlapping semantic resonances of the phrase.
12 My analysis contests the argument that the "God of the fathers" in the non-P sources of Exodus did not originally invoke the God of the patriarchs; see recently T. Römer, "The Revelation of the Divine Name to Moses and the Construction of a Memory About the Origins of the Encounter Between Yhwh and Israel," in *Israel's Exodus in Transdisciplinary Perspective* (eds. T.E. Levy *et. al.*; New York 2015), 309–310.

ing of this passage. As commentators have noted,[13] the verbal sequence of God's call to Moses is stylistically identical to two passages in Genesis where God or his angel calls Abraham and Jacob:

וַיֹּאמֶר מֹשֶׁה מֹשֶׁה וַיֹּאמֶר הִנֵּנִי

And He said, "Moses, Moses." And he said, "Here am I." (Exod 3:4)

וַיֹּאמֶר אַבְרָהָם אַבְרָהָם וַיֹּאמֶר הִנֵּנִי

And He said, "Abraham, Abraham." And he said, "Here am I." (Gen 22:11)

וַיֹּאמֶר יַעֲקֹב יַעֲקֹב וַיֹּאמֶר הִנֵּנִי

And He said, "Jacob, Jacob." And he said, "Here am I." (Gen 46:2)

These are the only passages with this particular emphatic style, with the name of the person doubled, followed by the deictic, הִנֵּנִי ("Here am I").

There are also two variations on this style in Genesis, where God or his angel calls Abraham and Jacob, but the name is called only once:

וַיֹּאמֶר אֵלָיו אַבְרָהָם וַיֹּאמֶר הִנֵּנִי

And he said to him, "Abraham." And he said, "Here am I." (Gen 22:1)

וַיֹּאמֶר אֵלַי מַלְאַךְ הָאֱלֹהִים בַּחֲלוֹם יַעֲקֹב וָאֹמַר הִנֵּנִי

And the angel of God said to me in a dream, "Jacob." And I said, "Here am I." (Gen 31:11)

God's call to Abraham in Gen 22:1 is echoed and intensified by the angel's dramatic call in Gen 22:11.[14] Similarly, the angelic call to Jacob in Gen 31:11 is echoed and, in a sense, resumed in God's final call in Gen 46:2.

---

13 See M. Köckert, *Vätergott und Väterverheissungen* (Göttingen 1988), 321–322, who emphasizes the verbal links between Exod 3:4–12 and Gen 46:2–4; E. Blum, *Die Komposition der Vätergeschichte* (Neukirchen-Vluyn 1984), 247, who emphasizes the links between Gen 46:2–4 and Gen 31:11,13.; and Schmid, *Moses Story* (see n. 6), 55–57, who discounts the link with Exod 3:4.
14 The speaker in Gen 22:11 is arguably the מלאך אלהים ("angel of God"), a reading preserved in the Peshitta. The reading מלאך יהוה ("angel of YHWH") in MT, SP, and LXX is likely a scribal harmonization with the מלאך יהוה in the second angelic speech in Gen 22:15 (the latter is generally recognized as an editorial expansion); see J. Skinner, *A Critical and Exegetical Commentary on Genesis* (Edinburgh ²1930), 330. The reading אלהים in 4QGen-Exod[a] of Gen 22:14 (vs. יהוה in MT, SP, and LXX) adds substance to this argument; see J.R. Davila, "The Name of God at Moriah: An Unpublished Fragment from 4QGenExod[a]," *JBL* 110 (1991), 577–582.

Only one of these passages contains "promise" language (Gen 46:3, כִּי־לְגוֹי גָּדוֹל אֲשִׂימְךָ שָׁם, "For there I will make you into a great nation "),[15] but the others do not, so we cannot consign these to a "promises" stratum.[16]

Each of these verses from the E source describes a divine revelation. It seems evident that these dramatic moments in the E narrative stylistically echo each other. These moments illuminate E's literary style and long-range compositional structure. In the divine revelation to Moses, the language of God's call implicitly links the scene with the previous revelations to the patriarchs, subtly announcing that Moses is the new chosen patriarch or leader, whom God calls to be the agent of major events in Israelite religious history.

The stylistic echo or allusion to the Jacob passage in Gen 46:2–4 is particularly intriguing, since in it God promises Jacob a personal Exodus from Egypt:

וַיֹּאמֶר יַעֲקֹב יַעֲקֹב וַיֹּאמֶר הִנֵּנִי: וַיֹּאמֶר אָנֹכִי הָאֵל אֱלֹהֵי אָבִיךָ אַל־תִּירָא מֵרְדָה מִצְרַיְמָה כִּי־לְגוֹי גָּדוֹל אֲשִׂימְךָ שָׁם: אָנֹכִי אֵרֵד עִמְּךָ מִצְרַיְמָה וְאָנֹכִי אַעַלְךָ גַם־עָלֹה וְיוֹסֵף יָשִׁית יָדוֹ עַל־עֵינֶיךָ:

And He said, "Jacob, Jacob." And he said, "Here am I." And He said, "I am God, the God of your father. Do not be afraid of going down to Egypt. For I will make you into a great people there. I will go down with you to Egypt, and I will surely bring you up. And Joseph will set his hand on your eyes." (Gen 46:2–4)

God's self-identification as אֱלֹהֵי אָבִיךָ ("the God of your father") is the same as the self-identification to Moses in Exodus 3. The promise of a personal Exodus – "I will go down with you to Egypt, and I will surely bring you up" – is a subtle foreshadowing of the Exodus story.[17] In Genesis the promise concerns the return of Jacob (or, as God seems to hint, his embalmed corpse) from Egypt to be buried in his ancestral land. The language of this promise to Jacob oscillates between the individual patriarch and his collective offspring, since God will make Jacob into a גוֹי גָּדוֹל ("great people") in Egypt. The Exodus of an individual will expand into the Exodus of Jacob's descendants, whom God will "bring up from this land" (Exod 3:8).

---

15 The alliterative phrase, גּוֹי גָּדוֹל ("great nation"), occurs elsewhere in E: Gen 21:18; Exod 32:10. It also occurs in J (Gen 12:2; 18:18; Num 14:2) and P (Gen 17:20).

16 See recently J.S. Baden, *The Promise to the Patriarchs* (New York 2013), 119–126, who emphasizes the distinctive E language in the promise passages located in the E source, e.g. אַל־תִּירָא ("Fear not") in Gen 46:3 and אַל־תִּירְאִי (ditto, to Hagar) in Gen 21:17.

17 So Blum, *Komposition* (see n. 13), 247; Köckert, *Vätergott* (see n. 13), 322; Gertz, *Tradition* (see n. 9), 278. But cf. Schmid, *Moses Story* (see n. 6), 56, who argues that "Gen 46:1–5a has been formulated for the purpose of encompassing only the ancestral story in Genesis 12–50" and does "not [look forward] to the return of Israel in Exodus."

The Mosaic revelation in Exod 3:3–6 echoes and alludes to previous revelations to Jacob and Abraham in Genesis, deepening the content of the new revelation and constructing the progression of the history of religion in the E narrative. God's promises to the patriarchs are activated by these allusions, but these promises seem to have been forgotten by the Israelites during the Egyptian bondage. The wording of God's revelation to Moses explicitly and implicitly activates these narrative memories. When God says to Moses, "I am the God of your father, God of Abraham, God of Isaac, and god of Jacob… I have come down to rescue them from the hand of Egypt and to bring them up from this land" (Exod 3:6, 8); the history of Israelite religion is renewed. God reminds Moses of the past history of religion, and the language of the narration evokes the literary memory of past revelations in the E text.

The native history constructed by this web of allusions and echoes is supplemented by another key event in E. Gen 35:1–7 presents an earlier renewal of Israelite religion. In this passage, God commands Jacob to dwell in Bethel and "build there an altar to the God who appeared to you when you fled from Esau, your brother," referring to the divine revelation recounted in Gen 28:10–22.[18] Then Jacob turns to address his family and household, commanding them to abandon the foreign gods that they served in Haran:

הָסִרוּ אֶת־אֱלֹהֵי הַנֵּכָר אֲשֶׁר בְּתֹכְכֶם וְהִטַּהֲרוּ וְהַחֲלִיפוּ שִׂמְלֹתֵיכֶם: וְנָקוּמָה וְנַעֲלֶה בֵּית־אֵל וְאֶעֱשֶׂה־שָּׁם מִזְבֵּחַ לָאֵל הָעֹנֶה אֹתִי בְּיוֹם צָרָתִי וַיְהִי עִמָּדִי בַּדֶּרֶךְ אֲשֶׁר הָלָכְתִּי:

Put aside the foreign gods that are in your midst, and purify yourselves and change your clothes. And we will arise and go up to Bethel, and there I will make an altar to the God who answered me on the day of my distress, and who has been with me on the road on which I have walked. (Gen 35:2–3)

This is the only mention of אֱלֹהֵי הַנֵּכָר ("foreign gods") in the Tetrateuch. In order to serve the God who revealed himself to Jacob at Bethel (בֵּית אֵל, lit. "House of God"), Jacob's household must set aside other gods from foreign lands and purify themselves. These rites of separation prepare for a key moment in E's history of religion. The renewal of the worship of God at Bethel seems to represent, for Jacob's family, a transformation from a polytheism that includes foreign gods to the worship of God alone. This is E's rite of passage to Israelite monotheism (or perhaps better, monolatry). The presumption is that Jacob's family had been wor-

---

18 This revelation is primarily E, with J or J-like material in 28:13–15; see recently R. Hendel, "Cultural Memory," in *Reading Genesis: Ten Methods* (ed. R. Hendel; New York 2010), 33–38; and the alternative analysis of E. Blum, "The Jacob Tradition," in *The Book of Genesis: Composition, Reception, and Interpretation* (eds. C.A. Evans *et al.*; Leiden 2012), 197–203.

shiping other gods – either exclusively or alongside the God of Jacob – and have brought their divine icons back with them. An explicit illustration is Rachel's possession of her father's household gods. In Gen 31:19 we learn that "Rachel stole the Teraphim that belonged to her father," and later in the story Laban clarifies what these stolen go(o)ds are: לָמֶּה גָנַבְתָּ אֶת־אֱלֹהָי ("Why did you steal my gods?" Gen 31:30). Before rededicating themselves to Israelite religion, Jacob's family must put away these foreign gods, which Laban identifies as *his* gods.[19]

What is the relationship between God and these foreign gods? Clearly Jacob's family must abandon them in order to serve the God of the patriarchs. But are they to do so because they are false gods, or simply because they are other people's gods? The emphasis in E seems to be on the latter. There are two indications that it is the "otherness" of these gods, and not their divinity, that is the issue. First, Jacob provides the foreign gods with a decent burial at a sacred place. Second, elsewhere the E source seems to acknowledge the gods of other peoples. Let us examine these two points further.

When Jacob commands his household to put aside their foreign gods, they immediately oblige: "They gave to Jacob all the foreign gods that were in their hands and the rings that were in their ears. And Jacob buried them beneath the oak tree near Shechem" (Gen 35:4). This burial site, the אֵלָה ("oak, terebinth") near Shechem, is known elsewhere. In the J source the tree is called the אֵלוֹן מוֹרֶה ("oak of the teacher[?]") and is the site of YHWH's revelation to Abram where He promises: "To your seed I will give this land" (Gen 12:6 – 7). In the Deuteronomistic History, Joshua renews the covenant at this site and quotes Gen 35:2: הָסִירוּ אֶת־אֱלֹהֵי הַנֵּכָר אֲשֶׁר בְּקִרְבְּכֶם ("Put aside the foreign gods that are in your midst," Josh 24:23). This command is identical to Gen 35:2 with the exception of the last word, which is a synonym. The burial of foreign gods at the sacred site of Shechem seems to convey a sense of respect, even reverence, for these cultic objects. Elsewhere in the ancient Near East, there are indications that religious objects were ritually "terminated" by burial at or near a shrine.[20] This scene at Bethel is not a violent destruction of a foreign icon, as when Moses burns and

---

19 It is possible that these objects represent deified ancestors, as argued by T. J. Lewis and K. van der Toorn, "Teraphim," *TDOT* XV (eds. G.J. Botterweck *et al.*; Grand Rapids 2006), 783. However, Laban does not make this distinction, simply calling them "my gods," the normal locution for family gods.

20 For examples of (presumably intentionally) damaged statuary buried at cultic sites from Late Bronze Age Megiddo and Hazor, interpreted as "termination rituals," see S. Zuckerman, "Anatomy of a Destruction: Crisis Architecture, Termination Rituals and the Fall of Canaanite Hazor," *JMA* 20 (2007), 3 – 32. My thanks to Marian Feldman for this reference.

pulverizes the Golden Calf (Exod 32:20; see below), but apparently a sacred burial. The denunciations of foreign icons in the prophets and the Deuteronomic History condition us to read this burial in a negative light. But the narrative tone and the ancient Near Eastern context suggests that polytheistic worship is here put aside respectfully.

The oddity of this peaceful transition from foreign polytheism to Israelite monotheism is underscored by a textual plus in the Septuagint of Gen 35:4. After the sentence, "And Jacob buried them under the oak tree near Shechem," the Septuagint reads "and he destroyed them until today." The Greek plus, καὶ ἀπώλεσεν αὐτὰ ἕως τῆς σήμερον ἡμέρας, presupposes a Hebrew *Vorlage* that was, approximately, ויאבד אתם עד היום. This piece of scribal exegesis indicates the troubling nature of the burial rite in Gen 35:4. The Deuteronomic command to destroy foreign icons (e.g. Deut 12:2–3) is harmonized into this text, which – to the dismay of the proto-LXX scribe – seems to take a fairly irenic view of the gods of Haran.

Elsewhere the E source also seems to have a tolerant attitude toward foreign gods. In the covenant between Jacob and Laban at the boundary-land in Gilead, Laban makes a binding oath: אֱלֹהֵי אַבְרָהָם וֵאלֹהֵי נָחוֹר יִשְׁפְּטוּ בֵינֵינוּ ("May the God of Abraham and the God of Nahor judge between us," Gen 31:53). The clear implication of this legal formula, with the verb יִשְׁפְּטוּ ("judge") in the plural, is that these are two different gods. In this oath by Laban – who is explicitly called "the Aramean" in this chapter (Gen 31:20, 24) and speaks Aramaic (31:47) – the god of his grandfather, Nahor, is likely also an implicitly Aramean god.[21] In his response to Laban's oath, Jacob characteristically sidesteps the dilemma of swearing by a foreign god by a clever ruse. He swears by neither the God of Nahor nor the God of Abraham, but by the God of his father, Isaac: וַיִּשָּׁבַע יַעֲקֹב בְּפַחַד אָבִיו יִצְחָק ("And Jacob swore by the Fear of his father, Isaac"). Jacob uses the intimidating divine epithet פַּחַד ("Fear, Terror") as a sly reminder of the power of Jacob's God, who had the previous night threatened Laban in a divine revelation (Gen 31:24, 29). In this exchange between Laban and Jacob, the God of Nahor seems to be a foreign god, distinct from the God of Abraham. But there is no hint of dangerous idolatry here, only an evasive response by Jacob, which ensures the truce with his father-in-law.

A comparable view of foreign polytheism in E is earlier evinced by Abraham when he explains to the Philistine king Abimelech why he had been duplicitous about his relationship to Sarah: "When the Gods caused me to wander from the house of my father, I said to her .... Say of me, "He is my brother"" (Gen 20:13).

---

21 See M.S. Smith, *God in Translation* (Tübingen 2008), 104–107.

Abraham is, of course, being polite to the foreign king, but the plural verb הִתְעוּ ("caused me to wander") makes it clear that the subject, אֱלֹהִים, ("God, gods"), is in the plural. In dealing with foreigners and foreign gods, Abraham is as discreet as Jacob is sly.

Beyond this apparently irenic position toward other peoples' gods, the E source has a more familiar harsh attitude toward Israelites who, after the rite of passage in Genesis 35, backslide and worship foreign gods. A curious detail in the ritual acts of Genesis 35 may signal this dangerous contingency. Along with setting aside their foreign icons, Jacob's household also sets aside הַנְּזָמִים אֲשֶׁר בְּאָזְנֵיהֶם ("the rings that were in their ears," Gen 35:4). Jacob then buries the earrings with the foreign gods. The curious link between earrings and foreign gods seems to be an anticipatory detail, which is taken up in the Golden Calf story, another key event in E's history of religion. There Aaron commands the Israelites: "Take off the gold rings that are in the ears of your wives, sons, and daughters (נִזְמֵי הַזָּהָב אֲשֶׁר בְּאָזְנֵי נְשֵׁיכֶם בְּנֵיכֶם וּבְנֹתֵיכֶם), and bring them to me" (Exod 32:2). From these gold earrings Aaron makes the Golden Calf, with disastrous results. Aaron here seems to be a kind of anti-Jacob, reconstituting a foreign icon from the earrings of the people. To worship a foreign god after having entered into the covenant with God is a dangerous sin, which provokes his deadly wrath. For Israelites to worship foreign gods is, at this point, a breach of sacred boundaries with deadly consequences.

As many commentators have noted, the Golden Calf story bears an obvious relationship to the depiction in of the sin of Jeroboam in 1 Kings 12, where he sets up "two golden calves" for the people to worship at the shrines of Bethel and Dan. Jeroboam proclaims: "These are your gods, O Israel, who brought you up from the land of Egypt" (1 Kgs 12:28). The plural verb הֶעֱלוּךְ ("brought you up") clarifies that the subject אֱלֹהֶיךָ ("God, gods") is plural. The same sentence occurs in the Golden Calf story (Exod 32:4), where it is spoken by the idolatrous Israelites. The allusion in Exodus to the northern cult is clear. As many scholars have noted, the Golden Calf story "can only be understood as a condemnation of the established religion of Northern Israel, and at the same time of the priests connected with it, who probably traced their descent from Aaron."[22]

---

22 A. Kuenen, *An Historico-Critical Inquiry into the Origin and Composition of the Hexateuch* (trans. P.H. Wicksteed; London 1886), 245; and more recently G.N. Knoppers, "Aaron's Calf and Jeroboam's Calves," in *Fortunate the Eyes that See: Essays in Honor of David Noel Freedman* (eds. A.B. Beck *et al.*; Grand Rapids 1995), 92–104; and C.E. Hayes, "Golden Calf Stories: The Relationship of Exodus 32 and Deuteronomy 9–10," in *The Idea of Biblical Interpretation: Essays in Honor of James L. Kugel* (eds. H. Najman and J.H. Newman; Leiden 2004), 45–93.

The danger of foreign gods for Israelites is here polemically attached to the religion of the Northern Kingdom and, in particular, the cultic sites of Bethel and Dan. The E source is arguing against his adversaries about the proper forms of Israelite religious worship. He does this by characterizing the God of his adversaries as foreign gods. This *translatio damnatio* is elegantly conveyed in parallelistic style in the introduction to the Covenant Code in E:[23]

לֹא תַעֲשׂוּן אִתִּי אֱלֹהֵי כֶסֶף
וַאלֹהֵי זָהָב לֹא תַעֲשׂוּ לָכֶם

Do not make with me gods of silver,
And gods of gold do not make for yourselves. (Exod 20:23)

By implicitly polemicizing against the worship of foreign gods at Bethel and Dan, the E source alleges a backsliding from the separation from foreign gods in Genesis 35, which was a necessary part of the founding of Bethel as a sacred shrine. The rite of passage of Jacob's household from foreign polytheism to Israelite monotheism has been undone. Like Pascal, the E source inveighs against his adversaries in the religious establishment, alleging an atavistic worship of foreign gods, not the God of Abraham, Isaac, and Jacob.

2 God and the Gods in J

The revelation at the burning bush in J is comparable to the revelation on the holy mountain in E, but with a key difference. The name of God has already been revealed in Genesis. The J description of the revelation to Moses in Exodus 3 begins as follows:

> An angel of YHWH appeared to him in a flaming fire in the midst of the bush. And he looked and behold – the bush was burning with fire, but the bush was not consumed. And Moses said, "Let me turn aside so I might see this great sight, why the bush is not burned." (Exod 3:2–3)

In the Leitwort style of biblical prose, the revelation to Moses at the סְנֶה ("bush") is a wordplay with the future revelation at סִינַי (Sinai), which also burns with fire: "Mount Sinai was all in smoke because YHWH had descended on it in fire" (Exod 19:18). The latter is a full-sensory theophany, accompanied by lightning, thunder,

---

23 On this text and its context, see S. Chavel, "A Kingdom of Priests and its Earthen Altars in Exodus 19–24," *VT* 65 (2015), 172–175, 181–185.

quaking, fire, and the sound of horns. YHWH will later again descend to Sinai in J to reveal himself to Moses (Exod 34:5 – 9), a revelation I will address below.

But the worship of YHWH, according to J's history of religion, is already ancient. According to Gen 4:26, the first to call on YHWH's name was Enosh, Adam's grandson. The text reads (with some uncertainty in the first phrase): אָז הוּחַל (M זֶה הֵחֵל) לִקְרֹא בְּשֵׁם יְהוָה ("He was first to call on the name of YHWH").[24] It is not entirely clear what the act of "calling on the name of YHWH" consists of, but it probably has a range of religious connotations, viz. speech of divine praise, thanks, lament, request, etc. The key point for J's history of religion is that the worship of YHWH is the first religion of primeval human-kind. Cain and Abel have offered sacrificial offerings to YHWH (מִנְחָה לַיהוָה, Gen 4:3 – 4), and now Enosh begins the worship of YHWH at the level of religious speech, including prayer and other practices.

The implications of these events for J's history of religion are far-reaching. YHWH seems to be the sole God in antiquity. After he wakes from his drunken-ness, Noah blesses "YHWH, the God of Shem" (Gen 9:26), indicating that YHWH is the God of all the "Semitic" peoples. The first great Mesopotamian king, Nimrod, is a proverbial "mighty hunter before YHWH" (Gen 10:9), which seems to present YHWH as the patron god of Babylonia and Assyria. The angel of YHWH conveys a promise of many descendants to Hagar the Egyptian, for "YHWH has heard your suffering" (Gen 16:11). Hagar's descendants are the Ishmaelites, nomadic Arabi-an tribes. All of these peoples are under YHWH's sole authority. They are also subject to his dispensation of justice, as various peoples discover, including the builders of Babylon (Gen 11:1 – 9), the Egyptian pharaoh (Gen 12:17) and the inhabitants of Sodom and Gomorrah (Genesis 19).

The "other gods" included in J's history of religion in Genesis and Exodus are divine beings who are subservient to YHWH. There are מַלְאָכִים ("angels"), who convey YHWH's messages, make inquiries on his behalf, and otherwise rep-resent YHWH to humans. There are also the בְּנֵי הָאֱלֹהִים ("Sons of God"), who ap-pear only once in J, in Gen 6:1 – 4, where they marry human women and father a race of mighty warriors. The Sons of God are divine beings known elsewhere in the Bible, and are cognate with divine collectives in other Northwest Semitic re-ligions.[25] Notably, in the Song of Moses in Deuteronomy 32, the Sons of God are

---

24 See R. Hendel, *The Text of Genesis 1 – 11: Textual Studies and Critical Edition* (New York 1998), 49; and generally C. Westermann, *Genesis 1 – 11* (Minneapolis 1984), 339 – 341; M. Witte, *Die bib-lische Urgeschichte* (Berlin 1998), 61 – 65.

25 See R. Hendel, "The Nephilim Were On the Earth: Genesis 6:1 – 4 and Its Ancient Near East-ern Context," in *The Fall of the Angels* (eds. C. Auffarth and L. Stuckenbruck; Leiden 2004), 11 – 34.

the gods of other nations (Deut 32:8, reading with LXX and 4QDeut[q]; see similarly Deut 4:19 and Psalm 82).[26] But this is not the role of these deities in J. They are simply randy gods, subservient to Yhwh, who overstep their bounds in the chaotic times before the flood. Yhwh takes no direct action against them, and acts instead to secure a limit to human lifespan (Gen 6:3), so that these mixed marriages do not permanently blur the boundary between humans and gods.

In later times, the lure of Moabite gods is castigated in J, in particular a local Moabite deity, the Baal of Peor (Num 25:1–5). Moabite women seduce Israelite men to worship this god, combining the seduction of foreign women with that of foreign gods (cf. Solomon in 1 Kgs 11:1–5). For Israelite men as well as divine males, the lure of sex has the power to efface proper boundaries of religious practice, leaving the restoration of order to Yhwh's judgment and, on this and other occasions, his deadly wrath.

Enosh is the first to call on Yhwh, but there are others. The legacy of Enosh is taken up by the patriarchs, as the statement, "he called on the name of Yhwh," becomes a refrain.[27] These repetitions seem to signal an expansion (by founding new places of worship) or deepening (the Sinai theophany in Exodus 33–34) of Yhwh worship. The history of religion narrows to a particular lineage, but the global scope still obtains, since, as Yhwh promises Abraham: "all the peoples of the earth will be blessed through you" (Gen 12:3). Abraham calls on the name of Yhwh three times, twice at a cultic site he builds between Bethel and Ai, and once at a cultic site he founds at Beersheba. Notice the slight variations in the repetitions of the key words in these scenes of Abraham as cult-founder:

וַיִּבֶן־שָׁם מִזְבֵּחַ לַיהוָה וַיִּקְרָא בְּשֵׁם יְהוָה

And he built there an altar to Yhwh and he called on the name of Yhwh. (Gen 12:8)

וַיִּקְרָא שָׁם אַבְרָם בְּשֵׁם יְהוָה

And there Abram called on the name of Yhwh. (Gen 13:4)

וַיִּטַּע אֶשֶׁל בִּבְאֵר שָׁבַע וַיִּקְרָא־שָׁם בְּשֵׁם יְהוָה אֵל עוֹלָם

And he planted a tamarisk tree at Beersheba, and he called there on the name of Yhwh, God Most High. (Gen 21:33)

Later Isaac builds an altar at the cultic site at Beersheba:

---

26 On these texts, see recently P. Machinist, "How Gods Die, Biblically and Otherwise: A Problem of Cosmic Restructuring," in Pongratz-Leisten, *Monotheism* (see n. 3), 196–228.

27 See Blum, *Komposition* (see n. 13), 334–338, who focuses on the patriarchal altar passages; and Witte, *Urgeschichte* (see n. 24), 276–282; both of whom regard these as redactional layers.

וַיִּבֶן שָׁם מִזְבֵּחַ וַיִּקְרָא בְּשֵׁם יְהוָה

And he built there an altar, and he called on the name of YHWH. (Gen 26:25)

This Leitwort sequence culminates with YHWH's last revelation to Moses at the holy site of Sinai in J (Exodus 33:12–34:9).[28]

וְקָרָאתִי בְשֵׁם יְהוָה

And I will call on the name of YHWH. (Exod 33:19)

וַיִּקְרָא בְשֵׁם יְהוָה

And he called on the name of YHWH (Exod 34:5)

This last sequence requires further elucidation. At Sinai Moses asks YHWH: הַרְאֵנִי נָא אֶת־כְּבֹדֶךָ ("Please show me your Glory," Exod 33:18). The term, כְּבוֹד יְהוָה ("Glory of YHWH"), seems here to denote, as Benjamin Sommer states, "God's intensely bright body, which is normally surrounded by a cloud."[29] Moses wants a closer look.

YHWH replies positively: אֲנִי אַעֲבִיר כָּל־טוּבִי עַל־פָּנֶיךָ וְקָרָאתִי בְשֵׁם יְהוָה לְפָנֶיךָ ("I indeed will make all my goodness pass before you, and I will call on the name of YHWH before you," Exod 33:19). Here we have a repetition of the formula "calling on the name of YHWH," but now framed as a future intention and placed in the mouth of YHWH himself. This is a striking variation on previous uses of these key words – what does it mean for YHWH to call on the name of YHWH?

The question is answered, and the formula repeated twice with variation, when YHWH reveals himself to Moses the next day. In the first repetition:

וַיֵּרֶד יְהוָה בֶּעָנָן וַיִּתְיַצֵּב עִמּוֹ שָׁם וַיִּקְרָא בְשֵׁם יְהוָה וַיַּעֲבֹר יְהוָה עַל־פָּנָיו

YHWH descended in a cloud and he stood with him there. And he called on the name of YHWH. And YHWH passed before him (Exod 34:5–6)

YHWH is revealing himself literally – at least in part – to Moses (as promised in Exod 33:22–23). But the speaker who is calling on the name of YHWH here is not entirely clear – it could be Moses or YHWH. It seems more natural for Moses to be the one calling, since YHWH is standing next to him, and YHWH calls out his own name in the following sequence. But YHWH's previous promise, "I will call on the

---

28 On the source analysis of this text, see Baden, *Redaction* (see n. 4), 166–172. Note that Exod 34:11–26 (and portions of verse 10) are a later redaction; see S. Gesundheit, *Three Times a Year: Studies on Festival Legislation in the Pentateuch* (Tübingen 2012), 12–43.
29 B.D. Sommer, *The Bodies of God and the World of Ancient Israel* (Cambridge 2009), 61.

name of Yʜᴡʜ before you" (Exod 33:19), makes the identity of the speaker ambiguous. This ambiguity may be deliberate, perhaps evoking the awesome and
confusing aura of this scene. Calling on the name of Yʜᴡʜ in this final Sinaitic
revelation has multiple senses, as Yʜᴡʜ's name is called upon, but in different
ways.

Yʜᴡʜ proceeds to call out his name expansively, in a sense revealing the
deeper meaning of his name. This is a key moment in J's history of religion, comparable to the revelation of the divine name Yʜᴡʜ in the E and P sources.[30]

וַיִּקְרָא יְהֹוָה יְהֹוָה אֵל רַחוּם וְחַנּוּן אֶרֶךְ אַפַּיִם וְרַב־חֶסֶד וֶאֱמֶת נֹצֵר חֶסֶד לָאֲלָפִים נֹשֵׂא עָוֹן וָפֶשַׁע וְחַטָּאָה וְנַקֵּה לֹא
יְנַקֶּה פֹּקֵד עֲוֹן אָבוֹת עַל־בָּנִים וְעַל־בְּנֵי בָנִים עַל־שִׁלֵּשִׁים וְעַל־רִבֵּעִים

He called, "Yʜᴡʜ, Yʜᴡʜ, God compassionate and gracious, slow in anger and abundant in
kindness and truth, keeping kindness for thousands of generations, requiting iniquity,
transgression, and sin – yet not remitting punishment, visiting the sins of the fathers
upon the children and the children's children, upon the third and fourth generations."
(Exod 34:6–7)

This self-revelation culminates the long history of religious founders calling on
the name of Yʜᴡʜ. The formula, hearkening back to Enosh, Abraham, Isaac,
and (perhaps) Moses, takes on a new dimension when Yʜᴡʜ calls out his glorious name: "He called, "Yʜᴡʜ, Yʜᴡʜ ..." (Or, less likely, "Yʜᴡʜ called, "Yʜᴡʜ
...") This is not a revelation of the כְּבוֹד יְהֹוָה ("Glory of Yʜᴡʜ") as a fiery anthropomorphic body, but as, in William Propp's words, "a verbal portrait of Yʜᴡʜ's
personality."[31] The revelation does not focus on Yʜᴡʜ's bodily presence, and instead magnifies and elucidates the attributes of his glorious name. God's revelation is a verbal exegesis of his own essence. As Jean-Pierre Sonnet comments,
"the self-naming God ... stands out as the master of his own characterization."[32]
The ethical dialectic of justice and compassion – whose outworking has been
shown in many J texts (e. g. the Garden of Eden, Cain and Abel, Sodom and Go-

---

30 The last sequence quotes from Exod 20:5 and may be a secondary expansion. On recent interpretations of this passage, see R. Scoralick, *Gottes Güte und Gottes Zorn: Die Gottesprädikationen in Exodus 34,6f und ihre Intertextuellen Beziehungen zum Zwölfprophetenbuch* (Freiburg
2002).
31 W.H.C. Propp, *Exodus 19–40* (New Haven 2006), 611.
32 J.-P. Sonnet, "*Ehyeh asher ehyeh* (Exodus 3:14): God's 'Narrative Identity' among Suspense,
Curiosity, and Surprise," *Poetics Today* 31 (2010), 347.

morrah, the Joseph story) – is now shown to be the deep content of Yʜᴡʜ's character.[33]

The Leitwort formula, "he called on the name of Yʜᴡʜ," takes an unexpected turn and opens a new era in the history of religion when Yʜᴡʜ calls out his own name at Sinai. Yʜᴡʜ apparently exposes his physical Glory to Moses, but the focus is Yʜᴡʜ's verbal revelation of his ethical character. In J there is no giving of the law at Sinai,[34] but a revelation of Yʜᴡʜ's dialectical attributes of compassion and justice. The promise of seeing God's glorious body turns – surprisingly, with dramatic irony – into a revelatory discourse about Yʜᴡʜ's ethical essence.[35] In this theophany we are shown, at last, the deeper entailment of "calling on Yʜᴡʜ's name," which people have been doing intermittently since the time of Enosh.

3 Excursus: The Smallest Literary Unit

As I have acknowledged, the source-critical analysis presupposed by my discussion is highly contested in (primarily) European scholarship. The primary reason is as follows. In Rolf Rendtorff's programmatic work, particularly in Das überlieferungsgeschichtliche Problem des Pentateuch (1977), he argued that the methodology and presuppositions of source criticism conflict with that of form-criticism and tradition-historical criticism. He maintained that the two approaches "are opposed to each other in their starting point and in their statement of the question."[36] The isolation of the "smallest literary unit" (kleinste literarische Einheit) characteristic of the latter method, he maintained, should be translated into the procedures of source-criticism. Tradition and composition are thereby conflated. I maintain that there are several logical problems with this argument.

First, as Julius Wellhausen and Hermann Gunkel clearly articulated, the composers of the Pentateuchal sources arguably combined disparate narratives

---

33 On the dialectic of justice and compassion in Yʜᴡʜ's relationship to humans, see D.A. Lambert, How Repentance Became Biblical: Judaism, Christianity, and the Interpretation of Scripture (New York 2015), 24–28.
34 See B.J. Schwartz, "The Priestly Account of the Theophany and Lawgiving at Sinai," in Texts, Temples, and Traditions: A Tribute to Menahem Haran (eds. M.V. Fox et al.; Winona Lake 1996), 128; Baden, Composition (see n. 4), 77–78.
35 Cf. Yʜᴡʜ evocation of דֶּרֶךְ יְהוָה, "the way of Yʜᴡʜ," in the prelude to the Sodom and Gomorrah story (Gen 18:19).
36 R. Rendtorff, The Problem of the Process of Transmission in the Pentateuch (trans. J.J. Scullion; Sheffield 1990), 11.

that circulated in Israelite oral tradition. As Wellhausen writes: "In themselves, heterogenous components do not exclude the unity and naturalness of a written connection; it is possible that already the first [written] recording of the oral tradition associated all kinds of matter that had no internal connection."[37] Narrative units that may have at one time circulated separately (in oral and/or written traditions) were arguably combined episodically by the written composers.[38] Literary texts in the biblical and ancient Near Eastern world are often episodic and internally disparate.[39] It is a logical error to infer that the identification of a literary episode entails the identification of a separate literary composition.

Otto Eissfeldt made this point forcefully in an article on "The Smallest Literary Unit in the Narrative Books of the Old Testament." He writes: "it is not the "individual narrative" which is to be regarded as the smallest independent literary unit in the narrative books, but the larger context, whose extent must be determined by study of the horizon of the individual narratives."[40] He gives numerous examples where the literary horizon of an individual narrative is clearly discernible in the larger composition. This larger literary horizon is not contested nowadays for the P or D source, but it is in the non-P sources, due to Rendtorff's methodological rule. But the strict equation of "independent narrative" with "smallest independent literary unit" is unwarranted. Intertextual verbal links are evident in the J and E sources, as I have shown above, as they are in the P and D sources. One can have as a starting point the assumption that all intertextual verbal links between individual narratives are late redactional supplements, but in any given instance this assumption must be flexible and corrigible.

---

37 Trans. Baden, *Composition* (see n. 4), 271; J. Wellhausen, *Die Composition des Hexateuchs und der historischen Bücher des Alten Testaments* (Berlin ³1899), 7–8: "An sich schliessen heterogene Bestandteile die Einheit und Ursprünglichkeit eines schriftlichen Zusammenhanges nicht aus; es ist möglich, dass schon die erste Aufzeichnung der mündlichen Tradition allerlei in Verbindung brachte, was in keiner innerlichen Verwandtschaft stand."

38 An obvious analogy is the composition of the Old Babylonian Gilgamesh epic, based on the older cycle of Gilgamesh stories; see J.H. Tigay, "The Evolution of the Pentateuchal Narratives in the Light of the Evolution of the *Gilgamesh Epic*," in *Empirical Models for Biblical Criticism* (ed. J.H. Tigay; Philadelphia 1985), 21–52.

39 K. van der Toorn, *Scribal Culture and the Making of the Hebrew Bible* (Cambridge 2007), 14–15.

40 O. Eissfeldt, "The Smallest Literary Unit in the Narrative Books of the Old Testament," in *Old Testament Essays* (ed. D.C. Simpson; London 1927), 92; idem, "Die kleinste literarische Einheit in den Erzählungsbüchern des Alten Testaments," in *Kleine Schriften: Erster Band* (eds. R. Sellheim and F. Maass; Tübingen 1962), 148: "als kleinste selbständige literarische Einheit in den Erzählungsbüchern nicht die 'Einzel-Erzählung' anzusprechen ist, sondern der jeweilige grössere Zusammenhang, dessen Ausdehnung durch Untersuchung des Horizontes der einzelnen Erzählungen festgestellt werden muss."

The large-scale literary horizon of the narratives, in Eissfeldt's term, is a methodological imperative for identifying a literary composition. The conflation of the aims of form- and source-criticism is arguably a mistaken approach.

On the latter point, Erhard Blum has astutely noted that form criticism is not a single inquiry with a definable method, but an "amalgam of elements of independent lines of questioning." He concludes: "no specific 'form-critical method' exists."[41] If Blum is correct, then there is no specific form-critical method to be transferred into source criticism. Blum's critique of form-criticism as a single coherent discipline, I submit, renders questionable Rendtorff's insistence that form- and source-criticism are intrinsically at odds and must be reconceived.

Moreover, my specific observations above render problematic Rendtorff's conclusion – shared by many European scholars – that "there are no discernible links between the [non-P] patriarchal stories and the complexes of tradition that follow in the Pentateuch ... it is only with a layer of reworking that bears the Deuteronomic stamp that explicit cross references have been inset" [my emphasis].[42] None of the repetitions above bears a Deuteronomic stamp. But because they are implicit in the verbal texture rather than explicit cross-references (a distinction that seems irrelevant to the task of source criticism),[43] they may be to some degree invisible to this method.

4 God and the Gods in P

The history of religion in the P source is both familiar and strange to modern interpreters.[44] It is familiar because P's concept of God is the basis of the tradition-

---

41 E. Blum, "Formgeschichte – A Misleading Category? Some Critical Remarks," in *The Changing Face of Form Criticism for the Twenty-First Century* (eds. M.A. Sweeney and E. Ben Zvi; Grand Rapids 2003), 38, 45.

42 Rendtorff, *Problem* (see n. 36), 135.

43 On the primacy of explicit (versus implicit) cross-references in the Rendtorff-Blum method, see Schmid, *Moses Story* (see n. 6), 47–49. Schmid (ibid., 10 n. 60) attributes R. Kessler's dissertation, "Die Querverweise im Pentateuch: Überlieferungsgeschichtliche Untersuchung der expliziten Querverbindungen innerhalb des vorpriesterlichen Pentateuchs," (Diss. theol. Heidelberg 1972; *BEAT* 59, Frankfurt am Main et al 2015), with establishing this principle, which was taken up by Rendtorff, Blum, and others; see similarly D.M. Carr, "Changes in Pentateuchal Criticism," in *Hebrew Bible / Old Testament: The History of Its Interpretation. III/2: The Twentieth Century* (ed. M. Sæbø; Göttingen 2015), 441.

44 See recently K. Schmid, "The Quest for 'God': Monotheistic Arguments in the Priestly Texts of the Hebrew Bible," in Pongratz-Leisten, *Monotheism* (see n. 3), 271–289; idem, "Differenzierungen und Konzeptualisierungen der Einheit Gottes in der Religions- und Literaturgeschichte Isra-

al concept in Judaism, Christianity, and Islam – a transcendent, non-anthropo-morphic God who is more or less omniscient and all-powerful. This is the God who creates the cosmos by his word, and who creates humans to rule the earth. All this is familiar. But in comparison to the concepts of God in J and E, this God is quite strange. In P there are no angels, no Sons of God, and no foreign Gods. There is, to cite the Qur'an, no God but God.

The P text goes to some lengths to eliminate the possibility of other gods, including most of the varieties mentioned elsewhere in biblical writings. Konrad Schmid aptly calls this a "disenchantment" (Entzauberung) of the world (Max Weber's phrase).[45] In the creation story, several acts of creation seem to be worded in such a way as to preclude other divine beings. Consider the following passages:

וַיַּעַשׂ אֱלֹהִים אֶת־שְׁנֵי הַמְּאֹרֹת הַגְּדֹלִים

And God made the two great lights. (Gen 1:16)

וַיִּבְרָא אֱלֹהִים אֶת־הַתַּנִּינִם הַגְּדֹלִים

And God created the great sea monsters. (Gen 1:21)

וַיְכֻלּוּ הַשָּׁמַיִם וְהָאָרֶץ וְכָל־צְבָאָם

And heaven and earth and all their host were completed. (Gen 2:1)

Elsewhere in the Bible, Israelites make offerings of incense to the sun, moon, and stars. These celestial bodies were, as elsewhere in the ancient Near East, regarded as divine beings. Collectively they belong to "the host of heaven," which is sometimes a synonym for "the Sons of God." The heavenly host is God's heavenly army and, during peacetime, his celestial court. But in Genesis 1, the sun and moon are simply "two great lights" – they have no agency or personality, just part of the machinery of the cosmos. God creates light separately, and he assigns the celestial bodies the task regulating the cycle of light and darkness. The cosmos is like a watch, and they are the gears. Similarly, the phrase "host of heaven" is naturalized, as the "host" now refers to everything in heaven and earth that God has created. It no longer refers to the celestial gods or the Sons of God, but is a colorless noun for a group of things.

The תַּנִּינִם גְּדֹלִים ("great sea monsters") are usually elsewhere in the Bible divine monsters who are defeated by God in the primeval era or (in exilic and post-

---

els," in *Der eine Gott und die Götter. Polytheismus und Monotheismus im antiken Israel* (eds. M. Oeming and K. Schmid; Zürich 2003), 28–38.
45 Schmid, "Differenzierungen" (see n. 44), 36.

exilic writings) in the future eschatological era.[46] But in Genesis 1, the "great sea monsters" are explicitly created by God, and are the only individual animal species to be so honored, aside from humans, who are a separate creation. The verb בְּרָא ("created"), which is limited to God as subject, is used only for two particular creations: the great sea monsters and humans. Clearly these sea creatures are not God's primeval adversaries and they are not divine. They are a species of large water animal, created by God. They are great in size – probably identified with whales – but they are not gods.

The creation of humans in Genesis 1 also relates to the emptying of the cosmos of other gods. As Randall Garr observes:

> Without gods, there is a vacuum in God's world. God loses an entire administrative stratum with which he would otherwise share the governance of the world. So God adopts a replacement. He creates a new cooperative that will imitate and replace, at least in part, the functions of his divine comrades. P's God elects humankind as the community with which he will enter into a special binding relationship.[47]

Hence God creates humans בְּצֶלֶם אֱלֹהִים ("in the image of God") and assigns them to rule the earth. Humans are his co-regents. The possible existence of a divine assembly is raised when God says, נַעֲשֶׂה אָדָם בְּצַלְמֵנוּ ("Let us make humans in our image," Gen 1:26), but, as Garr observes, this possibility is foreclosed when God creates humans by himself: וַיִּבְרָא אֱלֹהִים אֶת־הָאָדָם בְּצַלְמוֹ ("And God created humankind in his image," 1:27).[48] The plural address, in retrospect, resolves retrospectively into a plural of majesty in a divine soliloquy. The absence of the divine hierarchy – no Host of Heaven, no angels – creates a vacuum that allows for a new concept of humans as God's partners in ruling the cosmos. In Assyrian ideology, the king was the high god's ṣalmu ("image") on earth, with divine authority to rule. As has often been observed, in P humans as a whole are assigned this privilege.

Because humans and animals pollute the earth with their violence, God cleanses the earth with the flood and begins a new era. Out of this primeval disruption begins a sequence of covenants, which structures P's history of religion. The covenants define the rules that various groups of humans must follow in order to maintain the proper order of the cosmos, and they are conjoined with a series of divine promises and natural or ritual signs that are reminders of

---

46 See J. Day, *God's Conflict with the Dragon and the Sea: Echoes of a Canaanite Myth in the Old Testament* (Cambridge 1985).
47 W.R. Garr, *In His Own Image and Likeness: Humanity, Divinity, and Monotheism* (Leiden 2003), 222.
48 Ibid., 202–212.

the covenant. Each covenant is initiated in a revelation by God, which consist primarily of divine speech. Only once does the grantee speak – when Abraham implores, "Would that Ishmael might live in your favor" (Gen 17:18). Although humans may rule the earth, God rules over them. In the sequence of covenants, this hierarchy is clear. The covenants are God's decrees, in which humans have no say.

God's name is progressively revealed in the series of covenants. From the beginning he is אֱלֹהִים ("God,"), which is grammatically a plural of intensification or majesty. To Abraham he reveals a new name, with a gesture to the reader of a future revelation:

וַיֵּרָא יְהוָה אֶל־אַבְרָם וַיֹּאמֶר אֵלָיו אֲנִי־אֵל שַׁדַּי

And Yhwh appeared to Abram, saying to him, "I am El Shaddai." (Gen 17:1)

In an elegant narratorial move, this verse doubly reveals God's name(s). God reveals his name El Shaddai to Abram, and the narrator subtly reveals the name Yhwh to the reader. (This is the first time the divine name Yhwh is used in P.) In a sense, the full revelation of God's name is intimated obliquely in this verse. The patriarchal designation, El Shaddai, may have originally been a name of the high god El.[49] But in P the name seems deliberately cryptic, an archaic designation of an unfathomable God. God's ultimate name is finally revealed to Moses, when God renews the covenant to Israel. He says:

אֲנִי יְהוָה וָאֵרָא אֶל־אַבְרָהָם אֶל־יִצְחָק וְאֶל־יַעֲקֹב בְּאֵל שַׁדָּי וּשְׁמִי יְהוָה לֹא נוֹדַעְתִּי לָהֶם

I am Yhwh. I appeared to Abraham, to Isaac, and to Jacob as El Shaddai, but my name Yhwh I did not reveal to them. (Exod 6:2–3)

God's final revelation of his name initiates the events of Exodus-Sinai, which build toward God's descent from heaven to dwell in the midst of his people (Exod 40:34). The narrative slows down to a crawl beginning with Exodus 25, when God proceeds to give precise instructions for the construction of the tabernacle, which is to be his earthly home. As Baruch Schwartz comments, "The Priestly narrative ... telegraphs early events and rushes to Sinai" where it finds its goal, "the eventual arrival of the immanent Presence of God to dwell upon earth in the midst of the Israelites."[50]

---

49 F.M. Cross, "Yahweh and El," in idem, *Canaanite Myth and Hebrew Epic: Essays in the History of the Religion of Israel* (Cambridge 1973), 52–60.
50 Schwartz, "Theophany" (see n. 34), 109, 122.

There is, however, a problem with God's new dwelling place on earth. Although humans are made in "the image of God," there is a vast metaphysical gap between God and humans. God's physical presence, the כְּבוֹד יְהוָה ("Glory of YHWH"), is an immaterial fiery mass that is intensely holy. In P's concept of God, this holy presence is antithetical to human bodies, particularly with respect to the all-too-human features of sex and death. God's holiness must be protected from contact with such bodily traits, lest the inherent danger of the intensely holy destroy the Israelites. This poses a paradox: God chooses to dwell in the midst of his people, yet God's holiness is dangerous to people. Many of the laws in Leviticus and Numbers are designed to regulate the dangerous proximity of God and Israel. As Propp comments, "God and Israel both want to live together, yet YHWH's attribute of Holiness is incompatible with earthly corruption. How can [He] 'tent among them amid their impurities' (Lev 16:16)?"[51]

The history of religion in P comes to fruition with these regulations. Just as the laws given to Noah control human violence, which otherwise would pollute the earth, the laws given to Moses and Israel in Leviticus and Numbers control the encroachment of human impurity onto divine space, which otherwise would pollute the Tabernacle and its court, causing death and devastation. Human impurities are conditions of embodied existence that are antithetical to God's metaphysical body. Sex and death are incompatible with the holy because YHWH's transcendent body does not have sex and does not die. The כְּבוֹד יְהוָה is metaphysically beyond eros and thanatos.[52]

The human impurities are, as David Wright observes, "natural and necessary."[53] They are not ethical transgressions, but conditions of the mortal body. God mandates sexual intercourse, which is explicitly described as a blessing: וַיְבָרֶךְ אֹתָם אֱלֹהִים וַיֹּאמֶר לָהֶם אֱלֹהִים פְּרוּ וּרְבוּ ("And God blessed them, and God said to them, "Be fruitful and multiply," Gen 1:28), and he reiterates this blessing in the Noachic and Abrahamic covenants (Gen 9:1,7; 17:2,6). Clearly this condition of impurity is not a transgression – it is a human attribute that simply is incom-

---

51 Propp, *Exodus* (see n. 31), 19 – 40, 686
52 D. Wright ("Unclean and Clean [OT]," *ABD* 6.730 – 733) divides the permitted human impurities into those related to sex, death, disease, and the cult. The latter involves incorrect performance of rites, and therefore is a different axis, which involves all the other categories. The only impurities relating to disease are those related analogically to sex (abnormal genital flows, Leviticus 15) or death (צָרַעַת, a skin disease in which the skin seems to die, Leviticus 13 – 14, cf. Num 12:12). Hence sex and death are sufficient categories for the human impurities in P. See further R. Hendel, "Purity and Danger in the Temple Court," forthcoming.
53 Wright, "Unclean" (see n. 52), 730.

mensurate with God's holy presence. So too for the impurity of corpse contact (Numbers 19) – such contact is inevitable among mortal species.

Beyond these conditions of ritual impurity that preclude Israelites entering the holy space of the Tabernacle court, there are also dangers for the priests who mediate between Israel and Yhwh in holy precincts. Only the priests may enter the zone from the sacrificial altar to the outer chamber of the Tabernacle. If a priest in this area accidentally exposes his penis, he dies (Exod 28:43). If he is intoxicated, he dies (Lev 10:9). If he is in a ritual state of mourning, with disheveled hair and torn clothes, he dies (Lev 10:6–7). If he is literally unclean, with unwashed hands and feet, he dies (Exod 30:20–21). The embodied traits of sex and death are conjoined here with bodily control and scrupulous cleanliness. To serve God, the priests must be initiated into a ritual state of holiness and maintain this high state in the ritual space. Otherwise, the fiery danger of God's holiness will kill them.

The concept of God in P is familiar and strange. He is the transcendent God of creation, who bestows his blessings on all living things. But he is also an awesome God whose dangerous holiness is antithetical to the physical bodies of humans, particularly in the carnal traits of sex and death. The laws regulate Israelite bodies so that He may dwell in the midst of his people without destroying them. In the absence of other gods, God's community is his people, but his presence comes at a price.

5 Conclusions: Histories of Religion and Cultural Memory

The histories of religion in J, E, and P represent three parallel yet, in some ways, incommensurate portraits of the past. Each portrays a history in which the God of the patriarchs reveals himself anew as the God of Moses and Israel, but each does so in the course of a distinctive narrative plot. Each has a different concept of the character and attributes of Yhwh, and each places him in a different kind of relationship to other gods. As I have observed above, these three native histories may be regarded as different constructions of cultural memory, that is, authoritative representations of the past with present relevance. I conclude with some reflections on how these narratives are animated by contemporary cultural issues and conflicts, and what positions the narrative takes within these wider discourses. Cultural memories are always in dialogue with other counter-memories, thereby allowing us to discern the interests that are at stake among various agents and groups. The key events of the past are typically, in cultural memory, windows onto the passions of the present.

In E's history of religion, we have already addressed the implicit argument with adversaries in the religious and political establishment of the Northern Kingdom. The transgression of the Golden Calf is, in some respects, a reversal of the original separation from foreign gods in the story of Jacob and his family. The buried earrings and icons have come back – in what Freud might call a return of the repressed – in the "foreign" cult at Bethel and Dan. The religious worship conducted by the northern priests and king, E seems to say, is abhorrent to the God of the patriarchs. If we read this implicit polemic rightly, this is a strong statement of current socio-religious conflict. It is important to observe that the attribution of worshiping foreign gods is a strategic way of "othering" this cult, which may not have been viewed by its practitioners as heterodox at all. The narrative does not provide access to the deeper issues that may have been at stake in this rhetorical assault. A kinship with Hosea's polemic against the Northern king and cult seems plausible, as many commentators have observed.[54]

The ritual separation from foreign gods in Gen 35:1–7 arguably has a further theo-political resonance. This line of separation articulates a boundary between Israel and other peoples. The institution of this separation celebrates the cultural identity of Israel as a people distinct from its genealogical kin in Haran and other locales. Israel's identity is now proclaimed to be geographically and religiously distinct. This rite of separation creates a red line in the past that maps onto the contemporary boundaries of national and religious identity.

In the context of its foreign neighbors, the relationship between God and the gods in E may be also described as a feature of cultural continuity. E's easy acknowledgement of foreign gods, with the caveat that Israelites do not serve them, is compatible with other native histories of religion from neighboring peoples in the Iron Age. The Mesha stele, a Moabite royal inscription from the mid-ninth century, is the prime example. In the stele's narration of the past conflicts between Moab and Israel, the Moabite god Chemosh is the divine agent of history, but YHWH is acknowledged as the God of the Israelites.[55] The difference between the efficacy of Chemosh and YHWH in these celebrated past events celebrates the ethnic and cultural identity of the two peoples. As Bruce Routledge observes, the rhetoric of differentiation – regarding land, king, and God – articulates the legiti-

---

54 See recently Chavel (see n. 23), "Kingdom of Priests," 197–201.

55 I infer this from Mesha's reference to the ‏כ]לי יהוה‎ ("vessels of YHWH"), which he captured and placed before Chemosh (line 17).

macy of the Moabite state. As he observes, "it is in opposition to Israel that Moab emerges as a workable, and independent, national identity."[56]

A similar dynamic obtains in E's portrait of the relationship between Israel's God and the foreign gods. Jacob acknowledges the existence of "foreign gods" in his household's possession and gives them an honorable burial. The gods of other peoples are acknowledged, but they seem to have no agency. Jacob acknowledges Laban's pledge to his ancestral god, the God of Nahor, but Jacob makes his oath only to the patriarchal god, "the Fear of his father Isaac." Other people have other gods, but Israel's God is the one with real agency. As in Moab, the national God is the powerful one, even though other nations have their gods too. The theology of the national god in Mesha and E creates a tangible religio-social identity in contrast to other nations, but it also has a residue of ambiguity, and perhaps anxiety, about other gods and nations.

An implicit anxiety about other gods and nations may also be evident in J's history of religion. Whereas E restricts the worship of YHWH to Israel alone, in J it seems that YHWH worship was widespread in the early generations of humanity, such that all early nations worshiped him. The prominence of Mesopotamian characters in these generations, including Nimrod, the first king of Babylonia and Assyria, and the builders of Babylon, indicates the kinds of cultural conflicts and anxieties that may be actuated here. I have previously argued that J's "Mesopotamian problem" in these stories may be a response to the political context of the contemporary Neo-Assyrian Empire.[57] Some of these stories and motifs may be, in some respects, a mimicry of imperial claims, a hybridizing discourse that inverts – at the level of cultural memory – the political power of the present. Babylon was destroyed and its builders scattered by YHWH's power, and King Nimrod ruled in all his cities – including the Assyrian imperial capital – by YHWH's favor. The international relations of the present are inverted in these stories of the formative past, which in turn reframes the religious and political contours of the present.

Numerous scholars have suggested that the impact of the Neo-Assyrian empire – including its imperial propaganda of the world-ruling god and king – may have been a stimulus in the rise of Israelite monotheism. As Mark Smith writes:

> "Israel lived under the shadow and threat of empire just as it was expressing its most explicit monotheistic formulations, and it was doing so in accordance with its own experience and traditions that at this point in its history distinguished it from its neighbors. Israel's

---

56 B. Routledge, *Moab in the Iron Age: Hegemony, Polity, Archaeology* (Philadelphia 2004), 150.
57 R. Hendel, "Genesis 1–11 and Its Mesopotamian Problem," in *Cultural Borrowings and Ethnic Appropriations in Antiquity* (ed. E. Gruen; Stuttgart 2005), 23–36.

monotheism emerged in the context of its lack of power in the face of empires, perhaps as a form of resistance to them."[58]

There are clear examples of the mimicry of Neo-Assyrian royal rhetoric in First Isaiah and Deuteronomy.[59] I suggest that J's history of religion in some respects mimics and inverts the ideology of Assyrian empire, such that YHWH is the original god of all peoples, to whom the Assyrians – and everyone else – owe fealty.

The history of religion in P is positioned differently. There are no foreign gods, and there are no other native gods beside YHWH – no angels, no heavenly host, no divine monsters to conquer. P's history of religion is animated by a critique of native Israelite religious concepts, what Baruch Halpern calls "a Sprachkritik, a philosophical assault on the relationship between symbols and the things they symbolize."[60] At the same time, P's history also grounds the authority of the priesthood in the necessary but dangerous relationship between YHWH and his people, in whose midst he dwells. The priests are elevated to the status of "holy" mediators, whose authority enables the cosmic order to operate harmoniously.

The nonexistence of other gods in P may be not only an inner-Israelite critique, but also a response to imperial theopolitics, particularly if the main part of the P source was composed during the Babylonian exile. There is no explicit mimicry of Neo-Babylonian gods, as one finds in Second Isaiah (Isa 46:1), so this remains a suggestive if not demonstrable undercurrent.[61] For P, it seems that other peoples have little role to play in religion except to abide by the Noachic covenant (to refrain from murder and ingesting blood). The burden and benefit of encountering God is wholly Israel's. In a context of imperial domination and

---

58 Smith, *Translation* (see n. 21), 178–180; see further E. Otto, "Assyria and Judean Identity: Beyond the Religionsgeschichtliche Schule," in *Literature as Politics, Politics as Literature: Essays on the Ancient Near East in Honor of Peter Machinist* (eds. D.S. Vanderhooft and A. Winitzer; Winona Lake 2013), 339–347; B. Levine, "Assyrian Ideology and Israelite Monotheism," *Iraq* 67 (2005), 411–427.
59 P. Machinist, "Assyria and Its Image in the First Isaiah," *JAOS* 103 (1983), 719–737; S.Z. Aster, "The Image of Assyria in Isaiah 2:5–22: The Campaign Motif Reversed," *JAOS* 127 (2007), 249–278; B.M. Levinson and J. Stackert, "Between the Covenant Code and Esarhaddon's Succession Treaty," *JAJ* 3 (2012), 128–140, and references.
60 B. Halpern, *From Gods to God: The Dynamics of Iron Age Cosmologies* (ed. M.J. Adams; Tübingen 2009), 3–4.
61 See E. Frahm, "Counter-texts, Commentaries, and Adaptations: Politically Motivated Responses to the Babylonian Epic of Creation in Mesopotamia, the Biblical World, and Elsewhere," *Orient* 45 (2010), 14–17.

the destruction of land, king, and nation, this may be a strategy of collective hope and survival.

The historical and cultural resonances of these native histories of religion allow us to discern the arguments and adversaries with which these histories are engaged. We can, at least in part, map these native histories onto a modern construction of the history of Israelite and ancient Near Eastern religions. There are many gaps in our knowledge, and much of the connective tissue of the modern historical model is tentative or hypothetical. In some respects the E portrayal seems more traditional in its concept of national gods, comparable to the conceptuality of the Mesha stele. The representation of religion in J seems innovative in its projection of YHWH religion to the primeval past. P's history of religion is also innovative: it is arguably the first – and perhaps only – monotheism in history, if we take the term as denoting one god with no remainder.[62] There are implications for a modern history of religion here, even if P's religious system was largely hypothetical or fictive in its formulation. But any history of religion has its fictive parts, which perhaps most clearly express the desires of the present.

In a sense the histories of religion in J, E, and P are counter-memories to each other, since they take different position on the events of the past and their relation to the present. But I do not presume that these sources knew each other. In this respect the concept of cultural memory allows us to discern their relationship as alternative discourses within the broader field of Israelite cultural memory. Even in the composite Pentateuch they operate as reservoirs of memory, which subsequent communities selectively recall, harmonize, and reinterpret to suit their present interests. The history of God and the gods is still being refashioned today, in part by modern historians of religion, and in part by those who take the Bible's histories as authoritative. The revelation of the God of Abraham, Isaac, and Jacob is still a topic of intense commitment and argument – by the pious, by the philosophers and scholars, and by the biblical authors themselves, whose narrative claims are still contested.

---

62 Note that even Second Isaiah has divine monsters and heavenly beings; see S.M. Olyan, "Is Isaiah 40–55 Really Monotheistic?" *JANER* 12 (2012), 190–201. Angels proliferate in subsequent Jewish, Christian, and Muslim traditions. The Egyptian religion of Akhenaten was in essence a ditheism, since Akhenaten was himself a god; see J.P. Allen, "The Natural Philosophy of Akhenaten," in *Religion and Philosophy in Ancient Egypt* (ed. W.K. Simpson; New Haven 1989), 89–102.

Juha Pakkala
The Origins of Yahwism
from the Perspective of Deuteronomism

1 Introduction

This paper seeks to sketch the origins and early development of Yahwism[1] as it appears from the perspective of Deuteronomistic texts.[2] They provide an excellent glimpse to the development of Yahwism from the sixth to fourth centuries BCE, when these texts were mainly written. This period was crucial for the eventual and later development of monotheistic conceptions that lie at the background of three world religions. Deuteronomistic literature may also be the most fruitful area for observing and understanding the reasons for the exceptional development that led Israel's religion to a trajectory away from the other religions of the Ancient Near East. Although the Deuteronomists were active from the sixth century BCE onwards, their sources also contain some information about the earlier development of Yahwism.[3]

The Hebrew Bible is not an unproblematic source for investigating the history of Israel's religion especially in the monarchic period. Most texts were written after the destruction of Jerusalem in 587 BCE, which meant the destruction of the main structures of the ancient Israelite society: the temple, monarchy, and other state institutions. This destruction necessitated and entailed a complete reorientation of Israel's religion, and this has to be taken into consideration when using the Hebrew Bible as a historical source. Consequently, there are considerable challenges when Israel's religion in the monarchic period is reconstructed on the basis of texts that were written later and largely represent a very different religion that had already adapted itself to the new situation without the temple

---

1 In this paper Yahwism refers to the worship and cult of YHWH.

2 Deuteronomism is here defined rather generally to include the Deuteronomic sections and redactions of Deuteronomy as well as the Deuteronomistic texts and redactions in the books from Deuteronomy to 2 Kings. It is necessary to acknowledge the uncertainties concerning Deuteronomism especially in the Book of Samuel but also in Joshua and Judges. See discussion in C. Edenburg and J. Pakkala (ed.), *Is Samuel Among the Deuteronomists? Current Views on the Place of Samuel in a Deuteronomistic History* (SBLAIL 16; Atlanta, GA 2013). Although not very specific, Deuteronomism is a usable concept for the purposes of the current paper.

3 Using other parts of the Hebrew Bible and beyond, the very early evidence for Yahwism will be discussed in much more detail in other papers of this volume.

DOI 10.1515/9783110448221-012

and the king. It seems probable that the Hebrew Bible only contains vestiges of the early and monarchic religion, for especially features that contradicted with later conceptions would have been left out or outright censored in the post–587 BCE texts. Parts of the old mythology featuring the monarchic religion are best preserved in the Psalms and other poetic literature, as their liturgical and hymnic contexts as well as the poetic form may have conserved ancient features better than the context and form of prose.

Methodologically this paper is based on literary and redaction critical analysis of the source texts. Although these methods have their limitations, it has become evident that the preserved texts were written by many authors, editors, and redactors in different times and contexts. It is therefore necessary to distinguish between different authors if we use the text as a source to reconstruct the history and religion of ancient Israel.[4] For the rise of Yahwism this approach is particularly fruitful, because it reveals crucial differences between Deuteronomistic literary layers, which implies the development of concepts during the time when these texts were produced.[5]

It should further be noted that the Deuteronomistic texts, as well as much of the rest of the Hebrew Bible, mainly deal with the state religion and the religion of the powerful. The Hebrew Bible was written by a group of people who probably represent only a small section of the society, the literate elite, who was close to the society's powerful. For example, the main source for the book of Kings was the royal annals, which recorded events from the perspective of the royal house. It is therefore probable that the Hebrew Bible provides only scanty evidence for the various forms of Yahwism practiced by the ordinary people on a local level. One also has to assume considerable local differences.

2 Pre-Deuteronomistic Yahwism

Although witnessed by the Deuteronomistic texts only in vestiges, it is necessary to give a brief overview of the development predating and leading to Deuteronomistic conceptions. Because sources are lacking or fragmentary, the very earliest Yahwism is controversial. Traditionally it has been assumed that YHWH did not

---

4 See discussion in R. Müller *et al.*, *Evidence of Editing. Growth and Change of Texts in the Hebrew Bible* (SBLRBS 75; Atlanta 2013). Failure to distinguish between different authors and editors would mean that we can only use the final texts as a very general source and then acknowledge that texts from very different contexts and centuries are intermingled.

5 For literary and redaction critical analysis of the texts discussed in this paper, see J. Pakkala, *Intolerant Monolatry in the Deuteronomistic History* (PFES 76; Helsinki and Göttingen 1999).

originate in Palestine but came from a region south of Judah perhaps at the end of the Bronze Age. There are some indications in support of this view. The giving of the law and the sojourn of the Israelites is strongly tied with the Sinai, an area outside of Israelite and Judean heartland, which begs for an explanation. Four short passages, often assumed to be early vestiges, point to the same geographical direction. These passages mention YHWH's coming from areas that can be located in the Sinai or Edom: Judg 5:4–5, 31 from Seir and Edom, Hab 3:3–4, 7 from Teman, Deut 33:2 from Seir and Paran, and Ps 68:8–9 from Sinai. It would be difficult to explain, why the national God of Israel and Judah had originated in an area of another nation, unless there was a strong tradition behind it.

There is also extra-biblical evidence to connect YHWH with the general area of Sinai and Edom. As many scholars have pointed out, some Late Bronze Age texts from Egypt link YHWH with Šasu, which have been assumed to be a people living in the approximate area south of Judah.[6] Moreover, the inscriptions from Kuntillet 'Ajrud in the Sinai could also be seen as argument to connect YHWH with this region. In addition to its southern location, some of the texts (KAgr 9:6, 9, 10) mention YHWH of Teman.[7] Incidentally, Teman is also mentioned in Hab 3:3, where it is paralleled with Paran, which may be connected with Edom (Deut 33:2) or is otherwise in the general area. Taking all this evidence together, many scholars have assumed that YHWH's origins are somehow connected with the general area in Edom and Sinai.[8]

Nevertheless, recently some scholars have challenged the southern origins of YHWH. Henrik Pfeiffer in particular has shown the weaknesses of using the biblical fragments as well as the extra-biblical references. He argues that the four short passages are literarily interdependent, Judg 5 being the oldest but still of post-monarchic origin.[9] If his analysis is correct, the passages are not a strong witness to the early origins of YHWH. Moreover, Reinhard Müller has provided

---

6 See S. Herrmann, "Der Alttestamentliche Gottesnahme" in *Gesammelte Studien zur Geschichte und Theologie des Alten Testaments* (TB 75; München 1966), 76–88.

7 According to Ernst A. Knauf, "Teman," *Das wissenschaftliche Bibellexikon im Internet* (2009), (https://www.bibelwissenschaft.de/de/stichwort/33170/), Teman primarily means "south", and since YHWH of Judah or Jerusalem is not otherwise mentioned in the Kuntillet 'Ajrud inscriptions, it is probable that YHWH of Teman refers to YHWH of Judah, the southern kingdom.

8 With many others, thus K. van der Toorn, "Yahweh," *DDD²* (ed. K. van der Toorn; Leiden ²1999), 910–919, especially pp. 911–913, and most recently M. Leuenberger, "*Jhwhs Herkunft aus dem Süden. Archäologische Befunde – biblische Überlieferungen – historische Korrelationen*," *ZAW* 122 (2010), 1–19.

9 See Pfeiffer's contribution in this volume; he also provides good arguments to be more cautious with the use of the extra-biblical sources for the early origins of YHWH.

an alternative solution to the southern origins and shown that Yhwh's early characteristics, preserved as vestiges in some poetic texts of the Hebrew Bible, correspond with those of a typical Syrian-type weather god.[10] This would make origins in the arid zones of Edom or Sinai unlikely.

In the end, the southern hypothesis remains a possibility, but for understanding Yhwh as a divinity it does not contain much substance. For the development of Yhwh, his clear characteristics as a weather god are much more important. Certainly, one can speculate that Yhwh, at least as the name of the divinity, came from outside Palestine, perhaps from the South. Having some similar characteristics with a local weather god, he would have retained an old name, but otherwise merged with an older Syro-Palestinian storm god.[11] At any rate, it seems probable that Yhwh, at least as the name of the deity, has an origin outside the conventional and known core-pantheons of Syria-Palestine.[12]

Regardless of his early origins, Yhwh was the main divinity worshipped in the kingdoms of Israel and Judah during most of the monarchic period, but the 10th and the first half of the 9th century BCE are uncertain. While the early history of Judah—and thereby also the history of Yhwh of Jerusalem—is poorly known and controversial, we are on a more solid ground with the kingdom of Israel. Historically it seems certain that Yhwh became the unquestioned dynastic and state God of Israel by mid–9th century BCE, during the time of Omri or Ahab. For example, the Mesha inscription, which can be dated to the second half of the 9th century BCE, refers to Yhwh as the divinity of the kingdom of Israel (line 18). Moreover, an inscription from Kuntillet 'Ajrud refers to the Yhwh of Samaria (KAgr 9:8), which implies that Samaria had become a significant location of Yhwh's cult already by beginning of the 8th century BCE, when the inscription was written.

It seems probable that the house of Omri was a strong proponent of Yahwism. This is suggested by the mostly Yahwistic names of kings after King Ahab. Before Ahab's son Ahaziah none of the Israelite kings had a Yahwistic name, which implies a dramatic shift in the time of Omri and Ahab. There may even

---

10 R. Müller, *Jahwe als Wettergott. Studien zur althebräischen Kultlyrik anhand ausgewählter Psalmen* (BZAW 387; Berlin), 241–244.

11 If one follows this line, a possible candidate would be Baal. This could explain why Baal is largely missing as a theophoric element in personal names as well as in the inscriptions. Nevertheless, there is very little evidence for this hypothesis.

12 The Amarna correspondence does not contain any personal name with Yhwh as a theophoric element, which suggests that Yhwh was either an insignificant local deity during the Late Bronze Age or that he came later from outside Palestine.

be indirect textual evidence in 1 Kings 16:32 that Ahab built a temple for YHWH in Samaria. According to the Masoretic text, "Ahab erected an altar for Baal in Baal's temple, which he had built in Samaria" (ויקם מזבח לבעל בית בעל אשר בנה בשמרון). This text can hardly be original, as the main sin illogically would be the erection of Baal's altar, while the building of the temple is mentioned merely as the place of the sin. It would be much more logical that the sin was the erection of Baal's altar in YHWH's temple. It is notable that the references to the temple differ considerably in the witnesses (for example, the LXX reads ἐν οἴκῳ τῶν προσοχθισμάτων αὐτοῦ "the house of his abominations"). The probable reason for the variant readings is that the original text contained an offensive or problematic reading that later scribes tried to avoid. A reference to the existence of YHWH's temple in Samaria would certainly have been a problematic reading causing many scribes to censor it. Consequently, the original text, which is not preserved in any witness, probably read "He (Ahab) erected an altar for Baal in the temple of YHWH, which he had built in Samaria" (ויקם מזבח לבעל בית יהוה אשר בנה בשמרון).[13]

The building of YHWH's temple in the new capital Samaria would have given a powerful boost to promote the state god of the new dynasty and its new capital. Considering the position of Samaria in the 9th century BCE, it would seem logical that the rise and eventual success of YHWH is the result of his elevation to the status of state God of the house of Omri. YHWH's characteristics as a Syrian type weather god may derive from or be a result of this period, for in the mid 9th century Israel was well connected with Syria and Lebanon.[14] Ironically, two of the most derided Israelite kings, Omri and Ahab, may have been essential in promoting early Yahwism.

The pre-Deuteronomistic remains in the Deuteronomistic literature give an impression of a strongly YHWH -centered religion during the monarchic period. Certainly this picture is partly a result of censoring, but only partly. The theophoric elements in personal names imply that YHWH was clearly the dominant deity who was not challenged after the 9th century BCE. Asherah had a role – as implied by the vestiges in the Hebrew Bible as well as by the inscriptions from Kuntillet 'Ajrud and Khirbet el-Kom – but this divinity seems to have been closely connected with YHWH's cult, probably as his consort. It is fair to assume that YHWH and El were originally separate divinities, but since most of the

---

13 For details, evidence, and arguments in favor of this hypothesis, see J. Pakkala, *God's Word Omitted. Omissions in the Transmission of the Hebrew Bible* (FRLANT 251; Göttingen 2013), 231–234.

14 For example, according to the Kurkh stela, Israel under Ahab was part of a military alliance with Damascus and Hamath against Assyria.

Hebrew Bible implicitly identifies them, it is probable that they had merged or were in the process of merging at least by end of the monarchic times.[15]

Baal's role has been subject of wide discussion, not the least because the Hebrew Bible criticizes the Israelites of worshipping this deity, but there is very little evidence that Baal had a significant position in Israel or Judah during the monarchic period. For example, Baal is met only seldom as a theophoric element of personal names on seals and inscriptions from the monarchic period.[16] The El Amarna correspondence similarly contains only a few personal names with Baal as a theophoric element. This would seem to suggest that Baal never had a similar position in Palestine as he had in Lebanon and (parts of) Syria. He is mentioned in a Kuntillet 'Ajrud inscription (KAgr 9:7), but so far there is not much evidence to suggest that he was a major deity in Israel or Judah during the monarchic time. This is understandable, since YHWH and Baal had very similar characteristics that would hardly fit the same pantheon or be both needed by the same worshipper.[17] In other words, YHWH's dominance explains why Baal is largely missing, at least in the monarchic period. Alternatively, YHWH and Baal could have been identified, but the evidence for this is meagre. There is some evidence for their worship in the same contexts—the original text of 2 Kings 10:23[18] and KAgr 9:7[19]—but they are too uncertain and open to interpretation to build a solid case.

---

15 Thus many, for example, van der Toorn, "Yahweh" (see n. 8), 917.

16 See J. H. Tigay, *You Shall Have No Other Gods. Israelite Religion in the Light of Hebrew Inscriptions* (HSM 31; Atlanta 1986). In the material discussed by Tigay, Baal is met only six times, out of which five are in the Samaria ostraca. Although new personal names have been found on seals and inscriptions after his analysis, personal names with Baal as the theophoric element still form a small fraction of all names. Nevertheless, J. Day, *Yahweh and the Gods and Goddesses of Canaan* (JSOTS 265; Sheffield 2002), 226–228, has criticized Tigay's conclusions and suggested that the worship of other gods may have been more common. Day writes: "My overall conclusion is that Yahweh was very much the chief god in ancient Israel, and the other gods and goddesses would have been worshipped as part of his pantheon, but the frequency of their worship has been underestimated by Tigay."

17 That YHWH was a Baal-Adad type weather god has been convincingly demonstrated by Müller, *Jahwe als Wettergott* (see n. 10), 241–244.

18 Second Kings 10:23 is a possible but quite uncertain source for a Baal-YHWH syncretism. The verse seems to imply that Baal and YHWH were worshipped in the same sanctuary. The original reference to a syncretistic cult has been censored in the Masoretic text by omitting the offensive section of the passage, but the Old Greek and Codex Vindobonensis, an Old Latin witness, have preserved the original reading. This position has been argued by J. T. Barrera, *Jehú y Joás: Texto y composición literaria de 2 Reyes 9–11* (Institución San Jerónimo 17; Valencia 1984), 147–157, 222–223. For discussion, see also Pakkala, *God's Word Omitted* (see n. 13), 234–237.

All in all, it is probable that Israel's monarchic religion was essentially polytheistic in its conceptions, but with a tendency towards YHWH-monolatry at least in Judah by the 7th century BCE. This provides the background for the later development towards the exclusive worship of YHWH that developed after the destruction of Jerusalem in 587 BCE. The reasons for the concentration on one divinity are unclear but they may be connected to the provincial and perhaps somewhat secluded location of Judah, its small size, and its relatively homogenous population.[20]

Many scholars have assumed that there was a party or group of people, who demanded the exclusive worship of YHWH already during the monarchic times.[21] The main evidence in support of a general attack on other gods before 587 BCE have been the religious reforms of Hezekiah and Josiah.[22] Especially Josiah's reform has often been regarded as a historical event where new ideas in Israel's religion were initiated.[23] The invention of Deuteronomy is often connected to the reform as well. However, it is very unlikely that any religious reforms in the sense intended by the authors of 2 Kings 18:4 and 23:1–24 took place. I have provided arguments for this position in a separate article, and will only refer to some arguments and considerations here.[24]

Rather than being historical events, it is more likely that the reform accounts are projections of later, post-monarchic BCE religious ideals into a monarchic context. This would explain the blatant contradiction between the reality, im-

---

19 Although the text is fragmentary and consists of a few lines only, El, YHWH and Baal seem to be mentioned in this hymn that is reminiscent of some theophanies of the Hebrew Bible.

20 Although there is very little information about the religion in Edom, Moab, and Ammon during the Iron Age, the scant evidence seems to suggest a concentration on the main god. It stands to reason that in areas with a heterogeneous population and wide international contacts the divine has the tendency to become more complex. It should be emphasized that our theories concerning this period are based on very little information, and thus a new significant find could considerably change the way we understand the monarchic religion of Israel.

21 Thus, among many others. M. Smith, *Palestinian Parties and Politics that Shaped the Old Testament* (New York 1971); B. Lang, "The Yahweh-Alone-Movement and the Making of Jewish Monotheism," in *Monotheism and the Prophetic Minority* (Sheffield 1983), 13–59; Day, *Yahweh and the Gods* (see n. 16), 228–229.

22 The criticism of other gods in some books of the prophets, especially in Hosea, has traditionally been used as an indicator that demands for the exclusive worship of YHWH were made already during the monarchic period.

23 For example, Day, *Yahweh and the Gods* (see n. 16), 230.

24 For discussion and arguments, see J. Pakkala, "Why the Cult Reforms in Judah Probably Did not Happen," – *One God – One Cult – One Nation. Archaeological and Biblical Perspectives* (Ed. R. Kratz and H. Spieckermann in collaboration with B. Corzilius and T. Pilger; BZAW 405; Berlin 2010), 201–235.

plied in the reforms accounts, and the religious ideals of the reforms. It would be very unusual that during the monarchic times the Israelites were almost constantly at war with the demands of their own religion and that only some kings defended the accepted religion. In addition to a strange conception that a nation always fails the demands of its God, the reforms would be a structural peculiarity during monarchic times.

From a textual and source-critical perspective, the reforms stand on a thin basis. Hezekiah's reform is only mentioned in one verse (2 Kings 18:4), which many scholars have argued to be a late addition. Josiah's reform in 2 Kings 23, on the other hand, is one of the most edited and debated texts in the Hebrew Bible. The reforms are not mentioned in any other passage in the Hebrew Bible or in other contemporary literature. Consequently, the evidence for a systematic attack on other gods during the monarchic times is too scanty to assume that demands for exclusive worship of YHWH were made before the destruction of 587 BCE.

Instead of relying on biblical texts that have been heavily edited in post–587 BCE contexts, one needs to find more fundamental reasons for a development that took Israel's religion into a path that eventually separated it from other religions of the Ancient Near East. Since a major reorientation in Israel's religion took place at some point in the 8th to 4th centuries BCE, it is most logical that it took place as a result of the events in 587 BCE. The destruction of the temple, monarchy, and state— the sudden loss of the main institutions of the religion —would have necessarily caused a dramatic change in Israel's religion.[25] For example, it is difficult to see that the temple cult in Jerusalem would not have been an essential part of any YHWH religion in monarchic Judah. With a possible image of YHWH and his ark,[26] the temple was also the presence and house of the divinity, with which the royal ideology and mythology would have been connected in some way. It also stands to reason that the monarchic institution was closely tied with Yahwism. Consequently, it is difficult to see how the monarchic religion could have continued without a fundamental change after the destruction of the temple.

---

25 Considering the importance of the royal house in other known religions of the Ancient Near East, the end of the Davidic dynasty would have brought about a similar crisis as the loss of the temple.
26 It seems increasingly probable that there was an image of YHWH in the temple. See, for example, the discussion by H. Niehr, "In Search of YHWH's Cult Statue in the First Temple," in *The Image and the Book: Iconic Cults, Aniconism, and the Rise of Book Religion in Israel and the Ancient Near East* (ed. K. van der Toorn; CBET 21; Leuven 1998), 73–95.

This leads us to the evidence preserved in the Deuteronomistic literature that provides a more solid ground to see what happened next in Israel's religion. The pre–587 BCE features of YHWH are mainly preserved as fragments, while much of the YHWH that the Hebrew Bible portrays was shaped by Deuteronomism.

3 Deuteronomistic History Writer and Deuteronomy

For the purposes of the current paper, the Deuteronomistic History writer[27] and the Deuteronomic author of Deuteronomy largely imply a similar picture of YHWH.[28] It is probable that both of these literary phases were written after the catastrophe of 587 BCE.[29] In their portrayal Israel has only one God, YHWH, and the intimate relationship between YHWH and the people of Israel neither needs nor gives much space to other divinities, but there does not seem to be any explicit exclusion of other gods. Although one cannot completely rule out the possibility that positive references to other gods were later censored from these literary phases, this seems improbable. The YHWH of these texts functions as the sole divinity to whom Israel is responsible and in relation to whom Israel should live. Israel's history and future is only determined by YHWH, who judges on the basis of how Israel obeys and follows him. In other words, there is a silent and *de facto* exclusion of other divinities, but no explicit command to reject or to condemn other gods can be connected with these literary phases. The position of the history writer and the Deuteronomic authors towards the other gods can be characterized as tolerant but within a clearly monolatric framework, where YHWH is the unquestioned God of Israel.

---

27 This author is conventionally called DtrH, but there are considerable problems related to the original theory that the same author edited all books from Joshua to 2 Kings. Nevertheless, it is possible to distinguish a history writer, who represents Deuteronomistic conceptions, at least in the book of Kings, but the Deuteronomistic contribution in Samuel in particular, and perhaps also in Judges, is more controversial.

28 Many controversial and debated issues are connected to the relationship between Deuteronomy and the books from Joshua to 2 Kings, but they are not directly relevant to the aims of this paper.

29 The post–587 BCE dating of the Deuteronomistic editors has been widely accepted in continental European scholarship, whereas the dating of the so-called *Urdeuteronomium* and the Deuteronomic authors is more debated. For arguments in favor of post-monarchic origin of *Urdeuteronomium*, see J. Pakkala "The Date of the Earliest Edition of Deuteronomy," *ZAW* 121/3 (2009), 388–401.

In comparison with the monolatric tendencies of the monarchic times, Israel's religion took a small step further, as it is probable that the roles other divinities had had before 587 BCE are largely missing in the Deuteronomic/Deuteronomistic tradition that emerged after 587 BCE. The reason for Asherah's disappearance or abandonment may have been the destruction of her main symbol in the temple in 587 BCE. In other words, there may not have been any active rejection of her or an attack on her cult; she would have been left out of the history writer's presentation because with the destruction of her physical symbol and representation, her main cult in the temple would have lost its basis. This does not mean that Asherah would have been abandoned in all contexts,[30] but since the history writer as well as the original authors of Deuteronomy were largely focused on the temple, its destruction would have mean the end of Asherah as an important divinity. Therefore, their conception of Yahwism did not need Asherah.

Although the temple had already been destroyed in 587 BCE, it remains the conceptual center of Yahwism.[31] For the history writer and Deuteronomic authors the main concern was the sacrificial cult of YHWH in many places; there may only be one place where the Israelites were allowed to sacrifice to YHWH. At the background was probably the concern of many YHWHs, because each temple and sacrificial cult potentially nurtured a different form of Yahwism. Instead of seeking the background of centralization in Josiah's time, a situation after 587 BCE is more probable. Jerusalem had ceased to be the unquestioned center of Yahwism, which inevitably increased the importance of local forms of Yahwism. The prohibition to sacrifice locally may thus have been an attempt to control them.

Although the exact reasons for the appearance of centralization are unclear and debated, it was a significant step towards defining and regulating Yahwism. It started a long tradition that gradually prohibited features that should not be-

---

30 Many scholars assume that Asherah continued to be worshipped after 587 BCE. Thus, for example, S. Ackerman, *Under Every Green Tree* (HSM 46; Atlanta 1992), 5–99 and H. Niehr, "Religio-Historical Aspects of the 'Early Post-Exilic' Period," in *The Crisis of Israelite Religion. Transformation of Religious Tradition in Exilic and Post-Exilic Times* (ed. B. Becking and M.C.A. Korpel; OTS 42; Leiden 1999) 228–244, here 240. This is very probably the case outside the Deuteronomistic tradition.

31 The author of Kings in particular is very centered on and interested in the Temple. From the annals he took several texts that mention the Temple: its repairs in 2 Kgs 12:5–16; 22:4–7, its blundering in 1 Kgs 14:25–28; 2 Kgs 16:8, and its violation in 2 Kgs 16:10–14; 21:4. He also evaluated the kings on the basis of how they related towards the Temple. Kings who repaired or contributed to the Temple were regarded as good (e.g., Asa, Hezekiah, Jehoash and Josiah), but its violators were regarded as bad (e.g., Ahaz and Manasseh).

long to Yahwism. The idea of excluding something from the legitimate cult is a prominent feature in early Deuteronomy and in the history writer's text, and this feature is further increased in later Deuteronomism. Moreover, the development towards oneness also begins in this phase, although it was still restricted to the oneness of the cult. The rise of these ideas were essential for the later development towards oneness of the entire divinity and the exclusion of other gods.

4 Intolerant Monolatry in the Nomistic Texts

One can see a clear change in attitude inside Deuteronomism. Whereas the history writer and the Deuteronomic author are largely silent about the other gods, this changes dramatically in the late Deuteronomistic texts, which for the purposes of this paper are called nomistic.[32]

The ideas of oneness and exclusivity were inherited from the history writer, but the nomists expanded them to include the other gods, while cult centralization recedes to the background. It was a consistent next step of the already implied monolatry, but now implicit became explicit, and the monolatric tendencies became intolerant. For the nomists Israel would only be allowed to worship one divinity, YHWH, while all others must be rejected. This idea is crystallized in the first commandment of the Decalogue: "You shall have no other gods before me," (Deut 5:7), and it is met in numerous different forms in commandments (e. g., Deut 12:2; 17:2–7), threats (e. g., Deut 29:21–27), and condemnations (e. g., 2 Kings 21:2–15). In many passages the danger posed by other gods is closely connected with cult items, objects, and religious phenomena that the nomists regard as illegitimate and foreign to their conception of pure Yahwism.[33] One receives the impression that the nomists have gradually limited the acceptable form of Yahwism to a form that strips it of as many aspects as possible that are shared with other religions and especially those practiced in Palestine. Exclusivity and oneness eventually become central features of nomistic Yahwism, although they were probably meant as a means to an end and not the end itself.

Although the texts do not specify the concrete reasons for the intolerance and exclusivity, the perceived external and/or internal threat would provide an

---

32 A central feature of the nomistic texts is the repeated reference to the Law that the Israelites should obey. It is often difficult to distinguish between different nomistic texts, and they are probable a group of successive editors with similar ideological conceptions.

33 Among many other similar examples, Deut 7:5 lists foreign altars, stone pillars/Massebot, the Asherahs, and idols as representatives of illegitimate cults of the foreign gods and foreign nations.

explanation. A group that feels its social identity threatened is more prone to attack and criticize other groups, especially those that are perceived to weaken the boundary between the ingroup and outgroup.[34] With significant institutions of Yahwism destroyed in 587 BCE, Yahwism would have been at a constant risk of losing its uniqueness and identity, and one strategy to survive would have been a protective attitude towards everything that may threaten the only fragments of individuality that were left. These would have been emphasized and perhaps expanded, whereas features that threatened to weaken the boundaries between Yahwism and other religions would have been diminished or prohibited. This would explain why the Canaanites and other native people of the land are the main target of religious polemic in the narrative fiction of Deuteronomistic texts. The Mesopotamian or Egyptian religions are not perceived threats but those religions that are much closer to Yahwism. In effect, the nomistic criticism is targeted at the religion that lies at the background of Israel's own religious conceptions.

That the development of exclusive Yahwism is closely connected with identity and its protection is seen in its profound relationship with nationalistic tendencies. YHWH is the God of Israel and of Israel only (e.g., Deut 4:19; Deut 7; 29:25), while other nations have their own gods. Israel is described as YHWH's possession (Deut 7:6: עַם סְגֻלָּה) that was chosen along the nations to be his special people (Deut 10:5). Israel will inherit the land if the Israelites follow his commandments (Deut 8; 9:1–6), the most important of which is the exclusive worship of YHWH. In the nomistic conception Israel's wellbeing as well as its relationship with YHWH is largely dependent on undivided loyalty towards YHWH as its God.

Although the idea of a law defining Yahwism is present already in earlier Deuteronomism, it becomes a prominent feature in the nomistic texts. The Law effectively replaced the temple as the main means to follow YHWH. Instead of sacrifices, the Israelites should approach YHWH by obeying his law. The transformation of Yahwism from preexilic conceptions to Deuteronomistic and nomistic conceptions is illustrated in this chart:[35]

---

34 As noted by J. N. Shelton et al., "Threatened Identities and Interethnic Interactions," *European Review of Social Psychology* 17 (2006), 321–358, here p. 353: "perceived threats to identity are a primary source for intergroup tension, prejudice, and hostility." For terminology of ingroup and outgroup, see, for example, H. Tajfel et al., "Social Categorization and Intergroup Behaviour," *European Journal of Social Psychology*, Vol. 1, Issue 2 (1971), 149–178.
35 For details and discussion, see J. Pakkala "The Nomistic Roots of Judaism," *Houses Full of All Good Things. Essays in Memory of Timo Veijola* (ed. J. Pakkala and M. Nissinen; PFES 95; Helsinki and Göttingen 2008), 251–268.

	Preexilic religion	History Writer	Nomistic religion
Core	Temple	Temple	Law
Mediator	King	King	Moses
Worship of YHWH	Sacrifices	Sacrifices	Obedience to the Law
Physical Symbol	YHWH's statue		Tablets of the Law

The exclusive relationship between Israel and YHWH was further inspired by vassal and/or succession treaties. Although many of the same elements were already present in earlier nomistic texts, later nomistic editors were strongly influenced by the ideology and conceptions of vassal treaties. The relationship between the lord and the vassal was defined and specified in the terms of a treaty that was made between the counterparts. In most cases, the exclusive devotion of the vassal towards the lord was the rationale and goal of the treaty, and the various stipulations and terms aimed at keeping the vassal from following other lords.[36] If the vassal was loyal, the lord promised to protect the vassal from its enemies. This scheme was largely adopted *mutatis mutandis* in late nomistic texts: YHWH represented the lord, Israel the vassal, and Deuteronomy the treaty. The influence of the vassal treaties is most clear in Deut 13 and 28, both of which may be literarily dependent on a vassal treaty,[37] but the ideas can be found in many other late nomistic passages as well.[38]

The Deuteronomists and nomists did not represent the entire society. We are mainly dealing with a small group of people, whose ideas were adopted by all Jewish communities only slowly, perhaps only after centuries. It is thus probable that the worship of other divinities continued in many Yahwistic contexts much after these texts were written. For example, it is unlikely that Asherah would have been abandoned in all contexts immediately after 587 BCE. For everyone her cult was not dependent on the temple in Jerusalem. Since her cult is so ve-

---

36 The main rationale of succession treaties was to guarantee the safe transfer of power within the dynasty; the vassal was expected to assist and contribute to this by hindering any potential threats.

37 For a detailed discussion of these passages in relation to vassal treaties, see C. Koch, *Vertrag, Treueid und Bund* (BZAW 383; Berlin and New York 2008). He has shown that both chapters derive from a post-587 BCE context. Koch also excludes the possibility—argued by H. U. Steymans, *Deuteronomium 28 und die adê zur Thronfolgeregelung Asarhaddons. Segen und Fluch im Alten Ound in Israel* (OBO 145; Fribourg 1995) – that the Succession Treaty of Esarhaddon could be used to date Deuteronomy or these chapters.

38 For example, T. Veijola, *Das fünfte Buch Mose (Deuteronomium) Kapitel 1,1–16,17* (ATD 8/1; Göttingen 2004), has found the same author's hand in many parts of Deuteronomy, especially in chapters 4 and 7–11, 29–30.

hemently condemned much later (Deut 16:21; 2 Kgs 23:6), it seems probable that her cult was rather wide-spread and continued at least on a local level. The Elephantine letters also show that other gods were worshipped alongside with YHWH in some Yahwistic contexts still in the fifth century BCE. Although the Elephantine context may not be the best representation of Yahwism in the Persian period, the community was in contact with Jerusalem (including the high priest) and Samaria, which shows that it was not merely a secluded and abnormal Jewish community. Yahwism of the Persian period was practiced in various contexts in different parts of the Near East and it is probable that it took many local forms.

5 Monotheistic Tendencies in Late Deuteronomistic Texts

Some of the youngest Deuteronomistic texts show a further development of Yahwism. Instead of a hostile attack on the other gods, there is a group of six texts that deny their existence: Deut 4:32–40; Deut 7:7–11; 2 Sam 7:22–29; 1 Kgs 8:54–61; 1 Kgs 18:21–40 and 2 Kgs 19:15–19. Although they may not derive from the same author, many scholars have shown that they are some of the latest additions to the books in question.[39]

It is clear that the conceptions in these texts are far from systematic monotheism. Without any arguments or discussion about its basis, the passages bluntly claim that there is only one God, YHWH, and all six passages share a core sentence that makes the claim: יהוה הוא האלהים (YHWH is the God) or אתה הוא האלהים (You are the God).[40] By adding אין עוד, Deut 4:35, 39; 1 Kgs 8:60 and 2 Kgs 19:15, 19 further specify that the phrase refers to the uniqueness of YHWH as God: יהוה הוא האלהים אין עוד.

Besides taking a step towards monotheism, these texts largely build on earlier nomistic conceptions. The nationalistic tendency is evident in Deut 4:32–40, 7:7–11 and 2 Sam 7:22–29, which is not entirely consistent if there are no other gods for other nations to worship. They refer to Israel's election from all the nations to be YHWH's own people. Israel's history is also used as proof that YHWH is the only God. Only 2 Kgs 19:15–19 is more open to the possibility that YHWH could be the God of all nations (cf. v. 15: לכל ממלכות הארץ), and it is possible that the author of 2 Kgs 19:15–19 was familiar with the monotheism of Deutero-

---

39 For discussion of the passages in question, see J. Pakkala, "The Monotheism of the Deuteronomistic History," *SJOT* 21/2 (2007), 159–178.
40 The first person address is due to the context.

Isaiah.[41] The passages also contain some other elements that could be connected with monotheistic ideas: For example, Deut 4:32 and 2 Kgs 19:15 directly refer to creation, which is a development in comparison with conventional Deuteronomistic conceptions.

6 Conclusions

We may observe an evolutionary development in the Deuteronomistic texts. At the background are theological conceptions common in the Levant during the monarchic period, but there is a slightly elevated tendency towards monolatry at least in Judah by the seventh century BCE. The idea of an early form of Yahwism that differed fundamentally from other religions of the Levant should be rejected. After the destruction of 587 BCE the religion of Israel began a new trajectory that eventually led to monotheistic conceptions and developed into Judaism. An exceptional drive for oneness and the demand for exclusivity separated Yahwism from other religions of the Ancient Near East, but there is no evidence that these features emerged during the monarchic period. Rather than assume the historicity of Josiah's reform, the destructions of 587 BCE provide a more logical background for the revolutionary conceptions to emerge. A literary and redaction critical approach of Deuteronomistic literature shows that crucial stages in the emergence of oneness and exclusivity took place when the Deuteronomistic texts were written and edited from the sixth century BCE onwards. One can observe the development of monolatric features from the earliest Deuteronomistic texts to monotheistic conceptions in latest Deuteronomistic additions.

---

41 This aspect is much more developed in the monotheism of Deutero-Isaiah (see, for example, Isa 45,18 – 23).

Friedhelm Hartenstein

The Beginnings of YHWH and "Longing for the Origin"

A historico-hermeneutical query

1 The book of beginnings and the starting point of Israel's history (of religion)

1.1 Biblical beginnings

In 2008, the Israeli author Meir Shalev published a reflective re-narration of biblical beginnings entitled *Pe'amim rishonot ba-Tanach* ("Beginnings ... Reflections on the Bible's Intriguing Firsts").[1] In his book, those beginnings are brought close to our everyday experience of the present and in this way, the arc of suspense of a narrative which provides everlasting insights is realised in a surprisingly unbroken new way. In Shalev's book, the biblical beginnings are "true" beginnings of our experience; quite unlike the famous first chapter of "Joseph and His Brothers" by Thomas Mann, "Prologue: The descent to the underworld," where the descent deeper and deeper to the "spring of past" makes the reader become dizzy in view of the ambivalence of the finally vain wherefrom and when question.[2] However, the fact that it is impossible to come back to a final point of aim and rest stimulates further narrations and research so that at least stories can be written with regard to a given revoked and amorphous condition. This span in the phenomenon of beginnings, between the presumably solid ground and the abyss which proves to be an uncrossable limit of cognition, characterises human thinking in myths as well as in philosophy and historiography. The religio-historical question regarding the beginnings of YHWH and Israel, i. e. the starting point of a "(religious) history of Israel," is no exception. As it appears from the following historico-hermeneutical outline, it is rather a model case for the ambivalence of such beginnings between the necessity of the ques-

---

1 M. Shalev, *Beginnings. The First Love, the First Hate, the First Dream... Reflections on the Bible's Intriguing Firsts* (New York 2011); German: *Aller Anfang. Die erste Liebe, das erste Lachen, der erste Traum und andere erste Male in der Bibel* (Zürich 2010).
2 T. Mann, *Joseph und seine Brüder (Joseph and His Brothers). The first part: Die Geschichten Jaakobs (The Tales of Jacob)* (Frankfurt 1991/1933), 9–54.

DOI 10.1515/9783110448221-013

tion and the inadequacy of the answers. The difficulties for the historico-critical reconstruction of the early history of the YHWH religion in Old Testament studies can be summarized mainly in two constellations of problems:

a) The problem of the reliability resp. the value as a source of biblical narratives in view of their intentions – different with regard to modern historiography – as ancient narrations with a founding purpose. Since archaeological and epigraphic evidence of the origin of YHWH is mostly lacking, the primary dependence on biblical texts still aggravates the problem.

b) The problem of representation of historical reconstruction in terms of a narrative which puts together single scholarly insights and shows by its plot according to the traditional scheme beginning – centre – end a "whole" that exists actually first of all within this form.[3] Ambiguity arises here due to the impression of a possibly excessive evidence of the representation as well as due to the intention of the narrating historian, which is not always deliberately clear, in view of the interpretation of the beginnings described. (The problem of the intentionality of the biblical narratives recurs on the level of modern historiography).

1.2 The biblical consciousness of a double "lateness" of the beginnings of Israel/YHWH

Especially Erhard Blum has recently pointed out that the "peculiarity of Old Testament historical tradition" can be attributed neither to historiography nor to fiction.[4] If biblical texts are frequently referred to as fiction or myths in Old Testament studies today, this is because of a modern understanding of truth which ultimately differs from the ancient conceptions." In the light of categories of literary studies however, Blum attaches great importance to the reliability of the biblical historical narratives for the authors / recipients at that time (and subsequently for the process of tradition leading to the "canon," too). This authority of the narratives leads to a credibility, which should be recognised also historically, of persons and events / traditions in the context of life at that time. The "Hebrew tales" do not depend on "the concepts of potential realities in the (deliberate)

---

3 Cf. H. White, *Die Bedeutung der Form. Erzählstrukturen in der Geschichtsschreibung* (Frankfurt 1990; English 1987); P. Ricœur, *Zeit und Erzählung, Vol. 1: Zeit und historische Erzählung* (Übergänge 18,1) (Munich 1988; French 1983).
4 E. Blum, "Historiographie oder Dichtung? Zur Eigenart alttestamentlicher Geschichtsüberlieferung," in *Das Alte Testament – ein Geschichtsbuch?* (ed. W. Johnstone and C. Markschies; ATM 10; Münster 2005), 65 – 86.

illusion of representation;"[5] therefore they are no intentional creative fiction. On the contrary, they claim to "serve a binding representation of historical reality."[6] Thus especially the "limits of our categories of description"[7] should be considered here. The biblical texts claim their own truth with recourse to historical experiences, which should be distinguished from the truth claim of myths as well as of modern historiography. This has consequences for the question of beginnings.

Above all, ancient Near Eastern myths did stabilise institutions and power structures. The Enuma Elish was the legitimising myth of the nation of Babylon; its cosmogony is a cratogony. There is an analogy in the Egyptian creation myth from Heliopolis, which legitimised the world order at last, in the centre of which the pharaoh in the role of the sun god defeats the enemies. The great biblical narrative from Gen to 2 Kgs also begins with a cosmogony in Gen 1. However, it neither serves to justify the rule by kings nor does it describe the origin of gods (ancient Near Eastern cosmogonies are often at the same time theogonies). On the contrary, the Creator God Yhwh has already been present before any narrated beginnings (in Gen 1, the priestly report, exilic at the earliest [6th/5th century BC] as well as in the following, in its core presumably pre-priestly creation narrative [from Gen 2:4b on, possibly 7th century BC]). There is no narration about a genesis of God. His origin is no object of the biblical query. This is as remarkable as the information given en passant in Gen 4:26 that "at that time," i.e. at the time of the first descendants of Cain and Seth, "they began to invoke the name of Yhwh."[8]

The Primeval History does not tell anything about the beginnings of God, but nonetheless about a first beginning of his worship. The fact that this beginning of worship was not attributed to Israel, but from primordial time to the time of Moses to related tribes, whose area of settlement was in southern Palestine, points to a twofold "delayed" historical consciousness against the backdrop of

---

5 Blum, *Historiographie* (see n. 4), 80.

6 Blum, *Historiographie* (see n. 4), 80.

7 Blum, *Historiographie* (see n. 4), 80.

8 In the canonical order of reading, Gen 4:26b ("non-P") appears to be multifaceted: On the one hand, this part of the verse links the beginnings of the worship of Yhwh with Enos ("man"), the son of Seth, who was born "in place of Abel" (Gen 4:25) and therefore also in contrast to the line of Cain, the fratricide. On the other hand, Cain himself was referred to as a worshipper of Yhwh in Gen 4:1–16 before; and God does not cut the connection with the fratricide (cf. the "protective mark" Gen 4:15). The note in 4:26b seems to provide information regarding the primeval, pre-Israelite worship of Yhwh altogether. Thus it precedes the encounter of Israel with Yhwh, which appears to be mediated by Moses' Midianite relatives in the Book of Exodus (cf. Exod 3 and Exod 18 with Jethro as a priest of Yhwh).

biblical stories: Unlike in the ancient Near East, the traditional literature of Israel is aware of its own ethnogenesis, which is in the centre of the Torah, as a late phenomenon in the world of nations (cf. Gen 10). And also the worship of YHWH in Israel has been established only in the course of an intricate history of rescue from enforced labour in Egypt and wandering in the wilderness as an essential element of the narrative about Israel's becoming a nation, associated with Moses and the mountain of God in the southern desert. In view of the binding and plausible character of the biblical texts of foundation, it would be probably wrong to interpret this altogether for newly planned inventions after the loss of nationhood. In fact, the texts that were developed into their "final form" mainly in the Persian period, are likely to link up especially with existing knowledge, which is plausible from a pragmatic point of view. Their awareness of the social and political marginality of their own existence as well as of a historically antecedent worship of YHWH by southern related tribes (Kenites, Midianites) contributed in the time after the loss of nationhood and in the diaspora to the establishment of a "portative homeland" (Heinrich Heine[9]) in the form of the Torah.

1.3 The starting point of Israel's history (of religion) and the hermeneutical question of beginnings

Therefore, Old Testament studies have mostly sketched a picture of Israel's early times and the beginnings of YHWH in consideration of the aspects mentioned: Exodus and Sinai as well as the associated origin of YHWH from outside of Palestine have been considered to be eventually inexplicable, taking into account that historically credible details can hardly be separated anymore from the later picture which was repainted by many literary layers. The attempt to remove glaze and colouration right up to the oldest contours quickly leads the historical-critical method to its limits. However, each (religio-)historical account on Israel begins with a more or less extensive passage about "early times" or "previous history." Often its function is not only that of a mere exposition, but it is meant to bear the burden – on thin ice – of justifying subsequent events, particularly the distinctiveness of Israel and its belief in God. There must be more weighty reasons than the necessity of a plot for the fact that Old Testament studies do not simply show restraint here and begin at a later point after which more

---

9 H. Heine, "Geständnisse (1854)," in *Sämtliche Schriften 11* (ed. K. Briegleb; Munich 1976), 443–501; 483.

probable things can be said instead of speculative descriptions of the beginning. There cannot be "proper" beginnings in history itself. These are always determined by the historian and based on a certain insight resp. determined by his choice of the subject (cf. below 2.3). Insofar it is remarkable that the most considerate scholar Herbert Donner even goes as far as emphasising the necessity to speculate about the "first things" of Israel in a supplement to the second edition of his standard work on "History of Israel" (here using the example of Ernst Axel Knauf's theory about Moses):

> "It is not a serious matter of argument if such things are allowed in historiography or not. Of course they are allowed, and what is more: they are necessary in cases where the sources are such as they are in the previous history of Israel – and besides, this has always been done like that when one did not want to confine oneself to a simple re-narration of the biblical story. Ignoring assertions on historical periods of this type would be the alternative to 'speculation.'"[10]

Probably, exponents of other disciplines of history would content themselves quicklier with a merely negative result in view of beginnings. At any rate, historiography of nations, institutions, and companies is (rightly) exposed to an ideologicaly critical questioning due to the emphasis of foundational beginnings. The latter is an important part of self-enlightenment in the circle of historical understanding. For that reason, Marc Bloch, one of the founders of the French school of historians of the "Annales," adopts in his "Apology of History" of 1949 right in the first chapter a particularly biting tone against his own guild, which in his opinion makes use of quasi-religious evaluations, considering its often exaggerated interest in beginnings:

> "It is never a mistake to start with an admission of guilt. Of course, the explanation of later times by earlier times means a lot to people whose main research topic is the past; sometimes however it is so dominant in our studies that we could be considered hypnotised. This tribal idol of historians in its most distinct form can be called 'obsession with origins'. There was a time in the development of historical thinking which was particularly devoted to it."[11]

---

10 H. Donner, *Geschichte des Volkes Israel und seiner Nachbarn in Grundzügen* (GAT 4,1; Göttingen ²1995), 132. – For the translation of this and the following quotations as well as of the whole article I would like to give many thanks to my secretary at the LMU Munich, Ms. Susanne Schleeger.
11 M. Bloch, *Apologie der Geschichte oder der Beruf des Historikers* (Stuttgart ²1980; French 1949), 47 f.

In order to clarify this issue, Bloch recommends to "analyse why precisely the [Christian FH] exegetes are so strikingly tormented by the question how something has come into existence."[12] And he gives a plausible answer instantly, pointing out that for Christianity as a "substantially historical religion," "the beginnings of faith are also its foundations."[13] As early as a hundred years ago, Johann Gustav Droysen assigned in his lecture on "Historik" (science of history) – to which I will come back in more detail shortly (2.3.) – the question of the beginnings to historical interpretation, not to historical critique. Among other things, he clarified this by the debates on Early Christianity in connection with "Baur's school:"

> "This illusion [sc. of a distinct and defining historical beginning FH] becomes even more questionable if one believes that the *essence* of the matter, the actually decisive quintessence can be found in this search of the beginning. A significant example for it is the one given by Baur's school in the field of theological studies. One is looking for early Christianity ["Urchristentum"], the rather true and right heart of Christian nature [...]."[14]

Bloch and Droysen discuss a conception of beginnings, which has remained stable through many transformations in history of theology and philosophy up to present forms of scholarly epistemological interests. Especially theology and historico-critical biblical studies remain open to judgement and determination of meaning, which reach far beyond "neutral" historical facts. If Bloch warns of the "obsession with beginnings" with a view to the guild of historians (in times of two world wars), this should be understood as critical wariness at the sight of an affirming "longing for origins." It is represented – in Bloch's time – by Mircea Eliade's phenomenology of religion (and particularly distinct in his "Kosmos und Geschichte" (Cosmos and History),[15] which was published in the same year as Bloch's "Apology of History," 1949).

In fact, it is the already mentioned tension in the quest and thinking of beginnings/origins between basis and abyss, continuity and disruption, which has been condensed to major historical experiences in Judaism and Christianity (epiphany of God in Exodus/Sinai and crucifixion/resurrection of Jesus). Then the beginnings/origins have had a continuing intense influence in occidental tradi-

---

12 Bloch, *Apologie* (see n. 11), 49.
13 Bloch, *Apologie* (see n. 11), 49.
14 J.G. Droysen, *Historik. Rekonstruktion der ersten vollständigen Fassung der Vorlesungen (1857), Grundriß der Historik in der ersten handschriftlichen (1857/1858) und in der letzten gedruckten Fassung (1882)* (ed. P. Leyh; Stuttgart 1977), 160 [emphasis and brackets in the original version].
15 M. Eliade, *Kosmos und Geschichte. Der Mythos der ewigen Wiederkehr* (Frankfurt 1986; French 1949).

tions of knowledge, liberated of Christian doctrine and up to a modern perception of history. In their own way, descriptions of the beginnings of YHWH and Israel by Old Testament scholars in the 19th and 20th century participated here, too. I would like to clarify this by the following selected examples, but not without specifying first some conceptual aspects of beginning and origin in contemporary philosophy and conception of history.

2 Beginning and origin in philosophy and conception of history

2.1 On the use of the terms "beginning" and "origin"

In his book "Die Frage nach dem Ursprung" (The question of origin), the philosopher Emil Angehrn explains by the language use of different constellations in occidental thinking that beginning and origin – despite a similar meaning in many respects – also show considerable differences:[16]

a) Whereas "beginning" from a temporal point of view describes a first initial point, "origin" is associated above all with the idea of an enduring foundation for the future: As for "beginning," the direction of view is prospective, as for "origin," it is mainly retrospective.

b) From a qualitative/ontological point of view, "beginning" is therefore often associated with an emphasis on something new and a break with the past, which can be more or less categorial (pathos of the beginning right up to a sudden revelation). On the other hand, "origin" is a point of reference for a thinking which wants to confirm traditions and thus to underline continuity (enduring foundation and effective deep layer).

c) The pathos of the (new) beginning therefore contrasts with an "eternal recurrence" of the same. A subjective aspect (human freedom to be able to begin) and an objective one (sudden change in an event) can be distinguished here.

d) Nevertheless, the idea of an "absolute" beginning proves to be uncertain: As soon as there is a consequent historical thinking, the initial point vanishes and mutual ambivalences of the conceptions of beginning and origin become visible:

---

16 E. Angehrn, *Die Frage nach dem Ursprung. Philosophie zwischen Ursprungsdenken und Ursprungskritik* (Munich 2007). Cf. with regard to the following ibid., 23–42 (Konstellationen und Zwiespältigkeiten des Ursprungsdenkens).

"The beginning is both ground and abyss, recognisable start and past which is lost in the dark; and return to the beginning means safety as well as threat, identity as well as diffusion."[17]

Since time immemorial, the securing of collective identities often took shape of a founding history of a founding history, which brings to mind "a way back that facilitates the understanding of subsequent constellations."[18] Also philosophic thinking tries to answer the question about the whence, wherefrom, and whereby of the contemporary world and its universal laws in a well founded way; this was already the prominent occupation of the Presocratics. From a philosophico-historical point of view, the general sequence of myth and metaphysics is referred to as typical for the constellations of occidental thinking, however simultaneously some of the time.[19] Positive definitions of beginnings/origins also can change to the contrary in both forms of thought. In view of the "significant unsteadiness in the epistemological state of the first one,"[20] "*Ursprungsdenken*" and "*Ursprungskritik*" are not mutually exclusive then but necessarily mutually dependent. This became particularly virulent in the 19th/20th century, when the understanding of the back and forth between the return to a solid ground and the awareness that there is a remaining hiddenness of final bases became more profound (critique of idealism) through the influence of a general historical consciousness.

Patterns of judgement which already existed in ancient times recur in the developmental logics of modern conceptions of history:[21] Yet ancient Near Eastern creation myths and Hesiod's Theogony include schemes of a graduated harmonious development as well as schemes of struggle and loss (successive genealogies of gods representing at the same time the emergence of the world elements, as well as antagonistic conflicts). Then the irreversible direction of a development is often a graduated sequence which includes a judgement: For example, the beginning (the "not yet" of all subsequent events) seems to be rudimentary, deficient, and small; history evolves to a higher level from there (history of progress). However, there is also the pattern of the lost and highly valued beginning, a "golden age," paradise or harmonious original condition (history of decay, frequently according to the pattern of a "Fall"). Due to such central figures in rep-

---

17 Angehrn, *Frage* (see n. 16), 30.
18 Angehrn, *Frage* (see n. 16), 28.
19 Cf. K. Hüber, *Die Wahrheit des Mythos* (Munich 1985); C. Jamme, *"Gott an hat ein Gewand". Grenzen und Perspektiven philosophischer Mythos-Theorien der Gegenwart* (Frankfurt 1991); E. Angehrn, *Die Überwindung des Chaos. Zur Philosophie des Mythos* (Frankfurt 1996).
20 Angehrn, *Frage* (see n. 16), 32.
21 The following according to Angehrn, *Frage* (see n. 16), 37 f.

resentations of history which reach far back and are often not apparent immediately, it is necessary to ask critical-hermeneutical questions and to unveil hidden premises to this day:

> "The normative or affective determination of a certain relation to the beginning is not a matter of course but requires clarification and discussion."[22]

2.2 Figures of modern conception of history

Once European thinkers have thematised history in contrast to a more and more unravelled nature as a decisive point of reference for occidental identity (starting in the 17th/18th and mainly in the 19th/20th century), the question of beginnings in a new form has proved to be determining:[23]

a) On the one hand in the 17th/18th century in images where nature was depicted as the early and original condition. In this context, the postulation of a "state of nature" was formulated, from which human development of civilisation had started (especially in Hobbes', Locke's, and Rousseau's theories of the state and legal theories, to a certain degree also in Herder's works). The discoveries of the "savage," uncivilised – from the Eurocentric perspective – peoples in America and Oceania caused this assumption, too. The gap between the own culture, which was estimated to be more developed, and the "primitives" became the "empirical" affirmation of the self-conception here.

b) On the other hand in the late 18th and particularly in the 19th century in the forms of historical thinking in the proper meaning of the word. Then extensive philosophies of history which aimed at the entire course of the becoming of the world (Kant and Hegel) were followed by the historiography of historicism with its academic ethos of a historical scholarship which is aware of its limits. In the 20th century, also fragmentary stories of the victims established themselves, reflecting the catastrophes of totalitarianism, genocides and world wars. In this context, historical thinking additionally places special emphasis on the interest in historical memory as an ethically imperative review.

---

22 Angehrn, *Frage* (see n. 16), 38.
23 With regard to the following cf. Angehrn, *Frage* (see n. 16), 135–157 (Konstellationen des neuzeitlichen Geschichtsdenkens).

2.3. The problematisation of beginnings in historiography in the light of Droysen's "Historik"

In the 19th century, single histories of cultures, empires, or nations were written in a more or less distinct divergence from the extensive explanatory claims of historico-philosophical speculation. They thematised important details of non-thematic comprehensive history. The idea of the genealogical explanation is central for these "particular histories" (contrary or referring to universal historical concepts) and it is meant to facilitate a "historical understanding in the genuine meaning"[24] even without the recourse to speculative first beginnings. The understanding itself is considered to be historical now (and thereby to be relative and limited). However, the claim to a quasi empirical representation of real processes, a "historical realism"[25] (exemplary in Leopold von Ranke) is connected to it, too. In addition to the perception of long-term structural "laws," a keen awareness of contingency and individuality in history is appearing – an aspect which is not only suited for contouring but also for a critique of historical imagination until today. In view of the questioning of an "empirical" conception of history in the 19th century, especially by Friedrich Nietzsche, Angehrn for example points to another hermeneutics of history which is aware of the fragmentarity of "historical reality" as well as of the fragility of its own narratives. The ability to dissociate is constitutive of it:

> "Authentic historical thinking, which emphasises the breaks and contingencies in becoming and enables to see what belongs to one's own from the exterior and to perceive what is different and unfamiliar, opposes the longing for the origin and the totalization of the beginning and the end."[26]

Hayden White, who devoted himself intensively to the forms of narration of historiography in the 19th century and to the claims to represent reality related to them, cites – in addition to Nietzsche – particularly Johann Gustav Droysen as the founder of such hermeneutics:[27]

> "Droysen clearly realised the weakness of the conception of realism based on an empirical epistemology. [...] What is historically real is never given by the mere 'experience'; it has

---

24 Angehrn, *Frage* (see n. 16), 156.
25 Cf. H. White, *Metahistory. Die historische Einbildungskraft im 19. Jahrhundert in Europa* (Frankfurt 1991; English 1973), 177–346 (Vier Formen des "Realismus" in der Geschichtsschreibung des 19. Jahrhunderts).
26 Angehrn, *Frage* (see n. 16), 157.
27 White, *Metahistory* (see n. 25).

always been worked on and formed by a specific organisation of experience, the praxis of society, from which the picture of reality is sketched. Undoubtedly, this is why he emphasised so much the possibility to sketch alternative, but equally valid pictures of historical reality [...]."[28]

Regarding our question, there is a remarkable treatise in Droysen's lecture on "Historik" published posthumously, which I have already mentioned above (cf. 1.). He ascribes the study of beginnings not to historical critique, but to interpretation (= the narrating representation), since a beginning cannot be won methodically-critically, but has always to be set and is therefore an element of an indispensable hermeneutic circle, "which helps *us* on, but not the matter."[29]

"That is the way all historical phenomena are; their beginning is not only a beginning, but at the same time the end and termination of a number of mediations, and it is just a methodical thoughtlessness to believe that by carrying out research you could reach a point which could be the beginning other than *relatively*, i.e. which proves to be a beginning other than in what it has become, }and therefore which we put as a beginning in relation to what it has become{. [...] For we can think speculatively and believe religiously in an unmediated, absolute beginning, but we cannot find it historically, and whoever wants to find it should not seek it historically; otherwise you will get into the boring discussion if the egg or the chicken was first."[30]

This is why Droysen refuses to accept the prevalent explanatory claims of historians which are analogous to natural sciences. It is problematic to make genetic deductions from original "seeds" or "organic growth" (use of metaphors of nature and plants) since these beginnings can only be asserted speculatively. On the other hand, the substance of "what our studies can accomplish"[31] is different:

"they are exact in so far as they get their results from this material [sc. their given sources FH] in correct syllogisms, that they do not deduce anything from hypothetical beginnings, that they do not try to explain empirical material by first seeds or origins which are *not* empirical. [...] We do not explain. Interpretation is not an explanation of later phenomena by earlier ones, of what has become as a}necessary{ result of historical conditions, but it is the reading of what is available, quasi a loosening and disentangling of this unimpressive ma-

---

28 H. White, "Droysens Historik. Geschichtsschreibung als bürgerliche Wissenschaft," in *Bedeu-tung* (see n. 3), 108–131; 126.

29 Droysen, *Historik* (see n. 14), 162 [emphasis in the original version].

30 Droysen, *Historik* (see n. 14), 160 [emphasis and brackets in the original version].

31 Droysen, *Historik* (see n. 14), 162.

terial according to the overabundance of its moments, the innumerable threads knotted together, just as if it became reanimated by the art of interpretation and finds its voice."[32]

As mentioned previously (cf. above 1.), Droysen cites the question regarding Early Christianity as a relevant example of how a "strong," highly significant conception of origin can guide and determine historical research with (latent or manifest) legitimising intent. For quite similar reasons, I would like to add the study of the beginnings of YHWH and Israel here.

3 "Originality" as a leitmotif in Wellhausen's conception of history

3.1 Measures of value in Wellhausen's conception of history

It is unnecessary to emphasise Julius Wellhausen's importance. Rudolf Smend referred to him as a "pioneer in three disciplines"[33] (Old and New Testament, Islamic studies). He fixed the relative order of the critically analysed sources of the Pentateuch/Hexateuch and the historical books of the Old Testament, which had been initiated by Wilhelm Martin Leberecht de Wette at the beginning of the 19th century and pursued in detail by scholars like Hermann Hupfeld and Abraham Kuenen, by conclusive historical means, i.e. source analysis[34] and above all in (religio-)historical longitudinal sections.[35]

Wellhausen clearly expresses personal appreciation and predilection in his texts, so that his approach is believed to be immediately recognisable. However, his basic intentions remain amazingly implicit. He joins the ranks of historiography of the 19th century mentioned above (2.2.) (history of single cultures, nations) and considers the (religious) history of Israel (or of the Arabs/Islam) quite naturally as part of the historiographic efforts of historical scholarship on the whole. On the other hand, he concludes his history of Israel/the Israelite-Jewish religion with Early Christianity including the formation of New Testament scriptures.

---

32 Droysen, *Historik* (see n. 14), 162f. [emphasis and brackets in the original version].
33 R. Smend, *Julius Wellhausen. Ein Bahnbrecher in drei Disziplinen* (Carl Friedrich von Siemens Stiftung Themen 82; Munich 2004).
34 J. Wellhausen, *Prolegomena zur Geschichte Israels* (1873) (Berlin ⁶1905); id., *Die Composition des Hexateuchs und der historischen Bücher des Alten Testaments* (1876f.) (Berlin ³1899).
35 J. Wellhausen, *Israelitische und jüdische Geschichte* (1894) (Berlin ⁶1907); id., *Israelitisch-jüdische Religion (Die Kultur der Gegenwart 1,4)* (Berlin and Leipzig 1905), 1–38 (= id., *Grundrisse zum Alten Testament* [TB 27; ed. R. Smend; Munich 1965], 65–109).

Thus his entire narrative is also guided by the interest in a deeper understanding of the matter in view of the own cultural and religious position. Studies on Wellhausen's images of history point out an as distanced as identifying attitude here (seeing himself in the role of an "heir" of history of Israel/Judaism and Christianity[36]). In view of the "culture of the present age," to which he belongs, he is characterising the "great importance" of the Israelite-Jewish religion as a "preliminary stage of the Christian one"[37] right in the first sentence of his description. At the end of the same description, he refers to the phenomenon of an emerging "religious individualism" in the late texts of the Old Testament, which "lays the ground on which Christianity is based from the start."[38] In his still illuminating study on "motifs and standards" of Wellhausen's historiography, Friedemann Boschwitz is interpreting this last passage of the "Israelite-Jewish religion" as one of two boundary posts between which the overall development of his concept is stretching:

> "thus we catch sight of the two extremely antithetical ends of his assessment of history: the Protestant 'religious individualism' on the one hand, and on the other hand, the enthusiastic appreciation of times when religion was 'patriotism' (IjGesch 55)."[39]

The development perceived by Wellhausen involves the way from a nation with a "national" faith in Yhwh to the individualisation of a more complex stage of religion which sets religion apart from nation. However, this is explicitly not narrated as a history of progress (and therefore no analogy with Hegel's philosophy of history is detectable). Opposed tendencies of esteem for Israel's simple, unadulterated, and strong beginnings close to nature rather become obvious. These beginnings were effaced by the later "overpainting" of the texts (e.g. David in Chronicles), and Wellhausen's reconstruction aims at the exposure of the "great simplicity" of the beginnings, here of cult:

> "The fact that Israelite religious service was of great simplicity at the beginning has to do with the general cultural stage; later it disappeared more and more, or just a minority kept to it basically and protestingly."[40]

---

36 Cf. F. Boschwitz, Julius Wellhausen. *Motive und Maßstäbe seiner Geschichtsschreibung* (1938) (Darmstadt ²1968), 32; and with reference to it L. Perlitt, *Vatke und Wellhausen. Geschichtsphilosophische Voraussetzungen und historiographische Motive für die Darstellung der Religion und Geschichte Israels durch Wilhelm Vatke und Julius Wellhausen* (BZAW 94; Berlin 1965), 181.

37 Wellhausen, *Religion* (see n. 35), 65.

38 Wellhausen, *Religion* (see n. 35), 109 (about Hiob and Psalms).

39 Boschwitz, *Wellhausen* (see n. 36), 31f. [emphasis in the original version].

40 Wellhausen, *Religion* (see n. 35), 77.

These and similar assertions can also be read as a history of decay, although this is not articulated explicitly. On the one hand, Boschwitz compares Wellhausen's emphasis of the simplicity and primordialism of the beginnings with Herder's idealisation of archaic peoples, from which it differs however because of the historical consciousness of the 19th century; on the other hand, he points to Wellhausen's closeness to Nietzsche's view that the preference of simpleness and earliness is the "somehow 'proper relation to all things'."[41] Wellhausen was also interested in pre-Islamic Arabs ("Arab paganism"), mainly because of the analogy with the "originality" of early Israelites:

"I have changed over from the Old Testament to the Arabs with intent to come to know the savage on whom priests and prophets have forced the Torah of YHWH. For I do not doubt that the easiest way to conceive an idea of the *original* features of the Hebrews when they entered into history is to compare them with the ancient Arab world."[42]

3.2 The beginnings of the Israelite religion and the hermeneutical question of Israel's/YHWH's distinctiveness

Regarding Wellhausen's description of the beginnings of Israel and its religion, the following aspects are important for our question:

a) The starting point of Israel's history (of religion) is Israel's becoming a nation, not its previous history.[43]

b) Wellhausen's narration about Israel's evolution begins with the change of place and status of the Hebrews, which leads to Israel's becoming a nation:

"From the steppe in southern Palestine the Hebrew families, who eventually became Israel, had moved to the adjacent eastern part of the Pharaonic kingdom."[44]

c) At first, Israel and YHWH formed a whole where the past history of God and His dwelling place on the mountain ("originally a weather god"[45]), of which traces are still perceptible, is not interesting anymore. Instead, the symbiotic union between God and nation, which according to Wellhausen has been con-

---

41 Boschwitz, *Wellhausen* (see n. 36), 31.
42 J. Wellhausen, *Muhammed in Medina. Das ist Vakidi's Kitab al Maghazi in verkürzter deutscher Wiedergabe herausgegeben* (Berlin 1882), 5 (emphasis FH).
43 Wellhausen, *Geschichte* (see n. 35), 11.
44 Wellhausen, *Geschichte* (see n. 35), 12.
45 Wellhausen, *Religion* (see n. 35), 74.

solidated by a "law" of the becoming of nations at war,[46] is considered to be the beginning and foundaticn for all subsequent events:

"At the time of Moses, the people of Israel grew together from related families and tribes and placed itself above them. The new unity was hallowed by YHWH, who had existed before indeed, but who became the ruler of this nation only now. YHWH God of Israel, Israel the nation of YHWH: this is the beginning and the enduring principle of the following politico-religious history."[47]

d) Despite the importance of beginnings for subsequent events, the explicitly open question remains how they allow Israel's distinctiveness to be completely understood. It is apriori an individual historical particularity and in that respect part of human history. However, it has also passed through an development of its own, which is not adequately explicable and perhaps has to do with the profile of the god (the particularity of cult does not concern the "manner" but the "dative to which it is dedicated,"[48] i.e. YHWH, not Baal):

"It is undeniably beneficial indeed that a development can be seen yet from hidden traces in the Old Testament; the history of Israel becomes a real history only as a result of it and is not left beyond all analogy with the history of the whole rest of mankind. But even if we could pursue this development in a more precise and more reliable way, it would explain only little after all. For instance, why did Chemosh of Moab not become the god of justice and creator of heaven and earth? A satisfactory answer to this cannot be given."[49]

The openness of the question of distinctiveness beyond historical individuality points to the deeper historico-hermeneutical significance of the question. Even though studies on biblical texts and their historical contexts follow the methods of historical scholarship, the difficult question in view of the assessment especially of beginnings (regarding the narrative description as well as the overall view) for the exegete – as a theologian or at least an "heir" of the Judaeo-Christian tradition – remains how he responds to the significant weight of historical beginnings in this tradition (e.g. to the central beliefs of crucifixion and resurrection of Jesus in Judaea under Roman administration in about 30 AD). The question cannot be avoided as soon as it is meant to be understood in a historical manner. Wellhausen expressed himself in a pleasantly reserved way and kept things in suspense. His contemporaries and successors have struggled more controversially down to the present day.

---

46 "It is war that creates nations" (Wellhausen, *Geschichte* [see n. 35], 25).
47 Wellhausen, *Geschichte* (see n. 35), 25.
48 Wellhausen, *Religion* (see n. 35), 79.
49 Wellhausen, *Religion* (see n. 35), 81.

4 Revelation and hermeneutics of history

4.1 The controversy regarding Israel's distinctiveness in the course of Wellhausen's perspective

Abraham Kuenen, Rudolf Smend senior, and Bernhard Stade assessed Israel's beginnings similarly to Wellhausen and partly in close agreement with his epoch-making point of view. Nevertheless, regarding the question of the distinctiveness of the Israelite religion, which has possibly already been underlying in these beginnings, also divergent opinions can be found in their studies and textbooks. In his "Religion of Israel," Kuenen drew a close analogy between the pre-prophetic ancient Israelite religion and what was known about the "Semites" (Moabites et al.) at that time. He emphasised the early polytheism ("At first the religion of Israel was polytheism"[50]) more strongly than Wellhausen. In this respect, he thought of the natural acceptance of similar gods of neighbouring peoples by early Israelites, as well as of the worship of other numina. At the same time, he emphasised the particularity of the "original idea of YHWH," from which Israel's later development towards "the highest and the best" arose:[51]

> "The relationship between YHWH and Israel is so thoroughly parallel to the relationship between Chemosh and Moab that there is no doubt about their similarity. [...] Please get me right: I am not saying that YHWH and Chemosh are identical. The later realised promise of the highest and best has already been lying in the original idea of YHWH, which is not at all the case with Chemosh. But I am asserting however that YHWH and Chemosh are sons of one house, branches of one line, and that it is not allowed to attribute a quite different origin to the one than to the other. It is this proposition which would have come to light also in comparative studies of the Semitic pantheon [...]."[52]

Theologians with a more traditional attitude disagreed. In the mentioned omnibus review of 1888 for example, Kuenen dealt above all with Friedrich Baethgen, who regarded "the scholars who think that traces of a former polytheism can be found in the narratives about Israel's forefathers"[53] contemptuously as "creators of myths:"

---

50 A. Kuenen, *The Religion of Israel to the Fall of the Jewish State I* (London 1874), (Dutch 1869–70: De godsdienst van Israël), 223, cf. further 223–249.
51 Regarding the "oldest and original Jahvism" (Kuenen, *Religion* [see n. 50], 231), he thought of YHWH as a god of the light or the sun (249).
52 A. Kuenen, "Drei Wege, ein Ziel (1888)," in *Gesammelte Abhandlungen zur Biblischen Wissenschaft* (trans. K. Budde; Freiburg 1894), 430–464; 461.
53 Kuenen, *Wege* (see n. 52), 450.

"But if Baethgen tries to make us believe that already the El Shaddai of the patriarchs and, *a fortiori*, the Mosaic Yʜwʜ constitute a higher stage of development than the Common Semitic El described by him there, we cannot possibly follow him. *The* El Shaddai and *the* Yʜwʜ, to whom this might apply, are products of imaginative fiction; imaginary figures, at their right place in dogmatics, but unverifiable historically."[54]

Therefore, Kuenen demands – which is surprisingly modern – a critical review of the own historico-hermeneutical presuppositions:

"Therefore a good deal depends on *the expectation* the study is approached with. Those who think that an original Israelite polytheism is *a priori* unlikely, even almost absurd, will not be impressed by the poor traces they encounter in the Old Testament, and they will easily succeed in deleting these traces, especially if they deal with each of them individually and do not care about their merging."[55]

According to Kuenen, the uniqueness of Yʜwʜ is only due to the individual character, which was nevertheless sufficient to predestine the later development. It certainly does not pertain to a categorial point of view – it would be unhistorical to claim that. Bernhard Stade, however, represented a somewhat "stronger" emphasis on the origin of the basic principle "Yʜwʜ, Israel's God" as exclusive worship (within the nation). He assumed that "the impulse for the particular development of Israel's religion had been set directly at the foundation of religion as a predisposition in Israel."[56] This shows how the question of Israel's finally inexplicable particularity, which Wellhausen had deliberately left in abeyance, has become a historico-hermeneutical problem for the historical representations in connection with him that cannot be simply put aside as a dogmatic relic. Indeed, the counterside tried to keep to the supra-natural singularity of the revelation. August Dillmann would be an example here. He posed the question differently, in a strictly rhetorical sense, since the answer was clear to him from the beginning:

"If the Old Testament religion is qualitatively and fundamentally different from all pagan religions, the question is: how is it to be understood according to its origin? By purely natural means or on the initiative and under the command of God?"[57]

---

54 Kuenen, *Wege*, 460 [emphasis in the original version].
55 Kuenen, *Wege*, 462 [emphasis in the original version]
56 B. Stade, *Biblische Theologie des Alten Testaments 1. Die Religion Israels und die Entstehung des Judentums* (GThW 2,2; Tübingen 1905), 46.
57 A. Dillmann, *Handbuch der alttestamentlichen Theologie* (ed. R. Kittel; Leipzig 1895), 52.

He accuses Kuenen, Duhm, Wellhausen, and Stade of misinterpreting Israel's beginnings as an "entirely indifferent Yahwism, which did not differ in the least from the popular religions of the other Canaanite tribes [...]."[58] He emphasises emphatically "that the nation joined the new religion all in all at the time of Moses."[59] Revelation with the "feature of originality"[60] is crucial to him. This shows how dealing with the hidden beginnings of Israel/YHWH made the exegetes position themselves in view of the relationship between revelation and history.

4.2 Influence of dialectical theology and the theory of the initial lack of analogy of Israel and YHWH

The category of revelation as God's self-revelation in and through history was attributed a new meaning also in Old Testament studies with the "dialectical theology" as an answer to the crisis of interpretation of history after World War I (and II). This did not remain without consequences for the dealing with the historico-hermeneutical question of the beginnings/origins of Israel/YHWH. It is revealing how religio-historical and literary-historical questions of the late 19th and early 20th century had been losing their impact. The traditio-historical approach took their place, trying to arbitrate between history and revelation by the category of a believed history of salvation in Israel (with a hermeneutic connection up to the present day; cf. Gerhard von Rad's approach regarding Israel's "historical credo"). Martin Noth, whose great traditio-historical reconstructions regarding the Pentateuch and historical books became the determining syntheses of the new approach, explained at the very beginning of his "Geschichte Israels" (History of Israel) of 1950, which served as a textbook for many generations of students, how he defined the relationship between history and revelation:

> "The true historicality of 'Israel' is not questioned by the fact that in its history, we also encounter the element of a condition which is not really perceptible anymore, and which is not attributable in any case to the coherences of established causes and effects anymore, and therefore which is not explicable anymore. For this element is part of *any* human history and must be a part of it [...]."[61]

---

58 Dillmann, *Theologie* (see n. 57), 55.
59 Dillmann, *Theologie* (see n. 57), 56.
60 Dillmann, *Theologie* (see n. 57), 65 [emphasis in the original version].
61 M. Noth, *Geschichte Israels* (1950) (Munich ³1956), 9 f. [emphasis in the original version].

Throughout history, an "element of what is not definable" and even "absolutely unfathomable, unhistorical," can be found.[62] Noth sees a clue to God's effectiveness "in history" in it, as the "ever-present Lord" (with reference to Karl Barth's "Kirchliche Dogmatik" (Ecclesiastical dogmatics) III,1 of 1945[63]). However, he does not only retain this possible regard to transcendency at the limits of cognition; in addition to it, the historian has to recognise Israel's lack of analogy, which is different in its own way:

"Yet still 'Israel' appears as a stranger in this world right in the light of these coherences and possibilities of comparison, who wore its clothes and behaved in its common manner, but was separated from it by its nature. This did not happen in such a way that every historical factor has its individual particularity and thus is never really equal to other historical factors, but rather in such a way that we encounter phenomena in the centre of the history of 'Israel' for which there are no more possibilities of comparison [...]."[64]

According to Noth, these phenomena without analogy are already present in Israel's beginnings, especially at Sinai, in the sense of a "strong" initial relationship. Instantly they appear to be "mysterious," since "we cannot name any human being who intervened in what is happening there, neither by acting nor by interpreting."[65] As is generally known, Noth had separated the figure of Moses traditio-historically from the Sinai tradition as being secondary. Thus, this tradition appears to be in "splendid isolation:"

"The *content and character of the act at Sinai* escapes from historical interpretation even more than the external circumstances and coherences. What we can understand historically is a testimony of an epiphany of God before the tribes pilgrimaging to Sinai, which is constantly repeated in liturgical presentation and preaching. The matter itself however extends into the sphere of what is not historically comprehensible anymore in the sense of p. 11 above. Nevertheless, this mystery and its consequences, the loyalty to the God who has become visible and the submission to His exclusive ('jealous') claims and will, has been emerging in historically determined forms."[66]

So it is a matter of revelation "in historically determined forms," where "that overall picture" (the union of Israel and God) "has been there in its major ele-

---

62 Noth, *Geschichte* (see n. 61), 10.

63 Noth, *Geschichte* (see n. 61), 10, with note 1 (K. Barth, KD III, 1, 84 ff.).

64 Noth, *Geschichte* (see n. 61), 11.

65 Noth, *Geschichte* (see n. 61), 128.

66 Noth, *Geschichte* (see n. 61), 126 [emphasis in the original version; regarding the hint on p. 11 cf. the quotation above, see n. 64].

ments very early."[67] Among others, Georg Fohrer, Werner H. Schmidt, and Rainer Albertz have taken a quite similar view of revelation in history, referring more or less distinctly to Noth. In W. H. Schmidt's successful textbook "Alttestamentlicher Glaube" (Old Testament belief), which is by definition a book between history of religion and theology, the pivotal commandment of the Decalogue (1st and 2nd commandment) referring to YHWH constitutes a beginning of Israel, which cannot be clarified by traditio-historical means anymore, and which was not effective "literally," but "first rather just in substance."[68] In his "Religionsgeschichte Israels" (Religious history of Israel) of 1992, which claimed to replace Old Testament theology by a socio-historical perspective, Rainer Albertz stands in the very tradition of the expounded determination of existing relationships between revelation and history in view of the particularity of Israel/YHWH, too, and he is influenced by dialectical theology when he interprets the Sinai theophany (without the Decalogue) as an experience which "completely breaks the course of history:"

> "In the liberation from their servitude in Egypt, they [sc. the Exodus group FH] had experienced YHWH in a historical process. They are confronted with the onset of His divine sphere of power coming into their reality at the mountain of God in a way that completely breaks the course of history."[69]

The mentioned interpretations of Israel's beginnings have in common that they read Israel's believed experiences of origins theologically in such a way that their claimed relevance for the present shines through and goes with an implicit and explicit demand for exegesis for the present. The tension of the beginnings between hiddenness and solid ground in view of what is historically not explicable (anymore) is not kept open here, but determined in the sense of a "strong" origin and new beginning (revelation). The hermeneutics of history, which is at the basis of it and hardly revealed in most cases (most clearly, however, in Noth), is salvation- and revelation-historical: closer to Dillmann (cf. 4.1.) than to Wellhausen and his followers. This has been changing again in the latest stage of representations of Israel's history (of religion).

---

67 Noth, *Geschichte* (see n. 61), 129.

68 W.H. Schmidt, *Alttestamentlicher Glaube* (Neukirchen-Vluyn [8]1996), 78.

69 R. Albertz, *Religionsgeschichte Israels in alttestamentlicher Zeit 1. Von den Anfängen bis zum Ende der Königszeit* (GAT 8,1; Göttingen 1992), 89.

5 The modern religio-historical approach and the beginnings of YHWH

5.1 State of discussion[70]

Especially due to intensive excavations and surveys in Palestine, material sources (archaeological remains, pictures and epigraphic evidence) have increased so significantly in the last decades that it is now a lot easier than before to correlate the analysis of biblical texts with (religio-) historical extrabiblical findings. However, the question of what is to be considered as a "primary" or "secondary" source cannot be answered generally but only with reference to each individual case and each specific issue (at any rate, it would be a mistake to regard the biblical texts a priori as historically irrelevant). The insight that Israel has come into being in the country itself is the major difference compared to former approaches to Israel's origins. The archaeological findings at Kuntillet 'Ajrud and Khirbet el-Kom made the assumption of polytheism in Israel and Judah (= Iron Age II) much more probable. Following Morton Smith and Bernhard Lang, the much-noticed theory of oppositional adherents of a "Sole-YHWH-movement,"[71] which could be deduced indirectly from the prophets of the 8th century BC, also was a turning away from von Rad's and Noth's traditio-historical school and a comeback of Wellhausen's and Kuenen's approach that prophecy was a major change in the religious development in Israel.

Like Kuenen, Manfred Weippert for example drew a religio-sociologically differentiated picture in a much-noticed paper of 1990, according to which a polytheism particularly of the nation had been determining for religion in the Iron Age states Israel and Judah. Only the archaeologically briefed, critical query behind the "final form" of the biblical texts makes it possible then – like in Wellhausen's "pagan relics" – to find traces of the former religion, which is deleted resp. only visible through later polemics:

> "This religion was polytheistic. The Old Testament is full of critical and polemical statements of the tenor that the Israelites worshiped a multitude of gods. Though I would not guarantee for all details of these statements, I still do not see any reason for doubting

---

70 Cf. also F. Hartenstein, "Religionsgeschichte Israels – ein Überblick über die Forschung seit 1990," *VF* 48 (2003), 2–28.

71 C.B. Lang (ed.), *Der einzige Gott. Die Geburt des biblischen Monotheismus* (Munich 1981).

about their fundamental validity. As a matter of course, Yʜwʜ, who even took a prominent position as the national god of Israel, was worshiped, too [...]."[72]

The particularity of the later theology/theologies of the Old Testament writings with its exclusive monotheism has then evolved – as in Wellhausen and Kuenen – first gradually, and, as Weippert is concerned, namely from Hosea on since the 8th century BC. However, in the end it remains doubtful where the criteria for that "internal religious process of distinction" come from. The question of the formative beginnings is shifting; nevertheless it is still beset by the same known problems. In Weippert's opinion, the pre-Israelite "original character of Yʜwʜ" is (quite similarly to Wellhausen) "inherently a god of the Hadad type,"[73] i.e. the weather god – a point of view which is broadly shared today. Quite traditionally, Weippert refers here to Yʜwʜ's first dwelling place in the mountains of the southern desert, the Sinai.

Important impulses not only for the reconstruction of the development of monotheism, but also in view of its beginnings/origins have come also from the short extra-biblical texts of Kuntillet 'Ajrud. Under the graffiti of the caravan station (8th century BC), "Yʜwʜ of Samaria" appears beside "Yʜwʜ of Teman," a location which refers to the territory of Edom. Scholars immediately linked it with the above (1.2.) mentioned biblical statements on the origin of Yʜwʜ from the South (Teman, [Mount] Paran, Seir, Sinai). Like almost all their followers in the 19th/20th century, Wellhausen and Kuenen have already considered the contact with the southern tribes of the Kenites/Kenizzites, Midianites, and Edomites as pre-Israelite worshippers of Yʜwʜ mentioned in the Bible to be historically reliable. In the light of the relevant biblical texts, most scholars consider nomadic groups from outside (the Shasu of the Egyptian sources) to be not exactly a directly verifiable, but crucial factor for the formation of tradition of emerging Israel. Possibly they introduced Yʜwʜ in Palestine – a theory which is held for example by Fritz Stolz, Mark S. Smith, and others.[74] However, this relative consent has recently been questioned, too.

In German-speaking Europe, there are more differentiated redaction-critical models than ever regarding the origin of biblical texts, in addition to religious

---

72 M. Weippert, "Synkretismus und Monotheismus. Religionsinterne Konfliktbewältigung im alten Israel (1990)," in *Jahwe und die anderen Götter. Studien zur Religionsgeschichte des antiken Israel in ihrem syrisch-palästinischen Kontext* (FAT 18; Tübingen 1997), 1–24; here 10.
73 Weippert, *Synkretismus* (see n. 72), 16.
74 F. Stolz, *Einführung in den biblischen Monotheismus* (Darmstadt 1996), 91; M.S. Smith, *The Origins of Biblical Monotheism. Israel's Polytheistic Background and the Ugaritic Texts* (Oxford 2001), 139–148.

history which works in close connection with archaeology of Palestine. In the context of relative chronologies of hypotheses about formation of texts (regarding which there is less consent than ever today), a distinct field of probabilities has appeared in so far as redaction criticism is often interpreted as tradition (and religious) history. This includes also the so-called "Berlin thesis" by Matthias Köckert and Henrik Pfeiffer, which contests the old age of Old Testament details on YHWH's southern origin.[75] Former studies had reckoned with an old tradition for the relevant texts about a theophany from the Southern desert (Judg 5 [The Song of Deborah]; Deut 33; Hab 3; Ps 68) since they had considered these motifs to be independent from their literary contexts. In his monograph "Jahwes Kommen von Süden" (YHWH's coming from the south) of 2005, Pfeiffer proposed the counter-thesis of a series of literary dependencies in postexilic times.[76] Even if the study is primarily conceived as a literary historical one, its intentions are linked to wide-ranging interests. It is about the destruction of the picture of "early Israel which – once again – was blessed with a *differentia specifica* in comparison to environmental religions."[77] The end result is clearly negative: YHWH did not come from the south. There were no such presumably early beginnings, including the unifying experiences of victory in early times, which have been strongly emphasised since Wellhausen:

> "For the religious history of early Israel, only one conclusion can be drawn: The texts which are being dealt with here are not suitable for the reconstruction of ancient profiles of YHWH. [...] There was no 'time of YHWH wars'. [...] Neither can the Song of Deborah in the sense of an ancient victory hymn be used as the original place of the theophany, nor is the Sinai the archetype of all theophanies."[78]

The book ends with the annotation that YHWH's "coming from the north"[79] is *e silentio* more probable even if there is no evidence at all for that. The fact that there are also supporting Egyptian and epigraphic sources for the above (1.2.) mentioned biblical consciousness of a double "lateness" of Israel/YHWH in the history of nations only plays a minor role in Pfeiffer's argumentation. This

---

75 M. Köckert, "Die Theophanie des Wettergottes Jahwe in Psalm 18," in *Kulturgeschichten (Festschrift V. Haas)* (ed. T. Richter *et al.*; Saarbrücken 2001), 209–226; 225 f.

76 H. Pfeiffer, *Jahwes Kommen von Süden. Jdc 5; Hab 3; Dtn 33 und Ps 68 in ihrem literatur- und theologiegeschichtlichen Umfeld* (FRLANT 211; Göttingen 2005).

77 Pfeiffer, *Jahwes Kommen* (see n. 76), 13; in view of the thesis by J. Jeremias (id., *Theophanie* [WMANT 10; Neukirchen-Vluyn, ²1977/1965]) about the old age of the tradition of theophany and its origin from victory celebrations of the early Israelites [emphasis in the original version].

78 Pfeiffer, *Jahwes Kommen* (see n. 77), 260.

79 Pfeiffer, *Jahwes Kommen* (see n. 77), 268.

has led to criticism expressed by Othmar Keel and Martin Leuenberger, who demand with good reason that the extrabiblical evidence is taken into account adequately.[80] If one follows them and the religio- and traditio-historical studies since Wellhausen, there are still more and better arguments for the point of view that Yhwh has unfathomable roots in the southern desert. Once again, Leuenberger puts the whole weight of the beginning on this result; it is "the fundamental point of origin of each representation of the Old Testament concepts of God, which remains of elementary interest beyond the limits of Old Testament studies."[81]

5.2 Conclusion

The question regarding the beginnings/origins of Israel and Yhwh still preoccupies historico-critical studies of the Old Testament and the (religious) history of Israel correlating with them. In a certain way, even the latest phase of the discussion is torn between idolisation and marginalisation of those beginnings, with hidden interests possibly being leading in each case. The general intention of the question regarding the beginnings/origins is still a deeper historical understanding of the unique character of Israel and its religion. At the same time, the old question of what is historically hidden and not explicable (anymore) is still as valid as important, even where it is not thematised explicitly. It is about Israel's/Yhwh's particularity, which can oscillate between individually historical and categorially different, depending on how it is interpreted. Therefore the position and subjective perception of those who are involved in the debate (even where these are denied!) should be reflected and publicly articulated in the circle of understanding.

Due to their special subject, Old Testament studies are obliged to work on the tension and connection between history of religion and theology. This can only succeed when they try to be conscious of their ways of understanding. Hence the ineluctable questions for the beginnings/origins should be considered in a historico-hermeneutical way. There can be no "correct" answers here, but the effort however to focus on historical and theological principles. The ambiv-

---

80 O. Keel, *Die Geschichte Jerusalems und die Entstehung des Monotheismus* 1 (OLB 4,1; Göttingen 2007), 200–202; M. Leuenberger, "JHWHs Herkunft aus dem Süden. Archäologische Befunde – biblische Überlieferungen – historische Korrelationen," in *Gott in Bewegung. Religions- und theologiegeschichtliche Beiträge zu Gottesvorstellungen im alten Israel* (FAT 76; Tübingen 2011), 10–33.
81 Leuenberger, *JHWHs Herkunft* (see n. 80), 33.

alences of the question regarding beginnings are constitutive and indissoluble – the historico-hermeneutical problem is deeper and thus cannot be finalised. In any case, this applies to a theologically reflected exegesis, but it also goes for studies which are deliberately "purely" historical. It wouldn't do any harm to the transparency of arguments to thematise frankly and precisely the specific difficulty within the frame of historical scholarship. In this sense and as a last point, I would like to refer again to Emil Angehrn (cf. 2.1.):

> "The normative or affective determination of a certain relation to the beginning is not a matter of course but requires clarification and discussion."[82]

---

82 Angehrn, *Frage*, 38 (= see n. 22).

Bibliography

Sources and editions

Ahituv, S., *Canaanite Toponyms in Ancient Egyptian Documents*. Jerusalem 1984.

Ahituv, S. et al., "The Inscriptions," Pages 73–142 in *Kuntillet 'Ajrud (Horvat Teman): An Iron Age II Religious Site on the Judah-Sinai Border*. Edited by Z. Meshel. Jerusalem 2012.

Ahituv, S., הכתב והמכתב. *Handbook of Ancient Hebrew Insricptions from the Land of Israel and the Kingdoms beyond the Jordan from the Period of the First Commonwealth*. Jerusalem 2005.

Allen, J. P., "A Report of Bedouin (Papyrus Anastasi VI)," (*COS* 3.16), Page 46 in *The Context of Scripture (Vol. 3)*. Edited by W. W. Hallo. Leiden 2002.

Allen, J. P., "The Craft of the Scribe (Papyrus Anastasi I)," (*COS* 3.2), Pages 9–14 in *The Context of Scripture (Vol. 3)*. Edited by W. W. Hallo. Leiden 2002.

Astour, M. C., "Mesopotamian and Transtigridian Place Names in the Medinet Habu Lists of Ramses III," *JAOS* 88 (1968), 733–752.

Avanzini, A., *Corpus of South Arabian Inscriptions I-III: Qatabanic, Marginal Qatabanic, Awsanite Inscriptions*. Arabica Antica 2. Pisa 2004.

Avigad, N. and B. Sass, *Corpus of West Semitic Stamp Seals*. Jerusalem 1997.

Avigad, N. et al., *West Semitic Seals. Eighth–Sixth Centuries BCE (The Reuben and Edith Hecht Museum Collection B)*. Haifa 2000.

Berlejung, A., "Die Inschriften von Kuntillet Ajrud," Pages 314–319 in *TUAT NF VI*. Edited by B. Janowski and D. Schwemer. Gütersloh 2011.

Cowley, A., *Aramaic Papyri of the Fifth Century B.C.* Oxford 1923.

Davies, G. I., *Ancient Hebrew Inscriptions. Corpus and Concordance*. Vol. 1–2. Cambridge 1991.2004.

Dietrich, M. and O. Loretz, "Mythen und Epen in ugaritischer Sprache," Pages 1091–1316 in *TUAT III/6*. Edited by O. Kaiser et al. Gütersloh 1987.

Dietrich, M. et al., *The Cuneiform Alphabetic Texts from Ugarit, Ras Ibn Hani and Other Places*. AOAT 360/1. Münster ³2013.

Dobbs-Allsopp, F. W. et al., *Hebrew Inscriptions. Texts from the Biblical Period of the Monarchy with Concordance*. New Haven 2005.

Donner, H. and W. Röllig, *Kanaanäische und aramäische Inschriften*. Vol. 1. Wiesbaden ⁵2002.

Edel, E. and M. Görg, *Die Ortsnamenlisten im nördlichen Säulenhof des Totentempels Amenophis' III*. ÄAT 50. Wiesbaden 2005.

Edel, E., *Die Ortsnamenlisten aus dem Totentempel Amenophis III*. BBB 25. Bonn 1966.

Edel, E., "Die Ortsnamenlisten in den Tempeln von Aksha, Amarah und Soleb im Sudan," *BN* 11 (1980), 63–79.

Frayne, D. R., *Sargonic and Gutian Periods The Royal Inscriptions of Mesopotamia*. Early Periods 2. Toronto 1993.

Giveon, R., "Toponymes ouest-asiatiques à Soleb," *VT* 14 (1964), 239–255.

Hawkins, J. D., *Corpus of Hieroglyphic Luwian Inscriptions, Vol. I: Inscriptions of the Iron Age*. Berlin 2000.

DOI 10.1515/9783110448221-014

Hölscher, M., *Die Personennamen der kassitischen Texte aus Nippur.* Münster 1996.
Kämmerer, T. R. and K. Metzler (eds.), *Das babylonische Weltschöpfungsepos Enûma elîš.* AOAT 375. Münster 2012.
Kitchen, K. A., "Karnak, Campaign from Sile to Pa-Canaan, Year 1," (*COS* 2.4 A), Pages 23 – 25 in *The Context of Scripture (Vol. 2).* Edited by W. W. Hallo. Leiden 2000.
Kitchen, K. A., *Ramesside Inscriptions II.* Oxford 1979.
Kitchen, K. A., *Ramesside inscriptions.* Translated and Annotated. Notes and Comments 2. Oxford 1999.
Kitchen, K. A., "The Battle of Qadesh – The 'Bulletin' Text," (*COS* 2.5B), Pages 38 – 40 in *The Context of Scripture (Vol. 2).* Edited by W. W. Hallo. Leiden 2000.
Meshel, Z. (ed.), *Kuntillet 'Ajrud (Ḥorvat Teman): An Iron Age II Religions Site on the Judah-Sinai Border.* Jerusalem 2012.
Niehr, H., "Mythen und Epen aus Ugarit," Pages 177 – 301 in *TUAT.NF VIII.* Edited by B. Janowski et al. Gütersloh 2015.
Pearce, L. E. and C. Wunsch, *Documents of Judean Exiles and West Semites in Babylonia in the Collection of David Sofer.* CUSAS 28. Bethesda 2014.
Porten, B. and A. Yardeni, *Textbook of Aramaic Documents from Ancient Egypt.* Newly Copied, Edited and Translated into Hebrew and English. Vol. 1–4. Jerusalem 1986–1999.
Porter, E. B. and R. L. B. Moss, *Topographical Bibliography of Ancient Egyptian Hieroglyphic Texts, Reliefs, and Paintings VII: Nubia, the Deserts, and Outside Egypt.* Oxford 1995.
Rainey, A., *The El-Amarna Correspondence.* HdO 110/1. Leiden and Boston 2015.
Renz, J. and W. Röllig, *Handbuch der althebräischen Epigraphik.* Vol. 1–3. Darmstadt 1995.2003.
Schneider, T., *Asiatische Personennamen in ägyptischen Quellen des Neuen Reiches.* OBO 114. Fribourg 1992.
Schwiderski, D. (ed.), *Die alt- und reichsaramäischen Inschriften. The Old and Imperial Inscriptions. Band 1: Konkordanz.* FoSub 4. Berlin 2008.
Schwiderski, D. (ed.), *Die alt- und reichsaramäischen Inschriften. The Old and Imperial Inscriptions. Band 2: Texte und Bibliographie.* FoSub 2. Berlin 2004.
Sethe, K., *Hieroglyphische Urkunden der griechisch-römischen Zeit.* UÄA II. Leipzig 1904.
Smith, M. S. and W. T. Pitard, *The Ugaritic Baal Cycle, vol. II: Introduction with Text, Translation and Commentary of KTU/CAT 1.3 – 1.4.* VTSup 114. Leiden 2009.
Smith, M. S., *The Ugaritic Baal Cycle, vol. I: Introduction with text. Translation and Commentary of KTU/CAT 1.1 – 1.2.* VTSup 55. Leiden 1994.
Weippert, M., *Historisches Textbuch zum Alten Testament.* GAT 10. Göttingen 2010.

Secondary literature

Ackerman, S., *Under Every Green Tree.* HSM 46. Atlanta 1992.
Ahituv, S., *Echoes from the Past. Hebrew and Cognate Inscriptions from the Biblical World.* Jerusalem 2008.
Ahituv, S., "The Sinai Theophany in the Psalm of Habakkuk," Pages 122 – 132 in *Birkat Shalom: Studies in the Bible, Ancient Near Eastern Literature, and Postbiblical Judaism*

Presented to Shalom M. Paul on the Occasion of his Seventieth Birthday. Edited by C. Cohen et al. Winona Lake 2008.

Ahlström, G. W., *The History of Ancient Palestine.* Minneapolis 1993.

Ahlström, G. W., *Who Were the Israelites?* Winona Lake 1986.

Albertz, R., *A History of Israelite Religion in the Old Testament Period: Volume I: From the Beginnings to the End of the Monarchy.* Translated by J. Bowden. OTL. Louisville 1994.

Albertz, R., *Religionsgeschichte Israels in alttestamentlicher Zeit, 1. Von den Anfängen bis zum Ende der Königszeit.* GAT 8.1. Göttingen 1992.

Albertz, R. and R. Schmitt (eds.), *Family and Household Religion in Ancient Israel and the Levant.* Winona Lake 2012.

Albright, W. F., *Yahweh and the Gods of Canaan: A Historical Analysis of Two Contrasting Faiths.* Winona Lake 1968.

Allen, J. P., "The Natural Philosophy of Akhenaten," Pages 89–102 in *Religion and Philosophy in Ancient Egypt.* Edited by W. K. Simpson. New Haven 1989.

Amzallag, N., "Some Implications of the Volcanic Theophany of YHWH on his Primeval Identity," *Antiguo Oriente* 12 (2014), 11–38.

Amzallag, N., "Yahweh, the Canaanite God of Metallurgy?" *JSOT* 33 (2009), 387–404.

Anderson, J. E., "Awaiting an Answered Prayer: The Development and Reinterpretation of Habakkuk 3 in its Contexts," *ZAW* 123 (2011), 57–71.

Anderson, J.S., *Monotheism and Jahweh's Appropiation of Baal.* LHBOTS 617. London 2015.

Angehrn, E., *Die Frage nach dem Ursprung. Philosophie zwischen Ursprungsdenken und Ursprungskritik.* München 2007.

Angehrn, E., *Die Überwindung des Chaos. Zur Philosophie des Mythos.* Frankfurt 1996.

Angerstorfer, A., "Ašerah als 'consort of Jahwe' oder Aširtah?" *BN* 17 (1982), 7–16.

Aro, J., "Der Abfall der kurzen Auslautvokale im Spätbabylonischen und seine Einwirkung auf die Formenlehre," *Studia Orientalia* 46 (1975), 11–20.

Assmann, J., *Ma'at: Gerechtigkeit und Unsterblichkeit im Alten Ägypten.* München ²1995.

Aster, S. Z., "The Image of Assyria in Isaiah 2:5–22: The Campaign Motif Reversed," *JAOS* 127 (2007), 249–278.

Astour, M. C., "Yahweh in Egyptian Topographical Lists," Pages 17–34 in *Festschrift Elmar Edel.* Edited by M. Görg and E. Pusch. ÄAT 1. Bamberg 1979.

Attinger, P. and M. Krebernik, "L'hymne à Ḫendursaĝa (Ḫendursaĝa A)," Pages 2–104 in *Von Sumer bis Homer. Festscnrift für Manfred Schretter zum 60. Geburtstag am 25. Februar 2004.* Edited by R. Rollinger. AOAT 325. Münster 2004.

Axelsson, L. E., *The Lord rose up from Seir. Studies in the History and Traditions of the Negev and Southern Judah.* CBOT 25. Stockholm 1987.

Ayali-Darshan, N., "The Other Version of the Story of the Storm-god's Combat with the Sea in Light of Egyptian, Ugaritic, and Hurro-Hittite Texts," *JANER* 15 (2015), 20–51.

Baden, J. S., *J, E, and the Redaction of the Pentateuch.* FAT 68. Tübingen 2009.

Baden, J. S., *The Composition of the Pentateuch: Renewing the Documentary Hypothesis.* New Haven 2012.

Baden, J. S., *The Promise to the Patriarchs.* New York 2013.

Barrera, J. T., *Jehú y Joás: Texto y composición literaria de 2 Reyes 9–11.* Institución San Jerónimo 17. Valencia 1984.

Bartlett, J. R., *Edom and the Edomites.* JSOTSup 77. JSOT/PEF Monograph series 1. Sheffield 1989.

Bartlett, J. R., "The brotherhood of Edom," *JSOT* 4 (1977), 2 – 27.

Barlett, J. R., "Yahweh and Qaus: a Response To Martin Rose," *JSOT* 5 (1978), 29 – 38

Batto, B. F., "Zedeq צדק," *DDD*[2] 929 – 934.

Baumgartner, W., *Geschichte der israelitischen Religion.* Debrecen 2004.

Bechmann, U., *Das Deboralied zwischen Geschichte und Fiktion. Eine exegetische Untersuchung zu Richter 5.* Diss. theol. 33. St. Ottilien 1989.

Beck, P., "Catalogue of Cult Objects and Study of the Iconography," Pages 27 – 197 in *Horvat Qitmit: An Edomite Shrine in the Biblical Negev.* Edited by I. Beit-Arieh. TAMS 11. Tel Aviv 1995.

Beck, P., "The Drawings and Decorative Designs," Pages 14 – 203 in *Kuntillet 'Ajrud (Horvat Teman): An Iron Age II Religious Site on the Judah-Sinai Border.* Edited by Z. Meshel. Jerusalem 2012.

Becker, U., "Das Exodus-Credo. Historischer Haftpunkt und Geschichte einer alttestamentlichen Glaubensformel," Pages 8 – 100 in *Das Alte Testament — Ein Geschichtsbuch?! Geschichtsschreibung oder Geschichtsüberlieferung im antiken Israel.* Edited by U. Becker and J. van Oorschot. ABG 17. Leipzig 2005.

Becker, U., "Die Reichsteilung in I Reg 12," *ZAW 112* (2000), 210 – 229.

Becker, U., *Exegese des Alten Testaments.* Tübingen [3]2011

Becking, B., "The Gods in Whom They Trusted ... Assyrian Evidence for Iconic Polytheism in Ancient Israel?" Pages 151 – 163 in *Only One God? Monotheism in Ancient Israel and the Veneration of the Goddess Asherah.* Edited by B. Becking et al. Sheffield 2001.

Bemporad, A., "I Habiru nella documentazione ittita," *SMEA* 51 (2009), 71 – 93.

Berges, U., *Die dunklen Seiten des guten Gottes. Zu Ambiguitäten im Gottesbild JHWHs aus religions- und theologiegeschichtlicher Perspektive.* Paderborn 2013.

Berlejung, A., *Die Theologie der Bilder: Das Kultbild in Mesopotamien und die alttestamentliche Bilderpolemik unter besonderer Berücksichtigung der Herstellung und Einweihung der Statuen.* OBO 162. Fribourg 1998.

Berlejung, A., "Geschichte und Religionsgeschichte des antiken Israel," Pages 5 – 192 in *Grundinformation Altes Testament.* Edited by J. C. Gertz et al. Göttingen [3]2009.

Berlejung, A., "History and Religion of Ancient Israel," Pages 5 – 234 in *T&T Clark Handbook of the Old Testament. An Introduction to the Literature, Religion and History of the Old Testament.* Edited by J. C. Gertz et al. London 2012.

Berlejung, A., "Masks in the Old Testament?" in *The Physicality of the Other: Masks as a Means of Encounter.* Edited by A. Berlejung and J. Filitz. ORA. Tübingen forthcoming.

Berlejung, A., "Twisting Traditions: Programmatic Absence-Theology for the Northern Kingdom in 1 Kgs 12:26 – 33* (the 'Sin of Jeroboam')," *JNSL* 35/2 (2009), 1 – 42.

Berner, C., "Abraham amidst Kings, Coalitions and Military Campaigns: Reflections on the Redaction History of Gen 14 and its Early Rewritings," Pages 23 – 60 in *The Reception of Biblical War Legislation in Narrative Contexts.* Edited by C. Berner and H. Samuel. BZAW 460. Berlin 2015.

Berner, C., *Die Exoduserzählung: Das literarische Werden einer Ursprungslegende Israels.* FAT 73. Tübingen 2010.

Berner, C., "Gab es einen vorpriesterlichen Meerwunderbericht?" *Bib 95* (2014), 1 – 25.

Berner, C., "The Egyptian Bondage and Solomon's Forced Labor. Literary Connections between Exod 1 – 15 and 1 Kgs 1 – 12," Pages 211 – 240 in *Pentateuch, Hexateuch or*

Enneateuch? Identifying Literary Works in Genesis through Kings. Edited by T. B. Dozeman et al. AIL 8. Atlanta 2011.

Bernett, M. and O. Keel, *Mond, Stier und der Kult am Stadttor: Die Stele von Betsaida (et-Tell).* OBO 161. Fribourg 1998.

Beyerle, S., *Der Mosesegen im Deuteronomium. Eine text-, kompositions- und formkritische Studie zu Deuteronomium 33.* BZAW 250. Berlin 1997.

Bietak, M., "On the Historicity of the Exodus: What Egyptology Today Can Contribute to Assessing the Biblical Account of the Sojourn in Egypt," Pages 1–37 in *Israel's Exodus in Transdisciplinary Perspective. Text, Archaeology, Culture, and Geoscience.* Edited by T. E. Levy et al. Heidelberg 2015.

Binger, T., Asherah. *Godesses in Ugarit, Israel and the Old Testament.* JSOT Suppl. Ser. 232. Sheffield 1997.

Blenkinsopp, J., "The Midianite-Kenite Hypothesis Revisited and the Origins of Judah," *JSOT* 33 (2008), 131–153.

Bloch, M., Apologie der Geschichte oder der Beruf des Historikers. Stuttgart ²1980.

Blum, E., "Der historische Mose und die Frühgeschichte Israels," *HeBAI* 1 (2012), 37–63.

Blum, E., "Die Wandinschriften 4.2 und 4.6 sowie die Pithos-Inschrift 3.9 aus Kuntillet 'Aǧrūd," *ZDPV* 129 (2013), 22–54.

Blum, E., "Formgeschichte – A Misleading Category? Some Critical Remarks," Pages 32–46 in *The Changing Face of Form Criticism for the Twenty-First Century.* Edited by M. A. Sweeney and E. Ben Zvi. Grand Rapids 2003.

Blum, E., "Historiographie oder Dichtung? Zur Eigenart alttestamentlicher Geschichtsüberlieferung," Pages 6–86 in *Das Alte Testament – ein Geschichtsbuch?* Edited by W. Johnstone and C. Markschies. ATM 10. Münster 2005.

Blum, E., "The Jacob Tradition," Pages 181–211 in *The Book of Genesis: Composition, Reception, and Interpretation.* Edited by C. A. Evans et al. Leiden 2012.

Blum, E., "The Literary Connection between the Books of Genesis and Exodus and the End of the Book of Joshua," Pages 89–106 in *A Farewell to the Yahwist? The Composition of the Pentateuch in Recent European Interpretation.* Edited by T. B. Dozeman and K. Schmid. Atlanta 2006.

Blum, E., *Die Komposition der Vätergeschichte.* WMANT 57. Neukirchen-Vluyn 1984.

Blum, E., *Studien zur Komposition des Pentateuch.* BZAW 189. Berlin 1990.

Bonnet, C. and H. Niehr, *Religionen in der Umwelt des Alten Testaments II: Phönizier, Punier, Aramäer.* Studienbücher Theologie 4,2. Stuttgart 2010.

Boschwitz, F., *Julius Wellhausen. Motive und Maßstäbe seiner Geschichtsschreibung.* Darmstadt ²1968.

Bray, J. S., *Sacred Dan: Religious Tradition and Cultic Practice in Judges 17–18.* LHBOTS 449. New York 2006.

Briggs, C. A. and E. G. Briggs, *The Book of Psalms.* ICC. Edinburgh 1909.

Brockelmann, C., *Grundriß der vergleichenden Grammatik der semitischen Sprachen, I: Laut– und Formenlehre.* Berlin 1908.

Brueggemann, W., *Theology of the Old Testament. Testimony, Dispute, Advocacy.* Minneapolis 1997.

Budde, K., *Religion of Isrcel to the Exile.* New York 1899.

Bunnens, G., *A New Luwian Stele and the Cult of the Storm-God at Til Barsib-Masuwari.* Publication de la Mission archéologique de'l Université de Liège en Syrie: Tell Ahmar 2. Leuven 2006.

Burney, C. F., *The Book of Judges.* London 1918.

Cancik, H., "Das ganze Land Ḫet," Pages 30–33 in *Die Hethiter und ihr Reich. Das Volk der 1000 Götter, Katalog der Ausstellung.* Edited by H. Wilinghöfer. Bonn 2002.

Carr, D. M., "Changes in Pentateuchal Criticism," Pages 433–466 in *Hebrew Bible / Old Testament: The History of Its Interpretation. III/2: The Twentieth Century.* Edited by M. Sæbø. Göttingen 2015.

Carr, D. M., "The Moses Story: Literary Historical Reflections," *HeBAI* 1 (2012), 7–36.

Carr, D. M., *The Formation of the Hebrew Bible: A New Reconstruction.* Oxford 2011.

Cavigneaux, A. and M. Krebernik, "Nungal," in *RlA* 9/7–8.615–618.

Chamaza, V., *Die Omnipotenz Aššurs. Entwicklungen in der Aššur-Theologie unter den Sargoniden Sargon II., Sanherib und Asarhaddon.* AOAT 295. Münster 2002.

Charlesworth, J. H., "Bashan, Symbology, Haplography, and Theology in Psalm 68," Pages 351–372 in *David and Zion: Biblical Studies in Honor of J. J. M. Roberts.* Edited by B. F. Batto and K. L. Roberts. Winona Lake 2004.

Chavel, S., "A Kingdom of Priests and its Earthen Altars in Exodus 19–24," *VT* 65 (2015), 169–222.

Clines, D. J. A., *The Dictionary of Classical Hebrew.* Sheffield 2011.

Cohen, D., *Dictionnaire des racines sémitiques ou attestées dans les langues sémitiques,* Fasc. 6. Leuven 1996.

Coogan, M. D., "A Structural and Literary Analysis of the Song of Deborah," *CBQ* 40 (1978), 143–166.

Coogan, M. D., *West Semitic Personal Names in the Murašû Documents.* HSM 7. Missoula 1976.

Cook, S. L., *The Social Roots of Biblical Yahwism.* SBL 8. Atlanta 2004.

Cross, F. M., *Canaanite Myth and Hebrew Epic: Essays in the History of the Religion of Israel.* Cambridge 1973.

Cross, F. M., "Yahweh and El," Pages 5–60 in *Canaanite Myth and Hebrew Epic: Essays in the History of the Religion of Israel.* Edited by F. M. Cross. Cambridge 1973.

Cross, F. M., "Yahweh and the God of the Patriarchs," *HThR* 55 (1962), 244–259.

Cross, F. M., and D. N. Freedman, *Studies in Ancient Yahwistic Poetry.* Grand Rapids 1997.

Crüsemann, F., *Der Widerstand gegen das Königtum: Die antiköniglichen Texte des Alten Testaments und der Kampf um den frühen israelitischen Staat.* WMANT 49. Neukirchen-Vluyn 1978.

Dalley, S., "Gods from north-eastern and northwestern Arabia in cuneiform texts from the First Sealand Dynasty, and a cuneiform inscription from Tell en-Naṣbeh, c. 1500 BC," *Arabian Archaeology and Epigraphy* 25 (2013), 177–185.

Dalley, S., *Yahweh in Hamath in the 8th Century BC,* VT 40 (1990), 2–32.

Danmanville, J., "Ḫepat," in *RlA* 4.326–329.

Darby, E., *Interpreting Judean Pillar Figurines: Gender and Empire in Judean Apotropaic Ritual.* FAT II/69. Tübingen 2014.

Davila, J. R., "The Name of God at Moriah: An Unpublished Fragment from 4QGenExod[a]," *JBL* 110 (1991), 577–582.

Day, J., *God's Conflict with the Dragon and the Sea: Echoes of a Canaanite Myth in the Old Testament*. Cambridge 1985.

Day, J., *In search of pre-exilic Israel. Proceedings of the Oxford Old Testament Seminar*. JSOT.S 406. London et al. 2006.

Day, J., *Yahweh and the Gods and Goddesses of Canaan*. JSOTSup 265. Sheffield 2000.

Dearman, A. (ed.), *Studies in the Mesha Inscription and Moab*. ASOR/SBL Archaeology and Biblical Studies 2. Atlanta 1989.

Delekat, L., "Yahō-Yahwáe und die alttestamentlichen Gottesnamenkorrekturen," Pages 23–75 in *Tradition und Glaube. Festgabe für K. G. Kuhn*. Edited by J. Jeremias et al. Göttingen 1971.

Delitzsch, F., *Biblischer Commentar über die Psalmen*. BC 4,1. Leipzig ⁵1894.

Dicou, B., *Edom, Israel's Brother and Antagonist*. JSOTSS 169. Sheffield 1994.

Diebner, B., "Wann sang Debcrah ihr Lied? Überlegungen zu zwei der ältesten Texte des TNK (Ri 4 und 5)," *ACEBT* (1995), 105–130.

Dietrich, W. and M. A. Klopfenstein (eds.), *Ein Gott allein? JHWH-Verehrung und biblischer Monotheismus im Kontext der israelitischen und altorientalischen Religionsgeschichte*. OBO 139. Göttingen 1994.

Dietrich, W., *Nahum, Habakuk, Zephanja*. IEKAT. Stuttgart 2014.

Dijkstra, M., "El, the God of Israel – Israel the People of Yнwн: On the Origins of Ancient Israelite Yahwism," Pages 81–126 in *Only One God? Monotheism in Ancient Israel and the Veneration of the Goddess Asherah*. Edited by B. Becking. Sheffield 2001.

Dillmann, A., *Handbuch der alttestamentlichen Theologie*. Edited by R. Kittel. Leipzig 1895.

Donner, H., *Geschichte des Volkes Israel und seiner Nachbarn in Grundzügen*. GAT 4,1. Göttingen ²1995.

Dothan T. and S. Gitin, "Tel Miqne/Ekron: The Rise and Fall of a Philistine City," *Qadmoniot* 105–106 (1994), 2–28.

Dozeman, T. B. and K. Schmid (eds.), *A Farewell to the Yahwist? The Composition of the Pentateuch in Recent European Interpretation*. SBLSymS 34. Atlanta 2006.

Dozeman, T. B. and K. Schmid (eds.), *The Book of Exodus: Composition, Reception, and Interpretation*. VT.S 164. Leiden 2014.

Dozeman, T. B et al. (eds.), *The Pentateuch: International Perspectives on Current Research*. FAT 78. Tübingen 2011.

Driver, G. R., "The Original Form of the Name 'Yahweh': Evidence and Conclusions," *ZAW 46* (1928), 7–25.

Droysen, J. G., *Historik. Rekonstruktion der ersten vollständigen Fassung der Vorlesungen (1857), Grundriß der Historik in der ersten handschriftlichen (1857/1858) und in der letzten gedruckten Fassung (1882)*. Edited by P. Leyh. Stuttgart 1977.

Dunn, J. E., "A God of Volcanoes: Did Yahwism Take Root in Volcanic Ashes?" *JSOT* 38 (2014), 387–424.

Durand, J. M., "Le mythologème du combat entre le dieu de l'Orage et la Mer en Mésopotamie," *MARI 7* (1993), 41–46.

Edenburg, C. and J. Pakkala (eds.), *Is Samuel Among the Deuteronomists? Current Views on the Place of Samuel in a Deuteronomistic History*. SBL AIL 16. Atlanta 2013.

Edzard, D. O., "Amarna und die Archive seiner Korrespondenten zwischen Ugarit und Gaza," Pages 248–259 in *Biblical Archaeology Today. Proceedings of the International*

Congress on Biblical Archaeology. Jerusalem, April 1984. Edited by J. Amitai. Jerusalem 1985.

Eissfeldt, O., "'ähᵉyäh 'ªšär 'ähᵉyäh und 'Ēl 'ôlām," Pages 193–198 in *Kleine Schriften. Vierter Band.* Tübingen 1966.

Eissfeldt, O. "Baʻalšamēm und Jahwe". Pages 171–198 in *Kleine Schriften. Zweiter Band.* Tübingen 1963.

Eissfeldt, O., "Die kleinste literarische Einheit in den Erzählungsbüchern des Alten Testaments," Pages 143–149 in *Kleine Schriften: Erster Band.* Tübingen 1962.

Eissfeldt, O., "El and Yahweh," *JSS* 1 (1965), 26–37.

Eissfeldt, O., "Jahve und Baal," Pages 1–12 in *Kleine Schriften: Erster Band.* Tübingen 1962.

Eissfeldt, O., "Jahwe, der Gott der Väter," Pages 79–91 in *Kleine Schriften: Vierter Band.* Tübingen 1966.

Eissfeldt, O., "Jahwe Zebaoth," Pages 103–123 in *Kleine Schriften: Dritter Band.* Tübingen 1966.

Eissfeldt, O., "Neue Zeugnisse für die Aussprache des Tetragramms als Jahwe," Pages 81–96 in *Kleine Schriften: Zweiter Band.* Tübingen 1963.

Eissfeldt, O., "The Smallest Literary Unit in the Narrative Books of the Old Testament," Pages 85–93 in *Old Testament Essays.* Edited by D. C. Simpson. London 1927.

Eliade, M., *Kosmos und Geschichte. Der Mythos der ewigen Wiederkehr.* Frankfurt 1986.

Emerton, J. A., "New Light on Israelite Religion. The Implications of the Inscriptions from Kuntillet ʻAjrud," *ZAW* 94 (1982), 2–20.

Emerton, J. A., "Some Notes on the Ugaritic Counterpart of the Arabic *ghain*," Pages 3–50 in *Studies in Philology in Honour of Ronald James Williams.* Edited by G. E. Kadish and G. E. Freeman. Toronto 1982.

Erichsen, W., *Demotisches Glossar.* Copenhagen 1945.

Erman, A., *Neuägyptische Grammatik.* Leipzig ²1933.

Erman, A. and H. Grapow, *Wörterbuch der aegyptischen Sprache I.* Berlin 1926.

Fairman, H. W., Review of Simons, Handbook, *JEA* 26 (1940), 165.

Faust, A., *Israel's Ethnogenesis: Settlement, Interaction, Expansion and Resistance.* London 2007

Faust, A., "The Emergence of Israel: On Origins and Habitus," Pages 467–482 in *Israel's Exodus in Transdisciplinary Perspective. Text, Archaeology, Culture, and Geoscience.* Edited by T. E. Levy et al. Heidelberg 2015.

Finkelstein, I., *The Archaeology of the Israelite Settlement.* Jerusalem 1988.

Fishbane, M., *Biblical Interpretation in Ancient Israel.* Oxford 1985.

Fitzgerald, A., *The Lord of the East Wind.* CBQMS 34. Washington 2002.

Fitzmyer, J. A., *The Aramaic Inscriptions of Sefire.* BibOr 19/A. Rome 1995.

Fohrer, G., *History of Israelite Religion.* Translated by D. E. Green. New York 1972.

Fowler, J. D., *Theophoric Personal Names in Ancient Hebrew. A Comparative Study.* JSOT.S 49. Sheffield 1988.

Frahm, E., "Counter-texts, Commentaries, and Adaptations: Politically Motivated Responses to the Babylonian Epic of Creation in Mesopotamia, the Biblical World, and Elsewhere," *Orient* 45 (2010), 1–17.

Frame, G., *Rulers of Babylonia.* RIMB 2. Toronto 1995.

Frankfort, H., *Kingship and the Gods: A Study of Ancient Near Eastern Religion as the Integration of Society and Nature.* Chicago 1948.

Freedman, D. N., "The Name of the God of Moses," *JBL* 79 (1960), 151–156.

Freedman, D. N., "Archaic Forms In Early Hebrew Poetry," *ZAW* 72 (1960), 101–107.

Freedman, D. N., "Early Israelite History in the Light of Early Israelite Poetry," Pages 131–166 in *Pottery, Poetry, and Prophecy. Studies in Early Hebrew Poetry*. Edited by D. N. Freedman. Winona Lake 1980.

Freedman, D. N., "Pottery, Poetry, and Prophecy. An Essay on biblical Poetry," Pages 1–22 in *Pottery, Poetry, and Prophecy. Studies in Early Hebrew Poetry*. Edited by D. N. Freedman. Winona Lake 1980.

Freedman, D. N. and P. O'Connor, "יהוה JHWH," in *ThWAT* 3.533–554

Frevel, C., *Aschera und der Ausschließlichkeitsanspruch YHWHs. Beiträge zu literarischen, religionsgeschichtlichen und ikonographischen Aspekten der Ascheradiskussion*. BBN 94. Weinheim 1995.

Frevel, C., "Grundriss der Geschichte Israels," Pages 587–717 in *Einleitung in das Alte Testament*. Edited by E. Zenger et al. KStTh 1/1. Stuttgart ⁷2008.

Fritz, V., *Die Entstehung Israels im 12. und 11. Jahrhundert v. Chr.* BE 2. Stuttgart 1996.

Frolov, S., "How old is the song of Deborah?" *JSOT* 36 (2011), 163–184.

Fuchs, A. and S. Parpola, "*Iaū-bi'di*," in *PNA* 2/I.497.

Gabriel, G., *enūma eliš – Weg zu einer globalen Weltordnung*. ORA 12. Tübingen 2014.

Galling, K., "Das Gemeindegesetz in Deuteronomium 23," Pages 176–191 in *Festschrift Alfred Bertholet*. Edited by W. Baumgartner et al. Tübingen 1950.

Gardiner, A. H., *Egyptian Grammar, Being an Introduction to the Study of Hieroglyphs*. Oxford ³1957.

Gardiner, A. H., "The Tomb of a Much-Travelled Theban Official," *JEA* 4 (1917), 28–38.

Garfinkel, Y. and C. Epstein, *Neolithic and Chalcolithic Pottery of the Southern Levant*. Jerusalem 1999.

Garr, W. R., *In His Own Image and Likeness: Humanity, Divinity, and Monotheism*. Leiden 2003.

Gaß, E., "Das Gebirge Manasse zwischen Bronze- und Eisenzeit," *ThQ* 186 (2006), 96–117.

Gauthier, H., *Dictionnaire des noms géographiques contenus dans les textes hiéroglyphiques I*. Cairo 1925.

Gelb, I. J., *Computer-Aided Analysis of Amorite*. Chicago 1980.

Gelb, I. J., *Glossary of Old Akkadian*. Materials for the Akkadian Dictionary No. 3. Chicago 1957.

George, A. R., "The Day the Earth Divided: A Geological Aetiology in the Babylonian Gilgameš Epic," *ZA* 80 (1990), 214–219.

Gertz, J. C., "Die Stellung des kleinen geschichtlichen Credos in der Redaktionsgeschichte von Deuteronomium und Pentateuch," Pages 30–45 in *Liebe und Gebot. Studien zum Deuteronomium. FS zum 70. Geburtstag von L. Perlitt*. Edited by R. G. Kratz and H. Spieckermann FRLANT 190. Göttingen 2000.

Gertz, J. C., "Mose und die Anfänge der jüdischen Religion," *ZThK* 99 (2002), 3–20.

Gertz, J. C., "The Literature of the Old Testament: Torah and Former Prophets," Pages 235–382 in *T&T Clark Handbook of the Old Testament. An Introduction to the Literature, Religion and History of the Old Testament*. Edited by J. C. Gertz et al. London 2012.

Gertz, J. C., "The Miracle at the Sea: Remarks on the Recent Discussion about Origin and Composition of the Exodus Narrative," Pages 91–120 in *The Book of Exodus: Composition, Reception, and Interpretation*. Edited by T. B. Dozeman et al. Leiden 2014.

Gertz, J. C., *Tradition und Redaktion in der Exoduserzählung. Untersuchungen zur Endredaktion des Pentateuch.* FRLANT 186. Göttingen 2000.

Gertz, J. C., "*Mose,*" in M. Bauks and K. Koenen (eds.), *Das wissenschaftliche Bibellexikon im Internet,* www.wibilex.de, 2008.

Gese, H., *Alttestamentliche Studien.* Tübingen 1991.

Gese, H., *Vom Sinai zum Zion. Alttestamentliche Beiträge zur biblischen Theologie.* BEvTh 64. Tübingen 1984.

Gesenius, W., *Hebräisches und Aramäisches Handwörterbuch über das Alte Testament.* Berlin [18]2012.

Gesundheit, S., *Three Times a Year: Studies on Festival Legislation in the Pentateuch.* FAT 82. Tübingen 2012.

Gibson, A., *Biblical Semantic Logic: A Preliminary Analysis.* The Biblical Seminar 75. London 2001.

Gitin, S., "Seventh Century BCE Cultic Elements at Ekron," *Biblical Archaeology Today* (1990), 248–253.

Giveon, R., "Toponymes ouest-asiatiques à Soleb," *VT* 14 (1964), 239–255.

Giveon, R., *Les Bédouins Shosou des documents Égyptiens.* DMOA 18. Leiden 1971.

Goedicke, H., "The Tetragram in Egyptian?" *JSSEA* 24 (1994), 24–27.

Goetze, A., "Die Pestgebete des Muršiliš," Pages 160–251 in *Kleinasiatische Forschungen.* Edited by F. Sommer and H. Ehelolf. Weimar 1929.

Gogel, S. L., *A Grammar of Epigraphic Hebrew.* SBLRBS 23. Atlanta 1998.

Goldingay, J., *Psalms I: 1–41.* Baker Commentary on the Old Testament. Grand Rapids 2006.

Gombrich, E. H., *Art and Illusion: A Study in the Psychology of Pictorial Representation.* Oxford [5]1977.

Gomes, J. F., *The Sanctuary of Bethel and the Configuration of Israelite Identity.* BZAW 368. Berlin 2006.

Gordon, R. P., "Introducing the God of Israel," Pages 3–19 in *The God of Israel.* Edited by R. P. Gordon. UCOP 64. Cambridge 2007.

Görg, M., "Jahwe – ein Toponym?" *BN* 1 (1976), 7–14. Reprinted in *Beiträge zur Zeitgeschichte der Anfänge Israels. Dokumente – Materialien -Notizen.* ÄAT 2. Wiesbaden 1989, 180–187.

Görg, M., "Jahwe," in *NBL* 2.265.

Görg, M., "Thutmosis III. und die š₃św-Region," *JNES* 38 (1979), 199–202.

Görg, M., "YHWH – ein Toponym? Weitere Perspektiven," *BN* 101 (2000), 12.

Görg, M., *Religionen in der Umwelt des Alten Testaments III: Ägyptische Religion. Wurzeln – Wege – Wirkungen.* Studienbücher Theologie 4,3. Stuttgart 2007.

Graefe, E., *Untersuchungen zur Wortfamilie bj-.* Diss. phil. Köln 1971.

Graf, F., "Hipta," in *DNP* 5.611.

Granerød, G., *Abraham and Melchizedek: Scribal Activity of Second Temple Times in Genesis 14 and Psalm 110.* BZAW 406. Berlin 2010.

Granerød, G., *Dimensions of Yahwism in the Persian Period. Studies in the Religion and Society of the Judaean Community at Elephantine.* BZAW 488. Berlin 2016.

Gray, J., "The Desert Sojourn of the Hebrews and the Sinai-Horeb Tradition," *VT* 4 (1954), 148–154.

Grdseloff, B., "Édôm, d'après les sources égyptiennes," *Revue del l'histoire juive en Égypte* 1 (1947), 69–99.

Greenfield,J. C., "Of Scribes, Scripts and Languages," Pages 173–185 in *Phoinikeia Grammata. Lire et écrire en Méditerranée*. Edited by C. Baurain et al. Namur 1991.

Greenstein, E. L., "The God of Israel and the Gods of Canaan: How Different Were They?" Pages 47–58 in *The Bible and Its World: Proceedings of the Twelfth World Congress of Jewish Studies Jerusalem. July 29 – August 5, 1997*. Edited by R. Margolin. Jerusalem 1999.

Gressmann, H., *Altorientalische Bilder zum Alten Testament*. Berlin ²1927.

Gressmann, H., *Die Lade Jahwes und das Allerheiligste des Salomonischen Tempels*. BWAT NF 1. Berlin 1920.

Gressmann, H., *Mose und seine Zeit. Ein Kommentar zu den Mose-Sage*. FRLANT 18. Göttingen 1913.

Grimal, N.-C., *Civilisation pharaonique: archéologie, philologie, histoire. Les Egyptiens et la géographie du monde*. Paris 2003.

Groß, W., "Die Herausführungsformel – Zum Verhältnis von Formel und Syntax," *ZAW* 86 (1974), 425–453.

Gross, W., *Richter*. HThKAT. Freiburg 2009.

Gruber, M. I., *Aspects of Nonverbal Communication in the Ancient Near East*. Translated by M. S. Smith. Studia Pohl 12,'I–II. Rome 1980.

Guichard, M., "Un David raté ou une histoire de habiru à l'époque amorrite. Vie et mort de Samsi-Erah, chef de guerre et homme du peuple," Pages 2–93 in *Le jeune héros*. Edited by J. M. Durand et al. OBO 250. Fribourg 2011.

Niehr, H., "Host of Heaven צבא השמים," in *DDD*² 428–430.

Haarmann, V., *JHWH-Verehrer der Völker: die Hinwendung von Nichtisraeliten zum Gott Israels in alttestamentlichen Überlieferungen*. AThANT 91. Zürich 2008.

Haas, V., *Geschichte der Hethitischen Religion*. HO I/15. Leiden 1994.

Haas, V., *Hethitische Berggötter und hurritische Steindämonen*. Mainz 1982.

Haas, V. and H. Koch, *Religionen des Alten Orients Teil 1: Hethiter und Iran*. GAT 1,1. Göttingen 2011.

Haas V. and I. Wegner, "Betrachtungen zu den Ḫabiru," Pages 197–200 in *Munuscula Mesopotamica. Festschrift für Johannes Renger*. Edited by B. Böck et al. AOAT 267. Münster 1999.

Hadley, J. M., *The Cult of Asherah in Ancient Israel and Judah. Evidence for a Hebrew Goddess*. Cambridge 2000.

Halpern, B., *From Gods to God: The Dynamics of Iron Age Cosmologies*. Edited by M. J. Adams. Tübingen 2009.

Hamilton, J. M., "Paran," in *ABD* 5.162.

Hartenstein, F., *Das Angesicht JHWHs: Studien zu seinem höfischen und kultischen Bedeutungshintergrund in den Psalmen und in Exodus 32–34*. FAT 55. Tübingen 2008

Hartenstein, F., "Die Geschichte JHWHs im Spiegel seiner Namen," Pages 73–95 in *Gott Nennen. Gottes Namen und Gott als Name*. Edited by I. U. Dalferth and P. Stoellger. RPT 35. Tübingen 2008.

Hartenstein, F., *Die Unzugänglichkeit Gottes im Heiligtum: Jesaja 6 und der Wohnort JHWHs in der Jerusalemer Kulttradition*. WMANT 75. Neukirchen-Vluyn 1997.

Hartenstein, F., "JHWH, Erschaffer des Himmels. Zu Herkunft und Bedeutung eines monotheistischen Kernarguments," *ZTK* 110 (2013), 383–409.

Hartenstein, F., "Religionsgeschichte Israels – ein Überblick über die Forschung seit 1990," *VF* 48 (2003), 2–28.

Hartenstein, F., "'Wach auf, Harfe und Leier, ich will wecken das Morgenrot' (Psalm 57,9): Musikinstrumente als Medien des Gotteskontakts im Alten Orient und im Alten Testament," Pages 101–127 in *Musik, Tanz und Gott: Tonspuren durch das Alte Testament*. Edited by M. Geiger and R. Kessler. SBS 207. Stuttgart 2007.

Hartenstein, F., "Wettergott – Schöpfergott – Einziger. Kosmologie und Monotheismus in den Psalmen," Pages 77–97 in *JHWH und die Götter der Völker. Symposion zum 80. Geburtstag von Klaus Koch*. Edited by F. Hartenstein and M. Rösel. Neukirchen-Vluyn 2009.

Hartenstein, F. and K. Schmid (eds.), *Abschied von der Priesterschrift? Zum Stand der Pentateuchdebatte*. VWGTh 40. Leipzig 2015.

Hayes, C. E., "Golden Calf Stories: The Relationship of Exodus 32 and Deuteronomy 9–10," Pages 4–93 in *The Idea of Biblical Interpretation: Essays in Honor of James L. Kugel*. Edited by H. Najman and J. H. Newman. Leiden 2004.

Hein, I., *Die ramessidische Bautätigkeit in Nubien*. GOF.B 22. Wiesbaden 1991.

Heine, H., "Geständnisse (1854)," Pages 443–501 in *Sämtliche Schriften 11*. Edited by K. Briegleb. München 1976.

Helck, W., "Die Bedrohung Palästinas durch einwandernde Gruppen am Ende der 18. und am Anfang der 19. Dynastie," *VT* 18 (1968), 472–480.

Helck, W., *Die Beziehungen Ägyptens zu Vorderasien im 3. und 2. Jahrtausend v. Chr.* ÄA 5. Wiesbaden ²1971.

Hemmer Gudme, A. K. de, *Before the God in this Place for Good Remembrance. A Comparative Analysis of the Aramaic Votive Inscriptions from Mount Gerizim*. BZAW 441. Berlin 2013.

Hendel, R., "Cultural Memory," Pages 3–38 in *Reading Genesis: Ten Methods*. Edited by R. Hendel. New York 2010.

Hendel, R., "Genesis 1–11 and Its Mesopotamian Problem," Pages 2–36 in *Cultural Borrowings and Ethnic Appropriations in Antiquity*. Edited by E. Gruen. Stuttgart 2005.

Hendel, R., "Is the 'J' Primeval Narrative an Independent Composition? A Critique of Crüsemann's 'Die Eigenständigkeit der Urgeschichte,'" Pages 181–205 in *The Pentateuch: International Perspectives on Current Research*. Edited by T. B. Dozeman et al. Tübingen 2011.

Hendel, R., *Literaturkritik and Literary Criticism of the Pentateuch*. forthcoming.

Hendel, R., *Purity and Danger in the Temple Court*. forthcoming.

Hendel, R., "The Exodus as Cultural Memory: Egyptian Bondage and the Song of the Sea," Pages 6–77 in *Israel's Exodus in Transdisciplinary Perspective: Text, Archaeology, Culture, and Geoscience*. Edited by T. E. Levy et al. Heidelberg 2015.

Hendel, R., "The Nephilim Were On the Earth: Genesis 6:1–4 and Its Ancient Near Eastern Context," Pages 1–34 in *The Fall of the Angels*. Edited by C. Auffarth and L. Stuckenbruck. Leiden 2004.

Hendel, R., "The Social Origins of the Aniconic Tradition in Early Israel," *CBQ* 50 (1988), 365–382.

Hendel, R., *The Text of Genesis 1–11: Textual Studies and Critical Edition*. New York 1998.

Hermann, A., *Die Stelen der thebanischen Felsgräber der 18. Dynastie*. ÄF 11. Glückstadt 1940.

Herrmann, S., "Der alttestamentliche Gottesname," Pages 76–88 in *Gesammelte Studien zur Geschichte und Theologie des Alten Testaments*. Edited by S. Herrmann. TB 75. München 1986.

Herrmann, S., "Der atl. Gottesname," *EvTh* 26 (1966), 281–293.

Herrmann, W., "Jahwes Triumph über Mot," *UF* 11 (1979), 371–377.

Herrmann, W., *Theologie des Alten Testaments. Geschichte und Bedeutung des israelitisch-jüdischen Glaubens*. Stuttgart 2004.

Herrmann, W., *Von Gott und den Göttern. Gesammelte Aufsätze zum Alten Testament*. BZAW 259. Berlin 1999.

Hess, R. S., "The Divine Name Yahweh in Late Bronze Age Sources," *UF* 23 (1991), 181–188.

Hess, R. S., *Amarna Personal Names*. ASORDS 9. Winona Lake 1993.

Hess, R. S., *Israelite Religions: An Archaeological and Biblical Survey*. Grand Rapids 2007.

Hiebert, T., *God of My Victory: The Ancient Hymn in Habakkuk 3*. HSM 38. Atlanta 1986.

Hoch, J. E., *Semitic Words in Egyptian Texts of the New Kingdom and Third Intermediate Period*. Princeton 1994.

Hoch, J. E., *Semitic Words in Egyptian Texts of the New Kingdom and Third Intermediate Period*. Princeton 1994.

Hoffman, Y., "A North Israelite Typological Myth and a Judaean Historical Tradition: the Exodus in Hosea and Amos," *VT* 39 (1989), 169–182.

Hoffmeier, J. K., *Israel in Egypt: The Evidence for the Authenticity of the Exodus Tradition*. New York 1996.

Holtz, S. E., "The Case for Adverbial *yaḥad*," *VT* 59 (2009), 211–221.

Horn, S. H., "Jericho in a Topographical List of Ramesses II," *JNES* 12 (1953), 201–203.

Horowitz, W., Cuneiform in Canaan. Cuneiform Sources from the Land of Israel in Ancient Times. Jerusalem 2006.

Hossfeld, F. L. and E. Zenger, *Psalmen 51–100: Übersetzt und ausgelegt*. HTKAT. Freiburg ²2000.

Hüber, K., *Die Wahrheit des Mythos*. München 1985.

Hutter, M., *Religionen in der Umwelt des Alten Testaments I: Babylonier, Syrer, Perser*. Studienbücher Theologie 4,1. Stuttgart 1996.

Hutton, J., "Local Manifestations of Yahweh and Worship in the Interstices: A Note on Kuntillet 'Ajrud," *JANER* 10 (2010), 177–210.

Hyatt, J. P., "The Treatment of Final Vowels in Early Neo-Babylonian," *YOSR* 23 (1941), 1–20.

Jamme, C., *"Gott an hat ein Gewand". Grenzen und Perspektiven philosophischer Mythos-Theorien der Gegenwart*. Frankfurt 1991.

Janowski, B., "Gottesvorstellungen," in *Handbuch theologischer Grundbegriffe zum Alten und Neuen Testament* 25.

Janowski, B., "JHWH und der Sonnengott. Aspekte der Solarisierung JHWHs in vorexilischer Zeit," Pages 192–219 in *Die rettende Gerechtigkeit. Beiträge zur Theologie des Alten Testaments 2*. Neukirchen-Vluyn 1999.

Janssens, G., *Studies in Hebrew Historical Linguistics Based on Origen's Secunda*. Orientalia Gandensia 9. Leuven 1982.

Jenkins, I., "The Masks of Dionysos/Pan – Osiris – Apis," *Jahrbuch des Deutschen Archäologischen Instituts* 109 (1994), 273–299.

Jeon, J., *The Call of Moses and the Exodus Story: A Redaction-Critical Study*. Tübingen 2013.

Jeremias, J., *Theologie des Alten Testaments*. GAT 6. Göttingen 2015.

Jeremias, J., *Theophanie: Die Geschichte einer alttestamentlichen Gattung.* WMANT 10. Neukirchen-Vluyn ²1977.

Jeremias, J. and F. Hartenstein, "'Jhwh und seine Aschera,' 'Offizielle Religion' und 'Volksreligion' zur Zeit der klassischen Propheten," Pages 79–138 in *Religionsgeschichte Israels. Formale und materiale Aspekte.* Edited by B. Janowksi and M. Köckert. Veröffentlichungen der Wissenschaftlichen Gesellschaft für Theologie 15. Gütersloh 1999.

Joannès, F. and A. Lemaire, "Trois tablettes cunéiformes à onomastique ouest-sémitique (collection Sh. Moussaïeff)," *Transeuphratène* 17 (1999), 1–34.

Jones, R., "Y. Garfinkel in an interview with Israel Today Magazine from May 15, 2012," http://www.israeltoday.co.il/NewsItem/tabid/178/nid/23224/language/en-US/Default.aspx (accessed 16/12/12).

Junge, F., *Neuägyptisch. Einführung in die Grammatik.* Wiesbaden 2008.

Kaiser, O., *Der eine Gott Israels und die Mächte der Welt. Der Weg Gottes im Alten Testamment vom Herrn seines Volkes zum Herrn der ganzen Welt.* FRLANT 249. Göttingen 2013.

Kaiser, O., *Glaube und Geschichte im Alten Testament. Das neue Bild der Vor- und Frühgeschichte Israels und das Problem der Heilsgeschichte.* BThSt 150. Neukirchen-Vluyn 2014.

Kampp, F., *Die Thebanische Nekropole zum Wandel des Grabgedankens von der XVIII. bis zur XX. Dynastie.* Theben XIII/1–2. Mayence 1996.

Keel, O., "Paraphernalia of Jerusalem Sanctuaries and Their Relation to Deities Worshiped Therein during the Iron Age IIA–C," Pages 317–342 in *Temple Building and Temple Cult: Architecture and Cultic Paraphernalia of Temples in the Levant (2.–1. Mill. B.C.E.). Proceedings of a Conference on the Occasion of the 50th Anniversary of the Institute of Biblical Archaeology at the University of Tübingen (28–30 May 2010).* Edited by J. Kamlah. ADPV 41. Wiesbaden 2012.

Keel, O., *Die Geschichte Jerusalems und die Entstehung des Monotheismus.* OLB 4.1. Göttingen 2007.

Keel, O., *Jerusalem und der eine Gott. Eine Religionsgeschichte.* Göttingen 2011.

Keel, O., "Seth-Baal und Seth-Baal-Jahweh – interkulturelle Ligaturen," Pages 87–107 in *Jerusalem und die Länder. Ikonographie – Topographie – Theologie. Festschrift für Max Küchler zum 65. Geburtstag.* Edited by I. J. Theißen et al. NTOA 70. Göttingen 2009.

Keel, O., *The Symbolism of the Biblical World: Near Eastern Iconography and the Book of Psalms.* Translated by T. J. Hallett. Winona Lake 1997.

Keel, O. and S. Schroer, *Die Ikonographie Palästinas/Israels und der Alte Orient: Eine Religionsgeschichte in Bildern, Band 1. Vom ausgehenden Mesolithikum bis zur Frühbronzezeit.* Fribourg 2005.

Keel, O. and C. Uehlinger, *Gods, Goddesses, and Images of God in Ancient Israel.* Translated by T. H. Trapp. Minneapolis 1998.

Keel, O. and C. Uehlinger, *Göttinnen, Götter und Gottessymbole: Neue Erkenntnisse zur Religionsgeschichte Kanaans und Israels aufgrund bislang unerschlossener ikonographischer Quellen.* QD 134. Freiburg ⁴1997.

Kessler, R., *Die Querverweise im Pentateuch: Überlieferungsgeschichtliche Untersuchung der expliziten Querverbindungen innhalb des vorpriesterlichen Pentateuchs.* Diss. theol. Heidelberg, 1972. BEAT 59. Frankfurt am Main 2015.

Kinyongo, J., *Origine et signification du nom divin Yahvé à la lumière travaux et de traditions sémitico-bibliques*. BBB 35. Bonn 1970.

Kitchen, K. A., The Egyptian Evidence on Ancient Jordan, in *Early Edom and Moab. The Beginning of the Iron Age in Southern Jordan*. Edited by P. Bienkowski. SAM 7. Sheffield 1992.

Klein, A., "Hymn and History in Ex 15," *ZAW* 124 (2012), 516–527.

Klein, A., *Geschichte und Gebet: die Rezeption der biblischen Geschichte in den Psalmen des Alten Testaments*. FAT 94. Tübingen 2014.

Kletter, R., *The Judean Pillar-Figurines and the Archaeology of Asherah*. BAR IS 636. Oxford 1996.

Knauf, E., "Exodus," in *Handbuch theologischer Grundbegriffe zum Alten und Neuen Testament* 176–178.

Knauf, E. A., "Deborah's Language. Judges Ch. 5 in its Hebrew and Semitic Context," Pages 167–182 in *Studia Semitica et Semitohamitica. FS für R. Voigt anläßlich seines 60. Geburtstages am 17. Januar 2004*. Edited by B. Burtea et al. AOAT 317. Münster 2005.

Knauf, E. A., *Midian: Untersuchungen zur Geschichte Palästinas und Nordarabiens am Ende des 2. Jahrtausends v. Chr.* ADPV 10. Wiesbaden 1988.

Knauf, E. A., "Teman," in M. Bauks and K. Koenen (eds.), *Das wissenschaftliche Bibellexikon im Internet*, www.wibilex.de, 2008.

Knauf, E. A., "Yahwe," *VT* 34 (1984), 467–472.

Knohl, I., "Pharaoh's War on the Israelites: The Untold Story," *AZURE* 41 (2010), http://www.azure.org.il/article.php?id=543 (accessed 23/04/2011).

Knoppers, G. N., "Aaron's Calf and Jeroboam's Calves," Pages 92–104 in *Fortunate the Eyes that See: Essays in Honor of David Noel Freedman*. Edited by A. B. Beck et al. Grand Rapids 1995.

Koch, C., *Vertrag, Treueid und Bund*. BZAW 383. Berlin 2008.

Koch, K., "Jahwäs Übersiedelung vom Wüstenberg nach Kanaan. Zur Herkunft von Israels Gottesverständnis," Pages 171–209 in *Der Gott Israels und die Götter des Orients. Religionsgeschichtliche Studien II*. FRLANT 216. Göttingen 2007.

Koch, K., "ŠADDAJ. Zum Verhältnis zwischen israelitischer Monolatrie und nordwest-semitischem Polytheismus," Pages 118–152 in *Studien zur alttestamentlichen und altorientalischen Religionsgeschichte*. Göttingen 1988.

Koch, K. et al., *Der Gott Israels und die Götter des Orients: Religionsgeschichtliche Studien II*. FRLANT 216. Göttingen 2007.

Köckert, M., "Die Theophanie des Wettergottes in Psalm 18," Pages 209–226 in *Kulturgeschichten: Altorientalische Studien für Volkert Haas zum 65. Geburtstag*. Edited by T. Richter et al. Saarbrücken 2001.

Köckert, M., "Von einem zum einzigen Gott. Zur Diskussion der Religionsgeschichte Israels," *BThZ* 15 (1998), 137–175.

Köckert, M., *Vätergott und Väterverheißungen. Eine Auseinandersetzung mit Albrecht Alt und seinen Erben*. FRLANT 142. Göttingen 1988.

Köckert, M., "Vom Kultbild Jahwes zum Bilderverbot. Oder: Vom Nutzen der Religionsgeschichte für die Theologie," *ZTK* 106 (2004), 371–406.

Köckert, M., "Wandlungen Gottes im antiken Israel," *BThZ* 22 (2005), 3–36.

Köckert, M., "YHWH in the Northern and Southern Kingdom," Pages 357–394 in *One God – One Cult – One Nation: Archeological and Biblical Perspectives*. Edited by R. G. Kratz and H. Spieckermann. BZAW 405. Berlin 2010.

Köhler, L. and W. Baumgartner, *Hebräisches und aramäisches Lexikon zum Alten Testament*. Leiden ³1990.

Köhlmoos, M., *Bet-El – Erinnerungen an eine Stadt*. FAT 49. Tübingen 2006.

Kottsieper, I., "El – ferner oder naher Gott? Zur Bedeutung einer semitischen Gottheit in verschiedenen sozialen Kontexten im 1. Jtsd. v. Chr," Pages 25–74 in *Religion und Gesellschaft: Studien zu ihrer Wechselbeziehung in den Kulturen des Antiken Vorderen Orients*. Edited by R. Albertz and S. Otto. AOAT 248. Münster 1997.

Kratz, R. G., "Der Mythos vom Königtum Gottes in Kanaan und Israel," Pages 141–155 in *Mythos und Geschichte. Kleine Schriften II*. Tübingen 2015.

Kratz, R. G., "Erkenntnis Gottes im Hosebuch," *ZThK 94* (1997), 1–24.

Kratz, R. G., "Israel als Staat und als Volk," *ZThK 97* (2000), 1–17.

Kratz, R. G., "Reste hebräischen Heidentums am Beispiel der Psalmen," Pages 156–189 in *Mythos und Geschichte. Kleine Schriften II*. FAT 102. Tübingen 2015.

Kratz, R. G., *Historical and Biblical Israel: The History, Tradition, and Archives of Israel and Judah*. Translated by P. M. Kurtz. Oxford 2015.

Kratz, R. G., *The Composition of the Narrative Books of the Old Testament*. Translated by J. Bowden. London 2005.

Kratz, R. G. and H. Spieckermann (eds.), *One God – One Cult – One Nation: Archaeological and Biblical Perspectives*. Berlin 2010.

Krebernik, M., "Richtergott(heiten)," in *RlA* 11/5–6.354–361.

Krebernik, M., "Sonnengott. A. I. In Mesopotamien. Philologisch," in *RlA* 12/7–8.599–611.

Krebernik, M. and J. van Oorschot (eds.), *Polytheismus und Monotheismus in den Religionen des Vorderen Orients*. AOAT 298. Münster 2002.

Kuenen, A., *An Historico-Critical Inquiry into the Origin and Composition of the Hexateuch*. Translated by P. H. Wicksteed. London 1886.

Kuenen, A., "*Drei Wege, ein Ziel* (1888)," Pages 430–464 in *Gesammelte Abhandlungen zur Biblischen Wissenschaft*. Translated by K. Budde. Freiburg 1894.

Kuenen, A., *The Religion of Israel to the Fall of the Jewish State I*. London 1874.

Laaf, P., *Die Pascha-Feier Israels: eine literar- und überlieferungsgeschichtliche Studie*. BBB 36. Bonn 1970.

Labuschange, C. J., *The Incomparability of Yahweh in the Old Testament*. Pretoria Oriental Series V. Leiden 1966.

Lambert, D. A., *How Repentance Became Biblical: Judaism, Christianity, and the Interpretation of Scripture*. New York 2015.

Lambert, W. G., *Babylonian Creation Myths*. Mesopotamian Civizations 16. Winona Lake 2013.

Lang, B., "The Yahweh-Alone-Movement and the Making of Jewish Monotheism," Pages 1–59 in *Monotheism and the Prophetic Minority*. Sheffield 1983.

Lang, B., *The Hebrew God: Portrait of an Ancient Deity*. New Haven 2002.

Lang, B. (ed.), Der einzige Gott. Die Geburt des biblischen Monotheismus. München 1981.

Leclant, J., "Fouilles et travaux en Égypte et au Soudan, 1961–1962," *Or*. 32 (1963), 184–219.

Leclant, J., "Fouilles et travaux en Égypte et au Soudan, 1962–1963," *Or*. 33 (1964), 337–404.

Leclant, J., "Les fouilles de Soleb (Nubie soudanaise), quelques remarques sur les écussons des peuples envoûtés de la salle hypostyle du secteur IV," Pages 205–216 in *Göttinger Vorträge*. NAWG.PH 13. Göttingen 1965.

Leclant, J., "Le 'Tétragramme' à l'époque d'Aménophis III," Pages 215–219 in *Near Eastern Studies dedicated to H. I. H. Prince Takahito Mikasa on the Occasion of His Seventy-Fifth Birthday*. Wiesbaden 1991.

Lehmann, R. G., "Typologie und Signatur. Studien zu einem Listenostrakon aus der Sammlung Moussaieff," *UF* 30 (1998), 397–459.

Lemaire, A., "Déesses et Dieux de Srie-Palestine d'après les inscriptions (c. 1000–500 av. n.è.)," Pages 127–158 in *Ein Gott allein? JHWH-Verehrung und biblischer Monotheismus im Kontext der israelitischen und altorientalischen Religionsgeschichte*. Edited by W. Dietrich and M. A. Klopfenstein. OBO 139. Göttingen 1994.

Lemaire, A., *Les écoles et la formation de la Bible dans L'ancient Israel*. OBO 39. Fribourg 1981.

Lemaire, A., "Les inscriptions de Khirbet El-Qôm et l'Ashér de Yhwh," *RB* 84 (1977), 597–608.

Lemaire, A., *The Birth of Monotheism. The Rise and Disappearance of Yahwism*. Washington 2007.

Lemche, N. P., *Die Vorgeschichte Israels: Von den Anfängen bis zum Ausgang des 13. Jahrhunderts v. Chr.* BE 1. Stuttgart 1996.

Leuenberger, M., "Jhwhs Herkunft aus dem Süden. Archäologische Befunde – biblische Überlieferungen – historische Korrelationen," *ZAW* 122 (2010), 1–19.

Leuenberger, M., "Noch einmal: Jhwh aus dem Süden. Methodische und religionsgeschichtliche Überlegungen in der jüngsten Debatte," Pages 267–287 in *Gott und Geschichte*. Edited by M. Meyer-Blanck. Veröffentlichungen der Wissenschaftlichen Gesellschaft für Theologie 44. Leipzig 2015.

Leuenberger, M., *Gott in Bewegung. Religions- und theologiegeschichtliche Beiträge zu Gottesvorstellungen im alten Israel*. FAT 76. Tübingen 2011.

Leuenberger, M., *Konzeptionen des Königtums Gottes im Psalter: Untersuchungen zu Komposition und Redaktion der theokratischen Bücher IV-V im Psalter*. ATANT 83. Zürich 2004.

Leuenberger, M., *Segen und Segenstheologien im alten Israel. Untersuchungen zu ihren religions- und theologiegeschichtlichen Konstellationen und Transformationen*. AThANT 90. Zürich 2008.

Levin, C., *Das Alte Testament*. München 2006.

Levin, C., "Altes Testament und Rechtfertigung," Pages 9–22 in *Fortschreibungen: Gesammelte Studien zum Alten Testament*. BZAW 316. Berlin 2003.

Levin, C., "Das Alter des Deboralieds," Pages 124–141 in *Fortschreibungen: Gesammelte Studien zum Alten Testament*. BZAW 316. Berlin 2003.

Levin, C., "Das Gebetbuch der Gerechten," Pages 291–313 in *Fortschreibungen: Gesammelte Studien zum Alten Testament*. BZAW 316. Berlin 2003.

Levin, C., "Das vorstaatliche Israel," *ZThK* 97 (2000), 385–403.

Levin, C., *Der Jahwist*. FRLANT 157. Göttingen 1993.

Levin, C., "Integrativer Monotheismus im Alten Testament," *ZThK* 109 (2012), 153–175.

Levin, C., "Old Testament Religion: Conflict and Peace," Pages 165–181 in *Re-Reading the Scriptures: Essays on the Literary History of the Old Testament*. FAT 87. Tübingen 2013.

Levine, B., "Assyrian Ideology and Israelite Monotheism," *Iraq* 67 (2005), 411–427.

Levinson, B. M. and J. Stackert, "Between the Covenant Code and Esarhaddon's Succession Treaty," *JAJ* 3 (2012), 128–140.

Levy, T. E. et al. (eds.), *Israel's Exodus in Transdisciplinary Perspective: Text, Archaeology, Culture, and Geoscience*. Heidelberg 2015.

Lewis, T. J., and K. van der Toorn, "Teraphim," *TDOT* 15.777–789.

Lewis, T. J., "Covenant and Blood Rituals: Understanding Exodus 24:3–8 in Its Ancient Near Eastern Context," Pages 341–350 in *Confronting the Past: Archaeological and Historical Essays on Ancient Israel in Honor of William G. Dever*. Edited by S. Gitin et al. Winona Lake 2006.

Lipiński, E., *La Royauté de Yahwé dans la poesie et la culte de l'ancien Israël*. Brüssel 1965.

Lipiński, E., *On the Skirts of Canaan in the Iron Age: Historical and Topographical Researches*. OLA 153. Leuven 2006.

Loretz, O., *Habiru-Hebräer. Eine sozio-linguistische Studie über die Herkunft des Gentiliziums 'ibrî vom Appellativum ḫabiru*. BZAW 160. Berlin 1984.

Loretz, O., *Ugarit-Texte und Thronbesteigungspsalmen: Die Metamorphose des Regenspenders Baal-Jahwe (Ps 24,7–10; 29; 47; 93; 95–100 sowie Ps 77,17–20; 114)*. UBL 7. Münster 1988.

Machinist, P., "Assyria and Its Image in the First Isaiah," *JAOS* 103 (1983), 719–737.

Machinist, P., "How Gods Die, Biblically and Otherwise: A Problem of Cosmic Restructuring," Pages 189–240 in *Reconsidering the Concept of Revolutionary Monotheism*. Edited by B. Pongratz-Leisten. Winona Lake 2011.

Mann, T., *Joseph und seine Brüder (Joseph and His Brothers). The first part: Die Geschichten Jaakobs (The Tales of Jacob)*. Frankfurt 1991.1933.

Maul, S., "Der Sieg über die Mächte des Bösen: Götterkampf, Triumphrituale und Torarchitektur in Assyrien," Pages 1–46 in *Gegenwelten zu den Kulturen Griechenlands und Roms in der Antike*. Edited by T. Hölscher. Leipzig 2000.

Mayer, R., "Der Gottesname Jahwe im Lichte der neuesten Forschung," *BZ NF* 2 (1958), 26–53.

Mazar, E., A Cuneiform Tablet from the Ophel in Jerusalem, *IEJ* 60 (2010), 4–21.

McCarter, P. K, "Aspects of the Religion of the Israelite Monarchy. Biblical and Epigraphic Data," Pages 137–156 in *Ancient Israelite Religion. Essays in Honor of Frank Moore Cross*. Edited by P. D. Miller et al. Reprint of the 1987 edition. Minneapolis 2009.

Meeks, W. A., *The First Urban Christians: The Social World of the Apostle Paul*. New Haven 1983.

Merlo, P., "L'Ašerah di YHWH a Kuntillet 'Ajrud. Rassegna critica degli studi e delle interpretazioni," *Studi Epigrafici e Linguistici* 11 (1994), 21–55.

Merwe, C. H. J. van der, "The Biblical Hebrew Particle *'ap*," *VT* 59 (2009), 266–283.

Mettinger, T. N. D., "Israelite Aniconism: Developments and Origins," Pages 173–204 in *The Image and the Book: Iconic Cults, Aniconism, and the Rise of Book Religion in Israel and the Ancient Near East*. Edited by K. van der Toorn. CBET 21. Leuven 1997.

Mettinger, T. N. D., "The Elusive Essence: YHWH, El and Baal and the Distinctiveness of Israelite Faith," Pages 393–417 in *Die Hebräische Bibel und ihre zweifache Nachgeschichte. Festschrift für Rolf Rendtorff zum 65. Geburtstag*. Edited by E. Blum et al. Neukirchen-Vluyn 1990.

Mettinger, T. N. D., "The Roots of Aniconism: An Israelite Phenomenon in Comparative Perspective," Pages 219–233 in *Congress Volume Cambridge 1995*. Edited by J. A. Emerton. VTSup 66. Leiden 1997.

Mettinger, T. N. D., *No Graven Image? Israelite Aniconism in its Ancient Near Eastern Context*. CBOT 42. Stockholm 1995.

Mettinger, T. N. D, "Yahweh Zebaoth יהוה צבאות," in *DDD*² 920–924.

Meyer, E., *Die Israeliten und ihre Nachbarstämme: Alttestamentliche Untersuchungen*. Halle 1906.

Meyer, R., *Hebräische Grammatik*. Berlin 1992.

Miano, D., "Yahweh," in *The Encyclopedia of Ancient History* 7156–7158.

Miller, P. D. Jr., "El the Warrior," *HTR* 60 (1967), 41–31.

Miller, P. D. Jr., *The Divine Warrior in Early Israel*. Cambridge 1973.

Miller, P. D. Jr., *The Religion of Ancient Israel*. Library of Ancient Israel. London 2000.

Mittmann, S., *Deuteronomium 1,1–6,3 literarkritisch und traditionsgeschichtlich untersucht*. BZAW 139. Berlin 1975.

Moor, J. C. de, "Standing Stones and Ancestor Worship," *UF* 27 (1995), 1–20.

Moor, J. C. de, *The Rise of Yahwism. The Roots of Israelite Monotheism*. BETL XCI. Leuven 1990.

Moore, F., *From Epic to Canon: History and Literature in Ancient Israel*. Baltimore 1998.

Moore, G. F., *A Critical and Exegetical Commentary on Judges*. ICC. Edinburgh 1895.

Moran, W. L., *The Amarna Letters*. Edited and Translated. Baltimore 1992.

Morson, G. S., *Narrative and Freedom: The Shadows of Time*. New Haven 1994.

Mosis, R., "'Ströme erheben Jahwe, ihr Tosen ...': Beobachtungen zu Ps 93," Pages 223–255 in *Ein Gott, eine Offenbarung: Beiträge zur biblischen Exegese, Theologie und Spiritualität*. Edited by F. V. Reiterer. Würzburg 1991.

Mowinckel, S., *Le décalogue*. EhPhR 16. Paris 1927.

Mowinckel, S., "The Name of the God of Moses," *HUCA* 32 (1961), 121–133.

Mowinckel, S., "Wann wurde der Jahwäkultus in Jerusalem offiziell bildlos?" *AcOr* 8 (1930), 257–279.

Müller, H.-P., "Ergative Constructions in Early Semitic Languages," *JNES* 54 (1995), 261–271.

Müller H.-P., "Gab es in Ebla einen Gottesnamen Ja?" *ZA* 70 (1981), 7–92.

Müller, H.-P., "Der Jahwename und seine Deutung Ex 3,14 im Lichte der Textpublikationen aus Ebla," *Bib* 62 (1981), 305–327.

Müller, H.-P., "Kolloquialsprache und Volksreligion in den Inschriften von Kuntillet 'Aǧrud und Ḥirbet el-Qōm," *ZAH* 5 (1992), 15–51.

Müller, H.-P., "Chemosh במוש," *DDD*² 186–189,

Müller, M., "Ägyptische Phonologie? Möglichkeiten und Grenzen linguistischer Modelle bei der Beschreibung des Lautsystems einer extinkten Sprache," Pages 509–531 in *Methodik und Didaktik in der Ägyptologie. Herausforderungen eines kulturwissenschaftlicher Paradigmenwechsels in den Altertumswissenschaften*. Edited by A. Verbovsek et al. Ägyptologie und Kulturwissenschaften IV. München 2011.

Müller, R. et al., *Evidence of Editing: Growth and Change of Texts in the Hebrew Bible*. SBLRBS 75. Atlanta 2014.

Müller, R., "Adad's Overflowing Scourge and the Weather God of Zion: Observations on Motif History in Isa 28:14–18," Pages 25–277 in *Thinking of Water in the Early Second Temple Period*. Edited by E. Ben Zvi and C. Levin. BZAW 461. Berlin 2014.

Müller, R., "Das befestigte Herz: Psalm 57 und die kosmologische Dimension der althebräischen Anthropologie," Pages 59–82 in *Die kleine Biblia: Beiträge zur Theologie der Psalmen und des Psalters*. BTS 148. Neukirchen-Vluyn 2014.

Müller, R., "Der finstere Tag Jahwes: Zum kultischen Hintergrund von Am 5,18–20," *ZAW* 122 (2010), 576–592.

Müller, R., "Der unvergleichliche Gott: Zur Umformung einer polytheistischen Redeweise im Alten Testament," Pages 304–319 in *Gott – Götter – Götzen: XIV. Europäischer Kongress für Theologie*. Edited by C. Schwöbel Veröffentlichungen der Wissenschaftlichen Gesellschaft für Theologie 38. Leipzig 2013.

Müller, R., *Jahwe als Wettergott: Studien zur althebräischen Kultlyrik anhand ausgewählter Psalmen*. BZAW 387. Berlin 2008.

Müller, R., et al., *Evidence of Editing. Growth and Change of Texts in the Hebrew Bible*. SBL RBS 75. Atlanta 2013.

Murtonen, A., *A Philogical and Literary Treatise on the Old Testament Divine Names אלוה, אל, אלהים and יהוה*. StOr 18.2. Helsinki 1952.

Na'aman, N., "King Mesha and the Foundation of the Moabite Monarchy," *IEJ* 47 (1997), 83–92.

Na'aman, N., "Out of Egypt or Out of Canaan? The Exodus Story Between Memory and Historical Reality," Pages 527–533 in *Israel's Exodus in Transdisciplinary Perspective. Text, Archaeology, Culture, and Geoscience*. Edited by T. E. Levy et al. Heidelberg 2015.

Na'aman, N., "The Exodus Story. Between Historical Memory and Historiographical Composition," *JANER* 11 (2011), 59–69.

Na'aman, N., Ḫabiru-like Bands in the Assyrian Empire and Bands in Biblical Historiography, *JAOS* 120 (2000), 621–624.

Na'aman, N. and N. Lissovsky, "Kuntillet 'Ajrud. Sacred Trees and the Ashera," *Tel Aviv* 35 (2008), 186–208.

Niehr, H., *Ba'alšamem: Studien zu Herkunft, Geschichte und Rezeptionsgeschichte eines phönizischen Gottes*. OLA 123/Studia Phoenicia 17. Leuven 2003.

Niehr, H., *Der höchste Gott: Alttestamentlicher JHWH-Glaube im Kontext syrisch-kanaanäischer Religion des 1. Jahrtausends v. Chr.* BZAW 190. Berlin 1990.

Niehr, H., Die Wohnsitze des Gottes El nach den Mythen aus Ugarit. Ein Beitrag zu ihrer Lokalisierung, Pages 325–360 in *Das biblische Weltbild und seine altorientalischen Kontexte*. Edited by Janowski, B. and B. Ego. FAT 32. Tübingen 2001.

Niehr, H., "He-of-the-Sinai יהוה סיני," in *DDD*[2] 287f.

Niehr, H., "In Search of YHWH's Cult Statue in the First Temple," Pages 7–95 in *The Image and the Book: Iconic Cults, Aniconism, and the Rise of Book Religion in Israel and the Ancient Near East*. Edited by K. van der Toorn. CBET 21. Leuven 1998.

Niehr, H., "JHWH in der Rolle des Baalšamem," Pages 307–326 in *Ein Gott allein? JHWH-Verehrung und biblischer Monotheismus im Kontext der israelitischen und altorientalischen Religionsgeschichte*. Edited by Dietrich, W., and Klopfenstein, M. A., OBO 139. Fribourg 1994.

Niehr, H., "Religio-Historical Aspects of the 'Early Post-Exilic' Period," Pages 228–244 in *The Crisis of Israelite Religion. Transformation of Religious Tradition in Exilic and Post-Exilic Times*. Edited by Becking, B. and M. C. A. Korpel, OTS 42. Leiden 1999.

Niehr, H., *Religionen in Israels Umwelt. Einführung in die mordwestsemitischen Religionen Syrien-Palästinas*. NEB.Erg 5. Würzburg 1998.

Niehr, H., "The Rise of Yнwн in Judahite and Israelite Religion: Methodological and Religi-Historical Aspects," Pages 23–36 in *Religious Diversity in Ancient Israel and Judah*. Edited by F. Stavrakopoulou and J. Barton. London 2010.

Niehr, H., "Zaphon צפון," DDD² 927–929.

Noth, M., *A History of Pentateuchal Traditions*. Translated by B. W. Anderson. Chico 1981.

Noth, M., *Das vierte Buch Mose. Numeri*. ATD 7. Göttingen 1966.

Noth, M., *Geschichte Israels* (1950). München³1956.

Noth, M., *Überlieferungsgeschichte des Pentateuch*. Stuttgart 1948.

Nowack, W., *Richter – Ruth übersetzt und erklärt*. HK 1/4.1. Göttingen 1900.

Nunn, A., "Aspekte der syrischen Religion im 2. Jahrtausend v.Chr," Pages 267–281 in *Götterbilder. Gottesbilder. Weltbilder. Vol. 1. Ägypten, Mesopotamien, Persien, Kleinasien, Syrien, Palästina. 2., durchgesehene Auflage*. Edited by R. G. Kratz and H. Spieckermann. FAT II/17. Tübingen 2009.

Oeming, M. and K. Schmid (eds.), *Der eine Gott und die Götter*. AThANT 82. Zürich 2003.

Olmo Lete, G. del and J. Sanmartín, *A Dictionary of the Ugaritic Language in the Alphabetic Tradition*. Translated by W. G. E. Watson. HdO I/112. Leiden ³2015.

Olyan, S. M., "Is Isaiah 4–55 Really Monotheistic?" *JANER* 12 (2012), 19–201.

Oswald, W., *Israel am Gottesberg. Eine Untersuchung zur Literargeschichte der vorderen Sinaiperikope Ex 19–24 und deren historischem Hintergrund*. OBO 159. Fribourg 1998.

Otto, E., "פסח," in *ThWAT* 6.659–682.

Otto, E., "Assyria and Judean Identity: Beyond the Religionsgeschichtliche Schule," Pages 339–347 in *Literature as Politics, Politics as Literature: Essays on the Ancient Near East in Honor of Peter Machinist*. Edited by D. S. Vanderhooft and A. Winitzer. Winona Lake 2013.

Otto, E., *Das Deuteronomium im Pentateuch und Hexateuch: Studien zur Literargeschichte von Pentateuch und Hexateuch im Lichte des Deuteronomiumsrahmens*. FAT 30. Tübingen 2000.

Otto, E., *Das Deuteronomium. Politische Theologie und Rechtsreform in Juda und Assyrien*. BZAW 284. Berlin 1999.

Otto, E., *Mose: Geschichte und Legende*. München 2006.

Otto, E. (ed.), *Mose: Ägypten und das Alte Testament*. SBS 189. Stuttgart 2000.

Pakkala, J., "Deuteronomy and 1–2 Kings in the Redaction of the Pentateuch and Former Prophets," Pages 133–162 in *Deuteronomy in the Pentateuch, Hexateuch, and the Deuteronomistic History*. Edited by K. Schmid and R. F. Person Jr. FAT 256. Tübingen 2012.

Pakkala, J., *God's Word Omitted. Omissions in the Transmission of the Hebrew Bible*. FRLANT 251. Göttingen 2013.

Pakkala, J., *Intolerant Monolatry in the Deuteronomistic History*. Publications of the Finnish Exegetical Society 76. Helsinki 1999.

Pakkala, J., "The Date of the Earliest Edition of Deuteronomy," *ZAW* 121/3 (2009), 388–401.

Pakkala, J., "The Monotheism of the Deuteronomistic History," *SJOT*, vol. 21/2 (2007), 159–178.

Pakkala, J., "The Nomistic Roots of Judaism," Pages 251–268 in *Houses Full of All Good Things. Essays in Memory of Timo Veijola*. Edited by J. Pakkala and M. Nissinen. PFES 95. Helsinki 2008.

Pakkala, J., "Why the Cult Reforms in Judah Probably Did not Happen," in Pages 201–235 *One God – One Cult – One Nation. Archaeological and Biblical Perspectives.* Edited by R. G. Kratz and H. Spieckermann. BZAW 405. Berlin 2010.

Pardee, D., "An Evaluation of the Proper Names from Ebla from a West Semitic Perspective: Pantheon Distribution According to Genre," Pages 119–151 in *Eblaite Personal Names and Semitic Name-Giving.* Edited by A. Archi. Archivi Reali di Ebla: Studi, I. Rome 1988.

Parke-Taylor, G. H., *Yahweh: The Divine Name in the Bible.* Waterloo 1975.

Parker, S. B. (ed.), *Ugaritic Narrative Poetry.* SBLWAW 9. Atlanta 1997.

Pascal, B., "Dios y los dioses en el Tetrateuco," Pages 4–66 in *Los rostros de Dios: Imágenes y experiencias de lo divino en la Biblia.* Edited by C. Bernabé. Estella 2013.

Perlitt, L., *Bundestheologie im Alten Testament.* WMANT 36. Neukirchen-Vluyn 1969.

Perlitt, L., *Deuteronomium.* BK V/2. Neukirchen-Vluyn 1991.

Perlitt, L., "Sinai und Horeb," Pages 32–49 in *Deuteronomium-Studien.* FAT 8. Tübingen 1994.

Perlitt, L., "Sinai und Horeb," Pages 302–322 in *Beiträge zur alttestamentlichen Theologie, Festschrift W. Zimmerli.* Edited by H. Donner et al. Göttingen 1977.

Perlitt, L., *Vatke und Wellhausen. Geschichtsphilosophische Voraussetzungen und historiographische Motive für die Darstellung der Religion und Geschichte Israels durch Wilhelm Vatke und Julius Wellhausen.* BZAW 94. Berlin 1965.

Pfeiffer, H., *Das Heiligtum von Bethel im Spiegel des Hoseabuches.* FRLANT 183. Göttingen 1999.

Pfeiffer, H., *Jahwes Kommen von Süden: Jdc 5; Hab 3; Dtn 33 und Ps 68 in ihrem literatur- und theologiegeschichtlichen Umfeld.* FRLANT 211. Göttingen 2005.

Pfitzmann, F., "Le 'maître des autruches' parmi le représentations de YHWH au Sud," in *Représenter dieux et hommes.* Edited by T. C. Römer. Paris forthcoming.

Pietsch, M., *Die Kultreform Josias. Studien zur Religionsgeschichte Israels in der späten Königszeit.* FAT 86. Tübingen 2013.

Podella, T., "Der 'Chaoskampfmythos' im Alten Testament: Eine Problemanzeige," Pages 283–329 in *Mesopotamica – Ugaritica – Biblica.* Edited by M. Dietrich and O. Loretz. AOAT 232. Kevelaer 1993.

Pongratz-Leisten, B., "A New Agenda for the Study of the Rise of Monotheism," Pages 1–40 in *Reconsidering the Concept of Revolutionary Monotheism.* Edited by B. Pongratz-Leisten. Winona Lake 2011.

Pongratz-Leisten, B., "Divine Agency and Astralization of the Gods," Pages 137–187 in *Reconsidering the Concept of Revolutionary Monotheism.* Edited by Pongratz-Leisten, B. Winona Lake 2011.

Pongratz-Leisten, B. (ed.), *Reconsidering the Concept of Revolutionary Monotheism.* Winona Lake 2011.

Popko, M., "Anikonische Götterdarstellungen in der altanatolischen Religion," Pages 319–327 in *Ritual and Sacrifice in the Ancient Near East: Proceedings of the International Conference organized by the Katholieke Universiteit Leuven from the 17th to the 20th of April 1991.* Edited by J. Quaegebeur. OLA 55. Leuven 1993.

Preuss, H. D., *Theologie des Alten Testaments, I–II.* Stuttgart 1991.1992.

Prinsloo, G. T. M., "Yahweh the Warrior: An Intertextual Reading of Habakkuk 3," *Old Testament Essays* 14 (2001), 475–493.

Propp, W. H. C., *Exodus 1–18.* New York 1999.

Propp, W. H. C., *Exodus 19–40*. New Haven 2006.

Propp, W. H. C., "On Hebrew śāde(h), 'Highland,'" *VT* 37 (1987), 230–236.

Rainey, A. F., *The El-Amarna Correspondence. A New Edition of the Cuneiform Letters from the Site of El-Amarna based on Collations of the Extant Texts*. HdO 110. 2015.

Rainey, A. F., "El-ʿAmarna Notes," *UF* 6 (1974), 297.

Rainey, A. F., "Toponymic Problems," *Tel Aviv* 2 (1975), 13–14.

Rainey, A. F., "Review of Hoch, Semitic Words," *IOS* 18 (1998), 431–453.

Redford, D. B., *Egypt, Canaan, and Israel in Ancient Times*. Princeton 1992.

Rendtorff, R., "El, Baʿal und Jahwe. Erwägungen zum Verhältnis von kanaanäischer und israelitischer Religion," Pages 172–187 in *Gesammelte Studien zum Alten Testament*. TB 57. München 1975.

Rendtorff, R., *The Problem of the Process of Transmission in the Pentateuch*. Translated by J. J. Scullion. Sheffield 1990.

Renz, J., "'Jahwe ist der Gott der ganzen Erde'. Der Beitrag der außerkanonischen althebräischen Texte zur Rekonstruktion der vorexilischen Religions- und Theologiegeschichte Palästinas," Pages 289–377 in *Israel zwischen den Mächten. Festschrift für Stefan Timm zum 65. Geburtstag*. Edited by F. Hartenstein and M. Pietsch. AOAT 364. Münster 2009.

Ricœur, P., *Zeit und Erzählung, Vol. 1: Zeit und historische Erzählung (Übergänge 18,1)*. München 1988. French 1983.

Ringgren, H., *Israelite Religion*. Translated by D. Green. Philadelphia 1966.

Roberts, J., *The Earliest Semitic Pantheon: A Study of the Semitic Deities Attested in Mesopotamia before Ur III*. Baltimore 1972.

Rofé, A., "Elders or Youngsters? Critical Remarks on 1 Kings 12," Pages 78–79 in *One God – One Cult – One Nation: Archaeological and Biblical Perspectives*. Edited by R. G. Kratz and H. Spieckermann. BZAW 405. Berlin 2010.

Rofé, A., Introduction to the Literature of the Hebrew Bible. JBS 9. Jerusalem 2009.

Röllig, W., "Bethel בת(י)אל," in *DDD²*. 173 f.

Römer, T., "The Revelation of the Divine Name to Moses and the Construction of a Memory About the Origins of the Encounter Between Yhwh and Israel," Pages 305–315 in *Israel's Exodus in Transdisciplinary Perspective*. Edited by T. E. Levy et. al. New York 2015.

Römer, T., *The So-Called Deuteronomistic History: A Sociological, Historical and Literary Introduction*. London 2007.

Römer, T., "Zwischen Urkunden, Fragmenten und Ergänzungen: Zum Stand der Pentateuchforschung," *ZAW* 125 (2013), 2–24.

Römer, T. C., "Le Baal d'Ougarit et le Yahvé biblique," Pages 33–44 in *Les écritures mises au jour sur le site antique d'Ougarit (Syrie) et leur déchiffrement*. Edited by P. Bordreuil et al. Paris 2013.

Römer, T. C., *L'invention de Dieu*. Paris 2014.

Römer, T. C., "The Revelation of the Divine Name to Moses and the Construction of a Memory about the Origins of the Encounter between Yhwh and Israel," Pages 305–315 in *Israel's Exodus in Transdisciplinary Perspective. Text, Archaeology, Culture, and Geoscience*. Edited by T. E. Levy et al. Heidelberg 2015.

Rose, M., *Jahwe. Zum Streit um den alttestamentlichen Gottesnamen*. ThSt(B) 122. Zürich 1978.

Rose, M., "Yahweh in Israel – Qaus in Edom?" *JSOT* 4 (1977), 28 – 34.

Routledge, B., *Moab in the Iron Age: Hegemony, Polity, Archaeology*. Philadelphia 2004.

Rudnig-Zelt, S., *Hoseastudien: Redaktionskritische Untersuchungen zur Genese des Hoseabuches*. FRLANT 213. Göttingen 2006.

Salvini, M., *The Ḫabiru Prism of King Tunip-Teššup of Tikunani*. Documenta Asiana 3. Rome 1996.

Sanders, S. L., "When the Personal Became Political: An Onomastic Perspective on the Rise of Yahwism," *HBAI* 4 (2015), 78–105.

Särkiö, P., *Exodus und Salomo. Erwägungen zur verdeckten Salomokritik anhand von Ex 1 – 2; 5; 14 und 32*. SESJ 71. Helsinki 1988.

Särkiö, P., "Hilferruf zu Jahwe aus dem Versteck. Eine neue Deutung der Inschrift yšr mḥr aus Ḥirbet Bēt Lēy," *ZDPV* 113 (1997), 39–60.

Sasse, H.-J., "Case in Cushitic, Semitic and Berber," Pages 111 – 125 in *Current Progress in Afro-Asiatic Linguistics. Papers of the Third International Hamito-Semitic Congress*. Edited by J. Bynon. Amsterdam 1984.

Schäfer, H., "Ein Phönizier auf einem ägyptischen Grabstein der Ptolemäerzeit," *ZÄS* 40 (1902 – 03), 31 – 35.

Schiff Giorgini, M. and C. Robichon, *Le temple—bas-reliefs et inscriptions*. Préparé et éd. par N. Beaux. Bibliothèque générale 19. Cairo 1998.

Schiff Giorgini, M. and C. Robichon, *Soleb* 3: *Le temple—description*. Préparé et éd. par N. Beaux. Bibliothèque générale 23. Cairo 2002.

Schipper, B. U., "Raamses, Pithom, and the Exodus: A Critical Evaluation of Ex 1:11," *VT* 65 (2015), 276 – 282.

Schloen, J. D., "Caravans, Kenites, and Casus Belli: Enmity and Alliance in the Song of Deborah," *CBQ* 55 (1993), 1 – 38.

Schmid, K., "Differenzierungen und Konzeptualisierungen der Einheit Gottes in der Religions- und Literaturgeschichte Israels," Pages 2 – 38 in *Der eine Gott und die Götter. Polytheismus und Monotheismus im antiken Israel*. Edited by M. Oeming and K. Schmid. Zürich 2003.

Schmid, K., *Genesis and the Moses Story: Israel's Dual Origins in the Hebrew Bible*. Winona Lake 2010.

Schmid, K., "Israel am Sinai. Etappen der Forschungsgeschichte zu Exod 32 – 34 in seinen Kontexten," Pages 9 – 39 in *Gottes Volk am Sinai. Untersuchungen zu Exod 32 – 34 und Dtn 9 – 10*. Edited by M. Köckert and E. Blum. VWGTh 18. Gütersloh 2001.

Schmid, K., "The Quest for 'God:' Monotheistic Arguments in the Priestly Texts of the Hebrew Bible," Pages 271 – 289 in *Reconsidering the Concept of Revolutionary Monotheism*. Edited by Pongratz-Leisten. Winona Lake 2011.

Schmid, K., *The Old Testament: A Literary History*. Translated by L. M. Maloney. Minneapolis 2012.

Schmidt, B. B., "The Aniconic Tradition: On Reading Images and Viewing Texts," Pages 75 – 105 in *The Triumph of Elohim: From Yahwisms to Judaisms*. Edited by D. V. Edelman. CBET 13. Kampen 1995.

Schmidt, L., "Die Berufung des Mose in Exodus 3 als Beispiel für Jahwist [J] und Elohist [E]," *ZAW* 85 (2014), 339 – 357.

Schmidt, W. H., *Alttestamentlicher Glaube*. Neukirchen–Vluyn [8]1996.

Schmidt, W. H., *Alttestamentlicher Glaube*. Neukirchen–Vluyn [11]2011.

Schmidt, W. H., *Das Königtum Gottes in Ugarit und Israel. Zur Herkunft der Königsprädikation Jahwes.* BZAW 60. Berlin ²1966.

Schmidt, W. H., "Die deuteronomisitsche Redaktion des Amosbuches," *ZAW* 77 (1965), 168–193.

Schmidt, W. H., *Exodus, Sinai und Mose.* EdF 191. Darmstadt ³1995.

Schneider, T., "Siptah und Beja: Neubeurteilung einer historischen Konstellation," *ZÄS* 130 (2003), 134–146.

Schneider, T., "The First Documented Occurrence of the God Yahweh? (Book of the Dead Princeton 'Roll 5')," *JANER* 7/2 (2008), 113–120.

Schneider, T., "Zur Interpretation des Eigennamens des Papyrus-Besitzers," Pages 102–110 in *Der Totenbuch-Papyrus Princeton Pharaonic Roll 5.* Edited by B. Lüscher. BAÄ 2. Basel 2008.

Schnutenhaus, F., "Das Kommen und Erscheinen Jahwes im Alten Testament," *ZAW* 76 (1974), 1–21.

Schorn, U., *Ruben und das System der zwölf Stämme Israels. Redaktionsgeschichtliche Untersuchungen zur Bedeutung des Erstgeborenen Jakobs.* BZAW 248. Berlin and New York 1997.

Schott, M., "Die Jakobpassagen in Hosea 12," *ZTK* 112 (2015), 1–26.

Schroer, S., *Die Ikonographie Palästinas/Israels und der Alte Orient: Eine Religionsgeschichte in Bildern, Band 2. Die Mittelbronzezeit.* Fribourg 2008.

Schroer, S., "Psalm 65 – Zeugnis eines integrativen JHWH-Glaubens?" *UF* 22 (1990).

Schulmeister, I., *Israels Befreiung aus Ägypten: Eine Formeluntersuchung zur Theologie des Deuteronomiums.* ÖBS 36. Frankfurt 2010.

Schwartz, B. J., "The Priestly Account of the Theophany and Lawgiving at Sinai," Pages 103–134 in *Texts, Temples, and Traditions: A Tribute to Menahem Haran.* Edited by M. V. Fox et al. Winona Lake 1996.

Schwartz, B. J., "The Torah: Its Five Books and Four Documents," Pages 161–226 in *The Literature of the Hebrew Bible: Introduction and Studies.* Edited by Z. Talshir. Jerusalem 2011.

Schwemer, D., "Das hethitische Reichspantheon: Überlegungen zu Struktur und Genese," Pages 241–265 in *Götterbilder, Gottesbilder, Weltbilder, Band 1: Ägypten, Mesopotamien, Persien, Kleinasien, Syrien, Palästina.* Edited by R. G. Kratz and H. Spieckermann. FAT II/17. Tübingen 2006.

Schwemer, D., *Die Wettergottgestalten Mesopotamiens und Nordsyriens im Zeitalter der Keilschriftkulturen. Materialien und Studien nach den schriftlichen Quellen.* Wiesbaden 2001.

Schwemer, D., "The Storm-Gods of the Ancient Near East: Summary, Synthesis, Recent Studies," Part I, *JANER* 7 (2008), 121–168; Part II, *JANER* 8 (2008), 1–44.

Scoralick, R., *Gottes Güte und Gottes Zorn: Die Gottesprädikationen in Exodus 34,6f und ihre Intertextuellen Beziehungen zum Zwölfprophetenbuch.* Freiburg 2002.

Scriba, A., *Die Geschichte des Motivkomplexes Theophanie: Seine Elemente, Einbindung in Geschehensabläufe und Verwendungsweisen in altisraelitischer, frühjüdischer und frühchristlicher Literatur.* FRLANT 167. Göttingen 1995.

Segal, J. B., *The Hebrew Passover: From Earliest Times to A.D. 70.* LOS 12. London 1963.

Segert, S., "Diptotic Geographical Feminine Names in the Hebrew Bible," *ZAH* 1/1 (Probeheft 1988), 3–37.

Seters, J. van, *The Life of Moses. The Yahwist as Historian in Exodus–Numbers*. CBET 10. Kampen 1994.

Sethe, K., *Spuren der Perserherrschaft in der späteren ägyptischen Sprache*. NGWG.PH. Berlin 1916.

Shalev, M., *Beginnings. The First Love, the First Hate, the First Dream… Reflections on the Bible's Intriguing Firsts*. New York 2011.

Shelton, J. N. et al., "Threatened Identities and Interethnic Interactions," *European Review of Social Psychology 17* (2006), 321–358.

Shupak, N., "The God from Teman and the Egyptian Sun God: A Reconsideration of Habakkuk 3,3–7," *JANES* 28 (2002), 97–116.

Simian-Yofre, H., "La teodicea del Deuteroisaías," *Bib* 62 (1981), 55–72.

Simons, J. J., *Handbook for the Study of Egyptian Topographical Lists relating to Western Asia*. Leiden 1937.

Singer, I., *Hittite Prayers*. SBLWAW 11. Atlanta 2002.

Ska, J.-L., "Questions of the 'History of Israel' in Recent Research," Pages 391–432 in *Hebrew Bible/Old Testament. The History of its Interpretation. Vol. III: From Modernism to Post-Modernism (The Nineteenth and Twentieth Centuries). Part 2: The Twentieth Century – From Modernism to Post-Modernism*. Edited by M. Sæbø. Göttingen 2015.

Skinner, J., *A Critical and Exegetical Commentary on Genesis*. Edinburgh ²1930.

Smend, R., *Die Bundesformel*. ThSt 68. Zürich 1963.

Smend, R., *Die Mitte des Alten Testaments*. Tübingen 2002.

Smend, R., "Jahwekrieg und Stämmebund: Erwägungen zur ältesten Geschichte Israels," Pages 116–199 in *Zur ältesten Geschichte Israels: Gesammelte Studien 2*. Edited by R. Smend. München 1987.

Smend, R., *Julius Wellhausen. Ein Bahnbrecher in drei Disziplinen*. Carl Friedrich von Siemens Stiftung Themen 82. München 2004.

Smith, M. S., *God in Translation. Deities in Cross-Cultural Discourese in the Biblical World*. FAT 57. Tübingen 2008.

Smith, M. S., *Palestinian Parties and Politics that Shaped the Old Testament*. New York 1971.

Smith, M. S., *Poetic Heroes: Literary Commemorations of Warriors and Warrior Culture in the Early Biblical World*. Grand Rapids 2014.

Smith, M. S., "The Baal Cycle," Pages 81–180 in *Ugaritic Narrative Poetry*. Edited by S. B. Parker. SBLWAW 9. Atlanta 1997.

Smith, M. S., *The Early History of God: Yahweh and the Other Deities in Ancient Israel*. BRS. Grand Rapids ²2002.

Smith, M. S., "The God Athtar in the Ancient Near East and His Place in KTU 1.6 I," Pages 627–640 in *Solving Riddles and Untying Knots: Biblical, Epigraphic, and Semitic Studies Presented to Jonas C. Greenfield*. Edited by Z. Zevit et al. Winona Lake 1995.

Smith, M. S., *The Memoirs of God: History, Memory, and the Experience of the Divine in Ancient Israel*. Minneapolis 2004.

Smith, M. S., *The Origins of Biblical Monotheism. Israel's Polytheistic Background and the Ugaritic Texts*. Oxford 2001.

Smith, M. S., *The Rituals and Myths of the FEAST OF THE GOODLY GODS of KTU/CAT 1.23: Royal Constructions of Opposition, Intersection, Integration, and Domination*. SBLRBS 51. Atlanta 2006.

Smith, M. S., "What is Prologue is Past: Composing Israelite Identity in Judges 5," Pages 43–58 in *Thus Says the Lord: Essays on the Former and Latter Prophets in Honor of Robert R. Wilson.* Edited by J. J. Ahn and S. L. Cook. LHBOTS 502. New York 2009.

Smith, M. S. and W. T. Pitard, *The Ugaritic Baal Cycle: Volume 2. Introduction with Text, Translation and Commentary of KTU 1.1–1.4.* SVT 114. Leiden 2009.

Sommer, B. D., *The Bodies of God and the World of Ancient Israel.* Cambridge 2009.

Sonnet, J.-P., "Ehyeh asher ehyeh (Exodus 3:14): God's 'Narrative Identity' among Suspense, Curiosity, and Surprise," *Poetics Today* 31 (2010), 331–351.

Sparks, K. L., "Israel and the Nomads of Ancient Palestine," Pages 9–26 in *Community Identity in Judean Historiography.* Edited by G. N. Knoppers and K. A. Ristau. Winona Lake 2009.

Spencer, P., *Amara West I: The architectural report.* With contributions by P. L. Shinnie, F. C. Fraser and H. W. Parker. MEES 63. London 1997.

Spieckermann, H., "'Des Herrn ist die Erde.' Ein Kapitel altsyrisch-kanaanäischer Religionsgeschichte," Pages 283–301 in *Götterbilder. Gottesbilder. Weltbilder. Band 1. Ägypten, Mesopotamien, Persien, Kleinasien, Syrien, Palästina. 2., durchgesehene Auflage.* Edited by R. G. Kratz and H. Spieckermann. FAT II/17. Tübingen 2009.

Spieckermann, H., "Der theologische Kosmos des Psalters," *BTZ* 21 (2004), 61–79.

Spieckermann, H., *Heilsgegenwart: Eine Theologie der Psalmen.* FRLANT 148. Göttingen 1989.

Spieckermann, H., "Schöpfung, Gerechtigkeit und Heil als Horizont alttestamentlicher Theologie," *ZTK* 100 (2003), 399–419.

Spiegelberg, W., *Demotische Grammatik.* Heidelberg 1925.

Stackert, J., *A Prophet Like Moses: Prophecy, Law, and Israelite Religion.* New York 2014.

Stade, B., *Biblische Theologie des Alten Testaments 1. Die Religion Israels und die Entstehung des Judentums.* GThW 2,2. Tübingen 1905.

Starke, F., "Sprachen und Schriften in Karkamiš," Pages 381–395 in *Ana šadî Labnāni lū allik. Beiträge zu altorientalischen und mittelmeerischen Kulturen. Festschrift für Wolfgang Röllig.* Edited by Pongratz-Leisten, B. et al. AOAT 247. Neukirchen-Vluyn 1997.

Staubli, T., *Das Image der Nomaden im Alten Israel und in der Ikonographie seiner sesshaften Nachbarn.* OBO 107. Fribourg 1991.

Stavrakopoulou, F. and J. Barton (eds.), *Religious Diversity in Ancient Israel and Judah.* London 2010.

Steymans, H. U., *Deuteronomium 28 und die adê zur Thronfolgeregelung Asarhaddons. Segen und Fluch im Alten Ound in Israel.* OBO 145. Fribourg 1995.

Stolz, F., *Einführung in den biblischen Monotheismus.* Darmstadt 1996.

Stolz, F., "River נהר," *DDD²* 707–709.

Stolz, F., "Sea ים," *DDD²* 737–742.

Strawn, B. A., *What is Stronger than a Lion?, Leonine Image and Metaphor in the Hebrew Bible and the Ancient Near East.* OBO 212. Fribourg 2005.

Streck, M. P., "Der Gottesname 'Jahwe' und das amurritische Onomastikon," *WO* 30 (1999), 3–38.

Streck, M. P., *Das amurritische Onomastikon der altbabylonischen Zeit. Die Amurriter: Die onomastische Forschung. Orthographie und Phonologie. Nominalmorphologie.* AOAT 271/1. Münster 2000.

Streck, M. P., Der Gottesname "Jahwe" und das amurritische Onomastikon, *WO* 30 (1999), 35–46.

Sürenhagen, D., *Paritätische Staatsverträge aus hethitischer Sicht.* Studia mediterranea 5. Pavia 1985.

Tadiello, R., "Il canto di Debora (Gdc 5): studio poetico e testuale," *RivBib* 61 (2013), 331–373.

Tajfel, H. et al., "Social Categorization and Intergroup Behaviour," *European Journal of Social Psychology,* Vol. 1, Issue 2 (1971), 149–178.

Taylor, J. G., *Yahweh and the Sun: Biblical and Archaeological Evidence for Sun Worship in Ancient Israel.* JSOTSup 111. Sheffield 1993.

Tazawa, K., *Syro-Palestinian Deities in New Kingdom Egypt: The Hermeneutics of Their Existence.* BAR 1965. Oxford 2009.

Tigay, J. H., "The Evolution of the Pentateuchal Narratives in the Light of the Evolution of the Gilgamesh Epic," Pages 21–52 in *Empirical Models for Biblical Criticism.* Edited by J. H. Tigay. Philadelphia 1985.

Tigay, J. H., *You Shall Have No Other Gods. Israelite Religion in the Light of Hebrew Inscriptions.* HSS 31. Atlanta 1986.

Tilly, M. and W. Zwickel, *Religionsgeschichte Israels: Von der Vorzeit bis zu den Anfängen des Christentums.* Darmstadt 2011.

Timm, S., "Gott kommt von Teman, der Heilige vom Berg Paran" (Habakuk 3:3) – und archäologisch Neues aus dem äußersten Süden (Tell el-Meharret)," *OTE N.S.* 9,2 (1996), 308–333.

Toorn, K. van der, Scribal Culture and the Making of the Hebrew Bible. Cambridge 2007.

Toorn, K. van der, "The Exodus as Charter Myth," Pages 113–127 in *Religious Identity and the Invention of Tradition.* Edited by J. W. van Henten and A. Houtepen. STAR 3. Assen 2001.

Toorn, K. van der, "The Iconic Book: Analogies between the Babylonian Cult of Images and the Veneration of the Torah," Pages 229–248 in *The Image and the Book, Iconic Cults, Aniconism, and the Rise of Book Religion in Israel and the Ancient Near East.* Edited by K. van der Toorn. CBET 21. Leuven 1997.

Toorn, K. van der,"Yahweh יהוה," in *DDD²* 910–919.

Trémouille, M.-C., *ᵈḪébat. Une divinité syro-anatolienne.* Eothen 7. Firenze 1997.

Tropper, J., "Die Endungen der semitischen Suffixkonjugation und der Absolutivkasus," *JSS* 44 (1999), 175–193.

Tropper, J., "Kasusverhältnisse in arabischen Ausnahmesätzen: Absolutiv nach 'illā," *ZAL* 37 (1999), 25–31.

Tropper, J., *Ugaritische Grammatik.* AOAT 273. Münster ²2012.

Uehlinger, C., "Anthropomorphic Cult Statuary in Iron Age Palestine and the Search for Yahweh's Cult Images," Pages 97–155 in *The Image and the Book: Iconic Cults, Aniconism, and the Rise of Book Religion in Israel and the Ancient Near East.* Edited by K. van der Toorn. CBET 21. Leuven 1997.

Uehlinger, C., "Arbeit an altorientalischen Gottesnamen. Theonomastik im Spannungsfeld von Sprache, Schrift und Textpragmatik," Pages 23–71 in *Gott Nennen. Gottes Namen und Gott als Name.* Edited by I. U. Dalferth and Ph. Stoellger. RPT 35. Tübingen 2008.

Uehlinger, C., "Distinctive or diverse? Conceptualizing ancient Israelite religion in its southern Levantine setting," *HBAI* 4 (2015), 1–24.

Uehlinger, C., "Götterbild," in *NBL* 1.871–892.

Uehlinger, C., "Israelite Aniconism in Context: Review of T. N. D. Mettinger, No Graven Image?" *Bib* 77 (1996), 540–549.

Uehlinger, C., "'... und wo sind die Götter von Samarien?' Die Wegführung syrisch-palästinischer Kultstatuen auf einem Relief Sargons II. in Ḫorṣābād/Dūr-Šarrukīn," Pages 739–776 in *Und Mose schrieb dieses Lied auf...*," Festschrift O. Loretz. Edited by M. Dietrich and I. Kottsieper. AOAT 250. Münster 1998.

Veen, P. van der, et al., "Israel in Canaan (Long) Before Pharaoh Merenptah? A Fresh Look at Berlin Statue Pedestal Relief 21687," *Journal of Ancient Egyptian Interconnections* 2/4 (2010), 15–25.

Veijola, T., *Das fünfte Buch Mose (Deuteronomium) Kapitel 1,1–16,17*. ATD 8/1. Göttingen 2004.

Vermeylen, J., "Les sections narratives de Deut 5–11 et leur relation à Exod 19–34," Pages 174–207 in *Das Deuteronomium. Entstehung, Gestalt und Botschaft*. Edited by N. Lohfink. BEThL 68. Leuven 1985.

Vielhauer, R., *Das Werden des Buches Hosea. Eine redaktionsgeschichtliche Untersuchung*. BZAW 349. Berlin 2007.

von Rad, G., "Das formgeschichtliche Problem des Hexateuch," Pages 9–86 in *Gesammelte Studien zum Alten Testament*. Edited by G. von Rad TB 8. München 1958 (originally published in 1938).

von Rad, G., *Old Testament Theology. Volume I: The Theology of Israel's Historical Traditions*. OTL. Louisville 2001.

von Soden, W., "Jahwe 'Er ist, Er erweist sich,'" *Die Welt des Orients* 3 (1966), 177–187.

Waltisberg, M., "Zum Alter der Sprache des Deboraliedes Ri 5*," *ZAH 13* (2000), 218–232.

Ward, W. A., "A New Look at Semitic Personal Names and Loanwords in Egyptian," *CEg* 71 (1996), 41–47.

Ward, W. A., *Index of Egyptian administrative and religious titles of the Middle Kingdom*. Beirut 1982.

Waschke, E. J., "תְּהוֹם *tᵉhôm*," in *ThWAT* 8.563–571.

Watson, W. G. E., "Fire אשׁ," in *DDD*[2] 331–332.

Weimar, P., *Die Meerwundererzählung: eine redaktionskritische Analyse von Ex 13,17–14,31*. ÄAT 9. Wiesbaden 1985.

Weinfeld, M., "Kuntillet 'Ajrud Inscriptions and Their Significance," *SEL* 1 (1984), 237–239.

Weippert, M., "'Heiliger Krieg' in Israel und Assyrien. Kritische Anmerkungen zu Gerhard von Rads Konzept des 'Heiligen Krieges in Israel,'" *ZAW* 84 (1972), 460–493.

Weippert, M., "Die Nomadenquelle. Ein Beitrag zur Topographie der Biqā' im 2. Jahrtausend v.Chr," Pages 259–272 in *Archäologie und Altes Testament. Festschrift für Kurt Galling zum 8. Januar 1970*. Edited by A. Kuschke and E. Kutsch. Tübingen 1970.

Weippert, M., "Edom und Israel," in *TRE* 9.291–299.

Weippert, M., *Edom. Studien und Materialien zur Geschichte der Edomiter auf Grund schriftlicher und archäologischer Quellen*. Diss. theol. Tübingen 1971.

Weippert, M., *Historisches Textbuch zum Alten Testament*. GAT 10. Göttingen 2010.

Weippert, M., "Jahwe," in *RlA* 5/3–4.246–253.

Weippert, M., *Jahwe und die anderen Götter: Studien zur Religionsgeschichte des antiken Israel in ihrem syrisch-palästinischen Kontext*. FAT 18. Tübingen 1997.

Weippert, M., *Palästina in vorhellenistischer Zeit. Mit einem Beitrag von L. Mildenberg*. Handbuch der Archäologie, Vorderasien 2,1. München 1988.

Weippert, M., "Semitische Nomaden des zweiten Jahrtausends," *Bib* 55 (1974), 265–280 and 427–433.

Weippert, M., "Synkretismus und Monotheismus: Religionsinterne Konfliktbewältigung im alten Israel," Pages 143–179 in *Kultur und Konflikt*. Edited by J. Assmann and D. Harth. Frankfurt 1990 (reproduced in *Jahwe und die anderen Götter: Studien zur Religionsgeschichte des antiken Israel in ihrem syrisch-palästinischen Kontext* [FAT 18. Tübingen 1997], 1–24).

Weiser, A., "Zur Frage nach den Beziehungen der Psalmen zum Kult. Die Darstellung der Theophanie in den Psalmen und im Festkult," Pages 513–531 in *Festschrift Alfred Bertholet zum 80. Geburtstag*. Edited by W. Baumgartner. Tübingen 1950.

Wellhausen, J., *Die Composition des Hexateuchs und der historischen Bücher des Alten Testaments*. Berlin ³1899. ⁴1963.

Wellhausen, J., *Israelitische und jüdische Geschichte* (1894). Berlin ⁶1907. ⁷1914.

Wellhausen, J., *Muhammed in Medina. Das ist Vakidi's Kitab al Maghazi in verkürzter deutscher Wiedergabe herausgegeben*. Berlin 1882.

Wellhausen, J., *Prolegomena to a History of Israel. With a Reprint of the Article 'Israel' from the Encyclopaedia Britannica*. Cambridge Library Collection. Cambridge 2013.

Wellhausen, J., *Prolegomena to the History of Ancient Israel*. New York 1957.

Wellhausen, J., *Prolegomena zur Geschichte Israels* (1873). Berlin ⁶1905.

Westermann, C., *Das Loben Gottes in den Psalmen*. Berlin ^repr^1953.

Westermann, C., *Genesis1–11*. Minneapolis 1984.

Wetsel, D., *Pascal and Disbelief: Catechesis and Conversion in the Pensées*. Washington 1994.

White, H., *Die Bedeutung der Form. Erzählstrukturen in der Geschichtsschreibung*. Frankfurt 1990.

White, H., *Metahistory. Die historische Einbildungskraft im 19. Jahrhundert in Europa*. Frankfurt 1991.

Wiggins, S. A., *A Reassessment of 'Asherah'*. AOAT 235. Kevelaer. 1993.

Willi, T., *Chronik, I. Teilband*. BK XXIV/1. Neukirchen-Vluyn 2009.

Wilson, K. A., *The Campaign of Pharaoh Shoshenq I into Palestine*. FAT 9/II. Tübigen 2005.

Wimmer, S. J. and K. Janaydeh, "Eine Mondgottstele aus *eṭ-Ṭurra*/Jordanien," *ZDPV* 127 (2011), 135–141.

Witte, M., *Die biblische Urgeschichte*. BZAW 265. Berlin 1998.

Witte, M., *Jesus Christus im Alten Testament. Eine biblisch-theologische Skizze*. SEThV 4. Münster 2013.

Witte, M., "Orakel und Gebete im Buch Habakuk," Pages 6–91 in *Orakel und Gebete. Interdisziplinäre Studien zur Sprache der Religion in Ägypten, Vorderasien und Griechenland in hellenistischer Zeit*. Edited by J. Diehl and M. Witte. FAT 2,38. Tübingen 2009.

Witte, M., "Vom EL SCHADDAJ zum PANTOKRATOR – Ein Überblick zur israelitisch-jüdischen Religionsgeschichte," Pages 211–256 in *Studien zur Hebräischen Bibel und ihrer Nachgeschichte*. Edited by J. F. Diehl and M. Witte. Kleine Untersuchungen zur Sprache des Alten Testaments und seiner Umwelt 12.13. Kamen 2011.

Witte, M., "Von der Weisheit des Glaubens an den einen Gott – eine Skizze zu historischen Anfängen und theologischen Ausgestaltungen des Monotheismus im Alten Testament," Pages 79–116 in *Die Gewalt des einen Gottes*. Edited by R. Schieder. Berlin 2014.

Wright, D., "Unclean and Clean [OT]," in *ABD* 6.730–733.

Xella, P., "Le dieu et 'sa' déesse. L'utilisation des suffixes pronominaux avec thélonyme d'Ebla à Ugarit et à Kuntillet 'Ajrud," *UF* 27 (1995), 599–610.

Zadok, R., *The Jews in Babylonia During the Chaldean and Achaemenid Periods Accordung to the Babylonian Sources*. Haifa 1979.

Zadok, R., *The Pre-Hellenistic Israelite Anthroponymy and Prosopography*. OLA 28. Leuven 1988.

Zakovitch, Y., *Jacob: Unexpected Patriarch*. Translated by V. Zakovitch. New Haven 2012.

Zauzich, K.-T., "Der ägyptische Name der Juden," Pages 409–416 in *In the Shadow of Bezalel. Aramaic, Biblical, and Ancient Near Eastern Studies in Honor of Bezalel Porten*. Edited by A. Botta. Culture and History of the Ancient Near East 60. Leiden 2013.

Zenger, E., "Der Psalter als Buch: Beobachtungen zu seiner Entstehung, Komposition und Funktion," Pages 1–57 in *Der Psalter in Judentum und Christentum*. HBS 18. Freiburg 1998.

Zevit, Z., "The Khirbet el-Qôm Inscription Mentioning a Goddess," *BASOR 255* (1984), 39–47.

Zevit, Z., "Yahweh worship and worshippers in the 8th century Syria," *VT* 41 (1991), 363–366.

Zobel, H.-J., "ארון," in *ThWAT* 1.391–404.

Zuckerman, S., "Anatomy of a Destruction: Crisis Architecture, Termination Rituals and the Fall of Canaanite Hazor," *Journal of Mediterranean Archaeology* 20 (2007), 3–32.

Zwickel, W., "Der Beitrag der Habiru zur Entstehung des Königtums," *UF* 28 (1996), 751–766.

Zwickel, W., *Einführung in die biblische Landes- und Altertumskunde*. Darmstadt 2002.

Authors

Adrom, Faried, Dr. phil. (2008), is research fellow (University of Basel Kings' Valley Project) at the University of Basel, Switzerland.

Berlejung, Angelika, Dr. theol. (1997), is professor of Old Testament at the Universität Leipzig, Germany, and extraordinary professor of Ancient Near Eastern Studies at the University of Stellenbosch, South Africa.

Berner, Christoph, Dr. theol. habil. (2006, 2010), is fellow in the Heisenberg program of the German National Research Foundation at the Georg-August-Universität Göttingen, Germany.

Hartenstein, Friedhelm, Dr. theol. habil. (1997, 2002), is professor of Old Testament at the Ludwig-Maximilians-Universität München, Germany.

Hendel, Ronald, Ph.D. (1985), is Norma and Sam Dabby professor of Hebrew Bible and Jewish Studies at the University of California, Berkeley, United States of America.

Jeremias, Jörg, Dr. theol. habil., Dr. h.c. (1964, 1969, 1993) is professor emeritus of Old Testament. He taught at the Ludwig-Maximilians-Universität München from 1972–1994 and from 1994–2005 at the Philipps-Universität Marburg, Germany.

Krebernik, Manfred, Dr. phil. habil. (1984, 1986), is professor of assyriology at the Friedrich-Schiller-Universität Jena, Germany.

Leuenberger, Martin, Dr. theol. habil. (2004, 2008), is professor of Old Testament at the Eberhard-Karls-Universität Tübingen, Germany.

Müller, Matthias, Dr. phil. (2003), is research fellow and lecturer at the University of Basel, Switzerland.

Müller, Reinhard, Dr. theol. habil. (2003, 2008), is professor of Old Testament at the Westfälische Wilhelms-Universität Münster, Germany.

Pakkala, Juha, Dr. theol. habil. (2000, 2005), is lecturer in Biblical Studies and Hebrew at the University of Helsinki, Finland

Pfeiffer, Henrik, Dr. theol. habil. (1997, 2003), is professor of Old Testament at the Friedrich-Alexander-Universität Erlangen-Nürnberg, Germany.

Smith, Mark S., Ph.D. (1985), is Helena Professor of Old Testament Literature and Exegesis at the Princeton Theological Seminary, United States of America.

Tropper, Josef, Dr. phil. habil. (1988, 1997), is extraordinary professor for Semitic Studies at the Freie Universität Berlin and lecturer for Semitic languages at the Humboldt-Universität zu Berlin, Germany.

Van Oorschot, Jürgen, Dr. theol. habil. (1986, 1991), is professor for Old Testament at the Friedrich-Alexander-Universität Erlangen-Nürnberg, Germany.

Witte, Markus, Dr. theol. habil. (1993, 1997), is professor of the Old Testament at the Humboldt-Universität zu Berlin, Germany.

Index of Modern Authors

Ackerman, S.   276
Adrom, F.   VII, IX, 23 – 24, 137, 169, 170, 209
Ahituv, S.   20, 23, 25 – 27, 41, 73, 88, 95, 97, 101 – 102, 105, 111
Ahlström, G.   24 – 25
Albertz, R.   38 – 39, 42 – 43, 158, 183 – 187, 229, 302
Albright, W.   38, 123, 173
Allen, J.   27, 43, 266
Amzallag, N.   162, 178
Anderson, J. E.   26
Angehrn, E.   289 – 292, 307
Angerstorfer, A.   18
Aro, J.   3
Assmann, J.   75, 225
Aster, S.   265
Astour, M.   25, 95, 99, 101, 104 – 107, 111, 142, 170
Attinger, P.   56
Avanzini, A.,   37, 43
Axelsson, L.   23, 26, 95, 106, 122, 156
Ayali-Darshan, N.   215

Baden, J.   190, 240, 242, 245, 253, 255 – 256
Barrera, J.   272
Bartlett, J.   27 – 28, 37 – 38, 150, 152
Barton, J.   XII
Batto, B.   29, 59, 210, 227
Baumgartner, W.   42, 122, 151
Bechmann, U.   124
Beck, P.   73, 84, 88
Becker, U.   52, 129, 185 – 186, 207, 211
Becking, B.   77, 90, 160, 276
Bemporad, A.   65
Berges, U.   161
Berlejung, A.   VII, IX, 73, 75, 78 – 79, 84 – 85, 88, 131, 161, 165, 196
Berner, C.   VII, X, 129 – 130, 133 – 135, 166, 186, 194, 198 – 201, 204
Bernett, M.   71, 84
Beyerle, S.   175
Bietak, M.   162, 171
Binger, T.   18
Blenkinsopp, J.   26

Bloch, M.   287 – 288
Blum, E.   37, 77, 116, 120, 122, 126 – 127, 129 – 130, 132 – 133, 136 – 139, 149 – 150, 155, 159, 161, 168, 172 – 173, 175 – 176, 187, 189, 193 – 196, 203, 205, 209, 242, 244 – 246, 252, 257, 284 – 285
Boschwitz, F.   295 – 296
Bray, J.   76
Briggs, C.   216
Briggs, E.   216
Brockelmann, C.   16
Budde, K.   37, 298
Bunnens, G.   220
Burney, C.   30

Cancik, H.   131
Carr, D.   30, 191, 203, 257
Cavigneaux, A.   56
Chamaza, V.   58
Charlesworth, J.   29
Chavel, S.   250, 263
Cohen, D.   11, 26
Coogan, M.   1, 2, 29
Cook, S.   35, 42
Cross, F.   1, 23 – 24, 26, 30 – 33, 37 – 39, 42, 77, 123, 173, 260
Crüsemann, F.   184, 241

Dalley, S.   61 – 62, 64
Danmanville, J.   64
Darby, E.   87
Davila, J.   244
Day, J.   38 – 39, 41, 50, 99, 259, 272 – 273
Dearman, A.   41
del Olmo Lete, G.   31
Delekat, L.   17
Delitzsch, F.   124
de Moor, J.   24, 27, 38 – 39, 41, 82, 106, 109, 111
Dicou, B.   150
Diebner, B.   124
Dietrich, M.   215, 219
Dietrich, W.   174
Dijkstra, M.   77, 160, 167

Dillmann, A.   299 – 300, 302
Dobbs-Allsopp, F.   25, 41
Donner, H.   2, 119, 131, 154, 287
Dothan, T.   20
Dozeman, T.   186, 190 – 191, 241 – 242
Driver, G.   8
Droysen, J.   288, 292 – 294
Dunn, J.   26
Durand, J.   50, 65

Edel, E.   25, 95, 97 – 99, 102 – 103, 105, 107,
       142, 170
Edenburg, C.   267
Edzard, D.   63
Eissfeldt, O.   52, 89, 256 – 257
Eliade, M.   288
Emerton, J.   17 – 18, 31, 82, 155
Epstein, C.   84
Erichsen, W.   109
Erman, A.   100 – 101

Fairman, H.   98, 113
Faust, A.   28, 162, 178
Finkelstein, I.   148
Fishbane, M.   29 – 30
Fitzgerald, A.   31
Fitzmyer, J.   210
Fohrer, G.   42, 302
Frahm, E.   265
Frame, G.   60
Frankfort, H.   230
Frayne, D.   62
Freedman, D.   8 – 10, 39, 123, 173, 249
Frevel, C.   20, 161
Fritz, V.   148, 304
Frolov, S.   174
Fuchs, A.   64

Gabriel, G.   58
Galling, K.   151
Gardiner, A.   94 – 97, 104 – 105
Garfinkel, Y.   83, 84
Gaß, E.   121, 148, 173
Gauthier, H.   108
Gelb, I.   5, 62
George, A.   222

Gertz, J.   130, 134, 158, 168, 191, 196, 200,
       202, 242, 245
Gese, H.   152, 176, 207
Gesenius, W.   2
Gesundheit, S.   198, 253
Gibson, A.   39
Gitin, S.   20, 42
Giveon, R.   24, 93, 97, 99, 101 – 104, 106,
       110, 113
Goedicke, H.   24, 95 – 96, 110, 141
Goetze, A.   131
Gogel, S.   14
Goldingay, J.   211
Gombrich, E.   77
Gomes, J.   77
Gordon, R.   42
Görg, M.   9 – 10, 23, 25, 60, 94 – 95, 98 –
       100, 102 – 108, 111, 141 – 142, 169 – 170,
       179
Graefe, E.   94
Graf, F.   64
Granerød, G.   194
Gray, J.   153
Grdseloff, B.   24 – 25, 93, 99 – 103, 110 – 111,
       170
Greenfield, J.   40, 59
Greenstein, E.   41
Gressmann, H.   80, 118, 135
Grimal, N.-C.   97
Groß, W.   30, 42, 121, 124, 126, 156, 173 –
       174, 181
Gruber, M.   219
Guichard, M.   65

Haarmann, V.   133, 193
Haas, V.   53, 65, 83 – 84, 220
Hadley, J.   55
Halpern, B.   265
Hamilton, J.   154
Hartenstein, F.   VII, X, 157, 161, 179, 190,
       208, 214, 223 – 224, 226, 228, 235, 303
Hawkins, J.   59
Hayes, C.   249
Hein, I.   96, 98
Heine, H.   286
Helck, W.   97, 103 – 104, 113

Hendel, R.   VII, X, 77, 201, 241, 246, 251, 261, 264
Hermann, A.   94, 140
Herrmann, S.   99, 110, 111, 140, 269
Herrmann, W.   50
Hess, R.   5–6, 19, 39, 41, 82–83, 93, 109
Hiebert, T.   26
Hoch, J.   7, 95, 101, 108
Hoffman, Y.   189, 206
Hoffmeier, J.   204
Hölscher, M.   61–62, 215
Holtz, S.   31
Horn, S.   112–113
Horowitz, W.   63
Hossfeld, F.   225, 236
Hüber, K.   290
Hutton, J.   25
Hyatt, J.   3

Jamme, C.   290
Janaydeh, K.   84
Janowski, B.   161
Janssens, G.   12
Jenkins, I.   84
Jeon, J.   242
Jeremias, J.   VII, IX–X, 119, 122–123, 173–174, 211, 233, 305
Joannès, F.   1–2
Junge, F.   100

Kaiser, O.   151, 158, 219
Kampp, F.   94
Keel, O.   25, 53–54, 60, 64, 68, 71–73, 75–76, 78–81, 83–89, 92, 116, 120, 122, 124, 132, 143, 155–156, 161, 163, 177, 208–209, 220, 223, 232–233, 306
Kessler, R.   226, 257
Kitchen, K.   27, 98–100, 112
Klein, A.   181, 201
Kletter, R.   88
Klopfenstein, M.   55, 89
Knauf, E.   9, 10, 37, 43, 60, 64, 95, 99, 106, 124, 128, 154–155, 173–174, 205, 208–209, 269, 287
Knohl, I.   29, 34
Knoppers, G.   249
Koch, C.   279

Koch, K.   93
Köckert, M.   IX, 18, 112, 115, 131, 144, 158–160, 186, 196, 205, 208–209, 244–245, 305
Köhlmoos, M.   185, 188
Kottsieper, I.   229
Kratz, R.   XII, 120, 130, 133–134, 136, 186, 188–189, 191, 193, 202–204, 208, 213, 226
Krebernik, M.   VII–VIII, X, 56, 59, 161, 165, 177–178, 209, 211
Kuenen, A.   249, 294, 298–300, 303–304

Laaf, P.   197, 199
Labuschange, C.   221
Lambert, D.   255
Lambert, W.   57
Lang, B.   273, 303
Leclant, J.   23, 95–97, 104, 108, 111
Lehmann, R.   15–16
Lemaire, A.   1–2, 41, 137, 146, 175
Lemche, N.   205
Leuenberger, M.   VII, IX–X, 99, 116, 120, 122, 124–126, 129, 131, 140–141, 143, 156, 158–160, 163–164, 167, 169–171, 173–175, 177–178, 195, 209, 213, 269, 306
Levin, C.   IX, 30, 115, 119–120, 124, 129, 133–136, 143, 145, 160, 167, 191, 201, 208, 210, 213, 216, 234
Levine, B.   265
Levinson, B.   265
Lewis, T.   42, 247
Lipiński, E.   27, 106, 213
Lissovsky, N.   137

Machinist, P.   53, 252, 265
Mann, T.   283
Maul, S.   215
Mazar, E.   63
Meeks, W.   26
Merlo, P.   18
Mettinger, T.   37, 53, 77, 80–81, 83–85, 88
Meyer, E.   118, 193
Meyer, R.   221
Miano, D.   161
Miller, P. Jr.   32, 39–40, 42, 173
Mittmann, S.   151

Moore, F.   23, 38, 123
Moore, G.   30
Moran, W.   63, 132
Morson, G.   243
Mosis, R.   224
Moss, R.   96, 98
Mowinckel, S.   3, 80, 118
Müller, C.   7
Müller, H.-P.   61, 159, 210
Müller, M.   VII, IX, 23–24, 100, 137, 142–144, 169–170, 209
Müller, R.   VII, IX–X, 38, 68, 75, 115, 160, 165–167, 207–213, 215–219, 221, 223–224, 226, 228–229, 233, 236, 268–270, 272

Na'aman, N.   17, 65, 137, 161–162
Niehr, H.   29, 38, 51, 53, 75, 89, 161, 208, 219, 230, 274, 276
Noth, M.   118, 131, 133, 135–136, 154, 158, 181–182, 190, 206, 300–303
Nowack, W.   124

Olyan, S.   266
Oswald, W.   116, 119, 120, 122,177, 192, 196, 200, 202, 205

Pakkala, J.   VII, X, 42, 188, 267–268, 271–273, 275, 278, 280
Parpola, S.   64
Pascal, B.   239, 240, 242, 250
Pearce, L.   60
Perlitt, L.   118–119, 122, 150–151, 154, 295
Pfeiffer, H.   VII, IX–X, 26, 68, 112, 115–116, 120–121, 124–126, 128–130, 156, 159–161, 164, 166, 173–178, 189, 196, 209, 269, 305
Pfitzmann, F.   162
Pitard, W.   32, 228
Podella, T.   215
Pongratz-Leisten, B.   55, 58, 240, 252
Popko, M.   83
Porter, E.   96, 98
Preuss, H.   151
Prinsloo, G.   26
Propp, W.   33, 162, 242, 254, 261

Rainey, A.   58, 63–64, 102, 105–106, 109
Redford, D.   130, 205
Rendtorff, R.   255–257
Renz, J.   8, 13, 18–19, 70–71, 88, 138–139
Ricoeur, P.   284
Ringgren, H.   37
Roberts, J.   40
Robichon, C.   96–97, 105
Rofé, A.   29, 34–35, 185
Röllig, W.   54, 70–71, 88
Römer, T.   161–162, 165, 170–171, 178, 185, 241, 243
Rose, M.   13, 17, 153
Routledge, B.   263–264
Rudnig-Zelt, S.   189

Salvini, M.   65
Sanmartín, J.   31
Särkiö, P.   184
Sasse, H.-J.   7
Schäfer, H.   108
Schiff Giorgini, M.   96–97, 105
Schipper, B.   169, 205
Schloen, J.   36
Schmid, K.   116, 119, 130, 190–191, 203, 241–242, 244–245, 257–258
Schmidt, B.   74
Schmidt, L.   134
Schmidt, W.   132–135, 146, 158, 189, 193, 197, 200, 204, 302
Schneider, T.   23–25, 99, 101, 108–109, 162
Schnutenhaus, F.   127
Schorn, U.   124
Schott, M.   136
Schroer, S.   78, 84, 217
Schulmeister, I.   181
Schwartz, B.   240, 255, 260
Schwemer, D.   83, 208–209, 212, 214–215, 223
Scoralick, R.   254
Scriba, A.   211
Segal, J.   197
Segert, S.   15
Sethe, K.   102, 108
Shalev, M.   283
Shelton, J.   278

Shupak, N. 26
Simian-Yofre, H. 216
Simons, J. 104–105
Ska, J.-L. 159
Skinner, J. 244
Smend, R. 145, 220, 294, 298
Smith, M. S. VII–VIII, IX–X, 32, 34–35, 37–38, 40–41, 49, 51, 64, 77, 161, 212, 228, 248, 264–265, 273, 304
Smith, M. 303
Sommer, B. 253
Sonnet, J.-P. 254
Sparks, K. 155
Spencer, P. 98
Spieckermann, H. 143–144, 186, 202, 207, 227, 230–231, 237
Spiegelberg, W. 109
Stackert, J. 240, 242, 265
Stade, B. 298–300
Starke, F. 59
Staubli, T. 79–80, 171
Steymans, H. 279
Stolz, F. 304
Strawn, B. 90
Streck, M. 4–5, 7, 10, 61
Sürenhagen, D. 131

Tadiello, R. 174
Tajfel, H. 278
Taylor, J. 41, 82–83
Tazawa, K. 32–33
Tigay, J. 256, 272
Tilly, M. 79–80, 84–85
Timm, S. 154
Trémouille, M.-C. 64
Tropper, J. VII–VIII, XII, 7, 14, 64

Uehlinger, C. 25, 70–73, 75, 81–92, 132

van der Merwe, C. 30
van der Toorn, K. 9, 23, 26, 37–39, 41, 43, 64, 80, 186, 247, 256, 269, 272
van der Veen, P. 26
van Seters, J. 122
Veijola, T. 279
Vermeylen, J. 119
Vielhauer, R. 189
von Rad, G. 117, 141, 182, 300, 303
von Soden, W. 10

Waltisberg, M. 124
Ward, W. 94–95
Waschke, E. 216
Watson, W. 210
Weimar, P. 202
Weippert, M. 1–2, 8, 11, 23–24, 55, 59–60, 64, 73, 75, 77, 99–102, 105–106, 112, 132, 137, 140–142, 145, 150, 152–153, 169–171, 208, 220, 303–304
Weiser, A. 122
Wellhausen, J. 38, 116–118, 122, 134, 158, 209, 255–256, 294–300, 302–306
Westermann, C. 122, 251
Wetsel, D. 239
White, H. 284, 292–293
Wiggins, S. 18, 20
Willi, T. 152
Wilson, K. 101
Wimmer, S. 84, 169
Witte, M. 160, 166, 251–252
Wright, D. 261

Zadok, R. 1, 3, 16
Zakovitch, Y. 35
Zauzich, K.-T. 109
Zenger, E. 207, 225, 236
Zevit, Z. 18
Zobel, H.-J. 80
Zuckerman, S. 247
Zwickel, W. 65, 79–80, 84–85, 87, 224

Index of Subjects and Names

Abimelech   248
Abraham   135, 148, 194, 239–266, 294, 298
Adad   52, 160, 164–166
Ahab   270–271
Ahaziah   270
Aleppo / Ḫalab   57, 63, 216–217
Altar   87–88, 246, 250, 252–253, 262, 271, 277
Amarna letters   5, 19, 63, 164
Ammon   58, 69, 210, 273
Anat   37, 49–50, 54–55, 64, 83, 164
Ancestor   16, 38, 71, 82, 88, 135, 147–150, 152, 243, 247
Angel   52, 56, 198, 244, 250–251, 258–259, 265–266
Arabah   102, 128, 150
Arad   69, 83, 87–88
Ark   59, 69, 79–80, 274
Asherah / ʾAṯiratu   18–20, 40, 51, 55, 70–71, 74, 77, 83, 86–91, 160, 164, 167, 172, 271, 276–277, 279
Assur   47–48, 53, 56–58, 111–112, 233
Assyrian empire / king   48, 53, 56, 64–65, 90, 150, 203, 264
Athtar   VIII, 39–43

Baal / Baʿal   VIII, IX, 31–42, 48–58, 64, 67–71, 74–78, 88–90, 139, 143–144, 160–166, 216, 228, 252, 270–273, 297
Baal cycle   32, 34, 49–51, 54, 228
Babylon   2, 56, 251, 264, 285
Babylonia   1, 3, 47, 49, 51, 58, 60–62, 251, 264
Baetyli   71, 80, 84, 88
Barak   125
Beersheba   77, 166, 252
Benjamin   147–148
Bes   70, 73
Bet Mirsim   85
Bet Shean   63
Bethel / Bet-El   53–55, 59, 77, 79, 130, 140, 148–149, 185, 188–189, 246, 249–252, 263
Betsaida / et-Tell   71

Blessing   18–19, 74, 138–139, 199, 231, 261–262
Blessing formulae   155, 172
Bronze Age   VIII, IX, 43, 63–64, 75, 78, 93, 129–132, 141, 148, 157–158, 162–165, 168–172, 178, 247, 269–270
Bull   49, 53, 68, 71–84, 90, 92, 188
Burial   147, 247–248, 264
Burning bush   134–135, 192, 239, 250

Canaan / Canaanite   5, 11, 23–27, 30, 32–33, 36–41, 48–50, 63–65, 77, 95, 97, 101–102, 105–106, 111, 123, 125, 127, 129–132, 144, 157–159, 162–164, 168, 177–178, 182, 191, 194–195, 247, 259, 260, 272, 278, 300
Charter myth   186–189
Cherub   56, 69, 81, 85–86, 214–215, 234
Cosmology   47, 57, 223, 237, 265
Cosmos   127, 212, 227, 236–237, 258–259, 288
Covenant   42, 59, 116, 118, 120, 181, 199, 247–250, 259–261, 265
Creation   XII, 47, 51–53, 57, 188–189, 201–202, 258–261, 265, 281, 285, 290
Cultic stand   82, 85

Dagan   47, 51, 57–58
Dan   53, 79, 140, 250 263
David   29, 58, 60, 65, 69, 80, 150, 152, 274, 295
Deborah   29, 30, 36, 117, 120, 124–128, 147, 174, 305
Desert   52, 68, 96–97, 117, 121, 135–136, 146, 154, 196, 199, 286, 304–306
Deuteronomism   267–281
Dumuzi / Tammuz   50

E(lohist)   190, 242–250, 266
Earth   14, 17, 30–33, 36, 39, 49, 51–52, 56–57, 76, 88, 121, 124, 174, 176, 203, 210–237, 250–252, 258–261, 297
Edom   24–30, 34–38, 42–43, 58–59, 69, 108, 121–122, 125–128, 140, 142, 150,

152–156, 174–178, 195, 210, 269, 270,
   273, 304
Edomite   IX–X, 84, 99, 102, 107, 112, 131,
   141, 147, 149, 151–157, 167–171, 178,
   209
El / 'Ilu   31, 37–42, 47–54, 57–61, 64, 67–
   71, 74–80, 89, 145, 147, 156, 160, 163–
   164, 167, 228–229, 271, 273
El Shaddai   260, 299
Elephantine   17, 54, 55, 280
Enki / Ea   56, 57
Enlil   47, 51–52, 56–57
Epiphany   124, 127–128, 135, 144, 211, 214,
   218, 233, 301
Esau   35, 104, 149–153, 246
Exodus   VII, X, 40, 110, 115–117, 129–136,
   142–143, 161–162, 171, 181–207, 240–
   245, 249–254, 260, 286, 288, 302
Exodus creed   166, 181–183, 186–189
Exodus formula   79, 187–188
Exodus group   131–132, 143, 182, 195, 302
Exodus narrative   93, 120, 133–136, 192,
   194, 196–206
Exodus tradition   129–132, 143, 172, 174,
   184–186, 190, 192, 195, 198, 200, 204–
   206

Faithfulness   227
Family   47, 51, 54–57, 152, 194, 197, 243,
   246–247, 263
Flood   215, 216, 218, 221–224, 228–229,
   235, 237, 252, 259
Forced labour   184, 286

Genealogy   XI, 36, 47, 243
Gilead   147–148, 248
Grace   227–229

Ḫab/piru   65, 129, 130, 167
Hadad   IX, 49, 53, 67–71, 74–78, 88–89,
   143, 154, 166, 208, 304
Ham   132
Hazor   63, 247
Heaven   30–33, 36, 41, 47, 52–53, 57, 83,
   89, 121, 174, 177, 208, 210, 212, 214,
   225–228, 234, 236, 258–260, 265–
   266, 297

Heavenly court   52
Hebron   63, 70, 148
Ḫepa(t)   63–65
Hexateuch   42, 117–118, 120, 122, 124, 151,
   182, 186, 193, 249, 256, 294
Hezekia   VII, 81, 273–276
Historical consciousness   285, 290
Historiography   65, 155, 284–287, 291–292,
   295
History   VII–XI, 23–26, 38–43, 45, 47, 54,
   68–69, 74–77, 93, 95, 110, 113, 115–
   118, 121–125, 129–132, 145–156, 158–
   161, 166, 168, 170–171, 175–179, 181–
   191, 197, 201, 203–206, 209, 237, 240–
   246, 249, 251–255, 257, 259–266, 268,
   270, 280, 283–306
History writer   275–277, 279
Horus   70

Identity   35, 58, 77, 103, 109, 130, 162, 186,
   203–204, 206, 220, 243, 254, 263–
   265, 278, 290–291
Ideology   171, 183, 186–187, 203, 205–206,
   259, 265, 274, 279
Idol   80, 277, 287
Idolatry   187, 248
Image   IX, 25, 53, 57, 67–70, 73–85, 88–
   91, 98, 105, 132, 187–189, 210, 213,
   228, 235–238, 259, 261, 265, 274, 291,
   295
Imagery   38–41, 213, 228, 235
Inanna   50, 57, 58
Inscription   VIII, 1–2, 13–14, 17–20, 25–
   26, 33, 37, 40–41, 43, 46, 55, 59–62,
   69, 71, 73–74, 88, 93, 96, 98, 100, 112,
   116, 137–140, 155–156, 175, 178, 195–
   196, 208, 210, 213, 230, 233, 263, 269–
   272
Iron Age   IX, 25, 27, 43, 59, 68, 71, 73, 77–
   78, 85, 88–99, 109, 128–130, 157, 172,
   263–265, 273, 303
Isaac   148, 239, 242–243, 246, 248, 250,
   252, 254, 260, 264, 266
Ishtar / Ištar   50, 56–58, 90, 139–140

J(ahwist) / Y(ahwist)   190, 250–255, 266
Jacob   IX, 35, 147–150, 152–153, 155, 194,
   239, 242–250, 260, 263–264, 266, 283
Jehoram   149
Jehovist   117–118
Jemmeh   63
Jeroboam   53, 79, 183–189, 249
Jerusalem   X, 20, 27, 35–36, 41, 50, 54–55,
   58–64, 68–70, 73, 75, 79–81, 84–87,
   90, 116, 118, 127, 129, 148, 150, 155–
   156, 159, 161, 166, 168, 174, 176–177,
   188, 196, 207, 209, 215, 217, 220, 223,
   229–230, 267, 269–270, 273–276,
   279–280, 306
Jezreel   35, 36, 148
Jethro   27, 133–134, 192–194, 285
Joseph   147–149, 185, 245, 255, 283
Joshua   118, 147, 149, 181, 189, 191, 242,
   247, 267, 275
Josiah   VII, 273–276, 281
Judgment of the nations   127–128, 288
Justice   59, 81, 126, 225, 251, 254–255, 297

Kemosh / Chemosh   79, 90, 210, 220, 263,
   297–298
Kenite hypothesis   26, 28, 89, 146, 159, 178
Khirbet Beit Layy   70
Khirbet Qeiyafa   83
Kingship   47, 57, 77, 136, 218, 220, 223, 225,
   227, 230–233, 237
Kumarbi   51
Kuntillet 'Ajrud   VIII, 8, 13–14, 17–20, 25,
   33, 41, 55, 59–60, 69–74, 88, 116, 128,
   137–140, 143, 155, 172, 175, 178, 195–
   196, 230, 269–272, 303, 304

Laban   101, 102, 178, 194, 247, 248, 264
Leah tribes   147, 156
Lebanon   38, 131, 143–144, 221–222, 271–
   272

Maṣṣot   196–199
Merenptah / Merneptah   26, 130, 145, 163
Mesha-stele   VIII, 43, 59, 90, 220, 263, 266
Midian / Midianites   IX, 10, 26–28, 39, 43,
   60, 62, 99, 106, 116, 118, 121, 132–136,
143, 146, 154–155, 159, 173, 178, 192–
   196, 201–202, 208, 285–286, 304
Midianite hypothesis   116, 133, 134, 146,
   159, 178, 193–196
Milkom / Milcom   58, 69, 210
Miracle at the sea   191, 200–203, 237, 242
Moab / Moabites   VIII, 13–14, 17, 58–59,
   69, 90, 93, 99, 130, 151–152, 210, 220,
   252, 263–264, 273, 297–298
Monolatry   210, 246, 268, 273, 277–281
Moon / moon-god   49, 57, 71, 79, 258
Moses   VII, X, 3, 27, 39, 43, 48, 109, 119–
   122, 132–136, 143, 146, 149, 151, 154–
   155, 162, 175, 184, 191–198, 201–205,
   239–247, 250–255, 257, 260–262, 279,
   285–287, 297, 300–301
Mot   50
Mountain   24, 26, 30–34, 37, 41, 47–53,
   56, 68, 88–90, 94, 100, 105, 108, 110–
   111, 117, 119, 121, 130, 146, 154, 174,
   176–178, 192–196, 212, 222, 225–229,
   234, 242, 250, 286, 296, 302, 304
Mountain of God   68, 146, 177, 192–196,
   286, 302

Nabonid   1, 126
Nabû   47, 56–57
Nahor   248, 264
Naphtali   124, 148
Negev   23, 60, 84, 87, 95, 122, 126, 128,
   154–155, 171
New Document Hypothesis   130, 133–134
New Year festival   50, 118, 212
Ninurta   51, 56–57, 60, 64, 233
Noah   251, 261
Northern Kingdom   9, 58, 78–79, 91, 130–
   131, 159, 183–190, 196, 203–206, 230,
   250, 263

Oath-deities   54
Omri / Omrides   89, 270–271

Passover (Pessaḥ)   196–199
P(riestly Code / Writer)   190, 254, 257–262,
   265–266
Paran   25, 28, 42, 117, 121–122, 128, 154–
   155, 175, 269, 304

Peace   94, 134, 210, 216, 227, 248, 258

Pharaoh   26, 29, 34, 63, 80, 94, 101, 130, 132–133, 145, 193, 199–200, 225, 232, 251, 285, 296

Polytheism   XI, 36, 46–48, 54, 90, 156, 187, 246, 248, 250, 258, 298–299, 303

Primeval history   266, 285

Qaus / Qōs   58, 69, 153

Rachel   147, 149, 247

Rachel tribes   148–149, 153, 155

Rameses   204

Rameses II / Ramesses II   24, 26–27, 98, 100, 103–104, 107, 112–113, 130, 140, 156, 204

Ramesses III   33, 102–103, 107, 171

Revelation   VII, X, 45, 116, 162, 170–171, 198, 239–255, 260, 266, 289, 298–302

Righteousness   5, 15, 210, 225–227

Ritual   42, 83, 85, 87, 146, 196–199, 212, 215, 218, 226, 229–231, 247, 249, 259, 262–263

River   36, 47, 51–52, 103, 210, 219, 223–224, 226

Sacred stones   71

Sacrifice   83, 133, 164, 192, 196, 199–200, 276, 278–279

Şædæq / Şidq(u)   59

Salvation   14, 203–204, 206, 300, 302

Samaria   18, 55, 59, 69–71, 74, 89–90, 137, 139–140, 155, 172, 190, 195, 204, 230, 270–272, 280, 304

Satan   52, 56, 198

Sea / Yamm / Yammu   5–6, 9, 49, 64, 164, 219–220

Sebulon   125

Seir / Seïr   23–30, 34, 42, 95, 99, 108, 117, 121–122, 124, 128, 141–142, 150, 153, 155–156, 159, 170–171, 174–175, 269, 304

Shamash / Šamš / Šæmæš   59, 64

Shasu / Šasu   24, 27–28, 43, 60, 68, 99–100, 103, 105–112, 131, 140–142, 167, 169–172, 178, 195–196, 269, 304

Shechem   63, 118, 129, 148–149, 247–248

Shrine   24, 80, 83–84, 112, 148, 247, 249–250

Sinai   25–30, 33–34, 36, 46, 48, 53, 68, 73, 94, 111, 115–125, 128, 132, 142–143, 154, 159, 172–177, 181, 192–193, 242, 250–255, 260, 269–270, 286, 288, 301, 305

Sisera   36, 125, 146

Soleb   IX, 24, 93, 96–98, 102–113, 116, 137, 140–143, 156, 169–170

Solomon   58, 69, 80, 85, 118, 183–186, 203, 252

Song of Deborah   29, 36, 117, 120, 124–126, 128, 174, 305

Song of Miriam   130, 201–202

Song of Moses   120, 201–202, 251

Sons of God / Gods   52, 167, 251, 258

Sphinx   56, 82, 85–86, 214

Standing stones   54, 68, 71, 74, 81–88, 92, 284

Stelae   71, 83–84, 88, 94

Storm-god / storm god   VIII, 38, 48, 52, 57, 63, 75–76, 90, 115, 131, 143–144, 165–166, 208–209, 212–213, 215–220, 223–225, 227–228, 232–233, 235, 270

Sun / sun-god / sun-goddess   VIII, 26, 41, 50, 56–57, 59, 64, 71, 80–83, 121, 258, 285, 298

Taanach   82–83, 85, 158, 164

Tabernacle   261–262

Tabor   144, 148

Teman   25–26, 28, 33, 41–42, 55, 59, 60, 70, 73, 121–122, 128, 137, 139–140, 153–155, 172, 175, 178, 195, 269, 304

Temple   X, 13, 24, 33, 47, 50, 54, 57–59, 64, 69, 80, 85, 87–89, 93, 96, 98, 113, 116, 120, 140, 156, 159, 166, 169, 187, 194, 196, 207, 216–217, 219, 222–223, 226, 228–229, 234–235, 255, 261, 267, 271, 274, 276, 278–279

Teššub   51, 63

Tetragrammaton   VII–VIII, 2, 10, 12–13, 17, 20, 23, 69, 94–113, 138–139, 164, 169

Tetrateuch   190, 239–266

Theophany   26, 68, 116, 119, 122–126, 128, 142–143, 146, 153, 155, 156, 159–160,

166, 173, 175–178, 195–196, 213, 221–222, 224–225, 232, 235, 250, 252, 255, 260, 302, 305

Throne 56, 69–70, 75–77, 81–82, 85–87, 92, 176, 219, 221–228, 230, 232, 235–237

Tiamat 52

Torah X, 80, 130, 240, 286, 296

Treaty 131, 210, 265, 279

Ugarit VIII, 14, 18, 31–32, 37, 39–40, 46–52, 54–58, 63–64, 93, 158, 162, 164–165, 212, 215–16, 219–220, 228–230, 304

Uruk 57–58

Utu 57, 59

Vassal 231, 279

Water 30, 45, 51–52, 57, 143, 174, 200, 210–212, 214–217, 221, 223–224, 228, 234–235, 259

Weather-god / weather god 49, 75, 78, 88–89, 160, 165, 167, 233, 270–272, 296, 304

Worship / worshipper VII–XI, 24–25, 41, 47, 54, 60, 62, 65, 67–92, 108, 111, 116, 118, 129, 132–133, 137, 145–147, 153, 156, 161, 165, 181–183, 188, 190, 192–193, 195–196, 199, 201, 204, 206, 208, 210, 237, 242, 246, 248–252, 263–264, 267, 270, 272–274, 276–277, 279–280, 285–286, 298, 303–304

Yhwh of hosts 53, 80, 218, 220

Zaphon / Ṣapānū 139, 144, 229–230

Zion 29, 48, 70, 159, 176–177, 229–230, 234

Index of Ancient Sources

HEBREW BIBLE

Genesis

1	237, 285
1:1	52
1:6	51–52
1:16	258
1:21	258
1:26	53, 259
1:28	261
2:1	258
4:3–4	251
4:26	X, 146, 251, 285
6:1–4	251
6:3	252
9:1	261
9:7	261
9:26	251
10	286
10:6	132
10:9	251
11:1–9	251
12:2	245
12:3	252
12:6–7	247
12:8	252
12:10–20	194
12:17	251
13:4	252
14:18–22	XI, 194
17:1	260
17:18	260
17:20	245
18:18	245
19:30–38	151
21:17	245
21:18	245
21:21	154
21:33	252
24	133
26:25	35, 253
28:10–22	246
29	133
29:30	147
30	147
32:4	35, 150
32:31	242
33:3	153
33:20	145
35:1–7	246, 263
35:2–3	246–247
35:4	247–249
36	151–152
36:8	35
36:12	152
36:13, 33	152
36:10–14	147
36:11, 15, 42	152
36:13, 17	102
36:26	105
36:38–39	37
36:43	38
46:3	245
46:2–4	244–245
49:25–26	40

Exodus

1–15	312
1:11	204–205
2:11–4:20a	133
2:15*	135
2:15–20	132, 146, 193–194
3	245
3:1	192–193
3:1–6*	134–136
3:2a	198
3:2–3	239, 250
3:3–6	246
3:4–6	242, 244
3:4–12	244
3:6	239, 246
3:8	246
3:12	192, 242
3:13–15	239
3:16–20	199
3:18b, 19a, 20	200
4:17, 18	135, 192
4:24–26	135, 136

4:27	192
5:1–4	199
5:22	192
6:2–3	260
8:4b	199
8:21b–24a	199
12–13	199, 200
12	198
12:1–13:16	196
13:21–23	197–198
14	191, 200–202
14–15	191, 202, 237
14:5a	184
14:19a	198
15	123, 201
15:1–19	202
15:5.8	124
15:16	15
15:21	130, 202
15:22	120
17:6	192
18	133, 194–195, 285
18:1–12	133, 192–193
18:5	192
18:12	146, 193
18:13–27	133
19–24	116
19	VII, 88, 116, 119–120, 125, 192
19:2	119–120
19:2–3	119
19:11, 18, 20	120, 250
19:15–19	53, 124–125, 250
20:2	166, 181, 188
20:5	206, 254
20:16	242
20:23	250
20:24 ff.	120
23:15	197, 199
24:18	119
25	260
28:43	262
30:20–21	262
32	208, 249
32:4	187, 249
33–34	252
33:18	253

33:19	253–254
34:5–9	251
34:5	253
34:6–7	254
40:34	260

Leviticus

10:6–7	262
10:9	262
13–14	261
16:16	261

Numeri

12:1	146, 154, 193, 195
12:12	261
13:3, 17, 26	154
24:18	25, 27–28
25:1–5	195, 252
25:6	146

Deuteronomium

1:1	101, 154
4:19	252, 278
4:32–40	280–281
5:6	181, 188, 206
5:7	277
7	VII, 278
7:5	277
7:6	278
7:7–11	280
8	278
9:1–6	278
10:5	278
12:2	277
12:2–3	248
13	279
16:1	199
16:13	50
16:21	280
16:22	91
17:2–7	277
23:2–9	151
28	279
29:21–27	277
29:25	278
32	123
32:8–9	156, 210, 252

33	IX–X, 117, 119. 124, 128–129, 153, 173, 176, 305
33:2	25–26, 28, 32, 34, 41, 81, 116, 121–124, 137, 146, 153–154, 156, 173–175, 195–196, 269
33:2–5, 26–29	32–33, 120
33:29	232

Joshua

14:6, 14;	
15:17	152
19:43	15
19:45	16
24	118
24:23	247
24:30	149

Judges

5	IX–X, 68, 88, 117, 119–120, 124, 127–129, 159–160, 166, 173–178, 269, 305
5:4–5	23–30, 32–34, 37, 116, 121–124, 126–128. 137, 146, 153–154, 156, 159, 173, 175–176, 195–196, 269
5:2–30	29, 125
5:20	41
5:24	27
5:31a	121, 127
6–9	135, 146

1 Samuel

15:6	146
18:6	219
27:10	146
30:29	146

2 Samuel

5:24	31
7:22–19	280
8:13–14	149
11:1	31
15:7	70
21:17	31
23:9, 24	17
24:1	198

1 Kings

1:39	226
7	90
7:23–26	223
8:6	69
8:54–61	280
11–12	184–185, 190
11:1–5	252
11:18	154
11:26–12:24	183
11:27–28	185–186
11:29–39	185
12	68, 79, 185, 249
12:1–19	185–186
12:25–33	187
12:26 ff.	68, 79
12:28	79, 130, 186–188, 249
12:29	140, 189
14:25–28	276
16:32	271
18:11	154
18:21–40	280
18:44–45	212
19:8	33
28–30	53

2 Kings

8:20	149
9:13	226
10:23	272
11:12	226
12:5–16	276
16:8	276
18:4	90–91, 273–274
19:15	280–281
19:15–19	280
21:2–15	277
22:4–7	276
23	274–275
23:1–24	273
23:6	280
23:11	81, 83

1 Chronicles

1	152
1:31 ff.	104, 135
1:35, 37	104

1:41	105	68:18	26
2:55	102	72	81, 230
5:19	102	77	216, 218, 237
11:12, 26	17	77:17 – 20	124, 215 – 216
14:15	31	77:17	124
21:1	198	77:19	233
		82	53, 156, 252
Job		83	135
1:6	52, 56	84:12	81
9:8	232	85	227
		85:11 – 14	210
Psalms		89	144
3:3	14	89:7 – 8	210, 222,
12:1	15	92:10	124, 126
13:4	229	92:16	15
18	X, 123 – 216, 218, 230 – 235, 237	93	X, 210, 216, 223 – 224, 230 – 231, 235, 237
18:4 – 20	235	93 – 100	216, 237
18:8 ff.	213, 233, 235	94:17	15
20	237	97	X, 213, 218, 235, 237
21	230 – 232	97:2 – 5	224
24	X, 210	97:3	210, 227
24:7, 9	219	97:4	233
24:8, 10	209	97:7	222
27:4	208	98	X, 226, 237
27:5	235,	99	70
24	218 – 219	101	230
24:7 – 10	216, 220	104:4	210
29	VIII, X, 38, 52, 144, 156, 209 – 213, 216, 219 – 220, 222, 224, 227, 230, 235, 237	108	207
		114	216, 237
		132	237
29:5 – 7	233	137:7	126, 150
31:21	235	144	237
36	X, 228 – 229	148	237
43:3	210	149	237
45	230	150	237
46	81, 224		
46:7	122	Proverbs	
47	216	26:27	236
48	X, 229 – 230		
48:3	50	Isaiah	
57	236	1:26	81
63:8	15	8:18	176
65	X, 217	9:3	135
68	X, 29, 32 – 37, 43, 120, 122, 124, 129	9:5	40
		18:4	81
68:8 – 9	29, 34	21:1	128

21:11	25
28:14 – 18	233 – 234
34	126 – 127, 150
38:11	12
43:16 – 17	124
45:18 – 23	281
46:1	265
51:9 – 10	124
59:9	81
60:1 – 3	81
63:1 – 6	126 – 127, 150, 156
63:19	122

Jeremiah	
7:12	X
20:9	239
49:7 – 22	126, 150
49:8	150
49:10	150
49:20	153

Ezekiel	
25:12 – 13	150, 153
35:1 – 15	150
35:15	25
47:1 – 12	228

Hosea	
2:17	189
8	68
8:5 – 6	68, 79
8:9, 10	138
10:5	79
10:12	129
11:1	189
12	136
12:4	189
12:10	189
12:14	136, 189
13	68
13:2	68, 79
13:4 – 5	129, 189

Amos	
1:2	122
1:11 – 12	126, 128
4:13	232

Obadiah	
6	150
8 ff.	150
9	150, 153
10 – 14	150
10	149, 151
12	149, 151

Micah	
1:3	232
1:4	88

Habakkuk	
3	IX–X, 26, 33 – 34, 117, 119 – 124, 128 – 129, 156, 173, 196, 209, 305
3:3	25, 41, 81, 116, 122, 128, 137, 146, 153 – 154, 173, 175, 195 – 196, 269
3:4	174
3:7	26 – 27, 116, 137, 195 – 196, 269
3:12	31
4:7	121

Zechariah	
3:1	56
9:14	128

New Testament

Galatians	
4:25	26

Hebrews	
7:3	XI

Ancient Near Eastern Texts
Amara–West topographical list   24, 116, 137, 140 – 143, 156, 169 – 171
Berlin Statue Pedestal Relief 21687   26
Egyptian Book of the Dead   23, 25, 99, 108
Khirbet el–Kom inscription   VIII, 18 – 19, 55, 69, 271, 303

Kuntillet 'Ajrud inscriptions   VIII, 25, 33, 41, 73, 128, 137–140, 143, 155, 172, 175, 178

Merneptah stele   26–27

Mesha stele/ inscription   VIII, 13, 17, 20, 43, 90, 93, 263, 266, 270

Enuma Elish   285

Soleb topographical list   IX, 93, 96–98, 102–113, 116, 137, 140–143, 169–170